THE JOSEPH SMITH PAPERS

Dean C. Jessee

Ronald K. Esplin

Richard Lyman Bushman

GENERAL EDITORS

PREVIOUSLY PUBLISHED

Journals, Volume 1: 1832–1839

Revelations and Translations: Manuscript Revelation Books, Facsimile Edition

Revelations and Translations, Volume 1: Manuscript Revelation Books

THE JOSEPH SMITH PAPERS

REVELATIONS AND TRANSLATIONS
VOLUME 2: PUBLISHED REVELATIONS

Robin Scott Jensen
Richard E. Turley Jr.
Riley M. Lorimer

VOLUME EDITORS

THE CHURCH
HISTORIAN'S
PRESS

The Church Historian's Press is an imprint of the Church History Department
of The Church of Jesus Christ of Latter-day Saints, Salt Lake City, Utah,
and a trademark of Intellectual Reserve, Inc.

www.josephsmithpapers.org

The Joseph Smith Papers Project is endorsed by
the National Historical Publications and Records Commission.

Art direction: Richard Erickson.
Cover design: Scott Eggers. Interior design: Richard Erickson and Riley M. Lorimer.
Typography: Riley M. Lorimer and Alison Palmer.

Library of Congress Cataloging-in-Publication Data

Smith, Joseph, 1805–1844.
Manuscript revelation books / Robin Scott Jensen, Robert J. Woodford, Steven C. Harper, volume editors.
p. cm. — (The Joseph Smith papers. Revelations and translations; v. 1)
Includes bibliographical references.
ISBN 978-1-60641-909-0 (hardbound: alk. paper; v. 1)
ISBN 978-1-60641-942-7 (hardbound: alk. paper; v. 2)
1. Smith, Joseph, 1805–1844—Manuscripts. 2. Book of Commandments—Manuscripts.
3. Doctrine and Covenants—Manuscripts. 4. Church of Jesus Christ of Latter-day Saints—Doctrines.
5. Mormon Church—Doctrines. I. Jensen, Robin Scott. II. Woodford, Robert J. (Robert John)
III. Harper, Steven Craig IV. Title. V. Series: Smith, Joseph, 1805–1844.
Joseph Smith papers. Revelations and translations; v. 1.

BX8621.S53 2010   289.3'2—dc22   2010027446

Printed in the United States of America on acid-free paper.
10 9 8 7 6 5 4 3 2 1

The Joseph Smith Papers

Contents

Detailed Contents

The following table lists all revelations and other items presented in this volume, in the order in which they appear in their respective publications: the Book of Commandments, *The Evening and the Morning Star,* and the first and second editions of the Doctrine and Covenants. Revelations printed in *Evening and Morning Star,* the later, reprinted version of *The Evening and the Morning Star,* can be found on the same pages as their earlier counterparts. The table also includes the items presented in Appendix 1: Proposed Sixth Gathering of the Book of Commandments. Because Appendix 2 includes only incomplete excerpts from Oliver Cowdery's copy of the Book of Commandments, the specific revelations that appear therein are not listed here.

The first column in the table below lists the chapter number, section number, or issue date of each item. The second column gives the standard date of each item, based on careful study of original sources. The "standard date" is the date a revelation or other item was originally dictated or recorded. If that date is ambiguous or unknown, the standard date is the best approximation of that date, based on existing evidence. These standard dates do not always correspond to the dates printed in the various publications. In cases in which two or more items bear the same date, such as April 1829, a letter of the alphabet has been appended, providing each item a unique editorial title—for example, April 1829–A or April 1829–B. A bracketed "D&C" reference to the 1981 edition of the Doctrine and Covenants is included for each item that was later canonized by The Church of Jesus Christ of Latter-day Saints. The page numbers in the third column correspond to page numbers in this published volume, not to original page numbers printed in the various publications. Readers wishing to locate a particular revelation or other item may also consult the table titled Corresponding Published Versions of Revelations (pages 719–724 herein), which lists the items in chronological order.

BOOK OF COMMANDMENTS

APPENDIX 1: PROPOSED SIXTH GATHERING OF THE BOOK OF COMMANDMENTS

Revelations Printed in
The Evening and the Morning Star

Doctrine and Covenants, 1835

Part One: Lectures on Faith

APPENDIX 2: SELECTIONS FROM OLIVER COWDERY'S COPY OF THE BOOK OF COMMANDMENTS

Doctrine and Covenants, 1844

Timeline of Joseph Smith's Life

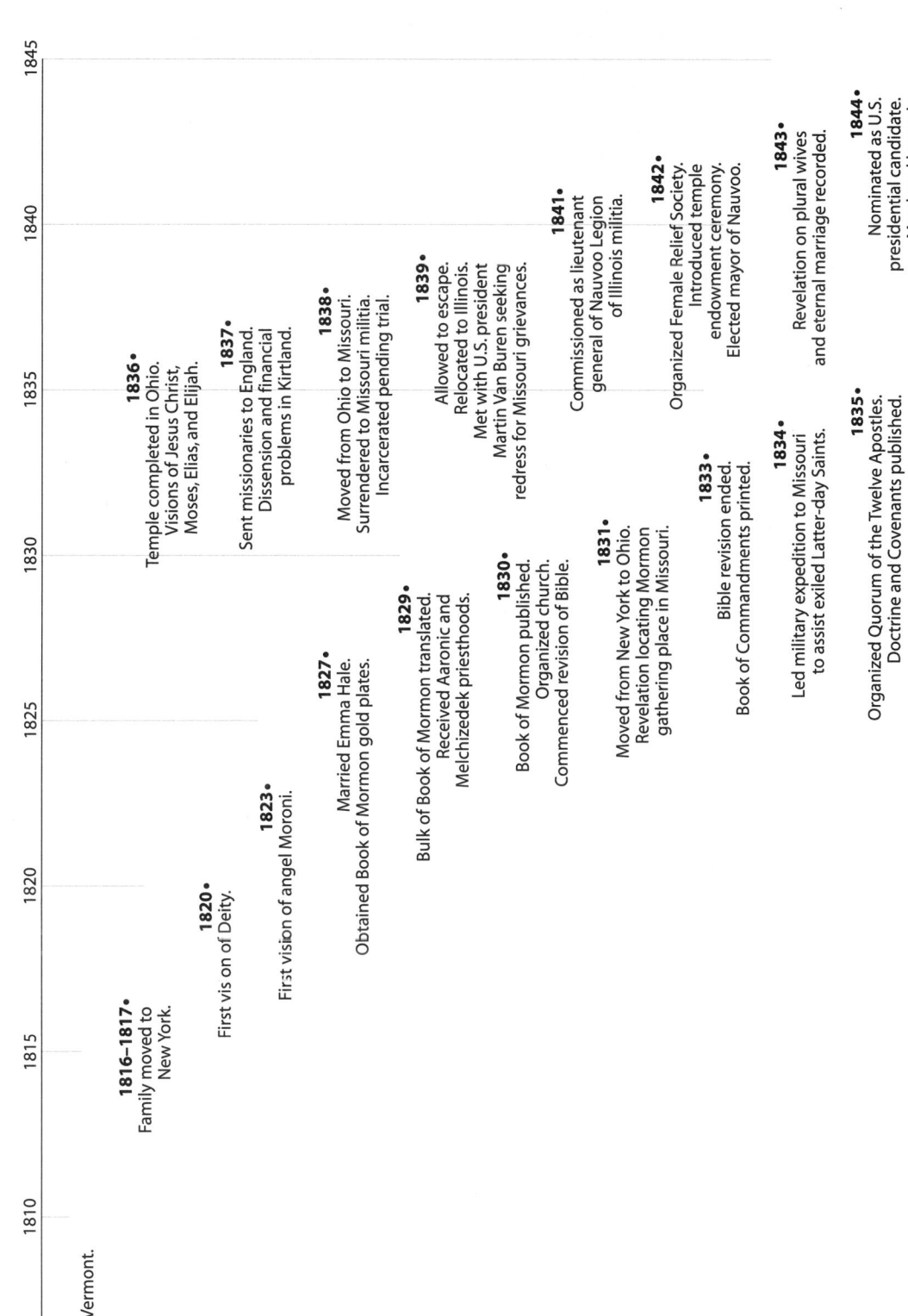

1805
Born in Vermont.

1816–1817
Family moved to New York.

1820
First vis on of Deity.

1823
First vision of angel Moroni.

1827
Married Emma Hale.
Obtained Book of Mormon gold plates.

1829
Bulk of Book of Mormon translated.
Received Aaronic and Melchizedek priesthoods.

1830
Book of Mormon published.
Organized church.
Commenced revision of Bible.

1831
Moved from New York to Ohio.
Revelation locating Mormon gathering place in Missouri.

1833
Bible revision ended.
Book of Commandments printed.

1834
Led military expedition to Missouri to assist exiled Latter-day Saints.

1835
Organized Quorum of the Twelve Apostles.
Doctrine and Covenants published.

1836
Temple completed in Ohio.
Visions of Jesus Christ, Moses, Elias, and Elijah.

1837
Sent missionaries to England.
Dissension and financial problems in Kirtland.

1838
Moved from Ohio to Missouri.
Surrendered to Missouri militia.
Incarcerated pending trial.

1839
Allowed to escape.
Relocated to Illinois.
Met with U.S. president Martin Van Buren seeking redress for Missouri grievances.

1841
Commissioned as lieutenant general of Nauvoo Legion of Illinois militia.

1842
Organized Female Relief Society.
Introduced temple endowment ceremony.
Elected mayor of Nauvoo.

1843
Revelation on plural wives and eternal marriage recorded.

1844
Nominated as U.S. presidential candidate.
Murdered by mob.

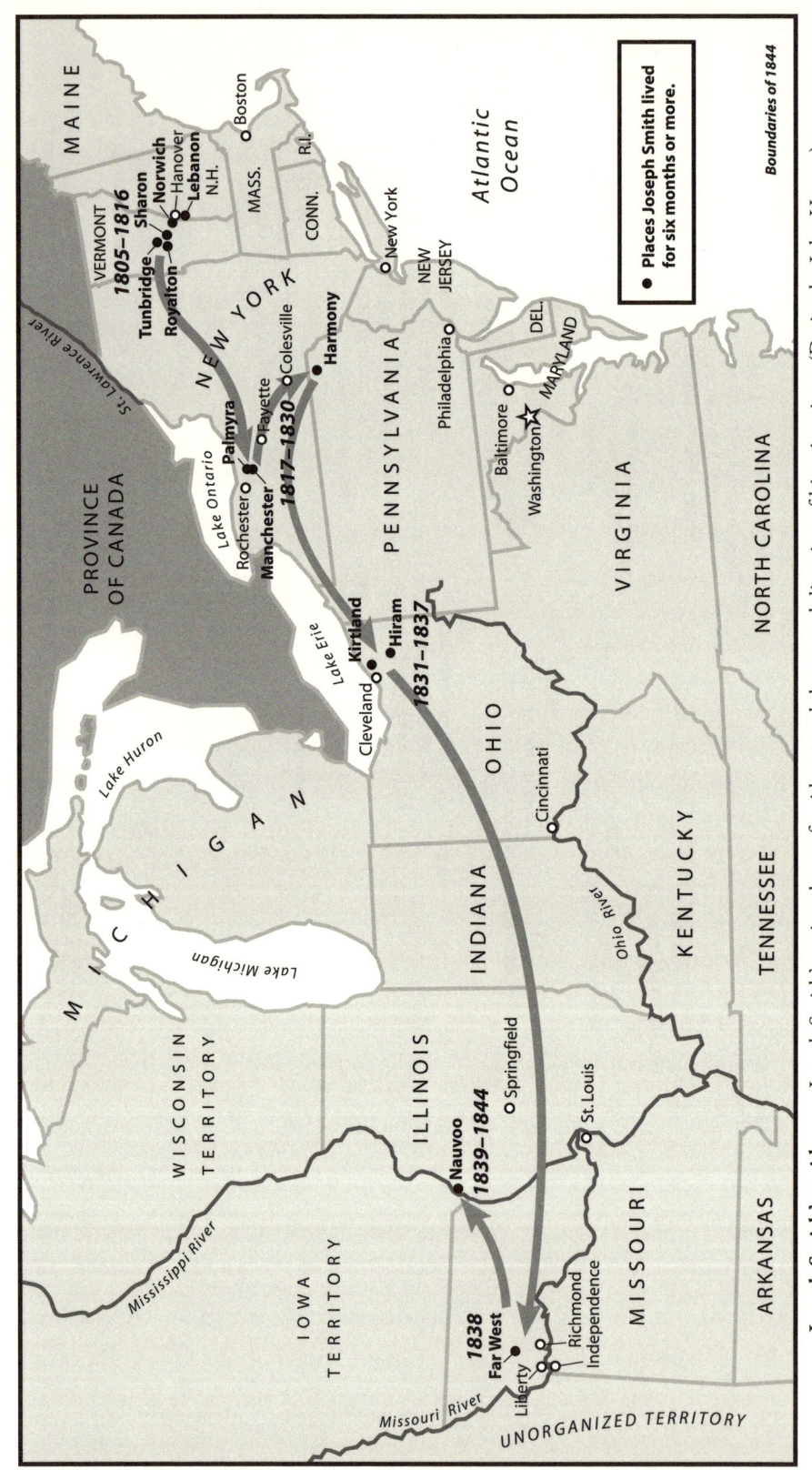

Joseph Smith's residences. Joseph Smith's major places of residence and the general direction of his migrations. (Design by John Hamer.)

Joseph Smith–Era Publications of Revelations

"The commandments of the Lord are sacred, and above the inventions of men," declared William W. Phelps in a February 1833 editorial in the Mormon newspaper *The Evening and the Morning Star.*[1] Phelps's pronouncement referred to more than just the commandments found in the Bible: only a few months earlier, he and others had begun setting type for the Book of Commandments, a compilation of sacred texts dictated by Joseph Smith and believed by Smith's followers to be communications from God. "When we remember," Phelps continued, "that the commandments of God, came by the gift and power of God: or, in other words, holy men spoke moved by the Holy Ghost, we ought to rejoice with great joy: for in this manner spake the prophets for the saint's good, even in these last days."[2] Phelps and other Latter-day Saints found great comfort—even great joy—in the continuation of God's interaction with man. These commandments, or revelations, as they were also called,[3] imparted theological guidance, spiritual comfort, and practical direction to the Saints.

This second volume of the Revelations and Translations series of *The Joseph Smith Papers* presents Joseph Smith's revelations in the format that early Latter-day Saints most often experienced them. Reproduced herein are the most significant printed versions of the revelations that were published or in the process of being published during Joseph Smith's lifetime. The publications containing these revelations are the Book of Commandments (1833); the church newspaper *The Evening and the Morning Star* (1832–1833) and its later, reprinted version, *Evening and Morning Star* (1835–1836); and the first and second editions of the Doctrine and Covenants (1835, 1844), the latter of which was begun in 1841 but not completed until late summer 1844—shortly after Joseph Smith's death on 27 June.[4] This volume is a companion to the first volume in this series, which

---

1. "Commandments," *The Evening and the Morning Star,* Feb. 1833, [4].

2. "Commandments," *The Evening and the Morning Star,* Feb. 1833, [5].

3. See *JSP,* MRB:xxvn3.

4. Other church-sanctioned publications and some non-Mormon ones printed revelations during Joseph Smith's lifetime. Though these publications are important textual sources, they are not included herein either because they were not official church publications or because they are not as significant in terms of quantity as the publications featured herein. (See, for example, *Verily, I say unto you, concerning your brethren who have been afflicted,* [Kirtland, OH: ca. Jan. 1834], copy at CHL [D&C 101]; "An Extract of Revelation," *Elders' Journal,* Aug. 1838, 52–53; "The Mormon Creed," *Painesville Telegraph,* 19 Apr. 1831, [4];

Joseph Smith–era publications of revelations. The present volume reproduces the most significant printed versions of Joseph Smith's revelations that were published or in the process of being published during his lifetime. The Book of Commandments is the smallest book in the photograph. Beneath it is a bound collection of both volumes (twenty-four issues) of *Evening and Morning Star,* and beneath that collection, in the marbled cover, is a bound collection of both volumes of *The Evening and the Morning Star.* On the right side of the photograph, the 1844 edition of the Doctrine and Covenants rests on top of the 1835 edition of the same book. Church History Library, Salt Lake City.

presents the contents of two large manuscript books into which revelation texts were hand copied. Together, these volumes provide the most important primary sources needed to study the revelation texts and their development during Joseph Smith's lifetime.

The Book of Commandments and the first edition of the Doctrine and Covenants are represented herein by photographs of the printed pages of a surviving copy of each original volume. The second edition of the Doctrine and Covenants is also represented by photographs of an original copy, but because the second edition was essentially a reprint of the first, only seven sections

Ezra Booth, "Mormonism—Nos. VIII–IX," *Ohio Star,* 8 Dec. 1831, [1]; and "Highly Important from the Far West," *New York Weekly Herald,* 3 July 1841, 340.)

added to the later compilation (sections 101–107) are included here. The items that appeared in *The Evening and the Morning Star* (Independence, Missouri; and Kirtland, Ohio) and its reprint, *Evening and Morning Star* (Kirtland, Ohio), are printed in a two-column format to facilitate comparison of the texts with one another. Two appendixes provide related materials: The first is a proposed sixth gathering of the Book of Commandments, which is a transcript of the thirteen additional items that would likely have been included in that volume had vigilantes not halted publication by destroying the print shop. The second appendix presents photographs of selected pages from Oliver Cowdery's copy of the Book of Commandments. These photographs show marks editors made in that volume while compiling and editing revelations for the first edition of the Doctrine and Covenants.

Both Joseph Smith–era editions of the Doctrine and Covenants were formally divided into two parts. The first part, "on the doctrine of the church," comprised seven lectures or essays on the subject of faith that were delivered to the Elders School in Kirtland, Ohio, in the winter of 1834–1835.[5] The lectures, though categorically different from revelations and probably authored by persons other than Joseph Smith, are included in their entirety herein to provide a complete presentation of the first edition of the Doctrine and Covenants.[6] Regardless of authorship, the lectures can be considered Joseph Smith documents in the sense that he and other members of the church presidency introduced them in a signed preface as being among "the leading items of the religion which we have professed to believe."[7] The second, or "covenants and commandments," part made up the bulk of the volume and included the revelations, a few other similar items, and several statements respecting church polity and practice.

As in the first volume of this series, the document introductions and annotation in this volume focus on textual matters, though the introductions also provide historical context for the documents. A central objective of the footnotes is to identify, wherever possible, the immediate source text or texts for the printed revelations included in this volume. In this regard, the chart on the next page may provide a convenient overview.

---

5. The first, fifth, and sixth lectures were available in printed form before they were published in the Doctrine and Covenants, the first as a broadside and the fifth and sixth in the church's newspaper. (*Theology. Lecture First,* [Kirtland, OH: ca. Feb. 1835], copy at CHL; "Lecture Fifth" and "Lecture Sixth," *LDS Messenger and Advocate,* May 1835, 1:122–126.)

6. The scholarship respecting authorship of the lectures is summarized in Reynolds, "Authorship Debate Concerning *Lectures on Faith,*" 355–382; and Partridge, *Notes on the Authorship of the Lectures on Faith,* 21–29.

7. "Preface," Doctrine and Covenants, 1835 ed., [iii].

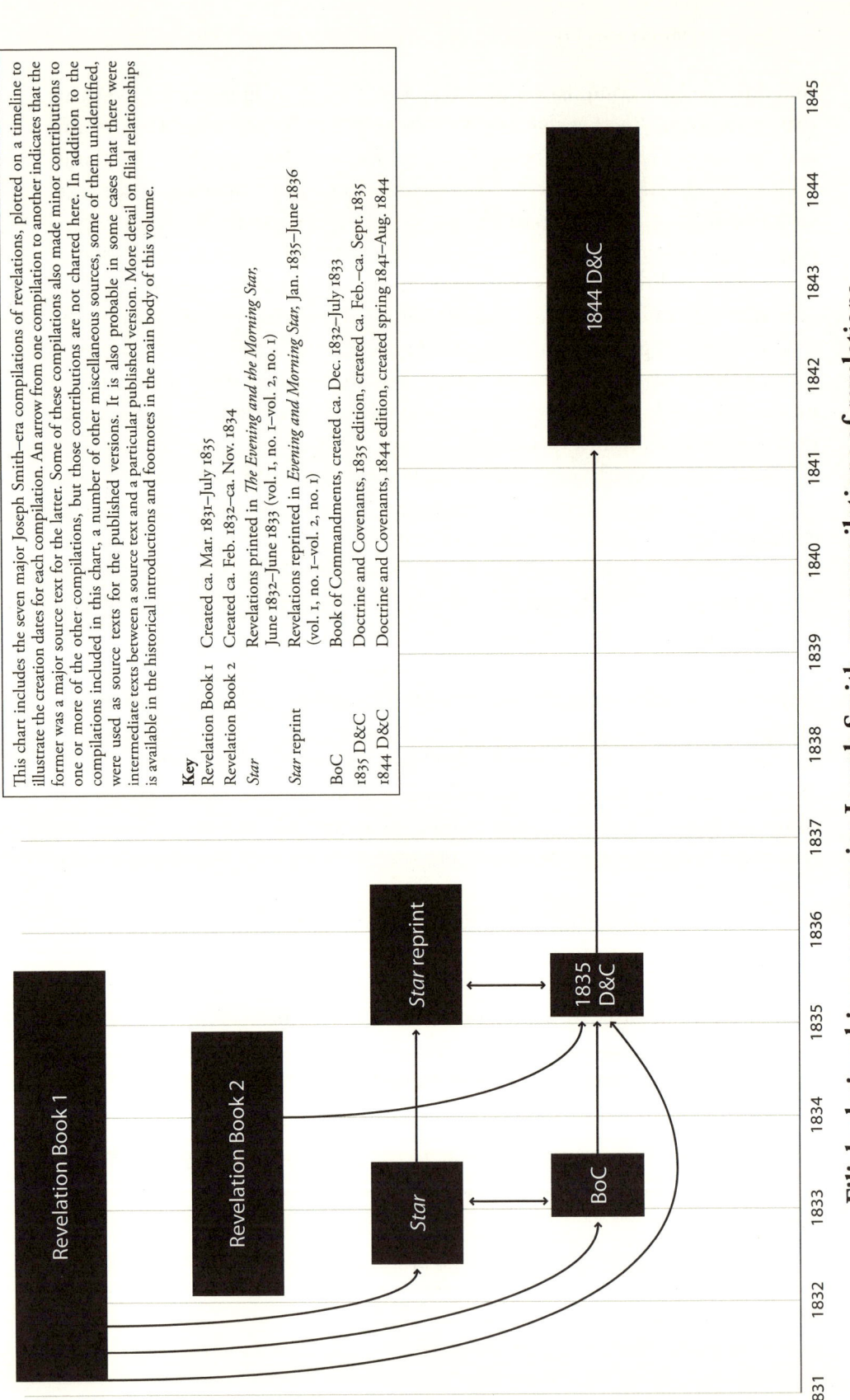

This chart includes the seven major Joseph Smith–era compilations of revelations, plotted on a timeline to illustrate the creation dates for each compilation. An arrow from one compilation to another indicates that the former was a major source text for the latter. Some of these compilations also made minor contributions to one or more of the other compilations, but those contributions are not charted here. In addition to the compilations included in this chart, a number of other miscellaneous sources, some of them unidentified, were used as source texts for the published versions. It is also probable in some cases that there were intermediate texts between a source text and a particular published version. More detail on filial relationships is available in the historical introductions and footnotes in the main body of this volume.

Key

Revelation Book 1	Created ca. Mar. 1831–July 1835
Revelation Book 2	Created ca. Feb. 1832–ca. Nov. 1834
Star	Revelations printed in *The Evening and the Morning Star*, June 1832–June 1833 (vol. 1, no. 1–vol. 2, no. 1)
Star reprint	Revelations reprinted in *Evening and Morning Star*, Jan. 1835–June 1836 (vol. 1, no. 1–vol. 2, no. 1)
BoC	Book of Commandments, created ca. Dec. 1832–July 1833
1835 D&C	Doctrine and Covenants, 1835 edition, created ca. Feb.–ca. Sept. 1835
1844 D&C	Doctrine and Covenants, 1844 edition, created spring 1841–Aug. 1844

Filial relationships among major Joseph Smith–era compilations of revelations

Users of the present volume should also consult the Documents series of *The Joseph Smith Papers,* which will publish the earliest and best extant version of each revelation, arranged in chronological order with other Joseph Smith documents of various genres. Volumes in the Documents series will include a historical introduction for each revelation, as well as rich contextual annotation and supplementary resources.

Oral and Print Cultures of Early Mormonism

On 1 November 1831, a conference at Hiram, Ohio, of leading elders of the Church of Christ voted to publish ten thousand copies of a compilation of Joseph Smith's revelations.[8] The preceding year, Joseph Smith had published the Book of Mormon, which his followers viewed as an inspired translation of an ancient narrative. But church leaders at the 1831 conference were authorizing, for the first time, publication of Smith's revelations—messages expressed in the first-person voice of Deity that Smith dictated to his scribes.

Publishing the revelations would not only expand their availability but also represent a change in practice because access to the revelations had, to that point, been limited. Early revelations cautioned leaders against sharing the texts widely. A March 1830 revelation, for example, gave the explicit command to "shew not these things neither speak these things unto the World."[9] A 3 November 1831 revelation, dictated immediately following the aforementioned conference, reminded listeners that Smith's revelations had been "commanded to be kept from the world in the day that they were given." With the newly authorized publication, however, the revelations were now "to go forth unto all flesh & this according to the mind & the will of the Lord."[10]

Practical and cultural considerations also played important roles in limiting access to the revelations. Joseph Smith's earliest visions and other communications with the divine, which began in 1820, were likely not recorded when they occurred. In part, Smith was personally reluctant to publicize his sacred experiences. He was also reared in a family and a society that were emerging from a predominantly oral culture to one increasingly reliant on written texts.[11] Initially, the young Joseph Smith seemed to view the divine communications he received as oral and private texts, to be shared with others only by word of mouth, if at all. Though many of Smith's earliest spiritual experiences would eventually be seen by followers as the genesis of a new religion and as worthy

---

8. Minute Book 2, 1 Nov. 1831.

9. Revelation, Mar. 1830, in Revelation Book 1, p. 27, in *JSP,* MRB:25 [D&C 19:21].

10. Revelation, 3 Nov. 1831, in Revelation Book 1, p. 120, in *JSP,* MRB:213 [D&C 133:60–61].

11. See Jensen, "Rely upon the Things Which Are Written," chap. 2, esp. 44–49.

of recording and retelling widely, they were at first largely personal experiences that answered private questions.[12]

By the late 1820s, after attracting a few followers, Joseph Smith began recording revelation texts in writing, both to preserve them and to transmit them more widely.[13] As he recorded more revelations, interest in them grew, and early converts made copies by hand either for personal reference or for use in proselytizing. The limitations of hand copying ensured that, even without an official policy, only Smith's closest associates had regular and unrestricted access to the revelations.

As the early recorded revelations were disseminated, *written* texts were accompanied by *oral* contexts. When possible, traveling missionaries made handwritten copies of revelations for themselves and then showed or read these texts to others while verbally conveying information about the origins or meaning of the texts. Early church leader Orson Hyde referenced the interplay between oral and written texts in his journal. Shortly after ordaining Simeon Waymouth an elder, Hyde wrote, "[I] instructed him[,] wrote the articles Laws and commands for him and gave him all the information [I] could."[14] Orson Pratt, another early convert, described the same interplay in a reminiscent account: "We often had access to the manuscripts [of the revelations] when boarding with the Prophet; and it was our delight to read them over and over again, before they were printed . . . and a few we copied for the purpose of reference in our absence on missions; and also to read them to the saints for their edification."[15]

Many revelation texts were recorded in such a way that their message could not have been fully understood without additional information. For example, the earliest extant text of an October 1830 revelation commands Parley P. Pratt to "go with my servant Oliver and Peter into the wilderness among the Lamanites and Ziba also shall go with them."[16] Including surnames was unnecessary because those within the small community of believers were personally acquainted with the individuals being referenced. Members of that community would also have understood what was meant by "wilderness" and "Lamanites."

---

12. See Allen, "Emergence of a Fundamental," 43–61; Bushman, *Rough Stone Rolling,* 39–41; and Bushman, "Joseph Smith's Many Histories," 12–15.

13. See "Joseph Smith as Revelator and Translator," in *JSP,* MRB:xxi–xxii.

14. Hyde, Journal, 15 Nov. 1832. Hyde may have been referring to the texts dated 10 April 1830 and 9 and 23 February 1831, which early members often called "the articles and covenants" and "the Law," respectively. (See Articles and covenants, 10 Apr. 1830, in Doctrine and Covenants 2, 1835 ed. [D&C 20], and Revelation, 9 and 23 Feb. 1831, in Doctrine and Covenants 13, 1835 ed. [D&C 42].)

15. Orson Pratt, "Explanation of Substituted Names in the Covenants," *The Seer,* Mar. 1854, 228.

16. Revelation, Oct. 1830–A, in Revelation Book 2, pp. 83–84, in *JSP,* MRB:583–585 [D&C 32:1–3].

Later, if Pratt and others shared the written text outside the community, they would have verbally communicated the missing or implied information.[17] Before print publication and while the Mormon community remained intimate, oral subtext or context conveyed more information than was actually written on paper.

Printing the revelations put greater distance between the reader of the text and the persons who originally dictated and recorded it. Before publication, hearers or readers likely would have learned about a text's creation or accepted interpretation from Joseph Smith or from his close associates. Once the text was printed, however, it generally had to stand on its own. Those who prepared the revelations for publication, therefore, sometimes provided additional contextual information. For example, they often inserted surnames[18] and brief introductions. Nevertheless, because no oral and little written introduction accompanied the individual printed revelation texts, the revelations became more autonomous, meaning that members could increasingly interpret the texts outside of their original context and intended meaning.

Though published texts could potentially lead to misinterpretation or heresy, they also provided Latter-day Saints and potential converts with a banner to rally around. Believing they were guided by commandments issued directly from God to Joseph Smith endowed early Mormons with a sense of exceptionalism that helped bind converts to the community of Saints. Early in his ministry, before the revelations had been published widely, Joseph Smith was fairly accessible to his followers. As the church grew, however, he necessarily became less so, and a smaller proportion of the church membership had regular contact with him and therefore with the community-building, faith-affirming power of his revelations. Publication allowed more people to access and interpret the revelations—the element of the new religion that drove every aspect of its doctrine and practice.

The Book of Commandments

Following the November 1831 conference, a revelation established a group of men, later called the Literary Firm, to oversee publication of the revelations.[19] Members of the Literary Firm were to benefit from the profits of its printing endeavors, with any surplus going into church coffers.[20] The United

---

17. For additional analysis of the oral context related to the October 1830 revelation, see Jensen, "Rely upon the Things Which Are Written," 1–5.

18. See, for example, Revelation, 30 Aug. 1831, in Revelation Book 1, pp. 107–108, in *JSP*, MRB:187–189 [D&C 63:39–66].

19. Revelation, 12 Nov. 1831, in Doctrine and Covenants 26, 1835 ed. [D&C 70].

20. Revelation, 26 Apr. 1832, in Revelation Book 1, p. 129, in *JSP*, MRB:231 [D&C 82:17–18].

Firm, an economic arm of the church, was to provide monetary support for the Literary Firm.[21] While the Literary Firm originally had plans to publish a number of works, including a hymnal and an almanac, its primary focus was the Book of Commandments.[22]

In the winter of 1831–1832, two Literary Firm members, Oliver Cowdery and John Whitmer, carried a manuscript book titled "Book of Commandments and Revelations" (known in this edition as Revelation Book 1) to Independence, Jackson County, Missouri. Using Revelation Book 1 as their primary source, Cowdery, Whitmer, and fellow Literary Firm member William W. Phelps, who had been appointed church printer, began printing what came to be called the Book of Commandments.[23] Church leaders expected the Book of Commandments to aid members in living their religion. "We hope," began one notice announcing the forthcoming book, "that while they [the Saints] are thus blessed with the precious word of their Lord from heaven, in these last days, . . . they will hearken to his counsels and lend an ear to all his precepts."[24] Anticipation for the Book of Commandments spread beyond church headquarters, in part through the ministry of missionaries, who saw the revelations as central to the gospel message they were sent to preach. In 1832, Orson Hyde, then preaching in Massachusetts, took advance orders for copies of the Book of Commandments.[25] The members who ordered books from Hyde were recent converts who purchased the book sight unseen, evidencing both the members' excitement about the book and their conviction that the revelations contained therein were crucial to improving their understanding of the doctrines of their newfound faith.

Printing was halted in July 1833 when tensions between Missouri Mormons and their neighbors came to a head over religious, economic, cultural, and political issues. That month Missouri vigilantes destroyed Phelps's printing office and demanded that the Mormons leave the county. A small number of sheets from the unfinished printing of the Book of Commandments were salvaged and later bound, but few copies of the volume survived the violence. Besides being scarce, the surviving volumes were also incomplete, since the vigilante activity prevented the printing of several additional revelations that appear to have been slated for inclusion.[26] Nevertheless, some early Latter-day

---

21. JS et al., Kirtland, OH, to Edward Partridge et al., Independence, MO, 25 June 1833, JS Collection, CHL.

22. Minute Book 2, 30 Apr. 1832.

23. See *JSP*, MRB:4–7.

24. "Revelations," *The Evening and the Morning Star*, May 1833, [1].

25. Hyde, Journal, 11 Sept. 1832.

26. See Appendix 1, p. 173 herein.

Saints did obtain and use the volume. Orson Pratt, for example, read from it at an 1834 baptism meeting, and in 1835, William W. Phelps counseled his wife based on a revelation found in the Book of Commandments.[27]

The Evening and the Morning Star

Though the Book of Commandments did not succeed in making the revelations widely available, printed versions of some revelations had become publicly available as early as 1832. In June of that year, before the Missouri printers began editing the revelations for the Book of Commandments, they launched the first official church newspaper, *The Evening and the Morning Star*. The *Star*'s prospectus announced it would "be devoted to the revelations of God as made known to his servants by the Holy Ghost."[28] The first three items published in the first issue of the newspaper, under the heading "Revelations," were the church's founding articles, an April 1830 revelation regarding baptism, and a March 1831 revelation on the Second Coming of Christ.[29] Ultimately, twenty-six full or partial revelation texts appeared in the *Star* between June 1832 and June 1833, reaching perhaps a few hundred subscribers. Textual studies and other evidence indicate that the versions of some revelations published in the *Star* were used as source texts when those same revelations were typeset for the Book of Commandments. The reverse was also true: printers used the typeset versions of some Book of Commandments texts as sources when typesetting revelations for the newspaper. In short, each publishing initiative in the small print shop leveraged the work being done on the other.

The paper was a crucial resource for Latter-day Saints because it was, at the time, the most accessible source for the revelations. During his ministry as a missionary, Orson Hyde recorded teaching from the account of Joseph Smith and Sidney Rigdon's vision of the degrees of heavenly glory, which was printed in the *Star*: "[I] visited a number of the Sisters and strengthened them by the word of Exhortation[.] [We] came together in the evening and we read and explained the vision to them, as the Second no. of the Star had come and it strengthened them verry much."[30] That the revelations were a prominent feature of the newspaper is evidenced by an October 1834 letter to Oliver Cowdery,

---

27. Pratt, Diary, 2 Apr. 1834; William W. Phelps, Kirtland, OH, to Sally Phelps, 11 Sept. 1835, William W. Phelps, Papers, BYU.

28. William W. Phelps, *The Evening and the Morning Star* Prospectus, *Evening and Morning Star,* June 1832 (Jan. 1835), 1–2; see also Crawley, *Descriptive Bibliography,* 1:32.

29. Articles and covenants, 10 Apr. 1830 [D&C 20]; Revelation, 16 Apr. 1830 [D&C 22]; and excerpt of Revelation, ca. 7 Mar. 1831 [D&C 45:1–67, 71], were printed in "Revelations," *The Evening and the Morning Star,* June 1832, [1]–[2].

30. Hyde, Journal, 13 Aug. 1832.

editor of the later church newspaper the *Latter Day Saints' Messenger and Advocate,* which published revelations only infrequently. "Some of our neighbors, who read your paper with us," wrote a church member, "ask why so many revelations in the papers of your predecessor, Mr. Phelps, and none in yours?"[31] The revelations were so central to the purpose of the *Star* that their absence was noted and their presence missed by readers both within the church and without.

In September 1833, two months after the destruction of the Missouri printing office, members of the United Firm met in Kirtland, Ohio, and established a press operated by the firm F. G. Williams & Co.[32] An April 1834 revelation transferred the responsibility of printing the revelations and other sacred works to this firm, under the direction of Oliver Cowdery and Frederick G. Williams.[33] F. G. Williams & Co. was largely made up of Literary Firm members, but the Literary Firm appears to have slowly faded out of existence after the expulsion of church members from Jackson County, though occasional later references to it do exist.[34]

F. G. Williams & Co. resumed publication of *The Evening and the Morning Star* in Kirtland. Although ten new issues of the *Star* were printed in Kirtland, editors did not publish any additional revelations in the paper. The twenty-fourth and final issue of the *Star* was published in Kirtland in September 1834. On the final page of that issue, a prospectus announced a forthcoming edited reprint of the newspaper, explaining that *The Evening and the Morning Star* had been valuable not only in providing access to the revelations but in documenting the growth of the church and recounting the suffering of the Mormons in Missouri. A reprint would make all these materials more widely available. The prospectus for the new publication, which was given the slightly modified title *Evening and Morning Star,* contemplated that editorial work in the reprint would be limited to the correction of typographical and other errors.[35] While editor Oliver Cowdery and others who assisted with printing *Evening and Morning Star* did take most of the text from the previously published issues, they also made substantive changes to the revelation texts.

---

31. Eli Gilbert, Huntington, CT, 24 Sept. 1834, Letter to the editor, *LDS Messenger and Advocate,* Oct. 1834, 1:10.

32. Minute Book 1, 11 Sept. 1833.

33. Revelation, 23 Apr. 1834, in Doctrine and Covenants 98:5, 1835 ed. [D&C 104:29–30].

34. For instance, David Whitmer and Samuel Smith were appointed in 1835 to be agents to the Literary Firm. (Minute Book 1, 16 Sept. 1835.) For more information on the Literary Firm, see Parkin, "Joseph Smith and the United Firm," 11–12, 31–33; and Cook, *Law of Consecration,* chap. 4.

35. "Prospectus," *The Evening and the Morning Star,* Sept. 1834, 192.

First Edition of the Doctrine and Covenants

Just as printers in Missouri had published revelations in the church newspaper at the same time they were preparing a book-length compilation of revelations, the Ohio editors who issued reprints of the *Star* were simultaneously preparing an updated compilation of revelations to succeed the Book of Commandments. Church leaders may have begun planning a successor volume as early as fall 1833, but work on the book, called the Doctrine and Covenants, did not begin in earnest until a year later. In September 1834, Joseph Smith, Sidney Rigdon, Frederick G. Williams, and Oliver Cowdery were appointed as a committee to select and arrange materials for a compilation of "items of the doctrine of Jesus Christ for the government of the church." These items were "to be taken from the bible, book of mormon, and the revelations which have been given to the church up to this date or shall be, until such arrangement is made."[36]

The committee eventually modified its approach: though revelations were printed as planned, doctrinal lectures delivered to the 1834–1835 Elders School were published instead of excerpts from the Bible and the Book of Mormon. In compiling and preparing the revelations for the Doctrine and Covenants, the committee drew primarily on Revelation Books 1 and 2 and on the Book of Commandments. As had been the case in the Missouri printing office, some cross-pollination also occurred between the newspaper and the book-length compilation: the first six issues of the reprinted *Star,* which were published from January 1835 to September 1835, contained the full or partial texts of thirteen revelations that were revised before or in connection with the publication of the Doctrine and Covenants.[37] Some revisions, therefore, appeared in *Evening and Morning Star* before they appeared in the Doctrine and Covenants, which was bound and on the market by September 1835.[38] Similarly, the eleven full or partial revelation texts that appeared in *Evening and Morning*

---

36. Minute Book 1, 24 Sept. 1834; see also pp. 303–304 herein.

37. Articles and covenants, 10 Apr. 1830 [D&C 20], and excerpt of Revelation, ca. 7 Mar. 1831 [D&C 45:1–67, 71], were printed in the June 1832 (Jan. 1835) issue of *Evening and Morning Star*. Revelation, 9 and 23 Feb. 1831 [D&C 42:12–77]; Revelation, 7 Aug. 1831 [D&C 59]; and Vision, 16 Feb. 1832 [D&C 76], were printed in the July 1832 (Feb. 1835) issue. Revelation, ca. 8 Mar. 1831–A [D&C 46], and Revelation, 9 May 1831 [D&C 50], were printed in the Aug. 1832 (Mar. 1835) issue. Revelation, Sept. 1830–A [D&C 29], and Revelation, 30 Oct. 1831 [D&C 65], were printed in the Sept. 1832 (Apr. 1835) issue. Revelation, 23 Feb. 1831 [D&C 42:78–93]; excerpt of Revelation, Feb. 1831–A [D&C 43:15–35]; and Revelation, 1 Nov. 1831–A [D&C 68], were printed in the Oct. 1832 (June 1835) issue. Revelation, 7 May 1831 [D&C 49], was printed in the Nov. 1832 (Sept. 1835) issue.

38. The seventh issue of the reprinted newspaper was not printed until April 1836, well after the publication of the Doctrine and Covenants. (*Evening and Morning Star,* Dec. 1832 [Apr. 1836], 97–112.)

Star after September 1835 corresponded with the versions previously published in the Doctrine and Covenants.

What might be seen as a purpose statement for the Doctrine and Covenants comes from the minutes of a general assembly of the church that met on 17 August 1835 to examine an advance copy of the Doctrine and Covenants. The minutes read, "It was deemed necessary to call the general assembly of the Church to see whether the book be approved or not by the authoroties of the church, that it may, if approved, become a law unto the church, and a rule of faith and practice unto the same."[39] As evidenced by the full title of the earlier compilation, *A Book of Commandments, for the Government of the Church of Christ,* the printed revelations were expected to inform church government. The destruction of the Missouri printing office had left that need largely unfulfilled, necessitating another volume that could serve as "a law unto the church" and "a rule of faith and practice." As the church grew numerically and geographically, as the ranks of leadership expanded, and as previously created leadership bodies began to assume more formal roles, expanding the revelations' availability became indispensable.

Because the 1835 volume was meant in part as a current guide to how Latter-day Saints should live their religion, some earlier revelations needed updating to reflect the latest developments in organization, doctrine, and practice. These were not the first changes to the revelations; manuscript versions of the revelations had been edited in preparation for publication in *The Evening and the Morning Star* and the Book of Commandments in 1832 and 1833. The majority of the earlier changes were intended to polish the texts for publication: versification was inserted, punctuation was added or modified, grammar was corrected, and some language was standardized. More significant alterations were also made to the revelations in 1832 and 1833, though most were limited to the addition of an occasional phrase or substitution of a word or two and largely had the effect of clarifying the language.[40]

The same patterns held true for modifications made in preparation for the 1835 volume, with most of the corrections being in the nature of copyediting. A minor subset of corrections made for the Doctrine and Covenants was more substantive in nature and often reflected changes in church government, structure, and doctrine that had occurred since the time the revelations were first

---

39. Minute Book 1, 17 Aug. 1835. The minutes were published in a condensed version as "General Assembly," in *LDS Messenger and Advocate,* Aug. 1835, 1:161–164; and "General Assembly," in Doctrine and Covenants, 1835 ed., 255–257.

40. See, for example, Revelation Book 1, pp. 42–43, in *JSP,* MRB:55–57. For further discussion of the process of editing the revelations for initial publication and analysis of the changes made, see Underwood, "Revelation, Text, and Revision," 67–84.

dictated. For instance, the church's founding articles, first recorded in April 1830, describe the roles of certain church officers.[41] New to the 1835 printing of the articles were instructions for ordaining men to the office of "president of the high priesthood, (or presiding elder,) bishop, high counsellor, and high priest."[42] When this document was voted upon by the church in June 1830, none of these offices had yet been established. As a second example, a revelation recorded circa August 1830 was greatly expanded when it was printed in the 1835 Doctrine and Covenants. The material added to the 1835 version included updated and expanded doctrine on priesthood keys that was not known at the time the revelation was originally dictated.[43] If the printed revelations were truly to be "a law unto the church, and a rule of faith and practice unto the same," only a book with the latest instruction on church government and practice would be useful.[44] The Doctrine and Covenants was intended as a living handbook, containing up-to-date instruction.

Some members of the Latter-day Saint community resisted the publication of the Doctrine and Covenants on the grounds that such a codification of belief too closely resembled a formal creed. These members believed they should rely only on inspiration and existing scripture, or as Almon Babbitt asserted, that "we have no articles of faith except the Bible."[45] The church presidency gave a firm response to these concerns in the preface to the 1835 edition: "There may be an aversion in the minds of some," they acknowledged, "against receiving any thing purporting to be articles of religious faith, in consequence of there being so many now extant." But, they wrote, "if men believe a system, and profess that it was given by inspiration, certainly the more intelligibly they can present it, the better. It does not make a principle untrue to print it."[46]

Second Edition of the Doctrine and Covenants

A few months after Joseph Smith and many church members migrated to northern Missouri in the first half of 1838, hostilities erupted between Mormons and Missouri vigilante and militia forces. The conflict led to the expulsion of virtually all practicing Mormons from Missouri. Many church members took refuge in Illinois, eventually founding a city they named Nauvoo along the banks of the Mississippi River. These hardships led some to

---

41. Articles and covenants, 10 Apr. 1830, in Revelation Book 1, pp. 52–58, in *JSP*, MRB:75–87 [D&C 20].

42. Articles and covenants, 10 Apr. 1830, in Doctrine and Covenants 2:17, 1835 ed. [D&C 20:67].

43. Compare the version of Revelation, ca. Aug. 1830 [D&C 27], found in Revelation Book 1 (*JSP*, MRB:41–43) with the version in Doctrine and Covenants 50, 1835 ed.

44. Minute Book 1, 17 Aug. 1835.

45. Minute Book 1, 19 Aug. 1834.

46. "Preface," Doctrine and Covenants, 1835 ed., [iii].

abandon the faith, even as hundreds and then thousands continued to convert in the British Isles and elsewhere. By mid-1844, there were roughly twelve thousand Mormons in Nauvoo and many others elsewhere, including nearly eight thousand in the British Isles.[47] These converts too needed access to the revelations.

In the late 1830s and early 1840s, published versions of revelations continued to appear in Latter-day Saint newspapers, pamphlets, and broadsides, though not at the same rate as in *The Evening and the Morning Star.* By early 1841, Nauvoo-based printer Ebenezer Robinson began stereotyping a second edition of the Doctrine and Covenants in the same office where the church newspaper *Times and Seasons* was published.[48] The decision to stereotype the second edition, especially in light of the struggle to sell the complete run of the first edition, speaks to leaders' conviction of the importance of the revelations.[49] In the mid-nineteenth century, books were not normally stereotyped unless they were expected to sell more than a few thousand copies or require multiple reprints.[50] Such optimism regarding the potential sales of the second edition recalls the earliest days of publishing the revelations, when the conference of 1 November 1831 determined to print ten thousand copies of the Book of Commandments. Sources indicate that one thousand copies of the 1844 edition were eventually printed, and the stereotyped plates were used again in 1845 and 1846 to print subsequent runs.[51]

Editors of the first edition of the Doctrine and Covenants were influenced by multiple source texts and in some cases made significant changes to the revelations. The second edition, in contrast, was largely a reprint of the first, with very few changes. Robinson and successors to his role drew on the 1835 edition as their only source text for most of the 1844 edition, except in the case of eight items they added, six of which were not recorded until after 1835. In 1842 Robinson sold the printing concern to Joseph Smith, who placed all

47. See May, "Demographic Portrait of the Mormons," 43; Cannon, "Migration of English Mormons to America," 441; and "General Conference," *LDS Millennial Star,* Apr. 1844, 4:194–195.

48. Stereotyping, a common nineteenth-century printing practice, was intended to speed up the process of mass printing. After setting type for a page, the printer created a mold of the type, into which he poured hot lead, thereby creating a plate from which to print each page. This allowed the individual pieces of type to be reused to set additional pages. The plates could be reused for later printings. (See Gaskell, *New Introduction to Bibliography,* 201–204.)

49. By 1836, at least five hundred copies of the first print run remained unsold. (Minute Book 1, 2 Apr. 1836.)

50. Gaskell, *New Introduction to Bibliography,* 294.

51. John Taylor, Carthage, IL, to Leonora Taylor, Nauvoo, IL, 25 June 1844, John Taylor, Collection, CHL; General Church Minutes, 8 Aug. 1844; Crawley, *Descriptive Bibliography,* 1:277–280; see also p. 641 herein.

aspects of the operation under the direction of the Quorum of the Twelve.[52] Work on the second edition of the Doctrine and Covenants was delayed such that the book was not published and available for purchase until late July or early August 1844, several weeks after Joseph Smith was killed.

Epilogue

A brief review of the question of prophetic succession that arose after Joseph Smith's death highlights two significant consequences of publishing the revelations. First, publication of the revelations led to their being increasingly subject to a wide variety of interpretations, outside of the guidance of central authorities. Second, upon Smith's death the Doctrine and Covenants increasingly emerged as a symbol of Smith's spiritual legacy and of the foundation he had laid for the church.

Several individuals or groups eventually claimed authority to succeed Joseph Smith as head of the church he founded. The primary contenders for that position in the immediate aftermath of Smith's death were Sidney Rigdon, who had been Smith's first counselor in the First Presidency, and the Quorum of the Twelve Apostles, led by quorum president Brigham Young. The formal resolution of the dispute came at an 8 August 1844 conference in Nauvoo at which the vast majority of those in attendance voted to accept the Twelve as leaders of the church. Rigdon nevertheless continued to assert his leadership claims, which led to a public excommunication proceeding held before Bishop Newel K. Whitney and the high council of Nauvoo on 8 September. The primary charges were that Rigdon had claimed to receive revelation for the church and had secretly performed ordinations.

Opening the arguments, Brigham Young explained that the trial was authorized by texts in the Doctrine and Covenants.[53] Throughout the proceedings against Rigdon, accusers grounded their remarks in Joseph Smith's revelations. They consistently argued that a protocol established during Smith's lifetime required new revelation to be presented to the quorums and approved by the leadership of the church. Rigdon, they argued, had refused to submit

---

52. See p. 639 herein.

53. "Trial of Elder Rigdon," *Times and Seasons,* 15 Sept. 1844, 5:648. Young was likely referring to Instruction on priesthood, ca. April 1835, in Doctrine and Covenants 3:37, 1844 ed. [D&C 107:82–84]. The trial was held at a public meeting area in Nauvoo with many onlookers, and the proceedings were published in *Times and Seasons,* the church's official newspaper, over the course of three issues. A summary of the trial was published in the *Nauvoo Neighbor,* the weekly newspaper of Nauvoo. ("Trial of Elder Rigdon," *Times and Seasons,* 15 Sept. 1844, 5:647–655; "Continuation of Elder Rigdon's Trial," *Times and Seasons,* 1 Oct. 1844, 5:660–667; "Conclusion of Elder Rigdon's Trial," *Times and Seasons,* 15 Oct. 1844, 5:685–687; "Trial of Elder Rigdon," *Nauvoo Neighbor,* 11 Sept. 1844, [2].)

his revelations to this process. Apostle Orson Hyde described the protocol succinctly: "There is a way by which all revelations purporting to be from God through any man can be tested. Brother Joseph gave us the plan . . . when all the quorums are assembled and organized in order, let the revelation be presented to the quorums . . . and if it pass the whole without running against a snag, you may know it is of God."[54] Another member of the Twelve, Parley P. Pratt, asserted that any new revelation or church action should be tested against the revelations given through Joseph Smith: "the old revelations require us to build this temple. . . . The new revelation [from Rigdon] is to draw the people to Pittsburg, and scatter them abroad; and do any thing and every thing but that which the old revelations bid us do."[55] The "old revelations," as Smith's dictated texts were called at the trial, were to be a gauge for any newly advanced doctrine, teaching, or revelation, and their availability in published form created a churchwide standard by which members could measure their understanding of church doctrine and practice.

In criticizing Rigdon's approach, the Twelve argued that their present focus was not to obtain new revelations but to implement the revelations already received by Joseph Smith. Pratt stated, "Now the quorum of the Twelve have not offered a new revelation from the time of the massacre of our beloved brethren, Joseph and Hyrum, but we have spent all our time, early and late, to do the things the God of heaven commanded us to do through brother Joseph."[56] But while emphasizing Joseph Smith's initiatives, the Twelve asserted that they would also be entitled to receive revelation by the means established by the martyred prophet. "Now we dont expect ever to move without revelation and they that have the keys of the kingdom can get revelation," Brigham Young declared.[57]

The importance the Twelve placed on Joseph Smith's revelations was reflected throughout the church. Local church members and congregations who supported the Twelve found justification for their positions in the revelation texts and emphasized the importance of adhering to Smith's revelations.[58]

---

54. "Trial of Elder Rigdon," *Times and Seasons,* 15 Sept. 1844, 5:649.

55. "Trial of Elder Rigdon," *Times and Seasons,* 15 Sept. 1844, 5:653. William W. Phelps made a similar statement at the trial: "The devil has blinded his [Rigdon's] eyes, and he has endeavored to blind the minds of the people against those revelations that have been our guide since we came into this church. Those revelations that said we should build the temple, in order to save ourselves and our dead, and bring to pass those keys and blessings which will secure to ourselves and our posterity the blessings which all, since the days of Adam, had lived and died for." ("Continuation of Elder Rigdon's Trial," *Times and Seasons,* 1 Oct. 1844, 5:663.)

56. "Trial of Elder Rigdon," *Times and Seasons,* 15 Sept. 1844, 5:653.

57. "Continuation of Elder Rigdon's Trial," *Times and Seasons,* 1 Oct. 1844, 5:664.

58. For example, one editorial in the New York City publication *The Prophet* quoted from several

A conference in Michigan representing fourteen church branches resolved "that we who compose the north eastern conference of Michigan, viewing the present situation of the church of Jesus Christ of Latter-day Saints, feel to sustain the present authorities of the church, the quorum of the Twelve, and others in carrying out the commandments of God, that have been given thorugh Joseph Smith, our martyred prophet."[59]

It should be noted, however, that for leaders like Brigham Young, interpretation of the printed revelations did not give sufficient authority to lead the church. The revelations, though of undeniable importance, were secondary in authority to the men who had been ordained to the priesthood and called to speak in the name of God. The minutes of Rigdon's trial record Young as saying, "As to a person not knowing more than the written word, let me tell you that there are keys that the written word never spoke of, nor never will."[60] Young later recounted a meeting in which he, at the urging of Joseph Smith, stated his views on the relative importance of the printed word of God, as revealed in the Bible, Book of Mormon, and Doctrine and Covenants: "I would not give the ashes of a rye straw for these 3 books for the salvation of any man . . . if we hadn't living oracles in our midst we had nothing [more than the] sectarian world."[61]

Nevertheless, the Doctrine and Covenants served as a proof text for several groups who traced their faith back to Smith, not just for those who followed Brigham Young and the Twelve. Sidney Rigdon's new newspaper, *Messenger and Advocate of the Church of Christ,* opened with a letter written by a Rigdon supporter that used almost a dozen quotations or citations from the 1844 edition of the Doctrine and Covenants to argue for Rigdon's authority. Citing passages regarding the role of the Twelve, the letter's author, John Forgeus, interpreted Smith's revelations in Rigdon's favor. Speaking of followers of the Twelve generally, Forgeus asserted they were "honest, industrious and good citizens, but nevertheless, I know they have been duped in regard to following the counsel of men, instead of following the commandments of God, as given through Joseph Smith."[62] Other individuals claiming rightful succession or authority to lead also relied on revelations in the Doctrine and Covenants to

passages of the Doctrine and Covenants to support an argument in favor of the Twelve and against Rigdon. ("Church Government," *The Prophet,* 2 Nov. 1844, [2].)

59. "Minutes of a Conference," *Times and Seasons,* 1 Dec. 1844, 5:726.

60. "Continuation of Elder Rigdon's Trial," *Times and Seasons,* 1 Oct. 1844, 5:667.

61. George D. Watt, Sermon shorthand notes, 8 Oct. 1866, George D. Watt, Papers, CHL, as transcribed by LaJean Purcell Carruth.

62. John A. Forgeus to Samuel L. Forgeus, 25 Sept. 1844, *Messenger and Advocate of the Church of Christ,* 15 Oct. 1844, 10.

justify their positions. James J. Strang presented an "Epistle" to the "Elders of the Church" in which he cited the Doctrine and Covenants over twenty times and quoted a dozen excerpts from the revelations. Strang counseled the elders to remember "the words of the Lord by the mouth of the Prophet Joseph: that you be not deceived, that you receive not the teachings of any that come before you as revelations and commandments, except they come in at the gate and be ordained according to the command of God."[63] Other groups or individuals also relied on their interpretations of revelations in the Doctrine and Covenants to justify following (or not following) various leaders.[64]

Despite the wide variety of conflicting arguments advanced by or on behalf of would-be successors to Joseph Smith, individuals who wrote or talked about succession matters did agree that church government and practice should follow the revelations. As Mormons chose new leaders and continued their practice of the faith Joseph Smith had founded, they grounded decisions in the revelations he had left behind. In the absence of the founding revelator, they followed the textual witness of Joseph Smith's calling: the published revelations.

---

63. "An Epistle," *Voree Herald,* Jan. 1846, [1]–[3].

64. A survey of the use of the Doctrine and Covenants by the different branches of Mormonism has yet to be produced, but the practice of looking to the revelations for justification was widespread. One individual recalled, "I have been in different organizations at different times . . . but when in each of these organizations I supposed I was under the church. When I found out that they were teaching or practice-ing anything that was not authorized by the church prior to 1844 as the law is set forth in the bible, the book of Mormon, and the book of doctrine and covenants, why I left it at once." (Jason W. Briggs, Testimony, Denver, CO, 8 June 1892, p. 606, question 377, in United States Circuit Court [8th Circuit], *Reorganized Church of Jesus Christ of Latter Day Saints v. Church of Christ of Independence, Missouri, et al.,* typescript at CHL.)

Editorial Method

The goal of the Joseph Smith Papers Project is to present verbatim transcripts of Joseph Smith's papers in their entirety, making available the most essential sources of Smith's life and work and preserving the content of aging manuscripts from damage or loss. The papers include documents that were created by Joseph Smith, whether written or dictated by him or created by others under his direction, or that were owned by Smith, that is, received by him and kept in his office (as with incoming correspondence). Under these criteria—authorship and ownership—the project intends to publish, either in letterpress volumes or electronic form, every extant Joseph Smith document to which its editors can obtain access. This volume—the second in the Revelations and Translations series—presents the most significant early published versions of the revelations dictated by Joseph Smith.

Texts Presented as Photographic Facsimiles

Three texts featured in this volume are presented as photographic facsimiles: the Book of Commandments (1833), the first edition of the Doctrine and Covenants (1835), and seven sections of the second edition of the Doctrine and Covenants (1844) not found in the first edition. Because these printed texts can be easily read, the photographic facsimiles presented in this volume are not transcribed. For these texts, line numbers have been editorially supplied to the left of each photograph, and annotation on the bottom of the page is keyed to specific line numbers. This volume also includes, as Appendix 2, photographic facsimiles of selected pages of Oliver Cowdery's copy of the Book of Commandments.

Though a number of original copies of the Book of Commandments and the first and second editions of the Doctrine and Covenants are extant, of necessity only one copy of each publication was selected for presentation in this volume. In each case, the editors selected a copy with a completely intact text block and with a binding that would not be damaged from wear during photography. The selected copies of these publications, besides being featured herein, are the copies cited or referenced throughout *The Joseph Smith Papers*.

Though this volume includes many photographic facsimiles, it has not been designated as a "Facsimile Edition." That label, first used for the oversize version of the initial volume in the Revelations and Translations series, is reserved for volumes of *The Joseph Smith Papers* that are printed in full color and that present a photographic facsimile of a manuscript on the left page of each spread with a corresponding typographic facsimile on the right. The purpose of this volume is to reproduce the original typeset text within the selected copies, not to feature the selected copies as artifacts or to fully identify the characteristics that make them unique apart from all other copies.

The textual photographs herein were created specifically for this publication and its web counterpart by Welden C. Andersen, a lead photographer for the Audiovisual Department of The Church of Jesus Christ of Latter-day Saints. The process Andersen used to create the photographs was the same as that described in the facsimile edition of the first volume of the Revelations and Translations series (see *JSP*, MRB:xxxvii). During photography, many pages of the original artifacts were held flat with a microspatula (see figure below).

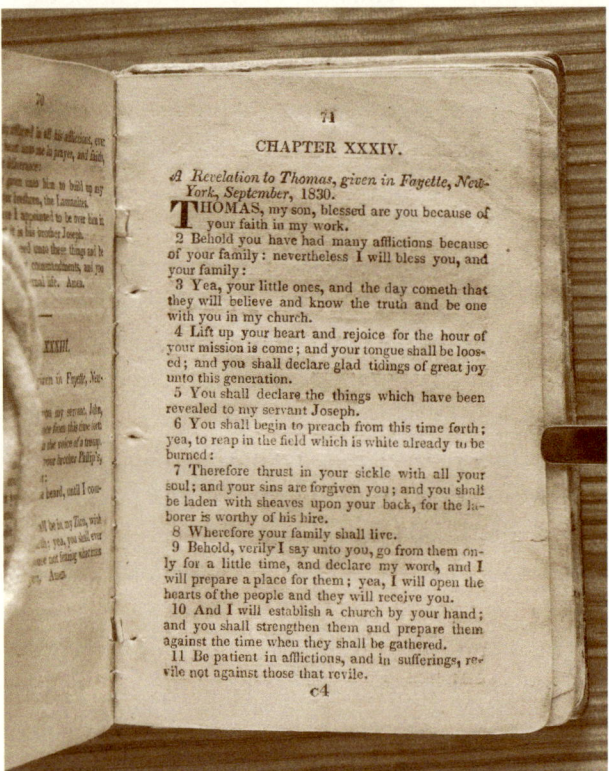

Creating texual photographs. Many pages of the original artifacts featured herein were held flat with a microspatula during photography. In this photograph, the opposite side of the volume can be seen opened to just beyond ninety degrees, with a weighted string holding the pages back. In the images published in this volume, the spatula was digitally removed and the image was cropped to the page being photographed. Book of Commandments, p. 71, Church History Library, Salt Lake City.

Charles M. Baird, a prepress specialist with the Materials Management Department of The Church of Jesus Christ of Latter-day Saints, and Riley M. Lorimer, a typesetter and production editor for the Joseph Smith Papers Project, prepared the images for printing. They used a process similar to that used for the facsimile edition of the first volume of the Revelations and Translations series (see *JSP*, MRB:xxxviii–xxxix), but with two differences. First, whereas the images in the earlier volume were printed in full color, Baird prepared this volume's images to be printed in duotone, a format that combines two colors (in this case, Pantone brown 1545 and Pantone yellow 123). While these duotone images do not precisely match the colors of the original pages, they are an approximate match and convey the richness and depth of the original documents much better than black-and-white images. Second, for the earlier volume, Baird used photo-editing software to crop the images to the edge of the manuscript book, which allowed users to see each page in the context of the book as a whole. For this volume, Lorimer applied a template to each image to crop each page to its edges. For aesthetic reasons, the template uses slightly rounded, rather than square, page corners. The photographic facsimiles in this volume are enlarged beyond the original document dimensions to aid in readability. For the original dimensions, consult the source notes preceding each document herein.

Except as described in this note, the textual photographs in this volume have not been altered.

Additional Texts

While Appendix 1 contains what appears to be the transcript of an existing text, this appendix is in fact a reconstruction of the text that likely would have been included as the sixth and final gathering of the Book of Commandments if the Missouri printing office had not been destroyed. For the editorial conventions related to this proposed sixth gathering, see the Note on Editorial Method that precedes the reconstructed text (pages 176–177 herein).

The revelations published in *The Evening and the Morning Star* and its reprint, *Evening and Morning Star,* are transcribed in this volume. Presenting these revelations as transcripts allows a side-by-side format to facilitate comparison. For the guidelines editors followed in transcribing these revelations, see the Note on Editorial Method that precedes the transcripts (pages 199–201 herein).

Transcription Symbols

Most of the information related to transcription methodology, including the meaning of transcription symbols, is detailed in the two aforementioned editorial notes in the body of this volume. A few transcription symbols, however, are used in source notes and other annotation:

[roman]	Brackets enclose editorial insertions that expand, correct, or clarify the text.
[roman]	Stylized brackets represent brackets used in the original text.
|	A line break artificially imposed in the original manuscript is rendered as a vertical line in editorial matter.

Annotation Conventions

This volume is a textual and not a historical study. Annotation in this volume focuses on explaining the production and printing history of the publications and on identifying each discrete revelation text within a publication. For extensive historical analysis and context, readers should consult the Documents series under the date of each item.

A footnote at the beginning of each discrete revelation text supplies the standard editorial title and date for the revelation or other item. A footnote also identifies, when known, the source text or texts that editors and printers used for that particular item. When identifying a source text for a particular item, footnotes often state that the version at hand "corresponds" or "closely corresponds" to an earlier text, suggesting that the earlier version was used as a source text for the version at hand. "Corresponds" and "closely corresponds" are editorial shorthand. If a text "corresponds" to another text, the versions match enough to establish a filial relationship, but at least two substantive changes appear in the later version. A substantive change—an addition, deletion, substitution, or other revision that alters meaning—can be as small as substituting one word for another or can be larger, encompassing the revision of a phrase or even the addition of one or more paragraphs. If a text "closely corresponds" to another text, the versions are essentially identical, with the exception of changes in capitalization, minor changes in punctuation, and no more than one word- or phrase-level revision. Some textual elements tend to vary so much between versions that they were not taken into account when establishing filial relationships between texts. These elements are introductory headings, versification, and the inclusion of surnames. Detailed discussion of the analysis that led to the determination of any particular source text is outside the scope of this volume.

Annotation clarifies the text only rarely. Marginalia is explained when the meaning of the inscription is known and is especially relevant. In the two cases in which entire lines of text are missing because of an original printing error, the missing text is transcribed from another copy of the publication and provided in a footnote (see pages 461 and 464 herein). When the dates and places associated with the original dictation of a revelation are incorrect in the original publications, the errors are corrected in annotation. The Documents series provides additional information on creation dates and places of dictation. In referring to people, the Book of Commandments usually includes first names only. For the full names, readers should consult the corresponding texts in the 1835 Doctrine and Covenants. In both editions of the Doctrine and Covenants, the original compilers sometimes replaced personal names, place names, and other words with substitute words, in order to obscure certain information from the public. For detailed information on the location of substitute words and on the original words they replaced, see pages 708–711 herein.

Certain conventions simplify the presentation of the annotation. Joseph Smith is usually referred to by the initials JS. The terms *Saint, Latter-day Saint,* and *Mormon*—all used by mid-1834 in reference to church members—are employed interchangeably here. Most sources are referred to by a shortened citation form, with a complete citation given in the Works Cited. Some documents are referred to by editorial titles rather than by their original titles or the titles given in the catalogs of their current repositories. The editorial titles are listed in the Works Cited along with the complete citations by which the documents can be found in repositories.

The annotation extensively cites Joseph Smith's revelations. In the 1830s, Smith and his followers used the terms *commandment* and *revelation* to refer to these dictations that they viewed as divine communications. Usage patterns in early documents suggest that in the earliest years, Latter-day Saints may have seen subtle differences in the meaning of these terms: *commandment* may have denoted communications that required action or obedience, whereas *revelation* may have referred to communications on doctrinal topics. During the mid-1830s, *revelation*—the term used throughout *The Joseph Smith Papers* to refer to these works—became standard. Many of these revelations were first collected and published in 1833, with numbered chapters and paragraphs (or verses), as the Book of Commandments. An expanded collection, organized into sections and with new versification, was published in 1835 as the Doctrine and Covenants. In 1844, at the time of his death, Joseph Smith was overseeing publication of a revised edition of the Doctrine and Covenants, which was published later that year. Since then, the Doctrine and Covenants has been published in several editions, some including newly canonized revelations or other items.

Source citations in this volume identify revelations by their original date and by a citation of the version most relevant to the particular instance of annotation (usually a version found in one of the publications featured in this volume). In cases in which two or more revelations bear the same date, such as April 1829, a letter of the alphabet is appended so that each revelation has a unique editorial title—for example, April 1829–A or April 1829–B. Revelation citations also include a bracketed "D&C" reference that provides the Doctrine and Covenants section and verse numbers that have been standard in The Church of Jesus Christ of Latter-day Saints since 1876 (see figure on following page).

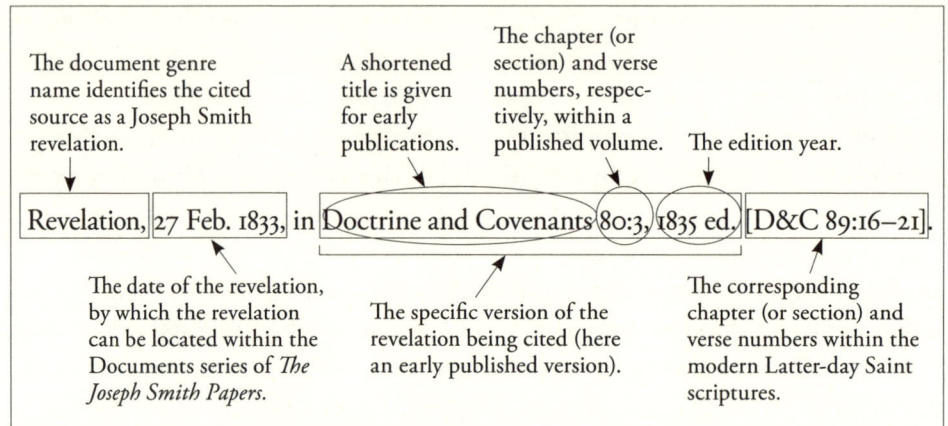

The document genre name identifies the cited source as a Joseph Smith revelation.

A shortened title is given for early publications.

The chapter (or section) and verse numbers, respectively, within a published volume.

The edition year.

Revelation, 27 Feb. 1833, in Doctrine and Covenants 80:3, 1835 ed. [D&C 89:16–21].

The date of the revelation, by which the revelation can be located within the Documents series of *The Joseph Smith Papers.*

The specific version of the revelation being cited (here an early published version).

The corresponding chapter (or section) and verse numbers within the modern Latter-day Saint scriptures.

Citation format for Joseph Smith revelations.

Bracketed D&C references are provided for the benefit of Latter-day Saints, who can easily access the revelations in their familiar canon of scriptural works, and other students of early Mormonism who may wish to access the most widely available editions of these revelations. A table titled Corresponding Published Versions of Revelations is provided following the Works Cited to help readers refer from the cited version of a revelation to other published versions of the same revelation.

This volume includes a Directory of Printers that identifies many of the people who assisted in compiling, editing, and printing the publications featured in this volume and provides brief biographies of some of these people. Other people whose names appear in this volume are not identified in the directory. Readers seeking more information about such individuals should consult the biographical directory on the Joseph Smith Papers website, josephsmithpapers.org, or in other printed volumes of *The Joseph Smith Papers.* Complete documentation for the reference material in the back of the volume will be made available at the Joseph Smith Papers website, as will other resources, including a complete calendar of Joseph Smith's papers.

PUBLISHED
REVELATIONS

Book of Commandments. In 1832, William W. Phelps, Oliver Cowdery, and John Whitmer began printing a book-length compilation of Joseph Smith's revelations. By July 1833, they had printed sixty-five chapters on 160 pages, but the work was never completed because the printing office was destroyed. Church members saved sheets of the unbound volume and later had copies individually bound. The copy shown here and reproduced in this volume was owned by Wilford Woodruff. Church History Library, Salt Lake City.

BOOK OF COMMANDMENTS

Source Note

A Book of Commandments, for the Government of the Church of Christ, Organized according to Law, on the 6th of April, 1830; *Zion [Independence], MO: W. W. Phelps & Co., 1833; incomplete (printing interrupted); [1]–160 pp.; includes typeset signature marks and copyright notice. The copy presented herein is held at CHL; includes 22 pages of handwritten texts; also includes early and later marginalia as well as archival stamps and notations.*

This book was printed in sextodecimo format on five sheets and folded into five gatherings of sixteen leaves (thirty-two pages) each, making a text block of 160 pages. The sheets were probably printed using a work-and-turn technique, yielding two copies of the same gathering for each sheet. In the copy of the book featured in this volume, three nonprinted gatherings were also bound with the printed gatherings: two folio gatherings of two leaves each, and an octavo gathering of eight leaves, which includes the back pastedown. The pages of the book featured herein measure 4½ × 3⅛ inches (11 × 8 cm), but these dimensions vary somewhat in other extant copies of the volume. The book's final printed gathering ends on page 160, partway through the revelation labeled "CHAPTER LXV." That at least one more gathering was intended is evident from several sources, including editing marks made in Revelation Book 1, which was the source text for much of the Book of Commandments.[1] Changes made during printing resulted in variations among known copies of the Book of Commandments, the most obvious of which are the differences found on the title page.[2]

Because destruction of the print shop halted printing and destroyed most of the stock before any books were bound, the bindings of the surviving copies vary. The copy presented in this volume, which belonged to early church member and leader Wilford Woodruff, measures 4½ × 3¼ × ⅞ inches (11 × 8 × 2 cm). The cover is made from heavy paperboard material and bound in brown leather, which is now worn. In both the material and the manner of binding, the binding is similar to that of Woodruff's first journal, which was begun sometime in late 1834, suggesting both books were bound at the same time.[3] The thread used in sewing the volume is visible along the spine of the book. A piece of blue-lined paper, measuring 1⅞ × 2⅛ inches (5 × 5 cm), is pasted to the outside front cover of this copy of the Book of Commandments. "No. 1" is written in red ink on this label, and an additional notation, reading "Book of Commandments", is written in graphite. On the inside front cover, a notation written in black ink

---

1. See Appendix 1, p. 173 herein; see also Phelps, "Short History," [3]; and Frederick G. Williams, Kirtland, OH, to John Murdock, 10 Oct. 1833, in JS Letterbook 1, pp. 61–62.

2. The title page of the Book of Commandments appears in two different formats, the first without a decorative border. Sometime during the printing, a border was inserted, forcing the compositor to compress the spaces between and within the lines of text. See pages 13 and 600 herein for examples of the two iterations. A systematic analysis of printing variants among extant copies of the Book of Commandments is beyond the scope of this volume.

3. Wilford Woodruff, Journal, 1834–1838, Wilford Woodruff, Journals and Papers, CHL.

in Thomas Bullock's hand reads "Presented to the | Historian's Office | by Wilford Woodruff | July 19 54 [July 19, 1854]". In the center of the same page, a library notation that was written in ink but has since been erased reads "No 904". The recto of the front flyleaf bears a notation in graphite, apparently in Woodruff's handwriting: "Wilford | Woodruff | Woodruff". On this same page, a stamp applied sideways in purple ink reads "HISTO[RI]AN'S OFFICE. | Chur[ch] of Jesus Christ | of Latter-day Saints." The same stamp appears on the copyright page three pages later, at the bottom of page 60, and on the inside back cover. The flyleaf's verso bears several inscriptions: Woodruff's signature (with the first name spelled "Willford") in black ink near the top of the page; "Tuskalusa | Allabama" in graphite in the middle of the page; and "6" followed by an illegible character, both written sideways in black ink roughly three-quarters down the page. On eleven of the twelve blank leaves he bound into the back of this book, Woodruff copied the remaining text of the partially printed chapter 65, another revelation, and several hymns.[4] Because this volume of *The Joseph Smith Papers* presents the revelations in their printed form, Woodruff's later handwritten additions are not included herein.

Woodruff likely acquired this copy of the Book of Commandments on 12 August 1834.[5] He appears to have retained this volume until he donated it to the Church Historian's Office on 19 July 1854. Library markings indicate the volume has remained in continuous church custody.[6]

Historical Introduction

Church leaders took the first formal step toward printing the Book of Commandments at a conference of elders at Hiram, Ohio, on 1 November 1831. The minutes for this conference open with a request from Oliver Cowdery that the conference determine "the mind of the Lord" on the subject of how many copies to print. The conference decided to publish ten thousand copies.[7] This resolution was likely the product of prior discussion, but no record of any such discussion exists.

A July 1831 revelation had already appointed William W. Phelps to be church printer and Cowdery to assist him.[8] Phelps acquired a printing press and type in Cincinnati, Ohio, en route to Independence, Jackson County, Missouri, where he and his family settled in early 1832.[9] The previous summer, Edward Partridge purchased a lot near the center of town

---

4. The twelfth leaf is the back pastedown, which Woodruff left blank. He completed Revelation, 11 September 1831 [D&C 64], and copied in full Revelation, 27 February 1833 [D&C 89], after which he copied eight hymns, four of which he gave headings. Each hymn was printed in *The Evening and the Morning Star*, and all four of Woodruff's hymn headings match the headings given in the *Star*. The hymn that begins "Age after age has roll'd away" was printed in the May 1833 issue of the *Star;* "The great and glorious gospel light," in July 1833; "Ere long the vail will rend in twain," in May 1833; "Come ye children of the kingdom," in April 1833; "My soul is full of peace and love," in June 1833; "The happy day has rolled on," in June 1833; "Beyond these earthly scenes in sight," in July 1832; and "There is a land the Lord will bless," in September 1834.

5. Whitmer, Daybook, 12 Aug. 1834.

6. "1303" is written in black ink on the bottom of page [3]. This number corresponds to an entry made sometime after 1930 in an early Church Historian's Office catalog book. In addition, the Church Historian's Office stamp used to mark several pages of the volume appears to have been in use in the late nineteenth century and possibly in the early twentieth century. ("Library Record," book no. 1303.)

7. Minute Book 2, 1 Nov. 1831.

8. Revelation, 20 July 1831, in Doctrine and Covenants 27:5, 1835 ed. [D&C 57:11–13]. An earlier revelation appointed Phelps to assist Cowdery in printing the revelations. (Revelation, 14 June 1831, in Doctrine and Covenants 68:2, 1835 ed. [D&C 55:4].)

9. JS History, vol. A-1, 154. After the Independence printing office was destroyed in summer 1833,

upon which the building that likely became the printing office already stood.[10] Cowdery, who arrived in Missouri shortly before Phelps, wrote to JS on 28 January 1832 that they were nearly ready to begin printing and hoped that Martin Harris could supply the paper.[11] The following month, Phelps issued a printed prospectus for an official church newspaper to be titled *The Evening and the Morning Star*,[12] indicating that by this time the press was functional despite a shortage of paper.[13] A revelation dictated by JS in Ohio on 20 March 1832, in response to the above letter from Cowdery, directed Bishop Newel K. Whitney to purchase printing paper—by credit if necessary—and JS and his associates to transport it to Missouri. They did so, purchasing paper in Wheeling, Virginia (now West Virginia), around the first of April 1832 and arriving in Missouri later that month.[14] In May, after JS had departed on the return journey to Ohio, Phelps, Cowdery, John Whitmer, and several others met at the printing office, which was located south of the courthouse and public square, to formally dedicate the building and the materials.[15] Active publishing began the following month, when issues of the *Star* first began to appear. Around this same time, the Mormon printing office also began to publish issues of the *Upper Missouri Advertiser*, a community newspaper.[16]

While JS and other leaders were in Missouri in April 1832, the Literary Firm met. Acting in their capacity as overseers of church publications, the firm decided to reduce the

---

Phelps claimed that five thousand pounds of type had been lost, which would have been about five times the amount normally on hand in a printing office at this time. (Declaration, in Missouri Circuit Court [5th Circuit], Feb. 1834 term, *Phelps and Cowdery v. Olmstead et al.*, Jackson County Records Center, Independence, MO; Stower, *Printer's Grammar*, 57, as excerpted in Rummonds, *Nineteenth-Century Printing Practices*, 1:232.)

10. Jackson Co., MO, Deed Records, bk. A, pp. 111–113, microfilm 1,017,978, U.S. and Canada Record Collection, FHL; see also Berrett, *Sacred Places*, 4:51–52.

11. Oliver Cowdery, Independence, MO, to JS, Kirtland Mills, OH, 28 Jan. 1832, JS Collection, CHL. In a postscript and a now-missing notation to be used as a bill or receipt, Cowdery apparently informed JS how much paper should be purchased in order to provide enough stock for ten thousand copies of the Book of Commandments.

12. The prospectus for *The Evening and the Morning Star*, dated 23 February 1832 and no longer extant, was included as the first item in the first issue of the later, Ohio-based *Evening and Morning Star*. (William W. Phelps, *The Evening and the Morning Star* Prospectus, *Evening and Morning Star*, June 1832 [Jan. 1835], 1–2; see also Phelps, "Short History," [2]–[3]; and "To Man," *The Evening and the Morning Star*, June 1832, [6].)

13. The next known publication of the press was a political circular (no longer extant) dated 21 May 1832. (Lilburn W. Boggs, "To the People of Missouri," *Missouri Intelligencer*, 2 June 1832, [2]; Crawley, *Descriptive Bibliography*, 1:33.)

14. Revelation, 20 Mar. 1832, in Newel K. Whitney, Papers, BYU; Newel K. Whitney, Statement, ca. 1842, Historian's Office, JS History Documents, CHL; Minute Book 2, 30 Apr. 1832. It is unknown exactly how much paper JS and his associates brought to Missouri, but Phelps and Cowdery listed the total amount of paper lost in the July 1833 destruction of the printing office at one hundred reams. If Phelps and Cowdery's accounting is accurate, it is unclear whether the listed one hundred reams of paper was only the amount that was lost or was the total amount of paper brought to Missouri. (Declaration, in Missouri Circuit Court [5th Circuit], Feb. 1834 term, *Phelps and Cowdery v. Olmstead et al.*, Jackson County Records Center, Independence, MO.)

15. Minute Book 2, 29 May 1832; Berrett, *Sacred Places*, 4:51–52.

16. Crawley, *Descriptive Bibliography*, 1:34–35.

original print run of ten thousand copies to three thousand, a decision probably based on the amount of paper that had been purchased and brought to Missouri.[17] The firm appointed a committee of three individuals—William W. Phelps, Oliver Cowdery, and John Whitmer—"to review the Book of Commandmants [that is, the "Book of Commandments & Revelations," or Revelation Book 1] & select for printing such as shall be deemed by them proper, as dictated by the Spirit & make all necessary verbal corrections."[18] The committee acted upon that instruction by both selecting and revising manuscripts, using Revelation Book 1 as their primary source text. The committee did not include all items found in Revelation Book 1; some items therein were explicitly marked for exclusion from the Book of Commandments, and some others bear no such mark but were nonetheless excluded.[19] The title page of the Book of Commandments indicates that the book was printed by W. W. Phelps & Co., and while Phelps is traditionally recognized as the publisher and printer, all three individuals appointed to review the revelations contributed to the work of printing the Book of Commandments.[20]

Many of the revelations in the Book of Commandments appear in Revelation Book 1 with editing marks that were made in preparation for the publication. Revelation Book 1 was not, however, the sole source for the Book of Commandments. One revelation and part of another that appear in the Book of Commandments do not appear in Revelation Book 1; the manuscript sources for these revelations are unknown.[21] Furthermore, some revelations that appeared in the Book of Commandments had been printed earlier in *The Evening and the Morning Star.* When revelations had already been printed in the *Star,* the editors appear to have used the newspaper, rather than Revelation Book 1, to set type for the Book of Commandments.[22]

---

17. Minute Book 2, 30 Apr. 1832. Assuming that the Book of Commandments was to comprise six gatherings (with two identical gatherings printed on each sheet), and assuming five hundred sheets per ream, a print run of ten thousand copies of the Book of Commandments would require sixty reams, whereas a print run of three thousand copies would require eighteen reams. Paper was expensive and in short supply and would need to be divided among several printing projects. Besides the Book of Commandments and the two newspapers, an almanac and a hymnal were also planned (but ultimately neither was published in Missouri). It is possible JS and his companions purchased the paper on credit, which could suggest they did not have sufficient funds to purchase the amount of paper originally contemplated. (See Revelation, 20 Mar. 1832, in Newel K. Whitney, Papers, BYU.)

18. Minute Book 2, 30 Apr. 1832.

19. See, for example, Explanation of scripture, ca. Dec. 1830, in Revelation Book 1, pp. 60–61, in *JSP,* MRB:91–93 [D&C 74], which bears the notation "Not to be printed." Revelation, ca. early 1830, in Revelation Book 1, pp. 30–31, in *JSP,* MRB:31–33, which bears no such notation, was also omitted from the Book of Commandments. That there was a systematic review of Revelation Book 1 is suggested by a notation on page 76 of Revelation Book 1: "Compared thus far by J[ohn Whitmer] & O[liver Cowdery]."

20. Late in his life Phelps stated, "I was ordained and appointed to take the lead in printing, as printer to the church . . . with Oliver Cowdery and John Whitmer as my assistants." (Phelps, "Short History," [2]–[3]; see also Oliver Cowdery, Kirtland, OH, to William W. Phelps, [Clay Co., MO], [30 Mar. 1834], in Cowdery, Letterbook, 36–38; and Declaration, in Missouri Circuit Court [5th Circuit], Feb. 1834 term, *Phelps and Cowdery v. Olmstead et al.,* Jackson County Records Center, Independence, MO.)

21. Revelation, May 1829–B, in Book of Commandments 11 [D&C 12]; Revelation, 23 Feb. 1831, in Book of Commandments 47 [D&C 42:78–93].

22. See "Table 1: Relationship between Items in Revelation Book 1 and *The Evening and the Morning*

The incomplete Book of Commandments contains most of the revelations known to have been dictated by JS through September 1831, organized largely chronologically. Seven items that were dictated before September 1831 and copied into Revelation Book 1 were not published in the Book of Commandments.[23]

The apparent intent of editorial work on the revelations—and in any case, the result of that work—was primarily to polish the revelations for publication. Most of the editorial revisions were in the nature of copyediting changes: inserting versification; standardizing language; correcting punctuation, capitalization, grammar, and spelling. A smaller subset of revisions was significant, usually involving the addition of a phrase or the substitution of a word or two.[24] In a few cases, revisions served to update the revelations to reflect changes that had occurred in church government or policy since the time the revelations were first dictated, but such updating was not done systematically. In the majority of cases, revelations that could have been up-

Source texts. The principal source texts for the Book of Commandments (top of stack) were Revelation Book 1 (middle) and various issues of *The Evening and the Morning Star* (bound collection, bottom). Church History Library, Salt Lake City.

dated were not. For example, although the first ordinations to the office of high priest had occurred in June 1831,[25] the editors preparing the Book of Commandments for publication did not introduce the term "high priest" into revelations predating June 1831 where it would have been logical to do so. A 9 February 1831 revelation, for instance, states that the bishop

---

Star," in *JSP,* MRB.695–697. In most cases, the revelations as published in the *Star* were typeset from Revelation Book 1.

23. Within Revelation Book 1, see the following: Revelation, ca. June 1829, pp. 23–24, in *JSP,* MRB:21–23; Revelation, ca. early 1830, pp. 30–31, in *JSP,* MRB:31–33; Explanation of scripture, ca. Dec. 1830, pp. 60–61, in *JSP,* MRB:91–93 [D&C 74]; Revelation, 15 May 1831, p. 85, in *JSP,* MRB:143; Revelation, 20 May 1831, pp. 86–87, in *JSP,* MRB:145–147 [D&C 51]; and Revelation, 20 July 1831, pp. 93–94, in *JSP,* MRB:159–161 [D&C 57]. The seventh revelation in this category is Revelation, June 1829–E [D&C 17]. A partial index to Revelation Book 1 indicates that this revelation was copied on page 25 of the manuscript book, but the page on which it was inscribed is among those now missing. (See Revelation Book 1, p. [207], in *JSP,* MRB:385.) There is no apparent pattern among these seven items to explain why they were not published.

24. See p. xxx herein. For a list of revelations published in the Book of Commandments identifying the types of editing marks made in Revelation Book 1 to prepare each revelation for publication, see "Table 2: Relationship between Items in Revelation Book 1 and the Book of Commandments," in *JSP,* MRB:697–700.

25. Minute Book 2, 3 June 1831.

is to be assisted in certain duties by the elders. In 1835, as part of an effort to update the revelations to reflect changes in church government and policy, this language was expanded to clarify that the high priests are also to assist in these duties.[26] The update presumably could have been made earlier, for inclusion in the Book of Commandments, but was not. In fact, the office of high priest is not mentioned anywhere in the Book of Commandments. More systematic updating of the revelations to reflect changes in church government and policy occurred two years later in connection with the publication of the Doctrine and Covenants.[27]

Printing standards of the day called for printers to recopy heavily edited manuscripts to provide a clean copy for typesetting.[28] Some of the text of Revelation Book 1 was almost certainly recopied before the Book of Commandments was typeset, as evidenced by differences between the text in the marked-up Revelation Book 1 and the final printed Book of Commandments.[29]

The Independence print shop was small enough that it likely carried only one size of paper. Considering this, the Book of Commandments was likely printed on royal-size paper, which measures approximately 25 × 20 inches (64 × 51 cm), because *The Evening and the Morning Star* was printed on royal quarto (a royal-size sheet folded twice, yielding four leaves approximately 12½ × 10 inches [32 × 25 cm] each).[30] Had the Book of Commandments, which was printed in sextodecimo format, been printed on royal-size paper with a sheetwise technique (one gathering per sheet), the process would have yielded sixteen leaves measuring approximately 6¼ × 5 inches (16 × 13 cm) each, a page size significantly larger than was needed for the Book of Commandments, which measures approximately 4½ × 3⅛ inches (11 × 8 cm) (allowing for small variations in page size for different copies). This is not an impossibility, because the excess paper around the margins could have been trimmed. However, some untrimmed or partially untrimmed extant copies of the Book of Commandments have roughly half an inch (1 cm) of excess paper (beyond the point where the edge should be trimmed) on the bottom of the leaves, suggesting a far more likely scenario: If a work-and-turn technique (printing two copies of the same gathering per sheet)

---

26. Revelation, 9 Feb. 1831, in Book of Commandments 44:26, 54 [D&C 42:31, 71]; Revelation, 9 Feb. 1831, in Doctrine and Covenants 13:8, 19, 1835 ed. [D&C 42:31, 71].

27. See p. 306 herein.

28. De Vinne, *Printer's Price-List,* 402, as excerpted in Rummonds, *Nineteenth-Century Printing Practices,* 2:822–823.

29. The mark-up of Revelation Book 1, including versification, does not always match the final version of the text printed in the Book of Commandments. While it is technically possible that the discrepancies between the texts as edited in Revelation Book 1 and as printed in the Book of Commandments could have resulted from corrections introduced in the galley proof stage (the stage at which the typeset page was proofed for the last time), the amount of labor that would be involved in changing versification and paragraphing in galleys strongly suggests that these discrepancies were introduced on an interim copy rather than in galleys.

30. MacKellar, *American Printer,* 271, as excerpted in Rummonds, *Nineteenth-Century Printing Practices,* 1:459. The paper size for *The Evening and the Morning Star* was noted in its prospectus, and measurements of extant copies confirm that the paper was indeed printed on royal quarto–size paper. (William W. Phelps, *The Evening and the Morning Star* Prospectus, *Evening and Morning Star,* June 1832 [Jan. 1835], 1–2.)

had been used, each sheet would have yielded thirty-two leaves measuring 5 × 3⅛ inches (13 × 8 cm) each, leaving only half an inch to be trimmed from each leaf.

Textual and other sources suggest time frames in which the individual gatherings of the Book of Commandments were likely typeset and printed. In this regard, analyzing the filial relationship between common texts in Revelation Book 1, the Book of Commandments, and *The Evening and the Morning Star* is especially useful.[31] Though editors of the Book of Commandments could have started printing that volume in late April 1832 (after the paper arrived from Virginia) or June 1832 (when the first issue of the *Star* was printed), analysis of typefaces used at the Missouri printing office suggests that typesetting for the first gathering (pages 1–32) began no earlier than November 1832.[32] At the latest, typesetting and printing began in December 1832, the month a notice in the *Star* stated that the Book of Commandments was "now Printing" and would "be published as soon as the Lord will."[33]

The second gathering (pages 33–64) was of course printed after the first, meaning after December 1832. Moreover, independent textual evidence definitively places the typesetting date of the second gathering after September 1832.[34] The third gathering (pages 65–96) was printed sometime after January 1833 and before circa May 1833.[35] The fourth (pages

---

31. Because the Book of Commandments and *The Evening and the Morning Star* share a common source (Revelation Book 1) for many texts, and because different layers of editing within Revelation Book 1 clearly pertain to one published version or the other, it is often possible to determine whether a particular text was first printed in the Book of Commandments or in the *Star*.

32. The first six issues of *The Evening and the Morning Star* (June through November 1832) were printed in two sizes of type: long primer (about 10 point) and brevier (about 8 point). Beginning with the December 1832 issue and continuing for the remainder of the Missouri publication, the newspaper was printed in only long primer. Because the Book of Commandments was printed in brevier size, it is likely that the printers stopped using brevier for the newspaper in November 1832 so they could use it instead for the Book of Commandments. While it is not known how much type the Missouri printers began the operation with, they apparently started running out of brevier while typesetting two different gatherings of the Book of Commandments (see pp. 106 and 138 herein), suggesting a supply limited enough that it could not support two printing projects at once.

33. Notice, *The Evening and the Morning Star,* Dec. 1832, [8]. JS noted in his journal on 1 December 1832 that he "wrote and corrected revelations." If typesetting for the Book of Commandments did not begin until at least November 1832, a proof of the first gathering probably could not have been printed and delivered to Ohio in time for JS to be reviewing it on 1 December. (JS, Journal, 1 Dec. 1832, in *JSP,* J1:10.)

34. A comparison of the different layers of editing marks in Revelation Book 1 clearly indicates that Revelation, September 1830–A [D&C 29], was typeset for the September 1832 issue of *The Evening and the Morning Star* before it was typeset for chapter 29 of the Book of Commandments, which begins on page 61, in the second gathering, and continues into the third.

35. A comparison of the respective versions of Revelation, 2 January 1831 [D&C 38], in Revelation Book 1, the January 1833 issue of *The Evening and the Morning Star,* and chapter 40 of the Book of Commandments indicates that the newspaper version was typeset before the Book of Commandments version. JS and others wrote a letter dated 25 June 1833 in which they made corrections to a proof sheet of the third gathering, likely sent to them sometime in late May. A letter from JS and others dated a week later, 2 July, responded to a 7 June letter from Independence, suggesting that the galley sheet was put in the mail to Ohio no later than circa 31 May. (JS et al., Kirtland, OH, to Edward Partridge et al., Independence, MO, 25 June 1833, JS Collection, CHL; JS et al., Kirtland, OH, to "Brethren," [Independence, MO], 2 July 1833, in JS Letterbook 1, pp. 51–54.)

97–128) and fifth (pages 129–160) gatherings were printed after the third gathering (circa May 1833) and before the destruction of the printing office (July 1833). Additionally, independent textual evidence places the typesetting date of the fifth gathering after February 1833.[36]

By mid-1833, a reported seven individuals were working in the Independence printing office[37] and were likely close to completing their work on the Book of Commandments. On 13 February 1833, W. W. Phelps & Co. filed for a copyright on the book, depositing a copy of the title page with the federal district court in Missouri, as required by law.[38] In May, *The Evening and the Morning Star* published a revelation intended as the last revelation, or "appendix," for the new book.[39] In the same issue, editors of the paper announced that the finished volume would "be published in the course of the present year" and cost "from 25, to 50 cents a copy."[40]

In a letter dated 25 June, JS and his associates in Ohio responded to questions from the Missouri printers about binding the books and authorized them to release books without binding in order to get them into circulation sooner.[41] The same letter gave minor corrections to chapters 40 and 44 of the Book of Commandments.[42] Inasmuch as chapter 44 ends on page 96 and the book was being printed on gatherings comprising thirty-two pages each, these corrections suggest that JS and his associates in Ohio had probably received copies of the first three gatherings of the volume, either to proofread or as a courtesy.[43] The corrections, however, arrived in Missouri too late to be incorporated into the printed

---

36. Editing marks in Revelation Book 1 indicate that Revelation, 30 August 1831 [D&C 63], was typeset for the February 1833 issue of *The Evening and the Morning Star* before it was typeset for chapter 64 of the Book of Commandments, which is in the fifth gathering.

37. "To His Excellency, Daniel Dunklin," *The Evening and the Morning Star,* Dec. 1833, 114–115; see also pp. 700–701 herein.

38. The original copyright registration has not been located. A certified copy was made in 1921 by H. C. Geisberg. (Woodford, "Development of the Doctrine and Covenants," 1:31; Wheaton and Wheaton, *Book of Commandments Controversy Reviewed,* 52–53.)

39. Revelation, 3 Nov. 1831, in Revelation Book 1, pp. 116–121, in *JSP,* MRB:205–215 [D&C 133]; "Revelations," *The Evening and the Morning Star,* May 1833, [1]–[2].

40. "Revelations," *The Evening and the Morning Star,* May 1833, [1].

41. JS et al., Kirtland, OH, to Edward Partridge et al., Independence, MO, 25 June 1833, JS Collection, CHL.

42. JS et al., Kirtland, OH, to Edward Partridge et al., Independence, MO, 25 June 1833, JS Collection, CHL. The corrections were as follows: "The following errors we have found in the commandments as printed 40th Chap 10th verse third line, instead of corruptable put corrupted 14 verse of the same chapter 5th line instead of respecter to persons, put respecter of persons, 21st verse 2nd line of the same chapter, instead of respecter to, put respecter of 44 Chapter 12 verse last line, instead of hands, put heads." In the Woodruff copy of the Book of Commandments (featured herein), these corrections are marked in an unidentified hand. (See pp. 93, 94, and 103 herein.)

43. William E. McLellin, who lived in Independence in 1833 and therefore may have had firsthand knowledge of some details of the printing operation, later stated that the Missouri editors sent a gathering of the Book of Commandments to Kirtland for correction. (William E. McLellin, Independence, MO, to Joseph Smith III, [Plano, IL], July 1872, typescript, Letters and Documents Copied from Originals in the Office of the Church Historian, Reorganized Church, CHL.)

volume.[44] Letters could take anywhere from about ten days to a month to make the journey between northeastern Ohio and Independence, Missouri, depending on the mode of delivery and other factors.[45] The delay in communication between JS and those printing the revelations prevented JS from maintaining a close supervisory role over the press. That JS saw advance sheets of the Book of Commandments, however, indicates Phelps, Cowdery, and Whitmer made efforts to keep him informed.

What proved to be the final known communication from church headquarters in Ohio to the printers in Missouri regarding the printing of the Book of Commandments was given 2 July 1833. On that date, in response to a letter of 7 June that is no longer extant, JS and counselors Sidney Rigdon and Frederick G. Williams sent instructions for shipping copies of the Book of Commandments to Kirtland.[46]

By the time that letter could reach Independence, the printing project had come to an abrupt end. On 20 July 1833, a group of four to five hundred Missouri vigilantes stormed the printing office, destroyed or confiscated much of the contents, and halted the printing of not only the Book of Commandments but of all Mormon publications in Independence. According to claims Phelps and Cowdery made in a lawsuit filed against several dozen of the vigilantes early the following year, the mob "forced open the door [to the print shop], tore down the same, forced and tore off the roof from the said printing office[,] forced . . . and tore down the walls of the same and then and there totally and wholly demolished tore down and destroyed the said printing office." Furthermore, the Missourians "seised [seized,] tore down and forcibly took and carried aw[ay] and converted to their[—]the said defendants[—]own use a certain printing press of the plaintiffs then and there set up and in use in the said printing office." Phelps and Cowdery valued the printing office at three thousand dollars and the press at five hundred dollars.[47] The assailants gave the press, which had apparently been pushed out of the second-story window and damaged in the fall, to Robert Kelly and William Davis, who used it beginning in early January 1834 to publish a newspaper in Liberty, Missouri, titled the *Upper Missouri Enquirer.*[48]

Several Latter-day Saints were able to save sheets of the unbound Book of Commandments, and copies were later individually bound for private use. It is unclear how many copies were saved and bound, but fewer than three dozen are currently known to exist. Also unclear is how those who saved the sheets from the attackers were able to salvage sheets from all five gatherings. Inside the print shop, each sheet would have been placed in an

---

44. The 25 June 1833 letter with the corrections arrived in Independence 29 July 1833, by which time the first five gatherings had been printed and the printing office had been destroyed by vigilantes. (John Whitmer with William W. Phelps postscript, Independence, MO, to JS and Oliver Cowdery, Kirtland Mills, OH, 29 July 1833, in JS Letterbook 2, pp. 52–56; see also Hartley, "Postal History," 185.)

45. Hartley, "Postal History," 176.

46. JS et al., Kirtland, OH, to "Brethren," [Independence, MO], 2 July 1833, in JS Letterbook 1, pp. 51–54.

47. Declaration, in Missouri Circuit Court (5th Circuit), Feb. 1834 term, *Phelps and Cowdery v. Olmstead et al.,* Jackson County Records Center, Independence, MO.

48. Missouri Writers' Project, *Missouri,* 108; JS History, vol. A-1, 412. One author has tracked the press to mid- and late-nineteenth-century newspapers published in Colorado and New Mexico. (Gladden, "An Early Printing Press Used in Colorado.")

uncollated stack, with one stack for each gathering, meaning that the salvagers would have had to hurriedly gather a sample from each of the stacks after the stacks were thrown from the print shop.[49] If the process of folding and collating the sheets had already begun, however, it would have been easier to collect all five sheets.[50]

John Whitmer's daybook documents that he sold six copies of the Book of Commandments to various individuals for twenty-five cents each.[51] Whether official agents were appointed to sell copies is unknown, but it appears that church leaders gathered known copies and distributed them.[52] The scarcity of the volume likely contributed to church leaders' prompt renewal of interest in printing a compilation of revelations—an objective that would not be realized until the 1835 publication of the Doctrine and Covenants in Kirtland, Ohio.

---

49. For an overview of folding and collating practices of the time, see Gaskell, *New Introduction to Bibliography*, 6, 143–145.

50. Another possible explanation for why so many volumes contain all five sheets is that a small number of advance copies may have been nearly completed, in which case it is possible that the majority of the surviving copies come from this advance collation. A David Whitmer reminiscence suggests as much, though he evidently misunderstood or misremembered what state the volume was in when he received it: "I received my Book of Commandments, complete before the press was destroyed by the mob, as did many other brethren." It is also possible that those gathering sheets collected many redundant sheets that were later discarded after complete volumes were assembled. (Whitmer, *Address to Believers in the Book of Mormon*, 5.)

51. Whitmer, Daybook, 6 and 13 July 1834; 3 and 12 Aug. 1834; 16 Sept. 1834.

52. For example, Mary Elizabeth Lightner recalled later that Oliver Cowdery took the several sheets saved by Lightner and her sister Caroline and bound them, giving one assembled copy to Lightner. (Mary Elizabeth Rollins Lightner, "Ran from the Mob," *Deseret Evening News,* 20 Feb. 1904, 24.)

line 1

A

BOOK

OF

COMMANDMENTS,

FOR THE GOVERNMENT OF THE

Church of Christ,

ORGANIZED ACCORDING TO LAW, ON THE

6th of April, 1830.

ZION:

PUBLISHED BY W. W. PHELPS & CO.

....

1833.

---

line 1. Two versions of the Book of Commandments title page are extant: a version without an ornamental border (as seen here) and a more common version with an ornamental border (see p. 600 herein). It appears that the original version was the borderless one and that printing was interrupted at some point to insert the border. On the version with the border, the text is shifted to the right and some of the spacing between the words and lines is compressed, suggesting the printers were making room for the inserted border.

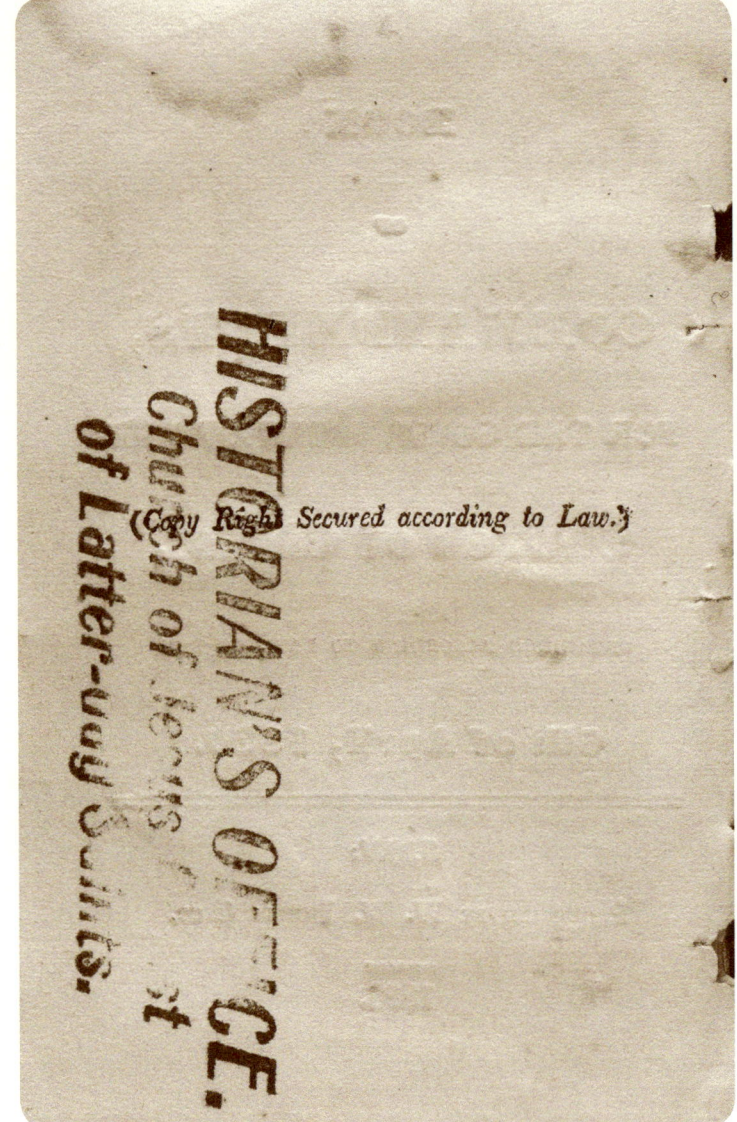

line 1

----

line 1. The Church Historian's Office stamp, here applied in purple ink, was in use sometime in the late nineteenth century and possibly in the early twentieth century. This volume was donated to the Church Historian's Office by Wilford Woodruff in 1854; the stamp suggests that the book underwent library processing in the late nineteenth or early twentieth century. (See p. 4 herein.)

CHAPTER I.

1 *A Preface or instruction unto the Book of Com-*
mandments, which were given of the Lord unto
his church, through him whom he appointed to
this work, by the voice of his saints through the
prayer of faith: The church being organized
according to the will of him, who rules all things,
on the sixth day of April, in the year of our
Lord, one thousand eight hundred and thirty:
HEARKEN, O ye people of my church, saith
the voice of Him who dwells on high, and
whose eyes are upon all men; yea, verily I say,
hearken ye people from afar, and ye that are upon
the islands of the sea, listen together; for verily the
voice of the Lord is unto all men, and there is none
to escape, and there is no eye that shall not see,
neither ear that shall not hear, neither heart that
shall not be penetrated; and the rebellious shall be
pierced with much sorrow, for their iniquties shall
be spoken upon the house-tops, and their secret acts
shall be revealed; and the voice of warning shall
be unto all people, by the mouths of my disciples,
whom I have chosen in these last days, and they
shall go forth and none shall stay them, for I the
Lord have commanded them.

2 Behold, this is mine authority, and the authority
of my servants, and my Preface unto the Book of
my Commandments, which I have given them to
publish unto you, O inhabitants of the earth:—
Wherefore fear and tremble, O ye people for what
I the Lord have decreed, in them, shall be fulfilled.

A2

1303

line 1. Revelation, 1 Nov. 1831–B [D&C 1]. Revelation Book 1 bears no editing marks that are reflected in this version. The chapter's italicized heading, however, matches the heading found only in Revelation Book 1, suggesting that Revelation Book 1 was used as a source text for this version. (See *JSP*, MRB:223–227.)

line 32. "A2" is the first of seven signature marks found on the rectos of this leaf and the next six leaves of this gathering. These marks were used in collating the gatherings after the sheets were folded.

line 33. "1303", here inscribed in black ink, was the number assigned to this volume in an early Church Historian's Office library catalog book, in use circa 1930. (See 4n6 herein.)

4

line *1* And verily, I say unto you, that they who go forth,
bearing these tidings unto the inhabitants of the
earth, to them is power given, to seal both on earth
and in heaven, the unbelieving and rebellious; yea,
5 verily, to seal them up unto the day when the wrath
of God shall be poured out upon the wicked, without measure, unto the day when the Lord shall
come to recompence unto every man according to
his work, and measure to every man according to
10 the measure which he has measured to his fellow
man.

3 Wherefore the voice of the Lord is unto the
ends of the earth, that all that will hear may hear:
Prepare ye, prepare ye for that which is to come,
15 for the Lord is nigh; and the anger of the Lord is
kindled, and his sword is bathed in heaven, and it
shall fall upon the inhabitants of the earth; and
the arm of the Lord shall be revealed; and the day
cometh, that they who will not hear the voice of
20 the Lord, neither the voice of his servants, neither
give heed to the words of the prophets, and apostles,
shall be cut off from among the people: For
they have strayed from mine ordinances, and have
broken mine everlasting covenant; they seek not
25 the Lord to establish his righteousness, but every
man walketh in his own way, and after the image
of his own god, whose image is in the likeness of the
world, and whose substance is that of an idol, which
waxeth old and shall perish in Babylon, even Baby-
30 lon the great, which shall fall:

4 Wherefore I the Lord, knowing the calamity
which should come upon the inhabitants of the earth,
called upon my servant Joseph, and spake unto
him from heaven, and gave him commandments;
35 and also gave commandments to others, that they

5

line 1

should proclaim these things unto the world, and all this that it might be fulfilled, which was written by the prophets: The weak things of the world should come forth and break down the mighty and strong ones: that man should not counsel his fellow man, neither trust in the arm of flesh, but that every man might speak in the name of God, the Lord, even the Savior of the world; that faith also might increase in the earth; that mine everlasting covenant might be established; that the fulness of my gospel might be proclaimed by the weak and the simple, unto the ends of the world; and before kings and rulers.

5 Behold I am God and have spoken it: these commandments are of me, and were given unto my servants in their weakness, after the manner of their language, that they might come to understanding; and inasmuch as they erred, it might be made known: and inasmuch as they sought wisdom, they might be instructed: and inasmuch as they sinned, they might be chastened, that they might repent; and inasmuch as they were humble, they might be made strong, and blessed from on high, and receive knowledge from time to time: after they, having received the record of the Nephites; yea, even my servant Joseph might have power to translate through the mercy of God, by the power of God, the book of Mormon: And also, those to whom these commandments were given, might have power to lay the foundation of this church, and to bring it forth out of obscurity, and out of darkness, the only true and living church upon the face of the whole earth, with which I the Lord am well pleased, speaking unto the church collectively and not individually, for I the Lord can not look upon sin

A3

6

line 1
with the least degree of allowance: Nevertheless
he that repenteth and doeth the commandments of
the Lord, shall be forgiven, and he that repenteth
not from him shall be taken even the light which he
hath received, for my Spirit shall not always strive
with man, saith the Lord of hosts.

6 And again, verily I say unto you, O inhabitants
of the earth, for I the Lord am willing to make
these things known unto all flesh, for I am no respecter to persons, and willeth that all men shall
know that the day speedily cometh, the hour is not
yet, but is nigh at hand, when peace shall be taken
from the earth, and the devil shall have power over
his own dominion; and also, the Lord shall have
power over his saints and shall reign in their midst,
and shall come down in judgment upon Idumea, or
the world.

7 Search these commandments, for they are true
and faithful, and the prophecies and promises which
are in them, shall all be fulfilled. What I the Lord
have spoken, I have spoken, and I excuse not myself, and though the heavens and the earth pass
away, my word shall not pass away, but shall all
be fulfilled, whether by mine own voice, or by the
voice of my servants, it is the same: For behold,
and lo, the Lord is God, and the Spirit beareth record, and the record is true, and the truth abideth
forever and ever: Amen.

7

CHAPTER II.

line 1

1 *A Revelation given to Joseph, in Harmony, Pennsylvania, July, 1828, after Martin had lost the Manuscript of the forepart of the book of Mormon, translated from the book of Lehi, which was abridged by the hand of Mormon, saying:*

THE works, and the designs, and the purposes of God, can not be frustrated, neither can they come to nought, for God doth not walk in crooked paths; neither doth he turn to the right hand nor to the left; neither doth he vary from that which he hath said: Therefore his paths are strait and his course is one eternal round.

2 Remember, remember, that it is not the work of God that is frustrated, but the work of men: for although a man may have many revelations, and have power to do many mighty works, yet, if he boasts in his own strength, and sets at nought the counsels of God, and follows after the dictates of his own will, and carnal desires, he must fall and incur the vengeance of a just God upon him.

3 Behold, you have been intrusted with these things, but how strict were your commandments; and remember, also, the promises which were made to you, if you did not transgress them; and behold, how oft you have transgressed the commandments and the laws of God, and have gone on in the persuasions of men: for behold, you should not have feared man more than God, although men set at naught the counsels of God, and despise his words, yet you should have been faithful and he would have extended his arm, and supported you against all the fiery darts of the adversary; and he would have been with you in every time of trouble.

A4

---

line 1. Revelation, July 1828 [D&C 3]. This version reflects editing marks made in Revelation Book 1, indicating that the latter was used as a source text for the former. (See *JSP*, MRB:9–11.)

8

line 1   4 Behold thou art Joseph, and thou wast chosen
to do the work of the Lord, but because of transgression, if thou art not aware thou wilt fall, but remember God is merciful: Therefore, repent of that
5   which thou hast done, and he will only cause thee
to be afflicted for a season, and thou art still chosen,
and wilt again be called to the work; and except
thou do this, thou shalt be delivered up and become
as other men, and have no more gift.

10   5 And when thou deliveredst up that which God
had given thee sight and power to translate, thou deliveredst up that which was sacred, into the hands of
a wicked man, who has set at nought the counsels
of God, and has broken the most sacred promises,
15   which were made before God, and has depended
upon his own judgment, and boasted in his own
wisdom, and this is the reason that thou hast lost
thy privileges for a season, for thou hast suffered the
counsel of thy director to be trampled upon from
20   the beginning.

6 Nevertheless, my work shall go forth and accomplish my purposes, for as the knowledge of a
Savior has come into the world, even so shall
the knowledge of my people, the Nephites,
25   and the Jacobites, and the Josephites, and the
Zoramites, come to the knowledge of the Lamanites, and the Lemuelites and the Ishmaelites, which
dwindled in unbelief, because of the iniquities of
their fathers, who have been suffered to destroy
30   their brethren, because of their iniquities, and their
abominations: and for this very purpose are these
plates preserved which contain these records, that
the promises of the Lord might be fulfilled, which
he made to his people; and that the Lamanites
35   might come to the knowledge of their fathers, and

9

line 1 that they might know the promises of the Lord, and
that they may believe the gospel and rely upon
the merits of Jesus Christ, and be glorified through
faith in his name; and that through their repentance
5 they might be saved: Amen.

CHAPTER III.

1 *A Revelation given to Joseph, the father of Joseph, in Harmony, Pennsylvania, February,
1829. saying:*

10 NOW, behold, a marvelous work is about to
come forth among the children of men, therefore, O ye that embark in the service of God, see
that ye serve him with all your heart, might, mind
and strength, that ye may stand blameless before
15 God at the last day: Therefore, if ye have desires
to serve God, ye are called to the work, for behold,
the field is white already to harvest, and lo, he that
thrusteth in his sickle with his might, the same layeth up in store that he perish not, but bringeth sal-
20 vation to his soul, and faith, hope, charity, and
love, with an eye single to the glory of God, qualifies him for the work.

2 Remember temperance, patience, humility, diligence, &c., ask and ye shall receive, knock and it
25 shall be opened unto you: Amen.

45

---

line 6. Revelation, Feb. 1829 [D&C 4]. Other than a correction of the date of this revelation, no editing marks corresponding to this version are found in the extant portion of Revelation Book 1. The source text for this version is unknown. (See *JSP,* MRB:11.)

CHAPTER IV.

A Revelation given to Joseph and Martin, in Harmony, Pennsylvania, March, 1829, when Martin desired of the Lord to know whether Joseph had, in his possession, the record of the Nephites.

BEHOLD, I say unto you, that my servant Martin has desired a witness from my hand, that my servant Joseph has got the things of which he has testified, and borne record that he has received of me.

2 And now, behold, this shall you say unto him:—I the Lord am God, and I have given these things unto my servant Joseph, and I have commanded him that he should stand as a witness of these things, nevertheless I have caused him that he should enter into a covenant with me, that he should not show them except I command him, and he has no power over them except I grant it unto him; and he has a gift to translate the book, and I have commanded him that he shall pretend to no other gift, for I will grant him no other gift.

3 And verily I say unto you, that wo shall come unto the inhabitants of the earth, if they will not hearken unto my words, for, behold, if they will not believe my words, they would not believe my servant Joseph, if it were possible that he could show them all things. O ye unbelieving, ye stiffnecked generation, mine anger is kindled against you!

4 Behold, verily I say, I have reserved the things of which I have spoken, which I have intrusted to my servant, for a wise purpose in me, and it shall be made known unto future generations: But this generation shall have my words, yea and the testi-

line 1

5

10

15

20

25

30

---

line 1. Revelation, Mar. 1829 [D&C 5]. The pages containing the text of this revelation are missing from Revelation Book 1. The source text for this version is unknown.

11

mony of three of my servants shall go forth with my
words unto this generation ; yea, three shall know of
a surety that these things are true, for I will give
them power, that they may behold and view these
5 things as they are, and to none else will I grant this
power, to receive this same testimony among this
generation.   And the testimony of three witnesses
will I send forth and my word, and behold, whosoever believeth in my word, them will I visit with the
10 manifestation of my Spirit, and they shall be born
of me, and their testimony shall also go forth.

5 And thus, if the people of this generation harden
not their hearts, I will work a reformation among
them, and I will put down all lyings, and deceiv-
15 ings, and priestcrafts, and envyings, and strifes, and
idolatries, and sorceries, and all manner of iniquities, and I will establish my church, like unto the
church which was taught by my disciples in the
days of old.

20 6 And now if this generation do harden their
hearts against my word, behold I will deliver them
up unto satan, for he reigneth and hath much power at this time, for he hath got great hold upon the
hearts of the people of this generation : and not far
25 from the iniquities of Sodom and Gomorrah, do
they come at this time : and behold the sword of
justice hangeth over their heads, and if they persist
in the hardness of their hearts, the time cometh that
it must fall upon them.   Behold I tell you these
30 things even as I also told the people of the distruc-
tion of Jerusalem, and my word shall be verified at
this time as it hath hitherto been verified.

7 And now I command my servant Joseph to repent, and walk more uprightly before me, and yield
35 to the persuasions of men no more ; and that he be

12

line 1
firm in keeping the commandments wherewith I
have commanded him; and if he doeth this, behold
I grant unto him eternal life, even if he should be
slain.

8 And now I speak again concerning the man that
desireth a witness: behold I say unto him, he exalteth himself and doth not humble himself sufficiently
before me, but if he will go out and bow down before me, and humble himself in mighty prayer and
faith, in the sincerity of his heart, then will I grant
unto him a view of the things which he desireth to
know: and then he shall say unto the people of this
generation, behold I have seen the things and I
know of a surety that they are true, for I have seen
them, and they have been shown unto me by the
power of God and not of man. And I command
him that he shall say no more unto them, concerning
these things, except he shall say, I have seen them,
and they have been shown unto me by the power of
God.

9 And these are the words which he shall say.—
But if he deny this he will break the covenant which
he has before covenanted with me, and behold he
is condemned. And now except he humble himself and acknowledge unto me the things that he
has done, which are wrong, and covenant with me
that he will keep my commandments, and exercise
faith in me, behold I say unto him, he shall have
no such views, for I will grant unto him no views
of the things of which I have spoken. And if this
be the case, I command him that he shall do no
more, nor trouble me any more concerning this
matter.

10 And if this be the case, behold I say unto you,
Joseph, when thou hast translated a few more pages,

13

line 1 thou shalt stop for a season, even until I command
thee again: then thou mayest translate again. And
except thou do this, behold thou shalt have no more
gift, and I will take away the things which I have
5 intrusted with thee.

11 And now, because I foresee the lying in wait
to destroy thee: Yea, I foresee that if my servant humbleth not himself, and receive a witness
from my hand, that he will fall into transgression;
10 and there are many that lie in wait to destroy thee
from off the face of the earth: And for this cause,
that thy days may be prolonged, I have given unto
thee these commandments; yea, for this cause I
have said, stop and stand still until I command thee,
15 and I will provide means whereby thou mayest accomplish the thing which I have commanded thee;
and if thou art faithful in keeping my commandments, thou shalt be lifted up at the last day:—
Amen.

20 A7

14

CHAPTER V.

¶ *A Revelation to Oliver, given in Harmony, Pennsylvania, April,* 1829, *when employed a scribe for Joseph, while translating the book of Mormon.*

A GREAT and marvelous work is about to come forth unto the children of men : behold I am God, and give heed unto my word, which is quick and powerful, sharper than a two-edged sword, to the dividing asunder of both joints and marrow :— Therefore give heed unto my words.

2 Behold the field is white already to harvest, therefore whoso desireth to reap, let him thrust in his sickle with his might and reap while the day lasts, that he may treasure up for his soul everlasting salvation in the kingdom of God : Yea, whosoever will thrust in his sickle and reap, the same is called of God ; therefore, if you will ask of me you shall receive ; if you will knock it shall be opened unto you.

3 Now as you have asked, behold I say unto you, keep my commandments, and seek to bring forth and establish the cause of Zion : seek not for riches but for wisdom, and behold the mysteries of God shall be unfolded unto you, and then shall you be made rich. Behold he that hath eternal life is rich.

4 Verily, verily I say unto you, even as you desire of me, so shall it be unto you ; and, if you desire, you shall be the means of doing much good in this generation. Say nothing but repentance unto this generation ; keep my commandments and assist to bring forth my work according to my commandments, and you shall be blessed.

line 1

5

10

15

20

25

30

---

line 1. Revelation, Apr. 1829–A [D&C 6]. The pages containing the text of this revelation are missing from Revelation Book 1. The source text for this version is unknown.

line 1

5 Behold thou hast a gift, and blessed art thou because of thy gift.   Remember it is sacred and cometh from above; and if thou wilt inquire, thou shalt know mysteries which are great and marvelous: therefore thou shalt exercise thy gift, that thou mayest find out mysteries, that thou mayest bring many to the knowledge of the truth; yea, convince them of the error of their ways.   Make not thy gift known unto any, save it be those which are of thy faith.— Trifle not with sacred things.   If thou wilt do good, yea and hold out faithful to the end, thou shalt be saved in the kingdom of God, which is the greatest of all the gifts of God; for there is no gift greater than the gift of salvation.

6 Verily, verily I say unto thee, blessed art thou for what thou hast done, for thou hast inquired of me, and behold as often as thou hast inquired, thou hast received instruction of my Spirit.   If it had not been so, thou wouldst not have come to the place where thou art at this time.

7 Behold thou knowest that thou hast inquired of me, and I did enlighten thy mind; and now I tell thee these things, that thou mayest know that thou hast been enlightened by the Spirit of truth; yea, I tell thee, that thou mayest know that there is none else save God, that knowest thy thoughts and the intents of thy heart: I tell thee these things as a witness unto thee, that the words or the work which thou hast been writing is true:

8 Therefore be diligent, stand by my servant Joseph faithfully in whatsoever difficult circumstances he may be, for the word's sake.   Admonish him in his faults and also receive admonition of him.   Be patient; be sober; be temperate; have patience, faith, hope and charity.

48

16

9 Behold thou art Oliver, and I have spoken unto thee because of thy desires, therefore, treasure up these words in thy heart. Be faithful and diligent in keeping the commandments of God, and I will incircle thee in the arms of my love.

10 Behold I am Jesus Christ, the Son of God. I am the same that came unto my own and my own received me not. I am the light which shineth in darkness, and the darkness comprehendeth it not.

11 Verily, verily I say unto you, if you desire a further witness, cast your mind upon the night that you cried unto me in your heart, that you might know concerning the truth of these things; did I not speak peace to your mind concering the matter?— What greater witness can you have than from God? And now behold, you have received a witness, for if I have told you things which no man knoweth, have you not received a witness? And behold I grant unto you a gift if you desire of me, to translate even as my servant Joseph.

12 Verily, verily I say unto you, that there are records which contain much of my gospel, which have been kept back because of the wickedness of the people; and now I command you, that if you have good desires, a desire to lay up treasures for yourself in heaven, then shall you assist in bringing to light, with your gift, those parts of my scriptures which have been hidden because of iniquity.

13 And now behold I give unto you, and also unto my servant Joseph, the keys of this gift, which shall bring to light this ministry; and in the mouth of two or three witnesses, shall every word be established.

14 Verily, verily I say unto you, if they reject my words, and this part of my gospel and ministry, bles-

17

sed are ye, for they can do no more unto you than
unto me; and if they do unto you, even as they have
done unto me, blessed are ye, for you shall dwell
with me in glory: but if they reject not my words,
which shall be established by the testimony which
shall be given, blessed are they; and then shall ye
have joy in the fruit of your labors.

15 Verily, verily I say unto you, as I said unto
my disciples, where two or three are gathered together in my name, as touching one thing, behold there
will I be in the midst of them: even so am I in the
midst of you. Fear not to do good my sons, for
whatsoever ye sow, that shall ye also reap: therefore, if ye sow good, ye shall also reap good for your
reward:

16 Therefore fear not little flock, do good, let earth
and hell combine against you, for if ye are built upon my Rock, they cannot prevail. Behold I do not
condemn you, go your ways and sin no more: perform with soberness the work which I have commanded you: look unto me in every thought, doubt
not, fear not: behold the wounds which pierced my
side, and also the prints of the nails in my hands
and feet: be faithful; keep my commandments, and
ye shall inherit the kingdom of heaven: Amen.

18

CHAPTER VI.

line 1

1 *A Revelation given to Joseph and Oliver, in Harmony, Pennsylvania, April, 1829, when they desired to know whether John, the beloved disciple, tarried on earth. Translated ·from parchment, written and hid up by himself.*

5

AND the Lord said unto me, John my beloved, what desirest thou? and I said Lord, give unto me power that I may bring souls unto thee.— And the Lord said unto me: Verily, verily I say unto thee, because thou desiredst this, thou shalt tarry till I come in my glory:

10

2 And for this cause, the Lord said unto Peter:— If I will that he tarry till I come, what is that to thee? for he desiredst of me that he might bring souls unto me: but thou desiredst that thou might speed- ily come unto me in my kingdom: I say unto thee, Peter, this was a good desire, but my beloved has undertaken a greater work.

15

3 Verily I say unto you, ye shall both have accor- ding to your desires, for ye both joy in that which ye have desired.

20

---

line 1. Account of John, Apr. 1829–C [D&C 7]. This version reflects editing marks made in Revelation Book 1, indicating that the latter was used as a source text for the former. (See *JSP,* MRB:17–19.)

19

CHAPTER VII.

line 1

1 *A Revelation given to Oliver, in Harmony, Pennsylvania, April,* 1829.

OLIVER, verily, verily I say unto you, that assuredly as the Lord liveth, which is your God and your Redeemer, even so sure shall you receive a knowledge of whatsoever things you shall ask in faith, with an honest heart, believing that you shall receive a knowledge concerning the engravings of old records, which are ancient, which contain those parts of my scripture of which have been spoken, by the manifestation of my Spirit; yea, behold I will tell you in your mind and in your heart by the Holy Ghost, which shall come upon you and which shall dwell in your heart.

2 Now, behold this is the Spirit of revelation :— behold this is the Spirit by which Moses brought the children of Israel through the Red sea on dry ground : therefore, this is thy gift; apply unto it and blessed art thou, for it shall deliver you out of the hands of your enemies, when, if it were not so, they would slay you and bring your soul to destruction.

3 O remember, these words and keep my commandments. Remember this is your gift. Now this is not all, for you have another gift, which is the gift of working with the rod : behold it has told you things : behold there is no other power save God, that can cause this rod of nature, to work in your hands, for it is the work of God; and therefore whatsoever you shall ask me to tell you by that means, that will I grant unto you, that you shall know.

4 Remember that without faith you can do noth-

---

line 1. Revelation, Apr. 1829–B [D&C 8]. This version reflects editing marks made in Revelation Book 1, indicating that the latter was used as a source text for the former. (See *JSP*, MRB:15–17.)

20

line 1 ing. Trifle not with these things. Do not ask for
that which you ought not. Ask that you may know
the mysteries of God, and that you may translate
all those ancient records, which have been hid up,
5 which are sacred, and according to your faith shall
it be don unto you.

5 Behold it is I that have spoken it, and I am the
same which spake unto you from the beginning:—
Amen.

——————————

10 CHAPTER VIII.

1 *A Revelation given to Oliver, in Harmony,*
Pennsylvania, April, 1829.

BEHOLD I say unto you, my son, that, because
you did not translate according to that which
15 you desired of me, and did commence again to write
for my servant Joseph, even so I would that you
should continue until you have finished this record,
which I have intrusted unto you: and then behold,
other records have I, that I will give unto you pow-
20 er that you may assist to translate.

2 Be patient my son, for it is wisdom in me, and
it is not expedient that you should translate at this
present time. Behold the work which you are called to do, is to write for my servant Joseph; and
25 behold it is because that you did not continue as
you commenced, when you begun to translate, that
I have taken away this privilege from you. Do not
murmur my son, for it is wisdom in me that I have
dealt with you after this manner.

3 Behold you have not understood, you have sup-
30 posed that I would give it unto you, when you took

----

line 10. Revelation, Apr. 1829–D [D&C 9]. This version reflects editing marks made in the extant portion of this text in Revelation Book 1, indicating that the latter was used as a source text for the former.
(See *JSP,* MRB:19.)

21

no thought, save it was to ask me; but behold I say unto you, that you must study it out in your mind; then you must ask me if it be right, and if it is right, I will cause that your bosom shall burn within you: therefore, you shall feel that it is right; but if it be not right, you shall have no such feelings, but you shall have a stupor of thought, that shall cause you to forget the thing which is wrong: therefore, you cannot write that which is sacred, save it be given you from me.

4 Now if you had known this, you could have translated: nevertheless, it is not expedient that you should translate now. Behold it was expedient when you commenced, but you feared and the time is past, that it is not expedient now: for, do you not behold that I have given unto my servant Joseph sufficient strength, whereby it is made up? and neither of you have I condemned.

5 Do this thing which I have commanded you, and you shall prosper. Be faithful, and yield to no temptation. Stand fast in the work wherewith I have called you, and a hair of your head shall not be lost, and you shall be lifted up at the last day: Amen.

22

CHAPTER IX.

*1 A Revelation given to Joseph, in Harmony,
Pennsylvania, May, 1829, informing him of the
alteration of the Manuscript of the fore part of
the book of Mormon.*

NOW, behold I say unto you, that because you
delivered up so many writings, which you had
power to translate, into the hands of a wicked man,
you have lost them, and you also lost your gift at the
same time, nevertheless it has been restored unto
you again : therefore, see that you are faithful and
go on unto the finishing of the remainder of the work
as you have begun. Do not run faster than you
have strength and means provided to translate, but
be diligent unto the end, that you may come off con-
querer; yea, that you may conquer satan, and those
that do uphold his work.

2 Behold they have sought to destroy you; yea,
even the man in whom you have trusted, and for
this cause I said, that he is a wicked man, for he has
sought to take away the things wherewith you have
been intrusted; and he has also sought to destroy
your gift, and because you have delivered the writings into his hands, behold they have taken them
from you: therefore, you have delivered them up;
yea, that which was sacred unto wickedness. And
behold, satan has put it into their hearts to alter the
words which you have caused to be written, or which
you have translated, which have gone out of your
hands; and behold I say unto you, that because they
have altered the words, they read contrary from that
which you translated and caused to be written; and
on this wise the devil has sought to lay a cunning

line 1

5

10

15

20

25

30

---

line 1. Revelation, ca. Apr. 1829 [D&C 10]. This version reflects editing marks made in the extant portion of this text in Revelation Book 1, indicating that the latter was used as a source text for the former.
This revelation should be dated circa April 1829. For more information on this dating, see the discussion
of this revelation in the Documents series. (See *JSP,* MRB:13–15.)

23

plan, that he may destroy this work; for he has put it into their hearts to do this, that by lying they may say they have caught you in the words which you have pretended to translate.

3 Verily I say unto you, that I will not suffer that satan shall accomplish his evil design in this thing, for behold he has put it into their hearts to tempt the Lord their God; for behold they say in their hearts, We will see if God has given him power to translate, if so, he will also give him power again; and if God giveth him power again, or if he translate again, or in other words, if he bringeth forth the same words, behold we have the same with us, and we have altered them: Therefore, they will not agree, and we will say that he has lied in his words, and that he has no gift, and that he has no power: therefore, we will destroy him, and also the work, and we will do this that we may not be ashamed in the end, and that we may get glory of the world.

4 Verily, verily I say unto you, that satan has great hold upon their hearts; he stirreth them up to do iniquity against that which is good, that he may lead their souls to destruction, and thus he has laid a cunning plan to destroy the work of God; yea, he stirreth up their hearts to anger against this work; yea, he saith unto them, Deceive and lie in wait to catch, that ye may destroy: behold this is no harm, and thus he flattereth them and telleth them that it is no sin to lie, that they may catch a man in a lie, that they may destroy him, and thus he flattereth them, and leadeth them along until he draggeth their souls down to hell; and thus he causeth them to catch themselves in their own snare; and thus he goeth up and down, to and fro in the earth, seeking to destroy the souls of men.

24

5 Verily, verily I say unto you, wo be unto him that lieth to decieve, because he supposeth that another lieth to decieve, for such are not exempt from the justice of God.

6 Now, behold they have altered those words, because satan saith unto them, He hath decieved you, and thus he flattereth them away to do iniquity, to tempt the Lord their God.

7 Behold I say unto you, that you shall not translate again those words which have gone forth out of your hands; for behold, they shall not lie any more against those words; for behold, if you should bring forth the same words, they would say that you have lied; that you have pretended to translate, but that you have contradicted your words; and behold they would publish this, and satan would harden the hearts of the people, to stir them up to anger against you, that they might not believe my words: thus satan would overpower this generation, that the work might not come forth in this generation: but behold here is wisdom, and because I show unto you wisdom, and give you commandments concerning these things, what you shall do, show it not unto the world until you have accomplished the work.

8 Marvel not that I said unto you, here is wisdom, show it not unto the world, for I said, show it not unto the world, that you may be preserved. Behold I do not say that you shall not show it unto the righteous; but as you cannot always judge the righteous, or as you cannot always tell the wicked from the righteous: therefore, I say unto you, hold your peace until I shall see fit to make all things known unto the world concerning the matter.

9 And now, verily I say unto you, that an account of those things that you have written, which have

25

gone out of your hands, are engraven upon the plates
of Nephi; yea, and you remember, it was said in
those writings, that a more particular account was
given of these things upon the plates of Nephi.

10 And now, because the account which is engraven upon the plates of Nephi, is more particular concerning the things, which in my wisdom I would
bring to the knowledge of the people in this account:
therefore, you shall translate the engravings which
are on the plates of Nephi, down even till you come
to the reign of king Benjamin, or until you come to
that which you have translated, which you have retained; and behold, you shall publish it as the record of Nephi, and thus I will confound those who
have altered my words. I will not suffer that they
shall destroy my work; yea, I will show unto them
that my wisdom is greater than the cunning of the
devil.

11 Behold they have only got a part, or an abridgment of the account of Nephi. Behold there are
many things engraven on the plates of Nephi, which
do throw greater views upon my gospel: therefore,
it is wisdom in me, that you should translate this
first part of the engravings of Nephi, and send forth
in this work. And behold, all the remainder of this
work, does contain all those parts of my gospel which
my holy prophets; yea, and also my disciples desired in their prayers, should come forth unto this
people. And I said unto them, that it should be
granted unto them according to their faith in their
prayers; yea, and this was their faith, that my gospel which I gave unto them, that they might preach
in their days, might come unto their brethren, the
Lamanites, and also, all that had become Lamanites, because of their dissensions.

26

12 Now this is not all, their faith in their prayers were, that this gospel should be made known also, if it were possible that other nations should possess this land; and thus they did leave a blessing upon this land in their prayers, that whosoever should believe in this gospel, in this land, might have eternal life; yea, that it might be free unto all of whatsoever nation, kindred, tongue, or people, they may be.

13 And now, behold, according to their faith in their prayers, will I bring this part of my gospel to the knowledge of my people. Behold, I do not bring it to destroy that which they have received, but to build it up.

14 And for this cause have I said, if this generation harden not their hearts, I will establish my church among them. Now I do not say this to destroy my church, but I say this to build up my church: therefore, whosoever belongeth to my church need not fear, for such shall inherit the kingdom of heaven: but it is they who do not fear me, neither keep my commandments, but buildeth up churches unto themselves, to get gain; yea, and all those that do wickedly, and buildeth up the kingdom of the devil; yea, verily, verily I say unto you, that it is they that I will disturb, and cause to tremble and shake to the centre.

15 Behold, I am Jesus Christ, the Son of God: I came unto my own, and my own received me not. I am the light which shineth in darkness, and the darkness comprehendeth it not. I am he who said other sheep have I which are not of this fold, unto my disciples, and many there were that understood me not.

16 And I will show unto this people, that I had

27

other sheep, and that they were a branch of the
house of Jacob; and I will bring to light their marvelous works, which they did in my name; yea, and
I will also bring to light my gospel, which was ministered unto them, and behold they shall not deny
that which you have received, but they shall build
it up, and shall bring to light the true points of my
doctrine: Yea, and the only doctrine which is in
me; and this I do, that I may establish my gospel,
that there may not be so much contention: Yea,
satan doth stir up the hearts of the people to contention, concerning the points of my doctrine; and in
these things they do err, for they do wrest the scriptures, and do not understand them: therefore, I
will unfold unto them this great mystery, for behold,
I will gather them as a hen gathereth her chickens
under her wings, if they will not harden their hearts:
Yea, if they will come, they may, and partake of
the waters of life freely.

17 Behold this is my doctrine: whosoever repenteth, and cometh unto me, the same is my church:
whosoever declareth more or less than this, the same
is not of me, but is against me: therefore, he is not
of my church.

18 And now, behold whosoever is of my church,
and endureth of my church to the end, him will I establish upon my Rock, and the gates of hell shall not
prevail against them.

19 And now, remember the words of him who is
the life and the light of the world, your Redeemer,
your Lord and your God: Amen.

28

CHAPTER X.

line 1

1 *A Revelation given to Hyrum, in Harmony, Pennsylvania, May,* 1829.

A GREAT and marvelous work is about to come forth among the children of men : behold I am God and give heed to my word, which is quick and powerful, sharper than a two-edged sword, to the dividing asunder of both joints and marrow : therefore, give heed unto my word.

2 Behold the field is white already to harvest, therefore, whoso desireth to reap, let him thrust in his sickle with his might, and reap while the day lasts, that he may treasure up for his soul everlasting salvation in the kingdom of God ; yea, whosoever will thrust in his sickle and reap, the same is called of God : therefore, if you will ask of me, you shall receive ; if you will knock, it shall be opened unto you.

3 Now as you have asked, behold I say unto you, keep my commandments, and seek to bring forth and establish the cause of Zion. Seek not for riches but for wisdom, and behold the mysteries of God shall be unfolded unto you, and then shall you be made rich ; behold he that hath eternal life is rich.

4 Verily, verily I say unto you, even as you desire of me, so shall it be done unto you ; and, if you desire you shall be the means of doing much good in this generation. Say nothing but repentance unto this generation. Keep my commandments, and assist to bring forth my work according to my commandments, and you shall be blessed.

5 Behold thou hast a gift, or thou shalt have a gift, if thou wilt desire of me in faith, with an honest

---

line 1. Revelation, May 1829–A [D&C 11]. The pages containing the text of this revelation are missing from Revelation Book 1. The source text for this version is unknown.

29

heart, believing in the power of Jesus Christ, or in
my power which speaketh unto thee: for behold it
is I that speaketh: behold I am the light which shineth in darkness, and by my power I give these words
unto thee.

6 And now, verily, verily I say unto thee, put
your trust in that Spirit which leadeth to do good:
Yea, to do justly; to walk humbly; to judge righteously; and this is my Spirit.

7 Verily, verily I say unto you, I will impart unto you of my Spirit, which shall enlighten your
mind, which shall fill your soul with joy, and then
shall you know, or by this shall you know, all things
whatsoever you desire of me, which is pertaining
unto things of righteousness, in faith believing in
me that you shall receive.

8 Behold I command you, that you need not suppose that you are called to preach until you are called: wait a little longer, until you shall have my
word, my Rock, my church, and my gospel, that
you may know of a surety my doctrine; and then
behold, according to your desires, yea, even according to your faith, shall it be done unto you.

9 Keep my commandments; hold your peace; appeal unto my Spirit: Yea, cleave unto me with all
your heart, that you may assist in bringing to light
those things of which have been spoken: Yea, the
translation of my work: be patient until you shall
accomplish it.

10 Behold this is your work, to keep my commandments: Yea, with all your might, mind, and
strength: seek not to declare my word, but first seek
to obtain my word, and then shall your tongues be
loosed; then, if you desire you shall have my Spirit,
and my word: Yea, the power of God unto the

30

convincing of men : but now hold your peace ; study
my word which hath gone forth among the children
of men ; and also study my word which shall come
forth among the children of men ; or that which
you are translating : Yea, until you have obtained
all which I shall grant unto the children of men in
this generation ; and then shall all things be added
thereunto.

11 Behold thou art Hyrum, my son ; seek the
kingdom of God and all things shall be added according to that which is just.　Build upon my Rock,
which is my gospel ; deny not the Spirit of revelation, nor the Spirit of prophecy, for wo unto him
that denieth these things : therefore, treasure up in
your hearts until the time which is in my wisdom,
that you shall go forth :　Behold I speak unto all
who have good desires, and have thrust in their
sickles to reap.

12 Behold I am Jesus Christ, the Son of God : I
am the life and the light of the world : I am the
same which came unto my own, and my own received me not : but verily, verily I say unto you,
that as many as receiveth me, them will I give
power to become the sons of God, even to them that
believe on my name :　Amen.

31

CHAPTER XI.

1 *A Revelation given to Joseph (K.,) in Harmony, Pennsylvania, May, 1829, informing him
how he must do, to be worthy to assist in the
work of the Lord.*

A GREAT and marvelous work is about to come
forth among the children of men : behold I am
God, and give heed to my word, which is quick and
powerful, sharper than a two-edged sword, to the
dividing asunder of both joints and marrow : therefore, give heed unto my word.

2 Behold the field is white already to harvest,
therefore whoso desireth to reap, let him thrust in
his sickle with his might, and reap while the day
lasts, that he may treasure up for his soul everlasting salvation in the kingdom of God : Yea, whosoever will thrust in his sickle and reap, the same is
called of God : therefore, if you will ask of me you
shall receive ; if you will knock it shall be opened
unto you.

3 Now as you have asked, behold I say unto you,
keep my commandments, and seek to bring forth
and establish the cause of Zion.

4 Behold I speak unto you, and also to all those
who have desires to bring forth and establish this
work, and no one can assist in this work, except he
shall be humble and full of love, having faith, hope
and charity, being temperate in all things, whatsoever shall be intrusted to his care.

5 Behold I am the light and the life of the world,
that speaketh these words : therefore, give heed
with your might, and then you are called : Amen.

---

line 1. Revelation, May 1829–B [D&C 12]. Unlike most revelations printed in the Book of Commandments, the text of this revelation was never copied into Revelation Book 1. The source text for this version
is unknown.

32

CHAPTER XII.

line 1

1 *A Revelation given to David, in Fayette, New York, June,* 1829.

A GREAT and marvelous work is about to come forth unto the children of men: behold I am God, and give heed to my word, which is quick and powerful, sharper than a two-edged sword, to the dividing asunder of both joints and marrow: therefore, give heed unto my word.

2 Behold the field is white already to harvest, therefore, whoso desireth to reap, let him thrust in his sickle with his might, and reap while the day lasts, that he may treasure up for his soul everlasting salvation in the kingdom of God: Yea, whosoever will thrust in his sickle and reap, the same is called of God: therefore, if you will ask of me you shall receive; if you will knock it shall be opened unto you.

3 Seek to bring forth and establish my Zion.— Keep my commandments in all things, and if you keep my commandments, and endure to the end, you shall have eternal life; which gift is the greatest of all the gifts of God.

4 And it shall come to pass, that if you shall ask the Father in my name, in faith believing, you shall receive the Holy Ghost, which giveth utterance, that you may stand as a witness of the things of which you shall both hear and see; and also, that you may declare repentance unto this generation.

5 Behold I am Jesus Christ the Son of the living God, which created the heavens and the earth; a light which cannot be hid in darkness: wherefore, I must bring forth the fulness of my gospel from the

5

10

15

20

25

30

---

line 1. Revelation, June 1829–A [D&C 14]. The pages containing the text of this revelation are missing from Revelation Book 1. The source text for this version is unknown.

33

line 1
Gentiles unto the house of Israel.   And behold thou
art David, and thou art called to assist: Which
thing if ye do, and are faithful, ye shall be blessed
both spiritually and temporally, and great shall be
your reward: Amen.

———

CHAPTER XIII.

1 *A Revelation given to John, in Fayette, New-*
York, June, 1829.

HEARKEN my servant John, and listen to
the words of Jesus Christ, your Lord and
your Redeemer, for behold I speak unto you with
sharpness and with power, for mine arm is over all
the earth, and I will tell you that which no man
knoweth save me and thee alone: for many times
you have desired of me to know that which would
be of the most worth unto you.

2 Behold, blessed are you for this thing, and for
speaking my words which I have given you, according to my commandments:

3 And now behold I say unto you, that the thing
which will be of the most worth unto you, will be to
declare repentance unto this people, that you may
bring souls unto me, that you may rest with them
in the kingdom of my Father.   Amen.

B1

---

line 6. Revelation, June 1829–C [D&C 15]. The pages containing the text of this revelation are missing
from Revelation Book 1. The source text for this version is unknown.

line 25. This page begins the second gathering of the book. "B1" is the first of eight signature marks
found on the rectos of the first eight leaves of this gathering. These marks were used in collating the gatherings after the sheets were folded.

84

CHAPTER XIV.

line 1

1. *A Revelation given to Peter, in Fayette, New York, June, 1829.*

HEARKEN my servant Peter, and listen to the words of Jesus Christ, your Lord and your Redeemer, for behold I speak unto you with sharpness and with power, for mine arm is over all the earth, and I will tell you that which no man knoweth save me and thee alone: for many times you have desired of me to know that which would be of the most worth unto you.

2 Behold, blessed are you for this thing, and for speaking my words which I have given you, according to my commandments:

3 And now behold I say unto you, that the thing which will be of the most worth unto you, will be to declare repentance unto this people, that you may bring souls unto me, that you may rest with them in the kingdom of my Father.   Amen

----

CHAPTER XV.

line 20

1 *A Revelation to Joseph, Oliver and David, making known the calling of twelve disciples in these last days, and also, instructions relative to building up the church of Christ, according to the fulness of the gospel: Given in Fayette, New-York, June, 1829.*

NOW behold, because of the thing which you have desired to know of me, I give unto you these words:

2 Behold I have manifested unto you, by my

----

line 1. Revelation, June 1829–D [D&C 16]. The page containing the text of this revelation is missing from Revelation Book 1. The source text for this version is unknown.

line 20. Revelation, June 1829–B [D&C 18]. The pages containing the text of this revelation are missing from Revelation Book 1. The source text for this version is unknown.

35

line 1
Spirit in many instances, that the things which you have written are true:

3 Wherefore you know that they are true; and if you know that they are true, behold I give unto you a commandment, that you rely upon the things which are written; for in them are all things written, concerning my church, my gospel, and my rock.

4 Wherefore if you shall build up my church, and my gospel, and my rock, the gates of hell shall not prevail against you.

5 Behold the world is ripening in iniquity, and it must needs be, that the children of men are stirred up unto repentance, both the Gentiles, and also the house of Israel:

6 Wherefore as thou hast been baptized by the hand of my servant, according to that which I have commanded him:

7 Wherefore he hath fulfilled the thing which I commanded him.

8 And now marvel not that I have called him unto mine own purpose, which purpose is known in me:

9 Wherefore if he shall be diligent in keeping my commandments, he shall be blessed unto eternal life, and his name is Joseph.

10 And now Oliver, I speak unto you, and also unto David, by the way of commandment:

11 For behold I command all men every where to repent, and I speak unto you, even as unto Paul mine apostle, for you are called even with that same calling with which he was called.

12 Remember the worth of souls is great in the sight of God:

13 For behold the Lord your God suffered death

B2

36

line 1

in the flesh: wherefore he suffered the pain of all men, that all men might repent and come unto him.

14 And he hath risen again from the dead, that he might bring all men unto him on conditions of repentance.

15 And how great is his joy in the soul that repenteth.

16 Wherefore you are called to cry repentance unto this people.

17 And if it so be that you should labor in all your days, in crying repentance unto this people, and bring save it be one soul only unto me, how great shall be your joy with him in the kingdom of my Father?

18 And now if your joy will be great with one soul, that you have brought unto me into the kingdom of my Father, how great will be your joy, if you should bring many souls unto me?

19 Behold you have my gospel before you, and my rock, and my salvation:

20 Ask the Father in my name in faith believing that you shall receive, and you shall have the Holy Ghost which manifesteth all things, which is expedient unto the children of men.

21 And if you have not faith, hope and charity, you can do nothing.

22 Contend against no church, save it be the church of the devil.

23 Take upon you the name of Christ, and speak the truth in soberness, and as many as repent, and are baptized in my name, which is Jesus Christ, and endure to the end, the same shall be saved.

24 Behold Jesus Christ is the name which is given of the Father, and there is none other name given whereby man can be saved:

37

25 Wherefore all men must take upon them the name which is given of the Father, for in that name shall they be called at the last day:

26 Wherefore if they know not the name by which they are called, they cannot have place in the kingdom of my Father.

27 And now behold, there are others which are called to declare my gospel, both unto Gentile and unto Jew: Yea, even unto twelve:

28 And the twelve shall be my disciples, and they shall take upon them my name:

29 And the twelve are they which shall desire to take upon them my name, with full purpose of heart:

30 And if they desire to take upon them my name, with full purpose of heart, they are called to go into all the world to preach my gospel unto every creature:

31 And they are they which are ordained of me to baptize in my name, according to that which is written; and you have that which is written before you:

32 Wherefore you must perform it according to the words which are written.

33 And now I speak unto the twelve:

34 Behold my grace is sufficient for you: You must walk uprightly before me and sin not.

35 And behold you are they which are ordained of me to ordain priests and teachers to declare my gospel, according to the power of the Holy Ghost which is in you, and according to the callings and gifts of God unto men:

36 And I Jesus Christ, your Lord and your God, have spoken it.

37 These words are not of men, nor of man, but of me:

38

38 Wherefore you shall testify they are of me, and not of man; for it is my voice which speaketh them unto you:

39 For they are given by my Spirit unto you:

40 And by my power you can read them one to another; and save it were by my power, you could not have them:

41 Wherefore you can testify that you have heard my voice, and know my words.

42 And now behold I give unto you, Oliver, and also unto David, that you shall search out the twelve which shall have the desires of which I have spoken; and by their desires and their works, you shall know them:

43 And when you have found them you shall show these things unto them.

44 And you shall fall down and worship the Father in my name:

45 And you must preach unto the world, saying, you must repent and be baptized in the name of Jesus Christ:

46 For all men must repent and be baptized; and not only men, but women and children, which have arriven to the years of accountability.

47 And now, after that you have received this, you must keep my commandments in all things:

48 And by your hands I will work a marvelous work among the children of men, unto the convincing of many of their sins, that they may come unto repentance; and that they may come unto the kingdom of my Father:

49 Wherefore the blessings which I give unto you are above all things.

50 And after that you have received this, if you keep not my commandments, you cannot be saved

89

line 1 in the kingdom of my Father. Behold I Jesus Christ, your Lord and your God, and your Redeemer, by the power of my Spirit, have spoken it. Amen.

————

CHAPTER XVI.

5 1 *A commandment of God and not of man to you, Martin, given (Manchester, New-York, March, 1830,) by him who is eternal:*

YEA, even I, I am he, the beginning and the *10* end: Yea, Alpha and Omega, Christ the Lord, the Redeemer of the world:

2 I having accomplished and finished the will of him whose I am, even the Father:

3 Having done this, that I might subdue all things *15* unto myself:

4 Retaining all power, even to the destroying of satan and his works at the end of the world, and the last great day of judgment, which I shall pass upon the inhabitants thereof, judging every man according *20* to his works, and the deeds which he hath done.

5 And surely every man must repent or suffer, for I God am endless:

6 Wherefore, I revoke not the judgments which I shall pass, but woes shall go forth, weeping, wailing *25* and gnashing of teeth:

7 Yea, to those who are found on my left hand, nevertheless, it is not written, that there shall be no end to this torment; but it is written endless torment.

30 8 Again, it is written eternal damnation: wherefore it is more express than other scriptures, that it

B4

————

line 5. Revelation, Mar. 1830 [D&C 19]. This version reflects editing marks made in the extant portion of this text in Revelation Book 1, indicating that the latter was used as a source text for the former. (See *JSP,* MRB:25–27.)

40

might work upon the hearts of the children of men, altogether for my name's glory:

9 Wherefore, I will explain unto you, this mystery, for it is mete unto you, to know even as mine apostles.

10 I speak unto you that are chosen in this thing, even as one, that you may enter into my rest.

11 For behold, the mystery of Godliness how great is it? for behold I am endless, and the punishment which is given from my hand, is endless punishment, for endless is my name:

12 Wherefore—

Eternal punishment ⎫ Endless punishment
is God's punishment:⎬ is God's punishment:

13 Wherefore, I command you by my name, and by my Almighty power, that you repent: repent, lest I smite you by the rod of my mouth, and by my wrath, and by my anger, and your sufferings be sore:

14 How sore you know not!

15 How exquisite you know not!

16 Yea, how hard to bear you know not!

17 For behold, I God have suffered these things for all, that they might not suffer, if they would repent, but if they would not repent, they must suffer even as I:

18 Which suffering caused myself, even God, the greatest of all, to tremble because of pain, and to bleed at every pore, both body and spirit:

19 And would that I might not drink the bitter cup and shrink:

20 Nevertheless, glory be to the Father, and I partook and finished my preparations unto the children of men:

21 Wherefore, I command you again by my Al-

41

mighty power, that you confess your sins, lest you suffer these punishments of which I have spoken, of which in the smallest, yea, even in the least degree you have tasted at the time I withdrew my Spirit.

22 And I command you, that you preach nought but repentance; and show not these things, neither speak these things unto the world, for they can not bear meat, but milk they must receive:

23 Wherefore, they must not know these things lest they perish:

24 Wherefore, learn of me, and listen to my words; walk in the meekness of my Spirit and you shall have peace in me, Jesus Christ by the will of the Father.

25 And again: I command you, that thou shalt not covet thy neighbor's wife.

26 Nor seek thy neighbor's life.

27 And again: I command you, that thou shalt not covet thine own property, but impart it freely to the printing of the book of Mormon, which contains the truth and the word of God, which is my word to Gentile, that soon it may go to the Jew, of which the Lamanites are a remnant; that they may believe the gospel, and look not for a Messiah to come which has already come.

28 And again: I command you, that thou shalt pray vocally as well as to thyself:

29 Yea, before the world as well as in secret; in public as well as in private.

30 And thou shalt declare glad tidings; yea, publish it upon the mountains, and upon every high place, and among every people which thou shalt be permitted to see.

31 And thou shalt do it with all humility, trusting in me, reviling not against revilers.

B5

42

32 And of tenets thou shalt not talk, but thou shalt declare repentance and faith on the Savior and remission of sins by baptism and by fire; yea, even the Holy Ghost.

33 Behold this is a great and the last commandment which I shall give unto you:

34 For this shall suffice for thy daily walk even unto the end of thy life.

35 And misery thou shalt receive, if thou wilt slight these counsels; Yea, even destruction of thyself and property.

36 Impart a portion of thy property; Yea, even a part of thy lands and all save the support of thy family.

37 Pay the printer's debt.

38 Release thyself from bondage.

39 Leave thy house and home, except when thou shalt desire to see them.

40 And speak freely to all: Yea, preach, exhort, declare the truth, even with a loud voice; with a sound of rejoicing, crying hosanna! hosanna! blessed be the name of the Lord God.

41 Pray always and I will pour out my Spirit upon you, and great shall be your blessing:

42 Yea, even more than if you should obtain treasures of earth, and corruptibleness to the extent thereof.

43 Behold, canst thou read this without rejoicing, and lifting up thy heart for gladness; or canst thou run about longer as a blind guide; or canst thou be humble and meek and conduct thyself wisely before me:

44 Yea, come unto me thy Savior. Amen.

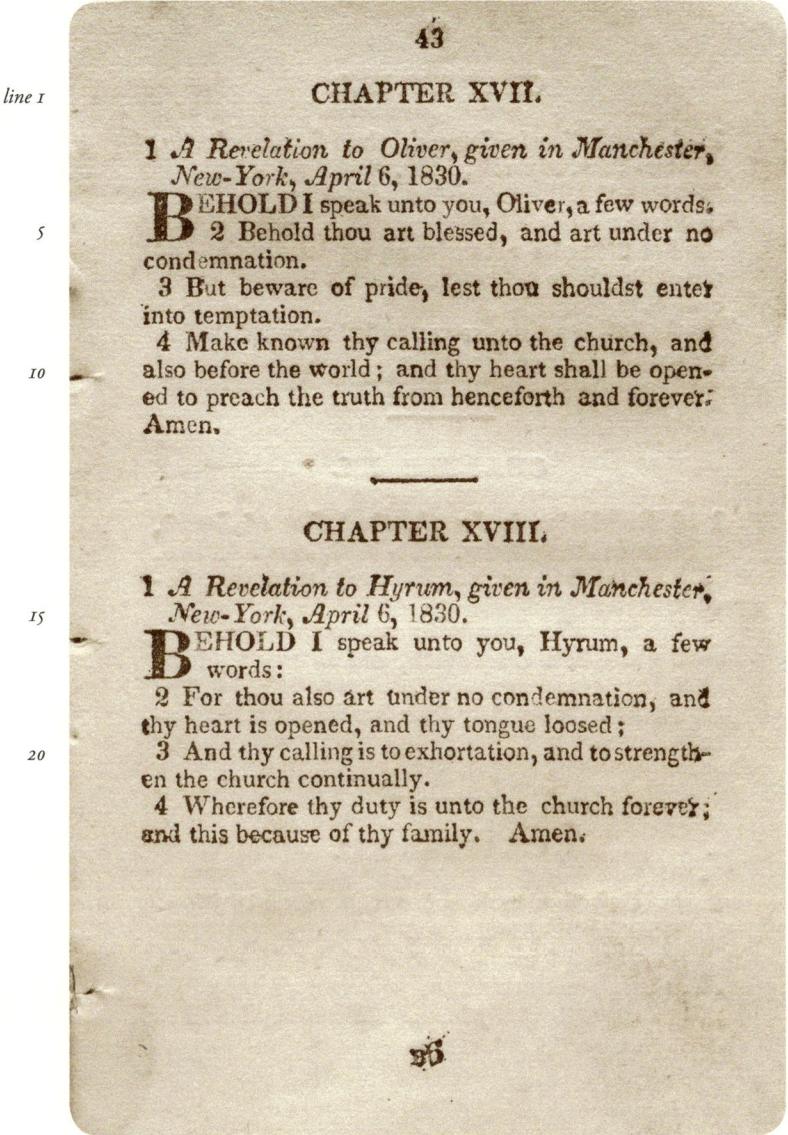

43

line 1

CHAPTER XVII.

1 *A Revelation to Oliver, given in Manchester, New-York, April 6, 1830.*

BEHOLD I speak unto you, Oliver, a few words.
2 Behold thou art blessed, and art under no condemnation.

3 But beware of pride, lest thou shouldst enter into temptation.

4 Make known thy calling unto the church, and also before the world; and thy heart shall be opened to preach the truth from henceforth and forever. Amen.

CHAPTER XVIII.

1 *A Revelation to Hyrum, given in Manchester, New-York, April 6, 1830.*

BEHOLD I speak unto you, Hyrum, a few words:

2 For thou also art under no condemnation, and thy heart is opened, and thy tongue loosed;

3 And thy calling is to exhortation, and to strengthen the church continually.

4 Wherefore thy duty is unto the church forever; and this because of thy family. Amen.

line 1. Revelation, Apr. 1830–A [D&C 23:1–2]. This version reflects editing marks made in Revelation Book 1, indicating that the latter was used as a source text for the former. The two chapters on this page are among seven (17–22 and 28) in the Book of Commandments that carry day-specific dates. The specific dates found in these two chapters were not originally recorded in or added to the text of Revelation Book 1. (See *JSP,* MRB:29.)

line 13. Revelation, Apr. 1830–B [D&C 23:3]. This version reflects editing marks made in Revelation Book 1, indicating that the latter was used as a source text for the former. (See *JSP,* MRB:29.)

line 1

44

CHAPTER XIX.

1 *A Revelation to Samuel, given in Manchester, New-York, April 6, 1830.*

BEHOLD I speak a few words unto you, Samuel:

5

2 For thou also art under no condemnation, and thy calling is to exhortation, and to strengthen the church.

3 And thou art not as yet called to preach before the world.   Amen.

10

CHAPTER XX.

1 *A Revelation to Joseph, the father of Joseph, given in Manchester, New-York, April 6, 1830.*

BEHOLD I speak a few words unto you, Joseph:

15

2 For thou also art under no condemnation, and thy calling also is to exhortation, and to strengthen the church.

3 And this is thy duty from henceforth and forever.   Amen.

20

CHAPTER XXI.

1 *A Revelation to Joseph (K.,) given in Manchester, New-York, April 6, 1830.*

BEHOLD I manifest unto you by these words, that you must take up your cross, in the which you must pray vocally before the world, as well as

25

---

line 1. Revelation, Apr. 1830–C [D&C 23:4]. This version reflects editing marks made in Revelation Book 1, indicating that the latter was used as a source text for the former. The three chapters on this page are among seven (17–22 and 28) in the Book of Commandments that carry day-specific dates. The specific dates found in these three chapters were not originally recorded in or added to the text of Revelation Book 1. (See *JSP*, MRB:29–31.)

line 11. Revelation, Apr. 1830–D [D&C 23:5]. This version reflects editing marks made in Revelation Book 1, indicating that the latter was used as a source text for the former. (See *JSP*, MRB:31.)

line 21. Revelation, Apr. 1830–E [D&C 23:6–7]. This version reflects editing marks made in Revelation Book 1, indicating that the latter was used as a source text for the former. (See *JSP*, MRB:31.)

45

line 1 in secret, and in your family, and among your friends, and in all places.

2 And behold it is your duty to unite with the true church, and give your language to exhortation continually, that you may receive the reward of the laborer. Amen.

5

CHAPTER XXII.

1 *A Revelation to Joseph, given in Manchester, New-York, April 6, 1830.*

10 BEHOLD there shall be a record kept among you, and in it thou shalt be called a seer, a translator, a prophet, an apostle of Jesus Christ, an elder of the church through the will of God the Father, and the grace of our Lord Jesus Christ;

15 2 Being inspired of the Holy Ghost to lay the foundation thereof, and to build it up unto the most holy faith;

3 Which church was organized and established, in the year of our Lord eighteen hundred and thirty, *20* in the fourth month, and on the sixth day of the month, which is called April.

4 Wherefore, meaning the church, thou shalt give heed unto all his words, and commandments, which he shall give unto you, as he receiveth them, walk-*25* ing in all holiness before me:

5 For his word ye shall receive, as if from mine own mouth, in all patience and faith;

6 For by doing these things, the gates of hell shall not prevail against you:

30 7 Yea, and the Lord God will disperse the powers of darkness from before you; and cause the

B7

---

line 7. Revelation, 6 Apr. 1830 [D&C 21]. This version reflects editing marks made in Revelation Book 1, indicating that the latter was used as a source text for the former. This chapter is one of seven (17–22 and 28) in the Book of Commandments that carry day-specific dates. Revelation Book 1 states that this revelation was received in Fayette, New York. (See *JSP,* MRB:27–29.)

46

heavens to shake for your good, and his name's glory.

8 For thus saith the Lord God, him have I inspired to move the cause of Zion in mighty power for good; and his diligence I know, and his prayers I have heard:

9 Yea, his weeping for Zion I have seen, and I will cause that he shall mourn for her no longer, for his days of rejoicing are come unto the remission of his sins, and the manifestations of my blessings upon his works.

10 For behold, I will bless all those who labor in my vineyard, with a mighty blessing, and they shall believe on his words, which are given him through me, by the Comforter:

11 Which manifesteth that Jesus was crucified by sinful men for the sins of the world;

12 Yea, for the remission of sins unto the contrite heart.

13 Wherefore, it behooveth me, that he should be ordained by you, Oliver, mine apostle;

14 This being an ordinance unto you, that you are an elder under his hand, he being the first unto you, that you might be an elder unto this church of Christ, bearing my name;

15 And the first preacher of this church, unto the church, and before the world; yea, before the Gentiles:

16 Yea, and thus saith the Lord God, lo, lo, to the Jews, also. Amen.

47

CHAPTER XXIII.

1 *A Commandment unto the church of Christ, which was established in these last days, in the year of our Lord one thousand eight hundred and thirty: Given in Fayette, New-York, April, 1830, in consequence of some desiring to unite with the church without re-baptism, who had previously been baptized.*

BEHOLD I say unto you, that all old covenants have I caused to be done away in this thing, and this is a new and an everlasting covenant; even that which was from the beginning.

2 Wherefore although a man should be baptized an hundred times, it availeth him nothing;

3 For you cannot enter in at the straight gate by the law of Moses, neither by your dead works;

4 For it is because of your dead works, that I have caused this last covenant, and this church to be built up unto me; even as in days of old.

5 Wherefore enter ye in at the gate, as I have commanded, and seek not to counsel your God. Amen.

CHAPTER XXIV.

1 *The Articles and Covenants of the church of Christ, given in Fayette, New-York, June, 1830:*

THE rise of the church of Christ in these last days, being one thousand eight hundred and thirty years since the coming of our Lord and Saviour Jesus Christ, in the flesh;

28

---

line 1. Revelation, 16 Apr. 1830 [D&C 22]. This version closely corresponds to the version in the June 1832 issue of *The Evening and the Morning Star,* suggesting that the latter was used as a source text for the former.

line 23. Articles and covenants, 10 Apr. 1830 [D&C 20]. This version reflects editing marks made in Revelation Book 1, indicating that the latter was used as a source text for the former. This item should be dated 10 April 1830. For more information on this dating, see the discussion of this item in the Documents series. (See *JSP,* MRB:75–87.)

48

2 It being regularly organized and established agreeable to the laws of our country, by the will and commandments of God in the fourth month and on the sixth day of the month, which is called April:

3 Which commandments were given to Joseph, who was called of God and ordained an apostle of Jesus Christ, an elder of this church;

4 And also to Oliver, who was also called of God an apostle of Jesus Christ, an elder of this church, and ordained under his hand:

5 And this according to the grace of our Lord and Savior Jesus Christ, to whom be all glory both now and fo ever. Amen.

6 For, after that it truly was manifested unto this first elder, that he had received a remission of his sins, he was entangled again in the vanities of the world;

7 But after truly repenting, God ministered unto him by an holy angel, whose countenance was as lightning, and whose garments were pure and white above all whiteness, and gave unto him commandments which inspired him from on high, and gave unto him power, by the means which were before prepared, that he should translate a book;

8 Which book contained a record of a fallen people, and also the fulness of the gospel of Jesus Christ to the Gentiles;

9 And also to the Jews, proving unto them, that the holy scriptures are true;

10 And also, that God doth inspire men and call them to his holy work, in these last days as well as in days of old, that he might be the same God forever. Amen.

11 Which book was given by inspiration, and is called the book of Mormon, and is confirmed to

49

others by the ministering of angels, and declared unto the world by them:

12 Wherefore having so great witnesses, by them shall the world be judged, even as many as shall hereafter receive this work, either to faith and righteousness, or to the hardness of heart in unbelief, to their own condemnation, for the Lord God hath spoken it, for we, the elders of the church, have heard and bear witness to the words of the glorious Majesty on high; to whom be glory forever and ever. Amen.

13 Wherefore, by these things we know that there is a God in heaven, who is infinite and eternal, from everlasting to everlasting, the same unchangeable God, the maker of heaven and earth and all things that in them is, and that he created man male and female, and after his own image, and in his own likeness created he them;

14 And that he gave unto the children of men commandments, that they should love and serve him the only being whom they should worship, but by the transgression of these holy laws, man became sensual and devilish, and became fallen man.

15 Wherefore, the Almighty God gave his only begotten Son, as it is written in those scriptures, which have been given of him, that he suffered temptations, but gave no heed unto them;

16 That he was crucified, died, and rose again the third day, and that he ascended into heaven to sit down on the right hand of the Father, to reign with Almighty power according to the will of the Father.

17 Therefore, as many as would believe and were baptized in his holy name, and endured in faith to the end, should be saved;

56

18 Yea, even as many as were before he came in the flesh, from the beginning, who believed in the words of the holy prophets, who were inspired by the gift of the Holy Ghost, which truly testified of him in all things, as well as those who should come after, who should believe in the gifts and callings of God, by the Holy Ghost, which beareth record of the Father and of the Son, which Father and Son and Holy Ghost, is one God, infinite and eternal, without end.   Amen.

19 And we know, that all men must repent and believe on the name of Jesus Christ, and worship the Father in his name, and endure in faith on his name to the end, or they cannot be saved in the kingdom of God.

20 And we know, that justification through the grace of our Lord and Savior Jesus Christ, is just and true;

21 And we know, also, that sanctification through the grace of our Lord and Savior Jesus Christ, is just and true, to all those who love and serve God with all their mights, minds, and strength, but there is a possibility that men may fall from grace and depart from the living God.

22 Therefore, let the church take heed and pray always, lest they fall into temptation;

23 Yea, and even he that is sanctified also.

24 And we know, that these things are true and agreeable to the revelation of John, neither adding to, nor diminishing from the prophecy of his book;

25 Neither to the holy scriptures;

26 Neither to the revelations of God which shall come hereafter, by the gift and power of the Holy Ghost;

27 Neither by the voice of God;

line 1

28 Neither by the ministering of angels, and the Lord God hath spoken it; and honor, power, and glory, be rendered to his holy name both now and ever. Amen.

5   29 And again, by way of commandment to the church, concerning the manner of baptism;

30 Behold whosoever humbleth himself before God and desireth to be baptized, and comes forth with a broken heart and a contrite spirit, and wit-

10 nesseth unto the church, that they have truly repented of all their sins and are willing to take upon them the name of Christ, having a determination to serve him unto the end, and truly manifest by their works that they have received the Spirit of Christ

15 unto the remission of their sins, then shall they be received unto baptism into the church of Christ.

31 The duty of the elders, priests, teachers, deacons and members of the church of Christ.

32 An apostle is an elder, and it is his calling to

20 baptize and to ordain other elders, priests, teachers and deacons, and to administer the flesh and blood of Christ according to the scriptures;

33 And to teach, expound, exhort, baptize, and watch over the church;

25 34 And to confirm the church by the laying on of the hands, and the giving of the Holy Ghost, and to take the lead of all meetings.

35 The elders are to conduct the meetings as they are led by the Holy Ghost.

30 36 The priest's duty is to preach, teach, expound, exhort and baptize, and administer the sacrament, and visit the house of each member, and exhort them to pray vocally and in secret, and also to attend to all family duties;

35 37 And ordain other priests, teachers and deacons,

52

and take the lead of meetings; but none of these offices is he to do when there is an elder present, but in all cases is to assist the elder.

38 The teacher's duty is to watch over the church always, and be with them, and strengthen them, and see that there is no iniquity in the church, neither hardness with each other, neither lying nor backbiting, nor evil speaking;

39 And see that the church meet together often, and also see that all the members do their duty;

40 And he is to take the lead of meetings in the absence of the elder or priest, and is to be assisted always, and in all his duties in the church by the deacons;

41 But neither the teachers nor deacons have authority to baptize nor administer the sacrament, but are to warn, expound, exhort and teach, and invite all to come unto Christ.

42 Every elder, priest, teacher or deacon, is to be ordained according to the gifts and callings of God unto him, by the power of the Holy Ghost which is in the one who ordains him.

43 The several elders composing this church of Christ, are to meet in conference once in three months, or from time to time as they shall direct or appoint, to do church business whatsoever is necessary.

44 And each priest or teacher, who is ordained by a priest, is to take a certificate from him at the time, which when presented to an elder, he is to give him a license, which shall authorize him to perform the duty of his calling.

45 The duty of the members after they are received by baptism.

46 The elders or priests are to have a sufficient

line 1 time to expound all things concerning this church of
Christ to their understanding, previous to their partaking of the sacrament, and being confirmed by the
laying on of the hands of the elders;

5 47 So that all things may be done in order.

48 And the members shall manifest before the
church, and also before the elders, by a godly walk
and conversation, that they are worthy of it, that
there may be works and faith agreeable to the holy
10 scriptures, walking in holiness before the Lord.

49 Every member of this church of Christ having
children, is to bring them unto the elders before the
church, who are to lay their hands upon them in
the name of the Lord, and bless them in the name
15 of Christ.

50 There can not any one be received into this
church of Christ, who has not arrived to the years
of accountability before God, and is not capable of
repentance.

20 51 And baptism is to be administered in the following manner unto all those who repent:

52 Whosoever being called of God and having
authority given them of Jesus Christ, shall go down
into the water with them, and shall say, calling
25 them by name:

53 Having authority given me of Jesus Christ, I
baptize you in the name of the Father, and of the
Son, and of the Holy Ghost. Amen.

54 Then shall he immerse them in the water, and
30 come forth again out of the water.

55 And it is expedient that the church meet together oft to partake of bread and wine, in remembrance of the Lord Jesus;

56 And the elder or priest shall administer it, and
35 after this manner shall he do, he shall kneel with

line 1 the church, and call upon the Father in mighty prayer, saying:

57 O God the Eternal Father, we ask thee in the name of thy Son Jesus Christ, to bless and sanctify this bread to the souls of all those who partake of it, that they may eat in remembrance of the body of thy Son. and witness unto thee O God the Eternal Father, that they are willing to take upon them the name of thy Son, and always remember him, and keep his commandments which he hath given them, that they may always have his Spirit to be with them. Amen.

58 The manner of administering the wine:

59 Behold they shall take the cup and say, O God, the Eternal Father, we ask thee in the name of thy Son Jesus Christ, to bless and sanctify this wine to the souls of all those who drink of it, that they may do it in remembrance of the blood of thy Son, which was shed for them, that they may witness unto thee, O God the Eternal Father, that they do always remember him, that they may have his Spirit to be with them. Amen.

60 Any member of this church of Christ, transgressing or being overtaken in a fault, shall be dealt with according as the scriptures direct.

61 It shall be the duty of the several churches, composing this church of Christ, to send one or more of their teachers to attend the several conferences, held by the elders of this church, with a list of the names of the several members, uniting themselves to the church since the last conference, or send by the hand of some priest, so that there can be kept a regular list of all the names of the members of the whole church, in a book kept by one of the elders;

55

line 1

62 Whomsoever the other elders shall appoint from time to time:

63 And also, if any have been expelled from the church, so that their names may be blotted out of the general church record of names.

64 Any member removing from the church where he resides, if going to a church where he is not known, may take a letter certifying that he is a regular member and in good standing;

65 Which certificate may be signed by any elder or priest, if the member receiving the letter is personally acquainted with the elder or priest, or it may be signed by the teachers or deacons of the church.

CHAPTER XXV.

1 *A Revelation to Joseph, and also to Oliver, given in Harmony, Pennsylvania, July, 1830.*
BEHOLD thou wast called and chosen to write the book of Mormon, and to my ministry;

2 And I have lifted thee up out of thine afflictions, and have counseled thee, that thou hast been delivered from all thine enemies, and thou hast been delivered from the powers of satan, and from darkness!

3 Nevertheless, thou art not excusable in thy transgressions; nevertheless go thy way and sin no more.

4 Magnify thine office;

5 And after thou hast sowed thy fields and secured them go speedily unto the church, which is in Colesville, Fayette and Manchester, and they shall

---

line 15. Revelation, July 1830–A [D&C 24]. This version reflects editing marks made in Revelation Book 1, indicating that the latter was used as a source text for the former. (See *JSP*, MRB:35–39.)

56

support thee; and I will bless them both spiritually and temporally;

6 But if they receive thee not, I will send upon them a cursing instead of a blessing.

7 And thou shalt continue in calling upon God in my name, and writing the things which shall be given thee by the Comforter;

8 And expounding all scriptures unto the church, and it shall be given thee in the very moment, what thou shalt speak and write;

9 And they shall hear it, or I will send unto them a cursing instead of a blessing:

10 For thou shalt devote all thy service in Zion.

11 And in this thou shalt have strength.

12 Be patient in afflictions, for thou shalt have many:

13 But endure them, for lo, I am with you, even unto the end of thy days.

14 And in temporal labors thou shalt not have strength, for this is not thy calling.

15 Attend to thy calling and thou shalt have wherewith to magnify thine office, and to expound all scriptures.

16 And continue in the laying on of the hands, and confirming the churches.

17 And thy brother Oliver shall continue in bearing my name before the world; and also to the church.

18 And he shall not suppose that he can say enough in my cause;

19 And lo I am with him to the end.

20 In me he shall have glory, and not of himself, whether in weakness or in strength, whether in bonds or free:

21 And at all times and in all places, he shall

57

open his mouth and declare my gospel as with the voice of a trump, both day and night.

22 And I will give unto him strength such as is not known among men.

23 Require not miracles, except I shall command you; except casting out devils; healing the sick; and against poisonous serpents; and against deadly poisons:

24 And these things ye shall not do, except it be required of you, by them who desire it, that the scriptures might be fulfilled, for ye shall do according to that which is written.

25 And in whatsoever place ye shall enter, and they receive you not, in my name, ye shall leave a cursing instead of a blessing, by casting off the dust of your feet against them as a testimony, and cleansing your feet by the wayside.

26 And it shall come to pass, that whosoever shall lay their hands upon you by violence, ye shall command to be smitten in my name, and behold I will smite them according to your words, in mine own due time.

27 And whosoever shall go to law with thee shall be cursed by the law.

28 And thou shalt take no purse, nor scrip, neither staves, neither two coats, for the church shall give unto thee in the very hour what thou needest for food, and for raiment, and for shoes, and for money, and for scrip:

29 For thou art called to prune my vineyard with a mighty pruning, yea, even for the last time.

30 Yea, and also, all those whom thou hast ordained.

31 And they shall do even according to this pattern, Amen.

68

CHAPTER XXVI.

line 1

1 *A Revelation to Emma, given in Harmony, Pennsylvania, July,* 1830.

EMMA, my daughter in Zion, a revelation I give unto you, concerning my will:

2 Behold thy sins are forgiven thee, and thou art an elect lady, whom I have called.

3 Murmur not because of the things which thou hast not seen, for they are withheld from thee, and from the world, which is wisdom in me in a time to come.

4 And the office of thy calling shall be for a comfort unto my servant Joseph, thy husband, in his afflictions with consoling words, in the spirit of meekness.

5 And thou shalt go with him at the time of his going, and be unto him for a scribe, that I may send Oliver whithersoever I will.

6 And thou shalt be ordained under his hand to expound scriptures, and to exhort the church, according as it shall be given thee by my Spirit:

7 For he shall lay his hands upon thee, and thou shalt receive the Holy Ghost, and thy time shall be given to writing, and to learning much.

8 And thou needest not fear, for thy husband shall support thee from the church:

9 For unto them is his calling, that all things might be revealed unto them, whatsoever I will according to their faith.

10 And verily I say unto thee, that thou shalt lay aside the things of this world, and seek for the things of a better.

11 And it shall be given thee, also, to make a selection of sacred Hymns, as it shall be given thee,

---

line 1. Revelation, July 1830–C [D&C 25]. This version reflects editing marks made in Revelation Book 1, indicating that the latter was used as a source text for the former. (See *JSP,* MRB:39–41.)

59

which is pleasing unto me, to be had in my church?

12 For my soul delighteth in the song of the heart: Yea, the song of the righteous is a prayer unto me.

13 And it shall be answered with a blessing upon their heads.

14 Wherefore lift up thy heart and rejoice, and cleave unto the covenants which thou hast made.

15 Continue in the spirit of meekness, and beware of pride.

16 Let thy soul delight in thy husband, and the glory which shall come upon him.

17 Keep my commandments continually, and a crown of righteousness thou shalt receive.

18 And except thou do this, where I am you cannot come.

19 And verily, verily I say unto you, that this is my voice unto all. Amen.

CHAPTER XXVII.

1 *A Revelation to Joseph, Oliver and John, given in Harmony, Pennsylvania, July, 1830.*

BEHOLD, I say unto you, that you shall let your time be devoted to the studying of the scriptures, and to preaching, and to cofirming the church at Colesville;

2 And to performing your labors on the land, such as is required, until after you shall go to the west, to hold the next conference; and then it shall be made known what you shall do.

3 And all things shall be done by common consent in the church, by much prayer and faith;

4 For all things you shall receive by faith. Amen.

---

line 18. Revelation, July 1830–B [D&C 26]. This version reflects editing marks made in Revelation Book 1, indicating that the latter was used as a source text for the former. (See *JSP*, MRB:39.)

60

CHAPTER XXVIII.

line 1

1 *A Commandment to the church of Christ, given in Harmony, Pennsylvania, September 4, 1830.*

LISTEN to the voice of Jesus Christ, your Lord, your God and your Redeemer, whose word is quick and powerful.

2 For behold I say unto you, that it mattereth not what ye shall eat, or what ye shall drink, when ye partake of the sacrament, if it so be that ye do it with an eye single to my glory;

3 Remembering unto the Father my body which was laid down for you, and my blood which was shed for the remission of your sins:

4 Wherefore a commandment I give unto you, that you shall not purchase wine, neither strong drink of your enemies:

5 Wherefore you shall partake of none, except it is made new among you, yea, in this my Father's kingdom which shall be built up on the earth.

6 Behold this is wisdom in me, wherefore marvel not, for the hour cometh that I will drink of the fruit of the vine with you, on the earth, and with all those whom my Father hath given me out of the world:

7 Wherefore lift up your hearts and rejoice, and gird up your loins and be faithful until I come:— even so. Amen.

5

10

15

20

25

ISTORIAN'S OFFICE.
Church of Jesus Christ
of Latter-day Saints.

---

line 1. Revelation, ca. Aug. 1830 [D&C 27]. Editing marks made in Revelation Book 1 are reflected both in this version and the version in the March 1833 issue of *The Evening and the Morning Star*. Because the newspaper version and the version printed here were set in type at approximately the same time, it is difficult to tell which was set in type first. This chapter is one of seven (17–22 and 28) in the Book of Commandments that carry a day-specific date. The specific date found in this chapter was not originally recorded in or added to the text of Revelation Book 1. This revelation should be dated circa August 1830. For more information on this dating, see the discussion of this revelation in the Documents series. (See *JSP,* MRB:41–43.)

line 27. The Church Historian's Office stamp, here applied in purple ink, was in use sometime in the late nineteenth century and possibly in the early twentieth century. (See p. 14 herein.)

61

CHAPTER XXIX.

line 1

1 *A Revelation to the church of Christ, given in the presence of six elders, in Fayette, New-York, September,* 1830.

LISTEN to the voice of Jesus Christ, your Redeemer, the Great I AM, whose arm of mercy hath atoned for your sins;

2 Who will gather his people even as a hen gathereth her chickens under her wings, even as many as will hearken to my voice, and humble themselves before me, and call upon me in mighty prayer.

3 Behold, verily, verily I say unto you, that at this time your sins are forgiven you; therefore ye receive these things:

4 But remember to sin no more, lest perils shall come upon you.

5 Verily I say unto you, that ye are chosen out of the world to declare my gospel with the sound of rejoicing, as with the voice of a trump:

6 Lift up your hearts and be glad for I am in your midst, and am your advocate with the Father; and it is his good will to give you the kingdom;

7 And as it is written, Whatsoever ye shall ask in faith, being united in prayer according to my command, ye shall receive;

8 And ye are called to bring to pass the gathering of mine elect, for mine elect hear my voice and harden not their hearts:

9 Wherefore the decree hath gone forth from the Father, that they shall be gathered in unto one place, upon the face of this land, to prepare their hearts, and be prepared in all things, against the day when tribulation and desolation are sent forth upon the wicked:

---

line 1. Revelation, Sept. 1830–A [D&C 29]. This version reflects editing marks made in Revelation Book 1, indicating that the latter was used as a source text for the former. (See *JSP,* MRB:43–51.)

82

line 1

10 For the hour is nigh, and the day soon at hand, when the earth is ripe:

11 And all the proud, and they that do wickedly, shall be as stubble, and I will burn them up, saith the Lord of Hosts, that wickedness shall not be upon the earth:

12 For the hour is nigh, and that which was spoken by mine apostles must be fulfilled; for as they spoke so shall it come to pass;

13 For I will reveal myself from heaven with power and great glory, with all the hosts thereof, and dwell in righteousness with men on earth a thousand years, and the wicked shall not stand.

14 And again, verily, verily I say unto you, and it hath gone forth in a firm decree, by the will of the Father, that mine apostles, the twelve which were with me in my ministry at Jerusalem, shall stand at my right hand at the day of my coming in a pillar of fire, being clothed with robes of righteousness, with crowns upon their heads, in glory even as I am, to judge the whole house of Israel, even as many as have loved me and kept my commandments, and none else;

15 For a trump shall sound both long and loud, even as upon mount Sinai, and all the earth shall quake, and they shall come forth:

16 Yea, even the dead which died in me, to receive a crown of righteousness, and to be clothed upon, even as I am, to be with me, that we may be one.

17 But behold, I say unto you, that before this great day shall come, the sun shall be darkened, and the moon shall be turned into blood, and the stars shall fall from heaven;

18 And there shall be greater signs in heaven

63

above, and in the earth beneath; and there shall be
weeping and wailing among the hosts of men;

19 And there shall be a great hailstorm sent forth
to destroy the crops of the earth:

20 And it shall come to pass, because of the wickedness of the world, that I will take vengeance upon the wicked, for they will not repent:

21 For the cup of mine indignation is full; for
behold, my blood shall not cleanse them if they
hear me not.

22 Wherefore I the Lord God will send forth flies
upon the face of the earth, which shall take hold of
the inhabitants thereof, and shall eat their flesh, and
shall cause maggots to come in upon them, and their
tongues shall be stayed that they shall not utter
again t me, and their flesh shall fall from off their
bones, and their eyes from their sockets:

23 And it shall come to pass, that the beasts of
the forests, and the fowls of the air, shall devour
them up:

24 And that great and abominable church, which
is the whore of all the earth, shall be cast down by
devouring fire, according as it was spoken by the
mouth of Ezekiel the prophet, which spoke of these
things, which have not come to pass, but surely
must, as I live, for abominations shall not reign.

25 And again, verily, verily I say unto you, that
when the thousand years are ended, and men again
begin to deny their God, then will I spare the earth
but for a little season;

26 And the end shall come, and the heaven and
the earth shall be consumed, and pass away, and
there shall be a new heaven and a new earth;

27 For all old things shall pass away, and all
things shall become new, even the heaven and the

64

earth, and all the fulness thereof, both men and
beasts;

28 The fowls of the air, and the fishes of the sea,
and not one hair, neither mote, shall be lost, for it
is the workmanship of mine hand.

29 But behold, verily I say unto you, before the
earth shall pass away, Michael mine archangel,
shall sound his trump, and then shall all the dead
awake, for their graves shall be opened, and they
shall come forth; yea, even all;

30 And the righteous shall be gathered on my right
hand unto eternal life;

31 And the wicked on my left hand will I be
ashamed to own before the Father:

32 Wherefore I will say unto them, depart from
me ye cursed into everlasting fire, prepared for the
devil and his angels.

33 And now behold I say unto you, never at any
time, have I declared from mine own mouth, that
they should return, for where I am they cannot
come, for they have no power;

34 But remember, that all my judgments are not
given unto men;

35 And as the words have gone forth out of my
mouth, even so shall they be fulfilled, that the first
shall be last, and that the last shall be first in all
things, whatsoever I have created by the word of
my power, which is the power of my Spirit;

36 For by the power of my Spirit, created I them:

37 Yea, all things both spiritual and temporal:

38 Firstly spiritual, secondly temporal, which is
the beginning of my work:

39 And again, firstly temporal, and secondly spiritual, which is the last of my work:

40 Speaking unto you, that you may naturally

65

line 1 understand, but unto myself my works have no end, neither beginning; but it is given unto you, that ye may understand, because ye have asked it of me and are agreed.

5 41 Wherefore, verily I say unto you, that all things unto me are spiritual, and not at any time have I given unto you a law which was temporal, neither any man, nor the children of men:

42 Neither Adam your father, whom I created; *10* behold I gave unto him that he should be an agent unto himself;

43 And I gave unto him commandment, but no temporal commandment gave I unto him; for my commandments are spiritual;

15 44 They are not natural, nor temporal, neither carnal nor sensual.

45 And it came to pass, that Adam being tempted of the devil, for behold the devil was before Adam, for he rebelled against me saying, Give me *20* thine honor, which is my power: and also a third part of the hosts of heaven turned he away from me because of their agency:

46 And they were thrust down, and thus came the devil and his angels; and behold, there is a place *25* prepared for them from the beginning, which place is hell:

47 And it must needs be that the devil should tempt the children of men, or they could not be agents unto themselves, for if they never should *30* have bitter, they could not know the sweet.

48 Wherefore, it came to pass, that the devil tempted Adam and he partook the forbidden fruit, and transgressed the commandment, wherein he became subject to the will of the devil, because he *35* yielded unto temptation.

c1

---

line 36. This page begins the third gathering of the book. "C1" is the first of eight signature marks found on the rectos of the first eight leaves of this gathering. These marks were used in collating the gatherings after the sheets were folded.

66

49 Wherefore, I the Lord God caused that he should be cast out from the garden of Eden, from my presence, because of his transgression;

50 Wherein he became spiritually dead; which is the first death, even that same death, which is the last death, which is spiritual, which shall be pronounced upon the wicked when I shall say, Depart ye cursed.

51 But behold I say unto you, that I the Lord God gave unto Adam and unto his seed, that they should not die as to the temporal death, until I the Lord God should send forth angels to declare unto them repentance and redemption, through faith on the name of mine only begotten Son:

52 And thus did I the Lord God appoint unto man the days of his probation; that by his natural death he might be raised in immortality unto eternal life, even as many as would believe, and they that believe not, unto eternal damnation, for they cannot be redeemed from their spiritual fall, because they repent not, for they will love darkness rather than light, and their deeds are evil, and they receive their wages of whom they list to obey.

53 But behold I say unto you, that little children are redeemed from the foundation of the world, through mine only Begotten:

54 Wherefore they cannot sin, for power is not given unto satan to tempt little children, until they begin to become accountable before me;

55 For it is given unto them even as I will, according to mine own pleasure, that great things may be required at the hand of their fathers.

56 And again I say unto you, that whoso having knowledge, have I not commanded to repent? and he that hath no understanding, it remaineth in me

67

line 1 to do according as it is written. And now, I declare no more unto you at this time. Amen.

CHAPTER XXX.

1 *A Revelation to Oliver, given in Fayette, New York, September, 1830.*

BEHOLD I say unto you, Oliver, that it shall be given unto thee, that thou shalt be heard by the church, in all things whatsoever thou shalt teach them by the Comforter, concerning the revelations and commandments which I have given.

2 But behold, verily, verily I say unto you, no one shall be appointed to receive commandments and revelations in this church, excepting my servant Joseph, for he receiveth them even as Moses:

3 And thou shalt be obedient unto the things which I shall give unto him, even as Aaron, to declare faithfully the commandments and the revelations, with power and authority unto the church.

4 And if thou art led at any time by the Comforter to speak or teach, or at all times by the way of commandment unto the church, thou mayest do it.

5 But thou shalt not write by way of commandment, but by wisdom:

6 And thou shalt not command him who is at thy head, and at the head of the church, for I have given him the keys of the mysteries and the revelations which are sealed, until I shall appoint unto them another in his stead.

7 And now, behold I say unto you, that you shall go unto the Lamanites and preach my gospel unto them, and cause my church to be established among

c2

---

line 3. Revelation, Sept. 1830–B [D&C 28]. This version reflects editing marks made in Revelation Book 1, indicating that the latter was used as a source text for the former. (See *JSP,* MRB:51–53.)

68

them. And thou shalt have revelations but write them not by way of commandment.

8 And now behold I say unto you, that it is not revealed, and no man knoweth where the city shall be built, but it shall be given hereafter.

9 Behold I say unto you, that it shall be on the borders by the Lamanites.

10 Thou shalt not leave this place until after the conference, and my servant Joseph shall be appointed to rule the conference by the voice of it, and what he saith to thee, that thou shalt tell.

11 And again, thou shalt take thy brother Hiram between him and thee alone, and tell him that those things which he hath written from that stone are not of me, and that satan deceiveth him :

12 For behold these things have not been appointed unto him :

13 Neither shall any thing be appointed unto any of this church contrary to the church covenants, for all things must be done in order and by common consent in the church, by the prayer of faith.

14 And thou shalt settle all these things according to the covenants of the church before thou shalt take thy journey among the Lamanites.

15 And it shall be given thee from the time that thou shalt go, until the time that thou shalt return, what thou shalt do.

16 And thou must open thy mouth at all times declaring my gospel with the sound of rejoicing.— Amen.

69

CHAPTER XXXI.

A Revelation to David, given in Fayette, New-York, September, 1830.

BEHOLD I say unto you, David, that you have feared man and have not relied upon me for strength, as you ought:

2 But your mind has been on the things of the earth more than on the things of me, your Maker, and the ministry whereunto you have been called; and you have not given heed unto my Spirit, and to those who were set over you, but have been persuaded by those whom I have not commanded:

3 Wherefore you are left to inquire for yourself, at my hand, and ponder upon the things which you have received.

4 And your home shall be at your father's house, until I give unto you further commandments.

5 And you shall attend to the ministry in the church, and before the world, and in the regions round about. Amen.

———

CHAPTER XXXII.

A Revelation to Peter, given in Fayette, New-York, September, 1830.

BEHOLD I say unto you, Peter, that you shall take your journey with your brother Oliver, for the time has come, that it is expedient in me, that you shall open your mouth to declare my gospel:

2 Therefore, fear not but give heed unto the words and advice of your brother, which he shall give you,

68

---

line 1. Revelation, Sept. 1830–C [D&C 30:1–4]. This version reflects editing marks made in Revelation Book 1, indicating that the latter was used as a source text for the former. (See *JSP,* MRB:55.)

line 2. From this page through the end of the book, the verse number "1" is no longer included at the beginning of each chapter heading.

line 21. Revelation, Sept. 1830–D [D&C 30:5–8]. This version reflects editing marks made in Revelation Book 1, indicating that the latter was used as a source text for the former. (See *JSP,* MRB:55.)

70

line 1
3 And be you afflicted in all his afflictions, ever lifting up your heart unto me in prayer, and faith, for his and your deliverance :

4 For I have given unto him to build up my
5 church among your brethren, the Lamanites.

5 And none have I appointed to be over him in the church, except it is his brother Joseph.

6 Wherefore give heed unto these things and be diligent in keeping my commandments, and you
10 shall be blessed unto eternal life.   Amen.

———

CHAPTER XXXIII.

A Revelation to John, given in Fayette, New-York, September, 1830.

BEHOLD I say unto you my servant, John,
15 that thou shalt commence from this time forth to proclaim my gospel, as with the voice of a trump.

2 And your labor shall be at your brother Philip's, and in that region round about :

3 Yea, wherever you can be heard, until I com-
20 mand you to go from hence.

4 And your whole labor shall be in my Zion, with all your soul, from henceforth ; yea, you shall ever open your mouth in my cause not fearing what man can do, for I am with you.   Amen.

———

line 11. Revelation, Sept. 1830–E [D&C 30:9–11]. This version reflects editing marks made in Revelation Book 1, indicating that the latter was used as a source text for the former. (See *JSP,* MRB:57.)

71

CHAPTER XXXIV.

A Revelation to Thomas, given in Fayette, New-York, September, 1830.

THOMAS, my son, blessed are you because of your faith in my work.

2 Behold you have had many afflictions because of your family: nevertheless I will bless you, and your family:

3 Yea, your little ones, and the day cometh that they will believe and know the truth and be one with you in my church.

4 Lift up your heart and rejoice for the hour of your mission is come; and your tongue shall be loosed; and you shall declare glad tidings of great joy unto this generation.

5 You shall declare the things which have been revealed to my servant Joseph.

6 You shall begin to preach from this time forth; yea, to reap in the field which is white already to be burned:

7 Therefore thrust in your sickle with all your soul; and your sins are forgiven you; and you shall be laden with sheaves upon your back, for the laborer is worthy of his hire.

8 Wherefore your family shall live.

9 Behold, verily I say unto you, go from them only for a little time, and declare my word, and I will prepare a place for them; yea, I will open the hearts of the people and they will receive you.

10 And I will establish a church by your hand; and you shall strengthen them and prepare them against the time when they shall be gathered.

11 Be patient in afflictions, and in sufferings, revile not against those that revile.

c4

line 1

5

10

15

20

25

30

35

---

line 1. Revelation, Sept. 1830–F [D&C 31]. This version reflects editing marks made in Revelation Book 1, indicating that the latter was used as a source text for the former. (See *JSP,* MRB:57–59.)

line 1

12 Govern your house in meekness, and be stead-fast.

13 Behold I say unto you, that you shall be a physician unto the church, but not unto the world, for they will not receive you.

14 Go your way whithersoever I will, and it shall be given you by the Comforter what you shall do, and whither you shall go.

15 Pray always, lest you enter into temptation, and loose your reward.

16 Be faithful unto the end, and lo, I am with you.

17 These words are not of man nor of men, but of me, even Jesus Christ, your Redeemer, by the will of the Father. Amen.

CHAPTER XXXV.

A Revelation to Ezra, and Northrop, given in Fayette, New-York, October, 1830.

BEHOLD I say unto you, my servants Ezra, and Northrop, open ye your ears and hearken to the voice of the Lord your God, whose word is quick and powerful, sharper than a two-edged sword, to the dividing asunder of the joints and marrow, soul and spirit; and is a discerner of the thoughts and intents of the heart.

2 For verily, verily I say unto you, that ye are called to lift up your voices as with the sound of a trump, to declare my gospel unto a crooked and a perverse generation:

3 For behold the field is white already to harvest; and it is the eleventh hour, and for the last time

line *16*. Revelation, Oct. 1830–B [D&C 33]. This version reflects editing marks made in Revelation Book 1, indicating that the latter was used as a source text for the former. (See *JSP,* MRB:59–61.)

73

that I shall call laborers into my vineyard. And
my vineyard has become corrupted every whit:
and there is none which doeth good save it be a
few; and they err in many instances, because of
priestcrafts, all having corrupt minds.

4 And verily, verily I say unto you, that this
church have I established and called forth out of
the wilderness:

5 And even so will I gather mine elect from the
four quarters of the earth, even as many as will believe in me, and hearken unto my voice:

6 Yea, verily, verily I say unto you, that the field
is white already to harvest:

7 Wherefore thrust in your sickles, and reap with
all your might, mind, and strength.

8 Open your mouths and they shall be filled; and
you shall become even as Nephi of old, who journeyed from Jerusalem in the wilderness:

9 Yea, open your mouths and spare not, and you
shall be laden with sheaves upon your backs, for lo
I am with you:

10 Yea, open your mouths and they shall be filled, saying Repent, repent and prepare ye the way
of the Lord, and make his paths strait: for the kingdom of heaven is at hand:

11 Yea, repent and be baptized every one of you,
for a remission of your sins; yea, be baptized even
by water, and then cometh the baptism of fire and
of the Holy Ghost.

12 Behold, verily, verily I say unto you, this is
my gospel, and remember that they shall have faith
in me, or they can in no wise be saved:

13 And upon this Rock I will build my church;
yea, upon this Rock ye are built, and the gates of
hell shall not prevail against you; and ye shall re-

c5

74

line 1 member the church articles and covenants to keep
them :

14 And whoso having faith you shall confirm in
my church, by the laying on of the hands, and I
5 will bestow the gift of the Holy Ghost upon them.

15 And the book of Mormon, and the holy scriptures, are given of me for your instruction ; and the
power of my Spirit quickeneth all things :

16 Wherefore be faithful, praying always, hav-
10 ing your lamps trimmed and burning, and oil with
you, that you may be ready at the coming of the
Bridegroom ; for behold, verily, verily I say unto
you, that I come quickly ; even so : Amen.

CHAPTER XXXVI.

A Revelation to Orson (P.) given in Fayette,
15 *New-York, November, 1830.*

MY son Orson, hearken and hear and behold
what I the Lord God shall say unto you,
even Jesus Christ your Redeemer, the light and the
20 life of the world :

2 A light which shineth in darkness and the darkness comprehendeth it not :

3 Who so loved the world that he gave his own
life, that as many as would believe might become
25 the sons of God :

4 Wherefore you are my son, and blessed are you
because you have believed, and more blessed are
you because you are called of me to preach my gospel ; to lift up your voice as with the sound of a
30 trump, both long and loud, and cry repentance unto a crooked and perverse generation ; preparing

----

line 14. Revelation, 4 Nov. 1830 [D&C 34]. This version reflects editing marks made in Revelation Book 1,
indicating that the latter was used as a source text for the former. (See *JSP*, MRB:61–63.)

75

line 1 the way of the Lord for his second coming: for behold, verily, verily I say unto you, the time is soon
at hand, that I shall come in a cloud with power
and great glory, and it shall be a great day at the
5 time of my coming, for all nations shall tremble.

5 But before that great day shall come, the sun
shall be darkened, and the moon be turned into
blood, and the stars shall refuse their shining, and
some shall fall, and great destructions await the
10 wicked:

6 Wherefore lift up your voice and spare not, for
the Lord God hath spoken.

7 Therefore prophesy and it shall be given by the
power of the Holy Ghost; and if you are faithful
15 behold I am with you until I come:

8 And verily, verily I say unto you, I come quickly.

9 I am your Lord and your Redeemer; even so:
Amen.

CHAPTER XXXVII.

20 *A Revelation to Joseph, and Sidney, given in
Fayette, New-York, December, 1830.*

LISTEN to the voice of the Lord your God,
even Alpha and Omega, the beginning and
25 the end, whose course is one eternal round, the same
today as yesterday and forever.

2 I am Jesus Christ, the Son of God, who was
crucified for the sins of the world, even as many as
will believe on my name, that they may become
30 the sons of God, even one in me as I am in the Fa-
.ther, as the Father is one in me, that we may be one.

6

---

line 20. Revelation, 7 Dec. 1830 [D&C 35]. This version reflects editing marks made in Revelation Book 1, indicating that the latter was used as a source text for the former. (See *JSP,* MRB:63–67.)

76

3 Behold, verily, verily I say unto my servant Sidney, I have looked upon thee and thy works.

4 I have heard thy prayers and prepared thee for a greater work.

5 Thou art blessed for thou shalt do great things.

6 Behold thou wast sent forth, even as John, to prepare the way before me, and before Elijah which should come, and thou knew it not.

7 Thou didst baptize by water unto repentance, but they received not the Holy Ghost; but now I give unto thee a commandment, that thou shalt baptize by water, and they shall receive the Holy Ghost by the laying on of hands, even as the apostles of old.

8 And it shall come to pass, that there shall be a great work in the land even among the Gentiles, for their folly and their abominations shall be made manifest, in the eyes of all people:

9 For I am God and mine arm is not shortened and I will show miracles, signs and wonders, unto all those who believe on my name.

10 And whoso shall ask it in my name, in faith, they shall cast out devils; they shall heal the sick; they shall cause the blind to receive their sight, and the deaf to hear, and the dumb to speak, and the lame to walk:

11 And the time speedily cometh, that great things are to be shown forth unto the children of men:

12 But without faith shall not any thing be shown forth except desolations upon Babylon, the same which has made all nations drink of the wine of the wrath of her fornication.

13 And there are none that doeth good except those who are ready to receive the fullness of my gospel, which I have sent forth to this generation:

77

14 Wherefore, I have called upon the weak things of the world, those who are unlearned and despised, to thresh the nations by the power of my Spirit:

15 And their arm shall be mine arm, and I will be their shield and their buckler, and I will gird up their loins, and they shall fight manfully for me:

16 And their enemies shall be under their feet; and I will let fall the sword in their behalf; and by the fire of mine indignation will I preserve them.

17 And the poor and the meek shall have the gospel preached unto them, and they shall be looking forth for the time of my coming, for it is nigh at hand:

18 And they shall learn the parable of the fig-tree: for even now already summer is nigh, and I have sent forth the fulness of my gospel by the hand of my servant Joseph:

19 And in weakness have I blessed him, and I have given unto him the keys of the mystery of those things which have been sealed, even things which were from the foundation of the world, and the things which shall come from this time until the time of my coming, if he abide in me, and if not, another will I plant in his stead.

20 Wherefore watch over him that his faith fail not, and it shall be given by the Comforter, the Holy Ghost, that knoweth all things:

21 And a commandment I give unto thee, that thou shalt write for him:

22 And the scriptures shall be given even as they are in mine own bosom, to the salvation of mine own elect:

23 For they will hear my voice, and shall see me, and shall not be asleep, and shall abide the day of my coming, for they shall be purified even as I am

(line markers: 5, 10, 15, 20, 25, 30, 35)

78

line 1   pure. And now I say unto you, tarry with him
and he shall journey with you; forsake him not and
surely these things shall be fulfilled.

24 And inasmuch as ye do not write, behold it
5   shall be given unto him to prophesy.

25 And thou shalt preach my gospel, and call on
the holy prophets to prove his words, as they shall
be given him.

26 Keep all the commandments and covenants by
10   which ye are bound, and I will cause the heavens
to shake for your good:

27 And satan shall tremble; and Zion shall rejoice upon the hills, and flourish; and Israel shall
be saved in mine own due time.

15   28 And by the keys which I have given, shall they
be led and no more be confounded at all.

29 Lift up your hearts and be glad: your redemption draweth nigh.

30 Fear not little flock, the kingdom is yours un-
20   til I come.

31 Behold I come quickly; even so: Amen.

CHAPTER XXXVIII.

*A Revelation to Edward, given in Fayette, New
York, December, 1830.*

25   THUS saith the Lord God, the mighty One of
Israel, behold I say unto you, my servant Edward, that you are blessed, and your sins are forgiven you, and you are called to preach my gospel
as with the voice of a trump; and I will lay my
hand upon you by the hand of my servant Sidney,
30   and you shall receive my Spirit, the Holy Ghost,

---

line 22. Revelation, 9 Dec. 1830 [D&C 36]. This version reflects editing marks made in Revelation Book 1,
indicating that the latter was used as a source text for the former. (See *JSP*, MRB:67–69.)

line 1 even the Comforter, which shall teach you the peaceable things of the kingdom:

2 And you shall declare it with a loud voice saying, Hosanna, blessed be the name of the most high God.

3 And now this calling and commandment give I unto all men, that as many as shall come before my servant Sidney and Joseph, embracing this calling and commandment, shall be ordained and sent forth to preach the everlasting gospel among the nations, crying repentance, saying, Save yourselves from this untoward generation, and come forth out of the fire, hating even the garment spotted with the flesh.

4 And this commandment shall be given unto the elders of my church, that every man which will embrace it with singleness of heart, may be ordained and sent forth, even as I have spoken.

5 I am Jesus Christ, the Son of God:

6 Wherefore gird up your loins and I will suddenly come to my temple; even so: Amen.

CHAPTER XXXIX.

A Revelation to Joseph and Sidney, given in Canandaigua, New-York, December, 1830.

BEHOLD I say unto you, that it is not expedient in me that ye should translate any more until ye shall go to the Ohio; and this because of the enemy and for your sakes.

2 And again, I say unto you, that ye shall not go until ye have preached my gospel in those parts, and have strengthened up the church whithersoev-

---

line 22. Revelation, 30 Dec. 1830 [D&C 37]. This version reflects editing marks made in Revelation Book 1, indicating that the latter was used as a source text for the former. (See *JSP,* MRB:69.)

80

et it is found, and more especially in Colesville:
3 For behold they pray unto me in much faith.
4 And again a commandment I give unto the
church, that it is expedient in me that they should
assemble together at the Ohio, against the time that
my servant Oliver shall return unto them.
5 Behold here is wisdom, and let every man choose
for himself until I come; even so: Amen.

CHAPTER XL.

*A Revelation to the churches in New-York, com-
manding them to remove to Ohio, given in Fayette, New-York, January, 1831.*
THUS saith the Lord your God, even Jesus
Christ, the Great I AM, Alpha and Omega,
the beginning and the end, the same which looked
upon the wide expanse of eternity, and all the seraphic hosts of heaven, before the world was made,
the same which knoweth all things, for all things are
present before mine eyes:
2 I am the same which spake and the world was
made, and all things came by me:
3 I am the same which hath taken the Zion of
Enoch into mine own bosom:
4 And verily I say, even as many as have believed on my name, for I am Christ, and in mine own
name, by the virtue of the blood which I have spilt,
have I plead before the Father for them:
5 But behold the residue of the wicked have I kept
in chains of darkness until the judgment of the great
day, which shall come at the end of the earth, and
even so will I cause the wicked to be kept, that

---

line 9. Revelation, 2 Jan. 1831 [D&C 38]. This version reflects editing marks made in Revelation Book 1
and corresponds to the version in the January 1833 issue of *The Evening and the Morning Star,* suggesting
that both were used as source texts for this version. (See *JSP,* MRB:69–75.)

81

will not hear my voice but harden their hearts, and
wo, wo, wo is their doom.

6 But behold, verily, verily I say unto you, that
mine eyes are upon you; I am in your midst and
ye cannot see me, but the day soon cometh that ye
shall see me and know that I am:

7 For the vail of darkness shall soon be rent, and
he that is not purified shall not abide the day:

8 Wherefore gird up your loins and be prepared.

9 Behold the kingdom is yours and the enemy
shall not overcome.

10 Verily I say unto you, ye are clean but not all;
and there is none else with whom I am well pleased,
for all flesh is corruptible before me, and the powers
of darkness prevail upon the earth, among the children of men, in the presence of all the hosts of heav-
en, which causeth silence to reign, and all eternity
is pained, and the angels are waiting the great command, to reap down the earth, to gather the tares
that they may be burned:

11 And behold the enemy is combined.

12 And now I show unto you a mystery, a thing
which is had in secret chambers, to bring to pass
even your destruction, in process of time, and ye
knew it not, but now I tell it unto you, and ye are
blessed, not because of your iniquity, neither your
hearts of unbelief, for verily some of you are guilty
before me; but I will be merciful unto your weakness.

13 Therefore, be ye strong from henceforth; fear
not for the kingdom is yours:

14 And for your salvation I give unto you a commandment, for I have heard your prayers, and the
poor have complained before me, and the rich have
I made, and all flesh is mine, and I am no respect-

---

line 14. The inscriptions, written in graphite, that change "corruptible" to "corrupted" follow revisions recommended by JS in a letter to Missouri editors dated 25 June 1833. The markings on this page and on pages 82 and 91 of this copy of the Book of Commandments were likely made sometime after the letter was published in the 15 February 1845 issue of *Times and Seasons.* (JS et al., Kirtland, OH, to Edward Partridge et al., Independence, MO, 25 June 1833, JS Collection, CHL; "History of Joseph Smith," *Times and Seasons,* 15 Feb. 1845, 6:800–803; see also 10n42 herein.)

82

of

line 1 er to persons.   And I have made the earth rich,
and behold it is my footstool: wherefore, again I
will stand upon it:
15 And I hold forth and deign to give unto you
5 greater riches, even a land of promise; a land flowing with milk and honey, upon which there shall be
no curse when the Lord cometh, and I will give it
unto you for the land of your inheritance, if you
seek it with all your hearts:
10 16 And this shall be my covenant with you, ye
shall have it for the land of your inheritance, and
for the inheritance of your children forever, while
the earth shall stand, and ye shall possess it again
in eternity, no more to pass away:
15 17 But verily I say unto you, that in time ye shall
have no king nor ruler, for I will be your King and
watch over you.
18 Wherefore, hear my voice and follow me, and
you shall be a free people, and ye shall have no
20 laws but my laws, when I come, for I am your Lawgiver, and what can stay my hand.
19 But verily I say unto you, teach one another
according to the office wherewith I have appointed
you, and let every man esteem his brother as him-
25 self, and practice virtue and holiness before me.
20 And again I say unto you, let every man esteem his brother as himself:
21 For what man among you, having twelve sons,
and is no respecter to them, and they serve him obe-
30 diently, and he saith unto the one, be thou clothed
in robes and sit thou here; and to the other, be thou
clothed in rags and sit thou there, and looketh upon his sons and saith I am just.
22 Behold, this I have given unto you a parable,
35 and it is even as I am, I say unto you, be one:

of

---

lines 1 and 29. The inscriptions, written in graphite, that change "to" to "of" follow revisions recommended by JS in a letter to Missouri editors dated 25 June 1833. The markings on this page and on pages
81 and 91 of this copy of the Book of Commandments were likely made sometime after the letter was
published in the 15 February 1845 issue of *Times and Seasons.* (JS et al., Kirtland, OH, to Edward Partridge
et al., Independence, MO, 25 June 1833, JS Collection, CHL; "History of Joseph Smith," *Times and
Seasons,* 15 Feb. 1845, 6:800–803; see also 10n42 herein.)

83

line 1

and if ye are not one, ye are not mine. And again
I say unto you, that the enemy in the secret chambers, seeketh your lives:

23 Ye hear of wars in far countries, and you say
in your hearts there will soon be great wars in far
countries, but ye know not the hearts of them in
your own land:

24 I tell you these things because of your prayers:

25 Wherefore, treasure up wisdom in your bosoms,
lest the wickedness of men reveal these things unto
you, by their wickedness, in a manner which shall
speak in your ears, with a voice louder than that
which shall shake the earth:

26 But if ye are prepared, ye shall not fear.

27 And that ye might escape the power of the enemy, and be gathered unto me a righteous people,
without spot and blameless:

28 Wherefore, for this cause I gave unto you the
commandment, that ye should go to the Ohio: and
there I will give unto you my law, and there you
shall be endowed with power from on high, and
from thence, whomsoever I will shall go forth among
all nations, and it shall be told them what they
shall do, for I have a great work laid up in store:

29 For Israel shall be saved, and I will lead them
whithersoever I will, and no power shall stay my
hand.

30 And now I give unto the church in these parts,
a commandment, that certain men among them
shall be appointed, and they shall be appointed by
the voice of the church; and they shall look to the
poor and the needy, and administer to their relief,
that they shall not suffer; and send them forth to
the place which I have commanded them; and
this shall be their work, to govern the affairs of the

84

property of this church. And they that have farms,
that can not be sold, let them be left or rented as
seemeth them good.

31 See that all things are preserved, and when
men are endowed with power from on high, and
are sent forth, all these things shall be gathered unto the bosom of the church.

32 And if ye seek the riches which it is the will
of the Father to give unto you, ye shall be the richest of all people, for ye shall have the riches of eternity:

33 And it must needs be that the riches of the
earth is mine to give:

34 But beware of pride, lest ye become as the Nephites of old.

35 And again: I say unto you, I give unto you
a commandment, that every man both elder, priest,
teacher and also member, go to with his might, with
the labor of his hands, to prepare and accomplish
the things which I have commanded.

36 And let your preaching be the warning voice,
every man to his neighbor, in mildness and in meekness.

37 And go ye out from among the wicked. Save
yourselves.

38 Be ye clean that bear the vessels of the Lord;
even so: Amen.

85

CHAPTER XLI.

A Revelation to James (C.,) given in Fayette, New-York, January, 1831.

HEARKEN and listen to the voice of him who is from all eternity to all eternity, the Great I AM, even Jesus Christ, the light and the life of the world; a light which shineth in darkness and the darkness comprehendeth it not:

2 The same which came in the meridian of time unto my own, and my own received me not; but to as many as received me, gave I power to become my sons, and even so will I give unto as many as will receive me, power to become my sons.

3 And verily, verily I say unto you, he that receiveth my gospel, receiveth me; and he that receiveth not my gospel, receiveth not me.

4 And this is my gospel: Repentance and baptism by water, and then cometh the baptism of fire and the Holy Ghost, even the Comforter, which showeth all things, and teacheth the peaceable things of the kingdom.

5 And now behold I say unto you, my servant James, I have looked upon thy works and I know thee:

6 And verily I say unto thee, thine heart is now right before me at this time, and behold I have bestowed great blessings upon thy head:

7 Nevertheless thou hast seen great sorrow, for thou hast rejected me many times because of pride, and the cares of the world:

8 But behold the days of thy deliverance are come.

9 Arise and be baptized, and wash away your sins, calling on my name and you shall receive my Spirit, and a blessing so great as you never have

---

line 1. Revelation, 5 Jan. 1831 [D&C 39]. This version reflects editing marks made in Revelation Book 1, indicating that the latter was used as a source text for the former. (See *JSP,* MRB:87–91.)

line 1 known. And if thou do this, I have prepared thee
for a greater work.

10 Thou shalt preach the fulness of my gospel
which I have sent forth in these last days; the cov-
5 enant which I have sent forth to recover my people,
which are of the house of Israel.

11 And it shall come to pass that power shall rest
upon thee; thou shalt have great faith and I will be
with thee and go before thy face.

10 12 Thou art called to labor in my vineyard, and
to build up my church, and to bring forth Zion,
that it may rejoice upon the hills and flourish.

13 Behold, verily, verily I say unto thee, thou art
not called to go into the eastern countries, but thou
15 art called to go to the Ohio.

14 And inasmuch as my people shall assemble
themselves to the Ohio, I have kept in store a blessing such as is not known among the children of
men, and it shall be poured forth upon their heads.

20 15 And from thence men shall go forth into all
nations.

16 Behold, verily, verily I say unto you, that the
people in Ohio call upon me in much faith, thinking I will stay my hand in judgment upon the na-
25 tions, but I can not deny my word:

17 Wherefore lay to with your might and call
faithful laborers into my vineyard, that it may be
pruned for the last time.

18 And inasmuch as they do repent and receive
30 the fulness of my gospel, and become sanctified, I
will stay mine hand in judgment:

19 Wherefore go forth, crying with a loud voice,
saying, The kingdom of heaven is at hand; crying
Hosanna! blessed be the name of the most high
35 God.

87

line 1 20 Go forth baptizing with water, preparing the way before my face, for the time of my coming; for the time is at hand:

21 The day nor the hour no man knoweth, but it surely shall come, and he that receiveth these things receiveth me; and they shall be gathered unto me in time and in eternity.

22 And again, it shall come to pass, that on as many as ye shall baptize with water, ye shall lay your hands, and they shall receive the gift of the Holy Ghost, and shall be looking forth for the signs of my coming, and shall know me.

23 Behold I come quickly; even so: Amen.

CHAPTER XLII.

A Revelation to Joseph, and Sidney, given in Fayette, New-York, January, 1831, explaining why James (C.,) obeyed not the revelation which was given unto him.

BEHOLD, verily I say unto you, that his heart was right before me, for he covenanted with me, that he would obey my word.

2 And he received the word with gladness, but straitway satan tempted him; and the fear of persecution, and the cares of the world, caused him to reject the word:

3 Wherefore he broke my covenant, and it remaineth in me to do with him as seemeth me good. Amen.

line 14. Revelation, 6 Jan. 1831 [D&C 40]. This version reflects editing marks made in Revelation Book 1, indicating that the latter was used as a source text for the former. (See *JSP*, MRB:91.)

88

CHAPTER XLIII.

A Revelation to the church in Kirtland, Ohio, and also the calling of Edward to the office of bishop, given February, 1831.

HEARKEN and hear, O ye my people, saith your Lord and your God, ye whom I delight to bless with the greatest of blessings, ye that hear me:

2 And ye that hear me not will I curse, that have professed my name, with the heaviest of all cursings.

3 Hearken, O ye elders of my church whom I have called;

4 Behold I give unto you a commandment, that ye shall assemble yourselves together to agree upon my word, and by the prayer of your faith ye shall receive my law, that ye may know how to govern my church, and have all things right before me.

5 And I will be your Ruler when I come: and behold, I come quickly: and ye shall see that my law is kept.

6 He that receiveth my law and doeth it the same is my disciple;

7 And he that saith he receiveth it and doeth it not, the same is not my disciple, and shall be cast out from among you:

8 For it is not meet that the things which belong to the children of the kingdom, should be given to them that are not worthy, or to dogs, or the pearls to be cast before swine.

9 And again, it is meet that my servant Joseph should have a house built, in which to live and translate.

10 And again, it is meet that my servant Sidney should live as seemeth him good.

---

line 1. Revelation, 4 Feb. 1831 [D&C 41]. This version reflects editing marks made in Revelation Book 1, indicating that the latter was used as a source text for the former. (See *JSP*, MRB:93–95.)

89

line 1

11 And again, I have called my servant Edward, and give a commandment, that he should be appointed by the voice of the church, and ordained a bishop unto the church, to leave his merchandise and to spend all his time in the labors of the church; to see to all things as it shall be appointed unto him, in my laws in the day that I shall give them.

12 And this because his heart is pure before me; for he is like unto Nathaniel of old, in whom there is no guile.

13 These words are given unto you, and they are pure before me:

14 Wherefore beware how you hold them, for they are to be answered upon your souls in the day of judgment; even so: Amen.

CHAPTER XLIV.

A Revelation given to twelve elders assembled in Kirtland, Ohio; and also the law for the government of the church, given in the presence of the same, February, 1831.

HEARKEN, O ye elders of my church who have assembled yourselves together, in my name, even Jesus Christ, the Son of the living God, the Savior of the world;

2 Inasmuch as they believe on my name and keep my commandments;

3 Again I say unto you, hearken and hear and obey the law which I shall give unto you:

4 For verily I say, as ye have assembled yourselves together according to the commandment wherewith I commanded you, and are agreed as touch-

---

line 16. Revelation, 9 Feb. 1831 [D&C 42:1–72]. Verses 1–11 and 55–57 of this revelation reflect editing marks made in Revelation Book 1, and the remaining verses closely correspond to the version in the July 1832 issue of *The Evening and the Morning Star,* suggesting that both were used as source texts for the version printed here. (See *JSP,* MRB:95–105.)

90

ing this one thing, and have asked the Father in
my name, even so ye shall receive.

5 Behold, verily I say unto you, I give unto you
this first commandment, that ye shall go forth in my
name, every one of you, excepting my servants Joseph and Sidney.

6 And I give unto them a commandment that they
shall go forth for a little season, and it shall be giv-
en by the power of my Spirit when they shall return:

7 And ye shall go forth in the power of my Spirit, preaching my gospel, two by two, in my name,
lifting up your voices as with the voice of a trump,
declaring my word like unto angels of God:

8 And ye shall go forth baptizing with water, saying, Repent ye, repent ye, for the kingdom of
heaven is at hand.

9 And from this place ye shall go forth into the
regions westward, and inasmuch as ye shall find
them that will receive you, ye shall build up my
church in every region, until the time shall come
when it shall be revealed unto you, from on high,
when the city of the New Jerusalem shall be prepared that ye may be gathered in one, that ye may
be my people and I will be your God.

10 And again, I say unto you, that my servant
Edward shall stand in the office wherewith I have
appointed him.

11 And it shall come to pass that if he transgress
another shall be appointed in his stead; even so:
Amen.

12 Again I say unto you, that it shall not be giv-
en to any one to go forth to preach my gospel, or to
build up my church, except he be ordained by some
one who has authority, and it is known to the church

heads 31

that he has authority, and has been regularly ordained by the hands of the church.

13 And again, the elders, priests, and teachers of
this church, shall teach the scriptures which are in
the bible, and the book of Mormon, in the which is
the fulness of the gospel; and they shall observe the
covenants and church articles to do them; and
these shall be their teachings.

14 And they shall be directed by the Spirit, which
shall be given them by the prayer of faith; and if
they receive not the Spirit, they shall not teach.

15 And all this they shall observe to do, as I have
commanded concerning their teaching, until the fulness of my scriptures are given.

16 And as they shall lift up their voices by the
Comforter, they shall speak and prophesy as seemeth me good; for behold the Comforter knoweth all
things, and beareth record of the Father, and of the
Son.

17 And now behold I speak unto the church:

18 Thou shalt not kill; and he that killeth, shall
not have forgiveness, neither in this world, nor in
the world to come.

19 And again, thou shalt not kill; he that killeth
shall die.

20 Thou shalt not steal; and he that stealeth and
will not repent, shall be cast out.

21 Thou shalt not lie; he that lieth and will not
repent, shall be cast out.

22 Thou shalt love thy wife with all thy heart,
and shall cleave unto her and none else; and he
that looketh upon a woman to lust after her, shall
deny the faith, and shall not have the Spirit, and if
he repent not, he shall be cast out.

23 Thou shalt not commit adultery; and he that

---

line 2. The inscriptions, written in graphite, that change "hands" to "heads" follow revisions recommended by JS in a letter to Missouri editors dated 25 June 1833. The markings on this page and on pages
81 and 82 of this copy of the Book of Commandments were likely made sometime after the letter was
published in the 15 February 1845 issue of *Times and Seasons*. (JS et al., Kirtland, OH, to Edward Partridge
et al., Independence, MO, 25 June 1833, JS Collection, CHL; "History of Joseph Smith," *Times and
Seasons,* 15 Feb. 1845, 6:800–803; see also 10n42 herein.)

92

committeth adultery and repenteth not, shall be
cast out; and he that committeth adultery and repenteth with all his heart, and forsaketh and doeth
it no more, thou shalt forgive him; but if he doeth
5   it again, he shall not be forgiven, but shall be cast
out.

24 Thou shalt not speak evil of thy neighbor, or
do him any harm.

25 Thou knowest my laws, they are given in my
10   scriptures, he that sinneth and repenteth not, shall
be cast out.

26 If thou lovest me, thou shalt serve me and keep
all my commandments; and behold, thou shalt consecrate all thy properties, that which thou hast un-
15   to me, with a covenant and a deed which can not
be broken; and they shall be laid before the bishop
of my church, and two of the elders, such as he shall
appoint and set apart for that purpose.

27 And it shall come to pass, that the bishop of
20   my church, after that he has received the properties
of my church, that it can not be taken from the
church, he shall appoint every man a steward over
his own property, or that which he has received, inasmuch as is sufficient for himself and family:

25   28 And the residue shall be kept to administer to
him who has not, that every man may receive according as he stands in need:

29 And the residue shall be kept in my storehouse,
to administer to the poor and needy, as shall be ap-
30   pointed by the elders of the church and the bishop;
and for the purpose of purchasing lands, and the
building up of the New Jerusalem, which is hereafter to be revealed; that my covenant people may
be gathered in one, in the day that I shall come to
35   my temple;

93

30 And this I do for the salvation of my people.

31 And it shall come to pass, that he that sinneth and repenteth not shall be cast out, and shall not receive again that which he has consecrated unto me:

32 For it shall come to pass, that which I spake by the mouths of my prophets shall be fulfilled; for I will consecrate the riches of the Gentiles, unto my people which are of the house of Israel.

33 And again, thou shalt not be proud in thy heart; let all thy garments be plain, and their beauty the beauty of the work of thine own hands, and let all things be done in cleanliness before me.

34 Thou shalt not be idle; for he that is idle shall not eat the bread, nor wear the garments of the laborer.

35 And whosoever among you that are sick, and have not faith to be healed, but believeth, shall be nourished in all tenderness with herbs and mild food, and that not of the world; and the elders of the church, two or more shall be called, and shall pray for, and lay their hands upon them in my name, and if they die, they shall die unto me; and if they live they shall live unto me.

36 Thou shalt live together in love, insomuch that thou shalt weep for the loss of them that die, and more especially for those that have not hope of a glorious resurrection.

37 And it shall come to pass, that those that die in me shall not taste of death, for it shall be sweet unto them; and they that die not in me, wo unto them; for their death is bitter.

38 And again, it shall come to pass, that he that has faith in me to be healed, and is not appointed unto death, shall be healed.

94

line 1

39 He who has faith to see, shall see; he who has faith to hear, shall hear; the lame who have faith to leap, shall leap; and they who have not faith to do these things, but believe in me, have power to become my sons, and inasmuch as they break not my laws, thou shalt bear their infirmities.

40 Thou shalt stand in the place of thy stewardship:

41 Thou shalt not take thy brother's garment; thou shalt pay for that which thou shalt receive of thy brother.

42 And if thou obtainest more than that which would be for thy support, thou shalt give it into my storehouse, that all things may be done according to that which I have spoken.

43 Thou shalt ask and my scriptures shall be given as I have appointed; and for thy safety it is expedient that thou shouldst hold thy peace concerning them, until ye have received them:

44 Then I give unto you a commandment that ye shall teach them unto all men; and they also shall be taught unto all nations, kindreds, tongues and people.

45 Thou shalt take the things which thou hast received, which thou knowest to have been my law, to be my law, to govern my church; and he that doeth according to these things shall be saved, and he that doeth them not shall be damned, if he continue.

46 If thou shalt ask, thou shalt receive revelation upon revelation, knowledge upon knowledge, that thou mayest know the mysteries, and the peaceable things of the kingdom; that which bringeth joy, that which bringeth life eternal.

47 Thou shalt ask and it shall be revealed unto

5

10

15

20

25

30

35

---

line 13. From this point to the end of the gathering (Book of Commandments page 96), the compositor used a lowercase italic *y* in place of a roman one, indicating that he had run out of roman *y* type. In both this and the following gathering, the compositor switched to italic *y*'s after approximately the nine-hundredth roman *y*.

95

you in my own due time where the New Jerusalem
shall be built.

48 And behold, it shall come to pass, that my servants shall be sent both to the east, and to the west,
to the north, and to the south; and even now let
him that goeth to the east, teach them that shall be
converted to flee to the west; and this in consequence of that which is to come on the earth, and
of secret combinations.

49 Behold, thou shalt observe all these things, and
great shall be thy reward.

50 Thou shalt observe to keep the mysteries of the
kingdom unto thyself, for it is not given to the world
to know the mysteries.

51 The laws which ye have received, and shall
hereafter receive, shall be sufficient for you both
here, and in the New Jerusalem.

52 Therefore, he that lacketh knowledge, let him
ask of me and I will give him liberally and upbraid
him not.

53 Lift up your hearts and rejoice, for unto you
the kingdom has been given; even so: Amen.

54 The priests and teachers, shall have their stewardship given them even as the members; and the
elders are to assist the bishop in all things, and he
is to see that their families are supported out of the
property which is consecrated to the Lord, either a
stewardship, or otherwise, as may be thought best
by the elders and bishop.

55 Thou shalt contract no debts with the world,
except thou art commanded.

56 And again, the elders and bishop, shall counsel together, and they shall do by the direction of
the Spirit as it must needs be necessary.

57 There shall be as many appointed as must

26

line 1

needs be necessary to assist the bishop in obtaining
places for the brethren from New-York, that they
may be together as much as can be, and as they are
directed by the Holy Spirit; and every family shall
have a place, that they may live by themselves.—
And every church shall be organized in as close bodies as they can be; and this for a wise purpose;—
even so.   Amen.

CHAPTER XLV.

*A Revelation to the elders of the church, assem-
bled in Kirtland, Ohio, given February, 1831.*
O HEARKEN, ye elders of my church, and
give ear to the words which I shall speak unto you:
2 For behold, verily, verily I say unto you, that
ye have received a commandment for a law unto
my church, through him whom I have appointed
unto you, to receive commandments and revelations
from my hand.
3 And this ye shall know assuredly, that there is
none other appointed unto you to receive commandments and revelations until he be taken, if he abide
in me.
4 But verily, verily I say unto you, that none else
shall be appointed unto this gift except it be through
him, for if it be taken from him he shall not have
power, except to appoint another in his stead:
5 And this shall be a law unto you, that ye receive not the teachings of any that shall come before you as revelations or commandments:
6 And this I give unto you, that you may not be

line 9. Revelation, Feb. 1831–A [D&C 43]. This version reflects editing marks made in Revelation Book 1, indicating that the latter was used as a source text for the former. (See *JSP,* MRB:105.)

97

deceived; that you may know they are not of me.

7 For verily I say unto you, that he that is ordained of me shall come in at the gate and be ordained as I have told you before, to teach those revelations which you have received, and shall receive through him whom I have appointed.

8 And now behold I give unto you a commandment, that when ye are assembled together ye shall note with a pen how to act, and for my church to act upon the points of my law and commandments, which I have given:

9 And thus it shall become a law unto you, being sanctified by that which ye have received, that ye shall bind yourselves to act in all holiness before me; that inasmuch as ye do this, glory shall be added to the kingdom which ye have received.

10 Inasmuch as ye do it not, it shall be taken even that which ye have received.

11 Purge ye out the iniquity which is among you; sanctifiy yourselves before me and if ye desire the glories of the kingdom, appoint ye my servant Joseph and uphold him before me by the prayer of faith.

12 And again, I say unto you, that if ye desire the mysteries of the kingdom, provide for him food and raiment and whatsoever thing he needeth to accomplish the work, wherewith I have commanded him:

13 And if ye do it not, he shall remain unto them that have received him, that I may reserve unto myself a pure people before me.

14 Again I say, hearken ye elders of my church, whom I have appointed:

15 Ye are not sent forth to be taught, but to teach the children of men the things which I have put in-

D1

---

line 36. This page begins the fourth gathering of the book. "D1" is the first of eight signature marks found on the rectos of the first eight leaves of this gathering. These marks were used in collating the gatherings after the sheets were folded.

98

line 1 tö your hands by the power of my Spirit: and ye
are to be taught from on high.

16 Sanctify yourselves and ye shall be endowed
with power, that ye may give even as I have spo-
5 ken.

17 Hearken ye, for behold the great day of the
Lord is nigh at hand.

18 For the day cometh that the Lord shall utter
his voice out of heaven; the heavens shall shake
10 and the earth shall tremble, and the trump of God
shall sound both long and loud, and shall say to the
sleeping nations:

19 Ye saints arise and live:

20 Ye sinners stay and sleep until I shall call
15 again:

21 Wherefore gird up your loins, lest ye be found
among the wicked.

22 Lift up your voices and spare not.

23 Call upon the nations to repent, both old and
20 young, both bond and free; saying, Prepare yourselves for the great day of the Lord:

24 For if I, who am a man, do lift up my voice
and call upon you to repent, and ye hate me, what
will ye say when the day cometh when the thun-
25 ders shall utter their voices from the ends of the
earth, speaking in the ears of all that live, saying,
Repent, and prepare for the great day of the Lord;

25 Yea, and again, when the lightnings shall streak
forth from the east unto the west, and shall utter
30 forth their voices unto all that live, and make the
ears of all tingle, that hear, saying these words:

26 Repent ye, for the great day of the Lord is
come.

27 And again, the Lord shall utter his voice out
35 of heaven, saying:

99

28 Hearken, O ye nations of the earth, and hear the words of that God who made you.

29 O ye nations of the earth, how often would I have gathered you, together as a hen gathereth her chickens under her wings, but ye would not?

30 How oft have I called upon you by the mouth of my servants; and by the ministering of angels; and by mine own voice; and by the voice of thunderings; and by the voice of lightnings; and by the voice of tempests; and by the voice of earthquakes; and great hail-storms; and by the voice of famines, and pestilences of every kind; and by the great sound of a trump; and by the voice of judgment; and by the voice of mercy all the day long; and by the voice of glory, and honor, and the riches of eternal life; and would have saved you with an everlasting salvation, but ye would not?

31 Behold the day has come, when the cup of the wrath of mine indignation, is full.

32 Behold, verily I say unto you, that these are the words of the Lord your God:

33 Wherefore, labor ye, labor ye, in my vineyard for the last time:

34 For the las time call ye upon the inhabitants of the earth, for in mine own due time will I come upon the earth in judgment:

35 And my people shall be redeemed and shall reign with me on earth:

36 For the great Millennial, which I have spoken by the mouth of my servants, shall come;

37 For satan shall be bound; and when he is loosed again, he shall only reign for a little season, and then cometh the end of the earth:

38 And he that liveth in righteousness, shall be changed in the twinkling of an eye;

D 2

100

line 1

39 And the earth shall pass away so as by fire;

40 And the wicked shall go away into unquench-able fire; and their end no man knoweth, on earth, nor ever shall know, until they come before me in judgment.

5

41 Hearken ye to these words; behold I am Je-sus Christ, the Savior of the world.

42 Treasure these things up in your hearts, and let the solemnities of eternity rest upon your minds.

10

43 Be sober.

44 Keep all my commandments; even so: Amen.

CHAPTER XLVI.

A Revelation to Joseph, and Sidney, given in Kirtland, Ohio, February, 1831.

15

BEHOLD thus saith the Lord unto you my ser-vants, it is expedient in me that the elders of my church should be called together, from the east and from the west, and from the north and from the south, by letter or some other way.

20

2 And it shall come to pass, that, inasmuch as they are faithful, and exercise faith in me, I will pour out my spirit upon them in the day that they assemble themselves together.

3 And it shall come to pass that they shall go forth into the regions round about, and preach repentance unto the people;

25

4 And many shall be converted, insomuch that ye shall obtain power to organize yourselves, according to the laws of man;

30

5 That your enemies may not have power over you, that you may be preserved in all things;

---

line 12. Revelation, Feb. 1831–B [D&C 44]. This version reflects editing marks made in Revelation Book 1, indicating that the latter was used as a source text for the former. (See *JSP,* MRB:113–115.)

101

6 That you may be enabled to keep my laws, that every band may be broken wherewith the enemy seeketh to destroy my people.

7 Behold I say unto you, that ye must visit the poor and the needy and administer to their relief, that they may be kept until all things may be done according to my law which ye have received: Amen.

CHAPTER XLVII.

A Revelation to seven elders of the church, assembled in Kirtland, Ohio, given February 1831.

EVERY person who belongeth to this church of Christ, shall observe to keep all the commandments and covenants of the church;

2 And it shall come to pass, that if any persons among you shall kill, they shall be delivered up and dealt with according to the laws of the land;

3 For remember, that he hath no forgiveness;

4 And it shall be proven according to the laws of the land.

5 But if any man shall commit adultery, he shall be tried before two elders of the church or more, and every word shall be established against him by two witnesses of the church, and not of the world.

6 But if there are more than two witnesses it is better:

7 But he shall be condemned by the mouth of two witnesses, and the elders shall lay the case before the church, and the church shall lift up their hands against them, that they may be dealt with according to the law.

8 And if it can be, it is necessary that the bishop

DB

---

line 8. Revelation, 23 Feb. 1831 [D&C 42:78–93, 74–77]. The source text for this version is unknown.

102

is present also.   And thus ye shall do in all cases
which shall come before you.

9 And if a man shall rob, he shall be delivered
up unto the law.

10 And if he shall steal, he shall be delivered up
unto the law.

11 And if he lie, he shall be delivered up unto the
law.

12 If he do any manner of iniquity, he shall be
delivered up unto the law, even that of God.

13 And if thy brother offend thee, thou shalt take
him between him and thee alone; and if he confess,
thou shalt be reconciled.

14 And if he confess not, thou shalt take another
with thee; and then if he confess not, thou shalt deliver him up unto the church, not to the members
but to the elders.

15 And it shall be done in a meeting, and that
not before the world.

16 And if thy brother offend many, he shall be
chastened before many.

17 And if any one offend openly, he shall be
rebuked openly, that he may be ashamed.

18 And if he confess not, he shall be delivered up
unto the law.

19 If any shall offend in secret, he shall be rebuked
in secret, that he may have opportunity to confess
in secret to him whom he has offended, and to God,
that the brethren may not speak reproachfully of
him.

20 And thus shall ye conduct in all things.

21 Behold, verily I say unto you, that whatsoever
persons among you having put away their companions, for the cause of fornication, or in other words,
if they shall testify before you, in all lowliness of

line 1 heart, that this is the case, ye shall not cast them
out from among you:

22 But if ye shall find that any persons, have left
their companions, for the sake of adultery, and they
5 themselves are the offenders, and their companions
are living, they shall be cast out from among you,

23 And again I say unto you, that ye shall be
watchful and careful, with all inquiry, that ye receive none such among you, if they are married.

10 24 And if they are not married, they shall repent
of all their sins, or ye shall not receive them. Amen:

CHAPTER XLVIII.

*A Revelation to the church, given in Kirtland,
Ohio, March 1831.*

15 HEARKEN, O ye people of my church to
whom the kingdom has been given:

2 Hearken ye and give ear to him who laid the
foundation of the earth; who made the heavens and
all the hosts thereof, and by whom all things were
20 made which live and move and have a being.

3 And again I say, hearken unto my voice, lest
death shall overtake you:

4 In an hour when ye think not, the summer shall
be past, and the harvest ended, and your souls not
25 saved.

5 Listen to him who is the Advocate with the
Father, who is pleading your case before him:

6 Saying Father behold the sufferings and death
of him who did no sin, in whom thou wast well
30 pleased; behold the blood of thy Son which was
shed, the blood of him whom thou gavest that thy-

D4

---

line 12. Revelation, ca. 7 Mar. 1831 [D&C 45]. This version reflects editing marks made in Revelation Book 1, indicating that the latter was used as a source text for the former. (See *JSP*, MRB:115–125.)

104

self might be glorified : wherefore Father spare these my brethren that believe on my name, that they may come unto me and have everlasting life.

7 Hearken O ye people of my church, and ye elders listen together, and hear my voice while it is called today, and harden not your hearts :

8 For verily I say unto you that I am Alpha and Omega, the beginning and the end, the light and the life of the world, a light that shineth in darkness and the darkness comprehendeth it not :

9 I came unto my own and my own received me not :

10 But unto as many as received me, gave I power to do many miracles, and to become the sons of God, and even unto them that believed on my name gave I power to obtain eternal life.

11 And even so I have sent mine everlasting covenant into the world, to be a light to the world, and to be a standard for my people, and for the Gentiles to seek to it ;

12 And to be a messenger before my face to prepare the way before me.

13 Wherefore come ye unto it, and with him that cometh I will reason as with men in days of old, and I will show unto you my strong reasoning ;

14 Wherefore hearken ye together and let me show it unto you, even my wisdom, the wisdom of him whom ye say is the God of Enoch, and his brethren, who were separated from the earth, and were reserved unto myself, a city reserved until a day of righteousness shall come, a day which was sought for by all holy men, and they found it not because of wickedness and abominations, and confessed that they were strangers and pilgrims on the earth ;

105

15 But obtained a promise that they should find
it, and see it in their flesh.

16 Wherefore hearken and I will reason with you,
and I will speak unto you and prophesy as unto
men in days of old, and I will show it plainly as I
showed it unto my disciples, as I stood before them
in the flesh and spake unto them saying:

17 As ye have asked of me concerning the signs
of my coming, in the day when I shall come in my
glory, in the clouds of heaven, to fulfil the promises that I have made unto your fathers;

18 For as ye have looked upon the long absence
of your spirits from your bodies to be a bondage, I
will show unto you how the day of redemption shall
come and also the restoration of the scattered Israel.

19 And now ye behold this temple which is in Jerusalem, which ye call the house of God, and your
enemies say that this house shall never fall.

20 But verily I say unto you, that desolation shall
come upon this generation as a thief in the night,
and this people shall be destroyed and scattered
among all nations.

21 And this temple which ye now see, shall be
thrown down that there shall not be left one stone
upon another.

22 And it shall come to pass, that this generation
of Jews shall not pass away, until every desolation
which I have told you concerning them, shall come
to pass.

23 Ye say that ye know, that the end of the world
cometh; ye say also that ye know, that the heavens
and the earth shall pass away; and in this ye say
truly, for so it is;

24 But these things which I have told you, shall
not pass away until all shall be fulfilled.

D5

105

25 And this I have told you concerning Jerusalem, and when that day shall come, shall a remnant be scattered among all nations, but they shall be gathered again; but they shall remain until the times of the Gentiles be fulfilled.

26 And in that day shall be heard of wars and rumors of wars, and the whole earth shall be in commotion, and men's hearts shall fail them, and they shall say that Christ delayeth his coming until the end of the earth.

27 And the love of men shall wax cold, and iniquity shall abound; and when the time of the Gentiles is come in, a light shall break forth among them that sit in darkne, and it shall be the fulness of my gospel; but they receive it not, for they perceive not the light, and they turn their hearts from me because of the precepts of men; and in that generation shall the times of the Gentiles be fulfilled:

28 And there shall be men standing in that generation, that shall not pass, until they shall see an overflowing scourge; for a desolating sickness shall cover the land:

29 But my disciples shall stand in holy places, and shall not be moved; but among the wicked, men shall lift up their voices and curse God and die.

30 And there shall be earthquakes, also, in divers places, and many desolations, yet men will harden their hearts against me; and they will take up the sword one against another, and they will kill one another.

31 And now, when I the Lord had spoken these words unto my disciples, they were troubled; and I said unto them, be not troubled, for when all these

107

things shall come to pass, ye may know that the promises which have been made unto you, shall be fulfilled:

32 And when the light shall begin to break forth, it shall be with them like unto a parable which I will show you:

33 Ye look and behold the fig-trees, and ye see them with your eyes, and ye say when they begin to shoot forth and their leaves are yet tender, ye say that summer is now nigh at hand;

34 Even so it shall be in that day, when they shall see all these things, then shall they know that the hour is nigh.

35 And it shall come to pass that he that feareth me shall be looking for the great day of the Lord to come, even for the signs of the coming of the Son of man; and they shall see signs and wonders, for they shall be shown forth in the heavens above, and in the earth beneath; and they shall behold blood and fire, and vapors of smoke;

36 And before the day of the Lord shall come, the sun shall be darkened, and the moon be turned into blood, and stars fall from heaven;

37 And the remnant shall be gathered unto this place; and then they shall look for me, and behold I will come; and they shall see me in the clouds of heaven, clothed with power and great glory, with all the holy angels;

38 And he that watches not for me shall be cut off.

39 But before the arm of the Lord shall fall, an angel shall sound his trump, and the saints that have slept, shall come forth to meet me in the cloud.

40 Wherefore if ye have slept in peace, blessed

108

...are you, for as you now behold me and know that I am, even so shall ye come unto me and your souls shall live, and your redemption shall be perfected, and the saints shall come forth from the four quarters of the earth.

41 Then shall the arm of the Lord fall upon the nations, and then shall the Lord set his foot upon this mount, and it shall cleave in twain, and the earth shall tremble and reel to and fro, and the heavens also shall shake, and the Lord shall utter his voice and all the ends of the earth shall hear it, and the nations of the earth shall mourn, and they that have laughed shall see their folly, and calamity shall cover the mocker, and the scorner shall be consumed, and they that have watched for iniquity, shall be hewn down and cast into the fire.

42 And then shall the Jews look upon me, and say, What are these wounds in thine hands, and in thy feet?

43 Then shall they know that I am the Lord; for I will say unto them, These wounds, are the wounds with which I was wounded in the house of my friends.

44 I am he who was lifted up.

45 I am Jesus that was crucified.

46 I am the Son of God.

47 And then shall they weep because of their iniquities; then shall they lament because they persecuted their King.

48 And then shall the heathen nations be redeemed, and they which knew no law shall have part in the first resurrection;

49 And it shall be tolerable for them; and satan shall be bound that he shall have no place in the hearts of the children of men.

109

50 And at that day when I shall come in my glory, shall the parable be fulfilled which I spake concerning the ten virgins:

51 For they that are wise and have received the truth, and have taken the Holy Spirit for their guide, and have not been deceived;

52 Verily I say unto you, they shall not be hewn down and cast into the fire, but shall abide the day, and the earth shall be given unto them for an inheritance:

53 And they shall multiply and wax strong, and their children shall grow up without sin unto salvation, for the Lord shall be in their midst, and his glory shall be upon them, and he will be their King and their Lawgiver.

54 And now, behold I say unto you, it shall not be given unto you to know any farther than this, until the new testament be translated, and in it all these things shall be made known;

55 Wherefore I give unto you that ye may now translate it, that ye may be prepared for the things to come;

56 For verily I say unto you, that great things await you;

57 Ye hear of wars in foreign lands, but behold I say unto you they are nigh even unto your doors, and not many years hence ye shall hear of wars in your own lands.

58 Wherefore I the Lord have said gather ye out from the eastern lands, assemble ye yourselves together ye elders of my church;

59 Go ye forth into the western countries, call upon the inhabitants to repent, and inasmuch as they do repent, build up churches unto me; and with one heart and with one mind, gather up your riches

D7

110

line 1 that ye may purchase an inheritance which shall
hereafter be appointed unto you, and it shall be
called the New Jerusalem, a land of peace, a city
of refuge, a place of safety for the saints of the most
high God:

60 And the glory of the Lord shall be there, and
the terror of the Lord also shall be there, insomuch
that the wicked will not come unto it:

61 And it shall be called Zion:

62 And it shall come to pass, among the wicked,
that every man that will not take his sword against
his neighbor, must needs flee unto Zion for safety.

63 And there shall be gathered unto it out of every nation under heaven:

64 And it shall be the only people that shall not
be at war one with another.

65 And it shall be said among the wicked, let us
not go up to battle against Zion, for the inhabitants
of Zion are terrible:

66 Wherefore we can not stand.

67 And it shall come to pass that the righteous
shall be gathered out from among all nations, and
shall come to Zion singing, with songs of everlasting
joy.

68 And now I say unto you, keep these things
from going abroad unto the world, until it is expedient in me, that ye may accomplish this work in
the eyes of the people, and in the eyes of your enemies, that they may not know your works until ye
have accomplished the thing which I have commanded you:

69 That when they shall know it, that they may
consider these things, for when the Lord shall appear he shall be terrible unto them, that fear may
seize upon them, and they shall stand afar off and

111

tremble : and all nations shall be afraid because of the terror of the Lord, and the power of his might; even so : Amen.

CHAPTER XLIX.

A Revelation to the church, given in Kirtland, Ohio, March, 1831.

HEARKEN, O ye people of my church, for verily I say unto you, that these things were spoken unto you for your profit and learning;

2 But notwithstanding those things which are written, it always has been given to the elders of my church, from the beginning, and ever shall be, to conduct all meetings as they are directed and guided by the Holy Spirit:

3 Nevertheless ye are commanded never to cast any one out from your public meetings, which are held before the world :

4 Ye are also commanded not to cast any one, who belongeth to the church, out of your sacrament meetings:

5 Nevertheless, if any have trespassed, let him not partake until he makes reconciliation.

6 And again I say unto you, ye shall not cast any one out of your sacrament meetings, who is earnestly seeking the kingdom;

7 I speak this concerning those who are not of the church.

8 And again I say unto you, concerning your confirmation meetings, that if there be any that is not of the church, that is earnestly seeking after the kingdom, ye shall not cast them out;

D8

-----

line 4. Revelation, ca. 8 Mar. 1831–A [D&C 46]. This version reflects editing marks made in Revelation Book 1, indicating that the latter was used as a source text for the former. (See *JSP*, MRB:125–129.)

112

9 But ye are commanded in all things to ask of God who giveth liberally, and that which the Spirit testifies unto you, even so I would that ye should do in all holiness of heart, walking uprightly before me, considering the end of your salvation, doing all things with prayer and thanksgiving, that ye may not be seduced by evil spirits, or doctrines of devils, or the commandments of men, for some are of men, and others of devils.

10 Wherefore, beware lest ye are deceived! and that ye may not be deceived, seek ye earnestly the best gifts, always remembering for what they are given;

11 For verily I say unto you, they are given for the benefit of those who love me and keep all my commandments, and him that seeketh so to do, that all may be benefitted, that seeketh or that asketh of me, that asketh and not for a sign that he may consume it upon his lusts.

12 And again, verily I say unto you, I would that ye should always remember, and always retain in your minds what those gifts are, that are given unto the church, for all have not every gift given unto them: for there are many gifts, and to every man is given a gift by the Spirit of God;

13 To some it is given one, and to some is given another, that all may be profited thereby;

14 To some it is given by the Holy Ghost to know that Jesus Christ is the Son of God, and that he was crucified for the sins of the world; to others it is given to believe on their words, that they also might have eternal life, if they continue faithful.

15 And again, to some it is given by the Holy Ghost to know the differences of administration, as it will be pleasing unto the same Lord, according

113

line 1 as the Lord will, suiting his mercies according to the conditions of the children of men.

16 And again it is given by the Holy Ghost to some to know the diversities of operations, whether it be of God, that the manifestations of the Spirit may be given to every man to profit withal.

17 And again, verily I say unto you, to some it is given, by the Spirit of God, the word of wisdom; to another it is given, the word of knowledge, that all may be taught to be wise and to have knowledge.

18 And again, to some it is given to have faith to be healed, and to others it is given to have faith to heal.

19 And again, to some it is given the working of miracles;

20 And to others it is given to prophesy, and to others the discerning of spirits.

21 And again, it is given to some to speak with tongues, and to another it is given the interpretation of tongues:

22 And all these gifts cometh from God, for the benefit of the children of God.

23 And unto the bishop of the church, and unto such as God shall appoint and ordain to watch over the church, and to be elders unto the church, are to have it given unto them to discern all those gifts, lest there shall be any among you professing and yet be not of God.

24 And it shall come to pass that he that asketh in spirit shall receive in spirit; that unto some it may be given to have all those gifts, that there may be a head, in order that every member may be profited thereby:

25 He that asketh in the spirit, asketh according

114

line 1

to the will of God, wherefore it is done even as he asketh.

26 And again I say unto you, all things must be done in the name of Christ, whatsoever you do in the spirit;

27 And ye must give thanks unto God in the spirit for whatsoever blessing ye are blessed with:

28 And ye must practice virtue and holiness before me continually; even so: Amen.

CHAPTER L.

A Revelation to Joseph and John, given in Kirtland, Ohio, March 1831.

BEHOLD it is expedient in me that my servant John should write and keep a regular history, and assist you, my servant Joseph, in transcribing all things which shall be given you.

2 Again, verily I say unto you, that he can also lift up his voice in meetings, whenever it shall be expedient.

3 And again, I say unto you, that it shall be appointed unto him to keep the church record and history continually, for Oliver I have appointed to another office:

4 Wherefore it shall be given him, inasmuch as he is faithful, by the Comforter, to write these things; even so: Amen.

---

line 10. Revelation, ca. 8 Mar. 1831–B [D&C 47]. This version reflects editing marks made in Revelation Book 1, indicating that the latter was used as a source text for the former. (See *JSP,* MRB:131–133.)

113

CHAPTER LI.

A Revelation to the bishop, and the church in Kirtland, given in Kirtland, Ohio, March, 1831.

IT is necessary that ye should remain, for the present time, in your places of abode, as it shall be suitable to your circumstances;

2 And inasmuch as ye have lands, ye shall impart to the eastern brethren,;

3 And inasmuch as ye have not lands, let them buy, for the present time, in those regions round about, as seemeth them good, for it must needs be necessary that they have places to live for the present time.

4 It must needs be necessary, that ye save all the money that ye can, and that ye obtain all that ye can in righteousness, that in time ye may be enabled to purchase lands for an inheritance, even the city.

5 The place is not yet to be revealed, but after your brethren come from the east, there are to be certain men appointed, and to them it shall be given to know the place, or to them it shall be revealed; and they shall be appointed to purchase the lands, and to make a commencement, to lay the foundation of the city;

6 And then ye shall begin to be gathered with your families, every man according to his family, according to his circumstances, and as is appointed to him by the bishop and elders of the church, according to the laws and commandments, which ye have received, and which ye shall hereafter receive; even so: Amen.

---

line 1. Revelation, 10 Mar. 1831 [D&C 48]. This version reflects editing marks made in Revelation Book 1, indicating that the latter was used as a source text for the former. (See *JSP*, MRB:131.)

·116·

CHAPTER LII.

A Revelation to Sidney, Parley, and Lemon, given in Kirtland, Ohio, March, 1831.

HEARKEN unto my word, my servant Sidney, and Parley, and Lemon, for behold, verily I say unto you, that I give unto you a commandment, that you shall go and preach my gospel, which ye have received, even as ye have received it, unto the Shakers.

2 Behold I say unto you, that they desire to know the truth in part, but not all, for they are not right before me, and must needs repent:

3 Wherefore I send you, my servants Sidney and Parley, to preach the gospel unto them; and my servant Lemon shall be ordained unto this work, that he may reason with them, not according to that which he has received of them, but according to that which shall be taught him by you, my servants, and by so doing I will bless him, otherwise he shall not prosper:

4 Thus saith the Lord, for I am God and have sent mine only begotten Son into the world, for the redemption of the world, and have decreed, that he that receiveth him shall be saved, and he that receiveth him not, shall be damned:

5 And they have done unto the Son of man even as they listed;

6 And he has taken his power on the right hand of his glory, and now reigneth in the heavens, and will reign till he descends on the earth to put all enemies under his feet:

7 Which time is nigh at hand: I the Lord God have spoken it:

8 But the hour and the day no man knoweth,

line 1

5

10

15

20

25

30

---

line 1. Revelation, 7 May 1831 [D&C 49]. This version closely corresponds to the version in the November 1832 issue of *The Evening and the Morning Star,* suggesting that the latter was used as a source text for the former. This revelation should be dated 7 May 1831. For more information on this dating, see the discussion of this revelation in the Documents series.

117

neither the angels in heaven, nor shall they know until he come:

9 Wherefore I will that all men shall repent, for all are under sin, except them which I have reserved unto myself, holy men that ye know not of:

10 Wherefore I say unto you, that I have sent unto you mine everlasting covenant, even that which was from the beginning, and that which I have promised I have so fulfilled, and the nations of the earth shall bow to it;

11 And, if not of themselves, they shall come down, for that which is now exalted of itself, shall be laid low of power:

12 Wherefore I give unto you a commandment, that ye go among this people and say unto them, like unto mine apostle of old, whose name was Peter:

13 Believe on the name of the Lord Jesus, who was on the earth, and is to come, the beginning and the end;

14 Repent and be baptized in the name of Jesus Christ, according to the holy commandment, for the remission of sins;

15 And whoso doeth this, shall receive the gift of the Holy Ghost, by the laying on of the hands of the elders of this church.

16 And again, I say unto you, that whoso forbiddeth to marry, is not ordained of God, for marriage is ordained of God unto man:

17 Wherefore it is lawful that he should have one wife, and they twain shall be one flesh, and all this that the earth might answer the end of its creation; and that it might be filled with the measure of man, according to his creation before the world was made.

118

line 1

18 And whoso forbiddeth to abstain from meats, that man should not eat the same, is not ordained of God;

19 For behold the beasts of the field, and the fowls of the air, and that which cometh of the earth, is ordained for the use of man, for food, and for raiment, and that he might have in abundance, but it is not given that one man should possess that which is above another:

20 Wherefore the world lieth in sin; and wo be unto man that sheddeth blood or that wasteth flesh and hath no need.

21 And again, verily I say unto you, that the Son of man cometh not in the form of a woman, neither of a man travelling on the earth:

22 Wherefore be not deceived, but continue in steadfastness, looking forth for the heavens to be shaken;

23 And the earth to tremble, and to reel to and fro as a drunken man; and for the valleys to be exalted; and for the mountains to be made low; and for the rough places to become smooth:

24 And all this when the angel shall sound his trumpet.

25 But before the great day of the Lord shall come, Jacob shall flourish in the wilderness; and the Lamanites shall blossom as the rose:

26 Zion shall flourish upon the hills, and rejoice upon the mountains, and shall be assembled together unto the place which I have appointed.

27 Behold I say unto you, go forth as I have commanded you;

28 Repent of all your sins; ask and ye shall receive; knock and it shall be opened unto you:

29 Behold I will go before you, and be your rere-

119

ward; and I will be in your midst, and you shall
not be confounded:

30 Behold I am Jesus Christ, and I come quickly; even so: Amen.

———

CHAPTER LIII.

*A Revelation to the elders of the church assembled
at Kirtland, Ohio, given May, 1831.*

HEARKEN, O ye elders of my church, and
give ear to the voice of the living God; and
attend to the words of wisdom which shall be giv-
en unto you, according as ye have asked and are
agreed as touching the church, and the spirits which
have gone abroad in the earth.

2 Behold verily I say unto you, that there are many spirits which are false spirits, which have gone
forth in the earth, deceiving the world:

3 And also satan hath sought to deceive you, that
he might overthrow you.

4 Behold I the Lord have looked upon you, and
have seen abominations in the church, which profess
my name;

5 But blessed are they who are faithful and endure,
whether in life or in death, for they shall inherit
eternal life.

6 But wo unto them that are deceivers, and hypocrites, for thus saith the Lord, I will bring them to
judgment.

7 Behold verily I say unto you, there are hypocrites among you, and have deceived some, which
has given the adversary power, but behold such shall
be reclaimed;

———

line 5. Revelation, 9 May 1831 [D&C 50]. This version reflects editing marks made in Revelation Book 1 and closely corresponds to the version in the August 1832 issue of *The Evening and the Morning Star,* suggesting that both were used as source texts for this version. (See *JSP,* MRB:137–143.)

130

8 But the hypocrites shall be detected and shall be cut off, either in life or in death, even as I will, and wo unto them who are cut off from my church, for the same are overcome of the world :

9 Wherefore, let every man beware lest he do that which is not in truth and righteousness before me.

10 And now come, saith the Lord, by the Spirit, unto the elders of his church, and let us reason together, that ye may understand :

11 Let us reason even as a man reasoneth one with another face to face :

12 Now when a man reasoneth, he is understood of man, because he reasoneth as a man; even so will I the Lord reason with you that you may understand :

13 Wherefore I the Lord asketh you this question, unto what were ye ordained ?

14 To preach my gospel by the Spirit, even the Comforter which was sent forth to teach the truth; and then received ye spirits which ye could not understand, and received them to be of God, and in this are ye justified ?

15 Behold ye shall answer this question yourselves, nevertheless I will be merciful unto you :

16 He that is weak among you hereafter shall be made strong.

17 Verily I say unto you, he that is ordained of me and sent forth to preach the word of truth by the Comforter, in the spirit of truth, doth he preach it by the spirit of truth, or some other way ? and if by some other way, it be not of God.

18 And again, he that receiveth the word of truth, doth he receive it by the spirit of truth, or some other way ? if it be some other way, it be not of God :

121

19 Therefore, why is it that ye can not understand and know that he that receiveth the word by the spirit of truth, receiveth it as it is preached by the spirit of truth?

20 Wherefore, he that preacheth and he that receiveth, understandeth one another, and both are edified and rejoice together; and that which doth not edify, is not of God, and is darkness:

21 That which is of God is light, and he that receiveth light and continueth in God, receiveth more light, and that light groweth brighter and brighter, until the perfect day.

22 And again, verily I say unto you, and I say it that you may know the truth, that you may chase darkness from among you, for he that is ordained of God and sent forth, the same is appointed to be the greatest, notwithstanding he is least, and the servant of all:

23 Wherefore he is possessor of all things, for all things are subject unto him, both in heaven and on the earth, the life, and the light, the spirit, and the power, sent forth by the will of the Father, through Jesus Christ, his Son;

24 But no man is possessor of all things, except he be purified and cleansed from all sin;

25 And if ye are purified and cleansed from all sin, ye shall ask whatsoever you will in the name of Jesus, and it shall be done:

26 But know this, it shall be given you what you shall ask, and as ye are appointed to the head, the spirits shall be subject unto you:

27 Wherefore it shall come to pass, that if you behold a spirit manifested that ye can not understand, and you receive not that spirit, ye shall ask of the Father in the name of Jesus, and if he give

122

not unto you that spirit, then you may know that
it is not of God:

28 And it shall be given unto you power over that
spirit, and you shall proclaim against that spirit
with a loud voice, that it is not of God;

29 Not with railing accusation, that ye be not overcome; neither with boasting, nor rejoicing, lest you
be seized therewith:

30 He that receiveth of God, let him account it of
God, and let him rejoice that he is accounted of
God worthy to receive, and by giving heed and doing these things which ye have received, and which
ye shall hereafter receive:

31 And the kingdom is given unto you of the Father, and power to overcome all things, which is not
ordained of him:

32 And behold, verily I say unto you, blessed are
you who are now hearing these words of mine from
the mouth of my servant, for your sins are forgiven
you.

33 Let my servant Joseph (W.) in whom I am
well pleased, and my servant Parley, go forth among
the churches and strengthen them by the word of
exhortation;

34 And also my servant John (C.,) or as many
of my servants as are ordained unto this office, and
let them labor in the vineyard;

35 And let no man hinder them of doing that
which I have appointed unto them:

36 Wherefore in this thing my servant Edward is
not justified, nevertheless let him repent and he
shall be forgiven.

37 Behold ye are little children, and ye can not
bear all things now; ye must grow in grace and in
the knowledge of the truth.

123

line 1
38 Fear not, little children, for you are mine, and I have overcome the world, and you are of them that my Father hath given me;

39 And none of them which my Father hath given me shall be lost:

5
40 And the Father and I are one; I am in the Father and the Father in me:

41 And inasmuch as ye have received me, ye are in me, and I in you: wherefore I am in your midst; and I am the good Shepherd;

10
42 And the day cometh that you shall hear my voice and see me, and know that I am.

43 Watch, therefore, that ye may be ready; even so: Amen.

15
CHAPTER LIV.

A Revelation to the elders of the church assembled in Kirtland, Ohio, given June, 1831.

BEHOLD, thus saith the Lord unto the elders whom he hath called and chosen, in these last
20
days, by the voice of his Spirit, saying, I the Lord will make known unto you what I will that ye shall do from this time until the next conference, which shall be held in Missouri, upon the land which I will consecrate unto my people, which are a rem-
25
nant of Jacob, and them who are heirs according to the covenant.

2 Wherefore, verily I say unto you, let my servants Joseph and Sidney take their journey as soon as preparations can be made to leave their homes, and journey to the land of Missouri.
30
3 And inasmuch as they are faithful unto me, it

---

line 15. Revelation, 6 June 1831 [D&C 52]. This version reflects editing marks made in Revelation Book 1, indicating that the latter was used as a source text for the former. (See *JSP,* MRB:147–151.)

124

line 1 shall be made known unto them what they shall
do:

4 And it shall also, inasmuch as they are faithful, be made known unto them the land of your inheritance.

5 And inasmuch as they are not faithful, they
shall be cut off, even as I will, as seemeth me good.

6 And again, verily I say unto you, let my servant Lyman (W.,) and my servant John (C.,)
take their journey speedily:

7 And also my servant John (M.) and my servant Hyrum, take their journey unto the same place
by the way of Detroit.

8 And let them journey from thence preaching
the word by the way, saying none other things than
that which the prophets and apostles have written,
and that which is taught them by the Comforter,
through the prayer of faith.

9 Let them go two by two, and thus let them
preach by the way in every congregation, baptizing
by water, and the laying on of the hands by the
water side:

10 For thus saith the Lord, I will cut my work
short in righteousness:

11 For the days cometh that I will send forth judgment unto victory.

12 And let my servant Lyman beware, for satan
desireth to sift him as chaff.

13 And behold, he that is faithful shall be made
ruler over many things.

14 And again, I will give unto you a pattern in
all things, that ye may not be deceived, for satan is
abroad in the land, and he goeth forth deceiving the
nations:

15 Wherefore he that prayeth whose spirit is con-

125

line 1 trite, the same is accepted of me, if he obey mine
ordinances:

16 He that speaketh, whose spirit is contrite,
whose language is meek, and edifieth, the same is
5 of God, if he obey mine ordinances.

17 And again, he that trembleth under my power,
shall be made strong, and shall bring forth fruits of
praise, and wisdom, according to the revelations,
and truths which I have given you.

10 18 And again, he that is overcome and bringeth
not forth fruits, even according to this pattern, is
not of me:

19 Wherefore by this pattern ye shall know the
spirits in all cases, under the whole heavens.

15 20 And the days have come, according to men's
faith it shall be done unto them.

21 Behold this commandment is given unto all
the elders whom I have chosen.

22 And again, verily I say unto you, let my ser-
20 vant Thomas, and my servant Ezra, take their
journey also, preaching the word by the way, unto
this same land.

23 And again, let my servant Isaac and my servant Ezra (B.,) take their journey, also preaching
25 the word by the way unto the same land.

24 And again, let my servant Edward and Martin take their journey with my servants Sidney and
Joseph.

25 Let my servant David and Harvey, also take
30 their journey, and preach by the way unto this same
land.

26 Let my servants Parley and Orson (P.) take
their journey, and preach by the way, even unto
this same land.

35 27 And let my servants Solomon and Simeon,

126

line 1 also take their journey unto this same land, and preach by the way.

28 Let my servants Edson and Jacob (S.,) also take their journey.

5 29 Let my servants Levi and Zebidee, also take their journey.

30 Let my servants Reynolds and Samuel, also take their journey.

31 Let my servants Wheeler and William (C.,)
10 also take their journey.

32 And let my servants Newel (K.) and Selah, both be ordained and also take their journey:

33 Yea, verily I say, let all these take their journey unto one place, in their several courses, and
15 one man shall not build upon another's foundation, neither journey in another's track.

34 He that is faithful, the same shall be kept and blessed with much fruit.

35 And again, I say unto you, let my servant
20 Joseph (W.) and Solomon (H.,) take their journey into the eastern lands.

36 Let them labor with their families, declaring none other things than the prophets and apostles, that which they have seen, and heard, and most as-
25 suredly believe, that the prophecies may be fulfilled.

37 In consequence of transgression, let that which was bestowed upon Heman, be taken from him, and placed upon the head of Simonds.

38 And again, verily I say unto you, let Jared be
30 ordained a priest, and also George be ordained a priest.

39 Let the residue of the elders watch over the churches, and declare the word in the regions among them.

35 40 And let them labor with their own hands, that

---

line 21. From this point to the end of the gathering (Book of Commandments page 128), the compositor used a lowercase italic *y* in place of a roman one, indicating that he had run out of roman *y* type. In both this and the previous gathering, the compositor switched to italic *y*'s after approximately the nine-hundredth roman *y*.

127

line 1 there be no idolatry nor wickedness practiced. And
remember in all things, the poor and the needy,
the sick and the afflicted, for he that doeth not these
things, the same is not my disciple.

5 41 And again, let my servants Joseph and Sidney
and Edward, take with them a recommend from
the church.

 42 And let there be one obtained for my servant
Oliver, also:

10 43 And thus, even as I have said, if ye are faithful, ye shall assemble yourselves together to rejoice
upon the land of Missouri, which is the land of your
inheritance, which is now the land of your enemies.

 44 But behold I the Lord will hasten the city in
15 its time;

 45 And will crown the faithful with joy and with
rejoicing.

 46 Behold I am Jesus Christ, the Son of God, and
I will lift them up at the last day; even so: Amen.

---

20 ## CHAPTER LV.

*A Revelation to Sidney (G.,) given in Kirtland,
Ohio, June, 1831.*

BEHOLD I say unto you, my servant Sidney,
that I have heard your prayers, and you have
25 called upon me, that it should be made known unto you, of the Lord your God, concerning your calling, and election in this church, which I the Lord
have raised up in these last days.

 2 Behold I the Lord, who was crucified for the
30 sins of the world, giveth unto you a commandment,
that you shall forsake the world.

---

line 20. Revelation, 8 June 1831 [D&C 53]. This version reflects editing marks made in Revelation Book 1, indicating that the latter was used as a source text for the former. (See *JSP,* MRB:151–153.)

128

line 1

3 Take upon *you* mine ordinances, even that of an elder, to preach faith and repentance, and remission of sins, according to *my* word, and the reception of the Holy Spirit by the laying on of hands.

5

4 And also to be an agent unto this church in the place which shall be appointed by the bishop, according to commandments which shall be given hereafter.

5 And again, verily I say unto *you*, *you* shall take *your* journey with *my* servants Joseph and Sidney.

10

6 Behold these are the first ordinances which *you* shall receive:

7 And the residue shall be made known unto *you* in a time to come, according to *your* labor in *my* vineyard.

15

8 And again, I would that *ye* should learn that it is he only who is saved, that endureth unto the end; even so: Amen.

———

CHAPTER LVI.

20

A Revelation to Newel (K.,) and the church in Thompson, given in Kirtland, Ohio, June, 1831.

BEHOLD, thus saith the Lord, even Alpha and Omega, the beginning and the end, even he who was crucified for the sins of the world.

25

2 Behold, verily, verily I say unto *you*, my servant Newel, *you* shall stand fast in the office wherewith I have appointed *you*:

3 And if *your* brethren desire to escape their enemies let them repent of all their sins, and become truly humble before me and contrite:

30

———

line 20. Revelation, 10 June 1831 [D&C 54]. This version reflects editing marks made in Revelation Book 1, indicating that the latter was used as a source text for the former. (See *JSP,* MRB:153–155.)

129

4 And as the covenant which they made unto me, has been broken, even so it has become void and of none effect;

5 And wo to him by whom this offence cometh, for it had been better for him that he had been drowned in the depth of the sea;

6 But blessed are they who have kept the covenant, and observed the commandment, for they shall obtain mercy:

7 Wherefore, go to now and flee the land, lest your enemies come upon you:

8 And take your journey, and appoint whom you will to be your leader, and to pay moneys for you.

9 And thus you shall take your journey into the regions westward, unto the land of Missouri, unto the borders of the Lamanites.

10 And after you have done journeying, behold I say unto you, seek ye a living like unto men, until I prepare a place for you.

11 And again, be patient in tribulation until I come:

12 And behold I come quickly, and my reward is with me, and they who have sought me early, shall find rest to their souls; even so: Amen.

CHAPTER LVII.

A Revelation to William, given in Kirtland, Ohio, June, 1831.

BEHOLD thus saith the Lord unto you, my servant William; yea, even the Lord of the whole earth,

2 Thou art called and chosen and after thou hast

E1

---

line 25. Revelation, 14 June 1831 [D&C 55]. This version reflects editing marks made in Revelation Book 1, indicating that the latter was used as a source text for the former. (See *JSP*, MRB:155.)

line 32. This page begins the fifth gathering of the book. "E1" is the first of eight signature marks found on the rectos of the first eight leaves of this gathering. These marks were used in collating the gatherings after the sheets were folded.

130

line 1
been baptized by water, which if you do with an eye single to my glory, you shall have a remission of your sins, and a reception of the Holy Spirit, by the laying on of hands:

3 And then thou shalt be ordained by the hand of my servant Joseph, to be an elder unto this church, to preach repentance and remission of sins by way of baptism in the name of Jesus Christ, the Son of the living God;

4 And on whomsoever you shall lay your hands, if they are contrite before me, you shall have power to give the Holy Spirit.

5 And again, you shall be ordained to assist my servant Oliver to do the work of printing, and of selecting, and writing books for schools, in this church, that little children also may receive instruction before me as is pleasing unto me.

6 And again verily I say unto you, for this cause you shall take your journey with my servants Joseph and Sidney, that you may be planted in the land of your inheritance, to do this work.

7 And again let my servant Joseph (C.) also take his journey with them.

8 The residue shall be made known hereafter; even as I will: Amen.

CHAPTER LVIII.

A Revelation to the church, and certain elders, given in Kirtland, Ohio, June, 1831.

HEARKEN O ye people which profess my name, saith the Lord your God, for behold mine anger is kindled against the rebellious, and they

---

line 26. Revelation, 15 June 1831 [D&C 56]. This version reflects editing marks made in Revelation Book 1, indicating that the latter was used as a source text for the former. (See *JSP,* MRB:155–159.)

131

line 1 shall know mine arm and mine indignation in the day of visitation and of wrath upon the nations.

2 And he that will not take up his cross and follow me, and keep my commandments, the same

5 shall not be saved.

3 Behold I the Lord commandeth, and he that will not obey shall be cut off in mine own due time:

4 And after that I have commanded and the commandment is broken, wherefore I the Lord com-

10 mand and revoke, as it seemeth me good; and all this to be answered upon the heads of the rebellious saith the Lord:

5 Wherefore I revoke the commandment which was given unto my servants Thomas and Ezra, and

15 give a new commandment unto my servant Thomas, that he shall take up his journey speedily to the land of Missouri;

6 And my servant Selah shall also go with him:

7 For behold I revoke the commandment which

20 was given unto my servants Selah and Newel, in consequence of the stiffneckedness of my people which are in Thompson; and their rebellions:

8 Wherefore let my servant Newel remain with them, and as many as will go may go, that are con-

25 trite before me, and be led by him to the land which I have appointed.

9 And again, verily I say unto you, that my servant Ezra must repent of his pride, and of his selfishness, and obey the former commandment which

30 I have given him concerning the place upon which he lives;

10 And if he will do this, as there shall be no divisions made upon the land, he shall be appointed still to go to the land of Missouri;

35 11 Otherwise he shall rece'v the money which he

E2

132

has paid, and shall leave the place, and shall be cut off out of my church, saith the Lord God of hosts:

12 And though the heaven and the earth pass away, these words shall not pass away, but shall be fulfilled.

13 And if my servant Joseph must needs pay the money, behold I the Lord will pay it unto him again in the land of Missouri, that those of whom he shall receive may be rewarded again, according to that which they do.

14 For according to that which they do, they shall receive; even in lands for their inheritance.

15 Behold thus saith the Lord unto my people, you have many things to do, and to repent of:

16 For behold your sins have come up unto me, and are not pardoned, because you seek to counsel in your own ways.

17 And your hearts are not satisfied.

18 And ye obey not the truth, but have pleasure in unrighteousness.

19 Wo unto you rich men, that will not give your substance to the poor, for your riches will canker your souls! and this shall be your lamentation in the day of visitation, and of judgment, and of indignation:

20 The harvest is past, the summer is ended, and my soul is not saved!

21 Wo unto you poor men, whose hearts are not broken, whose spirits are not contrite, and whose bellies are not satisfied, and whose hands are not stayed from laying hold upon other men's goods, whose eyes are full of greediness, who will not labor with their own hands!

22 But blessed are the poor, who are pure in heart, whose hearts are broken, and whose spirits are con-

133

line 1 trite, for they shall see the kingdom of God coming in power and great glory unto their deliverance:

23 For the fatness of the earth shall be theirs:

24 For behold the Lord shall come, and his rec-
5 ompense shall be with him, and he shall reward every man, and the poor shall rejoice: and their generations shall inherit the earth from generation to generation, for ever and ever.

25 And now I make an end of speaking unto you,
10 even so: Amen.

CHAPTER LIX.

*A Revelation to the elders of the church, assem-
bled on the land of Zion, gwen August, 1831.*

HEARKEN O ye elders of my church, and
15 give ear to my word, and learn of me what
I will concerning you, and also concerning this land
unto which I have sent you:

2 For verily I say unto you, blessed is he that keepeth my commandments, whether in life or in death;

20 3 And he that is faithful in tribulation the reward
of the same is greater in the kingdom of heaven.

4 Ye can not behold with your natural eyes, for
the present time, the design of your God concerning those things which shall come hereafter, and the
25 glory which shall follow, after much tribulation.

5 For after much tribulation cometh the blessings.

6 Wherefore, the day cometh that ye shall be
crowned with much glory, the hour is not yet but is
nigh at hand.

30 7 Remember this which I tell you before, that you
may lay it to heart, and receive that which shall

r3

---

line 11. Revelation, 1 Aug. 1831 [D&C 58]. This version reflects editing marks made in Revelation Book 1, indicating that the latter was used as a source text for the former. (See *JSP,* MRB:161–169.)

134

follow. Behold, verily I say unto you, for this cause
I have sent you that you might be obedient, and
that your hearts might be prepared to bear testimony of the things which are to come;

8 And also, that you might be honored of laying
the foundation, and of bearing record of the land
upon which the Zion of God shall stand;

9 And also, that a feast of fat things might be
prepared for the poor;

10 Yea a feast of fat things, of wine on the lees
well refined, that the earth may know that the mouths
of the prophets shall not fail;

11 Yea, a supper of the house of the Lord, well
prepared, unto which all nations shall be invited.

12 Firstly the rich, and the learned, the wise and
the noble;

13 And after that cometh the day of my power:

14 Then shall the poor, the lame and the blind,
and the deaf, come in unto the marriage of the Lamb,
and partake of the supper of the Lord, prepared for
the great day to come.

15 Behold I the Lord have spoken it.

16 And that the testimony might go forth from
Zion; yea from the mouth of the city of the heritage of God:

17 Yea, for this cause I have sent you hither;

18 And have selected my servant Edward and appointed unto him his mission in this land:

19 But if he repent not of his sins, which are unbelief and blindness of heart, let him take heed lest
he fall.

20 Behold his mission is given unto him and it
shall not be given again.

21 And whoso standeth in this mission, is appointed to be a judge in Israel, like as it was in ancient:

135

line 1

days, to divide the lands of the heritage of God unto his children; and to judge his people by the testimony of the just, and by the assistance of his counsellors, according to the laws of the kingdom which
are given by the prophets of God:

22 For verily I say unto you, my laws shall be
kept on this land.

23 Let no man think that he is ruler, but let God
rule him that judgeth, according to the counsel of his
own will:

24 Or in other words, him that counselleth, or sitteth upon the judgment seat.

25 Let no man break the laws of the land, for he
that keepeth the laws of God, hath no need to break
the laws of the land:

26 Wherefore be subject to the powers that be,
until He reigns whose right it is to reign, and subdues all enemies under his feet.

27 Behold the laws which ye have received from
my hand, are the laws of the church;

28 And in this light ye shall hold them forth.

29 Behold here is wisdom.

30 And now as I spake concerning my servant
Edward: this land is the land of his residence, and
those whom he has appointed for his counsellors.

31 And also the land of the residence of him
whom I have appointed to keep my storehouse:

32 Wherefore let them bring their families to this
land, as they shall counsel between themselves and
me:

33 For behold it is not meet that I should command in all things, for he that is compelled in all
things, the same is a slothful and not a wise servant:

34 Wherefore he receiveth no reward.

35 Verily I say, men should be anxiously engaged

E4

136

line 1
in a good cause, and do many things of their own
free will, and bring to pass much righteousness:

36 For the power is in them, wherein they are
agents unto themselves.

37 And inasmuch as men do good, they shall in
no wise loose their reward.

38 But he that doeth not any thing until he is commanded, and receiveth a commandment with doubtful heart, and keepeth it with slothfulness, the same
is damned.

39 Who am I that made man, saith the Lord,
that will hold him guiltless, that obey not my commandments?

40 Who am I, saith the Lord, that have promised
and have not fulfilled?

41 I command and a man obeys not, I revoke
and they receive not the blessing:

42 Then they say in their hearts, this is not
the work of the Lord, for his promises are not fulfilled.

43 But wo unto such, for their reward lurketh beneath, and not from above.

44 And now I give unto you further directions
concerning this land.

45 It is wisdom in me, that my servant Martin
should be an example unto the church, in laying his
moneys before the bishop of the church.

46 And also, this is a law unto every man that
cometh unto this land, to receive an inheritance;

47 And he shall do with his moneys according as
the law directs.

48 And it is wisdom also, that there should be
lands purchased in Independence, for the place of
the storehouse:

49 And also for the house of the printing.

137

50 And other directions, concerning my servant Martin, shall be given him of the Spirit, that he may receive his inheritance as seemeth him good. And let him repent of his sins, for he seeketh the praise of the world.

51 And also let my servant William stand in the office which I have appointed him, and receive his inheritance in the land.

52 And also, he hath need to repent, for I the Lord am not pleased with him, for he seeketh to excell, and he is not sufficiently meek before me.

53 Behold he who has repented of his sins the same is forgiven, and I the Lord remembereth them no more.

54 By this ye may know if a man repenteth of his sins.

55 Behold he will confess them and forsake them.

56 And now verily I say, concerning the residue of the elders of my church, the time has not yet come for many years, for them to receive their inheritance in this land; except they desire it through prayer, only as it shall be appointed unto them of the Lord.

57 For behold they shall push the people together from the ends of the earth:

58 Wherefore assemble yourselves together, and they who are not appointed to stay in this land, let them preach the gospel in the regions round about;

59 And after that, let them return to their homes.

60 Let them preach by the way, and bear testimony of the truth in all places, and call upon the rich, the high, and the low, and the poor, to repent;

61 And let them build up churches inasmuch as the inhabitants of the earth will repent.

62 And let there be an agent appointed by the

138

line 1 voice of the church, unto the church in Ohio, to receive moneys to purchase lands in Zion.

63 And I give unto my servant Sidney a commandment, that he shall write a description of the
5 land of Zion, and a statement of the will of God,
as it shall be made known by the Spirit, unto him;
and an epistle and subscription, to be presented unto all the churches, to obtain moneys, to be put into
the hands of the bishop, to purchase lands for an in-
10 heritance for the children of God, of himself or the
agent, as seemeth him good, or as he shall direct.

64 For behold, verily I say unto you, the Lord
willeth that the disciples, and the children of men,
should open their hearts, even to purchase this whole
15 region of country, as soon as time will permit.

65 Behold here is wisdom; let them do this lest
they receive none inheritance, save it be by the shedding of blood.

66 And again, inasmuch as there is land obtain-
20 ed, let there be workmen sent forth, of all kinds, unto this land, to labor for the saints of God.

67 Let all these things be done in order.

68 And let the privileges of the lands be made
known from time to time, by the bishop, or the agent
25 of the church.

69 And let the work of the gathering be not in
haste, nor by flight, but let it be done as it shall be
counselled by the elders of the church at the conferences, according to the knowledge which they re-
30 ceive from time to time.

70 And let my servant Sidney consecrate and dedicate this land, and the spot of the temple, unto the
Lord.

71 And let a conference meeting be called, and
35 after that, let my servant Sidney and Joseph return,

139

and also Oliver with them, to accomplish the residue of the work, which I have appointed unto them
in their own land:

72 And the residue as shall be ruled by the conferences.

73 And let no man return from this land, except
he bear record by the way, of that which he knows
and most assuredly believes.

74 Let that which has been bestowed upon Ziba,
be taken from him:

75 And let him stand as a member in the church,
and labor with his own hands, with the brethren,
until he is sufficiently chastened for all his sins, for
he confesseth them not, and he thinketh to hide
them.

76 Let the residue of the elders of this church,
which are coming to this land, some of whom are
exceedingly blessed even above measure, also, hold
a conference upon this land.

77 And let my servant Edward direct the conference, which shall be held by them.

78 And let them also return, preaching the gospel
by the way, bearing record of the things which are
revealed unto them:

79 For verily the sound must go forth from this
place into all the world;

80 And unto the uttermost parts of the earth,
the gospel must be preached unto every creature,
with signs following them that believe.

81 And behold the Son of man cometh: Amen!

E6

140

line 1

CHAPTER LX.

A Revelation to the church, given in Zion, August, 1831.

BEHOLD, blessed saith the Lord, are they who have come up unto this land with an eye single to my glory, according to my commandments:

2 For them that live shall inherit the earth, and them that die shall rest from all their labors, and their works shall follow them, and they shall receive a crown in the mansions of my Father, which I have prepared for them;

3 Yea, blessed are they whose feet stand upon the land of Zion, who have obeyed my gospel, for they shall receive for their reward the good things of the earth;

4 And it shall bring forth in its strength:

5 And they also shall be crowned with blessings from above;

6 Yea and with commandments not a few;

7 And with revelations in their time:

8 They that are faithful and diligent before me:

9 Wherefore I give unto them a commandment, saying thus:

10 Thou shalt love the Lord thy God with all thy heart, with all thy might, mind, and strength:

11 And in the name of Jesus Christ thou shalt serve him.

12 Thou shalt love thy neighbor as thyself.

13 Thou shalt not steal.

14 Neither commit adultery, nor kill, nor do any thing like unto it.

15 Thou shalt thank the Lord thy God in all things.

16 Thou shalt offer a sacrifice unto the Lord thy God in righteousness:

---

line 1. Revelation, 7 Aug. 1831 [D&C 59]. The source text for this version is unknown.

141

17 Even that of a broken heart and a contrite spirit.

18 And that thou mayest more fully keep thyself unspotted from the world, thou shalt go to the house of prayer and offer up thy sacraments upon my holy day:

19 For verily this is a day appointed unto you to rest from your labors, and to pay thy devotions unto the Most High;

20 Nevertheless thy vows shall be offered up in righteousness on all days, and at all times;

21 But remember that on this, the Lord's day, thou shalt offer thine oblations, and thy sacraments, unto the Most High, confessing thy sins unto thy brethren, and before the Lord.

22 And on this day thou shalt do none other thing, only let thy food be prepared with singleness of heart, that thy fasting may be perfect, or in other words, that thy joy may be full.

23 Verily this is fasting and prayer; or, in other words, rejoicing and prayer.

24 And inasmuch as ye do these things with thanksgiving, with cheerful hearts, and countenances, not with much laughter, for this is sin, but with a glad heart, and a cheerful countenance;

25 Verily I say, that inasmuch as ye do this the fulness of the earth is yours;

26 The beasts of the fields, and the fowls of the air, and that which climbeth upon the trees, and walketh upon the earth:

27 Yea, and the herb, and the good things which cometh of the earth, whether for food or for raiment, or for houses, or for barns, or for orchards, or for gardens, or for vineyards:

28 Yea, all things which cometh of the earth, in

n7

142

line 1
the season thereof, is made for the benefit and the
use of man, both to please the eye, and to gladden
the heart:

29 Yea, for food and for raiment, for taste, and
for smell, to strengthen the body, and to enliven the
soul.

30 And it pleaseth God that he hath given all
these things unto man:

31 For unto this end were they made, to be used
with judgment, not to excess, neither by extortion:

32 And in nothing doth man offend God, or against
none is his wrath kindled, save those who confess
not his hand in all things, and obey not his commandments.

33 Behold this is according to the law and the
prophets:

34 Wherefore trouble me no more concerning this
matter, but learn that he who doeth the works of
righteousness, shall receive his reward, even peace in
this world, and eternal life in the world to come.

35 I the Lord have spoken it and the spirit beareth record. Amen.

CHAPTER LXI.

*A Revelation to the elders of the church, given in
Zion, August, 1831.*

BEHOLD, thus saith the Lord unto the elders
of his church, who are to return speedily to
the land from whence they came.

2 Behold it pleaseth me, that you have come up
hither;

3 But with some I am not well pleased, for they

---

line 23. Revelation, 8 Aug. 1831 [D&C 60]. This version reflects editing marks made in Revelation Book 1, indicating that the latter was used as a source text for the former. (See *JSP,* MRB:173–175.)

line 25. "8" was written in graphite by an unidentified scribe, making the date "8 August, 1831". The first publicly available version bearing this date appeared in the 1 March 1844 issue of *Times and Seasons,* suggesting that this inscription was made sometime after that issue was printed. ("History of Joseph Smith," *Times and Seasons,* 1 Mar. 1844, 5:448–452.)

143

line 1 will not open their mouths, but hide the talent which
I have given unto them, because of the fear of
man.

4 Wo unto such, for mine anger is kindled against
5 them.

5 And it shall come to pass, if they are not more
faithful unto me, it shall be taken away, even that
which they have, for I the Lord ruleth in the heavens above, and among the armies of the earth;

10 6 And in the day when I shall make up my jewels, all men shall know what it is that bespeaketh
the power of God.

7 But verily I will speak unto you concerning your
journey unto the land from whence you came.

15 8 Let there be a craft made, or bought, as seemeth you good, it mattereth not unto me, and take
your journey speedily for the place which is called
St. Louis.

9 And from thence let my servants Sidney and
20 Joseph and Oliver, take their journey for Cincinnati:

10 And in this place let them lift up their voice,
and declare my word with loud voices, without
wrath or doubting, lifting up holy hands upon them.

25 11 For I am able to make you holy, and your sins
are forgiven you.

12 And let the residue take their journey from St.
Louis, two by two, and preach the word, not in
haste, among the congregations of the wicked, un-
30 til they return to the churches from whence they
came.

13 And all this for the good of the churches; for
this intent have I sent them.

14 And let my servant Edward impart of the mon-
35 ey which I have given him, a portion unto mine el-

E3

144

ders, which are commanded to return: and he that
is able, let him return it by the way of the agent,
and he that is not, of him it is not required.

15 And now I speak of the residue which are to
come unto this land.

16 Behold they have been sent to preach my gospel among the congregations of the wicked:

17 Wherefore, I give unto them a commandment,
thus:

18 Thou shalt not idle away thy time:

19 Neither shalt thou bury thy talent that it may
not be known.

20 And after thou hast come up unto the land of
Zion, and hast proclaimed my word, thou shalt
speedily return proclaiming the word among the congregations of the wicked.

21 Not in haste, neither in wrath, nor with strife:

22 And shake off the dust of thy feet against those
who receive thee not, not in their presence, lest thou
provoke them, but in secret, and wash thy feet as a
testimony against them in the day of judgment.

23 Behold this is sufficient for you, and the will of
him who hath sent you.

24 And by the mouth of my servant Joseph, it
shall be made known concerning Sidney and Oliver.

25 The residue hereafter; even so: Amen.

145

CHAPTER LXII.

A Revelation to eleven elders, given upon the bank of the Missouri river, August, 1831.

BEHOLD, and hearken unto the voice of him who has all power, who is from everlasting to everlasting, even Alpha and Omega, the beginning and the end.

2 Behold, verily thus saith the Lord unto you O ye elders of my church, who are assembled upon this spot, whose sins are now forgiven you, for I the Lord forgiveth sins, and am merciful unto those who confess their sins with humble hearts:

3 But verily I say unto you, that it is not needful for this whole company of mine elders, to be moving swiftly upon the waters, whilst the inhabitants on either side are perishing in unbelief:

4 Nevertheless, I suffered it that ye might bear record:

5 Behold there are many dangers upon the waters and more especially hereafter, for I the Lord have decreed, in mine anger, many destructions upon the waters;

6 Yea, and especially upon these waters;

7 Nevertheless, all flesh is in mine hand, and he that is faithful among you, shall not perish by the waters.

8 Wherefore it is expedient that my servant Sidney (G.) and my servant William be in haste upon their errand and mission:

9 Nevertheless I would not suffer that ye should part until you are chastened for all your sins, that you might be one;

10 That you might not perish in wickedness;

11 But now verily I say, it behooveth me that ye

---

line 1. Revelation, 12 Aug. 1831 [D&C 61]. This version corresponds to the version in the December 1832 issue of *The Evening and the Morning Star,* suggesting that the latter was used as a source text for the former.

146

line 1

should part: wherefore let my servants Sidney and Willliam, take their former company, and let them take their journey in haste that they may fill their mission, and through faith they shall overcome;

12 And inasmuch as they are faithful, they shall be preserved, and I the Lord will be with them.

13 And let the residue take that which is needful for clothing.

14 Let my servant Sidney take that which is not needful with him, as you shall agree.

15 And now behold, for your good I gave unto you a commandment concerning these things; and I the Lord will reason with you as with men in days of old.

16 Behold I the Lord in the beginning, blessed the waters, but in the last days by the mouth of my servant John, I cursed the waters:

17 Wherefore, the days will come that no flesh shall be safe upon the waters, and it shall be said in days to come, that none is able to go up to the land of Zion, upon the waters, but he that is upright in heart.

18 And, as I the Lord in the beginning cursed the land, even so in the last days have I blessed it, in its time, for the use of my saints, that they may partake the fatness thereof.

19 And now I give unto you a commandment, and what I say unto one I say unto all, that you shall forewarn your brethren concerning these waters, that they come not in journeying upon them, lest their faith fail and they are caught in her snares:

20 I the Lord have decreed, and the destroyer rideth upon the face thereof, and I revoke not the decree.

147

21 I the Lord was angry with you yesterday, but today mine anger is turned away:

22 Wherefore let those concerning whom I have spoken, that should take their journey in haste:

23 Again I say unto you, let them take their journey in haste, and it mattereth not unto me, after a little, if it so be that they fill their mission, whether they go by water or by land:

24 Let this be as it is made known unto them according to their judgments, hereafter.

25 And now, concerning my servants Sidney, and Joseph, and Oliver, let them come not again upon the waters, save it be upon the canal, while journeying unto their homes, or in other words they shall not come upon the waters to journey, save upon the canal.

26 Behold I the Lord have appointed a way for the journeying of my saints, and behold this is the way:

27 That after they leave the canal, they shall journey by land, inasmuch as they are commanded to journey and go up unto the land of Zion; and they shall do like unto the children of Israel, pitching their tents by the way.

28 And behold this commandment, you shall give unto all your brethren: nevertheless unto whom it is given power to command the waters, unto him it is given by the Spirit to know all his ways:

29 Wherefore let him do as the Spirit of the living God commandeth him, whether upon the land or upon the waters, as it remaineth with me to do hereafter;

30 And unto you it is given the course for the saints, or the way for the saints of the camp of the Lord, to journey.

148

31 And again, verily I say unto you, my servants Sidney, and Joseph, and Oliver, shall not open their mouths in the congregations of the wicked, until they arrive at Cincinnati;

32 And in that place they shall lift up their voices unto God against that people.

33 Yea, unto him whose anger is kindled against their wickedness; a people which is well nigh ripened for destruction;

34 And from thence let them journey for the congregations of their brethren, for their labors, even now, are wanted more abundantly among them, than among the congregations of the wicked.

35 And now concerning the residue, let them journey and declare the word among the congregations of the wicked, inasmuch as it is given, and inasmuch as they do this they shall rid their garments, and they shall be spotless before me;

36 And let them journey together, or two by two, as seemeth them good, only let my servant Reynolds, and my servant Samuel, with whom I am well pleased, be not separated until they return to their homes, and this for a wise purpose in me.

37 And now verily I say unto you, and what I say unto one I say unto all, be of good cheer little children for I am in your midst, and I have not forsaken you, and inasmuch as you have humbled yourselves before me, the blessings of the kingdom are yours:

38 Gird up your loins and be watchful, and be sober, looking forth for the coming of the Son of man, for he cometh in an hour you think not.

39 Pray always that you enter not into temptation, that you may abide the day of his coming, whether in life or in death; even so: Amen.

149

CHAPTER LXIII.

line 1

*A Revelation to certain elders, while journeying
to the land of Zion, given on the bank of the
Missouri river, August, 1831.*

BEHOLD and hearken, O ye elders of my
church, saith the Lord your God; even Jesus
Christ, your advocate who knoweth the weakness
of man and how to succor them who are tempted:

2 And verily mine eyes are upon those who have
not as yet gone up unto the land of Zion:

3 Wherefore your mission is not yet full:

4 Nevertheless ye are blessed, for the testimony
which ye have borne, is recorded in heaven for the
angels to look upon, and they rejoice over you; and
your sins are forgiven you.

5 And now continue your journey.

6 Assemble yourselves upon the land of Zion,
and hold a meeting and rejoice together, and offer
a sacrament unto the Most High;

7 And then you may return to bear record;

8 Yea, even all together, or two by two, as seemeth
you good;

9 It mattereth not unto me, only be faithful, and
declare glad tidings unto the inhabitants of the
earth, or among the congregations of the wicked.

10 Behold I the Lord have brought you together
that the promise might be fulfilled, that the faithful
among you should be preserved and rejoice together
in the land of Missouri.

11 I the Lord promised the faithful, and cannot
lie.

12 I the Lord am willing, if any among you desireth to ride upon horses, or upon mules, or in
chariots, shall receive this blessing, if he receive it

line 1. Revelation, 13 Aug. 1831 [D&C 62]. This version reflects editing marks made in Revelation Book 1,
indicating that the latter was used as a source text for the former. (See *JSP*, MRB:181.)

150

line 1
from the hand of the Lord, with a thankful heart
in all things.

13 These things remain with you to do according
to judgment and the directions of the Spirit.

5
14 Behold the kingdom is yours.

15 And behold, and lo I am with the faithful always; even so: Amen.

CHAPTER LXIV.

A Revelation given in Kirtland, Ohio, August,

10
1831.

HEARKEN O ye people, and open your
hearts, and give ear from afar:

2 And listen, you that call yourselves the people
of the Lord, and hear the word of the Lord, and

15
his will concerning you:

3 Yea, verily I say, hear the word of him whose
anger is kindled against the wicked, and rebellious;
who willeth to take even them whom he will take,
and preserveth in life them whom he will preserve:

20
4 Who buildeth up at his own will and pleasure;
and destroyeth when he please; and is able to cast
the soul down to hell.

5 Behold I the Lord uttereth my voice, and it
shall be obeyed.

25
6 Wherefore verily I say, let the wicked take
heed, and let the rebellious fear, and tremble.

7 And let the unbelieving hold their lips, for the
day of wrath shall come upon them as a whirlwind,
and all flesh shall know that I am God.

30
8 And he that seeketh signs shall see signs, but
not unto salvation.

---

line 8. Revelation, 30 Aug. 1831 [D&C 63]. This version reflects editing marks made in Revelation Book 1 and corresponds to the version in the February 1833 issue of *The Evening and the Morning Star,* suggesting that both were used as source texts for this version. (See *JSP,* MRB:181–189.)

151

9 Verily I say unto you, there are those among you, who seeketh signs; and there have been such even from the beginning.

10 But behold, faith cometh not by signs, but signs follow those that believe.

11 Yea, signs cometh by faith, not by the will of men, nor as they please; but by the will of God.

12 Yea, signs cometh by faith, unto mighty works, for without faith no man pleaseth God: and with whom God is angry, he is not well pleased:

13 Wherefore, unto such he sheweth no signs, only in wrath unto their condemnation.

14 Wherefore I the Lord am not pleased with those among you, who have sought after signs and wonders for faith, and not for the good of men unto my glory:

15 Nevertheless, I gave commandments and many have turned away from my commandments, and have not kept them.

16 There were among you adulterers and adulteresses; some of whom have turned away from you, and others remain with you, that hereafter shall be revealed.

17 Let such beware and repent speedily, lest judgments shall come upon them as a snare, and their folly shall be made manifest, and their works shall follow them in the eyes of the people.

18 And verily I say unto you, as I have said before, he that looketh on a woman to lust after her, or if any shall commit adultery in their hearts, they shall not have the spirit, but shall deny the faith and shall fear:

19 Wherefore I the Lord have said that the fearful and the unbelieving, and all liars, and whosoever loveth and maketh a lie, and the whoremonger, and

152

line 1

the sorcerer, should have their part in that lake which burneth with fire and brimstone, which is the second death.

20 Verily I say, that they shall not have part in the first resurrection.

21 And now behold, I the Lord saith unto you, that ye are not justified because these things are among you, nevertheless he that endureth in faith and doeth my will, the same shall overcome, and shall receive an inheritance upon the earth, when the day of transfiguration shall come;

22 When the earth shall be transfigured, even according to the pattern which was shown unto mine apostles upon the mount:

23 Of which account the fulness ye have not yet received.

24 And now, verily I say unto you, that as I said that I would make known my will unto you, behold I will make it known unto you, not by the way of commandment, for there are many who observe not to keep my commandments, but unto him that keepeth my commandments, I will give the mysteries of my kingdom, and the same shall be in him a well of living water, springing up unto everlasting life.

25 And now, behold this is the will of the Lord your God concerning his saints, that they should assemble themselves together unto the land of Zion, not in haste, lest there should be confusion, which bringeth pestilence.

26 Behold the land of Zion, I the Lord holdeth it in mine own hands:

27 Nevertheless, I the Lord rendereth unto Cæsar the things which are Cæsar's:

28 Wherefore I the Lord willeth, that you should

line 5

10

15

20

25

30

35

---

line 6. The inscriptions that change "saith" to "say" were written in ink by an unidentified scribe at an unknown time.

153

purchase the lands, that you may have advantage
of the world, that you may have claim on the
world, that they may not be stirred up unto anger:

29 For satan putteth it into their hearts to anger
against you, and to the shedding of blood:

30 Wherefore the land of Zion shall not be obtained but by purchase, or by blood, otherwise there
is none inheritance for you.

31 And if by purchase behold you are blessed;

32 And if by blood, as you are forbidden to shed
blood, lo, your enemies are upon you, and ye shall
be scourged from city to city, and from synagogue
to synagogue, and but few shall stand to receive an
inheritance.

33 I the Lord am angry with the wicked;

34 I am holding my Spirit from the inhabitants
of the earth.

35 I have sworn in my wrath and decreed wars
upon the face of the earth, and the wicked shall
slay the wicked, and fear shall come upon every
man and the saints also shall hardly escape:

36 Nevertheless, I the Lord am with them, and
will come down in heaven from the presence of God,
and consume the wicked with unquenchable fire.

37 And behold this is not yet, but by and by:

38 Wherefore seeing that I the Lord have decreed
all these things upon the face of the earth, I willeth
that my saints should be assembled upon the land
of Zion;

39 And that every man should take righteousness
in his hands, and faithfulness upon his loins, and
lift a warning voice unto the inhabitants of the
earth;

40 And declare both by word and by flight, that
desolation shall come upon the wicked.

154

line 1   41 Wherefore let my disciples in Kirtland, arrange their temporal concerns, which dwell upon this farm.

   42 Let my servant Titus, who has the care thereof dispose of the land, that he may be prepared in the coming spring, to take his journey up unto the land of Zion, with those that dwell upon the face thereof, excepting those whom I shall reserve unto myself, that shall not go until I shall command them.

   43 And let all the moneys which can be spared, it mattereth not unto me whether it be little or much, sent up unto the land of Zion, unto them whom I have appointed to receive.

   44 Behold I the Lord, will give unto my servant Joseph power, that he shall be enabled to discern by the Spirit those who shall go up unto the land of Zion, and those of my disciples who shall tarry.

   45 Let my servant Newel retain his store, or in other words, the store yet for a little season.

   46 Nevertheless let him impart all the money which he can impart, to be sent up unto the land of Zion.

   47 Behold these things are in his own hands, let him do according to wisdom.

   48 Verily I say, let him be ordained as an agent unto the disciples that shall tarry, and let him be ordained unto this power;

   49 And now speedily visit the churches, expounding these things unto them, with my servant Oliver.

   50 Behold this is my will, obtaining moneys even as I have directed.

   51 He that is faithful and endureth shall overcome the world.

   52 He that sendeth up treasures unto the land of Zion, shall receive an inheritance in this world, and

155

his works shall follow him; and also, a reward in the world to come;

53 Yea, and blessed are the dead that die in the Lord from henceforth, when the Lord shall come and old things shall pass away, and all things become new, they shall rise from the dead and shall not die, and shall receive an inheritance before the Lord, in the holy city, and he that liveth when the Lord shall come, and have kept the faith, blessed is he;

54 Nevertheless it is appointed to him to die at the age of man:

55 Wherefore children shall grow up until they become old, old men shall die;

56 But they shall not sleep in the dust, but they shall be changed in the twinkling of an eye:

57 Wherefore, for this cause preached the apostles unto the world, the resurrection of the dead:

58 These things are the things that ye must look for, and speaking after the manner of the Lord, they are now nigh at hand;

59 And in a time to come, even in the day of the coming of the Son of man, and until that hour, there will be foolish virgins among the wise, and at that hour cometh an entire separation of the righteous and the wicked;

60 And in that day will I send mine angels, to pluck out the wicked, and cast them into unquenchable fire.

61 And now behold, verily I say unto you, I the Lord am not pleased with my servant Sidney, he exalted himself in his heart, and received not counsel, but grieved the Spirit:

62 Wherefore his writing is not acceptable unto the Lord, and he shall make another;

156

63 And if the Lord receive it not, behold he standeth no longer in the office which I have appointed him.

64 And again: verily I say unto you, let those who desire in their hearts, in meekness, to warn sinners to repentance, let them be ordained unto this power;

65 For this is a day of warning, and not a day of many words.

66 For I the Lord am not to be mocked in the last days.

67 Behold I am from above, and my power lieth beneath.

68 I am over all, and in all, and through all, and searcheth all things:

69 And the days cometh that all things shall be subject unto me.

70 Behold I am Alpha and Omega, even Jesus Christ.

71 Wherefore let all men beware, how they take my name in their lips:

72 For behold, verily I say, that many there be who are under this condemnation;

73 Who useth the name of the Lord, and useth it in vain, having not authority.

74 Wherefore let the church repent of their sins, and I the Lord will own them, otherwise they shall be cut off.

75 Remember, that that which cometh from above is sacred, and must be spoken with care, and by constraint of the Spirit, and in this there is no condemnation; and ye receive the Spirit through prayer:

76 Wherefore without this, there remaineth condemnation:

77 Let my servants Joseph and Sidney, seek them

157

line 1

a home as they are taught through prayer, by the Spirit.

78 These things remain to overcome, through patience, that such may receive a more exceeding and eternal weight of glory;

5

79 Otherwise, a greater condemnation: Amen.

———————

CHAPTER LXV.

A Revelation to the elders of the church, given in Kirtland, Ohio, September, 1831.

10

BEHOLD, thus saith the Lord your God unto you, O ye elders of my church, hearken ye, and hear, and receive my will concerning you:

2 For verily I say unto you, I will that ye should overcome the world:

15

3 Wherefore I will have compassion upon you.

4 There are those among you who have sinned;

5 But verily I say, for this once, for mine own glory, and for the salvation of souls, I have forgiven you your sins.

20

6 I will be merciful unto you, for I have given unto you the kingdom:

7 And the keys of the mysteries of the kingdom, shall not be taken from my servant Joseph, while he liveth, inasmuch as he obeyeth mine ordinances.

25

8 There are those who have sought occasion against him without cause;

9 Nevertheless he has sinned, but verily I say unto you, I the Lord forgiveth sins unto those who confess their sins before me, and ask forgiveness, who have not sinned unto death.

30

10 My disciples, in days of old, sought occasion

———————

line 7. "see sec. 64" was written in graphite by an unidentified scribe sometime in or after 1876, the year the Doctrine and Covenants was published in Salt Lake City for the first time. (Revelation, 11 Sept. 1831, in Doctrine and Covenants 64, 1876 ed. [D&C 64].)

line 7. Revelation, 11 Sept. 1831 [D&C 64:1–36]. This version reflects editing marks made in Revelation Book 1, indicating that the latter was used as a source text for the former. (See *JSP,* MRB:189–195.)

158

against one another, and forgave not one another
in their hearts, and for this evil they were afflicted,
and sorely chastened:

11 Wherefore I say unto you, that ye ought to
forgive one another, for he that forgiveth not his
brother his trespasses, standeth condemned before
the Lord, for there remaineth in him the greater sin.

12 I the Lord will forgive whom I will forgive,
but of you it is required to forgive all men;

13 And ye ought to say in your hearts, Let God
judge between me and thee, and reward thee according to thy deeds.

14 And he that repenteth not of his sins, and confesseth them not, then ye shall bring him before the
church, and do with him as the Scriptures saith unto you, either by commandment, or by revelation.

15 And this ye shall do that God might be glorified, not because ye forgive not, having not compassion, but that ye may be justified in the eyes of the
law, that ye may not offend him who is your Lawgiver.

16 Verily I say, for this cause ye shall do these
things.

17 Behold I the Lord was angry with him who
was my servant Ezra (B.);

18 And also, my servant Isaac; for they kept not
the law, neither the commandment: they sought
evil in their hearts, and I the Lord withheld my
Spirit.

19 They condemned for evil, that thing in which
there was no evil:

20 Nevertheless I have forgiven my servant Isaac.

21 And also my servant Edward, behold he hath
sinned, and satan seeketh to destroy his soul;

22 But when these things are made known unto

150

them, they repent of the evil, and they shall be for-given.

23 And now verily I say, that it is expedient in me that my servant Sidney (G.) after a few weeks, should return upon his business, and to his agency in the land of Zion;

24 And that which he hath seen and heard may be made known unto my disciples, that they perish not.

25 And for this cause have I spoken these things.

26 And again, I say unto you, that my servant Isaac may not be tempted above that which he is able to bear, and counsel wrongfully to your hurt, I gave commandment that this farm should be sold.

27 I willeth not that my servant Frederick, should sell his farm, for I the Lord willeth to retain a strong hold in the land of Kirtland, for the space of five years, in the which I will not overthrow the wicked, that thereby I may save some;

28 And after that day, I the Lord will not hold any guilty, that shall go, with an open heart, up to the land of Zion:

29 For I the Lord requireth the hearts of the children of men.

30 Behold now it is called today, and verily it is a day of sacrifice, and a day for the tithing of my people;

31 For he that is tithed shall not be burned; for after today cometh the burning:

32 This is speaking after the manner of the Lord;

33 For verily I say, tomorrow all the proud and they that do wickedly shall be as stubble: and I will burn them up, for I am the Lord of hosts;

34 And I will not spare any that remaineth in Babylon.

160

line 1   35 Wherefore, if ye believe me, ye will labor while it is called today.

36 And it is not meet that my servants, Newel and Sidney (G.) should sell their store, and their
5   possessions here, for this is not wisdom until the residue of the church, which remaineth in this place, shall go up unto the land of Zion.

37 Behold it is said in my laws, or forbidden to get in debt to thine enemies;
10   38 But behold it is not said at any time, that the Lord should not take when he please, and pay as seemeth him good:

39 Wherefore as ye are agents, and ye are on the Lord's errand; and whatever ye do according to
15   the will of the Lord, is the Lord's business, and it is the Lord's business to provide for his saints in these last days, that they may obtain an inheritance in the land of Zion:

40 And behold I the Lord declare unto you, and
20   my words are sure and shall not fail, that they shall obtain it;

41 But all things must come to pass in its time;

42 Wherefore be not weary in well doing, for ye are laying the foundation of a great work.
25   43 And out of small things proceedeth that which is great.

44 Behold the Lord requireth the heart and a willing mind;

45 And the willing and obedient shall eat the good of the land of Zion in these last days;
30   46 And the rebellious shall be cut off out of the land of Zion, and shall be sent away and shall not inherit the land:

47 For verily I say that the rebellious are not of
35   the blood of Ephraim.

---

line 34. "36" was written in graphite in the left margin by an unidentified scribe sometime in or after 1876, the year the Doctrine and Covenants was published in Salt Lake City for the first time. In that edition, in which the earlier versification of many of the texts was changed, the sentence beginning on this line became the first part of verse 36. (Revelation, 11 Sept. 1831, in Doctrine and Covenants 64:36, 1876 ed. [D&C 64:36].)

line 35. Printing was halted at this point because of the destruction of the printing office in July 1833.

line 36. "Hist of Church I p 213" (and several illegible characters, possibly "& 14") was written in graphite by an unidentified scribe sometime in or after 1902. This notation refers to the full version of this revelation found in *History of the Church,* which was published in 1902. (Roberts, *History of the Church,* 1:211–214.)

APPENDIX 1:
PROPOSED SIXTH
GATHERING OF THE
BOOK OF COMMANDMENTS

Introduction

The Book of Commandments as it exists today is incomplete. When angry residents of Jackson County, Missouri, razed the printing office operated by William W. Phelps, Oliver Cowdery, and John Whitmer in July 1833, sheets from only the first five gatherings of the book were salvaged (see further discussion on pages 4–12 herein). While it is possible—even likely—that typesetting or printing of an additional gathering had begun, no known copy of such a gathering exists.

Book collectors, historians, and others have long speculated about the intended contents of the complete Book of Commandments. Widespread access to Revelation Book 1—the primary source text for the Book of Commandments—has recently moved this debate from the realm of conjecture to that of careful analysis, though a definitive reconstruction of the planned contents of the Book of Commandments remains impossible. This appendix presents the items that were likely intended for the sixth gathering of the Book of Commandments. In so doing, this appendix attempts to reconstruct the text that would have been included in that volume if the printing had not been interrupted.

Unlike other texts found in *The Joseph Smith Papers,* this appendix is not a transcript of an existing document; rather it is a conception, based on existing evidence, of the sixth gathering of the Book of Commandments. This appendix includes the conclusion of chapter 65 of the Book of Commandments, twelve additional revelations, and a signed statement affirming the inspired nature of the revelations. These texts were selected for inclusion in this appendix based on available evidence from Revelation Book 1, the physical makeup of the existing portion of the Book of Commandments, analysis of textual patterns found in the Book of Commandments, and other textual and historical sources. This introduction outlines the justification for inclusion of these items.

Several important pieces of evidence indicate that further material was slated for inclusion in the Book of Commandments. First, the final revelation printed in the unfinished Book of Commandments (chapter 65) ends abruptly on page 160. The version of Revelation, 11 September 1831 [D&C 64], that appears in Revelation Book 1 contains a take mark after the word "Ephraim," which is the final word in the fifth gathering of the printed Book of Commandments.[1] But "Ephraim" is not the final word of the revelation text found in Revelation Book 1: about 170 words were left unpublished.[2] Editing marks on the copy of this revelation that appears in Revelation Book 1 show that nine additional verses were marked, indicating an intent to publish the entire revelation. Doing so would have necessitated the printing of a sixth gathering but would not have filled its thirty-two pages. It is possible that the editors could have printed less than a full gathering (as was done for the final gathering in the 1844 edition of the Doctrine and Covenants), but Revelation Book 1 contains enough additional marked-up text to fill an entire gathering. Second, a revelation demonstrably intended to serve as an appendix to the Book of Commandments was not in fact printed therein. Editors printed this revelation in the May 1833 issue of *The Evening and the Morning Star* and promised to include it in the Book of Commandments.[3] That this revelation, which was clearly slated for publication, does not appear in the extant copies of the Book of Commandments is further evidence that printing was not complete.

Nine revelations not printed in the Book of Commandments were marked up in Revelation Book 1 in preparation for publication.[4] These nine revelations—dating from late October 1831 to late January 1832—pick up chronologically where the last revelation in the published Book of Commandments (dated 11 September 1831) leaves off. Assuming Phelps, Cowdery, and Whitmer would have maintained the chronological order of the Book of Commandments for the remainder of the volume, three additional revelations dating from this same time period would likely have been included, though none of these revelations were marked up for publication. It is possible that different copies of the revelations were used instead of Revelation Book 1 to prepare these three texts for publication,

---

1. Revelation Book 1 contains three other take marks that correspond to the final words of three gatherings in the Book of Commandments. (Revelation Book 1, p. 39, in *JSP*, MRB:49; Revelation Book 1, p. 90, in *JSP*, MRB:153; Revelation Book 1, p. 111, in *JSP*, MRB:195.)

2. Revelation, 11 Sept. 1831, in Revelation Book 1, p. 111, in *JSP*, MRB:195 [D&C 64].

3. Revelation, 3 Nov. 1831, in Revelation Book 1, pp. 116–121, in *JSP*, MRB:205–215 [D&C 133]. While this revelation appears in the body of Revelation Book 1, it also appears on a separate document that was inserted into Revelation Book 1 at a later date, thereby becoming associated with the book though not physically part of it. This second version of the revelation bears the endorsement "An appendix to Revelation." In reference to this revelation, the May 1833 issue of *The Evening and the Morning Star* stated, "Having given, in a previous number, the Preface to the book of Commandments now in press, we give below, the close, or as it has been called, the Appendix." The revelation was placed as the last revelation in the first edition of the Doctrine and Covenants (1835), preceding only three items that were added very late in the publication process. (Appendix 1: Revelation, 3 Nov. 1831, [6], in *JSP*, MRB:405 [D&C 133]; "Revelations," *The Evening and the Morning Star*, May 1833, [1]; Revelation, 3 Nov. 1831, in Doctrine and Covenants 100, 1835 ed. [D&C 133].)

4. Within Revelation Book 1, see Revelation, 29 Oct. 1831, pp. 111–112, in *JSP*, MRB:195–197 [D&C 66]; Revelation, 1 Nov. 1831–A, pp. 113–114, in *JSP*, MRB:199–201 [D&C 68]; Revelation, 2 Nov. 1831, pp. 114–115, in *JSP*, MRB:201–203 [D&C 67]; Revelation, 3 Nov. 1831, pp. 116–121, in *JSP*, MRB:205–215 [D&C 133]; Revelation, 11 Nov. 1831–A, p. 122, in *JSP*, MRB:217 [D&C 69]; Revelation, 11 Nov. 1831–B, pp. 122–123, in *JSP*, MRB:217–219 [D&C 107 (partial)]; Revelation, 12 Nov. 1831, pp. 124–125, in *JSP*, MRB:221–223 [D&C 70]; Revelation, 1 Dec. 1831, p. 134, in *JSP*, MRB:241 [D&C 71]; and Revelation, 25 Jan. 1832, pp. 129–132, in *JSP*, MRB:231–237 [D&C 75].

because two of the three revelations were published in *The Evening and the Morning Star*.[5] These three revelations are included herein because they were created during the same time period as the nine marked-up revelations, suggesting they would have been printed along with the other nine.

While it is clear, therefore, that some additional revelations were slated for inclusion, it is less clear how many gatherings beyond the current five would have been printed if printing had gone on uninterrupted. The average word count for the extant portion of the Book of Commandments is 270 words per page. At that rate, the aforementioned twelve revelations from Revelation Book 1 would fill approximately thirty printed pages, which would leave enough room in a thirty-two-page gathering to include the "Testimony of the witnesses to the Book of the Lords commandments."[6] This document, which is copied in Revelation Book 1, is a signed statement testifying of the revelations' divine origin. It was likely meant to be printed at the back of the Book of Commandments, following a precedent set in the first edition of the Book of Mormon, which included two witness statements on the last two pages of the volume.

Beyond the thirteen items identified above and featured herein, it is possible but unlikely that the editors of the Book of Commandments would have included additional revelations from Revelation Book 1 that were dated after 25 January 1832 (the latest date of any of these thirteen items) and before summer 1833 (the latest date that a copy of a new revelation dictated by JS in Kirtland could have reached Missouri before the printing office was destroyed). Revelation Book 1 contains twenty-one items that fall in this time period. It cannot necessarily be assumed that all had reached the Missouri editors before the printing office was destroyed. It is perhaps more plausible to assume a cutoff date of 3 January 1833, the latest date of any revelation published in *The Evening and the Morning Star* (in the March 1833 issue). With that earlier cutoff date, the number of available additional items is reduced to sixteen. Of those sixteen, eleven can be considered possible candidates.[7] The other five texts dated after 25 January 1832 and on or before 3 January 1833 likely would not have been considered, one because it was marked "Not to be published now"[8] and the other four because they were not published in the 1835 or the 1844 editions of the Doctrine and Covenants, suggesting that the editors of the Book of Commandments probably would not have published them either.[9]

---

5. Revelation, 30 Oct. 1831, in "Revelations," *The Evening and the Morning Star*, Sept. 1832, [2] [D&C 65]; Revelation, 4 Dec. 1831, in "A Revelation Given December 4, 1831," *The Evening and the Morning Star*, Dec. 1832, [5]–[6] [D&C 72].

6. Testimony, ca. 1 Nov. 1831, in Revelation Book 1, p. 121, in *JSP*, MRB:215.

7. Within Revelation Book 1, see Vision, 16 Feb. 1832, pp. 135–139, in *JSP*, MRB:243–255 [D&C 76]; Revelation, 1 Mar. 1832, pp. 145–146, in *JSP*, MRB:267–269 [D&C 78]; Revelation, 7 Mar. 1832, p. 147, in *JSP*, MRB:271 [D&C 80]; Revelation, 12 Mar. 1832, p. 147, in *JSP*, MRB:271 [D&C 79]; Revelation, 15 Mar. 1832, pp. 139–140, in *JSP*, MRB:255–257 [D&C 81]; Revelation, 30 Apr. 1832, p. 132, in *JSP*, MRB:237 [D&C 83]; Revelation, 29 Aug. 1832, p. 148, in *JSP*, MRB:273 [D&C 99]; Revelation, 22 and 23 Sept. 1832, pp. 149–156, in *JSP*, MRB:275–289 [D&C 84]; Revelation, 6 Dec. 1832, p. 177, in *JSP*, MRB:331 [D&C 86]; Revelation, 27 and 28 Dec. 1832, pp. 158–166, in *JSP*, MRB:293–309 [D&C 88:1–126]; and Revelation, 3 Jan. 1833, pp. 166–167, in *JSP*, MRB:309–311 [D&C 88:127–141].

8. Revelation, 26 Apr. 1832, in Revelation Book 1, pp. 128–129, in *JSP*, MRB:229–231 [D&C 82].

9. Within Revelation Book 1, see Answers to questions, ca. Mar. 1832, pp. 141–144, in *JSP*,

No editing marks for the 1833 publication exist in Revelation Book 1 on any revelations dated later than 25 January 1832. Furthermore, the editors appear to have marked up revelations in groups or batches as they were preparing to set type. That the "Appendix" (Revelation, 3 November 1831 [D&C 133]), which was almost certainly intended to be the final revelation in the book, was marked up with the group of items featured herein suggests that the editors had concluded the process of preparing the text and did not plan to include any more revelations. Sources also indicate that printing was drawing to a close.[10]

Note on Editorial Method

The goal of this appendix is to propose and to reconstruct what would have been the sixth and likely final gathering of the Book of Commandments. Unlike other texts found in *The Joseph Smith Papers*, this appendix is not a transcript of an existing document. The transcripts presented herein take their base texts from Revelation Book 1, the principal source text for the Book of Commandments. In cases where the revelations were marked up in Revelation Book 1 in preparation for the publication of the Book of Commandments, the transcript silently incorporates those corrections, without employing brackets or textual footnotes. Where verse numbers were inserted into Revelation Book 1, verse numbers and the formatting that typically accompanies versification have been silently added to the text. As in the latter part of the Book of Commandments, the first verse of each item is not preceded by a verse number. Readers wishing to see the source texts from which the following transcripts are taken should consult Revelation Book 1 in the first volume of the Revelations and Translations series of *The Joseph Smith Papers*.

Other silent modifications have been made to the texts presented herein. End-of-line hyphens in the original manuscript source are not transcribed herein. Because many end-of-line hyphens have been editorially introduced in the transcripts, a hyphen appearing at the end of a line may or may not be original to the document. Misspellings, grammatical errors, or capitalization irregularities in the handwritten text of Revelation Book 1 have been silently modified, using patterns from the printed Book of Commandments as a precedent when possible. In some cases, changes have been made that would be considered incorrect by modern standards. For instance, the vast majority of instances of "fullness" in the Book of Commandments are spelled "fulness." As such, the texts in this appendix use the latter spelling. As in the Book of Commandments, the first word of each revelation

---

MRB: 259–265 [D&C 77]; Sample of pure language, ca. Mar. 1832, p. 144, in *JSP*, MRB:265; Revelation, 20 Mar. 1832, p. 148, in *JSP*, MRB:273; and Revelation, 25 Dec. 1832, p. 157, in *JSP*, MRB:291 [D&C 87].

10. William W. Phelps recalled that the book was "nearly printed" at the time printing was violently interrupted. In a letter of 25 June 1833, JS and other Kirtland leaders gave directions about binding the book, suggesting that the book's release was close at hand: "First as respects getting the book of Commandments bound we think it is not necessary they will be sold as well without binding and there is no book binder to be had as we know off nor is there materials to be had for binding without keeping the books too long from circulation." A week later, a second letter from Kirtland provided explicit instructions on where to ship copies of the Book of Commandments, again suggesting that completion of the volume was imminent. (Phelps, "Short History," [3]; JS et al., Kirtland, OH, to Edward Partridge et al., Independence, MO, 25 June 1833, JS Collection, CHL; Sidney Rigdon et al., Kirtland, OH, to "Brethren," [Independence, MO], 2 July 1833, in JS Letterbook 1, pp. 51–54.)

in these transcripts is set in all caps, though this transcription does not reproduce the drop cap of the first letter of the chapter. Where Revelation Book 1 contains redacted punctuation made in preparation for the 1833 publication, that punctuation is silently incorporated in the transcripts herein, except in a few cases when that redacted punctuation is nonstandard and would impair readability.

Four of the items in this appendix contain no editing marks in Revelation Book 1. For these items, versification is based on a close adherence to patterns found in the Book of Commandments, and the editorially supplied verse numbers are enclosed within brackets. Capitalization follows patterns from the Book of Commandments, and the first word of each verse is also capitalized. Punctuation for these four items is taken from the text of the 1835 Doctrine and Covenants. The text, therefore, follows the heavily punctuated style of the early nineteenth century without any attempt to match exactly the pattern of the Book of Commandments. This policy occasionally leaves commas at the end of verses, which never occurred in the Book of Commandments but is nevertheless left to stand. The transcripts of these four items follow the 1835 punctuation exactly, even though it may occasionally conflict with a punctuation mark in Revelation Book 1.

The numbering of chapters has been continued throughout this appendix, and chapter headings have been supplied based on patterns of chapter headings found in the Book of Commandments. Rarely, wording in the revelations is unclear because of grammatical errors, missing words, or other problems. In these cases, other authoritative texts, including *The Evening and the Morning Star* and the 1835 edition of the Doctrine and Covenants, have been consulted. In some cases, missing words have been supplied in brackets.

CHAPTER LXV.[1]
[*concluded*]

48   Wherefore, they shall be plucked out.

49   Behold I the Lord have made my church in these last days like unto a judge, setting on an hill, or in an high place, to judge the nations:

50   For it shall come to pass, that the inhabitants of Zion, shall judge all things;

51   And all liars and hypocrites shall be proved by them;

52   And they which are not apostles and prophets shall be known.

53   And even the judge and his counsellors, if they are not faithful in their stewardships, shall be condemned, and others shall be planted in their stead:

54   For behold I say unto you, that Zion shall flourish, and the glory of the Lord shall be upon her, and she shall be an ensign unto the people.

55   And these shall come unto her out of every nation under heaven.

56   And the days shall come, when the nations of the earth shall tremble because of her, and shall fear, because of her terrible ones: the Lord hath spoken it. Amen.

CHAPTER LXVI.[2]

A Revelation to William (M.,) given in Hiram, Ohio, October, 1831.

BEHOLD thus saith the Lord unto you my servant William blessed are you, inasmuch as you have turned away from your iniquities, and have received my truths, saith the Lord, your Redeemer, the Savior of the world, even of as many as believe on my name.

2   Verily I say unto you, blessed are you for receiving mine everlasting covenant, even the fulness of my gospel, sent forth unto the children of men, that they might have life and be made partakers of the glories which are to be revealed in the last days, as it was written by the prophets and apostles in days of old.

3   Verily I say unto you, my servant William that you are clean but not all;

4   Repent therefore of those things which are not pleasing in my sight, saith the Lord, for the Lord will show them unto you.

5   Now verily I the Lord will show unto you what I will concerning you, or what is my will concerning you.

6   Behold, verily I say unto you, that it is my will that you should proclaim my gospel from land to land, and from city to city:

7   Yea, in those regions round about, where it hath not been proclaimed.

8   Tarry not many days in this place.

9   Go not up unto the land of Zion as yet, but inasmuch as you can send, send;

10   Otherwise think not of thy property.

11   Go unto the eastern lands.

12   Bear testimony in every place, unto every people, and in their synagogues, reasoning with the people.

---

1. Revelation, 11 Sept. 1831 [D&C 64:36–43]. This version is based on the version in Revelation Book 1, p. 111, in *JSP*, MRB:195.

2. Revelation, 29 Oct. 1831 [D&C 66]. This version is based on the version in Revelation Book 1, pp. 111–112, in *JSP*, MRB:195–197.

13   Let my servant Samuel go with you, and forsake him not, and give him thine instructions.

14   And he that is faithful shall be made strong in every place, and I the Lord will go with you.

15   Lay your hands upon the sick, and they shall recover.

16   Return not until I the Lord shall send you.

17   Be patient in afflictions.

18   Ask and ye shall receive; knock and it shall be opened unto you.

19   Seek not to be cumbered.

20   Forsake all unrighteousness.

21   Commit not adultery, a temptation with which thou hast been troubled.

22   Keep these sayings, for they are true and faithful, and thou shalt magnify thine office, and push many people to Zion with songs of everlasting joy upon their heads.

23   Continue in those things even unto the end and you shall have a crown of eternal life on the right hand of my Father, who is full of grace and truth.

24   Verily, thus saith the Lord your God, your Redeemer, even Jesus Christ. Amen.

CHAPTER LXVII.[3]

A Revelation to the church, given in Hiram, Ohio, October, 1831.

HEARKEN, and lo, a voice as one sent down from on high, who is mighty and powerful, whose going forth is unto the ends of the earth; yea, whose voice is unto men,

[2]   Prepare ye the way of the Lord make his paths strait.

[3]   The keys of the kingdom of God are committed unto man on the earth,

[4]   And from thence shall the gospel roll forth unto the ends of the earth, as the stone which is hewn from the mountain without hands shall roll forth, until it has filled the whole earth;

[5]   Yea, a voice crying, Prepare ye the way of the Lord, prepare ye the supper of the Lamb, make ready for the Bridegroom;

[6]   Pray unto the Lord; call upon his holy name; make known his wonderful works among the people,

[7]   Call upon the Lord, that his kingdom may go forth upon the earth;

[8]   That the inhabitants thereof may receive it, and be prepared for the days to come, in the which the Son of man shall come down in heaven, clothed in the brightness of his glory, to meet the kingdom of God which is set up on the earth:

[9]   Wherefore, may the kingdom of God go forth, that the kingdom of heaven may come, that thou O God may be glorified in heaven, so on earth, that thine enemies may be subdued;

[10]   For thine is the honor, power and glory, forever and ever: Amen.

---

3. Revelation, 30 Oct. 1831 [D&C 65]. This version is based on the version in Revelation Book 1, p. 112, in *JSP,* MRB:197. Punctuation in this chapter is taken from Doctrine and Covenants 24, 1835 ed.

CHAPTER LXVIII.[4]

*A Revelation to Orson (H.,) Luke, Lyman (J.,) and William (M.,) given in Hiram, Ohio,
   November, 1831.*

MY servant, Orson, was called, by his ordinance, to proclaim the everlasting gospel, by
the Spirit of the living God, from people to people, and from land to land, in the congregations of the wicked, in their synagogues, reasoning with and expounding all scriptures
unto them:

[2]   And behold and lo, this is an ensample unto all those who were ordained unto this
priesthood, whose mission is appointed unto them to go forth:

[3]   And this is the ensample unto them, that they shall speak as they are moved upon by
the Holy Ghost;

[4]   And whatsoever they shall speak when moved upon by the Holy Ghost, shall be
scripture; shall be the will of the Lord; shall be the mind of the Lord; shall be the word of
the Lord; shall be the voice of the Lord, and the power of God unto salvation;

[5]   Behold this is the promise of the Lord unto you, O ye my servants:

[6]   Wherefore, be of good cheer, and do not fear, for I the Lord am with you, and will
stand by you; and ye shall bear record of me even Jesus Christ, that I am the Son of the
living God; that I was; that I am; and that I am to come.

[7]   This is the word of the Lord unto you my servant, Orson; and also unto my servant,
Luke, and unto my servant, Lyman, and unto my servant, William; and unto all the faithful elders of my church:

[8]   Go ye into all the world; preach the gospel to every creature; acting in the authority
which I have given you; baptizing in the name of the Father, and of the Son, and of the
Holy Ghost,

[9]   And he that believeth, and is baptized, shall be saved,

[10]   He that believeth not shall be damned;

[11]   And he that believeth shall be blessed with signs following, even as it is written:

[12]   And unto you it shall be given to know the signs of the times, and the signs of the
coming of the Son of man;

[13]   And of as many as the Father shall bear record, to you it shall be given power to seal
them up unto eternal life: Amen.

[14]   And now concerning the items in addition to the laws and commandments, they
are these:

[15]   There remaineth hereafter in the due time of the Lord, other bishops to be set apart
unto the church to minister even according to the first:

[16]   Wherefore it shall be an high priest who is worthy, and he shall be appointed by
a conference of high priests.

[17]   And again, no bishop or judge, which shall be set apart for this ministry, shall be
tried or condemned for any crime save it be before a conference of high priests;

[18]   And inasmuch as he is found guilty before a conference of high priests, by testimony

---

4. Revelation, 1 Nov. 1831–A [D&C 68]. This version is based on the version in Revelation Book 1,
pp. 113–114, in *JSP*, MRB:199–201. Punctuation in this chapter is taken from Doctrine and Covenants 22,
1835 ed.

that cannot be impeached, he shall be condemned or forgiven, according to the laws of the church.

[19]   And again, inasmuch as parents have children in Zion that teach them not to understand the doctrine of repentance; faith in Christ the Son of the living God; and of baptism and the gift of the Holy Spirit by the laying on of the hands, when eight years old, the sin be upon the head of the parents,

[20]   For this shall be a law unto the inhabitants of Zion: and their children shall be baptized for the remission of their sins when eight years old, and receive the laying on of the hands:

[21]   And they also shall teach their children to pray, and to walk uprightly before the Lord.

[22]   And the inhabitants of Zion shall also observe the sabbath day to keep it holy.

[23]   And the inhabitants of Zion, also, shall remember their labors, inasmuch as they are appointed to labor, in all faithfulness, for the idler shall be had in remembrance before the Lord.

[24]   Now I the Lord am not well pleased with the inhabitants of Zion, for there are idlers among them; and their children are also growing up in wickedness:

[25]   They also seek not earnestly the riches of eternity, but their eyes are full of greediness.

[26]   These things ought not to be, and must be done away from among them:

[27]   Wherefore let my servant Oliver, carry these sayings unto the land of Zion.

[28]   And a commandment I give unto them, that he that observeth not his prayers before the Lord in the season thereof, let him be had in remembrance before the judge of my people.

[29]   These sayings are true and faithful: wherefore transgress them not, neither take therefrom.

[30]   Behold I am Alpha and Omega, and I come quickly: Amen.

CHAPTER LXIX.⁵

A Revelation to the elders of the church, assembled at Hiram, Ohio, given November, 1831.

BEHOLD and hearken, O ye elders of my church, who have assembled yourselves together, whose prayers I have heard, and whose hearts I know, and whose desires have come up before me.

2   Behold and lo mine eyes are upon you;

3   And the heavens and the earth are in mine hands, and the riches of eternity are mine to give.

4   Ye endeavored to believe that ye should receive the blessing which was offered unto you, but behold, verily I say unto you, there were fears in your hearts;

5   And verily this is the reason that ye did not receive.

6   And now I the Lord give unto you a testimony of the truth of those commandments which are lying before you.

---

5. Revelation, 2 Nov. 1831 [D&C 67]. This version is based on the version in Revelation Book 1, pp. 114–115, in *JSP*, MRB:201–203.

7 Your eyes have been upon my servant Joseph; and his language you have known, and his imperfections you have known, and you have sought in your hearts knowledge, that you might express beyond his language:

8 This you also know.

9 Now seek ye out of the Book of Commandments, even the least that is among them, and appoint him that is the most wise among you, or if there be any among you, that shall make one like unto it, then ye are justified in saying, that ye do not know that they are true;

10 But if you can not make one like unto it, ye are under condemnation if ye do not bear record that they are true:

11 For ye know that there is no unrighteousness in them;

12 And that which is righteous cometh down from above, from the Father of lights.

13 And again, verily I say unto you, that it is your privilege, and a promise I give unto you, that have been ordained unto the ministry, that inasmuch as ye strip yourselves from jealousies and fears, and humble yourselves before me, for ye are not sufficiently humble, the veil shall be rent and you shall see me and know that I am;

14 Not with the carnal, neither natural, but with the spiritual, for no man has seen God at any time in the flesh, but by the Spirit of God;

15 Neither can any natural man abide the presence of God;

16 Neither after the carnal mind ye are not able to abide the presence of God now;

17 Neither the ministering of angels:

18 Wherefore continue in patience until ye are perfected.

19 Let not your minds turn back, and when ye are worthy, in mine own due time, ye shall see and know that which was confirmed upon you by the hands of my servant Joseph: Amen.

CHAPTER LXX.[6]

A Revelation given in Hiram, Ohio, November, 1831.

HEARKEN unto me saith the Lord, for verily I say unto you, for my servant Oliver's sake, it is not wisdom in me, that he should be intrusted with the commandments and the moneys which he shall carry unto the land of Zion, except one go with him, who will be true and faithful;

2 Wherefore I the Lord willeth that my Servant John should go with my servant Oliver.

3 And also that he observe to continue in writing and making a history of all the important things which he shall observe and know, concerning my church;

4 And also that he receive counsel and assistance from my Servant Oliver, and others.

5 And also that my servants who are abroad in the earth, should send forth the accounts of their stewardship, to the land of Zion;

6 For the land of Zion shall be a seat and a place to receive and do all these things:

7 Nevertheless let my servant John travel many times, from place to place, and from church to church, that he may the more easily obtain knowledge;

---

6. Revelation, 11 Nov. 1831–A [D&C 69]. This version is based on the version in Revelation Book 1, p. 122, in *JSP,* MRB:217.

8 Preaching and expounding, writing, copying, selecting, and obtaining all things, which shall be for the good of the church, and for the rising generations which shall grow up on the land of Zion, to possess it from generation to generation, forever and ever. Amen.

CHAPTER LXXI.[7]

A Revelation given in Hiram, Ohio, November, 1831.

TO the church of Christ in the land of Zion in addition to the church laws respecting church business verily I say unto you, saith the Lord of Hosts there must needs be presiding elders to preside over those who are of the office of an elder:

2 And also priests over those who are of the office of a priest;

3 And also teachers over those who are of the office of a teacher, in like manner.

4 And also the deacons;

5 Wherefore from deacon to teacher, and from teacher to priest, and from priest to elder; severally as they are appointed, according to the church articles and covenants:

6 Then cometh the high priesthood, which is the greatest of all:

7 Wherefore it must needs be that one be appointed of the high priesthood to preside over the priesthood:

8 And he shall be called president of the high priesthood of the church;

9 Or in other words the presiding high priest over the high priesthood of the church;

10 From the same cometh the administering of ordinances and blessings upon the church, by the laying on of the hands:

11 Wherefore the office of a bishop is not equal unto it;

12 For the office of a bishop is in administering all temporal things:

13 Nevertheless a bishop must be chosen from the high priesthood, that he may be set apart unto the ministering of temporal things, having a knowledge of them by the spirit of truth;

14 And also to be a judge in Israel to do the business of the church, to sit in judgment upon transgressors upon testimony as it shall be laid before him, according to the laws, by the assistance of his counsellors whom he hath chosen or will choose among the elders of the church.

15 Thus shall he be a judge even a common judge among the inhabitants of Zion until the borders are enlarged, and it becomes necessary to have other bishops or judges.

16 And inasmuch as there are other bishops appointed, they shall act in the same office.

17 And again, verily I say unto you, the most important business of the church, and the most difficult cases of the church, inasmuch as there is not satisfaction upon the decision of the judge, it shall be handed over, and carried up unto the court of the church before the president of the high priesthood;

18 And the president of the court of the high priesthood shall have power to call other high priests, even twelve to assist as counsellors,

19 And thus the president of the high priesthood, and his counsellors, shall have power to decide upon testimony, according to the laws of the church;

---

7. Revelation, 11 Nov. 1831–B [D&C 107 (partial)]. This version is based on the version in Revelation Book 1, pp. 122–123, in *JSP*, MRB:217–219.

20   And after this decision it shall be had in remembrance no more before the Lord;

21   For this is the highest court of the church of God and a final decision upon controversies, there is not any person belonging to the church who is exempt from this court of the church:

22   And inasmuch as the president of the high priesthood shall transgress, he shall be had in remembrance before the common court of the church, who shall be assisted by twelve counsellors of the high priesthood, and their decision upon his head shall be an end of controversy concerning him.

23   Thus none shall be exempt from the justice and the laws of God, that all things may be done in order, and in solemnity before me, according to truth and righteousness. Amen.

24   A few more words in addition to the laws of the church.

25   And again, verily I say unto you, the duty of a president over the office of a deacon, is to preside over twelve deacons, to set in counsel with them, and to teach them their duty, edifying one another as it is given according to the covenants.

26   And also the duty of the president over the office of the teachers, is to preside over twenty-four of the teachers, and to set in counsel with them, teaching them the duties of their office as given in the covenants.

27   Also the duty of the president over the priesthood, is to preside over forty-eight priests, and to set in counsel with them, and to teach them the duties of their office, as given in the covenants.

28   And again the duty of the president over the office of the elders, is to preside over ninety-six elders, and to set in counsel with them, and to teach them according to the covenants.

29   And again the duty of the president of the office of the high priesthood, is to preside over the whole church, and to be like unto Moses.

30   Behold here is wisdom:

31   Yea, to be a seer, a revelator, a translator, and a prophet, having all the gifts of God, which he bestoweth upon the head of the church:

32   Wherefore now let every man learn his duty, and to act in the office in which he is appointed, in all diligence.

33   He that is slothful shall not be counted worthy to stand.

34   And he that learneth not his duty, and sheweth himself not approved, shall not be counted worthy to stand; even so: Amen.

CHAPTER LXXII.[8]

A Revelation to the church, given in Hiram, Ohio, November, 1831.

BEHOLD and hearken, O ye inhabitants of Zion, and all ye people of my church, which are far off, and hear the word of the Lord, which I give unto my servant Joseph;

2   And also unto my servant Martin;

3   And also unto my servant Oliver;

4   And also unto my servant John;

---

8. Revelation, 12 Nov. 1831 [D&C 70]. This version is based on the version in Revelation Book 1, pp. 124–125, in *JSP,* MRB:221–223.

5   And also unto my servant Sidney;

6   And also unto my servant William by the way of commandment unto them, for I give unto them a commandment: Wherefore hearken and hear, for thus saith the Lord unto them, I the Lord have appointed them, and ordained them to be stewards over the revelations and commandments which I have given unto them, and which I shall hereafter give unto them;

7   And an account of this stewardship will I require of them in the day of judgment:

8   Wherefore I have appointed unto them, and this is their business in the church of God, to manage them and the concerns thereof, yea the benefits thereof:

9   Wherefore a commandment I give unto them, that they shall not give these things unto the church, neither unto the world:

10   Nevertheless, inasmuch as they receive more than is needful for their necessities, and their wants, it shall be given into my storehouse, and the benefits thereof shall be consecrated unto the inhabitants of Zion, and unto their generations, inasmuch as they become heirs according to the laws of the kingdom.

11   Behold this is what the Lord requires of every man in his stewardship; even as I the Lord have appointed, or shall hereafter appoint unto any man.

12   And behold none is exempt from this law, who belong to the church of the living God;

13   Yea, neither the bishop, neither the agent, who keepeth the Lord's storehouse; neither he who is appointed in a stewardship over temporal things; he who is appointed to administer spiritual things, the same is worthy of his hire; even as those who are appointed to a stewardship to administer in temporal things;

14   Yea even more abundantly which abundance is multiplied unto them through the manifestations of the Spirit:

15   Nevertheless in your temporal things you shall be equal;

16   And this not grudgingly, otherwise the abundance of the manifestations of the Spirit, shall be withheld.

17   Now this commandment I give unto my servants, for their benefit while they remain, for a manifestation of my blessings upon their heads, and for a reward of their diligence;

18   And for their security for food and for raiment, for an inheritance; for houses and for lands, in whatsoever circumstances I the Lord shall place them, and whithersoever I the Lord shall send them:

19   For they have been faithful over many things, and have done well inasmuch as they have not sinned.

20   Behold I the Lord am merciful and will bless them and they shall enter into the joy of these things; even so: Amen.

CHAPTER LXXIII.[9]

A Revelation to Joseph and Sidney, given in Hiram, Ohio, December, 1831.

BEHOLD, thus saith the Lord unto you my servants, that the time has verily come, that

---

9. Revelation, 1 Dec. 1831 [D&C 71]. This version is based on the version in Revelation Book 1, p. 134[a], in *JSP,* MRB:241.

it is necessary and expedient in me, that you should open your mouths in proclaiming my gospel, the things of the kingdom, expounding the mysteries thereof out of the scriptures, according to that portion of Spirit and power, which shall be given unto you, even as I will.

2   Verily I say unto you, proclaim unto the world in the regions round about, and in the church also, for the space of a season, even until it shall be made known unto you.

3   Verily this is a mission for a season, which I give unto you:

4   Wherefore labor ye in my vineyard.

5   Call upon the inhabitants of the earth and bear record and prepare the way for the commandments and the revelations which are to come.

6   Now, behold this is wisdom;

7   Whoso readeth let him understand and receive also:

8   For unto him who receiveth it shall be given more abundantly, even power:

9   Wherefore confound your enemies;

10   Call upon them to meet you, both in public and in private, and inasmuch as ye are faithful their shame shall be made manifest.

11   Wherefore let them bring forth their strong reasons against the Lord.

12   Verily thus saith the Lord unto you, there is no weapon that is formed against you shall prosper;

13   And if any man lift his voice against you, he shall be confounded in mine own due time;

14   Wherefore keep these commandments.

15   They are true and faithful; even so: Amen.

CHAPTER LXXIV.[10]

A Revelation to the high priests of the church, assembled at Kirtland, Ohio, given December, 1831.

HEARKEN and listen to the voice of the Lord, O ye who have called yourselves together, who are the high priests of my church, to whom the kingdom and power have been given.

[2]   For verily thus saith the Lord, it is expedient in me, for a bishop to be appointed unto you, or of you unto the church in this part of the Lord's vineyard:

[3]   And verily in this thing ye have done wisely, for it is required of the Lord, at the hand of every steward, to render an account of his stewardship, both in time and in eternity.

[4]   For he who is faithful and wise in time, is accounted worthy to inherit the mansions prepared for them of my Father.

[5]   Verily I say unto you, the elders of the church in this part of my vineyard, shall render an account of their stewardship, unto the bishop which shall be appointed of me, in this part of my vineyard.

[6]   These things shall be had on record to be handed over unto the bishop in Zion; and

---

10. Revelation, 4 Dec. 1831 [D&C 72]. This version is based on the version in Revelation Book 1, pp. 132–134[a], in *JSP,* MRB:237–241. Punctuation in this chapter is taken from Doctrine and Covenants 89, 1835 ed.

the duty of the bishop shall be made known by the commandments which have been given, and by the voice of the conference.

[7]   And now, verily I say unto you, my servant Newel is the man who shall be appointed, and ordained unto this power: this is the will of the Lord your God, your Redeemer; even so. Amen.

[8]   The word of the Lord, in addition to the law which has been given, making known the duty of the bishop, which has been ordained unto the church in this part of the vineyard; which is verily this:

[9]   To keep the Lord's storehouse; to receive the funds of the church in this part of the vineyard; to take an account of the elders as before has been commanded, and to administer to their wants, who shall pay for that which they receive, inasmuch as they have wherewith to pay; that this also may be consecrated to the good of the church, to the poor and needy:

[10]   And he who has not wherewith to pay, an account shall be taken and handed over to the bishop in Zion, who shall pay the debt out of that which the Lord shall put into his hands: and the labors of the faithful who labor in spiritual things, in administering the gospel and the things of the kingdom, unto the church, and unto the world, shall answer the debt unto the bishop in Zion:

[11]   Thus it cometh out of the church, for according to the law every man that cometh up to Zion, must lay all things before the bishop in Zion.

[12]   And now, verily I say unto you, that as every elder in this part of the vineyard, must give an account of his stewardship unto the bishop in this part of the vineyard, a certificate from the judge or bishop in this part of the vineyard, unto the bishop in Zion, rendereth every man acceptable, and answereth all things, for an inheritance, and to be received as a wise steward, and as a faithful laborer; otherwise he shall not be acceptable of the bishop in Zion.

[13]   And now, verily I say unto you, let every elder who shall give an account unto the bishop of the church, in this part of the vineyard, be recommended by the church or churches, in which he labors, that he may render himself and his accounts approved in all things.

[14]   And again, let my servants who are appointed as stewards over the literary concerns of my church, have claim for assistance upon the bishop or bishops, in all things, that the revelations may be published, and go forth unto the ends of the earth,

[15]   That they also may obtain funds which shall benefit the church, in all things; that they also may render themselves approved in all things and be accounted as wise stewards.

[16]   And now, behold this shall be an ensample for all the extensive branches of my church, in whatsoever land they shall be established. And now I make an end of my sayings. Amen.

[17]   A few words in addition to the laws of the kingdom, respecting the members of the church; they that are appointed by the Holy Spirit to go up unto Zion; and they who are privileged to go up unto Zion.

[18]   Let them carry up unto the bishop a certificate from three elders of the church, or a certificate from the bishop, otherwise he who shall go up unto the land of Zion, shall not be accounted as a wise steward. This also [is] an ensample. Amen.

CHAPTER LXXV.[11]

A Revelation to Joseph and Sidney, given in Hiram, Ohio, January, 1832.

FOR verily thus saith the Lord, it is expedient in me, that they should continue preaching the gospel, and in exhortation to the churches, in the regions round about, until conference:

[2]   And behold then it shall be made known unto them, by the voice of the conference, their several missions.

[3]   Now verily I say unto my servants Joseph and Sidney, saith the Lord, it is expedient to translate again, and inasmuch as it is practicable, to preach in the regions round about until conference, and after that it is expedient to continue the work of translation, until it be finished.

[4]   And let this be a pattern unto the elders until further knowledge, even as it is written.

[5]   And now I give no more unto you at this time. Gird up your loins and be sober: even so. Amen.

CHAPTER LXXVI.[12]

A Revelation to the elders of the church, assembled at Amherst, Ohio, given January, 1832.

VERILY, Verily I say unto you, I who speak even by the voice of my Spirit; even Alpha and Omega, your Lord and your God:

2   Hearken, O ye who have given your names to go forth to proclaim my gospel, and to prune my vineyard.

3   Behold I say unto you, that it is my will that you should go forth and not tarry, neither be idle, but labor with your mights lifting up your voices as with the sound of a trump proclaiming the truth according to the revelations and commandments which I have given you.

4   And thus if ye are faithful ye shall be laden with many sheaves, and crowned with honor, and glory, and immortality, and eternal life:

5   Therefore verily I say unto my Servant William (M.,) I revoke the commission which I gave unto him, to go unto the eastern countries, and I give unto him a new commission and a new commandment, in the which I the Lord chasteneth him for the murmurings of his heart; and he sinned, nevertheless I forgive him and say unto him again, go ye into the south countries;

6   And let my servant Luke go with him and proclaim the things which I have commanded them, calling on the name of the Lord for the Comforter, which shall teach them all things that is expedient for them, praying always that they faint not;

7   And inasmuch as they do this, I will be with them even unto the end.

8   Behold this is the will of the Lord your God concerning you; even so: Amen.

---

11. Revelation, 10 Jan. 1832 [D&C 73]. This version is based on the version in Revelation Book 1, pp. 146–147, in *JSP,* MRB:269–271. Punctuation in this chapter is taken from Doctrine and Covenants 29, 1835 ed.

12. Revelation, 25 Jan. 1832 [D&C 75]. This version is based on the version in Revelation Book 1, pp. 129–132, in *JSP,* MRB:231–237.

9 And again, verily thus saith the Lord, let my servant Orson (H.) and my servant Samuel, take their journey into the eastern countries, and proclaim the things which I have commanded them;

10 And inasmuch as they are faithful, lo I will be with them even unto the end.

11 And again verily I say unto my servant Lyman (J.) and unto my servant Orson (P.,) they shall also take their journey into the eastern countries:

12 And behold and lo: I am with them also, even unto the end.

13 And again I say unto my servant Asa and unto my servant Calves, that they also shall take their journey unto the western countries, and proclaim my gospel even as I have commanded them.

14 And he who is faithful shall overcome all things, and shall be lifted up at the last day.

15 And again, I say unto my servant Major, and my servant Burr, let them take their journey also unto the south countries:

16 Yea, let all these take their journey as I have commanded them, going from house to house, and from village to village, and from city to city;

17 And in whatsoever house ye enter, and they receive you, leave your blessings upon that house;

18 And in whatsoever house ye enter, and they receive you not ye shall depart speedily from that house, and shake off the dust of your feet as a testimony against them:

19 And you shall be filled with joy and gladness and know this, that in the day of judgment you shall be judges of that house, and condemn them; and it shall be more tolerable for the heathen in the day of judgment, than for that house:

20 Therefore gird up your loins and be faithful and ye shall overcome all things and be lifted up at the last day; even so: Amen.

21 And again thus saith the Lord unto you, O ye elders of my church, who have given your names that you might know his will concerning you:

22 Behold I say unto you that it is the duty of the church to assist in supporting the families of those, and also to support the families of those who are called and must needs be sent unto the world to proclaim the gospel unto the world.

23 Wherefore I the Lord give unto you this commandment, that ye obtain places for your families inasmuch as your brethren are willing to open their hearts;

24 And let all such as can obtain places for their families, and support of the church for them, not fail to go into the world;

25 Whether to the east, or to the west, or to the north, or to the south, let them ask and they shall receive; knock and it shall be opened unto them, and made known from on high, even by the Comforter, whither they shall go.

26 And again verily I say unto you that every man who is obliged to provide for his own family, let him provide and he shall in no wise loose his crown;

27 And let him labor in the church.

28 Let every man be diligent in all things.

29 And the idler shall not have place in the church, except he repents and mends his ways. Wherefore let my servant Simeon, and my servant Emer, be united in the ministry.

30 And also my servant Ezra, and my servant Thomas.

31 Also my servant Hyrum, and my servant Reynolds;

32   And also my servant Daniel, and my servant Seymour;

33   And also my servant Sylvester, and my servant Gideon;

34   And also my servant Ruggles, and my servant Stephen;

35   And also my servant Micah, and also my servant Eden; even so: Amen.

CHAPTER LXXVII.[13]

An Appendix unto the Book of Commandments:

HEARKEN, O ye people of my church, saith the Lord your God, and hear the word of the Lord, concerning you; the Lord who shall suddenly come to his temple; the Lord who shall come down upon the world with a curse to judgment; yea, upon all the nations that forget God and upon all the ungodly among you:

2   For he shall make bare his holy arm in the eyes of all the nations, and all the ends of the earth shall see the salvation of their God:

3   Wherefore prepare ye, prepare ye, O my people: sanctify yourselves: gather ye together, O ye people of my church, upon the land of Zion, all you that have not been commanded to tarry.

4   Go ye out from Babylon. Be ye clean that bear the vessels of the Lord. Call your solemn assemblies, and speak often one to another.

5   And let every man call upon the name of the Lord; yea, verily I say unto you, again, the time has come when the voice of the Lord is unto you, go ye out of Babylon: gather ye out from among the nations, from the four winds, from one end of heaven to the other.

6   Send forth the elders of my church unto the nations which are afar off; unto the islands of the sea; send forth unto foreign lands: call upon all nations: firstly, upon the Gentiles, and then upon the Jews.

7   And behold and lo this shall be their cry, and the voice of the Lord unto all people: go ye forth unto the land of Zion, that the borders of my people may be enlarged, and that her stakes may be strengthened, and that Zion may go forth unto the regions round about:

8   Yea let the cry go forth among all people: awake and arise and go forth to meet the Bridegroom:

9   Behold and lo the Bridegroom cometh. Go ye out to meet him. Prepare yourselves for the great day of the Lord. Watch, therefore, for ye know neither the day nor the hour.

10   Let them, therefore, who are among the Gentiles flee unto Zion. And let them who be of Judah flee unto Jerusalem, unto the mountains of the Lord's house.

11   Go ye out from among the nations, even from Babylon from the midst of wickedness, which is spiritual Babylon.

12   But verily thus saith the Lord, let not your flight be in haste, but let all things be prepared before you: and he that goeth, let him not look back lest sudden destruction shall come upon him.

13   Hearken and hear O ye inhabitants of the earth. Listen ye elders of my church together, and hear the voice of the Lord, for he calleth upon all men and he commandeth all men every where to repent:

---

13. Revelation, 3 Nov. 1831 [D&C 133]. This version is based on the version in Revelation Book 1, pp. 116–121, in *JSP,* MRB:205–215.

14   For behold the Lord God hath sent forth the angel crying through the midst of heaven, saying: prepare ye the way of the Lord, and make his paths strait, for the hour of his coming is nigh, when the Lamb shall stand upon mount Zion, and with him an hundred and forty-four thousand, having his Father's name written in their foreheads:

15   Wherefore, prepare ye for the coming of the Bridegroom: go ye, go ye out to meet him, for behold he shall stand upon the mount of Olivet, and upon the mighty ocean, even the great deep, and upon the islands of the sea, and upon the land of Zion; and he shall utter his voice out of Zion, and he shall speak from Jerusalem, and his voice shall be heard among all people, and it shall be a voice as the voice of many waters, and as the voice of a great thunder, which shall break down the mountains, and the valleys shall not be found:

16   He shall command the great deep and it shall be driven back into the north countries, and the islands shall become one land, and the land of Jerusalem and the land of Zion, shall be turned back into their own place, and the earth shall be like as it was in the days before it was divided.

17   And the Lord even the Savior shall stand in the midst of his people, and shall reign over all flesh. And they who are in the north countries shall come in remembrance before the Lord, and their prophets shall hear his voice, and shall no longer stay themselves and they shall smite the rocks, and the ice shall flow down at their presence.

18   And an high way shall be cast up in the midst of the great deep. Their enemies shall become a prey unto them, and in the barren deserts there shall come forth pools of living water; and the parched ground shall no longer be a thirsty land; and they shall bring forth their rich treasures unto the children of Ephraim my servants.

19   And the boundaries of the everlasting hills shall tremble at their presence. And these shall they fall down and be crowned with glory, even in Zion, by the hands of the servants of the Lord, even the children of Ephraim; and they shall be filled with songs of everlasting joy.

20   Behold this is the blessing of the everlasting God upon the tribes of Israel, and the richer blessing upon the head of Ephraim and his fellows.

21   And they also of the tribe of Judah, after their pain, shall be sanctified in holiness before the Lord to dwell in his presence day and night forever and ever.

22   And now verily saith the Lord, that these things might be known among you, O inhabitants of the Earth, I have sent forth mine angel, flying through the midst of heaven having the everlasting gospel, who hath appeared unto some, and hath committed it unto man, who shall appear unto many that dwell on the earth, and this gospel shall be preached unto every nation, and kindred, and tongue, and people, and the servants of God shall go forth, saying, with a loud voice:

23   Fear God and give glory to him: for the hour of his judgment is come: and worship him that made heaven, and earth, and sea, and the fountains of waters, calling upon the Lord day and night, saying:

24   O that thou wouldst rend the heavens, that thou wouldst come down, that the mountains might flow down at thy presence. And it shall be answered upon their heads for the presence of the Lord shall be as the melting fire that burneth and as the fire which causeth the waters to boil.

25   O Lord, thou shalt come down to make thy name known to thine adversaries and all

nations shall tremble at thy presence. When thou doeth terrible things, things they look
not for; yea, when thou comest down and the mountains flow down at thy presence, thou
shalt meet him who rejoiceth and worketh righteousness, who remember thee in thy ways:

26   For since the beginning of the world have not man heard nor perceived by the ear,
neither hath any eye seen, O God, besides thee, how great things thou hast prepared for
him that waiteth for thee.

27   And it shall be said, who is this that cometh down from God in heaven with dyed
garments; yea, from the regions which are not known, clothed in his glorious apparel, traveling in the greatness of his strength?

28   And he shall say, I am he who spake in righteousness, mighty to save. And the Lord
shall be red in his apparel, and his garments like him that treadeth in the wine vat, and so
great shall be the glory of his presence, that the sun shall hide his face in shame; and the
moon shall with hold its light; and the stars shall be hurled from their place:

29   And his voice shall be heard, I have trodden the wine press alone, and have brought
judgment upon all people; and none were with me; and I have trampled them in my fury,
and I did tread upon them in mine anger, and their blood have I sprinkled upon my garments, and stained all my raiment: for this was the day of vengeance which was in my
heart.

30   And now the year of my redeemed is come, and they shall mention the loving kindness of their Lord; and all that he has bestowed upon them, according to his goodness, and
according to his loving kindness, forever and ever. In all their affliction he was afflicted.

31   And the angel of his presence saved them; and in his love, and in his pity, he redeemed them, and he bore them and carried them all the days of old; yea, and Enoch also,
and they who were with him; the prophets that were before him, and Noah also, and they
who were before him, and Moses also and they who were before him, and from Moses to
Elijah, and from Elijah to John, who were with Christ in his resurrection, and the holy
apostles, with Abraham, Isaac and Jacob, shall be in the presence of the Lamb.

32   And the graves of the saints shall be opened, and they shall come forth and stand on
the right hand of the Lamb, when he shall stand upon mount Zion, and upon the holy city,
the New Jerusalem, and they shall sing the song of the Lamb day and night forever and
ever.

33   And for this cause, that men might be made partakers of the glories which were to be
revealed the Lord sent forth the fulness of his gospel, his everlasting covenant, reasoning in
plainness, and simplicity, to prepare the weak for those things which are coming on the
earth: and for the Lord's errand in the day when the weak should confound the wise; and
the little one become a strong nation, and two should put their tens of thousands to flight;
and by the weak things of the earth, the Lord should thresh the nations by the power of his
Spirit. And for this cause these commandments were given; they were commanded to be
kept from the world in the day that they were given, but now are to go forth unto all flesh.

34   And this according to the mind and will of the Lord, who ruleth over all flesh and
unto him that repenteth and sanctifieth himself before the Lord shall be given eternal life.
And upon them that hearken not to the voice of the Lord, shall be fulfilled that which was
written by the prophet Moses, that they should be cut off from among the people.

35   And also that which was written by the prophet, Malachi, for behold the day cometh

that shall burn as an oven, and all the proud; yea, and all that do wickedly, shall be stubble; and the day that cometh shall burn them up saith the Lord of Hosts, that it shall leave them neither root nor branch.

36   Wherefore this shall be the answer of the Lord unto them in that day when I come unto my own. No man among you received me, and you were driven out. When I called again there was none of you to answer, yet my arm was not shortened at all, that I could not redeem, neither my power to deliver.

37   Behold at my rebuke I dry up the sea. I make the rivers a wilderness: their fish stinketh, and dieth for thirst. I clothe the heavens with blackness, and make sackcloth their covering:

38   And this shall ye have of my hand, ye shall lie down in sorrow.

39   Behold and lo there are none to deliver you, for ye obeyed not my voice, when I called to you out of the heavens, ye believed not my servants; and when they were sent unto you ye received them not: wherefore they sealed up the testimony and bound up the law, and ye were delivered over unto darkness: these shall go away into outer darkness, where there is weeping, and wailing, and gnashing of teeth. Behold the Lord your God hath spoken it. Amen.

THE TESTIMONY OF WITNESSES.[14]

The testimony of the witnesses to the Book of the Lord's commandments, which he gave to his church through Joseph Smith, Jr. who was appointed by the voice of the church for this purpose:

We the undersigners feel willing to bear testimony to all the world of mankind, to every creature upon the face of all the earth, and upon the islands of the sea, that God hath borne record to our souls, through the Holy Ghost shed forth upon us, that these commandments are given by inspiration of God, and are profitable for all men, and are verily true. We give this testimony unto the world, the Lord being our helper: and it is through the grace of God, the Father, and his Son Jesus Christ, that we are permitted to have this privilege of bearing this testimony unto the world, in the which we rejoice exceedingly, praying the Lord always, that the children of men may be profited thereby: Amen.

Sidney Rigdon	Lyman Wight
Orson Hyde	John Murdock
William E. McLellin	Calvin Beebe
Luke Johnson	Zebedee Coltrin
Lyman Johnson	Joshua Fairchild
Reynolds Cahoon	Peter Dustin
John Corrill	Newel Knight
Parley Pratt	Levi Hancock
Harvey Whitlock	Thomas B. Marsh

---

14. Testimony, ca. 1 Nov. 1831. This version is based on the version in Revelation Book 1, p. 121, in *JSP*, MRB:215. A version of this testimony without the signatures was published in the 1835 Doctrine and Covenants as "the written testimony of the Twelve." The punctuation of this text is based on that 1835 version. (See p. 566 herein.)

THE EVENING AND THE MORNING STAR.

Vol. I.   **Independence, Mo. June, 1832.**   **No. 1.**

Revelations.

THE ARTICLES AND COVENANTS OF THE CHURCH OF CHRIST.

THE rise of the Church of Christ in these last days, being one thousand eight hundred and thirty years since the coming of our Lord and Savior Jesus Christ, in the flesh; it being regularly organized and established agreeable to the laws of our country, by the will and commandments of God in the fourth month and on the sixth day of the month, which is called April: Which commandments were given to Joseph, who was called of God and ordained an Apostle of Jesus Christ, an Elder of this Church; and also to Oliver, who was called of God an Apostle of Jesus Christ, an Elder of this Church, and ordained under his hand; and this according to the grace of our Lord and Savior Jesus Christ to whom be all glory both now and forever. Amen.

For, after that it truly was manifested unto this first Elder, that he had received a remission of his sins, he was entangled again in the vanities of the world, but after truly repenting God ministered unto him by an holy angel, whose countenance was as lightning, and whose garments were pure and white above all whiteness, and gave unto him commandments which inspired him from on high, and gave unto him power, by the means which were prepared, that he should translate a Book, which Book contained a record of a fallen people, and also the fulness of the Gospel of Jesus Christ to the Gentiles; and also to the Jews, proving unto them, that the holy Scriptures are true; and also, that God doth inspire men and call them to his holy work, in these last days as well as in days of old, that he might be the same God forever. Amen.

Which Book was given by inspiration, and is called The Book of Mormon, and is confirmed to others by the ministering of angels, and declared unto the world by them: Wherefore, having so great witnesses, by them shall the world be judged, even as many as shall hereafter receive this work, either to faith and righteousness, or to the hardness of heart in unbelief, to their own condemnation, for the Lord God hath spoken it, for we, the Elders of the Church, have heard and bear witness to the words of the glorious Magesty on high; to whom be glory forever and ever. Amen.

Wherefore, by these things we know, that there is a God in Heaven, who is infinite and eternal, from everlasting to everlasting, the same unchangeable God, the maker of Heaven and earth and all things that in them is, and that he created man male and female, and after his own image, and in his own likeness created he them; and that he gave unto the children of men commandments, that they should love and serve him the only being whom they should worship, but by the transgression of these holy laws, man became sensual and devilish, and became fallen man: Wherefore the Almighty God gave his only begotten Son, as it is written in those Scriptures which have been given of him, that he suffered temptations, but gave no heed unto them; that he was crucified, died, and rose again the third day, and that he ascended into Heaven to sit down on the right hand of the Father, to reign with Almighty power, according to the will of the Father. Therefore, as many as would believe and were baptized in his holy name, and endured in faith to the end, should be saved; yea, even as many as were before he came in the flesh, from the beginning, who believed in the words of the holy Prophets, who were inspired by the gift of the Holy Ghost, which truly testifies of him in all things, as well as those who should come after, who should believe in the gifts and callings of God, by the Holy Ghost, which beareth record of the Father and of the Son, which Father and Son and Holy Ghost, is one God, infinite and eternal, without end. Amen.

And we know, that all men must repent and believe on the name of Jesus Christ, and worship the Father in his name, and endure in faith on his name to the end, or they cannot be saved in the Kingdom of God: And we know, that Justification through the grace of our Lord and Savior Jesus Christ, is just and true; and we know also, that Sanctification through the grace of our Lord and Savior Jesus Christ, is just and true, to all those who love and serve God with all their mights, minds, and strength, but there is a possibility that men may fall from grace and depart from the living God. Therefore let the Church take heed and pray always, lest they fall into temptation; yea, and even he that is sanctified also: and we know, that these things are true and agreeable to the Revelation of John, neither adding to, nor diminishing from the prophecy of his Book; neither to the holy Scriptures; neither to the Revelations of God which shall come hereafter, by the gift and power of the Holy Ghost; neither by the voice of God; neither by the ministering of angels, and the Lord God hath spoken it; and honor, power, and glory be rendered to his holy name both now and ever. Amen.

And again, by way of commandment to the Church, concerning the manner of baptism: Behold whosoever humbleth himself before God and desireth to be baptized, and comes forth with a broken heart and a contrite spirit, and witnesseth unto the Church, that they have truly repented of all their sins and are willing to take upon them the name of Christ, having a determination to serve him unto the end, and truly manifest by their works that they have received the spirit of Christ unto the remission of their sins; then shall they be received unto baptism into the Church of Christ.

The duty of the Elders, Priests, Teachers, Deacons and members of the Church of Christ. An Apostle is an Elder, and it is his calling to baptize and to ordain other Elders, Priests, Teachers and Deacons, and to administer the flesh and blood of Christ according to the Scriptures; and to teach, expound, exhort, baptize, and watch over the Church, and to confirm the Church by the laying on of the hands, and the giving of the Holy Ghost, and to take the lead of all meetings. The Elders are to conduct the meetings as they are led by the Holy Ghost. The Priests' duty is to preach, teach, expound, exhort and baptize, and administer the Sacrament, and visit the house of each member, and exhort them to pray vocally and in secret, and also to attend to all family duties; and ordain other Priests, Teachers and Deacons, and take the lead in meetings; but none of these offices is he to do when there is an Elder present, but in all cases is to assist the Elder. The Teachers' duty is to watch over the Church always, and be with them, and strengthen them, and see that there is no iniquity in the Church, neither hardness with each other, neither lying nor back-biting nor evil speaking; and see that the Church meet together often, and also see that all the members do their duty; and he is to take the lead of meetings in the absence of the Elder or Priest, and is to be assisted always, and in all his duties in the Church by the Deacons; but neither the Teacher nor Deacons, have authority to baptize nor administer the Sacrament, but are to warn, expound, exhort and teach, and invite all to come unto Christ.

Every Elder, Priest, Teacher, or Deacon, is to be ordained according to the gifts and callings of God unto him, by the power of the Holy Ghost which is in the one who ordains him.

The several Elders composing this Church of Christ, are to meet in Conference once in three months, to do Church business whatsoever is necessary. And each Priest or Teacher, who is ordained by a Priest, is to take a certificate from him at the time, which when presented to an Elder, he is to give him a License, which shall authorize him to perform the duty of his calling.

The duty of the members after they are received by baptism. The Elders or Priests are to have a sufficient time to expound all things concerning this Church of Christ to their understanding, previous to their partaking of the Sacrament, and being confirmed by the laying on of the hands of the Elders; so that all things may be done in order. And the members shall manifest before the Church, and also before the Elders, by a godly walk and conversation, that they are worthy of it, that there may be works and faith agreeable to the holy Scriptures, walking in holiness before the Lord. Every member of this Church of Christ having children, is to bring them unto the Elders before the Church, who are to lay their hands on them in the name of the Lord, and bless them in the name of Christ. There cannot any one be received into this Church of Christ, who has not arrived to the years of accountability before God, and is not capable of repentance.

And baptism is to be administered in the following manner unto all those who repent: Whosoever being called of God and having authority given them of Jesus Christ, shall go down into the water with them, and shall say, calling them by name: Having authority given me of Jesus Christ, I baptize you in the name of the Father, and of the Son, and of the Holy Ghost. Amen. Then shall he immerse them in the water, and come forth again out of the water. And it is expedient that the Church meet together oft to partake of Bread and Wine, in remembrance of the Lord Jesus; and the Elder or Priest shall administer it, and after this manner shall he do, he shall kneel with the Church, and call upon the Father in mighty prayer saying: O God the Eternal Father, we ask thee in the name of thy Son Jesus Christ, to bless and sanctify this bread to the souls of all those who partake of it, that they may eat in remembrance of the body of thy Son, and witness unto thee, O God the Eternal Father, that they are willing to take upon them the name of thy Son, and always remember him, and keep his commandments which he hath given them, that they may always have his spirit to be with them. Amen. The manner of administering the Wine: Behold they shall take the Cup and say, O God, the Eternal Father, we ask thee in the name of thy Son Jesus Christ, to bless and sanctify this Wine to the souls of all those who drink of it, that they may do it in remembrance of the blood of thy Son, which was shed for them, that they may witness unto thee, O God the Eternal Father, that they do always remember him, that they may have his spirit to be with them. Amen.

Any member of this Church of Christ, transgressing or being overtaken in a fault, shall be dealt with according as the Scriptures direct. It shall be the duty of the several churches, composing this Church of Christ, to send one or more of their Teachers to attend the several Conferences, held by the Elders of this Church, with a list of the names of the several members, uniting themselves to the Church since the last Conference, or send by the hand of some Priest; so that there can be kept a regular list of all the names of the members of the whole Church, in a Book kept by one of the Elders; whomsoever the other Elders shall appoint from time to time: and also, if any have been expelled from the Church, so that their names may be blotted out of the general Church Record of names. Any member removing from the Church where he resides, if going to a Church where he is not known, may take a letter certifying that he is a regular member and in good standing; which certificate may be signed by any Elder or Priest, if the member receiving the letter is personly acquainted with the Elder or Priest, or it may be signed by the Teachers or Deacons of the Church.

Behold, I say unto you, that all old Covenants have I caused to be done away in

REVELATIONS PRINTED IN
THE EVENING AND THE MORNING STAR

Source Notes

THE EVENING AND THE MORNING STAR

Revelations published in The Evening and the Morning Star *(Independence, MO), vol. 1, nos. 1–10 and 12, and vol. 2, no. 13; edited by William W. Phelps. The copy used for this transcription is currently part of a bound volume held at CHL; includes marginalia, archival notations, stamps, and bookplates.*

The initial issues of *The Evening and the Morning Star* present revelations prominently on the first or second page of the newspaper. Beginning with the November 1832 issue, however, revelations were placed near the end of each issue. Each issue comprises four leaves (eight pages) that measure 12½ × 9⅞ inches (32 × 25 cm). Each page is set in two columns. The volume used for this transcription was donated to the Salt Lake Temple by Lycurgus A. Wilson on 8 September 1894, according to a bookplate on the inside front cover of the volume. It was transferred to the library of the Church Historian's Office sometime before 1923.[1]

EVENING AND MORNING STAR

Revelations published in Evening and Morning Star *(Kirtland, OH), vol. 1, nos. 1–10 and 12, and vol. 2, no. 13; edited by Oliver Cowdery. The copy used for this transcription is currently part of a bound volume held at CHL; includes marginalia and archival notations.*

Evening and Morning Star, an edited reprint of *The Evening and the Morning Star,* presents revelations throughout its first thirteen issues, except for the April 1833 issue, which was printed in June 1836. When printing *Evening and Morning Star,* the editors revised the revelations found in *The Evening and the Morning Star,* changing wording and sometimes order and position on the page. One revelation printed in the earlier newspaper was not reprinted in this edition of the paper.[2] The page size of *Evening and Morning Star* was smaller than that of its predecessor. Each issue has eight leaves (sixteen pages), with two columns on each page, each page measuring 9¼ × 5¾ inches (23 × 15 cm). Because *Evening and Morning Star* was a reprint, its issues maintained the dating of the original issues; thus, the first issue of *Evening and Morning Star* is dated June 1832, though it was printed in January 1835, as indicated by a publisher's notice on the last page of the issue.

The original owner of the volume used for this transcription is unknown. The upper right corner of the second free endsheet is cut away, and based on a residual ink flourish on the recto near the cut,

---

1. "Library Record," book no. 1239.

2. Revelation, 16 Apr. 1830, in "The Articles and Covenants of the Church of Christ," *The Evening and the Morning Star,* June 1832, [1]–[2] [D&C 22].

it appears that a signature was removed from the book at some point. This volume is held at the Church History Library, but its provenance is unknown.

Historical Introductions

The Evening and the Morning Star

Soon after his baptism into the church in 1831, William W. Phelps was instructed by revelation to relocate to Independence, Missouri, "and be established as a printer unto the church." Oliver Cowdery, who had been previously appointed to work on church publications, was directed to assist him.[3] In early 1832, Phelps and his associates in Independence began work on the church's first newspaper, *The Evening and the Morning Star*. Because of the difficulty of getting paper and other supplies to Independence, however, months passed before the first issue of the newspaper was printed in June 1832.

The newspaper's prospectus announced that it would, in part, "be devoted to the revelations of God as made known to his servants by the Holy Ghost, at sundry times since the creation of man, but more especially in these last days."[4] Though a small number of JS's revelations appeared first in non-Mormon newspapers elsewhere,[5] the *Star* was the first official periodical of the church to print them. As the church's only periodical at the time, the *Star* also published counsel to church members, local and world news, editorials, hymns, and letters from missionaries. The *Star* regularly published general announcements to missionaries serving throughout the country and letters from church members in other states, evidencing that its circulation reached well beyond Independence.[6]

The press owned by W. W. Phelps & Co., which was operated under the direction of the Literary Firm, was the only press in Independence and indeed the only press for roughly one hundred miles.[7] Reading material was scarce on the frontier, and it is likely that the town's non-Mormon residents read the *Star* in addition to the *Upper Missouri Advertiser*, the secular paper Phelps published on the same press.[8] In July 1833, when religious and

---

3. Revelation, 20 July 1831, in Doctrine and Covenants 27:5, 1835 ed. [D&C 57:11, 13]; Revelation, 14 June 1831, in Doctrine and Covenants 68:2, 1835 ed. [D&C 55:4].

4. William W. Phelps, *The Evening and the Morning Star* Prospectus, *Evening and Morning Star,* June 1832 (Jan. 1835), 1–2; Crawley, *Descriptive Bibliography,* 1:32.

5. See, for example, Articles and covenants, 10 Apr. 1830, and Revelations, 16 Apr. 1830 and ca. Aug. 1830, in "The Mormon Creed," *Painesville Telegraph,* 19 Apr. 1831, [4] [D&C 20, 22, and 27:1–5, 14–15, 18]; Revelation, 7 Dec. 1830, in "Miscellaneous," *Painesville Telegraph,* 17 Jan. 1832, [1] [D&C 35]; Revelation, 9 Feb. 1831, in "Secret Bye Laws of the Mormonites," *Painesville Telegraph,* 13 Sept. 1831, [1] [D&C 42:1–69]; and Revelation, Sept. 1830–B, in Ezra Booth, "Mormonism—Nos. VIII–IX," *Ohio Star,* 8 Dec. 1831, [1] [D&C 28].

6. See, for example, Notice, *The Evening and the Morning Star,* Aug. 1832, [7]; "Letters," *The Evening and the Morning Star,* Nov. 1832, [4]; "Extract" and "Letters," *The Evening and the Morning Star,* Jan. 1833, [7]; and "Extracts of Letters from the Elders Abroad," *The Evening and the Morning Star,* Feb. 1833, [5]–[6]. JS, in a November 1832 letter to Phelps, added ten new subscribers to the *Star,* nine from Guyandotte, Virginia (now West Virginia), and one from Wooster Township, Ohio. (JS, Kirtland, OH, to William W. Phelps, [Independence, MO], 27 Nov. 1832, in JS Letterbook 1, pp. 1–4.)

7. Notice, *The Evening and the Morning Star,* June 1832, [6].

8. The only known surviving copy of the *Upper Missouri Advertiser*—no. 3, dated 11 July 1832—is located at the American Antiquarian Society, Worcester, MA.

political tensions between the Mormons and their neighbors had already created a tinder-box environment, an article titled "Free People of Color" appeared in *The Evening and the Morning Star,* quoting from Missouri statutes respecting the immigration of free persons of African descent. Many Missourians, largely sympathetic to the practice of slavery, inter-preted the article as an attempt to invite free black people to settle in Missouri and were outraged.[9] Four days after the editors of *The Evening and the Morning Star* printed a broad-side extra in an attempt to calm the situation by clarifying the message of the offending article,[10] a group of Missouri vigilantes destroyed the printing office and most of the sheets of the still-unfinished Book of Commandments.

The destruction of the printing office caused a six-month hiatus in the publication of the *Star.* In September 1833, F. G. Williams & Co. was established in Kirtland, Ohio, for the purpose of printing church materials, and Oliver Cowdery was sent to New York to purchase a printing press and type.[11] Upon his return, Cowdery resumed printing the *Star* in Kirtland from January until September 1834. Beginning in October 1834, the *Latter Day Saints' Messenger and Advocate* succeeded the *Star* as the official church periodical.

Over the course of the *Star*'s fourteen-month run in Missouri, the paper printed nine-teen full and seven partial revelation texts. Only two issues of the Missouri newspaper did not contain featured revelations: the April 1833 issue and the July 1833 issue, which was the final issue printed in Missouri. As in the Book of Commandments and the first edition of the Doctrine and Covenants (1835), little, if any, introduction or commentary accompa-nied the featured revelations. In addition to publishing the revelations as stand-alone pieces, *The Evening and the Morning Star* often published articles that quoted from the revelations—both from those printed as featured documents in the paper and from those that had not been published therein. Well before the Book of Commandments was ex-pected to be completed, the editors of the *Star* advised readers to "search the revelations which we publish," an admonition that presumed that the Latter-day Saints had access to earlier issues.[12] In fact, for Mormons in Independence, as well as those scattered around the country, the *Star* became the most accessible source for JS's revelatory texts.

The revelations published in *The Evening and the Morning Star* appear to have been selected for their importance. Many of the published revelations addressed topics relating to church government, such as the roles of specific church officers,[13] the laws and command-ments to be kept by church members,[14] and the proper administration of the sacrament of

---

9. "Free People of Color," *The Evening and the Morning Star,* July 1833, 109; "To His Excellency, Daniel Dunklin," *The Evening and the Morning Star,* Dec. 1833, 114–115.

10. *The Evening and the Morning Star,* Extra, 16 July 1833, [1].

11. See pp. 302–303 herein.

12. "To the Honorable Men of the World," *The Evening and the Morning Star,* Aug. 1832, [6].

13. See, for example, Articles and covenants, 10 Apr. 1830, in "The Articles and Covenants of the Church of Christ," *The Evening and the Morning Star,* June 1832, [1], and June 1833, 97–98 [D&C 20]; Revelation, 1 Nov. 1831–A, in "A Revelation, Given November 1831," *The Evening and the Morning Star,* Oct. 1832, [3] [D&C 68]; and Revelation, 4 Dec. 1831, in "A Revelation Given December 4, 1831," *The Evening and the Morning Star,* Dec. 1832, [5]–[6] [D&C 72].

14. See, for example, Revelation, 9 and 23 Feb. 1831, in "Extract from the Laws for the Government of the Church of Christ" and "Items of Law for the Government of the Church of Christ," *The Evening and the Morning Star,* July 1832, [1], and Oct. 1832, [2] [D&C 42:11–93].

the Lord's Supper.[15] Other published revelations announced newly received theological principles[16] or looked forward to the second coming of Christ.[17] Revelations that were given to specific individuals providing counsel or commandment were not published.[18] After the *Star* moved to Ohio, no revelations were included in the ten issues of the newspaper published there.

EVENING AND MORNING STAR

In December 1833, six months after the printing office in Independence, Missouri, was destroyed and publication efforts there were permanently halted, printing commenced on a newly acquired press in Kirtland, Ohio. That press, operated by F. G. Williams & Co., continued printing *The Evening and the Morning Star,* the newspaper begun in Missouri, through September 1834. The September 1834 issue of that paper contained a prospectus announcing that the paper's two volumes would be reprinted.[19]

The first issue of the reprinted newspaper, which appeared under the slightly modified title *Evening and Morning Star,* was published in January 1835.[20] Though touted as a reprint that would correct typographical and other errors,[21] *Evening and Morning Star* actually contained significant changes to the revelation texts. In the first issue, editor Oliver Cowdery explained the revisions he was making in the reprinted versions of the revelations:

> On the revelations we merely say, that we were not a little surprised to find the previous print so different from the original. We have given them a careful comparison, assisted by individuals whose known integrity and ability is uncensurable. Thus saying we cast no reflections upon those who were entrusted with the responsibility of publishing them in Missouri, as our own labors were included in that important service to the church, and it was our unceasing endeavor to have them correspond with the copy furnished us. We believe they are now correct. If not in every word, at least in principle.[22]

---

15. See, for example, Revelation, ca. Aug. 1830, in "Revelations," *The Evening and the Morning Star,* Mar. 1833, [6] [D&C 27].

16. See, for example, Vision, 16 Feb. 1832, in "A Vision," *The Evening and the Morning Star,* July 1832, [2]–[3] [D&C 76].

17. See, for example, excerpt of Revelation, ca. 7 Mar. 1831, in "A Prophecy Given to the Church of Christ, March 7, 1831," *The Evening and the Morning Star,* June 1832, [2] [D&C 45:1–67, 71].

18. Revelations addressed to individuals were officially restricted "to the parties concerned" until they could be published in the Book of Commandments. (Minute Book 2, 30 Apr. 1832.)

19. "Prospectus," *The Evening and the Morning Star,* Sept. 1834, 192.

20. The title that appears in the newspaper's nameplate was likely shortened because of a reduction in the newspaper's size. The longer original title, *The Evening and the Morning Star,* is printed at the middle and end of each issue with other publication information. For the sake of clarity, the reprinted paper is referred to by its shortened title for all references in *The Joseph Smith Papers.*

21. "Prospectus," *The Evening and the Morning Star,* Sept. 1834, 192.

22. Notice, *Evening and Morning Star,* June 1832 (Jan. 1835), 16. The prospectus to *Evening and Morning Star* also states "that in the first 14 numbers, in the Revelations, are many errors, typographical, and others, occasioned by transcribing manuscript; but as we shall have access to originals, we shall endeavor to make proper corrections." ("Prospectus," *The Evening and the Morning Star,* Sept. 1834, 192.)

Despite the implications of Cowdery's statement, very few of the changes in the reprint represent a restoration back to the earliest text, though Cowdery consulted early manuscript sources when reprinting some of the revelations.[23] Because the revelations were meant to be used as a guide for the current operations of the church, they were edited in 1835 to reflect current organization, doctrine, and practice, which had continued to develop since the revelations were first dictated. For example, the version of a 9 February 1831 revelation printed in *Evening and Morning Star* includes discussion of the duties of elders, priests, teachers, bishops, high priests, and the high council.[24] Early versions of the revelation, however, make no mention of the office of high priest, which did not exist until June 1831,[25] or of the high council, a body that was not organized until February 1834.[26] The revelation was revised in 1835 to reflect these additional roles. Most of the changes made to revelations in the early issues of *Evening and Morning Star* are also reflected in the same revelations as published in the first edition of the Doctrine and Covenants (1835), and the editing work on that volume, in turn, influenced the presentation of revelations in later issues of *Evening and Morning Star.*[27]

The first six issues of *Evening and Morning Star* present the full texts of thirteen revelations that were modified before or during the typesetting of the 1835 Doctrine and Covenants, meaning that the changes to some of the revelations were first made to the texts in *Evening and Morning Star* and later replicated in the 1835 Doctrine and Covenants. A notice in the issue printed in June 1835 apologized for the delay of that issue due to "the publication of a book of much importance"—that is, the Doctrine and Covenants.[28] The seventh issue was not available until April 1836, well after the publication of the Doctrine and Covenants. As was the case with *The Evening and the Morning Star,* no further revelations were published in *Evening and Morning Star* following the June 1833 (June 1836) issue.

Note on Editorial Method

As discussed above, editors of the reprinted *Evening and Morning Star* often made changes to the revelations that originally appeared in *The Evening and the Morning Star.* This portion of the volume is designed to show at a glance the differences between the versions of the revelations that appeared in the two newspapers. In order to facilitate comparison of the texts, the revelations printed herein are presented side by side in a parallel column

---

23. On 4 February 1835, Cowdery wrote to Newel K. Whitney requesting that the latter send "the original copy of the Revelation given to 12 elders Feb. 1831 called 'The Law of the Church.'" Cowdery explained, "We are preparing the old Star for re-printing, and have no copy from which to correct, and kno[w] of no other beside yours." (Oliver Cowdery, Kirtland, OH, to Newel K. Whitney, 4 Feb. 1835, Newel K. Whitney, Papers, BYU.)

24. Revelation, 9 Feb. 1831, in "Extract of Covenants for the Church of the Latter Day Saints," *Evening and Morning Star,* July 1832 (Feb. 1835), 30–31 [D&C 42].

25. See Minute Book 2, 3 June 1831.

26. Minute Book 1, 17 Feb. 1834; see also Minutes, 17 Feb. 1834, in Doctrine and Covenants 5, 1835 ed. [D&C 102].

27. For example, the updates made in Revelation, 9 February 1831, for publication in *Evening and Morning Star* were then introduced into Doctrine and Covenants 13:8, 10, 19, 1835 ed. [D&C 42:31, 34, 71].

28. Notice, *Evening and Morning Star,* Oct. 1832 (June 1835), 80.

format. The left column contains the revelations as they were published in *The Evening and the Morning Star* (*Star*), and the right column contains the revelations as they were published in the reprinted *Evening and Morning Star* (reprint).

Where words appear in one version that do not appear in the other, blank space has been added in place of the missing words in order to ensure that the line endings of the two columns match. For example, speaking of Jesus Christ, one line of the *Star* says that he "came in the flesh," while the corresponding line of the reprint says that he "came in the meridian of time in the flesh." In this case, a blank space roughly equivalent in size to the missing words ("in the meridian of time") was added to the *Star* transcript, between "came" and "in the flesh." Where words in one version have been replaced with different words in the other, similar ideas have been aligned as closely as possible. No effort has been made to maintain original line breaks. End-of-line hyphens printed in the newspapers are not transcribed herein, except where they split a word across a page break. Because many end-of-line hyphens have been editorially introduced in the transcripts, a hyphen appearing at the end of a line in the transcripts may or may not be original to the newspapers.

In order to maintain the line-to-line alignment, paragraph breaks have been editorially introduced and removed at different points in the transcript of the reprint. Where a paragraph break appears in the reprint but not in the *Star,* the break is removed from the reprint transcript but noted with a paragraph mark (¶). Where the opposite is true—a paragraph break appears in the *Star* but not in the reprint—a break is introduced in the reprint transcript, and a carriage return symbol (↵) is inserted to note the editorial reformatting.

The transcripts presented herein do not correct typographical errors. No attempt has been made to note or mimic pieces of type accidentally printed upside down. Incomplete characters resulting from partially inked or broken type are transcribed fully. In the case of uninked type, if the impression of the type on the page is visible, the character is transcribed. Editorially supplied brackets are employed when a character is wholly illegible because of completely uninked or broken type, smeared ink, or damage to the page. In as many cases as possible, multiple variant copies of the newspapers were compared in order to supply the correct character. When the character was missing in other copies, contemporary usage and typesetting practices, modern standards, and the source text from which the type was originally set were all taken into consideration when attempting to supply an unknown character. Spaces of varying length have been standardized in the transcripts to one space. Occasionally, a piece of space type that was incorrectly set created a solid, rectangular ink mark on the page. These stray ink marks are not noted or reproduced in the transcripts. Page numbers from the original documents are noted in brackets.

Revelations featured herein are grouped by issue and presented in the order in which they appeared in the *Star*. Original headlines or other titles are transcribed and presented herein, though any editorial introductions to the revelations are not. Horizontal rules and extra leading are neither reproduced nor noted. A footnote at the beginning of each revelation identifies it and provides relevant bibliographic information, including the section number under which the revelation appears in the 1981 Latter-day Saint edition of the Doctrine and Covenants. In the case of excerpted revelatory items, verse numbers from the 1981 edition accompany the section number. The table that follows lists each of the revelatory items printed in this section, along with its bibliographic information.

Key to column titles

Vol:Issue:	Volume and issue number
Star Print Date:	Month in which the item was printed in *The Evening and the Morning Star*
Star Pages:	Pages on which the item was printed in *The Evening and the Morning Star*
Reprint Print Date:	Month in which the item was printed in *Evening and Morning Star*
Reprint Pages:	Pages on which the item was printed in *Evening and Morning Star*
Date:	Date of item, followed by section number in Doctrine and Covenants, 1981 edition, The Church of Jesus Christ of Latter-day Saints

Vol: Issue	Star Print Date	Star Pages	Reprint Print Date	Reprint Pages	Date
1:1	June 1832	[1]	Jan. 1835	2–4	10 Apr. 1830 [D&C 20]
1:1	June 1832	[1]–[2]			16 Apr. 1830 [D&C 22]
1:1	June 1832	[2]	Jan. 1835	5–6	ca. 7 Mar. 1831 [D&C 45:1–67, 71]
1:2	July 1832	[1]	Feb. 1835	30–31	9 and 23 Feb. 1831 [D&C 42:11–77]
1:2	July 1832	[1]	Feb. 1835	26–27	7 Aug. 1831 [D&C 59]
1:2	July 1832	[2]–[3]	Feb. 1835	27–30	16 Feb. 1832 [D&C 76]
1:3	Aug. 1832	[1]	Mar. 1835	42–43	ca. 8 Mar. 1831–A [D&C 46]
1:3	Aug. 1832	[1]	Mar. 1835	43–44	9 May 1831 [D&C 50]
1:4	Sept. 1832	[2]	Apr. 1835	60–62	Sept. 1830–A [D&C 29]
1:4	Sept. 1832	[2]	Apr. 1835	62	30 Oct. 1831 [D&C 65]
1:5	Oct. 1832	[2]	June 1835	74	23 Feb. 1831 [D&C 42:78–93]
1:5	Oct. 1832	[2]–[3]	June 1835	74	Feb. 1831–A [D&C 43:15–35]
1:5	Oct. 1832	[3]	June 1835	73–74	1 Nov. 1831–A [D&C 68]
1:6	Nov. 1832	[7]	Sept. 1835	93–94	7 May 1831 [D&C 49]
1:7	Dec. 1832	[5]	Apr. 1836	105–106	12 Aug. 1831 [D&C 61]
1:7	Dec. 1832	[5]–[6]	Apr. 1836	106–107	4 Dec. 1831 [D&C 72]
1:8	Jan. 1833	[5]–[6]	Apr. 1836	125–126	2 Jan. 1831 [D&C 38]
1:8	Jan. 1833	[6]	Apr. 1836	126	30 Apr. 1832 [D&C 83]
1:9	Feb. 1833	[5]	May 1836	138	27 and 28 Dec. 1832 [D&C 88:117–126]
1:9	Feb. 1833	[6]–[7]	May 1836	140–141	30 Aug. 1831 [D&C 63:1–64]
1:10	Mar. 1833	[6]	May 1836	155	ca. Aug. 1830 [D&C 27]
1:10	Mar. 1833	[6]	May 1836	155–156	1 Nov. 1831–B [D&C 1]
1:10	Mar. 1833	[6]	May 1836	156–157	3 Jan. 1833 [D&C 88:127–137]
1:12	May 1833	[1]–[2]	June 1836	177–179	3 Nov. 1831 [D&C 133]
2:13	June 1833	97–98	June 1836	193–196	10 Apr. 1830 [D&C 20]

June 1832

Revelations.

[1]THE ARTICLES AND
COVENANTS OF THE
CHURCH OF CHRIST.

THE rise of the Church of Christ in these last days, being one thousand eight hundred and thirty years since the coming of our Lord and Savior Jesus Christ, in the flesh; it being regularly organized and established agreeable to the laws of our country, by the will and commandments of God in the fourth month and on the sixth day of the month, which is called April: Which commandments were given to Joseph,   who was called of God and ordained an Apostle of Jesus Christ,   an   Elder of this Church; and also to Oliver,   who was called of God an Apostle of Jesus Christ,   an   Elder of this Church, and ordained under his hand; and this according to the grace of our Lord and Savior Jesus Christ to whom be all glory both now and forever. Amen.

For, after that it truly was manifested unto this first Elder, that he had received a remission of his sins, he was entangled again in the vanities of the world, but after truly repenting

God ministered unto him by an holy angel, whose countenance was as lightning, and whose garments were pure and white above all   white-

[2]THE ARTICLES AND
COVENANTS OF THE
CHURCH OF CHRIST.
[*With a few items from other revelations.*]

The rise of the church of Christ in these last days, being one thousand eight hundred and thirty years since the coming of our Lord and Savior Jesus Christ in the flesh, it being regularly organized and established agreeably to the laws of our country, by the will and commandments of God in the fourth month, and on the sixth day of the month, which is called April: which commandments were given to Joseph Smith Jr. who was called of God and ordained an apostle of Jesus Christ, to be the first elder of this church: and

to Oliver Cowdery, who was also called of God an apostle of Jesus Christ, to be the second elder of this church, and ordained under his hand: and this according to the grace of our Lord and Savior Jesus Christ, to whom be all glory both now and forever. Amen.

After   it was truly manifested unto this first elder that he had received a remission of his sins he was entangled again in the vanities of the world; but after

repenting, and humbling himself, sincerely, through faith God ministered unto him by a holy angel whose countenance was as lightning, and whose garments were pure and white above all other white-

---

1. Articles and covenants, 10 Apr. 1830, in "The Articles and Covenants of the Church of Christ," *The Evening and the Morning Star,* June 1832, [1]–[2] [D&C 20]. This version reflects editing marks made in Revelation Book 1, indicating that the latter was used as a source text for the former. (See *JSP,* MRB:75–87.)

2. Articles and covenants, 10 Apr. 1830, in "The Articles and Covenants of the Church of Christ," *Evening and Morning Star,* June 1832 (Jan. 1835), 2–4 [D&C 20]. This version closely corresponds to the version in the June 1833 issue of *The Evening and the Morning Star,* indicating that the latter was used as a source text for the former.

ness, and gave unto him commandments which inspired him from on high, and gave unto him power, by the means which were prepared, that he should translate a Book, which Book contained a record of a fallen people, and also the fulness of the Gospel of Jesus Christ to the Gentiles; and also to the Jews,

proving unto them, that the holy Scriptures are true; and also, that God doth inspire men and call them to his holy work, in these last days as well as in days of old, that he might be the same God forever. Amen.

Which Book was given by inspiration, and is called The Book of Mormon, and is confirmed to others by the ministering of angels, and declared unto the world by them: Wherefore, having so great witnesses, by them shall the world be judged, even as many as shall hereafter receive this work, either to faith and righteousness, or to the hardness of heart in unbelief, to their own condemnation, for the Lord God hath spoken it, for we, the Elders of the Church, have heard and bear witness to the words of the glorious Magesty on high; to whom be glory forever and ever. Amen.

Wherefore, by these things we know, that there is a God in Heaven, who is infinite and eternal, from everlasting to everlasting, the same unchangeable God, the maker of Heaven and earth and all things that in them is, and that he created man male and female, and after his own image, and in his own likeness created he them; and that he gave unto the children of men command-

ness, and gave unto him commandments which inspired him, and gave him power from on high, by the means which were before prepared, to translate the book of Mormon. Which contains a record of a fallen people, and the fulness of the gospel of Jesus Christ to the Gentiles, and to the Jews also, which was given by inspiration, and is confirmed to others by the ministering of angels, and is declared unto the world by them, proving to the world that the holy scriptures are true, and that God does inspire men and call them to his holy work in this age and generation, as well as in generations of old, thereby showing that he is the same God yesterday, to day, and forever. Amen.

Therefore, having so great witnesses, by them shall the world be judged, even as many as shall hereafter come to a knowledge of this work; and those who receive it in faith and work righteousness, shall receive a crown of eternal life; but those who harden their hearts in unbelief and reject it, it shall turn to their own condemnation; for the Lord God has spoken it; and we the elders of the church have heard, and bear witness to the words of the glorious Majesty on high, to whom be glory forever and ever. Amen.

By these things we know that there is a God in heaven who is infinite and eternal, from everlasting to everlasting the same unchangable God, the framer of heaven and earth and all things which are in them, and that he created man male and female: after his own image and in his own likeness created he them, and gave unto them commandments, that they should love and serve him

the only being whom they should worship, but by the transgression of these holy laws, man became sensual and devilish, and became fallen man: Wherefore the Almighty God gave his only begotten Son, as it is written in those Scriptures, which have been given of him, that he suffered temptations, but gave no heed unto them; that he was crucified, died, and rose again the third day, and that he ascended into Heaven to sit down on the right hand of the Father, to reign with Almighty power, according to the will of the Father. Therefore, as many as would believe and were baptized in his holy name, and endured in faith to the end, should be saved; yea, even as many as were before he came   in the flesh, from the beginning,

who believed in the words of the holy Prophets, who were inspired by the gift of the Holy Ghost, which truly testifies of him in all things,   as well as those who should come after, who should believe in the gifts and callings of God, by the Holy Ghost, which beareth record of the Father and of the Son, which Father and Son and Holy Ghost, is one God, infinite and eternal, without end. Amen.

And we know, that all men must repent and believe on the name of Jesus Christ, and worship the Father in his name, and endure in faith on his name to the end, or they cannot be saved in   the Kingdom of God: And we know, that Justification through the grace of our Lord and Savior Jesus Christ, is just and true; and we know, also, that Sanctification through the grace of our Lord and Savior Jesus Christ, is just and true, to all those who love and serve

ments that they should love and serve him the only living and true God, and that he should be the only Being whom they should worship. But by the transgression of these holy laws, man became sensual and devilish, and became fallen man. ¶ Wherefore, the Almighty God gave his only begotten Son, as it is written in those scriptures which have been given of him;

he suffered temptations but gave no heed unto them;   he was crucified, died, and rose again the third day; and

ascended into heaven to sit down on the right hand of the Father, to reign with almighty power according to the will of the Father, that as many as would believe and be baptized, in his holy name, and endure in faith to the end should be saved: not only those who believed after he came in the meridian of time in the flesh, but all those from the beginning, even as many as were before he came, who believed in the words of the holy prophets, who spake as they were inspired by the gift of the Holy Ghost, who truly testified of him in all things, should have eternal life, as well as those who should come after, who should believe in the gifts and callings of God by the Holy Ghost which beareth record of the Father, and of the Son, which Father,   Son, and Holy Ghost are one God, infinite and eternal, without end. Amen.

And we know that all men must repent and believe on the name of Jesus Christ and worship the Father in his name, and endure in faith on his name to the end, or they cannot be saved in [p. 2] the kingdom of God. And we know that justification through the grace of our Lord and Savior Jesus Christ, is just and true: and we know, also, that sanctification through the grace of our Lord and Savior Jesus Christ, is just and true, to all those who love and serve

God with all their mights, minds, and strength, but there is a possibility that men may fall from grace and depart from the living God. Therefore let the Church take heed and pray always, lest they fall into temptation; yea, and even   he that is sanctified   also: and we know, that these things are true and agreeable to the Revelation of John, neither adding to, nor diminishing from the prophecy of his Book; neither to the holy Scriptures; neither to the Revelations of God which shal[l] come hereafter, by the gift and power of the Holy Ghost; neither by the voice of God; neither by the ministering of angels, and the Lord God hath spoken it; and honor, power, and glory be rendered to his holy name both now and ever. Amen.

And again, by way of commandment to the Church, concerning the manner of baptism: Behold whosoever humbleth himself before God and desireth to be baptized, and comes forth with a broken heart and a contrite spirit, and witnesseth unto the Church, that they have truly repented of all their sins and are willing to take upon them the name of   Christ, having a determination to serve him unto the end, and truly manifest by their works that they have received   the spirit of Christ unto the remission of their sins, then shall they be received unto baptism into the Church of Christ.

The duty of the Elders, Priests, Teachers, Deacons and members of the Church of Christ. An Apostle is an Elder, and it is his calling to baptize and to ordain other Elders, Priests, Teachers and Deacons, and to administer

the flesh and blood of Christ

according to the Scriptures, and to teach,

God with all their mights, minds, and strength; but there is a possibility that man may fall from grace and depart from the living God. Therefore let the church take heed and pray always, lest they fall into temptations; yea, and even let those who are sanctified, take heed also. And we know that these things are true and according to the revelations of John, neither adding to, nor diminishing from the prophecy of his book,   the holy scriptures, or the revelations of God which shall come hereafter by the gift and power of the Holy Ghost,   the voice of God,   or the ministering of angels: and the Lord God has spoken it; and honor, power, and glory, be rendered to his holy name, both now and ever. Amen.

And again by way of commandment to the church concerning the manner of baptism. ¶   All those who humble themselves before God and desire to be baptized, and come forth with broken hearts and contrite spirits, and witness before the church that they have truly repented of all their sins and are willing to take upon them the name of Jesus Christ, having a determination to serve him to the end, and truly manifest by their works that they have received of the Spirit of Christ unto the remission of their sins,   shall be received by baptism into his church.

The duty of the elders, priests, teachers, deacons, and members of the church of Christ. ¶ An apostle is an elder, and it is his calling to baptize, and to ordain other elders, priests, teachers, and deacons, and to administer bread and wine—the emblems of the flesh and blood of Christ—and to confirm those who are baptized into the church, by the laying on of hands for the baptism of fire and the Holy Ghost, according to the scriptures; and to teach, expound, exhort, baptize, and watch over the Church, and to confirm the Church by the laying on of the hands, and the giving of the Holy Ghost, and to take the lead of all meetings. The Elders are to conduct the meetings as they are led by the Holy Ghost.

The Priests' duty is to preach, teach, expound, exhort and baptize, and administer the Sacrament, and visit the house of each member, and exhort them to pray vocally and in secret, and also to attend to all family duties; and

ordain other Priests, Teachers and Deacons, and   take the lead in meetings; but none of these offices is he to do when there is an Elder present,

but in all   cases   is to assist the Elder[3]   The Teachers' duty is to watch over the Church always, and be with them, and strengthen them, and see that there is no iniquity in the Church, neither hardness with each other, neither lying nor back-biting nor evil speaking; and see that the Church meet together often, and also see that all the members do their duty; and he is to take the lead of meetings in the absence of the Elder or Priest, and is to be assisted always, and in all his duties in the Church by the Deacons;   but neither the Teacher nor Deacons, have authority to baptize nor administer the Sacrament,

but   are   to warn, expound, exhort and teach, and invite all to come unto Christ.

expound, exhort, baptize, and watch over the church; and to confirm the church by the laying on of the hands, and the giving of the Holy Ghost—and to take the lead of all meetings. ¶ The elders are to conduct the meetings as they are led by the Holy Ghost, according to the commandments and revelations of God. ¶ The priest's duty is to preach, teach, expound, exhort, and baptize, and administer the sacrament, and visit the house of each member, and exhort them to pray vocally and in secret, and

attend to all family duties: and he may also ordain other priests, teachers, and deacons—and he is to take the lead of meetings when there is no elder present, but when there is an elder present he is only to preach, teach, expound, exhort, and baptize, and visit the house of each member, exhorting them to pray vocally and in secret, and attend to all family duties.   In all these duties the priest is to assist the elder if occasion requires. ¶ The teacher's duty is to watch over the church always, and be with,   and strengthen them, and see that there is no iniquity in the church, neither hardness with each other; neither lying,   backbiting, nor evil speaking; and see that the church meet together often, and also see that all members do their duty—and he is to take the lead of meetings in the absence of the elder or priest—and is to be assisted always,

in all his duties in the church, by the deacons, if occasion requires: but neither teachers nor deacons have authority to baptize,   administer the sacrament, or lay on hands;   they are however to warn, expound, exhort, and teach, and invite all to come unto Christ.

---

3. An extra space after this word and before the capitalized "T" of the following word suggests that the publishers planned for punctuation here, but no type impression is visible.

Every Elder, Priest Teacher, or Deacon, is to be ordained according to the gifts and callings of God unto him,

by the power of the Holy Ghost which is in the one who ordains him.

The several Elders composing this Church of Christ, are to meet in Conference once in three months,

to do Church business whatsoever is necessary.

And each Priest or Teacher,   who is ordained by a Priest, is to take a cirtificate from him at the time, which when presented to an Elder, he is to give him a License, which shall authorize him to perform the duty   of his calling.

The duty of the members after they are received by baptism. The Elders or Priests are to have a sufficient time to expound all things concerning this Church of Christ to their understanding, previous to their partaking of the Sacrament, and being confirmed by the laying on of the hands of the Elders; so that all things may be done

Every elder, priest, teacher, or deacon, is to be ordained according to the gifts and callings of God unto him: and he is to be ordained by the power of the Holy Ghost which is in the one who ordains him.

The several elders composing this church of Christ are to meet in conference once in three months, or from time to time, as said conferences shall direct or appoint: and said conferences are to do whatever church business is necessary to be done at the time.

The elders are to receive their liscences from other elders by vote of the church to which they belong, or from the conferences.
¶   Each priest,   teacher, or deacon, who is ordained by a priest, may take a cirtificate from him at the time, which cirtificate when presented to an elder, shall entitle him to a license, which shall authorize him to perform the du-[p. 3]ties of his calling—or he may receive it from a conference.

No person is to be ordained to any office in this church, where there is a regularly organized branch of the same, without the vote of that church; but the presiding elders, travelling bishops, high counsellors, high priests, and elders, may have the privilege of ordaining, where there is no branch of the church, that a vote may be called.

Every president of the high priesthood, (or presiding elder,) bishop, high counsellor, and high priest, is to be ordained by the direction of a high counsel, or general conference.

The duty of the members after they are received by baptism: ¶ The elders or priests are to have a sufficient time to expound all things concerning the church of Christ to their understanding, previous to their partaking of the sacrament, and being confirmed by the laying on of the hands of the elders; so that all things may be done in order. And the members shall manifest before the Church, and also before the Elders, by a godly walk and conversation, that they are worthy of it, that there may be works and faith agreeable to the holy Scriptures, walking in holiness before the Lord. Every member of this Church of Christ having children, is to bring them unto the Elders before the Church, who are to lay their hands on them in the name of the Lord, and bless them in the name of Christ. There cannot any one be received into this Church of Christ, who has not arrived to the years of accountability before God, and is not capable of repentance.

And baptism is to be administered in the following manner unto all those who repent: Whosoever being called of God and having authority given them of Jesus Christ,   shall go down into the water with them,

and shall say, calling them by name: Having authority given me of Jesus Christ, I baptize you in the name of the Father, and of the Son, and of the Holy Ghost. Amen. Then shall he immerse them in the water, and come forth again out of the water. And it is expedient that the Church meet together oft to partake of Bread and Wine, in remembrance of the Lord Jesus; and the Elder or Priest shall administer it, and after this manner shall he do,   he shall kneel with the Church, and call upon the Father in mighty prayer saying: O God the Eternal Father, we ask thee in the name of thy Son Jesus Christ, to bless and sanctify this bread to the souls of all those who partake of it, that they may eat in remembrance of the body of thy Son, and witness unto thee, O God the Eternal Father, that they are willing to take upon them the name of thy Son, and always remember him, and keep his commandments which

in order. And the members shall manifest before the church and also before the elders, by a godly walk and conversation, that they are worthy of it, that there may be works and faith agreeable to the holy scriptures—walking in holiness before the Lord. ¶ Every member of the church of Christ having children, is to bring them unto the elders before the church, who are to lay their hands upon them in the name of Jesus Christ, and bless them in his name. ¶   No one can be received into the church of Christ unless he has arrived unto the years of accountability before God, and is   capable of repentance.

Baptism is to be administered in the following manner unto all those who repent: The person who is called of God and has authority   from Jesus Christ to baptize, shall go down into the water with the person who has presented him, or herself for baptism, and shall say, calling him or her by name: Having been commissioned of Jesus Christ, I baptize you in the name of the Father, and of the Son, and of the Holy Ghost. Amen. Then shall he immerse him or her in the water, and come forth again out of the water. ¶

It is expedient that the church meet together often to partake of bread and wine in remembrance of the Lord Jesus: and the elder or priest shall administer it: and after this manner shall he administer it: he shall kneel with the church and call upon the Father in solemn prayer, saying, O God, the eternal Father, we ask thee in the name of thy Son Jesus Christ to bless and sanctify this bread to the souls of all those who partake of it, that they may eat in remembrance of the body of thy Son, and witness unto thee O God, the eternal Father, that they are willing to take upon them the name of thy Son, and always remember him and keep his commandments which he hath given them, that they may always have his spirit to be with them. Amen. The manner of administering the Wine: Behold they shall take the Cup   and say, O God, the Eternal Father, we ask thee in the name of thy Son Jesus Christ, to bless and sanctify this Wine to the souls of all those who drink of it, that they may do it in remembrance of the blood of thy Son, which was shed for them, that they may witness unto thee, O God the Eternal Father, that they do always remember him, that they may have his spirit to be with them. Amen.

Any member of this Church of Christ, transgressing or being overtaken in a fault, shall be dealt with according as the Scriptures direct. It shall be the duty of the several churches, composing this Church of Christ, to send one or more of their Teachers to attend the several Conferences, held by the Elders of this Church, with a list of the names of the several members, uniting themselves to the Church since the last Conference, or send by the hand of some Priest, so that there can be kept a regular list of all the names of the members of the whole Church,   in a Book kept by one of the Elders; whomsoever the other Elders shall appoint from time to time: and also, if any have been expelled from the Church, so that their names may be blotted out of the general Church Record of names. Any member removing from the Church where he resides, if going to a Church where he is not known, may take a letter certifying that he is a regular member and in good standing; which certificate may be signed by any Elder or Priest, if the member receiving the letter is personly acquainted with the Elder or Priest, or it may be signed by the Teachers or Deacons of the Church.

he has given them, that they may always have his Spirit to be with them. Amen. ¶ The manner of administering the wine:

He shall take the cup also, and say, O God, the eternal Father, we ask thee in the name of thy Son Jesus Christ, to bless and sanctify this wine to the souls of all those who drink of it, that they may do it in remembrance of the blood of thy Son which was shed for them, that they may witness unto thee, O God, the eternal Father, that they do always remember him, that they may have his Spirit to be with them. Amen.

Any member of the church of Christ transgressing, or being overtaken in a fault, shall be dealt with   as the scriptures direct. ¶ It shall be the duty of the several churches composing the church of Christ, to send one or more of their teachers to attend the several conferences, held by the elders of the church, with a list of the names of the several members uniting themselves with the church since the last conference, or send by the hand of some priest, so that   a regular list of all the names   of the whole church may be kept in a book, by one of the elders, whoever the other elders shall appoint from time to time: and also, if any have been expelled from the church; so that their names may be blotted out of the general church record of names. ¶ All members removing from the church where they reside, if going to a church where they are not known, may take a letter certifying that they are regular members and in good standing; which certificate may be signed by any elder or priest, if the member receiving the letter is personally acquainted with the elder or priest, or it may be signed by the teachers, or deacons of the church. [p. 4]

⁴Behold, I say unto you, that all old Covenants have I caused to be done away in [p. [1]] this thing, and this is a new and an everlasting Covenant: even that which was from the beginning. Wherefore, although a man should be baptized an hundred times, it availeth him nothing, for ye cannot enter in at the straight gate by the law of Moses; neither by your dead works; for it is because of your dead works, that I have caused this last Covenant, and this Church to be built up unto me; even as in days of old. Wherefore, enter ye in at the gate as I have commanded, and seek not to counsel your God. Amen.

⁵A PROPHECY GIVEN TO THE CHURCH OF CHRIST, MARCH 7, 1831.

HEARKEN, O ye people of my church to whom the Kingdom has been given: Hearken ye and give ear to him who laid the foundation of the earth; who made the Heavens and all the host thereof, and by whom all things were made which live and move and have a being. And again I say, hearken unto my voice, lest death shall overtake you: in an hour when ye think not the summer shall be past, and the harvest ended, and your souls not saved. Listen to

⁶EXTRACT OF A PROPHECY GIVEN MARCH 7, 1831.

Hearken, O ye people of my church to whom the kingdom has been given: hearken ye and give ear to him who laid the foundation of the earth; who made the heavens and all the host thereof, and by whom all things were made which live and move and have a being. And again I say, hearken unto my voice, lest death shall overtake you: in an hour when ye think not the summer shall be past, and the harvest ended, and your souls not saved. Listen to

---

4. Revelation, 16 Apr. 1830 [D&C 22], begins here. This version reflects editing marks made in Revelation Book 1, indicating that the latter was used as a source text for the former. It is unclear why editors joined this revelation with the previous item. These two items and a third—Revelation, circa August 1830 [D&C 27]—were also consolidated in a non-Mormon publication, the *Painesville Telegraph.* A copy of the revelation in the handwriting of Sidney Gilbert also pairs the articles and covenants with the revelation of 16 April 1830, though Gilbert's is not a direct copy of the text from either newspaper. ("The Mormon Creed," *Painesville Telegraph,* 19 Apr. 1831, [4]; Gilbert, Notebook, [11]–[12]; see *JSP,* MRB:35.)

5. Excerpt of Revelation, ca. 7 Mar. 1831, in "A Prophecy Given to the Church of Christ, March 7, 1831," *The Evening and the Morning Star,* June 1832, [2] [D&C 45:1–67, 71]. This version reflects editing marks made in Revelation Book 1, indicating that the latter was used as a source text for the former. (See *JSP,* MRB:115–125.)

6. Excerpt of Revelation, ca. 7 Mar. 1831, in "Extract of a Prophecy Given March 7, 1831," *Evening and Morning Star,* June 1832 (Jan. 1835), 5–6 [D&C 45:1–71]. This version corresponds to the version in *The Evening and the Morning Star,* indicating that the latter was used as a source text for the former.

him who is the advocate with the Father, who is pleading your case before him; saying Father behold the sufferings and death of him who did no sin, in whom thou wast well pleased; behold the blood of thy Son which was shed, the blood of him whom thou gavest that thyself might be glorified; wherefore Father spare these my brethren that believe on my name, that they may come unto me and have everlasting life.

Hearken O ye people of my church, and ye Elders listen together, and hear my voice while it is called to-day and harden not your hearts; for verily I say unto you that I am Alpha and Omega, the beginning and the end, the light and the life of the world, a light that shineth in darkness and the darkness comprehendeth it not; I came unto my own and my own received me not; but unto as many as received me gave I power to do many miracles, and to become the sons of God, and even unto them that believed on my name gave I power to obtain eternal life.   And even so I have sent mine everlasting covenant into the world, to be a light to the world, and to be a standard for my people and for the Gentiles to seek to it; and to be a messenger before my face to prepare the way before me. Wherefore come ye unto it, and with him that cometh I will reason as with men in days of old, and I will show unto you my strong reasoning; wherefore hearken ye together and let me show it unto you, even my wisdom, the wisdom of him whom ye say is the God of Enoch, and his brethren, who were seperated from the earth, and were reserved unto myself, a city reserved until a day of righteousness shall come, a day which was sought for by all holy men, and they found it not because of wickedness and abominations, and confessed that they were strangers and pilgrims on the earth; but obtained a promise

him who is the advocate with the Father, who is pleading your cause before him; saying, Father behold the sufferings and death of him who did no sin, in whom thou wast well pleased: behold the blood of thy Son which was shed, the blood of him whom thou gavest that thyself might be glorified; wherefore, Father spare these my brethren that believe on my name, that they may come unto me and have everlasting life.

Hearken, O ye people of my church, and ye elders listen together, and hear my voice while it is called to-day and harden not your hearts; for verily I say unto you that I am Alpha and Omega, the beginning and the end, the light and the life of the world, a light that shineth in darkness and the darkness comprehendeth it not: I came unto my own and my own received me not; but unto as many as received me gave I power to do many miracles, and to become the sons of God, and even unto them that believed on my name, gave I power to obtain eternal life.— And even so I have sent mine everlasting covenant into the world, to be a light to the world, and to be a standard for my people and for the Gentiles to seek to it; and to be a messenger before my face to prepare the way before me. Wherefore come ye unto it, and with him that cometh I will reason as with men in days of old, and I will show unto you my strong reasoning; wherefore hearken ye together and let me show it unto you, even my wisdom, the wisdom of him whom ye say is the God of Enoch, and his brethren, who were separated from the earth, and were received unto myself—a city reserved until a day of righteousness shall come—a day which was sought for by all holy men, and they found it not because of wickedness and abominations: and confessed that they were strangers and pilgrims on the earth; but obtained a promise

that they should find it, and see it in their flesh. Wherefore hearken and I will reason with you, and I will speak unto you and prophesy as unto men in days of old, and I will show it plainly as I showed it unto my disciples, as I stood before them in the flesh and spake unto them saying: As ye have asked of me concerning the signs of my coming, in the day when I shall come in my glory, in the clouds of Heaven, to fulfil the promises that I have made unto your fathers; for as ye have looked upon the long absence of your
bodies to be a bondage, I will show unto you how the day of redemption shall come, and also the restoration of the scattered Israel.

And now ye behold this temple which is in Jerusalem, which ye call the house of God, and your enemies say that this house shall never fall. But verily I say unto you, that desolation shall come upon this generation as a thief in the night, and this people shall be destroyed and scattered among all nations, and this temple which ye now see, shall be thrown down that there shall not be left one stone upon another. And it shall come to pass, that this generation of Jews shall not pass away, until every desolation which I have told you concerning them, shall come to pass.

Ye say that ye know, that the end of the world cometh; ye say also that ye know, that the Heavens and the earth shall pass away; and in this ye say truly, for so it is; but these things which I have told you, shall not pass away until all shall be fulfiled.   And this I have told you concerning Jerusalem, and when that day shall come, shall a remnant be scattered among all nations, but they shall be gathered again; but they shall remain until the times of the Gentiles be fulfilled. And in that day shall be heard of wars and rumors of wars, and

that they should find it, and see it in their flesh. Wherefore hearken and I will reason with you, and I will speak unto you and prophesy as unto men in days of old; and I will show it plainly as I showed it unto my disciples, as I stood before them in the flesh, and spake unto them saying: As ye have asked of me concerning the signs of my coming, in the day when I shall come in my glory in the clouds of heaven, to fulfil the promises that I have made unto your fathers: for as you have looked upon the long absence of your spirits from your bodies to be a bondage, I will show unto you how the day of redemption shall come, and also the restoration of   scattered Israel.

And now ye behold this temple which is in Jerusalem, which ye call the house of God, and your enemies say that this house shall never fall. But verily I say unto you, that desolation shall come upon this generation as a thief in the night, and this people shall be destroyed and scattered among all nations, and this temple which ye now see, shall be thrown down that there shall not be left one stone upon another. And it shall come to pass, that this generation of Jews shall not pass away, until every desolation which I have told you concerning them, shall come to pass.

Ye say that ye know, that the end of the world cometh; ye say also that ye know, that the heavens and the earth shall pass away; and in this ye say truly, for so it is; but these things which I have told you, shall not pass away, but all shall be fulfilled.— And this I have told you concerning Jerusalem, and when that day shall come, a remnant shall be scattered among all nations, but they shall be gathered again; but they shall remain until the times of the Gentiles be fulfilled. And in that day shall be heard of wars and rumors of wars, and the whole earth shall be in commotion, and men's hearts shallfail them, and they shall say that Christ delay[7] eth his coming until the end of the earth. And the love of men shall wax cold, and iniquity shall abound; and when the time of the Gentiles is come in, a light shall break forth among them that sit in darkness, and it shall be the fulness of my Gospel; but they receive it not, for they perceive not the light, and they turn their hearts from me because of the precepts of men; and in that generation shall the times of the Gentiles be fulfilled : and there shall be men standing in that generation, that shall not pass until they shall see an overflowing scourge; for a desolating sickness shall cover the land; but my disciples shall stand in holy places and shall not be moved, but among the wicked, men shall lift up their voices and curse God and die; and there shall be earthquakes, also, in divers places, and   desolations, yet men will harden their hearts against me; and they will take up the sword one against another and they will kill one another: and now, when I the Lord had spoken these words unto my disciples, they were troubled, and I said unto them, be not troubled, for when all these things shall come to pass, yc may know that the prom ises which have been made unto you, shall be fulfilled, and when the light shall begin to break forth, it shall be with them like unto a parable which I will show you: ye look and behold the fig trees, and ye see them with your eyes, and ye say when they begin to shoot forth and their leaves are yet tender, ye say that summer is now nigh at hand; even so it shall be in that day, when they shall see all these things,   then shall they know that the hour is nigh.

the whole earth shall be in commotion, and men's hearts shall fail them, and they shall say that Christ delayeth his coming until the end of the earth. And the love of men shall wax cold, and iniquity shall abound; and when the time of the Gentiles is come in, a light shall break forth among them that sit in darkness, and it shall be the fulness of my gospel; but they receive it not, for they perceive not the light, and they turn their hearts from me because of the precepts of men; and in that generation shall the times of the Gentiles be fulfilled: and there shall be men standing in that generation, that shall not pass until they shall see an overflowing scourge; for a dessolating sicness shall cover the land; but my disciples shall stand in holy places and shall not be moved; but among the wicked men shall lift up their voices and curse God and die. And there shall be earthquakes, also, in divers places, and many desolations, yet men will harden their hearts against me; and they will take up the sword one against another and they will kill one another. ¶ And now, when I the Lord had spoken these words unto my disciples, they were troubled, and I said unto them, be not troubled, for when all these things shall come to pass, ye may know that the promises which have been made unto you, shall be fulfilled; and when the light shall begin to break forth, it shall be with them like unto a parable which I will show you: you look and behold the fig trees, and ye see them with your eyes, and ye say, when they begin to shoot forth and their leaves are yet tender,   that summer is now nigh at hand; even so it shall be in that day when they shall see all these things; for then shall they know that the hour is nigh.

---

7. The piece of type bearing the "y" is slanted, possibly forcing "eth" to separate from the word.

And it shall come to pass that he that feareth me shall be looking for the great day of the Lord to come, even for the signs of the coming of the son of man; and they shall see signs and wonders, for they shall be shown forth in the Heavens above and in the earth beneath; and they shall behold blood and fire, and vapors of smoke; and before the day of the Lord   come the sun shall be darkened, and the moon be turned into blood, and stars fall from Heaven; and the remnant shall be gathered unto this place; and then they shall look for me, and behold I will come; and they shall see me in the clouds of Heaven, clothed with power and great glory, with all the holy angels; and he that watches not for me shall be cut off.

But before the arm of the Lord shall fall, an angel shall sound his trump, and the saints that have slept, shall come forth to meet me in the cloud. Wherefore if ye have slept in peace blessed are you, for as you now behold me and know that I am, even so shall ye come unto me and your souls shall live, and your redemption shall be perfected, and the saints shall come forth from the four quarters of the earth; then shall the arm of the Lord fall upon the nations, and then shall the Lord set his foot upon this mount, and it shall cleave in twain, and the earth shall tremble and reel to and fro, and the Heavens also shall shake and the Lord shall utter his voice and all the ends of the earth shall hear it, and the nations of the earth shall mourn, and they that have laughed shall see their folly, and calamity shall cover the mocker, and the scorner shall be consumed, and they that have watched for iniquity, shall be hewn down and cast into the fire.

And then shall the Jews look upon me, and say what are these wounds in thine hands, and in thy feet, then shall they know

And it shall come to pass that he that feareth me shall be looking for the great day of the Lord to come, even for the signs of the coming of the son of man; and they shall see signs and wonders, for they shall be shown forth in the heavens above and in the earth beneath; and they shall behold blood and fire, and vapors of smoke; and before the day of the Lord shall come the sun shall be darkened, and the moon turned into blood, and stars fall from heaven; and the remnant shall be gathered unto this place, and then they shall look for me, and behold I will come; and they shall see me in the clouds of heaven, clothed with power and great glory, with all [p. [5]] the holy angels; and he that watcheth not for me shall be cut off.

But before the arm of the Lord shall fall, an angel shall sound his trump, and the saints that have slept, shall come forth to meet me in the cloud. Wherefore if ye have slept in peace blessed are you, for as you now behold me and know that I am, even so shall ye come unto me and your souls shall live, and your redemption shall be perfected; and the saints shall come forth from the four quarters of the earth: then shall the arm of the Lord fall upon the nations, and then shall the Lord set his foot upon this mount, and it shall cleave in twain, and the earth shall tremble and reel to and fro, and the heavens also shall shake, and the Lord shall utter his voice and all the ends of the earth shall hear it; and the nations of the earth shall mourn, and they that have laughed shall see their folly, and calamity shall cover the mocker, and the scorner shall be consumed, and they that have watched for iniquity, shall be hewn down and cast into the fire.

And then shall the Jews look upon me, and say what are these wounds in thy hands and in thy feet? then shall they know that I am the Lord; for I will say unto them, these wounds, are the wounds with which I was wounded in the house of my friends. I am he who was lifted up. I am Jesus that was crucified. I am the son of God. And then shall they weep because of their iniquities; then shall they lament because they persecuted their King. And then shall the heathen nations be redeemed, and they which knew no law shall have part in the first resurrection, and it shall be tolerable for them; and satan shall be bound that he shall have no place in the hearts of the children of men.

And at that day when I shall come in my glory, shall the parable be fulfilled which I spake concerning the ten virgins; for they that are wise and have received the truth and have taken the Holy Spirit for their guide, and have not been deceived; verily I say unto you, they shall not be hewn down and cast into the fire, but shall abide the day, and the earth shall be given unto them for an inheritance; and they shall multiply and wax strong, and their children shall grow up without sin unto salvation, for the Lord shall be in their midst, and his glory shall be upon them, and he will be their King and their lawgiver.

And now, behold I say unto you, it shall not be given unto you to know any farther than this until the New Testament be translated, and in it all these things shall be made known; wherefore I give unto you that ye may now translate it, that ye may be prepared for the things to come; for verily I say unto you that great things await you; ye hear of wars in foreign lands, but behold I say unto you they are nigh even at your doors, and not many years hence ye shall hear of wars in your own lands. Wherefore I the Lord have said

that I am the Lord; for I will say unto them, these wounds, are the wounds with which I was wounded in the house of my friends. I am he who was crucified. I am the Son of God. And then shall they weep because of their iniquities; then shall they lament because they persecuted their King. And then shall the heathen nations be redeemed, and they which knew no law shall have part in the first resurrect:on,[8] and it shall be tolerable for them; and satan shall be bound that he shall have no place in the hearts of the children of men.

And at that day when I shall come in my glory, shall the parable be fulfilled which I spake concerning the ten virgins; for they that are wise and have received the truth and have taken the Holy Spirit for their guide, and have not been deceived; verily I say unto you, they shall not be hewn down and cast into the fire, but shall abide the day, and the earth shall be given unto them for an inheritance; and they shall multiply and wax strong, and their children shall grow up without sin unto salvation, for the Lord shall be in their midst, and his glory shall be upon them, and he will be their King and their Lawgiver.

And now, behold I say unto you, it shall not be given unto you to know any further than this until the new testament be translated, and in it all these things shall be made known; wherefore I give unto you that ye may now translate it, that ye may be prepared for the things to come; for verily I say unto you that great things await you: ye hear of wars in foreign lands, but behold I say unto you they are nigh even at your doors, and not many years hence ye shall hear of wars in your own lands. Wherefore I the Lord have said,

---

8. The ":" was clearly meant to be an "i".

gather ye out from the eastern lands, assemble ye yourselves together ye Elders of my Church; go ye forth into the western countries, call upon the inhabitants to repent, and inasmuch as they do repent, build up churches unto me; and with one heart and with one mind, gather up your riches that ye may purchase an inheritance which shall hereafter be appointed unto you, and it shall be called the New Jerusalem, a land of peace, a city of refuge, a place of safety for the saints of the most high God; and the glory of the Lord shall be there, and the terror of the Lord also shall be there.

gather ye out from the eastern lands, assemble ye yourselves together ye elders of my church; go ye forth into the western countries, call upon the inhabitants to repent, and inasmuch as they do repent, build up churches unto me; and with one heart and with one mind, gather up your riches that ye may purchase an inheritance which shall hereafter be appointed you; and it shall be called the New Jerusalem; a land of peace; a city of refuge; a place of safety for the saints of the most high God; and the glory of the Lord shall be there, and the terror of the Lord also shall be there, insomuch that the wicked shall not come into it: and it shall be called Zion. And it shall come to pass among the wicked, that every man who will not take his sword against his neighbor, must needs flee unto Zion for safety. And there shall be gathered unto it out of every nation under heaven; and it shall be the only people that shall not be at war one with the other. And it shall be said among the wicked, let us not go up against Zion; for the inhabitants of Zion are terrible —wherefore, we cannot stand. ¶ And it shall come to pass that the righteous shall be gathered out from among all nations, and shall come to Zion, singing, with songs of everlasting joy. Even so. Amen.

And it shall come to pass, that the righteous shall be gathered out from among all nations, and shall come to Zion, singing with songs of everlasting joy, even so. Amen.

July 1832

Revelations.

⁹EXTRACT FROM THE LAWS FOR THE GOVERNMENT OF THE CHURCH OF CHRIST.

¹⁰EXTRACT OF COVENANTS FOR THE CHURCH OF THE LATTER DAY SAINTS.

AGAIN I say unto you, that it shall not be given to any one to go forth to preach my gospel, or to build up my church, except he be ordained by some one who has authority, and it is known to the church that he has authority, and has been regularly ordained by the hands of the church. And again, the elders, priests, and teachers of this church, shall teach the Scriptures which are in the Bible, and the Book of Mormon, in the which is the fulness of the Gospel; and they shall observe the Covenants and church Articles to do them; and this shall be their teachings. And they shall be directed by the Spirit, which shall be given them by the prayer of faith; and if they receive not the Spirit, they shall not teach. And all this they shall observe to do, as I have commanded concerning their teaching, until the fulness of my Scriptures are given. And as they shall lift up their voices by the Comforter, they shall speak and prophesy as seemeth me good; for behold,

And again, the elders, priests and teachers of this church, shall teach the principles of my gospel which are in the bible and the book of Mormon, in the which is the fulness of the gospel; and they shall observe the covenants and church articles to do them, and these shall be their teachings, as they shall be directed by the Spirit; and the Spirit shall be given unto you by the prayer of faith, and if ye receive not the Spirit ye shall not teach.— And all this ye shall observe to do as I have commanded, concerning your teaching, until the fulness of my scriptures are given. And as ye shall lift up your voices by the Comforter, ye shall speak and prophesy as seemeth me good; for behold,

---

9. Excerpt of Revelations, 9 and 23 Feb. 1831, in "Extract from the Laws for the Government of the Church of Christ," *The Evening and the Morning Star,* July 1832, [1] [D&C 42:11–77]. This version reflects editing marks made in Revelation Book 1, indicating that the latter was used as a source text for the former. This publication excludes the first paragraph and the final four paragraphs of Revelation, 9 February 1831 [D&C 42:1–72], as found in Revelation Book 1, but it includes the entire excerpt of Revelation, 23 February 1831 [D&C 42:74–77], that was recorded on a slip of paper attached to manuscript page 67 of Revelation Book 1. (See *JSP,* MRB:95–107.)

10. Excerpt of Revelations, 9 and 23 Feb. 1831, in "Extract of Covenants for the Church of the Latter Day Saints," *Evening and Morning Star,* July 1832 (Feb. 1835), 30–31 [D&C 42:12–77]. In February 1835, while preparing this item for publication, Oliver Cowdery requested from Newel K. Whitney a manuscript copy of this item. Only a few of the changes made in 1835, however, represent a restoration back to an earlier version of the text. The majority of this version corresponds to the version in *The Evening and the Morning Star,* indicating that the latter was used as a source text for the former. (Oliver Cowdery, Kirtland, OH, to Newel K. Whitney, 4 Feb. 1835, Newel K. Whitney, Papers, BYU.)

the Comforter knoweth all things, and
beareth record of the Father, and of the Son.

And now behold, I speak unto the
church: Thou shalt not kill; and he that
killeth, shall not have forgiveness, neither
in this world, nor in the world to come.
And again,   thou shalt not kill;   he
that killeth shall die. Thou shalt not steal;
and he that stealeth and will not repent,
shall be cast out. Thou shalt not lie; he that
lieth and will not repent, shall be cast
out.   Thou shalt love thy wife with all thy
heart, and shall cleave unto her and none
else; and he that looketh upon a women to
lust after her, shall deny the faith, and shall
not have the Spirit; and if he repent not, he
shall be cast out. Thou shalt not commit
adultery; and he that commiteth adultery
and repenteth not, shall be cast out; and he
that   commiteth adultery and repenteth
with all his heart, and forsaketh and doeth
it no more, thou shalt forgive him; but if he
doeth it again, he shall not be forgiven, but
shall be cast out.   Thou shalt not speak
evil of thy neighbor, or do him any harm.
Thou knowest my laws,
they are given in my Scriptures, he that
sinneth and repenteth not, shall be cast out.

If thou lovest me, thou shalt serve me
and keep all my commandments; and behold, thou shalt
consecrate   all thy properties,
          that which thou hast
unto me, with a covenant and a deed
which cannot be broken;

                              and they shall
be laid before the bishop of my church, and
          two of the elders,
     such as he shall   appoint
and set apart for that purpose. And it shall
come to pass, that
the bishop of my church,   after that he
has received

the Comforter knoweth all things, and
beareth record of the Father and of the Son.

And now, behold I speak unto the
church: Thou shalt not kill; and he that
kills shall not have forgiveness,
in this world, nor in the world to come. ¶
And again, I say, thou shalt not kill; but he
that killeth shall die. Thou shalt not steal;
and he that stealeth and will not repent,
shall be cast out. Thou shalt not lie; he that
lieth and will not repent, shall be cast
out.— Thou shalt love thy wife with all thy
heart, and shall cleave unto her and none
else; and he that looketh upon a woman to
lust after her, shall deny the faith, and shall
not have the Spirit, and if he repents not he
shall be cast out. Thou shalt not commit
adultery; and he that committeth adultery
and repenteth not, shall be cast out; but he
that has committed adultery and repents
with all his heart, and forsaketh it, and doeth
it no more, thou shalt forgive;   but if he
doeth it again, he shall not be forgiven, but
shall be cast out.— Thou shalt not speak
evil of thy neighbor, nor do him any harm.
Thou knowest my laws concerning these
things are given in my scriptures; he that
sinneth and repenteth not, shall be cast out.

If thou lovest me thou shalt serve me
and keep all my commandments. And behold, thou wilt remember the poor, and
consecrate of   thy properties for their
support, that which thou hast to impart
unto them, with a covenant and a deed
which cannot be broken—and in as much
as ye impart of your substance unto the
poor, ye will do it unto me—and they shall
be laid before the bishop of my church and
his counsellors, two of the elders, or high
priests, such as he shall or has appointed
and set apart for that purpose. ¶ And it shall
come to pass, that after they are laid before
the bishop of my church, and after that he
has received these testimonies concerning

the properties of my church, that it cannot be taken from the church,   he shall appoint every man

a steward over his own property, or that which he has received, inasmuch as shall be sufficient for himself and family; and

the residue

shall be kept to administer to him who has not, that every man may   receive according as he stands in need;   and the residue shall be kept in my storehouse, to administer to the poor and   needy, as shall be appointed by the elders   of the church and the bishop;   and for the purpose of purchasing lands,

and the building up of the New Jerusalem, which is hereafter to be revealed; that my covenant people may be gathered in one, in the day that I shall come to my temple: And this I do for the salvation of my people. And it shall come to pass, that he that sinneth and repenteth not shall be cast out,   and shall not receive again that which he has consecrated

unto me:

For it shall come to pass, that which I spake by the mouths of my prophets shall be fulfilled; for I will consecrate   the riches of the Gentiles, unto   my people which are of the house of Israel. And again, thou shalt not be proud in thy heart; let all thy garments be plain, and their beauty the beauty of the work of

the consecration of the properties of my church, that they cannot be taken from the church, agreeably to my commandments, every man shall be made accountable unto me, a steward over his own property, or that which he has received by consecration, in as much as   is sufficient for himself and family. ¶ And again, if their shall be properties in the hands of the church, or any individuals of it, more than is necessary for their support, after this first consecration, which is a residue, to be consecrated unto the bishop, it [p. 30] shall be kept to administer to those who have not, from time to time, that every man who has need may be amply supplied, and receive according to his wants. Therefore,   the residue shall be kept in my store house, to administer to the poor and the needy, as shall be appointed by the high council of the church, and the bishop and his counsel, and for the purpose of purchasing lands for the public benefit of the church, and building houses of worship, and   building up of the New Jerusalem which is hereafter to be revealed, that my covenant people may be gathered in one in that day when I shall come to my temple. And this I do for the salvation of my people. ¶ And it shall come to pass, that he that sinneth and repenteth not, shall be cast out of the church, and shall not recive again that which he has consecrated unto the poor and the needy of my church, or in other words, unto me, for in as much as ye do it unto the least of these ye do it unto me—for it shall come to pass, that which I spake by the mouths of my prophets, shall be fulfilled; for I will consecrate of the riches of those who embrace my gospel among the Gentiles, unto the poor of my people who are of the house of Israel. ¶ And again, thou shalt not be proud in thy heart, let all thy garments be plain, and their beauty the beauty of the work of thine own hands, and let all things be done in cleanliness before me.

Thou shalt not be idle; for he that is idle shall not eat the bread, nor wear the garments of the laborer. And whosoever among you that are sick, and have not faith to be healed, but believeth, shall be nourished in all tenderness with herbs and mild food, and that not   of the world; and the elders of the church, two or more shall be called, and shall pray for, and lay their hands upon them in my name, and if they die, they shall die unto me; and if they live, they shall live unto me.— Thou shalt live together in love, insomuch that thou shalt weep for the loss of them that die, and more especially for those that have not hope of a glorious resurrection. And it shall come to pass, that those that die in me shall not taste of death, for it shall be sweet unto them; and they that die not in me, wo unto them; for their death is bitter. And again, it shall come to pass, that he that has faith in me to be healed, and is not appointed unto death, shall be healed. He who has faith to see, shall see; he who has faith to hear, shall hear; the lame who have faith to leap, shall leap; and they who have not faith to do these things, but believe in me, have power to become my sons, and inasmuch as they break not my laws, thou shalt bear their infirmities. Thou shalt stand in the place of thy stewardship: Thou shalt not take thy brother's garment; thou shalt pay for that which thou shalt receive of thy brother. And if thou obtainest more than that which would be for thy support, thou shalt give it into my storehouse, that all things may be done according to that which I have spoken. Thou shalt ask and my Scriptures shall be given as I have appointed; and

for thy safety   it is expedient that thou shalt hold thy peace concerning

thine own hands; and let all things be done in cleanliness before me. ⏎

Thou shalt not be idle; for he that is idle shall not eat the bread, nor wear the garments of the laborer. And whosoever among you   are sick, and have not faith to be healed, but believeth, shall be nourished with all tenderness with herbs and mild food, and that not by the hand of an enemy. And the elders of the church, two or more, shall be called, and shall pray for and lay their hands upon them in my name, and if they die they shall die unto me, and if they live they shall live unto me.   Thou shalt live together in love, in so much that thou shalt weep for the loss of them that die, and more especially for those that have not hope of a glorious resurrection. And it shall come to pass, that those that die in me, shall not taste of death, for it shall be sweet unto them, and they that die not in me, wo unto them, for their death is bitter! ¶ And again, it shall come to pass, that he that has faith in me to be healed, and is not appointed unto death, shall be healed: he who has faith to see shall see; he who has faith to hear shall hear: the lame who have faith to leap shall leap; and they who have not faith to do these things, but believe in me, have power to become my sons: and in as much as they break not my laws, thou shalt bear their infirmities. ¶ Thou shalt stand in the place of thy stewardship: thou shalt not take thy brother's garment; thou shalt pay for that which thou shalt receive of thy brother; and if thou obtainest more than that which would be for thy support, thou shalt give it into my storehouse, that all things may be done according to that which I have said. ¶ Thou shalt ask, and my scriptures shall be given as I have appointed, and they shall be preserved in safety; and it is expedient that thou shouldst hold thy peace concerning them, until ye have received them; then I give unto you a commandment that ye shall teach them unto all men; and they also shall be taught unto all nations, kindreds, tongues and people.

Thou shalt take the things which thou hast received, which thou knowest to have been my law, to be my law, to govern my church; and he that doeth according to these things shall be saved, and he that doeth them not shall be damned, if he continue. If thou shalt ask, thou shalt receive revelation upon revelation, knowledge upon knowledge, that thou mayest know the mysteries, and the peaceable things of the kingdom; that which bringeth joy, that which bringeth life eternal. Thou shalt ask and it shall be revealed unto you in my own due time where the New Jerusalem shall be built. And behold, it shall come to pass, that my servants shall be sent both to the east, and to the west, to the north, and to the south; and even now let him that goeth to the east, teach them that shall be converted to flee to the west; and this in consequence of that which is to come on the earth, and of secret combinations. Behold, thou shalt observe all these things, and great shall by thy reward. Thou shalt observe to keep the mysteries of the kingdom unto thyself, for it is not given to the world to know the mysteries. The laws which ye have received, and shall hereafter receive, shall be sufficient for you both here, and in the New Jerusalem. Therefore, he that lacketh knowledge, let him ask of me and I will give him liberally, and upbraid him not. Lift up your hearts and rejoice, for unto you the kingdom has been given; even so. Amen.

them, and not teach them until ye have reeived them in full. And I give unto you a commandment, that then ye shall teach them unto all men; for they shall be taught unto all nations, kindreds, tongues and people.

Thou shalt take the things which thou hast received, which have been given unto thee in my scriptures for a law, to be my law, to govern my church; and he that doeth according to these things, shall be saved, and he that doeth them not shall be damned, if he continues. ¶ If thou shalt ask, thou shalt receive revelation upon revelation, knowledge upon knowledge, that thou mayest know the mysteries, and peaceable things; that which bringeth joy, that which bringeth life eternal. ¶ Thou shalt ask, and it shall be revealed unto you in my own due time, where the New Jerusalem shall be built. ¶ And behold, it shall come to pass, that my servants shall be sent forth to the east, and to the west, to the north, and to the south; and even now, let him that goeth to the east, teach them that shall be converted to flee to the west; and this in consequence of that which is coming on the earth, and of secret combinations. Behold thou shalt observe all these things, and great shall be thy reward; for unto you it is given to know the mysteries of the kingdom, but unto the world it is not given to know them. Ye shall observe the laws which ye have received, and be faithful. And ye shall hereafter receive church covenants, such as shall be sufficient to establish you, both here, and in the New Jerusalem. Therefore, he that lacketh wisdom, let him ask of me, and I will give him liberally, and apbraid him not. Lift up your hearts and rejoice, for unto you the kingdom, or in other words, the keys of the church, have been given; even so Amen.

The priests and teachers, shall have their stewardship given them even as the members; and the elders are to assist the bishop in all things, and he is to see that their families are supported out of the property which is consecrated to the Lord,

either a stewardship, or otherwise, as may be thought best by the elders & bishop.

[11]Behold, verily I say unto you, that whatever persons among you having put away their companions for the cause of fornication, or in other words, if they shall testify before you in all lowliness of heart that this is the case, ye shall not cast them out from among you; but if ye shall find that any persons have left their companions for the sake of adultery, and they themselves are the offenders, and their companions are living, they shall be cast out from among you. And again I say unto you, that ye shall be watchful and careful, with all inquiry, that ye receive none such among you if they are married, and if they are not married, they shall repent of all their sins, or ye shall not receive them.

The priests and teachers shall have their stewardships, even as the members, and the elders, or high priests who are appointed to assist the bishop as counsellors, in all things are to have their families supported out of the property which is consecrated to the bishop, for the good of the poor, and for other purposes, as before mentioned; or they are to receive a just remuneration for all their services; either a stewardship, or otherwise, as may be thought best, or decided by the councellors and bishop. And the bishop also, shall receive his support, or a just remuneration for all his services, in the church.

Behold, verily I say unto you, that whatever persons among you having put away their companions for the cause of fornication, or in other words, if they shall testify before you in all lowliness of heart that this is the case, ye shall not cast them out from among you; but if ye shall find that any persons have left their companions for the sake of adultery, and they themselves are the offenders, and their companions are living, they shall be cast out from among you. And again I say unto you, that ye shall be watchful and careful, with all inquiry, that ye receive none such among you if they are married, and if they are not married, they shall repent of all their sins, or ye shall not receive them.

---

11. The excerpt of Revelation, 23 Feb. 1831 [D&C 42:74–77], begins here. The slip of paper attached to manuscript page 67 of Revelation Book 1 was used as a source text for this version. (See *JSP,* MRB:107.)

[12] COMMANDMENT FOR KEEPING THE SABBATH, &c.

BEHOLD, saith the Lord, blessed are they who have come up unto this land with an eye single to my glory, according to my commandments; for them that live   shall inherit the earth,   and them that die   shall rest from all their labours, and their works shall follow them, and they shall receive a crown in the mansions of my father, which I have prepared for them; yea, blessed are they whose feet stand upon the land of Zion, who have obeyed my gospel, for they shall receive for their reward the good things of the earth, and it shall bring forth in its strength;

and they also, shall be crowned with blessings from above; yea and with commandments not a few; and with revelations in their time, they that are faithful and diligent before me. Wherefore I give unto them a commandment, saying thus: thou shalt love the Lord thy God with all thy heart, with all thy might, mind, and strength; and in the name of Jesus Christ thou shalt serve him.   Thou shalt love thy neighbour as thyself. Thou shalt not steal. Neither commit adultery, nor kill, nor do any thing like unto it. Thou shalt thank the Lord thy God in all things. Thou shalt offer a sacrifice unto the Lord thy God in righteousness, even that of a broken heart and a contrite spirit; and that thou mayest

REVELATIONS.
[13] COMMANDMENT FOR KEEPING THE SABBATH,

[*Given August 7, 1831.*]

Behold, saith the Lord, blessed are they who have come up unto this land with an eye single to my glory, according to my commandments; for they that live, and walk in them, faithfully, shall inherit the earth when it is prepared for them; and when they die they shall rest from all their labors and their works shall follow them: and they shall receive a crown in the mansions of my Father which I have prepared.

Yea, blessed are they whose feet stand upon the land of Zion, who have obeyed my gospel; for they shall receive for their reward the good things of the earth, and it shall bring forth in its strength for them: and they shall also be crowned with blessings from above, yea, and with commandments not a few, and with revelations in their time—they who are faithful and diligent before me. Wherefore I give unto them a commandment, saying, thus: ¶ Thou shalt love the Lord thy God with all thy heart, with all thy might mind and strength, and in the name of Jesus Christ thou shalt serve him.— Thou shalt love thy neighbor as thyself. Thou shall not steal, neither commit adultery, nor kill, nor do any thing like unto it. Thou shalt thank the Lord thy God in all things. Thou shalt offer a sacrifice unto the Lord thy God in righteousness; even that of a broken heart and a contrite spirit. And that thou mayest

---

12. Revelation, 7 Aug. 1831, in "Commandment for Keeping the Sabbath, &c.," *The Evening and the Morning Star,* July 1832, [1] [D&C 59]. This version reflects editing marks made in Revelation Book 1, indicating that the latter was used as a source text for the former. (See *JSP,* MRB:169–173.)

13. Revelation, 7 Aug. 1831, in "Commandment for Keeping the Sabbath," *Evening and Morning Star,* July 1832 (Feb. 1835), 26–27 [D&C 59]. This version corresponds to the version in *The Evening and the Morning Star,* indicating that the latter was used as a source text for the former.

more fully keep thy self unspoted from the world, thou shalt go to the house of prayer and offer up thy sacraments upon my holy day, for verily this is a day appointed unto you to rest from your labours, and to pay thy devotions unto the most high: nevertheless thy vows shall be offered up in righteousness on all days, and at all times, but remember that on this, the Lord's day, thou shalt offer thine oblations, and thy sacraments, unto the most high, confessing thy sins unto thy brethren, and before the Lord; and on this day thou shalt do none other thing, only let thy food be prepared with singleness of heart, that thy fasting may be perfect, or in other words, that thy joy may be full.   Verily this is fasting and prayer; or, in other words, rejoicing and prayer. And in as much as ye do these things with thanksgiving, with cheerful hearts, and countenances, (not with much laughter, for this is sin,) but with a glad heart, and a cheerful countenance: verily I say,   that in as much as ye do this the fulness of the earth is yours; the beasts of the fields, and the fowls of the air, and that which climbeth upon the trees, and walketh upon the earth, yea, and the herb, and the good things which cometh   of the earth, whether for food or for raiment, or for houses, or for barns, or for orchards, or for gardens, or for vineyards; yea, all things which cometh   of the earth, in the season thereof, is made for the benefit and the use of man, both to please the eye, and to gladden the heart; yea, for food and for raiment, for taste, and for smell, to strengthen the body, and to enliven the soul; and it pleaseth God that he hath given all these things unto man; for unto this end were they made, to be used with judgment, not to excess, neither by extortion; and in nothing doth man offend God or against none is his wrath kindled, save those who

more fully keep thyself unspotted from the world, thou shalt go to the house of prayer and offer up thy sacraments upon my holy day; for verily, this is a day appointed unto thee to rest from thy labors, and to pay thy devotions unto the Most High. Nevertheless, thy vows should be offered up in righteousness on all days, and at all times; but remember, that on this, the Lord's day, thou shalt offer thine oblations and thy sacraments unto the Most High, confessing thy sins unto thy brethren and before the Lord; and on this day thou shalt do none other work, only let thy food be prepared with singleness of heart, that thy fasting may be perfect, or in other words, that thy joy may be full; for verily, this is fasting and prayer; or, in other words, rejoicing and prayer. And inasmuch as ye do these things with thanksgiving, with cheerful hearts and countenances—not with much laughter for this is sin—but with a glad heart and a cheerful countenance: verily I say unto you, that inasmuch as ye do this, the fulness of the earth is yours; the beasts of the field, and the fowls of the air, and that which climbeth upon the trees, and walketh upon the earth, yea, and the herb, and the good things which come forth of the earth, whether for food or   raiment, or   houses, or   barns, or   orchards, or   gardens, or   vineyards; yea, all things which come forth of the earth, in the season thereof, are made for the benefit and the use of man, both to please the eye and to gladden the heart; yea, for food and raiment, for taste and   smell, to strenthen the body, and to enliven the soul; and it pleases God that he has given all these things unto man; for unto this end were they made, to be used with judgment, not to excess, neither by extortion: and in nothing does man offend God, or against none is his wrath kindled save those who confess not his hand in all things and obey not his commandments. Behold this is according to the law and the prophets.

Wherefore trouble me no more concerning this matter, but learn that he that doeth the works of righteousness, shall receive his reward, even peace in this world, and eternal life in the world to come. I the Lord have spoken it and the spirit beareth record. Amen. [p. [1]]

¹⁴A VISION.

HEAR, O ye Heavens, and give ear, O earth, and rejoice ye inhabitants thereof, for the Lord he is God, and beside him there is none else; and great is his wisdom; marvelous are his ways; and the extent of his doings, none can find out; his purposes fail not, neither are there any who can stay his hand: from eternity to eternity, he is the same, and his years never fail.

I the Lord am merciful and gracious unto them who fear me, and delight to honor them who serve me in righteousness, and in truth;

great shall be their reward, and eternal shall be their glory; and unto them will I reveal all mysteries; yea, all the hidden mysteries of my Kingdom from days of old; and for ages to come will I make known unto them the good pleasure of my will concerning all things;

yea, even the wonders of eternity shall they know, and things to come will I show them, even the things of many generations; their wisdom shall be great, and

confess not his hand in all things, and obey not his commandments. Behold this is according to the law and the prophets.— [p. 26] Wherefore, trouble me no more concerning this matter, but learn that he who does the works of righteousness shall receive his reward, even peace in this world, and eternal life in the world to come. ¶ I the Lord have spoken it, and the Spirit beareth record. Amen.

¹⁵A VISION.

Hear, O ye heavens, and give ear, O earth, and rejoice ye inhabitants thereof, for the Lord   is God, & beside him there is no Savior;   great is his wisdom; marvelous are his ways; and the extent of his doings, none can find out; his purposes fail not, neither are there any who can stay his hand: from eternity to eternity, he is the same, and his years never fail.

For thus saith the Lord, I the Lord am merciful and gracious unto those who fear me, and delight to honor those who serve me in righteousness, and in truth unto the end; great shall be their reward, and eternal shall be their glory; and to them will I reveal all mysteries; yea, all the hidden mysteries of my kingdom from days of old; and for ages to come will I make known unto them the good pleasure of my will concerning all things pertaining to my kingdom; yea, even the wonders of eternity shall they know, and things to come will I show them, even the things of many generations; their wisdom shall be great, and

---

14. Vision, 16 Feb. 1832, in "A Vision," *The Evening and the Morning Star,* July 1832, [2]–[3] [D&C 76]. This version reflects editing marks made in Revelation Book 1, indicating that the latter was used as a source text for the former. (See *JSP,* MRB:243–255.)

15. Vision, 16 Feb. 1832, in "A Vision," *Evening and Morning Star,* July 1832 (Feb. 1835), 27–30 [D&C 76]. This version reflects editing marks made in Revelation Book 2 and closely corresponds to the version in *The Evening and the Morning Star,* indicating that both were used as source texts for this version. (See *JSP,* MRB:415–433.)

their understanding reach to Heaven;
before them the wisdom of the wise shall
perish, and the understanding of the prudent shall come to nought; for by my Spirit
will I enlighten them, and by my power
will I make known unto them the secrets
of my will; yea, even those things which
eye has not seen, nor ear heard, nor yet entered into the heart of man.

We, Joseph   and Sidney,
      being in the Spirit on the sixteenth
of February, in the year of our Lord, one
thousand eight hundred and thirty two, and
through the power of the Spirit, our eyes
were opened, and our understandings were
enlightened, so as to see and understand
the things of God; even   things which
were from the biginning before the world
was, which was ordained of the Father,
through his only begotten Son, who was in
the bosom of the Father, even from the beginning, of whom we bear record, and the
record which we bear is the fulness of the
Gospel of Jesus Christ, which is in the Son
whom we saw and with whom we conversed in the Heavenly Vision; for as we
sat doing the work of translation, which
the Lord had appointed unto us, we came
to the twenty ninth verse of the fifth chapter of John, which was given unto us thus:
            speaking of the resurrection of
the dead   who should hear
the voice of the Son of man, and shall
come forth; they who have done good in
the resurrection of the just, and they who
have done evil in the resurrection of the
unjust. Now this caused us to marvel, for it
was given   us of the Spirit; and while
we meditated upon these things, the Lord
touched the eyes of our understandings,
and they were opened, and the glory of the
Lord shone round about; and we beheld
the glory of the Son, on the right hand
of the Father, and received of his fulness;

their understanding reach to heaven: and
before them the wisdom of the wise shall
perish, and the understanding of the prudent shall come to nought; for by my Spirit
will I enlighten them, and by my power
will I make known unto them the secrets
of my will; yea, even those things which
eye has not seen, nor ear heard, nor yet entered into the heart of man.

We, Joseph Smith jr. and Sidney
Rigdon, being in the Spirit on the sixteenth
of February, in the year of our Lord, one
thousand eight hundred and thirty two,
      by the power of the Spirit our eyes
were opened, and our understandings were
enlightened, so as to see and understand
the things of God; even those things which
were from the beginning before the world
was, which were ordained of the Father,
through his only begotten Son, who was in
the bosom of the Father, even from the beginning, of whom we bear record, and the
record which we bear is the fulness of the
gospel of Jesus Christ, who is   the Son,
whom we saw and with whom we conversed in the heavenly vision; for while we
were doing the work of translation, which
the Lord had appointed unto us, we came
to the twenty ninth verse of the fifth chapter of John, which was given unto us, as
follows:—speaking of the resurrection of
the dead, concerning those who shall hear
the voice of the Son of man—and shall
come forth; they who have done good in
the resurrection of the just, and they who
have done evil in the resurrection of the
unjust. Now this caused us to marvel, for it
was given unto us of the Spirit: and while
we meditated upon these things, the Lord
touched the eyes of our understandings,
and they were opened, and the glory of the
Lord shone round about; and we beheld
the glory of the Son, on the right hand
of the Father, and received of his fulness;

and saw the holy angels, and they who are sanctified before his throne, worshiping God and the Lamb   forever and ever. And now after the many testimonies which have been given of him, this is the testimony, last of all, which we give of him, that he lives; for we saw him, even on the right hand of God; and we heard the voice bearing record that he is the only begotten of the Father; that by him, and through him, and of him, the worlds are made, and were created; and the inhabitants thereof are begotten sons and daughters unto God.   This we saw also and bear record, that an angel of God, who was in authority in the presence of God, who rebelled against the only begotten Son, (whom the Father loved, and who was in the bosom of the Father,) and was thrust down from the presence of God and the Son, and was called Perdition; for the Heavens wept over him; for he was Lucifer, even the son of the morning; and we beheld and lo, he is fallen! is fallen! even the son of the morning. And while we were yet in the Spirit, the Lord commanded us that we should write the Vision; for   behold satan, that old serpant, even the devil, who rebelled against God, and sought to take

kingdoms of our God, and of his Christ; wherefore he maketh war with the saints of God, and encompasses them   about: And we saw   a vision of the eternal sufferings of those wtth whom he maketh war and overcometh, for thus came the voice of the Lord unto us.

Thus saith the Lord, concerning all those who know my power, and who have been made partakers thereof, and suffered themselves, through the power of the devil, to be overcome   unto the denying of the truth, and the defying of my power: they are they who are the sons of perdition, of whom I say it had been better for them

and saw the holy angels, and they who are sanctified before his throne, worshiping God and the Lamb, who worship him forever and ever. And now, after the many testimonies which have been given of him, this is the testimony, last of all, which we give of him, that he lives; for we saw him, even on the right hand of God; and we heard the voice bearing record that he is the only begotten of the Father; that by him, and through him, and of him, the worlds are   and were created; and the inhabitants thereof are begotten sons and daughters unto God. And this we saw also, and bear record, that an angel of God, who was in authority in the presence of God, who rebelled against the only begotten Son—whom the Father loved, and who was in the bosom of the Father—and was thrust down from the presence of God and the Son, and was called Perdition; for the heavens wept over him;   he was Lucifer, a son of the morning; and we beheld and lo, he is fallen! is fallen! even a son of the morning. And while we were yet in the Spirit, the Lord commanded us that we should write the vision; for we beheld satan, that old serpent, even the devil, who rebelled against God, and sought to take the kingdom of our God, and   his Christ; wherefore he maketh war with the saints of God, and encompasses them round about. And we saw [p. 27] a vision of the sufferings of those with whom he made war and overcame, for thus came the voice of the Lord unto us.

Thus saith the Lord, concerning all those who know my power, and   have been made partakers thereof, and suffered themselves, through the power of the devil, to be overcome, and to   deny   the truth, and   defy   my power: they are they who are the sons of perdition, of whom I say it had been better for them

never to have been born; for they are vessels of wrath doomed to suffer the wrath of God, with the devil and his angels, throughout eternity: concerning whom I have said there is no forgiveness for them in this world nor in the world to come; having denied the Holy Ghost after having received it, and having denied the only begotten Son of the Father,   crucifying him unto themselves, and putting him to an open shame: these are they who shall go away into the lake of fire and brimstone, with the devil and his angels, and the only ones on whom the second death shall have any power; yea, verily the only ones who shall not be redeemed in the due time of the Lord, after the sufferings of his wrath, who
shall be brought forth by the resurrection of the dead, through the triumph & the glory of the Lamb; who was slain, who was in the bosom of the Father before the worlds were made. And this is the Gospel, the glad tidings which the voice out of the heavens bore record unto us, that he came into the world, even Jesus to be crucified for the world, and to bear the sins of the world, and to sanctify the world, and to cleanse it from all unrighteousness; that through him all might be saved, whom the Father had put into his power; and made by him who glorifieth the Father; and saveth all the work of his hands, except those sons of perdition, who denieth the Son after the Father hath revealed him: wherefore he saveth all save them, and these shall go away into everlasting punishment, which is endless punishment, which is eternal punishment, to reign with the devil and his angels throughout eternity, where their worm dieth not and the fire is not quenched, which is their torment, but the end thereof, neither the place thereof, and their torment, no man knoweth, neither was   revealed, neither is, neither will be revealed unto man, save

never to have been born; for they are vessels of wrath doomed to suffer the wrath of God, with the devil and his angels, in
          eternity: concerning whom I have said there is no forgiveness   in this world nor in the world to come: having denied the Holy Spirit after having received it, and having denied the only begotten Son of the Father, having crucified him unto themselves, and put him to an open shame: these are they who shall go away into the lake of fire and brimstone, with the devil and his angels, and the only ones on whom the second death shall have any power; yea, verily the only ones who [s]hall not be redeemed in the due time of the Lord, after the sufferings of his wrath; for all the rest shall be brought forth by the resurrection of the dead, through the triumph and the glory of the Lamb, who was slain, who was in the bosom of the Father before the worlds were made. And this is the gospel, the glad tidings which the voice out of the heavens bore record unto us, that he came into the world, even Jesus to be crucified for the world, and to bear the sins of the world, and to sanctify the world, and to cleanse it from all unrighteousness; that through him all might be saved, whom the Father had put into his power, and made by him; who glorifies the Father, and saves all the works of his hands, except those sons of perdition, who denies the Son after the Father has revealed him: wherefore he saves all except them;   they shall go away into everlasting punishment, which is endless punishment, which is eternal punishment, to reign with the devil and his angels in
          eternity, where their worm dieth not and the fire is not quenched, which is their torment, and the end thereof, neither the place thereof, nor their torment, no man knows, neither was it revealed, neither is, neither will be revealed unto man, except

to them who are made partakers thereof: nevertheless I the Lord showeth it by vision unto many, but straihgtway shutteth it up again: wherefore the end, the width, the height, the depth, and the misery thereof, he understandeth not, neither any man save them who are ordained unto this condemnation. And we heard the voice saying, Write the Vision for lo, this is the end of the vision of the eternal sufferings of the ungodly!

And again, we bear record for we saw and heard, and this is the testimony of the Gospel of Christ, concerning them who come forth in the resurrection of the just: they are they who received the testimony of Jesus, and believed on his name, and were baptized after the manner of his burial, being buried in the water in his name, and this according to the commandment which he hath given, that, by keeping the commandment, they might be washed and cleansed from all their sins, and receive the Holy Ghost by the laying on of the hands of him who is ordained and sealed unto this power; and who overcome by faith, and are sealed by that Holy Spirit of promise, which the Father shedeth forth upon all those who are just and true: they are they who are the church of the first-born: they are they into whose hands the Father hath given all things: they are they who are priests and kings, who having received of his fulness, and of his glory,   are priests of the most High after the order of Melchisedek, which was after the order of Enoch, which was after the order of the only begotten Son: wherefore, as it is written, they are gods, even the sons of God: wherefore all things are theirs, whether life or death, or things present, or things to come, all are theirs, and they are Christ's, and Christ is God's; and they shall overcome all things: wherefore let no man glory

to them who are made partakers thereof: nevertheless I the Lord show it by vision unto many, but straitway shut it up again: wherefore the end, the width, the heighth, the depth, and the misery thereof, they understand not, neither any man except them who are ordained unto this condemnation. And we heard the voice saying, Write the vision, for lo! this is the end of the vision of the   sufferings of the ungodly!

And again, we bear record for we saw and heard, and this is the testimony of the gospel of Christ, concerning them who come forth in the resurrection of the just: they are they who received the testimony of Jesus, and believed on his name, and were baptized after the manner of his burial, being buried in the water in his name, and this according to the commandment which he has given, that, by keeping the commandments, they might be washed and cleansed from all their sins, and receive the Holy Spirit by the laying on of the hands of him who is ordained and sealed unto this power; and who overcome by faith, and are sealed by that Holy Spirit of promise, which the Father sheds forth upon all those who are just and true: they are they who are the church of the first-born: they are they into whose hands the Father has given all things: they are tbey who are priests and kings, who having received of his fulness, and of his glory, and are priests of the most High after the order of Melchisedek, which was after the order of Enoch, which was after the order of the only begotten Son: wherefore, as it is written, they are gods, even the sons of God: wherefore all things are theirs, whether life or death, or things present, or things to come, all are theirs, and they are Christ's, and Christ is God's; and they shall overcome all things: wherefore let no man glory in man, but rather let him glory in God, who shall subdue all enemies under his feet; these shall dwell in the presence of God and his Christ forever and ever: these are they whom he shall bring with him, when he shall come in the clouds of heaven, to reign on the earth over his people: these are they who shall have part in the first resurrection: these are they who shall come forth in the resurrection of the just: these are they who are come unto mount Zion, and unto the city of the living God, the heavenly place,   the holiest of all: these are they who have come to an innumerrable company of angels; to the general assembly and church of Enoch, and of the first born: these are they whose names are written in Heaven, where God and Christ is the judge of all: these are they who are just men made perfect through Jesus the Mediator of the new covenant, who wrought out this perfect atonement through the shedding of his own blood: these are they whose bodies are celestial, whose glory is that of the Son, even

     of God the highest of all; which glory the Sun of the firmament is written of as being typical.

     And again, we saw the Terrestrial world, and behold and lo! these are they who are of the terrestrial, whose glory differeth from that of the church of the first born, who have received of the fulness of the Father, even as that of the Moon differeth from the Sun of the firmament. Behold, these are they who died without law; and also they who are the spirits of men kept in prison, whom the Son visited and preached the Gospel unto them, that they might be judged according to men in the flesh, who received not the testimony of Jesus in the flesh, but afterwards received it: these are they who are honorable men of the earth, who were blinded by the craftiness of men:

in man, but rather let him glory in God, who shall subdue all enemies under his feet: these shall dwell in the presence of God and his Christ forever and ever: these are they whom he shall bring with him, when he shall come in the clouds of heaven, to reign on the earth over his people: these are they who shall have part in the first resurrection: these are they who shall come forth in the resurrection of the just: these are they who are come unto mount Zion, and unto the city of the living God, the heavenly place, [p. 28] the holiest of all: these are they who have come to an innumerable company of angels; to the general assembly and church of Enoch, and of the first born: these are they whose names are written in heaven, where God and Christ are the judge of all: these are they who are just men made perfect through Jesus the mediator of the new covenant, who wrought out this perfect atonement through the shedding of his own blood: these are they whose bodies are celestial, whose glory is that of the sun, even the glory of God the highest of all; whose glory the sun of the firmament is written of as being typical.

     And again, we saw the terrestrial world, and behold and lo! these are they who are of the terrestrial, whose glory differs from that of the church of the first born, who have received   the fulness of the Father, even as that of the moon differs from the sun of the firmament. Behold, these are they who died without law; and also they who are the spirits of men kept in prison, whom the Son visited and preached the gospel unto them, that they might be judged according to men in the flesh, who received not the testimony of Jesus in the flesh, but afterwards received it: these are they who are honorable men of the earth, who were blinded by the craftiness of men:

these are they who receive of his glory, but not of his fulness: these are they who receive of the presence of the Son, but not of the fulness of the Father: wherefore they are bodies terrestrial, and not bodies celestial, and differeth in glory as the Moon differeth from the Sun: these are they who are not valiant in the testimony of Jesus: wherefore they obtained not the crown over the kingdoms of our God. And now this is the end of the vision which we saw of the terrestrial, that the Lord commanded us to write while we were yet in the Spirit.

And again, we saw the glory of the Telestial, which glory is that of the lesser, even as the glory of the stars differeth from that of the glory of the Moon in the firmament: these are they who receive not the Gospel of Christ, neither the testimony of Jesus: these are they who deny not the Holy Ghost: these are they who are thrust down to hell: these are they who shall not be redeemed from the devil, until the last resurrection, until the Lord, even Christ the Lamb, shall have finished his work: these are they who receive not of his fulness in the eternal world, but of the Holy Ghost through the administration of the terrestrial; and the terrestrial through the administration of the celestial; and also the telestial receive it of the administering of angels, who are appointed to minister for them, or who are appointed to be ministering spirits for them, for they shall be heirs of salvation.— And thus we saw in the Heavenly vision, the glory of the telestial which surpasseth all understanding; and no man knoweth it except him to whom God hath revealed it. And thus we saw the glory of the terrestrial, which excelleth in all things the glory of the telestial, even in glory, and in power, and in might, and in dominion. And thus we saw the glory of the celestial, which excelleth in all things where God,

these are they who receive of his glory, but not of his fulness: these are they who receive of the presence of the Son, but not of the fulness of the Father: wherefore they are bodies terrestrial, and not bodies celestial, and differ in glory as the moon differs from the sun: these are they who were not valiant in the testimony of Jesus: wherefore they obtained not the crown over the kingdom of our God. And now this is the end of the vision which we saw of the terrestrial, that the Lord commanded us to write while we were yet in the Spirit.

And again, we saw the glory of the telestial, which glory is that of the lesser, even as the glory of the stars differ from that of the glory of the moon in the firmament; these are they who receive not the gospel of Christ, neither the testimony of Jesus: these are they who deny not the Holy Spirit: these are they who are thrust down to hell: these are they who shall not be redeemed from the devil, until the last resurrection, until the Lord, even Christ the Lamb, shall have finished his work: these are they who receive not of his fulness in the eternal world, but of the Holy Spirit through the ministration of the terrestrial; and the terrestrial through the ministration of the celestial; and also the telestial receive it of the administering of angels, who are appointed to minister for them, or who are appointed to be ministering spirits for them, for they shall be heirs of salvation. And thus we saw in the heavenly vision, the glory of the telestial which surpasses all understanding; and no man knows it except him to whom God has revealed it. And thus we saw the glory of the terrestrial, which excels in all things the glory of the telestial, even in glory, and in power, and in might, and in dominion. And thus we saw the glory of the celestial, which excels in all things where God, even the Father, reigneth upon his throne forever and ever: before whose throne all things bow in humble reverence and giveth him glory forever and ever. They who dwell in his presence are the church of the first born; and they see as they are seen, and know as they are known, having received of his fulness and of his grace; and he maketh them equal in power, and in might, and in dominion. And the glory of the celestial is one, even as the glory of the Sun is one. And the glory of the Terrestrial is one, even as the glory of the Moon is one. And the glory of the Telestial is one, even as the glory of the stars is one: for as one star differeth from another star in glory, even so differeth one from another in glory in the telestial world: for these are they who are of Paul, and of Apollos, and Cephas: they are they who say, there are some of one and some of annother; some of Christ; and some of John; and some of Moses; and some of Elias; and some of Esaias; and some of Isaiah; and some of Enoch, but received not the Gospel; neither the testimony of Jesus; neither the prophets; neither the everlasting covenant; last of all: these are they who will not be gathered with the saints, to be caught up into [p. [2]] the church of the first born, and received into the cloud: these are they who are liars, and sorcerers, and adulterers, and whore-mungers, and whosoever loveth and maketh a lie: these are they   who suffer the wrath of God on the earth: these are they who suffer the vengeance of eternal fire: these are they who are cast down to hell and suffer the wrath of Almighty God until the fulness of times, when Christ shall have subdued all enemies under his feet, and shall have perfected his work, when he shall deliver up the kingdom and present it unto his Father spotless, saying: I have overcome and   trodden the wine-

even the Father, reigns upon his throne forever and ever: before whose throne all things bow in humble reverence and give him glory forever and ever. They who dwell in his presence are the church of the first born; and they see as they are seen, and know as they are known, having received of his fulness and of his grace; and he makes them equal in power, and in might, and in dominion. And the glory of the celestial is one, even as the glory of the sun is one. And the glory of the terrestrial is one, even as the glory of the moon is one. And the glory of the telestial is one, even as the glory of the stars are one: for as one star differs from another star in glory, even so differs one from another in glory in the telestial world: for these are they who are of Paul, and of Apollos, and of Cephas: these are they who say, there are some of one and some of another; some of Christ; and some of John; and some of Moses; and some of Elias; and some of Esaias; and some of Isaiah; and some of Enoch, but received not the gospel; neither the testimony of Jesus; neither the prophets: neither the everlasting covenant; last of all, these all are they who will not be gathered with the saints, to be caught up unto   the church of the first born, and received into the cloud: these are they who are liars, and sorcerors, and adulterers, and whore-mungers, and whosoever loves and makes a lie: these are they [p. 29] who suffer the wrath of God on the earth: these are they who suffer the vengeance of eternal fire: these are they who are cast down to hell and suffer the wrath of Almighty God until the fulness of times, when Christ shall have subdued all enemies under his feet, and shall have perfected his work, when he shall deliver up the kingdom and present it unto the Father spotless, saying: I have overcome and have trodden the wine-press alone, even the wine-press of the fierceness of the wrath of Almighty God: then shall he be crowned with the crown of his glory, to sit on the throne of his power to reign forever and ever. But behold and lo, we saw   the inhabitants of the telestial world, that they were in number as innumerable as the stars in the firmament of Heaven, or as the sand upon the sea shore, and heard the voice of the Lord saying: These all shall bow the knee, and every tongue shall confess to him who sitteth upon the throne forever and ever: for they shall be judged according to their works; and every man shall receive according to his own works, and his own dominion, in the mansions which are prepared; and they shall be servants of the most High, but where God and Christ dwells they cannot come, worlds without end. This is the end of the vision which we saw, which we were commanded to write while we were yet in the Spirit.

But great and marvelous are the works of the Lord and the mysteries of his kingdom which he showed unto us, which surpasseth all understanding in glory, and in might, and in dominion, which he commanded us we should not write, while we were yet in the Spirit, and are not lawful for man to utter; neither is man capable to make them known, for they are only to be seen and understood by the power of the Holy Ghost; which God bestows on those who love him and purify themselves before him; to whom he grants this privilege of seeing and knowing for themselves; that through the power and manifestation of the Spirit, while in the flesh, they may be able to bear his presence in the world of glory. And to God and the Lamb be glory, and honor, and dominion, forever and ever. Amen.

press alone, even the wine-press of the fierceness of the wrath of Almighty God: then shall he be crowned with the crown of his glory, to sit on the throne of his power to reign forever and ever. But hehold and lo, we saw the glory and the inhabitants of the telestial world, that they were

as innumerable as the stars in the firmament of heaven, or as the sand upon the sea shore, and heard the voice of the Lord saying: These all shall bow the knee, and every tongue shall confess to him who sits upon the throne forever and ever: for they shall be judged according to their works; and every man shall receive according to his own works, and his own dominion, in the mansions which are prepared, and they shall be servants of the most High, but where God and Christ dwell they cannot come, worlds without end. This is the end of the vision which we saw, which we were commanded to write while we were yet in the Spirit.

But great and marvelous are the works of the Lord and the mysteries of his kingdom which he showed unto us, which surpases all understanding in glory, and in might, and in dominion, which he commanded us we should not write, while we were yet in the Spirit and are not lawful for man to utter; neither is man capable to make them known, for they are only to be seen and understood by the power of the Holy Spirit, which God bestows on those who love him and purify themselves before him; to whom he grants this privilege of seeing and knowing for themselves; that through the power and manifestation of the Spirit, while in the flesh, they may be able to bear his presence in the world of glory. And to God and the Lamb be glory, and honor, and dominion forever and ever. Amen.

August 1832

Revelations.
¹⁶COMMANDMENT, GIVEN
MARCH 8, 1831.

HEARKEN, O ye people of my church, for verily I say unto you, that these things are spoken unto you for your profit and learning; but notwithstanding these things which are written, it always has been given to the elders of my church, from the beginning, and ever shall be, to conduct all meetings as they are directed and guided by the Holy Spirit: nevertheless ye are commanded never to cast any one out from your public meetings, which are held before the world: ye are also commanded never to cast any one, who belongeth to the church, out of your sacrament meetings: nevertheless, if any has trespassed, let him not partake until he makes reconciliation. And again I say unto you, ye shall not cast any out of your sacrament meetings, who is earnestly seeking the kingdom; I speak this concerning those who are not of the church. And again I say unto you, concerning your confirmation meetings, that if there be any that is not of the church, that is earnistly seeking after the kingdom, ye shall not cast them out, but ye are commanded in all things to ask of God who giveth liberally, and that which the spirit testifies unto you, even so I would that ye should do in all

REVELATIONS.
¹⁷A REVELATION GIVEN
MARCH 8, 1831.

Hearken, O ye people of my church, for ver ily I say unto you, that these things are spoken unto you for your profit and learning; but notwithstanding these things which are written, it always has been given to the elders of my church, from the beginning, and ever shall be, to conduct all meetings as they are directed and guided by the Holy Spirit: nevertheless ye are commanded never to cast any one out from your public meetings, which are held before the world: ye are also commanded never to cast one, who belongs to the church, out of your sacrament meetings: nevertheless, if any have trespassed, let them not partake until they make recon,ciliation.¹⁸ And again I say unto you, ye shal-¹⁹ not cast any out of your sacrament meetings who are earnestly seeking the kingdom; I speak this concerning those who are not of the church. And again I say unto you, concerning your confirmation meetings, that if there be any that are not of the church, that are earnestly seeking after the kingdom, ye shall not cast them out, but ye are commanded in all things to ask of God who gives liberally, and that which the Spirit testifies unto you, even so I would that ye should do in all

---

16. Revelation, ca. 8 Mar. 1831–A, in "Commandment, Given March 8, 1831," *The Evening and the Morning Star,* Aug. 1832, [1] [D&C 46]. This version reflects editing marks made in Revelation Book 1, indicating that the latter was used as a source text for the former. (See *JSP,* MRB:125–129.)

17. Revelation, ca. 8 Mar. 1831–A, in "A Revelation Given March 8, 1831," *Evening and Morning Star,* Aug. 1832 (Mar. 1835), 42–43 [D&C 46]. This version corresponds to the version in *The Evening and the Morning Star,* indicating that the latter was used as a source text for the former.

18. The comma in the middle of this word comes at the end of a printed line. The comma was likely mistakenly used in place of a hyphen.

19. This hyphen comes at the end of a printed line. The typesetter may have mistakenly placed this hyphen in anticipation of the continuation of the word on the next line, or more likely, the hyphen was mistakenly used in place of a second "l".

holiness of heart, walking uprightly before me, considering the end of your salvation, doing all things with prayer and thanksgiving, that ye may not be seduced by evil spirits, or doctrines of devils ,or the commandments of men, for some are of men, and others of devils: Wherefore, beware lest ye are deceived? and that ye may not be deceived, seek ye earnestly the best gifts, always remembering for what they are given; for verily I say unto you, they are given for the benefit of those who love me and keep all my commandments, and him that seeketh so to do, that all may be benefited; that seeketh or that asketh of me, that asketh and not for a sign that he may consume it upou his lusts.

And again, verily I say unto you, I would that ye should always remember, and always retain in your minds what these gifts are, that are given unto the church, for all have   not every gift given unto them, for there are many gifts, and to every man is given a gift by the spirit of God; to some is given one, and to some is given another, that all may be profied thereby; to some is given by the Holy Ghost to know that Jesus Christ is the Son of God, and that he was crucified for the sins of the world; to others it is given to believe on their words, that they also might have eternal life if they continue faithful. And again, to some it is given by the Holy Ghost to know the differences of administration, as it will be pleasing unto the same Lord, according as the Lord will, suiting his mercies according to the conditions of the children of men. And again it is given by the Holy Ghost to some to know the diversities of opperations, whether it be of God or not, so that the manifestations of the spirit may be given to every man to profit with all. And again, verily I say unto you,to some it is given, by the spirit of God, the

holiness of heart, walking uprightly before me, considering the end of your salvation, doing all things with prayer and thanksgiving, that ye may not be seduced by evil spirits, or doctrines of devils, or the commandments of men, for some are of men, and others of devils: Wherefore, beware lest ye are deceived! and that ye may not be deceived, seek ye earnestly the best gifts, always remembering for what they are given; for verily I say unto you, they are given for the benefit of those who love me and keep all my commandments, and him that seeks so to do, that all may be benefitted; that seek or that ask of me, that ask and not for a sign that they may consume it upon their lusts.

And again, verily I say unto you, I would that ye should always remember, and always retain in your minds what these gifts are, that are given unto the church, for all have [p. 42] not every gift given unto them, for there are many gifts, and to every man is given a gift by the Spirit of God; to some is given one, and to some is given another, that all may be profited thereby; to some is given by the Holy Spirit to know that Jesus Christ is the Son of God, and that he was crucified for the sins of the world; to others it is given to believe on their words, that they also might have eternal life if they continue faithful. And again, to some it is given by the Holy Spirit to know the difference of administration, as it will be pleasing unto the same Lord, according as the Lord will, suiting his mercies according to the conditions of the children of men. And again it is given by the Holy Spirit to some to know the diversities of opperations, whether they be of God or no*t*, so that the manifestations of the Spirit may be given to every man to profit with all. And again, verily I say unto you, to some it is given, by the Spirit of God, the word of wisdom; to another it is given, the word of knowledge, that all may be taught to be wise and to have knowledge. And again, to some it is given to have faith to be healed, and to others it is given to have faith to heal. And again, to some it is given, the working of miracles; and to others it is given to prophesy, and to others the discerning of spirits. And again, it is given to some to speak with tongues, and to another it is given the interpretation of tongues: and all these gifts cometh from the Lord, for the benefit of the children of God. And unto the bishop of the church, and unto such as God shall appoint and ordain to watch over the church, and to be elders unto the church, are to have it given unto them to discern all those gifts, lest there shall be any among you professing and yet not be of God. Behold, it shall come to pass that he that asketh in spirit shall receive in spirit; that unto some it may be given to have all those gifts, that there may be a head, in order that every member may be profited thereby; he that asketh in spirit asketh according to the will of God, wherefore it is done even as he asketh. And again I say unto you, all things must be done in the name of Christ, whatsoever you do in the spirit; and ye must give thanks unto God in the spirit for whatsoever blessing ye are blessed with: and ye must practice virtue and holiness before me continually; even so; Amen.

word of wisdom: to another   is given the word of knowledge, that all may be taught to be wise and to have knowledge. And again, to some it is given to have faith to be healed, and to others it is given to have faith to heal. And again, to some it is given, the working of miracles; and to others it is given to prophesy, and to others the discerning of spirits. And again, it is given to some to speak with tongues, and to another it is given the interpretation of tongues: and all these gifts come from the Lord, for the benefit of the children of God. And unto the bishop of the church, and unto such as God shall appoint and ordain to watch over the church, and to be elders unto the church, are to have it given unto them to discern all those gifts, lest there shall be any among you professing and yet not be of God. Behold, it shall come to pass that he that asks in spirit shall receive in spirit; that unto some it may be given to have all those gifts, that there may be a head, in order that every member may be profited thereby: he that asks in spirit asks according to the will of God, wherefore it is done even as he asks. And again I say unto you, all things must be done in the name of Christ, whatsoever you do in the spirit; and ye must give thanks unto God in the spirit for whatsoever blessing ye are blessed with: and ye must practice virtue and holiness before me continually; even so; Amen.

20COMMANDMENT, GIVEN
MAY 9, 1831.

21A REVELATION GIVEN
MAY 9, 1831.

HEARKEN, O ye elders of my church, and give ear to the voice of the living God; and attend to the words of wisdom which shall be given unto you, according as ye have asked and are agreed as touching the church, and the spirits which have gone abroad in the earth. Behold verily I say unto you, that there are many spirits, which are false spirits, which have gone forth in the earth, deceiving the world: and also satan hath sought to deceive you, that he might overthrow you. Behold I the Lord have looked upon you and have seen abominations in the church, which profess my name; but blessed are they who are faithful and endure whether in life or in death, for they shall inherit eternal life. But wo unto them that are deceivers, and hypocrites, for thus saith the Lord, I will bring them to judgment. Behold verily I say unto you, there are hypocrits among you, and have deceived some which has given the adversary power; but behold such shall be reclaimed, but the hypocrites shall be detected & shall be cut off, either in life or in death, even as I will, and wo is unto them that is cut off from my church, for the same is overcome of the world: wherefore, let every man be aware lest he do that which is not in truth and righteousness before me.

And now come, saith the Lord, by the spirit, unto the elders of his church, and let us reason together, that ye may understand: let us reason even as a man reasoneth one

Hearken, O ye elders of my church, and give ear to the voice of the living, God; and attend to the words of wisdom which shall be given unto you, according as ye have asked and are agreed as touching the church, and the spirits which have gone abroad in the earth. Behold verily I say unto you, that there are many spirits, which are false spirits, which have gone forth in the earth, deceiving the world: and also satan has sought to deceive you, that he might overthrow you. Behold I the Lord have looked upon you and have seen abominations in the church, which profess my name; but blessed are they who are faithful and endure whether in life or in death, for they shall inherit eternal life. But wo unto them that are deceivers, and hypocrites, for thus saith the Lord, I will bring them to judgment. Behold verily I say unto you, there are hypocrites among you, and have deceived some which has given the adversary power: but behold such shall be reclaimed, but the hypocrites shall be detected and shall be cut off, either in life or in death, even as I will, and wo　unto them that are cut off from my church, for the same are overcome with the world: wherefore let every man be aware lest he do that which is not in truth and righteousness before me.

And now come, saith the Lord, by the spirit, unto the elders of his church, and let us reason together, that ye may understand: let us reason even as a man reasons one

---

20. Revelation, 9 May 1831, in "Commandment, Given May 9, 1831," *The Evening and the Morning Star,* Aug. 1832, [1] [D&C 50]. This version reflects editing marks made in Revelation Book 1, indicating that the latter was used as a source text for the former. (See *JSP,* MRB:137–143.)

21. Revelation, 9 May 1831, in "A Revelation Given May 9, 1831," *Evening and Morning Star,* Aug. 1832 (Mar. 1835), 43–44 [D&C 50]. This version corresponds to the version in *The Evening and the Morning Star,* indicating that the latter was used as a source text for the former.

with another face to face: now when a man reasoneth he is understood of man, because he reasoneth as a man, even so will I the Lord reason with you that you may understand; wherefore I the Lord asketh you this question, unto what was ye ordained: to preach my gospel by the spirit, even the comforter which was sent forth to teach the truth; and then received ye spirits which ye could not understand, & received them to be of God, & in this are ye justified? Behold ye shall answer this question yourselves, nevertheless I will be merciful unto you: he that is weak among you hereafter shall be made strong.   Verily I say unto you, he that is ordained of me and sent forth to preach the word of truth by the comforter, in the spirit of truth, doth he preach it by the spirit of truth, or some other way: and if by some other way, it be not of God; and again he that receiveth the word of truth doth he receive it by the spirit of truth, or some other way; if it be some other way it be not of God: Therefore, why is it that ye cannot understand and know that he that receiveth the word by the spirit of truth, receiveth it as it is preached by the spirit of truth, wherefore he that preacheth and he that receiveth understandeth one another and both are edified and rejoice together; and that which doth not edify is not of God and is darkness; that which is of God is light and he that receiveth light and continueth in God, receiveth more light, and that light groweth brighter and brighter until the perfect day. And again, verily I say unto you, and I say it that you may know the truth, that you may chase darkness from among you, for he that is ordained of God and sent forth, the same is appointed to be the greatest, notwithstanding he is least, and the servant of all: wherefore he is possessor of all things, for all things are subject unto him, both in heaven

with another face to face: now when a man reasons he is understood of man, because he reasons as a man: even so will I the Lord reason with you that you may understand; wherefore I the Lord ask you this question: Unto what were ye ordained: to preach my gospel by the spirit, even the comforter which was sent forth to teach the truth; and then receive ye spirits which ye could not understand, and received them to be of God, and in this are ye justified? Behold ye shall answer this question yourselves, nevertheless I will be merciful unto you: he that is weak among you hereafter shall be made strong.— Verily I say unto you, he that is ordained of me and sent forth to preach the word of truth by the comforter, in the spirit of truth, does he preach it by the spirit of truth, or some other way: and if by some other way, it be not of God; and again he that receives the word of truth does he receive it by the spirit of truth, or some other way; if it be some other way it be not of God: Therefore, why is it that ye cannot understand and know that he that receives the word by the spirit of truth, receives it as it is preached by the spirit of truth, wherefore he that preaches and he that receives understands one another and both are edified and rejoice together: and that which does not edify is not of God and is darkness; that which is of God is light, and he that receives light and continues in God, receives more light, and that light grows brighter and brighter until the perfect day. And again, verily I say unto you, and I say it that ye may know the truth, that you may chase darkness from among you, for he that is ordained of God and sent forth, the same is appointed to be the greatest, notwithstanding he is least, and the servant of all: wherefore he is possessor of all things, for all things are subject unto him, both in heaven and on earth, the li[f]e the light the spirit and the power, sent forth by the will of the Father, through Jesus Christ, his Son; but no man is possessor of all things except he be purified and and cleansed from all sin; and if ye are purified and cleansed from all sin, ye shall ask whatsoever you will in the name of Jesus and it shall be done: but know this, it shall be given you what you shall ask, and as ye are appointed to the head, the spirits shall be subject unto you: wherefore it shall come to pass, that if you behold a spirit manifested that ye cannot understand, and you receive not that spirit, ye shall ask of the Father in the name of Jesus and if he give not unto you that spirit, then you may know that it is not of God; and it shall be given unto you power over that spirit, and you shall proclaim against that spirit with a loud voice, that it is not of God; not with railing accusation that ye be not overcome; neither with boasting, nor rejoicing, lest you be siezed therewit[h]: he that receiveth of God, let him account it of God, & let him rejoice that he is accounted of God worthy to receive & by giving heed & doing these things which ye have received, and which ye shall hereafter receive, and the kingdom is given unto you of the Father, and power to overcome all things, which is not ordained of him: and behold, verily I say unto you, blessed are you that hear these words of mine from the mouth of my servant, for your sins are forgiven you. Let my servant Joseph,   in whom I am well pleased, and my servant Parley,   go forth among the churches and strengthen them by the word of exhortation; and also

and on earth, the life, the light, the spirit and the power, sent forth by the will of the Father, through Jesus Christ his Son; but no man is possessor of all things except he be purified and   cleansed from all sin; and if ye are purified and cleansed from all sin, ye shall ask whatsoever you will in the name of Jesus and it shall be done: but know this, it shall be given you what you shall ask, and as ye are appointed to the head, the spirits shall be subject unto you: wherefore it shall come to pass, that if you behold a spirit manifested that ye cannot understand, and you receive not that spirit, ye shall ask of the Father in the name of Jesus and if he give not unto you that spirit, then ye may know that it is not of God: and it shall be given unto you power [p. 43] over that spirit, and you shall proclaim against that spirit with a loud voice, that it is not of God; not with railing accusation that ye be not overcome; neither with boasting, nor rejoicing, lest you be seized therewith: he that receives of God let him account it of God, and let him rejoice that he is accounted of God worthy to receive; and by giving heed and doing these things which ye have received, and which ye shall hereafter receive, and the kingdom is given unto you of the Father, and power to overcome all things, which are not ordained of him: and behold, verily I say unto you blessed are you that hear these words of mine from the mouth of my servant, for your sins are forgiven you. Let my servant Joseph Smith jr.[22] in whom I am well pleased, and my servant Parley P. Pratt, go forth among the churches and strengthen them by the word of exhortation; and also

---

22. "Smith jr." was added to this version, though both Revelation Book 1 (where "Wakefield" was inserted in this location) and Book of Commandments chapter 53 (where "(W.)" was printed in this location) indicate that this "Joseph" does not refer to JS but Joseph Wakefield. (See *JSP*, MRB:141.)

my servant John,   or as many of my servants as are ordaided unto this office, and let them labor in the vineyard; and let no man hinder them of doing that which I have appointed unto them: wherefore in this thing my servant Edward   is not justified, nevertheless let him repent and he shall be forgiven. Behold ye are little children, and ye cannot bear all things now; ye must grow in grace and in the knowledge of the truth.   Fear not, little children, for you are mine, and I have overcome the world, and you are of them that my Father hath given me; and none of them which my Father hath given me shall be lost: and the Father and I are one: I am in the Father and the Father in me: and inasmuch as ye have received me ye are in me, and I in you: wherefore I am in your midst; and I am the good shepherd; and the day com[e]th that you shall hear my voice and see me, and know that I am. Watch, therefore, that ye may be ready; even so: Amen. [p. [1]]

my servant John Whitmer,[23] or as many of my servants as are ordained unto this office, and let them labor in the vineyard; and let no man hinder them of doing that which I have appointed unto them: wherefore in this thing my servant Edward Partridge is not justified, nevertheless let him repent and he shall be forgiven. Behold ye are little children, and ye cannot bear all things now; ye must grow in grace and in the knowledge of the truth.— Fear not, little children, for you are mine, and I have overcome the world, and you are of them that my Father has given me; and none of them which my Father has given me shall be lost: and the Father and I are one: I am in the Father and the Father in me: and inasmuch as ye have received me ye are in me, and I in you: wherefore I am in your midst; and I am the good Shepherd; and the day comes that you shall hear my voice and see me, and know that I am. Watch, therefore, that ye may be ready; even so: Amen.

September 1832

Revelations.
[24]A REVELATION, GIVEN
SEPTEMBER, 1830.

REVELATIONS.
[25]A REVELATION GIVEN
SEPTEMBER, 1830.

LISTEN to the voice of Jesus Christ, your Redeemer, the great I am, whose arm of mercy hath atoned for your sins; who will

Listen to the voice of Jesus Christ, your Redeemer, the great I am, whose arm of mercy has atoned for your sins; who will

---

23. "Whitmer" was added to this version, though both Revelation Book 1 (where "Carrill" was inserted in this location) and Book of Commandments chapter 53 (where "(C.,)" was printed in this location) indicate that this "John" does not refer to John Whitmer but John Corrill. (See *JSP*, MRB:141.)

24. Revelation, Sept. 1830–A, in "A Revelation, Given September, 1830," *The Evening and the Morning Star*, Sept. 1832, [2] [D&C 29]. This version reflects editing marks made in Revelation Book 1, indicating that the latter was used as a source text for the former. (See *JSP*, MRB:43–51.)

25. Revelation, Sept. 1830–A, in "A Revelation Given September, 1830," *Evening and Morning Star*, Sept. 1832 (Apr. 1835), 60–62 [D&C 29]. This version corresponds to the version in *The Evening and the Morning Star*, indicating that the latter was used as a source text for the former.

gather his people even as a hen gathereth her chickens under her wings, even as many as will hearken to my voice, and humble themselves before me, and call upon me in mighty prayer.— Behold, verily, verily I say unto you at this time your sins are forgiven you; therefore ye receive these things; but remember to sin no more, lest perils shall come upon you. Verily I say unto you, that ye are   chosen out of the world to declare my gospel with the sound of rejoicing, as with the voice of a trump: lift up your hearts and be glad for I am in your midst, and am your advocate with the Father; and it is his good will to give you the kingdom; and as it is written, Whatsoever ye shall ask in faith, being united in prayer according to my command, ye shall receive; and ye are called to bring to pass the gathering of mine elect, for mine elect hear my voice and harden not their hearts: Wherefore the decree hath gone forth from the Father, that they shall be gathered in unto one place, upon the face of this land, to prepare their hearts, and be prepared in all things, against the day when tribulation and desolation are sent forth upon the wicked: for the hour is nigh, and the day is soon at hand, when the earth will be ripe; and all the proud, and they that do wickedly, shall be as stubble, and I will burn them up, saith the Lord of hosts, that wickedness shall not be upon the earth; for the hour is nigh, and that which was spoken by mine apostles must be fulfilled; for as they spoke so shall it come to pass; for I will reveal myself from heaven with power and great glory, with all the hosts thereof, and dwell in righteousness with men on earth a thousand years, and the wicked shall not stand. And again, verily, verily I say unto you, and it hath gone forth in a firm decree, by the will of the Father, that mine apostles, the twelve which

gather his people even as a hen gathers her chickens under her wings, even as many as will hearken to my voice, and humble themselves before me, and call upon me in mighty prayer.   Behold, verily, verily I say unto you at this time your sins are forgiven you: therefore ye receive these things; but remember to sin no more, lest perils shall come upon you. Verily I say unto you, that ye are [p. 60] chosen out of the world to declare my gospel with the sound of rejoicing, as with the voice of a trump: lift up your hearts and be glad for I am in your midst, and am your advocate with the Father; and it is his good will to give you the kingdom; and as it is written, Whatsoever ye shall ask in faith, being united in prayer according to my command, ye shall receive; and ye are called to bring to pass the gathering of my elect, for my elect hear my voice and harden not their hearts: Wherefore the decree has gone forth from the Father, that they shall be gathered in unto one place, upon the face of this land, to prepare their hearts, and be prepared in all things, against the day when tribulation and desolation are sent forth upon the wicked: for the hour is nigh, and the day is soon at hand, when the earth will be ripe; and all the proud, and they that do wickedly, shall be as stuble, and I will burn them up, saith the Lord of hosts, that wickedness shall not be upon the earth; for the hour is nigh, and that which was spoken by my apostles must be fulfilled: for as they spoke so shall it come to pass: for I will reveal myself from heaven with power and great glory, with all the hosts thereof, and dwell in righteousness with men on earth a thousand years, and the wicked shall not stand. And again, verily, verily I say unto you, and it has gone forth in a firm decree, by the will of the Father, that my apostles, the twelve which were with me in my ministry at Jerusalem, shall stand at my right hand at the day of my coming in a pillar of fire, being clothed with robes of righteousness, with crowns upon their heads, in glory even as I am, to judge the whole house of Israel, even as many as have loved me and kept my commandments, and none else; for a trump shall sound both long and loud, even as upon mount Sinai, and all the earth shall quake, and they shall come forth, yea, even the dead which died in me, to receive a crown of righteousness, and to be clothed upon, even as I am, to be with me, that we may be one. But behold, I say unto you, that before this great day shall come, the sun shall be darkened, and the moon shall be turned into blood, and the stars shall fall from heaven; and there shall be great signs in the heavens above, and in the earth beneath; and there shall be weeping and wailing among the inhabitants of the earth; and there shall be a great hailstorm sent forth to destroy the crops of the earth: and it shall come to pass, because of the wickedness of the world, that I will take vengeance upon the wicked, for they will not repent: for the cup of mine indignation is full; for, behold my blood shall not cleanse them if they repent not: wherefore, I will send forth flies upon the face of the earth, which shall take hold of the inhabitants thereof, and shall eat their flesh, and shall cause maggots to come in upon them, and their tongues shall be stayed that they shall not utter against me, and their flesh shall fall from off their bones, and their eyes from their sockets: and it shall come to pass, that the beasts of the forests, and the fowls of the air, shall devour them up: and that great and abominable church, which is the whore of all the earth, shall be cast down by devouring fire, according as it was spoken by the mouth of Ezekiel the prophet,

were with me in my ministry at Jerusalem, shall stand at my right hand at the day of my coming in a pillar of fire, being clothed with robes of righteousness, with crowns upon their heads, in glory even as I am, to judge the whole house of Israel, even as many as have loved me and kept my commandments, and none else; for a trump shall sound both long and loud, even as upon mount Sinai, and all the earth shall quake, and they shall come forth, yea, even the dead who died in me, to receive a crown of righteousness, and to be clothed upon, even as I am, to be with me that we may be one. But behold, I say unto you, that before this great day shall come, the sun shall be darkened, and the moon shall be turned into blood, and the stars shall fall from heaven; and there shall be great signs in the heavens above, and in the earth beneath; and there shall be weeping and wailing among the inhabitants of the earth; and there shall be a great hailstorm sent forth to destroy the crops of the earth: and it shall come to pass, because of the wickedness of the world, that I will take vengeance upon the wicked, for they will not repent: for the cup of my indignation is full; for, behold my blood shall not cleanse them if they repent not: wherefore, I will send forth flies upon the face of the earth, which shall take hold of the inhabitants thereof, and shall eat their flesh, and shall cause maggots to come in upon them, and their tongues shall be stayed that they shall not utter against me, and their flesh shall fall from off their bones, and their eyes from their sockets: and it shall come to pass, that the beasts of the forests, and the fowls of the air, shall devour them up: and that great and abominable church, which is the whore of all the earth, shall be cast down by devouring fire, according as it was spoken by the mouth of Ezekiel the prophet, which spoke of these things, which have not come to pass as yet, but surely must, as I live, for abominations shall not reign.

And again, verily, verily I say unto you, that when the thousand years are ended, and men again begin to deny their God, then will I spare the earth but for a little season; and then the end shall come, and the heaven and the earth shall be consumed, and pass away, and there shall be a new heaven and a new earth; for all old things shall pass away, and all things become new, even the heaven and the earth, and all the fulness thereof, both men and beasts; the fowls of the air, and the fishes of the sea, and not one hair, neither moat, shall be lost, for it is the workmanship of mine hand. But verily I say unto you, before the earth shall pass away, Michael, mine archangel, shall sound his trump, and then shall all the dead awake, for the graves shall be opened, and they shall come forth, yea, even all; and the righteous shall be gathered on my right hand unto eternal life; and the wicked on my left hand will I be ashamed to own before the Father: wherefore I will say unto them, depart from me ye cursed into everlasting fire, prepared for the Devil and his angels. And now, behold I say unto you, never, at any time, have I declared from mine own mouth, that they should return, for where I am they can not come, for they have no power; but remember, that all my judgments are not given unto men, and as the words have gone forth out of my mouth, even so shall they be fulfilled, that the first shall be last, and that the last shall be first in all things, whatsoever I have created by the word of my power, which is the power of my spirit, for by the power of my spirit created I them, yea, all things both spiritual and temporal; firstly spiritual, secondly temporal, which is the beginning of my work: and

which spoke of these things, which have not come to pass as yet, but surely must, as I live, for abominations shall not reign.

And again, verily, verily I say unto you, that when the thousand years are ended, and men again begin to deny their God, then will I spare the earth but for a little season; and then the end shall come, and the heaven and the earth shall be consumed, and pass away, and there shall be a new heaven and a new earth; for all old things shall pass away, and all things become new, even the heaven and the earth, and all the fulness thereof, both men and beasts; the fowls of the air, and the fishes of the sea, and not one hair, neither moat, shall be lost, for it is the workmanship of my hand. But verily I say unto you, before the earth shall pass away, Michael, my archangel, shall sound his trump, and then shall all the dead awake, for the graves shall be opened, and they shall come forth, yea, even all; and the righteous shall be gathered on my right hand unto eternal life; and the wicked on my left hand will I be ashamed to own before the Father: wherefore I will say unto them, depart from me ye cursed into everlasting fire, prepared for the devil and his angels. And now, behold I say unto you, never, at any time, have I declared from my own mouth, that they should return, for where I am they can not come, for they have no power; but remember, that all my judgments are not given unto men, and as the words have gone forth out of my mouth, even so shall they be fulfilled, that the first shall be last, and the last shall be first in all things, whatsoever I have created by the word of my power, which is the power of my Spirit, for by the power of my Spirit created I them, yea, all things both spiritual and temporal; firstly spiritual, secondly temporal, which is the beginning of my work: and again, firstly temporal, and secondly spiritual, which is the last of my work, speaking unto you that ye may naturally understand, but unto myself my work hath no end, neither beginning; but it is given unto you, that ye may understand, because ye have asked it of me, and are agreed: wherefore, verily I say unto you, that all things unto me are spiritual, and not at any time have I given unto you a law which was temporal, neither any man, nor the children of men; neither Adam your father, whom I created; behold I gave unto him that he should be an agent unto himsilf; and I gave unto him a commandment, but no temporal commandment gave I unto him, for my commandments are spiritual; they are not natural, nor temporal, neither carnal nor sensual; and it came to pass, that Adam, being tempted of the Devil, for behold the Devil was before Adam, for he rebelled against me, saying, Give me thine honor, which is my power, and also a third part af the host of heaven turned he away from me because of their agency: and they were thrust down, and thus came the Devil and his angels; and behold, there is a place prepared for them from the beginning, which place is hell; & it must needs be that the Devil should tempt the children of men, or they could not be agents unto themselves, for if they never should have bitter, they could not know the sweet: Wherefore, it came to pass, that the Devil tempted Adam and he partook of the forbidden fruit, and transgressed the commandment, wherein he became subject to the will of the Devil, because he yielded unto temptation: wherefore, I the Lord God caused that he should be cast out from the garden of Eden, from my presence, because of his transgression; wherein he became spiritually dead, which is the first death, even that same death which, is the last death, which

again, firstly temporal, and secondly spiritual, which is the last of my work, speaking unto you that ye may naturally understand, but unto myself my work has no end, neither beginning; but it is given unto you, that ye may understand, because ye have asked it of me, and are agreed: wherefore, verily I say unto you, that all things unto me are spiritual, and not at any time have I given unto you a law which was temporal, neither any man, nor the children of men; neither Adam your father, whom I created; behold I gave unto him that he should be an agent unto himself; and I gave unto him a commandment, but no temporal commandment gave I unto him, for my commandments are spiritual; they are not natural, nor temporal, neither carnal nor sensual; and it came to pass, that Adam, being tempted of the devil, for behold the devil was before Adam, for he rebelled against me, saying, Give me thy honor, which is my power, and also a third part of the host of heaven turned he away from me because of their agency: and they were thrust down, and thus came the devil and his angels; and behold, there is a place prepared for them from the beginning, which place is hell; and it must needs be that the devil should tempt the children of men, or they could not be agents unto themselves, for if they never should have bitter, they could not know the sweet: Wherefore, it came to pass, that the devil tempted Adam and he partook of the forbidden fruit, and [p. 61] transgressed the commandment, wherein he became subject to the will of the devil, because he yielded unto temptation: wherefore, I the Lord God caused that he should be cast out from the garden of Eden, from my presence, because of his transgression; wherein he became spiritually dead, which is the first death, even that same death which, is the last death, which is spiritual, which shall be pronounced upon the wicked when I shall say, Depart ye cursed. But behold I say unto you, that I the Lord God gave unto Adam, and unto his seed, that they should not die as to the temporal death, until I the Lord God should send forth angels to declare unto them repentance and redemption through faith on the name of mine only begotton Son; aud thus did I the Lord God appoint unto man the days of his probation, that by his natural death he might be raised in immortality unto eternal life, even as many as would believe on my name, and they that believe not, unto eternal damnation, for they can not be redeemed from their spiritual fall, because they repent not, for they love darkness more than light, and their deads are evil, and they receive their wages of whom they list to obey. But behold, I say unto you, that little children are redeemed from the foundation of the world, through mine only begotton: Wherefore they can not sin, for power is not given to Satan to tempt little children until they begin to be accountable before me, for it is given unto them even as I will, according to mine own pleasure, that great things may be required at the hand of their fathers. And again, I say unto you, that whoso, having knowledge, have not I commanded to repent? and he that hath no understanding, it remaineth in me to do according as it is written. And now, behold, I declare no more unto you at this time. Amen.

is spiritual, which shall be pronounced upon the wicked when I shall say, depart ye cursed. But behold I say unto you, that I the Lord God gave unto Adam, and unto his seed, that they should not die as to the temporal death, until I the Lord God should send forth angels to declare unto them repentance and redemption through faith on the name of my only begotten Son; and thus did I the Lord God appoint unto man the days of his probation, that by his natural death he might be raised in immortality unto eternal life, even as many as would believe on my name, and they that believe not, unto eternal damnation, for they cannot be redeemed from their spiritual fall, because they repent not, for they love darkness more than light, and their deads are evil, and they receive their wages of whom they list to obey. But behold, I say unto you, that little children are redeemed from the foundation of the world, through my only begotton: Wherefore they cannot sin, for power is not given to satan to tempt little children until they begin to be accountable before me, for it is given unto them even as I will, according to my own pleasure, that great things may be required at the hand of their fathers. And again, I say unto you, that whoso, having knowledge, have not I commanded to repent? and he that has no understanding, it remains in me to do according as it is written. And now, behold, I declare no more unto you at this time.— Amen.

[26]A REVELATION ON PRAYER,
GIVEN OCTOBER 30, 1831.

HEARKEN, and lo, a voice as of one sent down from on high, who is mighty and powerful, whose going forth is unto the ends of the earth; yea, whose voice is unto men, Prepare ye the way of the Lord, make his paths strait. The keys of the kingdom of God, are committed unto man on the earth, and from thence shall the gospel roll forth unto the ends of the earth, as the stone which is hewn from the mountain without hands shall roll forth, until it has filled the whole earth; yea, a voice crying, Prepare ye the way of the Lord, prepare ye the supper of the Lamb, make ready for the bridegroom; pray unto the Lord; call upon his holy name; make known his wonderful works among the people; call upon the Lord; that his kingdom may go forth upon the earth; that the inhabitants thereof may receive it, and be prepared for the days to come, in the which the Son of man shall come down in heaven, clothed in the brightness of his glory, to meet the kingdom of God which is set up on the earth: Wherefore, may the kingdom of God go forth, that the kingdom of heaven may come, that thou O God may be glorified in heaven, so on earth, that thine enemies may be subdued; for thine is the honor, power and glory, forever and ever: Amen.

[27]A REVELATION ON PRAYER,
GIVEN OCTOBER 30, 1831.

Hearken, and lo, a voice as of one sent down from on high, who is mighty and powerful, whose going forth is unto the ends of the earth; yea, whose voice is unto men, Prepare ye the way of the Lord, make his paths strait. The keys of the kingdom of God, are committed unto man on the earth, and from thence shall the gospel roll forth unto the ends of the earth, as the stone which is hewn from the mountain without hands shall roll forth, until it has filled the whole earth; yea, a voice crying, Prepare ye the way of the Lord, prepare ye the supper of the Lamb, make ready for the bridegroom; pray unto the Lord; call upon his holy name; make known his wonderful works among the people; call upon the Lord; that his kingdom may go forth upon the earth; that the inhabitants thereof may receive it, and be prepared for the days to come, in the which the Son of man shall come down in heaven, clothed in the brightness of his glory, to meet the kingdom of God which is set up on the earth: Wherefore, may the kingdom of God go forth, that the kingdom of heaven may come, that thou O God may be glorified in heaven, so on earth, that thy enemies may be subdued; for thine is the honor, power and glory, forever and ever: Amen.

---

26. Revelation, 30 Oct. 1831, in "A Revelation on Prayer, Given October 30, 1831," *The Evening and the Morning Star,* Sept. 1832, [2] [D&C 65]. This version reflects editing marks made in Revelation Book 1, indicating that the latter was used as a source text for the former. (See *JSP,* MRB:197.)

27. Revelation, 30 Oct. 1831, in "A Revelation on Prayer, Given October 30, 1831," *Evening and Morning Star,* Sept. 1832 (Apr. 1835), 62 [D&C 65]. This version corresponds to the version in *The Evening and the Morning Star,* indicating that the latter was used as a source text for the former.

October 1832

Revelations.

[28]ITEMS OF LAW FOR THE GOVERNMENT OF THE CHURCH OF CHRIST, GIVEN FEBRUARY 23, 1831.

[29]EXTRACTS GIVEN 1831.

EVERY person who belongeth to this church of Christ, shall observe to keep all the commandments and covenants of the church; and it shall come to pass, that if any person among you shall kill, they shall be delivered up and dealt with according to the laws of the land; for remember that he hath no forgiveness; and it shall be proven according to the laws of the land. But if any man shall commit adultery, he shall be tried before two elders of the church or more; and every word shall be established against him by two witnesses of the church, and not of the world; but if there are more than two witnesses it is better; but he

shall be condemned by the mouth of two witnesses; and the elders shall lay the case before the church, and the church shall lift up their hands against them, that they may be dealt with according to the law; and if it can be, it is necessary that the bishop is present also. And thus ye shall do in all cases which shall come before you.

And if any man shall rob, he shall be delivered up unto the law; and if he shall steal, he shall be delivered up unto the law; and if he shall lie, he

And again, every person who belongeth to this church of Christ shall observe to keep all the commandments and covenants of the church: and it shall come to pass, that if any persons among you shall kill, they shall be delivered up and dealt with according to the laws of the land; for remember, that he hath no forgiveness; and it shall be proven according to the laws of the land. ¶ And if any man or woman shall commit adultery, he or she shall be tried before two elders of the church or more, and every word shall be established against him or her by two witnesses of the church, and not of the enemy. But if there are more than two witnesses it is better: but he or she shall be condemned by the mouth of two witnesses, and the elders shall lay the case before the church, and the church shall lift up their hands against him or her, that they may be dealt with according to the law of God. And if it can be, it is necessary that the bishop is present also. And thus ye shall do in all cases which shall come before you. ⏎

And if a man or woman shall rob, he or she shall be delivered up unto the law of the land. And if he or she shall steal, he or she shall be delivered up unto the law of the land. And if he or she shall lie, he

---

28. Excerpt of Revelation, 23 Feb. 1831, in "Items of Law for the Government of the Church of Christ, Given February 23, 1831," *The Evening and the Morning Star,* Oct. 1832, [2] [D&C 42:78–93]. This item is not found in Revelation Book 1; the source text for this item is unknown.

29. Excerpt of Revelation, 23 Feb. 1831, in "Extracts Given 1831," *Evening and Morning Star,* Oct. 1832 (June 1835), 74 [D&C 42:78–93]. This version corresponds to the version in *The Evening and the Morning Star,* indicating that the latter was used as a source text for the former.

shall be delivred up unto the law; if he do any manner of iniquity, he shall be delivered up unto the law, even that of God. And if thy brother offend thee, thou shalt take him between him & thee alone, and if he confess thou shalt be reconciled, and if he confess not, thou shalt deliver him up unto the church, not to the members, but to the elders; and it shall be done in a meeting and that not before the world. And if thy brother offend many, he shall be chastened before many; and if any one offend openly, he shall be rebuked openly, that he may be ashamed, and if he confess not, he shall be delivered up unto the law.

If any shall offend in secret, he shall be rebuked in secret, that he may have opportunity to confess in secret to him whom he has offended, and to God; that the brethren may not speak reproachfully of him. And thus shall ye conduct in all things.

or she shall be delivered up unto the law of the land. If he or she do any manner of iniquity, he or she shall be delivered up unto the law, even that of God. ¶ And if thy brother or sister offend thee, thou shalt take him or her between him or her and thee alone, and if he or she confess, thou shalt be reconciled. And if he or she confess not, thou shalt deliver him or her up unto the church, not to the members but to the elders. And it shall be done in a meeting, and that not before the world. And if thy brother or sister offend many, he or she shall be chastened before many. And if any one offend openly, he or she shall be rebuked openly, that he or she may be ashamed. And if he or she confess not, he or she shall be delivered up unto the law of God. If any shall offend in secret, he or she shall be rebuked in secret, that he or she may have opportunity to confess in secret to him or her whom he or she has offended, and to God, that the church may not speak reproachfully of him or her. And thus shall ye conduct in all things.

[30]EXTRACT OF A REVELATION GIVEN FEBRUARY, 1831.

AGAIN, I say hearken, ye elders of my church whom I have appointed: ye are not sent forth to be taught, but to teach the children of men the things which I have put into your hands, by the power of my spirit; and ye are to be taught from on high; sanctify yourselves and ye shall be

[31]Again I say, hearken ye elders of my church, whom I have appointed: ye are not sent forth to be taught, but to teach the children of men the things which I have put into your hands by the power of my Spirit; and ye are to be taught from on high. Sanctify yourselves and ye shall be

---

30. Excerpt of Revelation, Feb. 1831–A, in "Extract of a Revelation Given February, 1831," *The Evening and the Morning Star,* Oct. 1832, [2]–[3] [D&C 43:15–35]. This version reflects editing marks made in Revelation Book 1, indicating that the latter was used as a source text for the former. This publication excludes the initial portion of the revelation as copied into Revelation Book 1. (See *JSP,* MRB:109–113.)

31. Excerpt of Revelation, Feb. 1831–A, in "Extracts Given 1831," *Evening and Morning Star,* Oct. 1832 (June 1835), 74 [D&C 43:15–35]. This version closely corresponds to the version in chapter 45 of the Book of Commandments, suggesting that the latter was used as a source text for the former. This revelation is printed immediately following the preceding one, without a new title or any other demarcation.

endowed with power, that ye may give even as I have spoken: Hearken ye, for behold, the great day of the Lord is nigh at hand; for the day cometh that the Lord shall utter his voice out of heaven, the heavens shall shake and the earth shall tremble, and the trump of God shall sound, both long and loud, and shall say to the sleeping nations, Ye saints arise and live; ye sinners stay and sleep untill I shall call again. Wherefore, gird up your loins, lest ye are found among the wicked; lift up your voices and spare not, call upon the nations to repent, both old and young, both bond and free; saying, Prepare yourselves for the great day of the Lord, for if I, who am a man, do lift up my voice and call upon you to repent, and ye hate me, what will you say when the day cometh, when the thunders shall utter their voices from the ends of tbe earth, speaking in the ears of all that live, saying, Repent, and prepare [p. [2]] for the great day of the Lord; yea and again, when the lightnings shall streak forth from the east unto the west, and shall utter forth their voices unto all that live, and make the ears of all tingle that hear; saying these words, Repent ye, for the great day of the Lord is come.

And again, the Lord shall utter his voice out of heaven, saying, Hearken, O ye nations of the earth, and hear the words of that God who made you; O ye nations of the earth, how often would I have gathered you,　　　　as a hen gathereth her chickens under her wings, but ye would not; how oft have I called upon you by the mouth of my servants, and by the ministering of angels,

　　　　　　　　and by the voice of lightnings, and by the voice of tempests, and by the voice of earthquakes, and great hailstorms, and by the voice of famine and pestilence of every kind, and by the

endowed with power, that ye may give even as I have spoken. Hearken ye, for behold the great day of the Lord is nigh at hand. For the day cometh that the Lord shall utter his voice out of heaven; the heavens shall shake and the earth shall tremble, and the trump of God shall sound both long and loud, and shall say to the sleeping nations, Ye saints arise and live: ye sinners stay and sleep until I shall call again. Wherefore gird up your loins, lest ye be found among the wicked. Lift up your voices and spare not. Call upon the nations to repent, both old and young, both bond and free; saying, Prepare yourselves for the great day of the Lord: for if I, who am a man, do lift up my voice and call upon you to repent, and ye hate me, what will ye say when the day cometh when the thunders shall utter their voices from the ends of the earth, speaking to the ears of all that live, saying: Repent, and prepare　　　for the great day of the Lord? yea, and again, when the lightnings shall streak forth from the east unto the west, and shall utter forth their voices unto all that live, and make the ears of all tingle, that hear, saying these words: Repent ye, for the great day of the Lord is come!

And again, the Lord shall utter his voice out of heaven, saying: Hearken, O ye nations of the earth, and hear the words of that God who made you. O ye nations of the earth, how often would I have gathered you together as a hen gathereth her chickens under her wings, but ye would not? How oft have I called upon you by the mouth of my servants; and by the ministring of angels; and by mine own voice; and by the voice of thunderings; and by the voice of lightnings; and by the voice of tempests; and by the voice of earthquakes, and great hailstorms; and by the voice of famines, and pestilences of every kind; and by the great sound of a trump, and by the voice of judgments, and by the voice of mercy all the day long, and by the voice of glory, and honor, and the riches of eternal life; and would have saved you with an everlasting salvation, but ye would not; behold, the day has come when the cup of the wrath of mine indignation is full. Behold verily, I say unto you, that these are the words of the Lord your God. Wherefore labor ye, labor ye, in my vineyard for the last time, for the last time call ye upon the inhabitants of the earth; for in mine own due time will I come upon the earth in judgment, and my people shall be redeemed, and shall reign with me on earth, for the great millennial which I have spoken by the mouth of my servants, shall come; for satan shall be bound, and when he is loosed again, he shall only reign for a little season, and then cometh the end of the earth. And he that liveth in righteousness, shall be changed in the twinkling of an eye, and the earth shall pass away so as by fire and the wicked shall go away into unquenchable fire, and their end no man knoweth on earth, nor ever shall know until they come before me in judgment.— Hearken ye to these words, behold I am Jesus Christ, the Savior of the world; treasure these things up in your hearts, and let the solemnities of eternity rest upon your minds, be sober, keep all the commandments, even so: Amen.

great sound of a trump; and by the voice of judgment: and by the voice of mercy all the day long: and by the voice of glory, and honor, and the riches of eternal life; and would have saved you with an everlasting salvation, but ye would not? Behold the day has come, when the cup of the wrath of mine indignation is full. ¶ Behold, verily I say unto you, that these are the words of the Lord your God: wherefore, labor ye, labor ye, in my vineyard for the last time: for the last time call   upon the inhabitants of the earth, for in mine own due time will I come upon the earth in judgment: and my people shall be redeemed and shall reign with me on earth: for the great Millennial which I have spoken by the mouth of my servants, shall come; for satan shall be bound; and when he is loosed again, he shall only reign for a little season, and then cometh the end of the earth: and he that liveth in righteousness, shall be changed in the twinkling of an eye; and the earth shall pass away so as by fire; and the wicked shall go away into unquenchable fire; and their end no man knoweth, on earth, or ever shall know, until they come before me in judgment.   ¶ Hearken ye to these words; behold I am Jesus Christ the Savior of the world. Treasure these things up in your hearts, and let the solemnities of eternity rest upon your minds. Be sober. Keep all my commandments; even so: Amen. [p. 74]

[32]A REVELATION, GIVEN
NOVEMBER, 1831.

REVELATIONS.

[33]*A Revelation, given November, 1831, to
Orson Hyde, Luke Johnson, Lyman Johnson
and William E. McLelin. The mind and will
of the Lord, as made known by the voice of
the Spirit to a conference concerning certain
elders: and also certain items, as made
known, in addition to the covenants and
commandments:—*

MY servant, Orson, was called,
by his ordinance, to proclaim the everlasting gospel, by the spirit of the living God,
from people to people, and from land to
land, in the congregations of the wicked, in
their synagogues, reasoning with and expounding all scriptures unto them: And
behold and lo, this is an ensample unto all
those who were ordained unto this priesthood, whose mission is appointed unto
them to go forth: And this is the ensample
unto them, that they shall speak as they are
moved upon by the Holy Ghost; and whatsoever they shall speak, when moved upon
by the Holy Ghost, shall be scripture; shall
be the will of the Lord; shall be the mind
of the Lord; shall be the word of the Lord;
shall be the voice of the Lord, and the
power of God unto salvation; Behold this is
the promise of the Lord unto you, O ye my
servants: wherefore, be of good cheer, and
do not fear, for I the Lord am with you,
and will stand by you; and ye shall bear
record of me even Jesus Christ, that I am
the Son of the living God; that I was; that I
am; and that I am to come. This is the
word of the Lord unto you my servant,
Orson; and also unto my servant,

My servant, Orson Hyde, was called,
by his ordinance, to proclaim the everlasting gospel, by the spirit of the living God,
from people to people, and from land to
land, in the congregations of the wicked, in
their synagogues, reasoning with and expounding all scriptures unto them: And
behold and lo, this is an ensample unto all
those who were ordained unto this priesthood, whose mission is appointed unto
them to go forth: And this is the ensample
unto them, that they shall speak as they are
moved upon by the Holy Ghost; and whatsoever they shall speak, when moved upon
by the Holy Ghost, shall be scripture; shall
be the will of the Lord; shall be the mind
of the Lord; shall be the word of the Lord;
shall be the voice of the Lord, and the
power of God unto salvation; Behold this is
the promise of the Lord unto you, O ye my
servants: wherefore, be of good cheer, and
do not fear, for I the Lord am with you,
and will stand by you; and ye shall bear
record of me even Jesus Christ, that I am
the Son of the living God; that I was; that I
am; and that I am to come. This is the
word of the Lord unto you my servant,
Orson Hyde; and also unto my servant,

---

32. Revelation, 1 Nov. 1831–A, in "A Revelation, Given November, 1831," *The Evening and the Morning
Star*, Oct. 1832, [3] [D&C 68]. This version reflects editing marks made in Revelation Book 1, indicating
that the latter was used as a source text for the former. (See *JSP*, MRB:199–201.)

33. Revelation, 1 Nov. 1831–A, in "Revelations," *Evening and Morning Star*, Oct. 1832 (June 1835),
73–74 [D&C 68]. This version reflects editing marks made in Revelation Book 1, indicating that the latter was used as a source text for the former. (See *JSP*, MRB:199–201.)

Luke, and unto my servant,
Lyman, and unto my servant
William; and unto all the faithful elders of my church: Go ye into all the world; preach the gospel to every creature; acting in the authority which I have given you; baptizing in the name of the Father, and of the Son, and of the Holy Ghost; and he that believeth, and is baptized, shall be saved, and he that believeth not shall be damned; and he that believeth shall be blessed with signs following, even as it is written: And unto you it shall be given to know the signs of the times, and the signs of the coming of the Son of man; and of as many as the Father shall bear record, to you it shall be given power to seal them up unto eternal life: Amen.

And now, concerning the items in addition to the Laws and commandments, they are these: There remaineth hereafter in the due time of the Lord,other bishops to be set apart unto the church, to minister even according to the first; wherefore it shall be an high priest who is worthy; and he shall be appointed by a conference of high priests.

Luke Johnson, and unto my servant, Lyman Johnson, and unto my servant William E. McLelin; and unto all the faithful elders of my church: Go ye into all the world; preach the gospel to every creature; acting in the authority which I have given you; baptizing in the name of the Father, and of the Son, and of the Holy Ghost; and he that believeth, and is baptized, shall be saved, and he that believeth not shall be damned; and he that believeth shall be blessed with signs following, even as it is written: And unto you it shall be given to know the signs of the times, and the signs of the coming of the Son of man; and of as many as the Father shall bear record, to you it shall be given power to seal them up unto eternal life: Amen.

And now concerning the items in addition to the covenants and commandments, they are these; there remaineth hereafter, in the due time of the Lord, other bishops to be set apart unto the church to minister even according to the first: Wherefore they shall be high priests who are worthy, and they shall be appointed by the first presidency of the Melchisedek priesthood, except they be literal descendants of Aaron; and if they be literal descendants of Aaron, they have a legal right to the bishopric, if they are the first born among the sons of Aaron: for the first born holds the right of presidency over this priesthood, and the keys or authority of the same. No man has a legal right to this office, to hold the keys of this priesthood, except he be a literal descendant and the first born of Aaron: but as a high priest of the Melchizedek priesthood, has authority to officiate in all the lesser offices, he may officiate in the office of bishop when no literal descendant of Aaron can be found; provided he is called and set apart, and ordained unto this power under the hands of the first presi-

And again, no bishop or judge, which
shall be set apart for this ministry, shall be
tried or condemned for any crime, save it be
before a conference of high priests;
and in as much as he is found guilty before
a conference of highpriests, by testimony
that cannot be impeached, he shall be condemned   or forgiven, according to the laws
                              of the church. And again,
in as much as parents have children in Zion,

that teach them not to understand the doctrine of repentance; faith in Christ the Son
of the living God; and of baptism and the
gift of the Holy Ghost by the laying on of
the hands, when eight years old: the sin be
upon the head of the parents, for this shall
be a law unto the inhabitants of Zion,

                                        and
their children shall be baptized for the remission of their sins when eight years old, and
receive the laying on of the hands: and they
also shall teach their children to pray, and
to walk uprightly before the Lord. And the
inhabitants of Zion shall also observe the
sabbath day to keep it holy. And the inhabitants of Zion, also, shall remember their
labors, in as much as they are appointed to
labor, in all faithfulness, for the idler shall
be had in remembrance before the Lord.

dency of the Melchizedek priesthood. And
a literal descendant of Aaron, also, must be
designated by this presidency, and found
worthy, and annointed, and ordained under
the hands of this presidency, otherwise
they are not legally authorized to officiate
in their priesthood: but by virtue of the decree concerning their right of the priesthood descending from father to son, they
may claim their annointing, if at any time
they can prove their lineage, or do ascertain it by revelation from the Lord under
the hands of the above named presidency.
¶ And again, no bishop or high priest, who
shall be set apart for this ministry, shall be
tried or condemned for any crime save it be
before the first presidency of the church;
and inasmuch as he is found guilty before
this presidency,   by testimony
that cannot be impeached, he shall be condemned, and if he repents he shall be forgiven, according to the covenants and commandments of the church. ¶ And again,
inasmuch as parents have children in Zion,
or in any of her stakes which are organized,
that teach them not to understand the doctrine of repentance; faith in Christ the Son
of the living God; and of baptism and the
gift of the Holy Ghost by the laying on of
the hands, when eight years old: the sin be
upon the head of the parents, for this shall
be a law unto the inhabitants of Zion, or in
any of her stakes which are organized, and
their children shall be baptized for the remission of their sins when eight years old, and
receive the laying on of the hands: and they
shall also teach their children to pray, and
to walk uprightly before the Lord. And the
inhabitants of Zion shall also observe the
Sabbath day to keep it holy. And the inhabitants of Zion, also, shall remember their
labors, inasmuch as they are appointed to
labor, in all faithfulness, for the idler shall
be had in remembrance before the Lord.

Now I the Lord am not well pleased
with the inhabitants of Zion, for there are
idlers among them; and their children are
also growing up in wickedness: They also
seek not earnestly the riches of eternity, but
their eyes are full of greediness. These
things ought not to be, and must be done
away from among them: wherefore let my
servant Oliver,   carry these sayings unto the land of Zion. And a commandment I give unto them, that he that
observeth not his prayers before the Lord
in the season thereof, let him be had in
rememberance before the judge of my people. These sayings are true and faithful:
wherefore transgress them not, neither take
therefrom. Behold I am Alpha and Omega,
and I come quickly: Amen.

Now I the Lord am not well pleased [p. 73]
with the inhabitants of Zion, for there are
idlers among them; and their children are
also growing up in wickedness: They also
seek not earnestly the riches of eternity, but
their eyes are full of greediness. These
things ought not to be, and must be done
away from among them: wherefore let my
servant Oliver Cowdery, carry these sayings unto the land of Zion. And a commandment I give unto them, that he that
observeth not his prayers before the Lord
in the season thereof, let him be had in
remembrance before the judge of my people. These sayings are true and faithful:
wherefore transgress them not, neither take
therefrom. Behold I am Alpha and Omega,
and I come quickly: Amen.

November 1832

Revelations.
[34]REVELATION, GIVEN MAY, 1831.

HEARKEN unto my word, my servant
Sidney, and Parley, and Lemon, for behold,
verily I say unto you, that I give unto you a
commandment, that you shall go and
preach my gospel, which ye have received,
even as ye have received it, unto the Shakers.
Behold I say unto you, that they desire to
know the truth in part, but not all, for they
are not right before me, and must needs
repent: wherefore I send you, my servants
Sidney and Parley, to preach the gospel
unto them; and my servant Lemon shall be

REVELATION.
[35]*Revelation, to Sidney Rigdon, Parley P.
Pratt, and Lemon Copley, given May,* 1831.

Hearken unto my word, my servant
Sidney, and Parley, and Lemon, for behold,
verily I say unto you, that I give unto you a
commandment, that you shall go and
preach my gospel, which ye have received,
even as ye have received it, unto the shakers.
Behold I say unto you, that they desire to
know the truth in part, but not all, for they
are not right before me, and must needs
repent: wherefore I send you, my servants
Sidney and Parley, to preach the gospel
unto them; and my servant Lemon shall be

34. Revelation, 7 May 1831, in "Revelation, Given May, 1831," *The Evening and the Morning Star,* Nov. 1832, [7] [D&C 49]. This version reflects editing marks made in Revelation Book 1, indicating that the latter was used as a source text for the former. (See *JSP,* MRB:133–137.)

35. Revelation, 7 May 1831, in "Revelation," *Evening and Morning Star,* Nov. 1832 (Sept. 1835), 93–94 [D&C 49]. This version closely corresponds to the version in section 65 of the 1835 Doctrine and Covenants, suggesting that the latter was used as a source text for the former.

ordained unto this work, that he may reason with them, not according to that which he has received of them, but according to that which shall be taught him by you, my servants, and by so doing I will bless him, otherwise he shall not prosper: Thus saith the Lord, for I am God and have sent mine only begotten Son into the world, for the redemption of the world, and have decreed, that he that receiveth him shall be saved, and he that receiveth him not, shall be damned: and they have done unto the son of Man even as they listed; and he has taken his power on the right hand of his glory, and now reigneth in the heavens, and will reign till he descends on the earth to put all enemies under his feet: which time is nigh at hand: I the Lord God have spoken it; but the hour and the day no man knoweth, neither the angels in heaven, nor shall they know until he come: wherefore I will that all men shall repent, for all are under sin, except them which I have reserved unto myself, holy men that ye know not of: wherefore I say unto you, that I have sent unto you mine everlasting covenant, even that which was from the beginning, and that which I have promised I have so fulfilled, and the nations of the earth shall bow to it; and, If not of themselves, they shall come down, for that which is now exalted of itself, shall be laid low of power: wherefore I give unto you a commandment, that ye go among this people and say unto them, like unto mine apostle of old, whose name was Peter: Believe on the name of the Lord Jesus, who was on the earth and is to come, the beginning and the end; repent and be baptized in the name of Jesus Christ, according to the holy commandment, for the remission of sins; and whoso doeth this shall receive the gift of the Holy Ghost, by the laying on of the hands of the elders of this church.

ordained unto this work, that he may reason with them, not according to that which he has received of them, but according to that which shall be taught him hy you, my servants, and by so doing I will bless him, otherwise he shall not prosper: thus saith the Lord, for I am God and have sent mine only begotten Son into the world, for the redemption of the world, and have decreed that he that receiveth him shall be saved, and he that reciveth him not, shall be damned. ¶ And they have done unto the Son of man even as they listed; and he has taken his power on the right hand of his glory, and now reigneth in the heavens, and will reign till he descends on the earth to put all enemies under his feet: which time is nigh at hand: I the Lord God have spoken it: but the hour and the day no man knoweth, neither the angels in heaven, nor shall they know until he comes: wherefore I will that all men shall repent, for all are under sin, except them which I have reserved unto myself, holy men that ye know not of: wherefore I say unto you, that I have sent unto you mine everlasting covenant, even that which was from the beginning, and that which I have promised I have so fulfilled, and the nations of the earth shall bow to it; and, if not of themselves, they shall come down, for that which is now exalted of itself, shall be laid low of power: wherefore I give unto you a commandment, that ye go among this people and say unto them, like unto mine apostle of old, whose name was Peter: Believe on the name of the Lord Jesus, who was on the earth, and is to come, the beginning and the end; repent and be baptized in the name of Jesus Christ, according to the holy commandment, for the remission of sins; and whoso doeth this, shall receive the gift of the Holy Ghost, by the laying on of the hands of the elders of this church.

And again: I say unto you, that whoso forbideth to marry is not ordained of God, for marriage is ordained of God unto man: wherefore it is lawful that he should have one wife, and they twain shall be one flesh, and all this that the earth might answer the end of its creation; and that it might be filled with the measure of man, according to his creation before the world was made. And whoso forbiddeth to abstain from meats, that man should not eat,   is not ordained of God; for behold the beasts of the field, and the fowls of the air, and that which cometh of the earth, is ordained for the use of man, for food, and for raiment, and that he might   have in abundance, but it is not given that one man should possess that which is above another: wherefore the world lieth in sin; and wo be unto man that sheddeth blood, or that wasteth flesh and hath no need. And again: verily I say unto you, that the son of Man cometh not in the form of a woman, neither of a man travelling on the earth: wherefore be not deceived but continue in steadfastness, looking forth for the heavens to be shaken; and the earth to tremble, and to reel to and fro as a drunken man; and for the valleys to be exalted; and for the mountains to be made low; and for the rough places to become smooth; and all this when the angel shall sound his trumpet, but before the great day of the Lord shall come, Jacob shall flourish in the wilderness; and the Lamanites shall blossom as the rose; Zion shall flourish upon the hills, and rejoice upon the mountains, and shall be assembled together unto the place which I have appointed. Behold I say unto you, Go forth as I have commanded you; repent of all your sins; ask and ye shall receive; knock and it shall be opened unto you: Behold I will go before you, and be your rereward; and I will be in your midst,

And again, I say unto you, that whoso forbiddeth to marry, is not ordained of God, for marriage is ordained of God unto man: wherefore it is lawful that he should have one wife, and they twain shall be one flesh, and all this that the earth might answer the end of its creation; and that it might be filled with the measure of man, according to his creation before the world was made. And whoso forbiddeth to abstain from meats, that man should not eat the same, is not ordained of God; for behold the beasts of the field, and the fowls of the air, and that which cometh of the earth, is ordained for the use of man, for food, and for raiment, and that he might [p. 93] have in abundance, but it is not given that one man should possess that which is above another: wherefore the world lieth in sin: and wo be unto man that sheddeth blood or that wasteth flesh and hath no need. ¶ And again, verily I say unto you, that the Son of man cometh not in the form of a woman, neither of a man travelling on the earth: wherefore be not deceived, but continue in steadfastness, looking forth for the heavens to be shaken: and the earth to tremble, and to reel to and fro as a drunken man; and for the valleys to be exalted; and for the mountains to be made low; and for the rough places to become smooth: and all this when the angel shall sound his trumpet. ¶ But before the great day of the Lord shall come, Jacob shall flourish in the wilderness; and the Lamanites shall blossom as the rose; Zion shall flourish upon the hills, and rejoice upon the mountains, and shall be assembled together unto the place which I have apointed. Behold I say unto you, go forth as I have commanded you; repent of all your sins; ask and ye shall receive; knock and it shall be opened unto you: behold I will go before you, and be your re-reward; and I will be in your midst, and you shall not be confounded: Behold I am Jesus Christ, and I come quickly; even so: Amen.

and you shall not be confounded: behold I am Jesus Christ, and I come quickly; Even so. Amen.

December 1832

³⁶A REVELATION GIVEN AUGUST, 1831.

BEHOLD, and hearken unto the voice of him who has all power, who is from everlasting to everlasting, even Alpha and Omega, the beginning and the end. Behold, verily thus saith the Lord unto you O ye elders of my church, who are assembled upon this spot, whose sins are now forgiven you, for I the Lord forgiveth sins, and am merciful unto those who confess their sins with humble hearts:

But verily I say unto you, that it is not needful for this whole company of mine elders, to be moving swiftly upon the waters, whilst the inhabitants on either side are perishing in unbelief: nevertheless, I suffered it that ye might bear record: behold there are many dangers upon the waters and more especially hereafter, for I the Lord have decreed, in mine anger, many destructions upon the waters; yea, and especially upon these waters: nevertheless, all flesh is in mine hand, and he that is faithful among you, shall not perish by the waters.

Wherefore it is expedient that my servant Sidney (G.)   and my servant William, (P.)   be in haste upon their errand and mission: nevertheless I would not suffer that ye should part until you are

³⁷REVELATION GIVEN AUGUST, 1831.

Behold, and hearken unto the voice of him who has all power, who is from everlasting to everlasting, even Alpha and Omega, the beginning and the end. Behold, verily thus saith the Lord unto you O ye elders of my church, who are assembled upon this spot, whose sins are now forgiven you, for I the Lord forgiveth sins, and am merciful unto those who confess their sins with humble hearts: ↵

but verily I say unto you, that it is not needful for this whole company of mine elders, to be moving swiftly upon the waters, whilst the inhabitants on either side are perishing in unbelief: nevertheless, I suffered it that ye might bear record: behold there are many dangers upon the waters and more especially hereafter, for I the Lord have decreed, in mine anger, many destructions upon the waters; yea, and especially upon these waters: nevertheless, all flesh is in mine hand, and he that is faithful among you, shall not perish by the waters.

Wherefore it is expedient that my servant Sidney Gilbert, and my servant William W. Phelps, be in haste upon their errand and mission: nevertheless I would not suffer that ye should part until you are

---

36. Revelation, 12 Aug. 1831, in "A Revelation Given August, 1831," *The Evening and the Morning Star*, Dec. 1832, [5] [D&C 61]. This version reflects editing marks made in Revelation Book 1, indicating that the latter was used as a source text for the former. (See *JSP*, MRB:175–179.)

37. Revelation, 12 Aug. 1831, in "Revelation Given August, 1831," *Evening and Morning Star*, Dec. 1832 (Apr. 1836), 105–106 [D&C 61]. This version closely corresponds to the version in section 71 of the 1835 Doctrine and Covenants, suggesting that the latter was used as a source text for the former.

chastened for all your sins, that you might be one; that you might not perish in wickedness; but now verily I say, it behooveth me that ye should part: wherefore let them my servants, Sidney   and William,

take their former company, and let them take their journey in haste that they may fill their mission, and through faith they shall overcome; and inasmuch as they are faithful, they shall be preserved, and I the Lord will be with them.

And let the residue take that which is needful for clothing; let my servant Sidney   take that which is not needful with him, as you shall agree.

And now behold, for your good I gave unto you a commandment concerning these things: and I the Lord will reason with you as with men in days of old.

Behold I the Lord in the beginning, blessed the waters, but in the last days by the mouth of my servant John, I cursed the waters: Wherefore, the days will come that no flesh shall be safe upon the waters, and it shall be said in days to come, that none is able to go up to the land of Zion, upon the waters, but he that is upright in heart.

And, as I the Lord in the beginning cursed the land, even so in the last days have I blessed it, in its time, for the use of my saints, that they may partake the fatness thereof.

And now I give unto you a commandment, and what I say unto one I say unto all, that you shall forewarn your brethren concerning these waters, that they come not in journeying upon them, lest their faith fail and they are caught in her snares: I the Lord have decreed, & the Destroyer rideth upon the face thereof, and I revoke not the decree:

I the Lord was angry with you yesterday, but today mine anger is turned away: wherefore let those concerning whom I

chastened for all your sins, that you might be one; that you might not perish in wickedness; but now verily I say, it behooveth me that ye should part: wherefore let   my servants Sidney Gilbert and William W. Phelps, take their former company, and let them take their journey in haste that they may fill their mission, and through faith they shall overcome; and inasmuch as they are faithful, they shall be preserved, and I the Lord will be with them. ↵

And let the residue take that which is needful for clothing. Let my servant Sidney Gilbert take that which is not needful with him, as you shall agree. ↵

And now behold, for your good I gave unto you a commandment concerning these things; and I the Lord will reason with you as with men in days of old. [p. 105]

Behold I the Lord in the beginning, blessed the waters, but in the last days by the mouth of my servant John, I cursed the waters: wherefore, the days will come that no flesh shall be safe upon the waters, and it shall be said in days to come, that none is able to go up to the land of Zion, upon the waters, but he that is upright in heart. ↵

And, as I the Lord in the begininng cursed the land, even so in the last days have I blessed it, in its time, for the use of my saints, that they may partake the fatness thereof. ↵

And now I give unto you a commandment, and what I say unto one I say unto all, that you shall forewarn your brethren concerning these waters, that they come not in journeying upon them, lest their faith fail and they are caught in her snares: I the Lord have decreed, and the destroyer rideth upon the face thereof, and I revoke not the decree: ↵

I the Lord was angry with you yesterday, but to-day mine anger is turned away. Wherefore let those concerning whom I have spoken, that should take their journey in haste: again I say unto you, let them take their journey in haste, and it mattereth not to me, after a little, if it so be that they fill their mission, whether they go by water or by land: let this be as it is made known unto them according to their judgments, hereafter.

And now, concerning my servants Sidney,   and Joseph,   and Oliver,   let them come not again upon the waters, save it be upon the canal, while journeying unto their homes, or in other words they shall not come upon the waters to journey, save upon the canal.

Behold I the Lord have appointed a way for the journeying of my saints, and behold this is the way: That after they leave the canal, they shall journey by land, inasmuch as they are commanded to journey and go up unto the land of Zion; and they shall do like unto the children of Israel, pitching their tents by the way.

And behold this commandment, you shall give unto all your brethren: nevertheless unto whom it is given power to command the waters, unto him it is given by the Spirit, to know all his ways: wherefore let him do as the Spirit of the living God commandeth him, whether upon the land or upon the waters, as it remaineth with me to do hereafter; and unto you it is given the course for the saints, or the way for the saints of the camp of the Lord, to journey.

And again: verily I say unto you, my servants Sidney,   and Joseph,   and Oliver,   shall not open their mouths in the congregations of the wicked, until they arrive at Cincinnati; and in that place they shall lift up their voices unto God against that people; yea, unto him whose anger is kindled against their wickedness; a people which is well ripened for destruction; and from thence

have spoken, that should take their journey in haste, again I say unto you, let them take their journey in haste, and it mattereth not to me, after a little, if it so be that they fill their mission, whether they go by water or by land: let this be as it is made known unto them according to their judgments, hereafter.

And now, concerning my servants Sidney Rigdon, and Joseph Smith, jr. and Oliver Cowdery, let them come not again upon the waters, save it be upon the canal, while journeying unto their homes, or in other words, they shall not come upon the waters to journey, save upon the canal. ↵

Behold I the Lord have appointed a way for the journeying of my saints, and behold this is the way: that after they leave the canal, they shall journey by land, inasmuch as they are commanded to journey and go up unto the land of Zion; and they shall do like unto the children of Israel, pitching their tents by the way.

And behold this commandment you shall give unto all your brethren: nevertheless unto whom it is given power to command the waters, unto him it is given by the Spirit to know all his ways: wherefore let him do as the Spirit of the living God commandeth him, whether upon the land or upon the waters, as it remaineth with me to do hereafter; and unto you it is given the course for the saints, or the way for the saints of the camp of the Lord, to journey. ↵

And again, verily I say unto you, my servants Sidney Rigdon, and Joseph Smith, jr. and Oliver Cowdery, shall not open their mouths in the congregations of the wicked, until they arrive at Cincinnati; and in that place they shall lift up their voices unto God against that people: yea, unto him whose anger is kindled against their wickedness; a people who is well nigh ripened for destruction; and from thence let them journey for the congregations of their brethren, for their labors, even now, are wanted more abundantly among them, than among the congregations of the wicked.

And now concerning the residue, let them journey and declare the word among the congregations of the wicked, inasmuch as it is given, and inasmuch as they do this they shall rid their garments, and they shall be spotless before me; and let them journey together, or two by two, as seemeth them good, only let my servant Reynolds,
and my servant Samuel,
with whom I am well pleased, be not separated until they return to their homes, and this for a wise purpose in me.

And now, verily I say unto you, and what I say unto one I say unto all, be of good cheer little children for I am in your midst, and I have not forsaken you, and inasmuch as you have humbled yourselves before me, the blessings of the kingdom are yours: gird up your loins and be watchful, and be sober, looking forth for the coming of the Son of man, for he cometh in an hour you think not. Pray always that you enter not into temptation, that you may abide the day of his coming, whether in life or in death; even so: Amen.

let them journey for the congregations of their brethren, for their labors, even now, are wanted more abundantly among them, than among the congregations of the wicked.

And now concerning the residue, let them journey and declare the word among the congregations of the wicked, inasmuch as it is given, and inasmuch as they do this they shall rid their garments, and they shall be spotless before me; and let them journey together, or two by two, as seemeth them good, only let my servant Reynolds Cahoon, and my servant Samuel H. Smith, with whom I am well pleased, be not separated until they return to their homes, and this for a wise purpose in me. ⏎

And now verily I say unto you, and what I say unto one I say unto all, be of good cheer little children, for I am in your midst, and I have not forsaken you, and inasmuch as you have humbled yourselves before me, the blessings of the kingdom are yours. Gird up your loins and be watchful, and be sober, looking forth for the coming of the Son of man, for he cometh in an hour you think not. Pray always that you enter not into temptation, that you may abide the day of his coming, whether in life or in death; even so. Amen.

[38]A REVELATION GIVEN DECEMBER 4, 1831.

HEARKEN and listen to the voice of the Lord, O ye people who have assembled yourselves together, who are the high priests of my church, to whom the kingdom and power have been given.

For verily thus saith the Lord, it is expedient in me, for a bishop to be appointed unto you, or of you unto the church in this part of the Lord's vineyard: and verily in this thing ye have done wisely, for it is required of the Lord, at the hand of every steward, to render an account of his stewardship, both in time and in eternity.

For he who is faithful and wise in time, is accounted worthy to inherit the mansions prepared for them of my Father.

Verily I say unto you, the elders of the church in this part of my vineyard, shall render an account of their stewardship, unto the bishop which shall be appointed of me, in this part of my vineyard.

These things shall be had on record to be handed over unto the bishop in Zion; and the duty of the bishop shall be made known by the commandments which have been given, and the voice of the conference.

And now, verily I say unto you, my servant Newel   is the man who shall be ap-[p. [5]]pointed, and ordained unto this power: This is the will of the Lord your God, your Redeemer; even so: Amen

[40]THE word of the Lord, in addition to the law which has been given, making known the duty of the bishop, which has

[39]REVELATION GIVEN DECEMBER, 1831.

Hearken and listen to the voice of the Lord, O ye   who have assembled yourselves together, who are the high priests of my church, to whom the kingdom and power has been given. ↵

For verily thus saith the Lord, it is expedient in me, for a bishop to be appointed unto you, or of you unto the church in this part of the Lord's vineyard: and verily in this thing ye have done wisely, for it is required of the Lord, at the hand of every steward, to render an account of his stewardship, both in time and in eternity. ↵

For he who is faithful and wise in time, is accounted worthy to inherit the mansions prepared for them of my Father. ↵

Verily I say unto you, the elders of the church in this part of my vineyard, shall render an account of their stewardship, unto the bishop which shall be appointed of me, in this part of my vineyard. ↵

These things shall be had on record to be handed over unto the bishop in Zion; and the duty of the bishop shall be made known by the commandments which have been given, and the voice of the conference.

And now, verily I say unto you, my servant Newel K. Whitney is the man who shall be appointed,   and ordained unto this power: this is the will of the Lord your God, your Redeemer; even so. Amen.

The word of the Lord, in addition to the law which has been given, making known the duty of the bishop, which has

---

38. Revelation, 4 Dec. 1831, in "A Revelation Given December 4, 1831," *The Evening and the Morning Star,* Dec. 1832, [5]–[6] [D&C 72]. This version reflects editing marks made in Revelation Book 1, indicating that the latter was used as a source text for the former. (See *JSP,* MRB:237–241.)

39. Revelation, 4 Dec. 1831, in "Revelation Given December, 1831," *Evening and Morning Star,* Dec. 1832 (Apr. 1836), 106–107 [D&C 72]. This version closely corresponds to the version in section 89 of the 1835 Doctrine and Covenants, suggesting that the latter was used as a source text for the former.

40. Extra leading separates this portion of the revelation from the preceding portion.

been ordained unto the church in this part of the vineyard; which is verily this:

To keep the Lord's storehouse; to receive the funds of the church in this part of the vineyard; to take an account of the elders as before has been commanded, and to administer to their wants, who shall pay for that which they receive, inasmuch as they have wherewith to pay; that this also may be consecrated to the good of the church, to the poor and needy:

And he who hath not wherewith to pay, an account shall be taken and handed over to the bishop in Zion, who shall pay the debt out of that which the Lord shall put into his hands:

And the labors of the faithful who labor in spiritual things, in administering the gospel and the things of the kingdom, unto the church, and unto the world, shall answer the debt unto the bishop in Zion:

Thus it cometh out of the church, for according to the law, every man that cometh up to Zion, must lay all things before the bishop in Zion.

And now, verily I say unto you, that as every elder in this part of the vineyard, must give an account of his stewardship unto the bishop in this part of the vineyard, a cirtificate   from the judge or bishop in this part of the vineyard, unto the bishop in Zion, rendereth every man acceptable, and answereth all things, for an inheritance, and to be received as a wise steward, and as a faithful laborer; otherwise he shall not be accepted of the bishop in Zion.

And now, verily I say unto you, let every elder who shall give an account unto the bishop of the church, in this part of the vineyard, be recommended by the church or churches, in which he labors, that he may render himself and his accounts approved in all things.

And again, let my servants who are

been ordained unto the church in this part of the vineyard; which is verily this: ⏎

to keep the Lord's storehouse; to receive the funds of the church in this part of the vineyard; to take an account of the elders as before has been commanded, and to administer to their wants, who shall pay for that which they receive, inasmuch as they have wherewith to pay; that this also may be consecrated to the good of the church, to the poor and needy: ⏎

and he who hath not wherewith to pay, an account shall be taken and handed over to the bishop in Zion, who shall pay the debt out of that which the Lord shall put into his hands: ⏎

and the labors of the faithful who labor in spiritual things, in administering the gospel and the things of the kingdom, unto the church, and unto the world, shall answer the debt unto the bishop in Zion: ⏎

thus it cometh out of the church, for according to the law every man that cometh up to Zion, must lay all things before the bishop in Zion.

And now, verily I say unto you, that as every elder in this part of the vineyard, must give an account of his stewardship unto the bishop in this part of the vineyard, a certifi-[p. 106]cate from the judge or bishop in this part of the vineyard, unto the bishop in Zion, rendereth every man acceptable, and answereth all things, for an inheritance, and to be received as a wise steward, and as a faithful laborer; otherwise he shall not be accepted of the bishop in Zion. ⏎

And now, verily I say unto you, let every elder who shall give an account unto the bishop of the church, in this part of the vineyard, be recommended by the church or churches, in which he labors, that he may render himself and his accounts approved in all things. ⏎

And again, let my servants who are

appointed as stewards over the literary concerns of my church, have claim for assistance upon the bishop or bishops, in all things, that the revelations may be published, and go forth unto the ends of the earth, that they also may obtain funds which shall benefit the church, in all things; that they also may render themselves approved in all things and be accounted as wise stewards.

And now, behold this shall be an ensample for all the extensive branches of my church, in whatsoever land they shall be established. And now I make an end of my sayings: Amen.

[41]A FEW words in addition to the laws of the kingdom, respecting the members of the church; they that are appointed by the Holy Spirit to go up unto Zion; and they who are privileged to go up unto Zion.

Let them carry up unto the bishop a certificate from three elders of the church, or a certificate from the bishop, otherwise he who shall go up unto the land of Zion, shall not be accounted as a wise steward. This also is an ensample: Amen.

appointed   stewards over the literary concerns of my church, have claim for assistance upon the bishop or bishops, in all things, that the revelations may be published, and go forth unto the ends of the earth, that they also may obtain funds which shall benefit the church, in all things: that they also may render themselves approved in all things and be accounted as wise stewards. ↵

And now, behold this shall be an ensample for all the extensive branches of my church, in whatsoever land they shall be established. And now I make an end of my sayings.— Amen.

A few words in addition to the laws of the kingdom, respecting the members of the church; they that are appointed by the Holy Spirit to go up unto Zion; and they who are privileged to go up unto Zion. ↵

Let them carry up unto the bishop a certificate from three elders of the church, or a certificate from the bishop, otherwise he who shall go up unto the land of Zion, shall not be accounted as a wise steward. This is also an ensample. Amen.

January 1833

Revelations.
[42]REVELATION GIVEN,
JANUARY 1831.

THUS saith the Lord your God, even Jesus Christ, the Great I AM, Alpha and Omega, the beginning and the end, the

REVELATIONS.
[43]REVELATION GIVEN
JANUARY, 1831.

Thus saith the Lord your God, even Jesus Christ, the great I AM, Alpha and Omega, the beginning and the end, the

---

41. Extra leading separates this portion of the revelation from the preceding portion.

42. Revelation, 2 Jan. 1831, in "Revelation Given, January 1831," *The Evening and the Morning Star,* Jan. 1833, [5]–[6] [D&C 38]. This version reflects editing marks made in Revelation Book 1, indicating that the latter was used as a source text for the former. (See *JSP,* MRB:69–75.)

43. Revelation, 2 Jan. 1831, in "Revelation Given January, 1831," *Evening and Morning Star,* Jan. 1833 (Apr. 1836), 125–126 [D&C 38]. This version closely corresponds to the version in section 12 of the 1835 Doctrine and Covenants, suggesting that the latter was used as a source text for the former.

same which looked upon the wide expanse of eternity, and all the seraphic hosts of heaven, before the world was made, the same which knoweth all things, for all things are present before mine eyes:

I am the same which spake and the world was made, and all things came by me: I am the same which hath taken the Zion of Enoch into mine own bosom:

And verily I say, even as many as have believed on my name, for I am Christ, and in mine own name, by the virtue of the blood which I have spilt, have I plead before the Father for them:

But behold the residue of the wicked have I kept in chains of darkness until the judgment of the great day, which shall come at the end of the earth, and even so will I cause the wicked to be kept, that will not hear my voice but harden their hearts, and wo, wo, wo is their doom.

But behold, verily, verily I say unto you, that mine eyes are upon you; I am in your midst and ye cannot see me, but the day soon cometh that ye shall see me and know that I am, for the vail of darkness shall soon be rent, and he that is not purified shall not abide the day: wherefore, gird up your loins and be prepared.

Behold the kingdom is yours and the enemy shall not overcome.

Verily I say unto you, that ye are clean but not all; and there is none else with whom I am well pleased, for all flesh is corruptible before me, and the powers of darkness prevail upon the earth, among the children of men, in the presence of all the host of heaven, which causeth silence to reign, and all eternity is pained, and the angels are waiting the great command, to reap down the earth, to gather the tares that they may be burned:

And behold the enemy is combined.

And now I show unto you a mystery, a

---

same which looked upon the wide expanse of eternity, and all the seraphic hosts of heaven, before the world was made: the same who knoweth all things, for all things are present before mine eyes: ⏎

I am the same who spake and the world was made, and all things came by me: I am the sam[e] who have taken the Zion of Enoch into mine own bosom: ⏎

and verily I say, even as many as have believed on my name, for I am Christ, and in mine own name, by the virtue of the blood which I have spilt, have I plead before the Father for them: ⏎

But behold the residue of the wicked have I kept in chains of darkness until the judgment of the great day, which shall come at the end of the earth; and even so will I cause the wicked to be kept, that will not hear my voice but harden their hearts, and wo, wo, wo is their doom.

But behold, verily, verily I say unto you, that mine eyes are upon you; I am in your midst and ye cannot see me, but the day soon cometh that ye shall see me and know that I am: for the vail of darkness shall soon be rent, and he that is not purified shall not abide the day: wherefore gird up your loins and be prepared. ⏎

Behold the kingdom is yours and the enemy shall not overcome.

Verily I say unto you,   ye are clean but not all: and there is none else with whom I am well pleased, for all flesh is corruptible before me, and the powers of darkness prevail upon the earth, am[o]ng the children of men, in the presence of all the hosts of heaven, which causeth silence to reign, and all eternity is pained, and the angels are waiting the great command to reap down the earth, to gather the tares that they may be burned: ⏎

and behold the enemy is combined.

And now I show unto you a mystery, a

thing which is had in secret chambers, to bring to pass even your destruction, in process of time, and ye knew it not, but now I tell it unto you, and ye are blessed, not because of your iniquity, neither your hearts of unbelief, for verily some of you are guilty before me; but I will be merciful unto your weakness.

Therefore, be ye strong from henceforth; fear not, for the kingdom is yours; and for your salvation I give unto you a commandment, for I have heard your prayers, and the poor have complained before me, and the rich have I made, and all flesh is mine, and I am no respecter to persons.

And I have made the earth rich, and behold it is my footstool: wherefore, again I will stand upon it: and I hold forth and deign to give unto you greater riches, even a land of promise; a land flowing with milk and honey, upon which there shall be no curse when the Lord cometh, and I will give it unto you for the land of your inheritance, if you seek it with all your hearts:

And this shall be my covenant with you, ye shall have it for the land of your inheritance, and for the inheritance of your children forever, while the earth shall stand, and ye shall possess it again in eternity, no more to pass away: but verily I say unto you, that in time ye shall have no king nor ruler, for I will be your King and watch over you:

Wherefore, hear my voice and follow me, and you shall be a free people, and ye shall have no laws but my laws,

 for I am your Law-giver, and what can stay my hand.

But verily I say unto you, teach one another according to the office wherewith I have appointed you, and let every man esteem his brother as himself, and practice virtue and holiness before me.

And again I say unto you, let every

thing wh[i]ch is had in secret chambers, to bring to pass even your destruction, in process of time, and ye knew it not, but now I tell it unto you, and ye are blessed, not because of your iniquity, neither your hearts of unbelief, for verily some of you are guilty before me; but I will be merciful unto your weakness. ⏎

Therefore, be ye strong from henceforth; fear not for the kingdom is yours: and for your salvation I give unto you a commandment, for I have heard your prayers, and the poor have complained before me, and the rich have I made, and all flesh is mine, and I am no respecter of persons. ⏎

And I have made the earth rich, and behold it is my footstool: wherefore, again I will stand upon it, and I hold forth and deign to give unto you greater riches, even a land of promise; a land flowing with milk and honey, upon which there shall be no curse when the Lord cometh: and I will give it unto you for the land of your inheritance, if you seek it with all you hearts: ⏎

and this shall be my covenant with you, ye shall have it for the land of your inheritance, and for the inheritance of your children forever, while the earth shall stand, and ye shall possess it again in eternity, no more to pass away. ¶ But verily I say unto you, that in time ye shall have no king nor ruler, for I will be your king and watch over you. ⏎

Wherefore, hear my voice and follow me, and you shall be a free people, and ye shall have no laws but my laws, when I come, for I am your Lawgiver, and what can stay my hand? ⏎

But verily I say unto you, teach one another according to the office wherewith I have appointed you, and let every man esteem his brother as himself, and practice virtue and holiness before me. ⏎

And again I say unto you, let every

man esteem his brother as himself: for what man among you, having twelve sons, and is no respecter to them, and they serve him obediently, and he saith unto the one, be thou clothed in robes and sit thou here; and to the other, be thou clothed in rags and sit thou there, and looketh upon his sons and saith I am just.

Behold, this I have given unto you a parable, and it is even as I am, I say unto you, be one; and if ye are not one, ye are not mine.

And again I say unto you, that the enemy in the secret chambers, seeketh your lives: ye hear of wars in far countries, and you say in your hearts   there will soon be great wars in far countries, but ye know not the hearts of them in your own land: I tell you these things because of your prayers:

Wherefore, treasure up wisdom in your bosoms, lest the wickedness of men reveal these things unto you, by their wickedness in a manner, which shall speak in your ears, with a voice louder than that which shall shake the earth: but if ye are prepared, ye shall not fear. [p. [5]]

And that ye might escape the power of the enemy, and be gathered unto me a righteous people without spot and blameless:

Wherefore, for this cause I gave unto you the commandment, that ye should go to the Ohio; and there I will give unto you my law & there you shall be endowed with power from on high, and from thence, whomsoever I will shall go forth among all nations, and it shall be told them what they shall do, for I have a great work laid up in store:

For Israel shall be saved, and I will lead them whithersoever I will, and no power shall stay my hand.

And now I give unto the church in these parts, a commandment, that certain

man esteem his brother as himself: for what man among you having twelve sons, and is no respecter to them, and they serve him obediently, and he saith unto the one, be thou clothed in robes and sit thou here; and to the other, be thou clothed in rags and sit thou there, and looketh upon his sons and saith I am just. [p. 125]

Behold, this I have given unto you a parable, and it is even as I am: I say unto you, be one; and if ye are not one, ye are not mine. ⏎

And again I say unto you, that the enemy in the secret chambers seeketh your lives: Ye hear of wars in far countries, and you say   that there will soon be great wars in far countries, but ye know not the hearts of them in your own land: I tell you these things because of your prayers: ⏎

wherefore, treasure up wisdom in your bosoms, lest the wickedness of men reveal these things unto you, by their wickedness, in a manner which shall speak in your ears, with a voice louder than that which shall shake the earth: but if ye are prepared, ye shall not fear.

And that ye might escape the power of the enemy, and be gathered unto me a righteous people, without spot and blameless: ⏎

wherefore, for this cause I gave unto you the commandment, that ye should go to the Ohio: and there I will give unto you my law; and there you shall be endowed with power from on high, and from thence, whomsoever I will shall go forth among all nations, and it shall be told them what they shall do: for I have a great work laid up in store: ⏎

for Israel shall be saved, and I will lead them whithersoever I will, and no power shall stay my hand.

And now I give unto the church in these parts, a commandment, that certain men among them shall be appointed, and they shall be appointed by the voice of the church; and they shall look to the poor and the needy, and administer to their relief, that they shall not suffer; and send them forth to the place which I have commanded them; and this shall be their work, to govern the affairs of the property of this church.

And they that have farms, that cannot be sold, let them be left or rented as seemeth them good.

See that all things are preserved, and when men are endowed with power from on high, and are sent forth, all these things shall be gathered unto the bosom of the church.

And if ye seek the riches which it is the will of the Father to give unto you, ye shall be the richest of all people, for ye shall have the riches of eternity: And it must needs be that the riches of the earth is mine to give:

But beware of pride lest ye become as the Nephites of old.

And again: I say unto you, I give unto you a commandment, that every man both elder, priest, teacher and also member, go to with his might, with the labor of his hands, to prepare and accomplish these things, which I have commanded.

And let your preaching be the warning voice, every man to his neighbor, in mildness and in meekness.

And go ye out from among the wicked. Save yourselves.

Be ye clean that bear the vessels of the Lord. Even so: Amen.

men among them shall be appointed, and they shall be appointed by the voice of the church: and they shall look to the poor and the needy, and administer to their relief, that they shall not suffer; and send them forth to the place which I have commanded them; and this shall be their work, to govern the affairs of the property of this church. ⏎

And they that have farms that cannot be sold, let them be left or rented as seemeth them good. ⏎

See that all things are preserved, and when men are endowed with power from on high, and   sent forth, all these things shall be gathered unto the bosom of the church.

And if ye seek the riches which it is the will of the Father to give unto you, ye shall be the richest of all people; for ye shall have the riches of eternity: and it must needs be that the riches of the earth is mine to give: ⏎

but beware of pride, lest ye become as the Nephites of old. ⏎

And again I say unto you, I give unto you a commandment, that every man, both elder, priest, teacher and also member, go to with his might, with the labor of his hands, to prepare and accomplish the things which I have commanded. ⏎

And let your preaching be the warning voice, every man   his neighbor, in mildness and in meekness. ⏎

And go ye out from among the wicked. Save yourselves. ⏎

Be ye clean that bear the vessels of the Lord; even so: Amen.

[44]ITEMS IN ADDITION TO THE LAWS FOR THE GOVERNMENT OF THE CHURCH OF CHRIST, GIVEN APRIL, 1832.

VERILY thus saith the Lord, in addition to the laws of the church, concerning women and children,   who belong to the church, who have lost their husbands, or fathers:

Women have claim on their husbands until they are taken, and, if they are not found transgressors,

they   remain upon their inheritances:

All children have claim upon their parents   until they are of age, and after that they have claim upon the church, or in other words, the Lord's storehouse   for inheritances.

[45]REVELATION GIVEN APRIL, 1832.

Verily thus saith the Lord, in addition to the laws of the church concerning women and children, those who belong to the church, who have los[t] [t]heir husbands or fathers: ↵

women have claim on their husbands for their maintainance until their h[u]sbands are taken; and if they are not found transgressors they shall have fellowship in the church, and if they are not faithful, they shall not have fellowship in the church; yet they may remain upon their inheritances according to the laws of the land.

All children have claim upon their parents for their maintainance until they are of age; and after that, they have claim upon the church; or, in other words, upon the Lord's storehouse, if their parents have not wherewith to give them inheritances. And the storehouse shall be kept by the consecrations of the church, that widows and orphans shall be provided for, as also the poor. Amen.

---

44. Revelation, 30 Apr. 1832, in "Items in Addition to the Laws for the Government of the Church of Christ, Given April, 1832," *The Evening and the Morning Star,* Jan. 1833, [6] [D&C 83]. This version corresponds to several early versions. The source text for this version is unknown.

45. Revelation, 30 Apr. 1832, in "Revelation Given April, 1832," *Evening and Morning Star,* Jan. 1833 (Apr. 1836), 126 [D&C 83]. This version closely corresponds to the version in section 88 of the 1835 Doctrine and Covenants, suggesting that the latter was used as a source text for the former.

February 1833

46REVELATION:

Therefore, verily I say unto you, my friends, call your solemn assemblies as I have commanded you, and as all have not faith, seek ye diligently and teach one another, words of wisdom; yea, seek ye out of the best books, words of wisdom:

Seek learning   by study, and also by faith.

Organize yourselves.

Prepare every needful thing, and establish an house, even an house of prayer; an house of fasting; an house of faith; an house of learning; an house of glory; an house of order; an house of God: that your in-comings may be in the name of the Lord, and your out-goings may be in the name of the Lord; that all your salutations may be in the name of the Lord, with uplifted hands unto the Most High.

Therefore, cease from all your light speeches; from all laughter; from all your lustful desires; from all your pride, and high-mindedness, and from all your wicked doings.

Appoint among yourselves a teacher, and let not all be spokesman at once, but let one speak at a time, and let all listen to the sayings, that when all have spoken, that

47REVELATION:

Therefore, verily I say unto you, my friends, call your solemn assembly, as I have commanded you; and as all have not faith, seek ye diligently and teach one another words of wisdom; yea, seek ye out of the best books words of wisdom: ⏎

seek learning even by study, and also by faith. ⏎

Organize yourselves; ⏎

prepare every needful thing, and establish a house, even a house of prayer, a house of fasting, a house of faith, a house of learning, a house of glory, a house of order, a house of God; that your incomings may be in the name of the Lord; that your outgoings may be in the name of the Lord; that all your salutations may be in the name of the Lord, with uplifted hands unto the Most High.

Therefore, cease from all your light speeches; from all laughter: from all your lustful desires: from all your pride and lightmindedness, and from all your wicked doings.— ⏎

Appoint among yourselves a teacher, and let not all be spokemen at once; but let one speak at a time, and let all listen unto his sayings, that when all have spoken, that

---

46. Excerpt of Revelation, 27 and 28 Dec. 1832, in "Revelation," *The Evening and the Morning Star,* Feb. 1833, [5] [D&C 88:117–126]. Though a version of this revelation was copied into Revelation Book 1, it does not appear to have been used as a source text for this version; the source text for this item is unknown. This revelation is presented as part of an editorial titled "COMMANDMENTS." The word "REVELATION" precedes the text of the revelation and is centered as though it were a title, though it is also the final word of the editorial.

47. Excerpt of Revelation, 27 and 28 Dec. 1832, in "Revelation," *Evening and Morning Star,* Feb. 1833 (May 1836), 138 [D&C 88:117–126]. This version closely corresponds to the version in section 7 of the 1835 Doctrine and Covenants, suggesting that the latter was used as a source text for the former. This revelation is presented as part of an editorial titled "COMMANDMENTS." The word "REVELATION" precedes the text of the revelation and is centered as though it were a title, though it is also the final word of the editorial.

all may be edified of all; and that every man may have an equal privilege.

See that ye love one another.

Cease to be covetous; learn to impart one to another as the gospel requires.

Cease to be idle; cease to be unclean; cease to find fault, one with another; cease to sleep longer than is needful.

Retire to thy bed early, that ye may not be weary.

Arise early, that your bodies and minds may be invigorated; and above all things, clothe yourselves with the bonds of charity, as with a mantle, which is the bonds of perfectness and peace.

Pray always, that you may not faint, until I come.

Behold   I will come quickly, and receive you unto myself: Amen.

⁴⁸A REVELATION
GIVEN, AUGUST 30, 1831.

HEARKEN O ye people, and open your hearts, and give ear from afar: and listen, you that call yourselves the people of the Lord, and hear the word of the Lord, and his will concerning you:

Yea, verily I say, hear the word of him whose anger is kindled against the wicked, and rebellious; who willeth to take even them whom he will take; and preserveth in life them whom he will preserve:

Who buildeth up at his own will and pleasure, and destroyeth when he please; and is able to cast the soul down to hell.

all may be edified of all, and that every man may have an equal privilege.

See that ye love one another; ↵

cease to be covetous, learn to impart one to another as the gospel requires; ↵

cease to be idle, cease to be unclean; ceasc to find fault one with another; cease to sleep longer than is needful; ↵

retire to thy bed early, that ye may not be weary; ↵

arise early, that your bodies and your minds may be invigorated: and above all things, clothe yourselves with the bonds of charity, as with a mantle, which is the bond of perfectness and peace: ↵

pray always, that you may not faint till I come: ↵

behold, and lo, I will come quickly, and receive you unto myself: Amen.

REVELATION
⁴⁹Given in Kirtland, August, 1831.

Hearken, O ye people, and open your hearts, and give ear from afar; and listen, you that call yourselves the people of the Lord, and hear the word of the Lord, and his will concerning you: ↵

yea, verily, I say, hear the word of him whose anger is kindled against the wicked, and rebellious; who willeth to take even them whom he will take, and preserveth in life them whom he will preserve: ↵

who buildeth up at his own will and pleasure; and destroyeth when he please; and is able to cast the soul down to hell.

---

48. Excerpt of Revelation, 30 Aug. 1831, in "A Revelation Given, August 30, 1831," *The Evening and the Morning Star,* Feb. 1833, [6]–[7] [D&C 63:1–64]. This version reflects editing marks made in Revelation Book 1, indicating that the latter was used as a source text for the former. (See *JSP,* MRB:181–189.)

49. Excerpt of Revelation, 30 Aug. 1831, in "Revelation Given in Kirtland, August, 1831," *Evening and Morning Star,* Feb. 1833 (May 1836), 140–141 [D&C 63:1–64]. This version closely corresponds to the version in section 20 of the 1835 Doctrine and Covenants, suggesting that the latter was used as a source text for the former. Several items in the newspaper separate this revelation from the preceding revelation.

Behold I the Lord uttereth my voice, and it shall be obeyed.

Wherefore verily I say, let the wicked take heed: and let the rebellious fear, and tremble.

And let the unbelieving hold their lips, for the day of wrath shall come upon them as a whirlwind, and all flesh shall know that I am God.

And he that seeketh signs shall see signs, but not unto salvation.

Verily I say unto you, there are those among you, who seeketh signs; and there has been such even from the beginning.

But behold, faith cometh not by signs, but signs follow those that believe.

Yea, signs cometh by faith, not by the will of men, nor as they please, but by the will of God.

Yea, signs cometh by faith, unto mighty works, for without faith no man pleaseth God: and with whom God is angry, he is not well pleased: wherefore, unto such he sheweth no signs, only in wrath unto their condemnation.

Wherefore I the Lord am not pleased with those among you, who have sought after signs and wonders for faith, and not for the good of men unto my glory:— nevertheless, I gave commandments and many have turned away from my commandments, and have not kept them.

There were among you adulterers and adulteresses; some of whom have turned away from you, and others remain with you, that hereafter shall be revealed.

Let such beware and repent speedily, lest judgments shall come upon them as a snare, and their folly shall be made manifest, and their works shall follow them in the eyes of the people.

And verily I say unto you, as I have said before, he that looketh on a woman to lust after her, or if any shall commit adul-

Behold I the Lord utter my voice, and it shall be obeyed. ↵

Wherefore verily I say, let the wicked take heed, and let the rebellious fear, and tremble. ↵

And let the unbelieving hold their lips, for the day of wrath shall come upon them as a whirlwind, and all flesh shall know that I am God. ↵

And he that seeketh signs shall see signs, but not unto salvation.

Verily I say unto you, there are those among you who seek signs: and there have been such even from the beginning. ↵

But behold, faith cometh not by signs, but signs follow those that believe. ↵

Yea, signs cometh by faith, not by the will of men, nor as they please, but by the will of God. ↵

Yea, signs cometh by faith, unto mighty works, for without faith, no man pleaseth God: and with whom God is angry, he is not well pleased: wherefore, unto such he showeth no signs, only in wrath unto condemnation.

Wherefore I the Lord am not pleased with those among you, who have sought after signs and wonders for faith, and not for the good of men unto my glory;   nevertheless, I gave commandments and many have turned away from my commandments, and have not kept them. ↵

There were among you adulterers and adulteresses; some of whom have turned away from you, and others remain with you: that hereafter shall be revealed.— ↵

Let such beware and repent speedily, lest judgments shall come upon them as a snare, and their folly shall be made manifest, and their works shall follow them in the eyes of the people.

And verily I say unto you, as I have said before, he that looketh on a woman to lust after her, or if any shall commit adultery in their hearts, they shall not have the Spirit, but shall deny the faith and shall fear:

Wherefore I the Lord have said that the fearful and the unbelieving, and all liars, and whosoever loveth and maketh a lie, and the whoremonger, and the sorcerer, should have their part in that lake which burneth with fire and brimstone, which is the second death.

Verily I say, that they shall not have part in the first resurrection.

And now behold, I the Lord saith unto you, that ye are not justified because these things are among you, nevertheless, he that endureth in faith and doeth my will, the same shall overcome, and shall receive an inheritance upon the earth, when the day of transfiguration shall come; when the earth shall be transfigured, even according to the pattern which was shown unto mine apostles upon the mount: of which account the fulness ye have not yet received.

And now, verily I say unto you, that as I said that I would make known my will unto you, behold I will make it known unto you, not by the way of commandment, for there are many who observe not to keep my commandments, but unto him that keepeth my commandments, I will give the mysteries of my kingdom, and the same shall be in him a well of living water, spring-ing up unto everlasting life.

And now, behold this is the will of the Lord your God concerning his saints, that they should assemble themselves together unto the land of Zion, not in haste, lest there should be confusion, which bringeth pestilence.

Behold the land of Zion, I the Lord holdeth it in mine own hands: neverthe-less, I the Lord rendereth unto Caesar the things which are Caesar's:

Wherefore I the Lord willeth, that you

tery in their hearts, they shall not have the Spirit, but shall deny the faith and shall fear: ⏎

wherefore I the Lord have said that the fearful, and the unbelieving, and all liars, and whosoever loveth and maketh a lie, & the whoremonger, and the sorcerer, shall have their part in that lake which burneth with fire and brimstone, which is the second death. ⏎

Verily I say, that they shall not have part in the first resurrection.

And now behold, I the Lord saith unto you, that ye are not justified because these things are among you, nevertheless he that endureth in faith and doeth my will, the same shall overcome, and shall receive an inheritance upon the earth, when the day of transfiguration shall come; when the earth shall be transfigured, even according to the pattern which was shown unto mine apostles upon the mount: of which account the fulness ye have not yet received.

And now, verily I say unto you, that as I said that I would make known my will unto you, behold I will make it known unto you, not by the way of commandment, for there are many who observe not to keep my commandments, but unto him that keepeth my commandments, I will give the mysteries of my kingdom, and the same shall be in him a well of living water, spring-ing up unto everlasting life.

And now, behold this is the will of the Lord your God concerning his saints, that they should assemble themselves together unto the land of Zion, not in haste, lest there should be confusion, which bringeth pestilence. ⏎

Behold the land of Zion, I the Lord holdeth it in mine own hands: neverthe-less, I the Lord rendereth unto Caesar the things which are Caesar's; ⏎

wherefore I the Lord willeth, that you

should purchase the lands, that you may have advantage of the world, that you may have claim on the world, that they may not be stirred up unto anger:

For satan putteth it into their hearts to anger against you, and to the shedding of blood:

Wherefore the land of Zion shall not be obtained but by purchase, or by blood, otherwise there is none inheritance for you.

And if by purchase behold you are blessed; and if by blood, as you are forbidden to shed blood, lo, your enemies are upon you, and ye shall be scourged from city to city, and from synagogue to synagogue, and but few shall stand to receive an inheritance.

I the Lord am angry with the wicked; I am holding my Spirit from the inhabitants of the earth.

I have sworn in my wrath and decreed wars upon the face of the earth, and the wicked shall slay the wicked, and fear shall come upon every man and the saints also shall hardly escape:

Nevertheless, I the Lord am with them, and will come down in heaven from the presence of   God, and consume the wicked with unquenchable fire.

And behold this is not yet, but by and by:

Wherefore seeing that I the Lord have decreed all these things upon the face of the earth, I willeth that my saints should be assembled upon the land of Zion and that every man should take righteousness in his hands, and faithfulness upon his loins and lift a warning voice unto the inhabitants of the earth; and declare both by word and by flight, that desolation shall come upon the wicked. [p. [6]]

Wherefore let my disciples in Kirtland,

should purchase the lands, that you may have advantage of the world, that you may have claim on the world, that they may not be stirred up unto anger: ⏎

for satan putteth it into their hearts to anger against you, and to the shedding of blood: ⏎

wherefore the land of Zion shall not be obtained but by purchase, or by blood, otherwise there is none inheritance for you. ⏎

And if by purchase behold you are blessed: and if by blood, as you are forbidden to shed blood, lo, your enemies are upon you, and ye shall be scourged from city to city, and from synagogue to synagogue, and but few shall stand to receive an inheritance.

I the Lord am angry with the wicked; I am holding my Spirit from the inhabitants of the earth. ⏎

I have sworn in my wrath and decreed wars upon the face of the earth, and the wicked shall slay the wicked, and fear shall come upon every man and the saints also shall hardly escape: ⏎

nevertheless I the Lord am with them, and will come down in heaven from the presence of my Father, and consume the wicked with unquenchable fire. ⏎

And behold this is not yet, but by and by: ⏎

wherefore seeing that I the Lord have decreed all these things upon the face of the earth, I willeth that my saints should be assembled upon the land of Zion; and that every man should take righteousness in his hands, and faithfulness upon his loins, and lift a warning voice unto the inhabitants of the earth; and declare both by word and by flight, that desolation shall come upon the wicked. ⏎

Wherefore let my disciples in Kirtland,

arrange their temporal concerns, which
dwell upon this farm.

Let my servant Titus,   who has
the care thereof, dispose of the land, that he
may be prepared in the coming spring, to
take his journey up unto the land of Zion,
with those that dwell upon the face thereof,
excepting those whom I shall reserve unto
myself, that shall not go until I shall command them.

And let all the moneys which can be
spared, (it mattereth not unto me whether it
be little or much) sent up unto the land of
Zion, unto them whom I have appointed to
receive.

Behold I the Lord, will give unto my
servant Joseph   power, that he
shall   be enabled to discern by the
Spirit those who shall go up unto the land
of Zion, and those of my disciples that
shall tarry.

Let my servant Newel
retain his store, or in other words, the store
yet for a little season.

Nevertheless let him impart all the
money which he can impart, to be sent up
unto the land of Zion.

Behold these things are in his own
hands, let him do according to wisdom.

Verily I say, let him be ordained   an
agent unto the disciples that shall tarry,
and let him be ordained unto this power;
and now speedily visit the churches, expounding these things unto them, with my
servant Oliver.

Behold this is my will, obtaining moneys even as I have directed.

He that is faithful and endureth shall
overcome the world.

He that sendeth up treasures unto the
land of Zion, shall receive an inheritance in
this world, and his works shall follow him;
and also, a reward in the world to come;
yea, and blessed are the dead that die in the

arrange their temporal concerns, which
dwell on this farm.

Let my servant Titus Billings, who has
the care thereof dispose of the land, that he
may be prepared in the coming spring, to
take his journey up unto the land of Zion,
with those that dwell upon the face thereof,
excepting those whom I shall reserve unto
myself, that shall not go until I shall command them.— ↵

And let all the moneys which can be
spared, it mattereth not unto me whether it
be little or much, sent up unto the land of
Zion, unto them whom I have appointed to
receive.

Behold I the Lord will give unto my
servant Joseph Smith, Jr. power, that he
shall [p. 140] be enabled to discern by the
Splrit those who shall go up unto the land
of Zion, and those of my disciples who
shall tarry.

Let my servant Newel K. Whitney
retain his store, or in other words, the store
yet for a little season. ↵

Nevertheless let him impart all the
money which he can impart, to be sent up
unto the land of Zion. ↵

Behold these things are in his own
hands, let him do according to wisdom. ↵

Verily I say, let him be ordained as an
agent unto the disciples that shall tarry,
and let him be ordained unto this power;
and now speedily visiting the churches, expounding these things unto them, with my
servant Oliver Cowdery. ↵

Behold this is my wlll, obtaining moneys even as I have directed.

He that is faithful and endureth shall
overcome the world. ↵

He that sendeth up treasures unto the
land of Zion, shall receive an inheritance in
this world, and his works shall follow him;
and also, a reward in the world to come;
yea, and blessed are the dead that die in the

Lord from henceforth, when the Lord shall come and old things shall pass away, and all things become new, they shall rise from the dead and shall not die,   and shall receive an inheritance before the Lord, in the holy city, and he that liveth when the Lord shall come, and have kept the faith, blessed is he; nevertheless it is appointed to him to die at the age of man:

Wherefore children shall grow up until they become old, old men shall die; but they shall not sleep in the dust, but they shall be changed in the twinkling of an eye:

Wherefore, for this cause preached the apostles unto the world, the resurrection of the dead:

These things are the things that ye must look for, and speaking after the manner of the Lord, they are now nigh at hand; and in a time to come, even in the day of the coming of the Son of man, and until that hour, there will be foolish virgins among the wise, and at that hour cometh an entire separation of the righteous and the wicked; and in that day will I send mine angels, to pluck out the wicked, and cast them into unquenchable fire.

And now behold, verily I say unto you, I the Lord am not well pleased with my servant Sidney,   he exalteth himself in his heart, and received not counsel, but grieved the Spirit:

Wherefore his writing is not axceptable unto the Lord, and he shall make another; and if the Lord receiveth it not; behold he standeth no longer in the office which he hath appointed him.

And again: verily I say unto you, let those who desire in their hearts, in meekness, to warn sinners to repentance, let them be ordained unto this power; for this is a day of warning, and not a day of many words.

Lord from henceforth, when the Lord shall come and old things shall pass away, and all things become new, they shall rise from the dead and shall not die after, and shall receive an inheritance before the Lord, in the holy city, and he that liveth when the Lord shall come, and have kept the faith, blessed is he; nevertheless it is appointed to him to die at the age of man: ↵

wherefore children shall grow up until they become old, old men shall die; but they shall not sleep in the dust, but they shall be changed in the twinkling of an eye: ↵

wherefore for this cause preached the apostles unto the world, the resurrection of the dead: ↵

these things are the things that ye must look for, and speaking after the manner of the Lord, they are now nigh at hand; and in a time to come, even in the day of the coming of the Son of man, and until that hour, there will be foolish virgins among the wise, and at that hour cometh an entire separation of the righteous and the wicked; and in that day will I send mine angels, to pluck out the wicked, and cast them into unquenchable fire.

And now behold, verily I say unto you, I the Lord am not well pleased with my servant Sidney Rigdon, he exalted himself in his heart, and received not counsel, but grieved the Spirit: ↵

wherefore his writing is not acceptable unto the Lord, and he shall make another; and if the Lord receive it not, behold he standeth no longer in the office which I have appointed him.

And again, verily I say unto you, those who desire in their hearts, in meekness, to warn sinners to repentance, let them be ordained unto this power: for this is a day of warning, and not a day of many words. ↵

For I the Lord am not to be mocked in the last days.

Behold I am from above, and my power lieth beneath.

I am over all, and in all, and through all, and searcheth all things:

And the days cometh that all things shall be subject unto me.

Behold I am Alpha and Omega, even Jesus Christ:

Wherefore let all men beware, how they take my name in their lips:

For behold, verily I say, that many there be who are under this condemnation; who useth the name of the Lord and useth it in vain, having not authority:

Wherefore let the church repent of their sins, and I the Lord will own them, otherwise they shall be cut off.

Remember that, that which cometh from above is sacred, and must be spoken with care, and by constraint of the Spirit and in this there is no condemnation; and ye receive the Spirit through prayer:

Wherefore without this there remaineth condemnation:

Amen.

For I the Lord am not to be mocked in the last days. ⏎

Behold I am from above, and my power lieth beneath. ⏎

I am over all, and in all, and through all, and searcheth all things: ⏎

and the day cometh that all things shall be subject unto me. ⏎

Behold I am Alpha and Omega, even Jesus Chrst. ⏎

Wherefore let all men beware, how they take my name in their lips: ⏎

for behold verily I say, that many there be who are under this condemnation; who useth the name of the Lord, and useth it in vain, having not authority. ⏎

Wherefore let the church repent of their sins, and I the Lord will own them, otherwise they shall be cut off.

Rememember, that that which cometh from above is sacred, and must be spoken with care, and by constraint of the Spirit, and in this there is no condemnation; and ye receive the Spirit through prayer: ⏎

wherefore without this, there remaineth condemnation: Let my servant Joseph Smith, jr. and Siduey Rigdon, seek them a home as they are taught through prayer, by the Spirit. These things remain to overcome, through patience, that such may receive a more exceeding and eternal weight of glory; otherwise, a greater condemnation: Amen.

March 1833

REVELATIONS.
[50]A COMMANDMENT
GIVEN, SEPTEMBER 4, 1830.

LISTEN to the voice of Jesus Christ, your Lord, your God, and your Redeemer, whose word is quick and powerful.

For behold I say unto you, that it mattereth not what ye shall eat, or what ye shall drink, when ye partake of the sacrament, if it so be that ye do it with an eye single to my glory; remembering unto the Father my body which was laid down for you, and my blood which was shed for the remission of your sins:

Wherefore a commandment I give unto you, that you shall not purchase wine, neither strong drink of your enemies:

Wherefore you shall partake of none, except it is made new among you, yea, in this my Father's kingdom which shall be built up on the earth.

Behold this is wisdom in me, wherefore marvel not, for the hour cometh that I will drink of the fruit of the vine with you, on the earth,

REVELATIONS.
[51]REVELATION
Given September, 1830.

Listen to the voice of Jesus Christ, your Lord, your God and your Redeemer, whose word is quick and powerful. ↵

For behold I say unto you, that it mattereth not what ye shall eat, or what ye shall drink, when ye partake of the sacrament, if it so be that ye do it with an eye single to my glory: remembering unto the Father my body which was laid down for you, and my blood which was shed for the remission of your sins: ↵

wherefore a commandment I give unto you, that you shall not purchase wine, neither strong drink of your enemies: ↵

wherefore you shall partake of none, except it is made new among you, yea, in this my Father's kingdom which shall be built up on the earth.

Behold this is wisdom in me: wherefore marvel not for the hour cometh that I will drink of the fruit of the vine with you on the earth, and with Moroni, whom I have sent unto you to reveal the book of Mormon, containing the fulness of my everlasting gospel; to whom I have committed the keys of the record of the stick of Ephraim; and also with Elias, to whom I

---

50. Revelation, ca. Aug. 1830, in "A Commandment Given, September 4, 1830," *The Evening and the Morning Star,* Mar. 1833, [6] [D&C 27]. This version closely corresponds to the version in chapter 28 of the Book of Commandments. It is unknown whether this version or the version in the Book of Commandments was set in type first. Either the version in Revelation Book 1 or the version in the Book of Commandments was likely used as a source text for the version printed here. This revelation should be dated circa August 1830. For more information on this dating, see the discussion of this revelation in the Documents series. (See *JSP,* MRB:41–43.)

51. Revelation, ca. Aug. 1830, in "Revelation Given September, 1830," *Evening and Morning Star,* Mar. 1833 (May 1836), 155 [D&C 27]. This version closely corresponds to the version in section 50 of the 1835 Doctrine and Covenants, suggesting that the latter was used as a source text for the former. This revelation should be dated circa August 1830. For more information on this dating, see the discussion of this revelation in the Documents series.

have committed the keys of bringing to pass the restoration of all things, or the restorer of all things spoken by the mouth of all the holy prophets since the world began, concerning the last days: and also John the son of Zacharias, which Zacharias he (Elias) visited and gav[e] promise that h[e] should have a son, and his name should be John, and he should be filled with the spirit of Elias; which John I have sent unto you, my servants, Joseph Smith, jr. and Oliver Cowdery, to ordain you unto this first priesthood which you have received, that you might be called and ordained even as Aaron: and also Elijah, unto whom I have committed the keys of the power of turning the hearts of the fathers to the children and the hearts of the children to the fathers, that the whole earth may not be smitten with a curse: and also, with Joseph, and Jacob, and Isaac, and Abraham your fathers; by whom the promises remain: and also with Michael, or Adam, the father of all, the prince of all, the ancient of days.

And also with Peter, and James, and John, whom I have sent unto you, by whom I have ordained you and confirmed you to be apostles and especial witnesses of my name, and bear the keys of your ministry: and of the same things which I revealed unto them, unto whom I have committed the keys of my kingdom, and a dispensation of the gospel for the last times: and for the fulness of times, in the whi[c]h I will gather together in one all things both which are in heaven and which are on earth: and also with all those whom my Father hath given me out of the world: ⏎

wherefore lift up your hearts and rejoice, and gird up your loins, and take upon you my whole armor, that ye may be able to withstand the evil day, having done all ye may be able to stand. Stand, there-

and with all those whom my Father hath given me out of the world:

Wherefore lift up your hearts and rejoice, and gird up your loins and be faithful until I come:

even so. Amen.

[52]REVELATION GIVEN, HIRAM, OHIO, NOVEMBER 1, 1831.

HEARKEN, O ye people of my church, saith the voice of Him who dwells on high, and whose eyes are upon all men; yea, verily I say, hearken ye people from afar, and ye that are upon the islands of the sea, listen together; for verily the voice of the Lord is unto all men, and there is none to escape, and there is no eye that shall not see, neither ear that shall not hear, neither heart that shall not be penetrated; and the rebellious shall be pierced with much sorrow, for their iniquties shall be spoken upon the house-tops, and their secret acts shall be revealed; and the voice of warning shall be unto all people, by the mouths of my disciples, whom I have chosen in these last days, and they shall go forth and none

fore, having your loins girt about with truth; having on the breastplate of righteousness; and your feet shod with the preparation of the gospel of peace which I have sent mine angels to commit unto you, taking the shield of faith wherewith ye shall be able to quench all the fiery darts of the wicked; and take the helmet of salvation, and the sword of my Spirit, which I will pour out upon you, and my word which I reveal unto you, and be agreed as touching all things whatsoever ye ask of me, and be faithful until I come, and ye shall be caught up that where I am ye shall be also.   Amen.

[53]REVELATION
Given, Hiram, Ohio, November 1, 1831.

Hearken, O ye people of my church, saith the voice of him who dwells on high, and whose eyes are upon all men: yea, verily I say, hearken ye people from afar, and ye that are upon the islands of the sea, listen together; for verily the voice of the Lord is unto all men, and there is none to escape, and there is no eye that shall not see, neither ear that shall not hear, neither heart that shall not be penetrated: and the rebellious shall be pierced with much sorrow, for their iniquities shall be spoken upon the house-tops, and their secret acts shall be revealed; and the voice of warning shall be unto all people, by the mouths of my disciples, whom I have chosen in these last days, and they shall go forth and none

---

52. Revelation, 1 Nov. 1831–B, in "Revelation Given, Hiram, Ohio, November 1, 1831," *The Evening and the Morning Star,* Mar. 1833, [6] [D&C 1]. This version closely corresponds to the version in chapter 1 of the Book of Commandments, suggesting that the latter was used as a source text for the former.

53. Revelation, 1 Nov. 1831–B, in "Revelation Given, Hiram, Ohio, November 1, 1831," *Evening and Morning Star,* Mar. 1833 (May 1836), 155–156 [D&C 1]. This version closely corresponds to the version in section 1 of the 1835 Doctrine and Covenants, suggesting that the latter was used as a source text for the former.

shall stay them, for I the Lord have commanded them.

Behold, this is mine authority, and the
authority of my servants, and my Preface
unto the Book of my Commandments,
which I have given them to publish unto
you, O inhabitants of the earth:

Wherefore fear and tremble, O ye people for what I the Lord have decreed, in
them, shall be fulfilled.

And verily, I say unto you, that they
who go forth, bearing these tidings unto
the inhabitants of the earth, to them is
power given, to seal both on earth and in
heaven, the unbelieving and   rebellious;
yea, verily, to seal them up unto the day
when the wrath of God shall be poured out
upon the wicked, without measure, unto

the day when the Lord shall come to
recompence unto every man according to
his work, and measure to every man according to the measure which he has measured to his fellow man.

Wherefore the voice of the Lord is
unto the ends of the earth, that all that will
hear may hear:

Prepare ye, prepare ye for that which is
to come, for the Lord is nigh; and the
anger of the Lord is kindled, and his sword
is bathed in heaven, and it shall fall upon
the inhabitants of the earth; and the arm
of the Lord shall be revealed; and the day
cometh, that they who will not hear the
voice of the Lord, neither the voice of his
servants, neither give heed to the words of
the prophets, and apostles, shall be cut off
from among the people:

For they have strayed from mine ordinances, and have broken mine everlasting
covenant; they seek not the Lord to establish his righteousness, but every man walketh in his own way, and after the image of
his own god, whose image is in the likeness
of the world, and whose substance is that

shall stay them, for I the Lord have commanded them.

Behold, this is mine authority, and the
authority of my servants, and my preface
unto the book of my commandments,
which I have given them to publish unto
you O inhabitants of the earth: ⏎

wherefore fear and tremble, O ye people, for what I the Lord have decreed, in
them, shall be fulfilled. ⏎

And verily, I say unto you, that they
who go forth, bearing these tidings unto
the inhabitants of the earth, to them is
power given to seal both on earth and in
heaven, the unbelieving and the rebellious;
yea, verily, to seal them up unto the day
when the wrath of God shall be poured out
upon the wicked without measure; un-[p.
155]to the day when the Lord shall come to
recompense unto every man according to
his work, and measure to every man according to the measure which he has measured to his fellow man.

Wherefore the voice of the Lord is
unto the ends of the earth, that all that will
hear may hear: ⏎

prepare ye, prepare ye for that which is
to come, for the Lord is nigh; and the
anger of the Lord is kindled, and his sword
is bathed in heaven, and it shall [f]all upon
the inhabitants of the earth; and the arm
of the Lord shall be revealed: and the day
cometh, that they who will not hear the
voice of the Lord, neither the voice of his
servants, neither give heed to the words of
the prophets, and apostles, shall be cut off
from among the people: ⏎

for they have strayed from mine ordinances, and have broken mine everlasting
covenant; they seek not the Lord to establish his righteousness, but every man walketh in his own way, and after the image of
his own god, whose image is in the likeness
of the world, and whose substance is that

of an idol, which waxeth old and shall perish in Babylon, even Babylon the great,
which shall fall:

Wherefore I the Lord, knowing the
calamity which should come upon the
inhabitants of the earth, called upon my
servant Joseph,   and spake unto
him from heaven, and gave him commandments; and also gave commandments to
others, that they should proclaim these
things unto the world, and all this that it
might be fulfilled, which was written by
the prophets:

The weak things of the world should
come forth and break down the mighty
and strong ones; that man should not
counsel his fellow man, neither trust in the
arm of flesh, but that every man might
speak in the name of God, the Lord, even
the Savior of the world; that faith also
might increase in the earth; that mine everlasting covenant might be established that
the fulness of my gospel might be proclaimed by the weak and the simple, unto
the ends of the world; and before kings and
rulers. Behold I am God and have spoken
it:

These commandments are of me, and
were given unto my servants in their weakness, after the manner of their language,
that they might come to understanding;
and inasmuch as they erred, it might be
made known:

And inasmuch as they sought wisdom,
they might be instructed; and inasmuch as
they sinned, they might be chastened, that
they might repent; and inasmuch as they
were humble, they might be made strong,
and blessed from on high, and receive
knowledge from time to time:

After they, having received the

of an idol, which waxeth old and shall perish in Babylon, even Babylon the great,
which shall fall.

Wherefore I the Lord, knowing the
calamity which should come upon the
inhabitants of the earth, called upon my
servant Joseph Smith, jr. [a]nd spake unto
him from heaven, and gave him commandments[54] and also gave commandments to
others, that they should proclaim these
things unto the world; and all this that it
might be fulfilled, which was written by
the prophets: ⏎

the weak things of the world shall
come forth and break down the mighty
and strong ones, that man should not
counsel his fellow man, neither trust in the
arm of flesh, but that every man might
speak in the name of God, the Lord, even
the Savior of the world; that faith also
might increase in the earth; that mine everlasting covenant might be established: that
the fulness of my gospel might be proclaimed by the weak and the simple, unto
the ends of the world, and before kings and
rulers. ¶ Behold I am God and have spoken
it: ⏎

these commandments are of me, and
were given unto my servants in their weak-
n[e]ss, after the manner of their language,
that they might come to understanding
and inasmuch as they erred it might be
made known: ⏎

and inasmuch as they sought wisdom,
they might be instructed: and inasmuch as
they sinned they might be chastened, that
they might repent: and inasmuch as they
were humble, they might be made strong,
and blessed from on high, and receive
knowledge from time to time: ⏎

and after   having received the

---

54. There is a blank space after "commandments" where a comma or semicolon was probably set but
did not print.

record of the Nephites; yea, even my servant Joseph   might have power to translate through the mercy of God, by the power of God, the book of Mormon:

And also, those to whom these commandments were given, might have power to lay the foundation of this church, and to bring it forth out of obscurity, and out of darkness, the only true and living church upon the face of the whole earth, with which I the Lord am well pleased, speaking unto the church collectively and not individually, for I the Lord cannot look upon sin with the least degree of allowance:

Nevertheless, he that repenteth and doeth the commandments of the Lord, shall be forgiven, and he that repenteth not, from him shall be taken even the light which he hath received, for my Spirit shall not always strive with man, saith the Lord of hosts.

And again, verily I say unto you, O inhabitants of the earth, for I the Lord am willing to make these things known unto all flesh, for I am no respecter to persons, and willeth that all men shall know that the day speedily cometh, the hour is not yet, but is nigh at hand, when peace shall be taken from the earth, and the devil shall have power over his own dominion; and also, the Lord shall have power over his saints, and shall reign in their midst, and shall come down in judgment upon Idumea, or the world.

Search these commandments, for they are true and faithful, and the prophecies and promises which are in them, shall all be fulfilled.

What I the Lord have spoken, I have spoken, and I excuse not myself, and though the heavens and the earth pass away, my word shall not pass away, but shall all be fulfilled, whether by mine own

record of the Nephites, yea, even my servant Joseph Smith, jr. might have power to translate through the mercy of God, by the power of God, the book of Mormon: ↵

and also, those to whom these commandments were given, might have power to lay the foundation of this church, and to bring it forth out of obscurity, and out of darkness, the only true and living church upon the face of the whole earth, with which I the Lord am well pleased, speaking unto the church collectively and not individually: for I the Lord cannot look upon sin with the least degree of allowance: ↵

nevertheless he that repents and does the commandments of the Lord, shall be forgiven, and he that repents not, from him shall be taken even the light which he has received, for my Spirit shall not always strive with man, saith the Lord of hosts.

And again, verily I say unto you, O inhabitants of the earth,   I the Lor[d] am willing to make these things known unto all flesh, for I am no respe[c]ter of persons, and willeth that all m[e]n shall know that the day sp[e]edily cometh, the hour is not yet, but is nigh at hand, when peace shall be taken [f]rom the earth, and the devil shall have power over his   dominion: and also, the Lord shall have power over his saints, and shall reign in their midst, and shall come down in judgment upon Idumea, or the world.

Search these commandments, for they are true and faithful, and the prophecies and promises which are in them shall all be fulfilled.

What I the Lord have spoken, I have spoken, and I excuse not myself, and though the heavens and the earth pass away, my word shall not pass away, but shall   be fulfilled, whether by mine own voice, or by the voice of my servants, it is the same:

For behold, and lo, the Lord is God, and the Spirit beareth record, and the record is true, and the truth abideth forever and ever: Amen.

[55]REVELATION GIVEN KIRTLAND, OHIO, JANUARY 3, 1833.

THE order of the house prepared for the presidency and instruction in all things, that is expedient for the officers, or in other words them who are called to the ministry in the church, beginning at the highpriests even down to the deacons.

And this shall be the order of the house:

He that is appointed to be a teacher shall be found standing in his place, which shall be prepared for him in the house of God; in a place that the congregation in the house may hear his words correctly, and distinctly, not with loud speech.

And when he cometh into the house of God, for he should be first in the house:

Behold this is beautiful, that he may be an example, let him offer himself in prayer upon his knees before God, in token of the everlasting covenant.

And when any shall come in after him,

[56]REVELATION
Given December 27, 1832.

And again, the order of the house prepared for the presidency of the school of the prophets, establ[i]shed for their instruction in all things that are expedient for them, even for all the officers of the church, or in other words, those who are called to the ministry in the church, beginning at the high priests, even do[w]n to the deacons: ↵

and this shall be the order of the honse of the presid[e]ncy of the school: ↵

He that is appointed to be president, or teacher shall be found standing in his place, in the house, which shall be prepared [f]or him. Therefore, he shall be first in the house of God, in a place that the congregation in the house may hear his words carefully and distinctly, not with loud speech. ↵

And when he cometh into the house of God, (for he should be first in the house; ↵

behold this is beautiful, that he may be an example.) ¶ Let him off[e]r himself in prayer upon his knees before God, in token, or remembrance, of the everlast[i]ng covenant, ↵

and when any shall come in after him

---

55. Excerpt of Revelation, 3 Jan. 1833, in "Revelation Given Kirtland, Ohio, January 3, 1833," *The Evening and the Morning Star,* Mar. 1833, [6] [D&C 88:127–137]. Though a version of this revelation was copied into Revelation Book 1, it does not appear to have been used as a source text for this version; the source text for this item is unknown.

56. Excerpt of Revelation, 3 Jan. 1833, in "Revelation Given December 27, 1832," *Evening and Morning Star,* Mar. 1833 (May 1836), 156–157 [D&C 88:127–137]. This version closely corresponds to the version in section 7 of the 1835 Doctrine and Covenants, suggesting that the latter was used as a source text for the former. This revelation should be dated 3 January 1833. For more information on this dating, see the discussion of this revelation in the Documents series.

let the teacher arise and with uplifted
hands to heaven:

Yea even directly and salute his brother,
or brethren with these words, saying:

Art thou a brother or brethren, I salute
you in the name of the Lord Jesus Christ,
in token   of the everlasting covenant; in which covenant I receive
you to fellowship in a determination that is
fixed, immoveable and unchangeable to be
your friend and brother through the grace
of God, in the bonds of love, to walk in all
the commandments of God blameless, in
thanksgiving forever and ever.

And he that cometh in,
                and is a brother or
brethren,   shall salute the
              teacher with uplifted hands to
heaven, with this same prayer and covenant,
or by saying amen, in token of the same. '57

Behold, verily I say unto you, this is a
sample unto you for a salutation to one
another in the house of God.

And to you the called to the ministry
of the ordinances of the house of God; and
ye are called to do this by prayer and
thanksgiving, as the Spirit shall give utterance, in all your doings in the house of
the Lord,
that it may become a sanctuary, a tabernacle of the Holy Spirit, to your edification:
Amen.

let the teacher arise, and w[i]th u[p]lifted
hands to heaven: ↲

yea, even directly,   salute his brother
or brethren with these words:

Art thou a brother or brethren, I salute
you in the name of the Lord Jesus Christ,
in token, o[f] remembrance of the everlasting covenant, in which covenant I receive
you to fellowship in a determination that is
fixed, immovable and unchangable, to be
your friend and brother through the grace
of God, in the bonds of love, to walk in all
th[e] commandments of God blamel[e]ss, in
thanksgiving, forev[e]r and ever. Amen.

And he that is found unworthy of this
salutation, shall not have a place among
you; for ye shall not suffer that mine house
shall be polluted by them.

And he that cometh in and is faithful
before me, and is a brother, or if they be
breth[p. 156]r[e]n, they shall salute the president or teacher with uplifted hands to
heaven with this same prayer and covenant,
or by saying, Amen, in tok[e]n of the [s]ame.

Behold, verily I say unto you, this is a
sample unto you for a salutation to one
anot[h]er in the ho[u]se of God, in the
school of the prophets. ↲

An[d]
ye are call[e]d to do this by prayer and
thanksgiving as the Spirit shall give utterance, in all y[o]ur doings in the ho[u]se of
the Lord, in the school of the prophets,
that it may become a sanctuary, a tabernacle, of the Holy Spirit to your edification.

---

57. This apostrophe is found at the right edge of the gutter. It was likely mistakenly used in place of a
piece of type bearing a space.

May 1833

[58]HEARKEN, O ye people of my church, saith the Lord your God, and hear the word of the Lord concerning you; the Lord who shall suddenly come to his temple; the Lord who shall come down upon the world with a curse to judgment; yea, upon all the nations that forget God, and upon all the ungodly among you.

For he shall make bare his holy arm in the eyes of all the nations, and all the ends of the earth shall see the salvation of their God:

Wherefore, prepare ye, prepare ye, O my people; sanctify yourselves; gather ye together, O ye people of my church, upon the land of Zion, all you that have not been commanded to tarry.

Go ye out from Babylon. Be ye clean that bear the vessels of the Lord. Call your solemn assemblies, and speak often one to another.

And let every man call upon the name of the Lord; yea, verily I say unto you, again, the time has come when the voice of the Lord is unto you, Go ye out of Babylon; gather ye out from among the nations, from the four winds, from one end of heaven to the other.

Send forth the elders of my church unto the nations which are afar off; unto the islands of the sea; send forth unto foreign lands; call upon all nations; firstly, upon the Gentiles, and then upon the Jews.

And behold and lo, this shall be their cry, and the voice of the Lord unto all peo-

[59]Hearken, O ye people of my church, saith the Lord your God, and hear the word of the Lord concerning you; the Lord who shall suddenly come to his temple; the Lord who shall come down upon the world with a curse to judgment; yea, upon all the nations that forget God, and upon all the ungodly among you. ↵

For he shall make bare his holy arm in the eyes of all the nations, and all the ends of the earth shall see the salvation of their God. ↵

Wherefore, prepare ye, prepare ye, O my people; sanctify yourselves; gather ye together, O ye people of my church, upon the land of Zion, all you that have not been commanded to tarry.— ↵

Go ye out from Babylon. Be ye clean that bear the vessels of the Lord. Call your solemn assemblies, and speak often one to another. ↵

And let every man call upon the name of the Lord; yea, verily I say unto you, again, the time has come when the voice of the Lord is unto you. Go ye out of Babylon; gather ye out from among the nations, from the four winds, from one end of heaven to the other.

Send forth the elders of my church unto the nations which are afar off; unto the islands of the sea; send forth unto foreign lands, call upon all nations; firstly, upon the Gentiles, and then upon the Jews. ↵

And behold and lo, this shall be their cry, and the voice of the Lord unto all peo-

---

58. Revelation, 3 Nov. 1831, in "Revelations," *The Evening and the Morning Star,* May 1833, [1]–[2] [D&C 133]. This version reflects editing marks made in Revelation Book 1, indicating that the latter was used as a source text for the former. (See *JSP,* MRB:205–215.)

59. Revelation, 3 Nov. 1831, in "Revelations," *Evening and Morning Star,* May 1833 (June 1836), 177–179 [D&C 133]. This version closely corresponds to the version in section 100 of the 1835 Doctrine and Covenants, suggesting that the latter was used as a source text for the former.

ple: Go ye forth unto the land of Zion, that
the borders of my people may be enlarged,
and that her stakes may be strengthened,
and that Zion may go forth unto the regions
round about:

Yea let the cry go forth among all people: Awake and arise and go forth to meet
the Bride-groom:

Behold and lo the Bride-groom cometh,
go ye out to meet him. Prepare yourselves
for the great day of the Lord. Watch, therefore, for ye know neither   the day
nor the hour.

Let them, therefore, which are among
the Gentiles, flee unto Zion. And let them
who be of Judah, flee unto Jerusalem, unto
the mountains of the Lord's house.

Go ye out from among the nations,
even from Babylon, from the midst of wickedness, which is spiritual Babylon.

But verily thus saith the Lord, let not
your flight be in haste, but let all things be
prepared before you: and he that goeth, let
him not look back, lest sudden destruction
shall come upon him.

Hearken and hear O ye inhabitants of
the earth. Listen ye elders of my church
together, and hear the voice of the Lord,
for he calleth upon all men and he commandeth all men every where to repent: for
behold the Lord God hath sent forth the
angel crying through the midst of heaven,
saying: Prepare ye the way of the Lord, and
make his paths strait, for the hour of his
coming is nigh, when the Lamb shall stand
upon mount Zion, and with him a hundred and forty-four thousand, having his
Father's name written in their foreheads:

Wherefore, prepare ye for the coming
of the Bride-groom: go ye, go ye out to
meet him, for behold he shall stand upon
the mount of Olivet, and upon the mighty
ocean, even the great deep, and upon the
islands of the sea, and upon the land of

ple: Go ye forth unto the land of Zion, that
the borders of my people may be enlarged,
and that her stakes may be strengthened,
and that Zion may go forth unto the regions
round about: ↵

yea, let the cry go forth among all people; Awake and arise & go forth to meet
the Bridegroom: ↵

behold and lo the Bridegroom cometh,
go ye out to meet him. Prepare yourselves
for the great day of the Lord. Watch, therefore, for ye know neither [p. [177]] the day
nor the hour. ↵

Let them, therefore, who are among
the Gentiles, flee unto Zion. And let them
who be of Judah, flee unto Jerusalem, unto
the mountains of the Lord's house. ↵

Go ye out from among the nations,
even from Babylon, from the midst of wickedness, which is spiritual Babylon.— ↵

But verily thus saith the Lord, let not
your flight be in haste, but let all things be
prepared before you: and he that goeth, let
him not look back, lest sudden destruction
        come upon him.

Hearken and hear O ye inhabitants of
the earth. Listen ye elders of my church
together, and hear the voice of the Lord,
for he calleth upon all men & he commandeth all men every where to repent: for
behold the Lord God hath sent forth the
angel, crying thro' the midst of heaven,
saying: Prepare ye the way of the Lord, and
make his paths strait, for the hour of his
coming is nigh, when the Lamb shall stand
upon mount Zion, and with him a hundred and forty four thousand, having his
Father's name written in their foreheads: ↵

wherefore, prepare ye for the coming
of the Bridegroom: go ye, go ye out to
meet him, for behold he shall stand upon
the mount of Olivet, and upon the mighty
ocean, even the great deep, and upon the
islands of the sea, and upon the land of

Zion; and he shall utter his voice out of Zion, and he shall speak from Jerusalem, and his voice shall be heard among all people, and it shall be a voice as the voice of many waters, and as the voice of a great thunder, which shall break down the mountains, and the valleys shall not be found:

He shall command the great deep and it shall be driven back into the north countries, and the islands shall become one land, and the land of Jerusalem and the land of Zion, shall be turned back into their own place, and the earth shall be like as it was in the days before it was divided.

And the Lord even the Savior shall stand in the midst of his people, and shall reign over all flesh. And they who are in the north countries shall come in remembrance before the Lord, and their prophets shall hear his voice, and shall no longer stay themselves, and they shall smite the rocks, and the ice shall flow down at their presence.

And an high way shall be cast up in the midst of the great deep. Their enemies shall become a prey unto them, and in the barren deserts there shall come forth pools of living water; and the parched ground shall no longer be a thirsty land. And they shall bring forth their rich treasures unto the children of Ephraim my servants.

And the boundaries of the everlasting hills shall tremble at their presence.— And then shall they fall down and be crowned with glory, even in Zion, by the hands of the servants of the Lord, even the children of Ephraim; and they shall be filled with songs of everlasting joy[60]

Behold this is the blessing of the everlasting God upon the tribes of Israel, and

Zion; and he shall utter his voice out of Zion, and he shall speak from Jerusalem, and his voice shall be heard among all people, and it shall be a voice as the voice of many waters, and as the voice of a great thunder, which shall break down the mountains, and the vallies shall not be found: ⏎

he shall command the great deep and it shall be driven back into the north countries, and the islands shall become one land, and the land of Jerusalem and the land of Zion, shall be turned back into their own place, and the earth shall be like as it was in the days before it was divided. ⏎

And the Lord even the Savior shall stand in the midst of his people, and shall reign over all flesh. And they who are in the north countries shall come in remembrance before the Lord, and their prophets shall hear his voice, and shall no longer stay themselves, and they shall smite the rocks, and the ice shall flow down at their presence. ⏎

And an high way shall be cast up in the midst of the great deep. Their enemie s shal become a prey unto them, and in th[e] barren deserts there shall come forth pools of living water; and the parched ground shall no longer be a thirsty land. And they shall bring forth their rich treasures unto the children of Ephraim my servants. ⏎

And the boundaries of the everlasting hills shall tremble at their presence.   And then shall they fall down and be crowned with glory, even in Zion, by the hands of the servants of the Lord, even the children of Ephraim; and they shall be filled with songs of everlasting joy.— ⏎

Behold this is the blessing of the everlasting God upon the tribes of Israel, and

---

60. A light ink mark suggests that a broken piece of type bearing a period was probably set but did not print.

the richer blessing upon the head of Ephraim and his fellows.

And they also of the tribe of Judah, after their pain, shall be sanctified in holiness before the Lord to dwell in his presence day and night for ever and ever.

And now verily saith the Lord, that these things might be known among you, O inhabitants of the earth, I have sent forth mine angel, flying through the midst of heaven, having the everlasting gospel, who hath appeared unto some, and hath committed it unto man, who shall appear unto many that dwell on the earth, and this gospel shall be preached unto every nation, and kindred, and tongue, and people, and the servants of God shall go forth, saying, with a loud voice:

Fear God and give glory to him: for the hour of his judgment is come: and worship him that made heaven, and earth, and sea, and the fountain of waters, calling upon the name of the Lord day and night, saying:

O that thou wouldst rend the heavens, that thou wouldst come down, that the mountains might flow down at thy presence. And it shall be answered upon their heads, for the presence of the Lord shall be as the melting fire that burneth, and as the fire which causeth the waters to boil.

O Lord, thou shalt come down to make thy name known to thine adversaries, and all nations shall tremble at thy presence. When thou doeth terrible things, things they look not for; yea, when thou comest down and the mountains flow down at thy presence, thou shalt meet him who rejoiceth and worketh righteousness, who remember thee in thy ways:

For since the beginning of the world have not man heard nor perceived by the ear, neither hath any eye seen, O God, besides

the richer blessing upon the head of Ephraim and his fellows. ⏎

And they also of the tribe of Judah, after their pain, shall be sanctified in holiness before the Lord to dwell in his presence day and night forever and ever.

And now verily saith the Lord, that these things might be known among you, O inhabitants of the earth, I have sent forth mine angel, flying through the midst of heaven, having the everlasting gospel, who hath appeared unto some, and hath committed it unto man, who shall appear unto many that dwell on the earth: and this gospel shall be preached unto every nation, and kindred, and tongue, and people, and the servants of God shall go forth, saying, with a loud voice: ⏎

Fear God and give glory to him: for the hour of his judgment is come: and worship him that made heaven, and earth, and sea, and the fountain of waters, calling upon the name of the Lord day and night, saying: ⏎

O that thou wouldst rend the heavens, that thou wouldst come down, that the mountains might flow down at they presence. And it shall be answered upon their heads, for the presence of the Lord shall be as the melting fire that burneth, and as the fire which causeth the waters to boil. ⏎

O Lord, thou shalt come down to make thy name known to thine adversaries, and all nations shall tremble at thy presence. When thou doeth terrible things, things they look not for; yea, when thou comest down and the mountains flow down at thy presence, thou shalt meet him who rejoiceth and worketh righteousness, who remember thee in thy ways: ⏎

for since the beginning of the world have not men heard nor perceived by the ear, neither hath any eye seen, O God, besides thee, how   great things thou hast prepared for him that waiteth for thee.

And it shall be said, Who is this that cometh down from God in heaven with died garments; yea, from the regions which are not known, clothed in his glorious apparrel, travelling in the greatness of his strength?

And he shall say, I am he who spake in righteousness, mighty to save. And the Lord shall be red in his apparrel, and his garments like him that treadeth in the wine vat, and so great shall be the glory of his presence, that the sun shall hide his face in shame; and the moon shall withhold its light; and the stars shall be hurled from their places:

And his voice shall be heard, I have trodden the wine-press alone, and have brought judgment upon all people; and none was with me; and I have trampled them in my fury, and I did tread upon them in mine anger, and their blood have I sprinkled upon my garments, and stained all my raiment: for this was the day of vengeance which was in my heart.

And now the year of my redeemed is come, and they shall mention the loving kindness of their Lord, and all that he has bestowed upon them, according to his goodness, and according to his loving kindness, forever and ever. In all their afflictions he was afflicted.

And the angel of his presence saved them; and in his love, and in his pity, he redeemed them, and bare them, and carried them all the days of old; yea, and Enoch also, and they who were with him; the prophets which were before him, and Noah also, and they who were before him, and Moses also, and they who were before him, and from Moses to Elijah, and from Elijah to John, who were with Christ in his resurrection, and the holy apostles, with

thee, how [p. 178] great things thou hast prepared for him that waiteth for thee.

And it shall be said, Who is this that cometh down from God in heaven with died garments: yea, from the regions which are not known, clothed in his glorious apparel, travelling in the greatness of his strength? ⏎

And he shall say I am he who spake in righteousness, mighty to save. And the Lord shall be red in his apparrel, and his garments like him that treadeth in the wine vat, and so great shall be the glory of his presence, that the sun shall hide his face in shame; and the moon shall withhold its light; and the stars shall be hurled from their places: ⏎

and his voice shall be heard, I have trodden the wine-press alone, and have brought judgment upon all people; and none was with me; and I have trampled them in my fury, and I did tread upon them in mine anger, and their blood have I sprinkled upon my garments, and stained all my raiment: for this was the day of vengeance which was in my heart. ⏎

And now the year of my redeemed is come, and they shall mention the loving kindness of their Lord, & all that he has bestowed upon them, according to his goodness, and according to his loving kindness, forever and ever. In all their afflictions he was afflicted. ⏎

And the angel of his presence saved them; and in his love, and in his pity, he redeemed them, and bare them, and carried them all the days of old; yea, and Enoch also, and they who were with him; the prophets who were before him, and Noah also, and they who were before him, and Moses also, and they who were before him, and from Moses to Elijah, and from Elijah to John, who were with Christ in his resurrection, and the holy apostles, with

Abraham, Isaac and Jacob, shall be in the presence of the Lamb.

And the graves of the saints shall be opened, and they shall come forth and stand on the right hand of the Lamb, when he shall stand upon mount Zion, and upon the holy city, the New Jerusalem, and they shall sing the song of the Lamb day and night forever and ever. [p. [1]]

And for this cause, that men might be made partakers of the glories which were to be revealed, the Lord sent forth the fulness of his gospel, his everlasting covenant, reasoning in plainness, and simplicity, to prepare the weak for those things which are coming on the earth; and for the Lord's errand in the day when the weak should confound the wise, and the little one become a strong nation, and two should put their tens of thousands to flight; and by the weak things of the earth, the Lord should thresh the nations by the power of his Spirit. And for this cause these commandments were given; they were commanded to be kept from the world in the day that they were given, but now are to go forth unto all flesh.

And this according to the mind and will of the Lord, who ruleth over all flesh; and unto him that repenteth and sanctifieth himself before the Lord, shall be given eternal life. And upon them that hearken not to the voice of the Lord, shall be fulfilled that which was written by the prophet Moses, That they should be cut off from among the people.

And also that which was written by the prophet Malachi: For behold the day cometh that shall burn as an oven, and all the proud; yea, and all that do wickedly, shall be stubble: and the day that cometh shall burn them up saith the Lord of Hosts, that it shall leave them neither root nor branch.

Abraham, Isaac and Jacob, shall be in the presence of the Lamb. ⏎

And the graves of the saints shall be opened, and they shall come forth and stand on the right hand of the Lamb, when he shall stand upon mount Zion, and upon the holy city, the New Jerusalem, and they shall sing the song of the Lamb day and night forever and ever.

And for this cause, that men might be made partakers of the glories which were to be revealed, the Lord sent forth the fulness of his gospel, his everlasting covenant, reasoning in plainness, and simplicity, to prepare the weak for those things which are coming on the earth; and for the Lord's errand in the day when the weak should confound the wise, and the little one become a strong nation, and two should put their tens of thousands to flight; and by the weak things of the earth, the Lord should thresh the nations by the power of his Spirit. And for this cause these commandments were given; they were commanded to be kept from the world in the day that they were given, but now are to go forth unto all flesh. ⏎

And this according to the mind and will of the Lord, who ruleth over all flesh; and unto him that repenteth and sanctifieth himself before the Lord, shall be given eternal life. And upon them that hearken not to the voice of the Lord, shall be fulfilled that which was written by the prophet Moses, that they should be cut off from among the people.

And also that which was written by the prophet Malachi: For behold the day cometh that shall burn as an oven, and all the pround; yea, and all that do wickedly, shall be stubble: and the day that cometh shall burn them up saith the Lord of hosts, that it shall leave them neither root nor branch.— ⏎

Wherefore this shall be the answer of the Lord unto them: In that day when I came unto my own, no man among you received me, and you were driven out.— When I called again, there was none of you to answer, yet my arm was not shortened at all, that I could not redeem, neither my power to deliver.

Behold at my rebuke I dry up the sea. I make the rivers a wilderness: their fish stinketh, and dieth for thirst. I clothe the heavens with blackness, and make sackcloth their covering.

And this shall ye have of my hand, ye shall lay down in sorrow.

Behold and lo there are none to deliver you, for ye obeyed not my voice when I called to you out of the heavens, ye believed not my servants; & when they were sent unto you ye received them not: wherefore they sealed up the testimony and bound up the law, and ye were delivered over unto darkness: these shall go away into outer darkness, where there is weeping, and wailing, and gnashing of teeth.— Behold the Lord your God hath spoken it. Amen.

Wherefore this shall be the answer of the Lord unto them: In that day when I came unto my own, no man among you received me, and you were driven out. When I called again, there was none of you to answer, yet my arm was not shortened at all, that I could not redeem, neither my power to deliver. ↵

Behold at my rebuke I dry up the sea. I make the rivers a wilderness: their fish stinketh, and dieth for thirst. I clothe the heavens with blackness, and make sackcloth their covering. ↵

And this shall ye have of my hand, ye shall lay down in sorrow.

Behold and lo there are none to deliver you, for ye obeyed not my voice when I called to you out of the heavens, ye believed not my servants; and when they were sent unto you ye received them not: wherefore they sealed up the testimony and bound up the law, and ye were delivered over unto darkness: these shall go away into outer darkness, where there is weeping, and wailing, and gnashing of teeth.　Behold the Lord your God hath spoken it. Amen. [p. 179]

June 1833

[61]THE ARTICLES AND COVENANTS OF THE CHURCH OF CHRIST.

THE rise of the church of Christ in these last days, being one thousand eight

[62]ARTICLES AND COVENANTS OF THE CHURCH OF CHRIST.

The rise of the church of Christ in these last days, being one thousand eight

---

61. Articles and covenants, 10 Apr. 1830, in "The Articles and Covenants of the Church of Christ," *The Evening and the Morning Star,* June 1833, 97–98 [D&C 20]. Though this item was printed in an earlier issue of *The Evening and the Morning Star,* this version closely corresponds to the version in chapter 24 of the Book of Commandments, suggesting that the Book of Commandments was used as a source text for this version.

62. Articles and covenants, 10 Apr. 1830, in "Articles and Covenants of the Church of Christ," *Evening and Morning Star,* June 1833 (June 1836), 193–196 [D&C 20]. This version closely corresponds to the version in section 2 of the 1835 Doctrine and Covenants, suggesting that the latter was used as a source text for the former.

hundred and thirty years since the coming
of our Lord and Savior Jesus Christ, in the
flesh;

It being regularly organized and established agreeable to the laws of our country,
by the will and commandments of God in
the fourth month and on the sixth day of
the month, which is called April:

Which commandments were given to
Joseph,   who was called of God
and ordained an apostle of Jesus Christ

an   elder of this church:

And also to Oliver,   who was
also called of   God an apostle of Jesus
Christ,   an   elder of this church,
and ordained under his hand:

And this according to the grace of our
Lord and Savior Jesus Christ, to whom be
all glory both now and forever. Amen.

For, after that it truly was manifested
unto this first elder, that he had received a
remission of his sins, he was entangled
again in the vanities of the world;

But after truly repenting,

God
ministered unto him, by an holy angel,
whose countenance was as lightning, and
whose garments were pure and white above
all   whiteness, and gave unto
commandments which inspired him from
on high, and gave unto him power,

by the means which were before prepared, that he should translate a book;

Which book contained a record of a
fallen people, and also the fulness of the
gopel of Jesus Christ to the Gentiles;

And also to the Jews,

proving unto them,
that the holy scriptures are true;

And also, that God doth inspire men
and call them to his holy work, in these last

·hundred and thirty years since the coming
of our Lord and Savior Jesus Christ in the
flesh, ↵

it being regularly organized and established agreeably to the laws of our country,
by the will and commandments of God in
the fourth month, and on the sixth day of
the month which is called April: ↵

which commandments were given to
Joseph Smith, jr. who was called of God
and ordained an apostle of Jesus Christ, to
be the first elder of this church; ↵

and   to Oliver Cowdery, who was
also called of of God an apostle of Jesus
Christ, to be the second elder of this church,
and ordained under his hand: ↵

and this according to the grace of our
Lord and Savior Jesus Christ, to whom be
all glory both now and forever. Amen.

After   it was truly manifested
unto this first elder that he had received a
remission of his sins he was entangled
again in the vanities of the world; ↵

but after   repenting, and humbling himself, sincerely, through faith God
ministered unto him by an holy angel
whose countenance was as lightning, and
whose garments were pure and white above
all other whiteness, and gave unto him
commandments which inspired him,

and gave   him power from on
high, by the means which were before prepared,   to translate the book of
Mormon, ↵

which   contains a record of a
fallen people, and   the fulness of the
gospel of Jesus Christ to the Gentiles, ↵

and to the Jews also, which was given
by inspiration, and is confirmed to others
by the ministering of angels, and is declared
unto the world by them, proving to the world
that the holy scriptures are true, ↵

and   that God does inspire men
and call them to his holy work in this age

days   as well as in days of
old,   that he might be the same
God   forever. Amen.

Which book was given by inspiration, and is called the book of Mormon, and is confirmed to others by the ministering of angels, and declared unto the world by them:

Wherefore having so great witnesses, by them shall the world be judged, even as many as shall hereafter

receive this work,
either to faith and   righteousness,

or to the
hardness of heart in unbelief,

to their own condemnation, for the Lord God hath spoken it, for we, the elders of the church, have heard and bear witness to the words of the glorious Majesty on high; to whom be glory forever and ever.—Amen.

Wherefore, by these things we know that there is a God in heaven, who is infinite and eternal, from everlasting to everlasting, the same unchangeable God, the maker of heaven and earth and all things that in them is, and that he created man male and female, and after his own image, and in his own likeness created he them;

And that he gave unto the children of men commandments, that they should love and serve him the

only being whom they should worship: but by the transgression of these holy laws, man became sensual and devlish, and became fallen man.

Wherefore, the Almighty God gave his only begotten Son, as it is written in those scriptures, which have been given of him, that he suffered temptations, but gave no heed unto them;

That he was crucified, died, and rose again the third day, and that he ascended

and generation, as well as in generations of old, thereby showing that he   is the same God yesterday, to-day, and forever. Amen.

Therefore, having so great witnesses, by them shall the world be judged, even as many as shall hereafter come to a knowledge of this work; and those who receive it

in faith and work righteousness, shall receive a crown of eternal life; but those who harden their hearts in unbelief and reject it, it shall turn to their own condemnation, for the Lord God has spoken it; and we, the elders of the church, have heard and bear witness to the words of the glorious Majesty on high, to whom be glory forever and ever.   Amen.

By these things we know that there is a God in heaven who is infinite and eternal, from everlasting to everlasting the same unchangeable God, the framer of heaven and earth and all things which are in them, and that he created man male and female: after his own image and in his own likeness created he them, ↵

and   gave unto them commandments that they should love and serve him the only living and true God, and that he should be the only being whom they should worship. But by the transgression of these holy laws, man became sensual and devilish, and became fallen man.

Wherefore the Almighty God gave his only begotten Son, as it is written in those scriptures which have been given of him;

he suffered temptations but gave no heed unto them; ↵

he was crucified, died, and rose again the third day; and   ascended

into heaven to sit down on the right hand
of the Father, to reign with Almighty power
according to the will of the Father.

Therefore, as many as would believe
and were baptized in his holy name, and endured in faith to the end, should be saved;

Yea even as many as were before he
came   in the flesh,
          from the beginning,
                         who believed
in the words of the holy prophets who
                    were inspired by the gift of
the Holy Ghost, which truly testified of
him in all things,
as well as those who should come after,
who should believe in the gifts & callings
of God, by the Holy Ghost, which beareth
record of the Father and of the Son, which
Father & Son and Holy Ghost, is one God,
infinite and eternal, without end. Amen.

And we know, that all men must repent
and believe on the name of Jesus Christ,
and worship the Father in his name, and
endure in faith on his name to the end, or
they can not be saved in   the kingdom of God.

And we know, that justification
through the grace of our Lord and Savior
Jesus Christ, is just and true;

And we know, also that sanctification
through the grace of our Lord and Savior
Jesus Christ, is just and true, to all those
who love and serve God with all their
mights, minds, and strength, but there is a
possibility that men may fall from grace
and depart from the living God.

Therefore, let the church take heed and
pray always, lest they fall into temptation;

Yea, and even   he that is sanctified   also.

And we know, that these things are
true and agreeable to the revelation of
John, neither adding to nor diminishing
from the prophecy of his book;

into heaven to sit down on the right hand
of the Father, to reign with almighty power
according to the will of the Father, ⏎

that as many as would believe
and be baptized, in his holy name, and endure in faith to the end should be saved: ⏎

not only those who believed after he
came in the meridian of time in the flesh,
but all those from the beginning, even as
many as were before he came, who believed
in the words of the holy prophets, who
spake as they were inspired by the gift of
the Holy Ghost, who truly testified of
him in all things, should have eternal life,
as well as those who should come after,
who should believe in the gifts and callings
of God by the Holy Ghost, which beareth
record of the Father, and of the Son, which
Father,   Son, and Holy Ghost are one God,
infinite and eternal, without end. Amen.

And we know   all men must repent
and believe on the name of Jesus Christ
and worship the Father in his name, and
endure in faith on his name to the end, or
they cannot be saved in [p. [193]] the kingdom of God. ⏎

And we know that justification
through the grace of our Lord and Savior
Jesus Christ, is just and true: ⏎

and we know, also, that sanctification
through the grace of our Lord and Savior
Jesus Christ, is just and true, to all those
who love and serve God, with all their
mights, minds, and strength; but there is a
possibility that man may fall from grace
and depart from the living God. ⏎

Therefore let the church take heed and
pray always, lest they fall into temptations; ⏎

yea, & even let those who are sanctified, take heed also. ⏎

And we know that these things are
true and according to the revelations of
John, neither adding to, nor diminishing
from the prophecy of his book, ⏎

Neither to the holy scriptures;

Neither to the revelations of God which shall come hereafter, by the gift and power of the Holy Ghost;

Neither by the voice of God;

Neither by the ministering of angels and the Lord God hath spoken it; and honor, power, and glory, be rendered to his holy name both now and ever. Amen.

And again, by way of commandment to the church, concerning the manner of baptism; Behold whosoever humbleth himself before God and desireth to be baptized and comes forth with a broken heart and a contrite spirit, and witnesseth unto the church, that they have truly repented of all their sins and are willing to take upon them the name of   Christ, having a determination to serve him unto the end, and truly manifest by their works that they have received   the Spirit of Christ unto the remission of their sins, then shall they be received unto baptism into the church of Christ.

The duty of the elders, priests, teachers, deacons and members of the church of Christ. An apostle is an elder, and it is his calling to baptize and to ordain other elders, priests, teachers and deacons and to administer

the flesh and blood of Christ

                                   according to the scriptures;

And to teach, expound, exhort, baptize, and watch over the church; and to confirm the church by the laying on of the hands, & the giving of the Holy Ghost, and to take the lead of all meetings.

The elders are to conduct the meetings as they are led by the Holy Ghost.

the holy scriptures, ⏎
or the revelations of God which shall come hereafter by the gift and power of the Holy Ghost, ⏎
the voice of God, ⏎
or the ministering of angels: and the Lord God has spoken it; and honor, power, and glory, he rendered to his holy name, both now and forever. Amen.

And again by way of commandment to the church concerning the manner of baptism. ¶   All those who humble themselves before God and desire to be baptized, and come forth with broken hearts and contrite spirits, and witness before ths church that they have truly repented of all their sins and are willing to take upon them the name of Jesus Christ, having a determination to serve him to the end, and truly manifest by their works that they have received of the Spirit of Christ unto the remission of their sins,

shall   be received by baptism into his church.

The duty of the elders, priests, teachers, deacons, and members of the church of Christ. ¶ An apostle is an elder, and it is his calling to baptize, and to ordain other elders, priests, teachers, and deacons, and to administer bread and wine—the emblems of the flesh and blood of Christ—and to confirm those who are baptized into the church, by the laying on of hands for the baptism of fire and the Holy Ghost, according to the scriptures; ⏎

and to teach, expound, exhort, baptize, and watch over the church; and to confirm the church by the laying on of hands, and the giving of the Holy Ghost—and to take the lead of all meetings.

The elders are to conduct the meetings as they are led by the Holy Ghost, according to the commandments and revelations of God.

The priest's duty is to preach, teach, expound, exhort and baptize, and administer the sacrament, and visit the house of each member, and exhort them to pray vocally and in secret, and also to attend to all family duties;

And ordain other priests teachers and deacons, and take the lead of meetings; but none of these offices is he to do when there is an elder present,

but in all cases is to assist the elder.

The teacher's duty is to watch over the church always, and be with them, and strengthen them, and see that their is no iniquity in the church, neither hardness with each other, neither lying nor back-biting, nor evil speaking;

And see that the church meet together often, and also see that all the members do their duty; and he is to take the lead of meetings in the absence of the elder or priest, and is to be assisted always, and in all his duties in the church by the deacons;

But neither the teachers nor deacons have authority to baptize nor administer the sacrament, but are to warn, expound, exhort and teach, and invite all to come unto Christ. Every elder, priest, teacher or deacon, is to be ordained according to the gifts and callings of God unto him, by the power of the Holy Ghost which is in the one who ordains him.

The several elders composing this church of Christ, are to meet in conference once in three months, or from time to time as they shall direct or appoint to do church busi-

The priest's duty is to preach, teach, expound, exhort, and baptize, and administer the sacrament, and visit the house of each member, and exhort them to pray vocally and in secret, and attend to all family duties: ↵

and he may also ordain other priests, teachers, and deacons—and he is to take the lead of meetings when there is no elder present, but when there is an elder present he is only to preach, teach, expound, exhort, and baptize, and visit the house of each member, exhorting them to pray vocally and in secret, and attend to all family duties. In all all these duties the priest is to assist the elder if occasion requires.

The teacher's duty is to watch over the church always, and be with, and strengthen them, and see that there is no iniquity in the church, neither hardness with with each other; neither lying, backbiting, nor evil speaking; ↵

and see that the church meet together often, and also see that all the members do their duty—and he is to take the lead of meetings in the absence of the elder or priest—and is to be assisted always, in all his duties in the church, by the deacons, if occasion requires: ↵

but neither teachers nor deacons have authority to baptize, administer the sacrament, or lay on hands; they are however to warn, expound, exhort, and teach, and invite all to come unto Christ. ¶ Every elder, priest, teacher, or deacon, is to be ordained according to the gifts and callings of God unto him: and he is to be ordained by the power of the Holy Ghost which is in the one who ordains him.

The several elders composing this church of Christ are to meet in conference once in three months, or from time to time, as said conferences shall direct or appoint: and said conferences are to do whatever ness whatsoever is necessary.

And each priest or teacher,
who is ordained by a priest, is to take a certificate from him at the time, which
        when presented to an elder,
he is to give him a license which shall
authorize him to perform the duty of his
calling.

The duty of the members after they are
received by baptism.

The elders or priests are to have a sufficient time to expound all things concerning this church of Christ to their understanding, previous to their partaking of the
sacrament, and being confirmed by the laying on of the hands of the elders;

So that all things may be done in
order.

And the members shall manifest before
the church, and also before the elders, by a
godly walk and conversation, that they are
worthy of it, that there may be works and
faith agreeable to the holy scriptures, walking in holiness before the Lord. Every
member of this church of Christ having
children, is to bring them unto the elders

church business is necessary to be done at
the time.

The elders are to receive their licences
from other elders by vote of the church to
which they belong, or from the conferences.

        Each priest,   teacher, or deacon,
who is ordained by a priest, may take a certificate from him at the time, which certificate when presented to an elder, [p. 194]
shall entitle him to a license, which shall
authorize him to perform the duties of his
calling—or he may receive it from a
conference.

No person is to be ordained to any office in this church, where there is a regularly organized branch of the same, without
the vote of that church; but the presiding
elders, travelling bishops, high counsellors,
high priests, and elders, may have the privilege of ordaining, where there is no branch
of the church, that a vote may be called.

Every president of the high priesthood, (or presiding elder,) bishop, high
counsellor, and high priest, is to be ordained by the direction of a high counsel,
or general conference.

The duty of the members after they are
received by baptism:

The elders or priests are to have a sufficient time to expound all things concerning the church of Christ to their understanding, previous to their partaking of the
sacrament, and being confirmed by the laying on of the hands of the elders; ⏎

so that all things may be done in
order. ⏎

And the members shall manifest before
the church and also before the elders, by a
godly walk and conversation, that they are
worthy of it, that there may be works and
faith agreeable to the holy scripture—walking in holiness before the Lord. ¶ Every
member of the church of Christ having
children, is to bring them unto the elders

before the church, who are to lay their hands upon them in the name of the Lord, and bless them in the name of Christ.

There cannot any one be received into this church of Christ who has not arrived to the years of accountability before God, and is not capable of repentance.

And baptism is to be administered in the following manner unto all those who repent:

Whosoever being called ofGod & having authority given them of Jesus Christ, shall go down into the water with them and shall say, calling them by name:

Having authority given me of Jesus Christ, I baptize you in the name of the Father, and of the Son, and of the Holy Ghost. Amen.

Then shall he immerse them in the water, and come forth again out of the water.

And it is expedient that the church meet together oft to partake of bread and wine, in remembrance of the Lord Jesus;

And the elder or priest shall administer it, and after this manner shall he do,

he shall kneel with the church, and call upon the Father in mighty prayer, saying:

O God, the Eternal Father, we ask thee in the name of thy Son Jesus Christ, to bless and sanctify this bread to the souls of all those who partake of it, that they may eat in remembrance of the body of thy Son, & witness unto thee, O God the Eternal Father, that they are willing to take upon them the name of thy Son, and always remember him, and keep his commandments which he hath given them, that they may always have his Spirit to be with them. Amen.

before the church, who are to lay their hands upon them in the name of Jesus Christ, and bless them in his name.

No one can be received into the church of Christ unless he has arrived unto the years of accountability before God, and is   capable of repentance.

Baptism is to be administered in the following manner unto all those who repent: ↵

The person who is called of God and has authority   from Jesus Christ to baptize, shall go down into the water with the person who has presented him or herself for baptism, and shall say, calling him or her by name: ↵

Having been commissioned of Jesus Christ, I baptize you in the name of the Father, and of the Son, and of the Holy Ghost, Amen. ↵

Then shall he immerse him or her in the water, and come forth again out of the water.

It is expedient that the church meet together often to partake of bread and wine in remembrance of the Lord Jesus: ↵

and the elder or priest shall administer it: and after this manner shall he administer it: he shall kneel with the church and call upon the Father in solemn prayer, saying, ↵

O God, the eternal Father, we ask thee in the name of thy Son Jesus Christ to bless and sanctify[63] this bread to the souls of all who partake of it, that they may eat in remembrance of the body of thy Son, and witness unto thee, O God, the eternal Father, that they are willing to take upon them the name of thy Son, and always remember him and keep his commandments which he has given them, that they may always have his Spirit to be with them. Amen.

---

63. The typesetter mistakenly introduced the "fi" ligature instead of a standard "f".

The manner of administering the wine:

Behold they shall take the cup   and say, O God, the Eternal Father, we ask thee in the name of thy Son Jesus Christ, to bless and sanctify this wine to the souls of all those who drink of it, that they may do it in remembrance of the blood of thy Son, which was shed for them, that they may witness unto thee, O God the Eternal Father, that they do always remember him, that they may have his Spirit to be with them. Amen.

Any member of this church of Christ, transgressing or being overtaken in a [p. [97]] fault, shall be dealt with according as the scriptures direct. It shall be the duty of the several churches, composing this church of Christ, to send one or more of their teachers to attend the several conferences, held by the elders of this church, with a list of the names of the several members, uniting themselves to the church since the last conference, or send by the hand of some priest, so that there can be kept a regular list of all the names of the members of the whole church,   in a book kept by one of the elders;

Whomsoever the other elders shall appoint from time to time:

And also, if any have been expelled from the church, so that their names may be blotted out of the general church record of names.

Any member removing from the church where he resides, if going to a church where he is not known, may take a letter certifying that he is a regular member and in good standing; which certificate may be signed by any elder or priest, if the member receiving the letter is personally acquainted with the elder or priest, or it may   be signed by the teachers or deacons of the church.

The manner of administering the wine: ⏎

He shall take the cup also, and say, O God, the eternal Father, we ask thee in the name of thy Son Jesus Christ, to bless and sanctify this wine to the souls of all those who drink of it, that they may do it in remembrance of the blood of thy Son which was shed for them, that they may witness unto thee, O God, the eternal Father, that they do always remember him, that they may have his Spirit to be with them. Amen.

Any member of the church of Christ transgressing, or being overtaken in a fault, shall be dealt with   as the scriptures direct. ¶ It shall be the duty of the several churches composing the church of Christ, to send one or more of their teachers to attend the several conferences, held by the elders of the church, wiih a list of the names of the several members uniting themselves with the church since the last conference, or send by the hand of some priest, so that   a regular list of all the names   of the whole church may be kept in a book, by one of the elders, ⏎

whoever the other elders shall appoint from time to time: ⏎

and also, if any have been expelled from the church; so that their names may be blotted out of the general church record of names.

All members removing from the church where they reside, if going to a church where they are not known, may take a letter certifying that they are regular members & in good standing; which certificate may be signed by any elder or priest, if the member receiving the letter is personally acquainted with the elder or priest, or it may [p. 195] be signed by the teachers or deacons of the church.

First edition of the Doctrine and Covenants. In September 1834, Joseph Smith, Sidney Rigdon, Frederick G. Williams, and Oliver Cowdery were appointed to select and arrange revelation texts and other materials for publication. The result was the first edition of the Doctrine and Covenants, completed in fall 1835. The copy shown here and reproduced in this volume was owned by Newel K. Whitney. Church History Library, Salt Lake City.

DOCTRINE AND COVENANTS, 1835

Source Note

Doctrine and Covenants of the Church of the Latter Day Saints: Carefully Selected from the Revelations of God, and Compiled by Joseph Smith Junior. Oliver Cowdery, Sidney Rigdon, Frederick G. Williams, [Presiding Elders of said Church.] Proprietors.; Kirtland, OH: F. G. Williams & Co., 1835; i–iv, 5–257, 25 pages of back matter paginated i–xxv; includes typeset signature marks and copyright notice. The copy presented herein is held at CHL; includes marginalia and archival markings.

This book was printed in octavo format on eighteen sheets, which were folded to make eighteen gatherings of eight leaves (sixteen pages) each. The text block consists of 288 pages measuring 6 × 4 inches (15 × 10 cm).[1] The sheets were likely printed using a work-and-turn technique, yielding two copies of the same gathering for each sheet.[2]

Different bindings exist among the extant copies from this printing of the Doctrine and Covenants because copies were bound at different times.[3] The copy of the book featured herein, which belonged to early church member and leader Newel K. Whitney, measures 6¼ × 4⅜ × ⅞ inches (16 × 11 × 2 cm). The cover is made from brown leather, with gilt and blind tooling on the spine and around the edges of the front and back covers. "Doctrine & | Covenants" is stamped on the spine in gilt. The front and back pastedowns, the front flyleaf, and the back flyleaf are single-sided marbled leaves featuring a Spanish pattern with blue shell body and shell veins of red and yellow. The verso of the front flyleaf bears a notation in graphite in unidentified handwriting, which was later stricken: "Presented, By. The hand of his mother E[lizabeth] A[nn]. Whitney to her Son Joshua [Kimball Whitney] on Tuesday Nov 26th 1872 S[alt]. L[ake]. City". The recto of the subsequent unprinted page bears several

---

1. In addition to the 282 pages identified in the preceding paragraph, the text block includes six unnumbered pages not accounted for in the pagination: a blank page after page 257 and five blank pages at the end of the volume, after page xxv.

2. An uncut sheet of the first Kirtland issue (Dec. 1833) of *The Evening and the Morning Star,* which was printed on the same press as the 1835 Doctrine and Covenants, is super royal size, or approximately 27½ × 20 inches (70 × 51 cm). Had the 1835 Doctrine and Covenants, which was printed in octavo format, been printed on super royal–size paper with a sheetwise technique (one gathering per sheet), each sheet would have yielded eight leaves measuring approximately 10 × 6⅞ inches (25 × 17 cm) each, a page size significantly larger than was needed for the Doctrine and Covenants, which measures approximately 6 × 4 inches (15 × 10 cm). If a work-and-turn technique had been used, each sheet would have yielded sixteen leaves measuring approximately 6⅞ × 5 inches (17 × 13 cm) each, leaving about a quarter inch to be trimmed from the top and bottom of each leaf and about a half an inch to be trimmed from the outside edge.

3. Crawley, *Descriptive Bibliography,* 1:57.

notations, all in unidentified handwriting: "RN- 232438", "Vault | Book | M223.1 | D637 | 1835 | no.4", "E[lizabeth]. A[nn]. Whitneys | Book", "G. S. L. City | May 23d. 1858.", and "Sister Elia [4 *illegible characters*] | see me at [7 *illegible characters*]". The verso of that page is blank, as is the following leaf. The title page bears the signature of "N[ewel] K Whitney". The final gathering of the book ends with two blank leaves. Two additional blank leaves were included, followed by a single flyleaf and the pastedown. The recto of the back flyleaf bears a light graphite notation in unidentified handwriting: "Mrs Whitney".

After the death of Newel K. Whitney in 1850, his wife Elizabeth Ann took possession of the book and then gave it to her son Joshua Kimball Whitney in 1872. The book remained in the Whitney family until it was acquired by the Historical Department of The Church of Jesus Christ of Latter-day Saints in 1987.

Historical Introduction

Even before JS learned in August 1833 that the Latter-day Saint printing office in Independence, Missouri, had been destroyed a few weeks earlier, plans were under way in Kirtland, Ohio, to obtain an additional press to print JS's newly completed Bible revision manuscript and other works.[4] After word of the destruction of the printing office reached Ohio, members of the United Firm—an organization set up to oversee various businesses within the church—resolved to take temporary responsibility for printing materials for the church until the Missouri press could resume operation.[5] In accordance with that decision, members of the United Firm established a press operated by F. G. Williams & Co., whose responsibilities included publishing *The Evening and the Morning Star* until it could be "transfered to its former Location" (Missouri) and launching a second newspaper to be titled *Latter Day Saints' Messenger and Advocate*.[6] Frederick G. Williams, a member of the United Firm, also believed that the Book of Commandments would "probably be reprinted" in Ohio.[7]

In fall 1833, Oliver Cowdery purchased a printing press from White, Hagar & Co. of New York City for 190 dollars and type from Nathan Lyman of Albany for 360 dollars and had the new equipment shipped to Kirtland.[8] That December, JS and other leaders

---

4. Oliver Cowdery with JS postscript, Kirtland Mills, OH, to William W. Phelps et al., [Independence, MO], 10 Aug. 1833, CHL; Revelation, 2 Aug. 1833–B, in Doctrine and Covenants 83:3, 1835 ed. [D&C 94:10]; JS et al., Kirtland, OH, to Edward Partridge et al., Independence, MO, 25 June 1833, JS Collection, CHL.

5. Minute Book 1, 11 Sept. 1833. For more information on the United Firm, see Parkin, "Joseph Smith and the United Firm."

6. Minute Book 1, 11 Sept. 1833. Despite early expectations, Mormon printing operations at Independence never resumed, and the *Star* finished its print run in Ohio. Publication of the *Messenger and Advocate* was postponed until October 1834, when the *Star*'s second volume was complete.

7. Frederick G. Williams, Kirtland, OH, to John Murdock, 10 Oct. 1833, in JS Letterbook 1, p. 62.

8. F. G. Williams and Company, Account Book, 1; JS, Kirtland, OH, to Edward Partridge et al., Clay Co., MO, 30 Mar. 1834, in Cowdery, Letterbook, 30–36. Nathan Lyman learned the practice of typefoundry from Elihu White of White, Hagar & Co., suggesting that either Lyman or White recommended the other to Cowdery. By the end of October 1833, Cowdery had arrived in Kirtland, but the press and type had not. The press and type were ready for service at least by 6 December 1833 but may have been ready as early as 12 November, when Cowdery was "making arrangements for printing." (De Vinne, *Practice of Typography*, 104; Oliver Cowdery, Kirtland Mills, OH, to Ambrose Palmer, New

dedicated the press, which was initially housed on the second story of a brick building the church had recently acquired from Peter French.[9] The press soon published two broadsheets and a broadside containing the texts of four revelations, foreshadowing its important role in making the revelations widely available.[10]

Though church leaders considered the publication of the revelations to be a priority, other matters delayed the work. In the late winter and early spring of 1834, most Ohio church leaders were occupied preparing for the Camp of Israel expedition to Missouri (later known as Zion's Camp). Traveling together in mid-April, not long before the expedition departed, JS, Cowdery, Sidney Rigdon, and early church member Zebedee Coltrin paused to give one another blessings for their individual responsibilities. JS was blessed to lead the upcoming expedition, while Rigdon and Cowdery were blessed with divine assistance "in arranging the church covenants which are to be soon published."[11] A revelation dictated by JS shortly thereafter reemphasized the plan to print the newly revealed word of God: "for this purpose have I commanded you to organize yourselves, even to print my word, the fullness of my Scriptures, the revelations which I have given unto you, and which I shall hereafter, from time to time, give unto you."[12] Though Oliver Cowdery and Sidney Rigdon remained in Kirtland while JS and others marched to Missouri, they had to manage church operations in addition to printing *The Evening and the Morning Star*, leaving little time to advance work on the revelations.

When JS returned from Missouri to Ohio in August 1834, focus again turned to publishing the revelations. In September the Kirtland high council appointed a committee consisting of JS, Oliver Cowdery, Sidney Rigdon, and Frederick G. Williams to publish a work "arrange[d from] the items of the doctrine of Jesus Christ." This committee was assigned to draw "from the bible, book of mormon, and the revelations which have been given to the church up to this date."[13] While a single volume containing excerpts from the Bible, Book of Mormon, and revelation texts was the original intention, the concept was

---

Portage, OH, 30 Oct. 1833, in Cowdery, Letterbook, 4–5; JS Journal, 4–6 Dec. 1833, in *JSP*, J1:20; Oliver Cowdery, Kirtland Mills, OH, to Samuel Bent, [Michigan Territory], 12 Nov. 1833, in Cowdery, Letterbook, 9.)

9. JS, Journal, 18 Dec. 1833, in *JSP*, J1:21–24; see also Parkin, "Joseph Smith and the United Firm," 32. This brick building was located in the "flats," or lowlands, on the north end of Kirtland. The printing establishment moved south to a second location, the second story of the newly completed schoolhouse immediately west of the House of the Lord, before work on the Doctrine and Covenants commenced— likely in late 1834. (Oliver Cowdery, Kirtland, OH, to William W. Phelps and John Whitmer, Clay Co., MO, 21 Jan. 1834, in Cowdery, Letterbook, 22; Frederick G. Williams, Kirtland, OH, to "Dear brethren," 10 Oct. 1833, in JS Letterbook 1, pp. 56–60; Revelation, 23 Apr. 1834, in Revelation Book 1, p. 194, in *JSP*, MRB:365 [D&C 104:28]; Minute Book 1, 11 Aug. 1834; Lucy Mack Smith, History, 1844–1845, bk. 13, [10]–[11]; Notice, *LDS Messenger and Advocate*, Oct. 1834, 1:11.)

10. *Verily, I say unto you, concerning your brethren who have been afflicted,* [Kirtland, OH: ca. Jan. 1834], copy at CHL [D&C 101]; *Verily, thus saith the Lord unto you, who have assembled yourselves together,* [Kirtland, OH: ca. Jan. 1834], copy at BYU [D&C 88–89]; *Behold, blessed saith the Lord, are they who have come up unto this land,* [Kirtland, OH: ca. Jan. 1834], copy at CHL [D&C 59].

11. JS, Journal, 18–19 Apr. 1834, in *JSP*, J1:41.

12. Revelation, 23 Apr. 1834, in Revelation Book 2, p. 105, in *JSP*, MRB:627 [D&C 104:58].

13. Minute Book 1, 24 Sept. 1834.

later modified. As the bipartite title "Doctrine and Covenants" suggests, the new book was made up of two parts. The first part, on "the doctrine of the church,"[14] comprised a series of seven doctrinal lectures on the subject of faith, first prepared as a course of instruction for the School of the Elders held in the second Kirtland printing office in the winter of 1834–1835.[15] Lecture one was contemporaneously published as a broadside and lectures five and six were published in the May 1835 issue of the *Latter Day Saints' Messenger and Advocate*,[16] but there is no known manuscript copy of any of the lectures. Although no JS-era published version states who authored the lectures, they were traditionally attributed to JS. Modern scholars, however, largely agree that Rigdon authored most or all of the lectures.[17]

The second part of the Doctrine and Covenants contained the "covenants and commandments of the Lord,"[18] or revelations. Inasmuch as the revelations made up the majority of the volume and the volume's title indicated that the texts therein were "carefully selected from the revelations of God," it is curious that the revelations were placed in the second part of the book. The sequence of the book's two parts may have resulted from the order in which materials were ready to be typeset. Regardless, the revelations were considered to be of paramount importance, and the 1835 Doctrine and Covenants was the most important collection of revelations published to that point. It presented more revelations than the incomplete Book of Commandments and presented some previously published revelations in expanded form.

The major work of printing the revelations in Ohio actually began in January 1835 with the publication of the newspaper *Evening and Morning Star,* a reprint of *The Evening and the Morning Star.* The earlier newspaper had published twenty-six full or partial revelation texts in its first thirteen issues. Of those, thirteen appeared in the reprinted *Star* before they were available to the public in the Doctrine and Covenants. Though the prospectus for the reprinted *Star* announced the new paper would merely correct "errors" in the revelations that had resulted from "transcribing manuscript,"[19] in fact the editors of the reprint made significant changes to the revelation texts—changes that were generally maintained when those texts were republished in the Doctrine and Covenants.[20]

---

14. Doctrine and Covenants, 1835 ed., [5].

15. Editorial, *LDS Messenger and Advocate,* May 1835, 1:122; see also JS History, vol. B-1, 557–558, 562–563; and Dahl, "Authorship and History of the Lectures on Faith," 12–13.

16. *Theology. Lecture First,* [Kirtland, OH: ca. Feb. 1835], copy at CHL; "Lecture Fifth" and "Lecture Sixth," *LDS Messenger and Advocate,* May 1835, 1:122–126. Both versions of the first lecture appear to use the same typesetting, as indicated by identical placement of a few pieces of broken type and by the fact that the width of each of the three columns of text on the broadsheet matches the width of the text in the 1835 Doctrine and Covenants. Corrections and additions to the Doctrine and Covenants version indicate that the broadsheet version was set in type first. Lectures five and six were retypeset for publication in the *Messenger and Advocate* after they had already been typeset for the Doctrine and Covenants.

17. See, for example, Reynolds, "The Case for Sidney Rigdon as Author of the *Lectures on Faith*"; Reynolds, "Authorship Debate concerning *Lectures on Faith*"; Partridge, *Notes on the Authorship of the Lectures on Faith;* and Phipps, "Lectures on Faith: An Authorship Study."

18. Doctrine and Covenants, 1835 ed., [75].

19. "Prospectus," *The Evening and the Morning Star,* Sept. 1834, 192; see also Notice, *Evening and Morning Star,* June 1832 (Jan. 1835), 16.

20. See pp. xxix–xxx and 198–199 herein.

John Whitmer and William W. Phelps arrived in Kirtland in May 1835.[21] Their arrival significantly alleviated the heavy workload at the Kirtland printing office, which was printing the *Messenger and Advocate* and other miscellaneous publications in addition to *Evening and Morning Star*. Whitmer was appointed editor of the *Messenger and Advocate* and Phelps, who had been the printer for the Book of Commandments, lent his hand to work on the Doctrine and Covenants.[22] By this time, some half-dozen individuals, in addition to Phelps and Whitmer, worked in the printing office: foreman James Carrell was assisted by Don Carlos Smith, Ebenezer Robinson, Solomon Wilbur Denton, and Samuel Brannan.[23] Robinson's reminiscences indicate that Oliver Cowdery managed the business of the printing establishment.[24] Apart from Cowdery, Phelps, and Whitmer, these individuals were printing hands who likely had little to do with the composition, structure, or intellectual work of the Doctrine and Covenants. In addition to serving on the publication committee for the volume, JS solicited financial help for printing, helped secure the copyright, and signed the preface. He is listed on the title page, but his role in the day-to-day work of preparing the revelations for publication is not fully known.[25] Some corrections in his hand that are reflected in the Doctrine and Covenants are found on revelations in Revelation Books 1 and 2,[26] and three notations in Revelation Book 2 indicate that he did at least some of the work of selecting items for publication.[27] JS apparently relied on others to do the actual typesetting and printing and possibly the bulk of the editing, arranging, and other intellectual work needed to prepare the revelations for print.[28]

The committee who selected items for publication drew on both manuscript and printed sources. When an item had already been printed, such as the sixty-four revelations or other items printed in full in the Book of Commandments, corrections or changes were sometimes made on a copy of the printed version. Appendix 2 presents selections from a copy of the Book of Commandments once owned by Oliver Cowdery, which contains editing marks made in preparation for the publication of the 1835 Doctrine and Covenants.[29]

---

21. Phelps, Diary and Notebook, 16 May 1835; Whitmer, Daybook, 16 May 1835.

22. Oliver Cowdery, "Address," *LDS Messenger and Advocate*, May 1835, 1:120 122; Whitmer, Daybook, 18 May 1835.

23. Ebenezer Robinson, "Items of Personal History of the Editor," *The Return*, Apr. 1889, 58; July 1889, 104. On 14 November 1835, after the Doctrine and Covenants was published, Phelps wrote to his wife: "We have, when all are in the office, three apprentices and four journeymen, and we shall have to employ some more men, as our work is so far behind." (William W. Phelps, Kirtland, OH, to Sally Phelps, Liberty, MO, 14 Nov. 1835, in Historical Department, Journal History of the Church, 14 Nov. 1835, CHL.)

24. Ebenezer Robinson, "Items of Personal History of the Editor," *The Return*, May 1889, 75.

25. JS, Kirtland, OH, to "Dear brethren," [Missouri], 15 June 1835, JS Collection, CHL; Copyright for first edition of Doctrine and Covenants, 14 Jan. 1835, Copyright Records, Ohio, 1831–1848 (Department of State), unnumbered vol., Rare Book and Special Collections Division, Library of Congress, Washington DC; title page and "Preface," Doctrine and Covenants, 1835 ed., [i], [iii]–iv.

26. See, for example, Revelation Book 1, pp. 194–198, in *JSP*, MRB:365–373, and Revelation Book 2, pp. 20–25, 28–31, in *JSP*, MRB:453–461, 469–475.

27. Revelation Book 2, pp. 20, 31, 111, in *JSP*, MRB:453, 475, 639.

28. For example, it appears that Oliver Cowdery did much of the work of identifying which items would appear at the beginning of the second part of the 1835 Doctrine and Covenants. (See p. 596 herein.)

29. See Appendix 2, p. 595 herein. Similar editing work was probably done on some of the revelations

When a revelation had not been printed before, the editors turned to manuscript sources, the most authoritative and commonly used of which were Revelation Books 1 and 2.[30] As with the 1832–1833 printing effort in Missouri, the printers may have recopied some texts in order to provide clean copies for typesetting.[31]

As had been the case with editorial work on the Book of Commandments, the editors of the Doctrine and Covenants made numerous copyediting changes to many of the revelations as well as a smaller number of substantive changes.[32] In contrast with the earlier work, however, the editors of the Doctrine and Covenants also made a focused effort to update the revelations to reflect changes in church government, structure, and doctrine that had occurred since the revelations were first dictated. For example, the earliest extant version of a 9 February 1831 revelation describes certain duties of elders, priests, teachers, and bishops.[33] Naturally, early versions of the revelation made no mention of the office of high priest, which did not exist until June 1831,[34] or of the high council, a body that was not organized until February 1834.[35] For publication in 1835, the revelation was revised to reflect the role of high priests and the high council.[36]

Extant sources permit the reconstruction of a rough chronology of the production of the volume. In mid-January 1835, JS, Cowdery, Rigdon, and Williams registered the volume for copyright in the United States District Court in Ohio.[37] The dated preface to the Doctrine and Covenants suggests that typesetting began shortly thereafter.[38] By late May, the first six gatherings (one-third of the volume's total gatherings) were printed,[39] taking the work through page 96, which included the entire first part of the book and the first four sections of the second part. The editors of the *Messenger and Advocate* optimistically promised readers of the May 1835 issue that the Doctrine and Covenants would be completed

---

published in early issues of *The Evening and the Morning Star,* though no such marked-up copies have been located.

30. The later pages of Revelation Book 2 possibly reflect an attempt to collect and copy previously unpublished revelations into a single source. (See *JSP,* MRB:409–410.)

31. See p. 8 herein.

32. See pp. xxx–xxxi, 7–8 herein.

33. Revelation, 9 Feb. 1831, in Revelation Book 1, pp. 62–67, in *JSP,* MRB:95–105 [D&C 42:1–72].

34. See Minute Book 2, 3 June 1831.

35. Minute Book 1, 17 Feb. 1834; see also Minutes, 17 Feb. 1834, in Doctrine and Covenants 5, 1835 ed. [D&C 102].

36. These updates were first made when the revelation was published in *Evening and Morning Star,* July 1832 (Feb. 1835), 30–31. The same updates were then introduced into Doctrine and Covenants 13:8, 10, 19, 1835 ed. [D&C 42:31, 34, 71].

37. Copyright for first edition of Doctrine and Covenants, 14 Jan. 1835, Copyright Records, Ohio, 1831–1848 (Department of State), unnumbered vol., Rare Book and Special Collections Division, Library of Congress, Washington DC.

38. The preface is dated 17 February 1835. ("Preface," Doctrine and Covenants, 1835 ed., [iii]–iv.)

39. William W. Phelps, Kirtland, OH, to Sally Phelps, Liberty, MO, 26 May 1835, William W. Phelps, Papers, BYU. A notice in the fifth issue of *Evening and Morning Star,* printed sometime in June 1835, apologized for publication delays caused by work on "a book of much importance." As the fourth issue of *Evening and Morning Star* was dated April 1835, significant work on the Doctrine and Covenants evidently occurred between issues. (Notice, *Evening and Morning Star,* Oct. 1832 [June 1835], 80; Notice, *Evening and Morning Star,* Sept. 1832 [Apr. 1835], 64.)

soon.[40] However, a 15 June letter from JS asking for donations or loans to help underwrite the printing of the revelations suggests that financial difficulty may have delayed the completion of the book.[41] It appears that early, unfinished portions of the book circulated before the book was bound and made widely available. In an epistle to the Twelve Apostles dated 4 August 1835, JS referred to a revelation by its section and verse numbers in the new publication, indicating that JS and evidently the Twelve had access to partial advance copies of the Doctrine and Covenants.[42]

On 17 August 1835, a general assembly of the church met "for the purpose of Examining a book of commandments and covenants" that had been "compiled and written by" the publication committee. "This Committee having finished said Book according to the instructions given them," the minutes read, "it was deemed necessary to call the general assembly of the Church to see whether the book be approved or not by the authoroties of the church, that it may, if approved, become a law unto the church, and a rule of faith and practice unto the same."[43] Though the assembly was convened "by the presidency of the Church,"[44] JS and Frederick G. Williams, a member of the presidency, were in Michigan at the time of the assembly.[45] The responsibility of presenting the book to the conference therefore fell to Oliver Cowdery, a member of both the presidency and the four-man publication committee.[46] Sidney Rigdon, the other presidency member and committee member present, stood and "explained the manner by which they intended to obtain the voice of the assembly for or against said book."[47] Voting on the book proceeded by quorums and groups, with the leader of each group bearing witness of the truth of the volume before his group voted to accept it. After the voting by quorums, the entire church membership present, both male and female, voted to accept the book as "the doctrine and covenants of their faith."[48] After the general assembly accepted the new publication, William W. Phelps read an article on marriage that the assembly approved and added to the volume.[49] The congregation then voted to accept and add to the volume an article on government introduced by

---

40. Editorial, *LDS Messenger and Advocate,* May 1835, 1:122.

41. JS, Kirtland, OH, to "Dear brethren," [Missouri], 15 June 1835, JS Collection, CHL.

42. In counseling the Twelve regarding fundraising in branches of the church, JS stated: "We remind you of these things, in the name of the Lord, and refer you to the book of covenants, 2nd. Section, 2nd. part, and 12, paragraph and ask, did we not instruct you to remember first the house, secondly the cause of Zion, and then the publishing the word to the Nations?" Though the extant version of the letter refers to the "2nd" section of the 1835 Doctrine and Covenants, the third section was probably the intended reference. (JS, Kirtland, OH, to the Quorum of the Twelve Apostles, 4 Aug. 1835, in JS Letterbook 1, p. 91.)

43. Minute Book 1, 17 Aug. 1835. The minutes were published in a condensed and somewhat modified format as "General Assembly," in *LDS Messenger and Advocate,* Aug. 1835, 1:161–164, and "General Assembly," in Doctrine and Covenants, 1835 ed., 255–257.

44. Minute Book 1, 17 Aug. 1835.

45. JS History, vol. B-1, 600.

46. Minute Book 1, 17 Aug. 1835.

47. "General Assembly," in Doctrine and Covenants, 1835 ed., 256.

48. "General Assembly," in Doctrine and Covenants, 1835 ed., 257; see also Minute Book 1, 17 Aug. 1835.

49. Minute Book 1, 17 Aug. 1835; "Marriage," ca. Aug. 1835, in Doctrine and Covenants 101, 1835 ed.

Oliver Cowdery.[50] Besides the revelations and these additions, the finished volume also contained a condensed and somewhat modified set of the minutes of this 17 August 1835 meeting, an "Index" (actually a table of contents in modern terms), a list of "Contents" (actually an index), and a single page titled "Notes to the Reader" that contained errata.[51]

In contrast with the chapters in the Book of Commandments, many of the sections in the Doctrine and Covenants were presented out of chronological order. Analysis of the Doctrine and Covenants and its source texts yields some insights about how texts were selected and why the sections may have been arranged in the order they were. Sections 1 through 7, which date from April 1830 to February 1834 but which are not arranged in chronological order, appear to have been placed first in the volume because of their importance: section 1, which was also the first chapter in the Book of Commandments, was understood to be a divinely given "preface" to the compilation;[52] section 2 contains the founding articles and covenants of the church; sections 3, 4, and 6 are identified in large headings as being "ON PRIESTHOOD" and constitute something of a handbook on priesthood and church government; section 5 presents the minutes from the organizational meeting of the first high council of the church; and section 7, the "olive leaf" revelation,[53] presents instructions on preparing for a solemn assembly in the temple in Kirtland. Of these seven texts, the first two were marked in Oliver Cowdery's copy of the Book of Commandments with the word "Covenants"[54] and the fourth through sixth were marked "To go into the covenants" in Revelation Book 2.[55] For some of the texts, there are additional editing marks in Revelation Book 2 that likely relate to publication in the Doctrine and Covenants.[56]

Sections 8 through 21 of the volume, which date from April 1829 to September 1831, are arranged in chronological order. In his copy of the Book of Commandments, Oliver Cowdery marked these texts, except for the text of section 8, with the word "Covenants,"[57] indicating that he may have made a special pass through the Book of Commandments to identify texts to be included early in the Doctrine and Covenants. For a handful of these texts, there are also editing marks in Revelation Book 1 that likely relate to publication in

---

50. Minute Book 1, 17 Aug. 1835; "Of Governments and Laws in General," ca. Aug. 1835, in Doctrine and Covenants 102, 1835 ed. [D&C 134].

51. "General Assembly," in Doctrine and Covenants, 1835 ed., 256–257; "Index," Doctrine and Covenants, 1835 ed., i–iii; "Contents," Doctrine and Covenants, 1835 ed., v–xxiii; "Notes to the Reader," Doctrine and Covenants, 1835 ed., xxv.

52. Revelation, 1 Nov. 1831–B, in Revelation Book 1, p. 125, in *JSP*, MRB:223; "Index," Doctrine and Covenants, 1835 ed., i.

53. "Index," Doctrine and Covenants, 1835 ed., i.

54. See p. 598 herein.

55. Revelation Book 2, pp. 20, 111, 31, in *JSP*, MRB:453, 639, 475. In addition, the text of section 7 was marked in Revelation Book 2 with slashes apparently in the same ink flow as the notations that read "To go into the covenants." These slashes served an unknown purpose but indicate this revelation was being surveyed at the same time as the three sections with that notation. (See *JSP*, MRB:487n56.)

56. See "Table 3: Relationship between Items in Revelation Books 1 and 2 and the 1835 Doctrine and Covenants," in *JSP*, MRB:702.

57. See pp. 598–599 herein.

the Doctrine and Covenants.⁵⁸ Most of these texts had also been previously published in *The Evening and the Morning Star,* suggesting that texts that may have been perceived as especially important were published in that newspaper.

The texts in sections 22 through 29, dating from May 1831 to January 1832, are not arranged in chronological order, nor were they published in the Book of Commandments. John Whitmer marked seven of these eight texts sequentially in Revelation Book 1 with "No 1" through "No 8," omitting "No 2";⁵⁹ only section 23 is not so marked, but it evidently should have been marked as "No 2." Again, these markings in a source text show that the arrangement of sections was deliberate. For all eight of these texts, there are editing marks in Revelation Book 1, beyond the aforementioned numbering, that likely relate to publication in the Doctrine and Covenants.⁶⁰

Sections 30 through 72 are arranged chronologically, though they do not pick up where any former grouping left off. These sections, which date from July 1828 to August 1831, present in order the remaining texts published in the Book of Commandments and not already included in the earlier sections of the Doctrine and Covenants.⁶¹ For this group of texts, only one revelation, section 42, has editing marks in Revelation Book 1 or Revelation Book 2 that likely relate to publication in the Doctrine and Covenants.⁶² However, many of the sections in this group reflect editing marks made in Oliver Cowdery's copy of the Book of Commandments, and the wording of most of the sections closely mirrors the wording in the Book of Commandments.⁶³ It is probable, therefore, that the Cowdery volume was the source text for nearly all of the sections in this grouping. The heading "ON PRIESTHOOD AND CALLING," which immediately precedes section 30, may indicate that subsequent sections were seen as having a common theme, or the heading may have been intended to apply to section 30 only. Regardless of what was meant by the heading, the revelations in sections 30 to 72 do seem to cohere roughly as a unit. Most of these revelations are shorter texts addressed to specific individuals, usually directing a person to undertake a particular assignment, or calling, in the church or giving specific counsel related to an assignment already given. The revelations preceding section 30, in contrast, are typically lengthier texts on church government or doctrine addressed to audiences of church members or leaders generally.

A final group of texts, sections 73 through 100, have creation dates ranging from December 1830 to November 1834.⁶⁴ At times sections within this group are presented in

---

58. See "Table 3: Relationship between Items in Revelation Books 1 and 2 and the 1835 Doctrine and Covenants," in *JSP,* MRB:702–703.

59. See *JSP,* MRB:159n196.

60. See "Table 3: Relationship between Items in Revelation Books 1 and 2 and the 1835 Doctrine and Covenants," in *JSP,* MRB:703.

61. Two revelations not published in the Book of Commandments were also included in this grouping: sections 42 and 54.

62. See "Table 3: Relationship between Items in Revelation Books 1 and 2 and the 1835 Doctrine and Covenants," in *JSP,* MRB:703–704.

63. See pp. 598–599 herein.

64. The final two sections in the volume, sections 101 and 102, present articles on marriage and government, respectively, that were created circa August 1835 as work on the volume was concluding. (See Minute Book 1, 17 Aug. 1835.)

chronological order (sections 90 through 94, for example); usually, however, they are out of chronological order. The principle by which the sections in this group were arranged is not evident, except that section 100 is labeled in large type as an "APPENDIX" to the work.[65] Most of these texts were marked up in Revelation Book 1, Revelation Book 2, or both for publication in the Doctrine and Covenants.[66]

William W. Phelps, who saw the first efforts to print the revelations hindered in Missouri, eagerly anticipated the publication of the Doctrine and Covenants. In the same issue of the *Messenger and Advocate* that printed the minutes of the 17 August 1835 assembly meeting, he announced that the Doctrine and Covenants was "nearly ready for sale" and "may be expected in the course of a month, as one thousand copies have already been delivered to the binder."[67] By September 1835, some copies of the book had been bound in Cleveland and were available for sale.[68] It appears that advance payments for the book were taken as early as 26 June 1835.[69] David Whitmer and Samuel Smith were appointed by the presidency of the church as official agents to sell copies of the volume, which were priced at one dollar.[70] From the first, the Doctrine and Covenants was more accessible to church members than the scarce and incomplete Book of Commandments had been, but it appears the volume was not as widely disseminated as church leaders had hoped. No definite information about the total size of the 1835 printing is extant, but in the first two months after the volume was available, just over eighty copies were sold by F. G. Williams & Co.[71] The F. G. Williams & Co. account book ends in early November 1835, and no other records have been located that provide a clearer picture of total sales. In April 1836, at least five hundred unbound copies remained unsold.[72] Any volumes not sold by 1838 and stored in Kirtland were likely destroyed when the Kirtland printing office burned in the early part of 1838.[73]

---

65. Revelation, 3 Nov. 1831, in Doctrine and Covenants 100, 1835 ed. [D&C 133], was referred to as an "appendix" as early as May 1833. ("Revelations," *The Evening and the Morning Star,* May 1833, [1]–[2]; see also Appendix 1: Revelation, 3 Nov. 1831, p. [6], in *JSP,* MRB:405 [D&C 133], and 174n3 herein.)

66. See "Table 3: Relationship between Items in Revelation Books 1 and 2 and the 1835 Doctrine and Covenants," in *JSP,* MRB:704–705.

67. [William W. Phelps], "Doctrine and Covenants," *LDS Messenger and Advocate,* Aug. 1835, 1:170.

68. Phelps wrote to his wife on 18 September 1835: "We got some of the commandments from Cleveland last week." (William W. Phelps, Kirtland Mills, OH, to Sally Phelps, Liberty, MO, 16–18 Sept. 1835, private possession, copy in CHL.)

69. F. G. Williams and Company, Account Book, 2 (second numbering).

70. Minute Book 1, 16 Sept. 1835; William W. Phelps, Kirtland Mills, OH, to Sally Phelps, Liberty, MO, 16–18 Sept. 1835, private possession, copy in CHL.

71. F. G. Williams and Company, Account Book, 5–6 (second numbering). While other individuals and perhaps other committees or groups within the church would have sold copies of the book, that the printer sold only about eighty copies within the first two months of its availability suggests that sales were disappointing.

72. Minute Book 1, 2 Apr. 1836.

73. John Smith, Kirtland, OH, to George A. Smith, Shinnston, VA, 15–17 Jan. 1838, George Albert Smith, Papers, CHL; Johnson, "A Life Review," 24. A published notice of a sheriff's sale lists "a quantity of Covenants" as part of the inventory of the printing office just before it was destroyed. ("Sheriff Sale," *Painesville Telegraph,* 5 Jan. 1838, [3].)

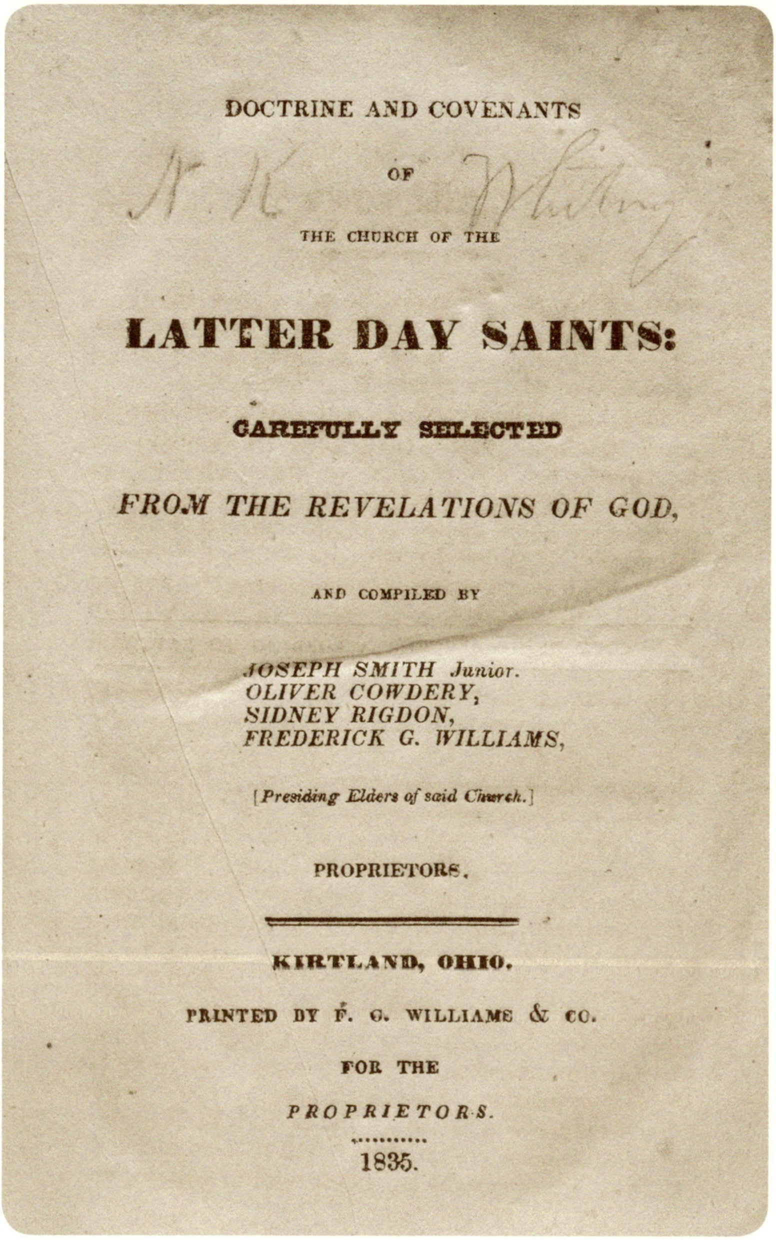

line 1

DOCTRINE AND COVENANTS

OF

THE CHURCH OF THE

LATTER DAY SAINTS:

5

CAREFULLY SELECTED

FROM THE REVELATIONS OF GOD,

AND COMPILED BY

JOSEPH SMITH Junior.
OLIVER COWDERY,
10 *SIDNEY RIGDON,*
FREDERICK G. WILLIAMS,

[*Presiding Elders of said Church.*]

PROPRIETORS.

KIRTLAND, OHIO.

15 PRINTED BY F. G. WILLIAMS & CO.

FOR THE

PROPRIETORS.

1835.

---

line 2. This signature was inscribed in graphite by Newel K. Whitney. This page begins the first gathering of the book.

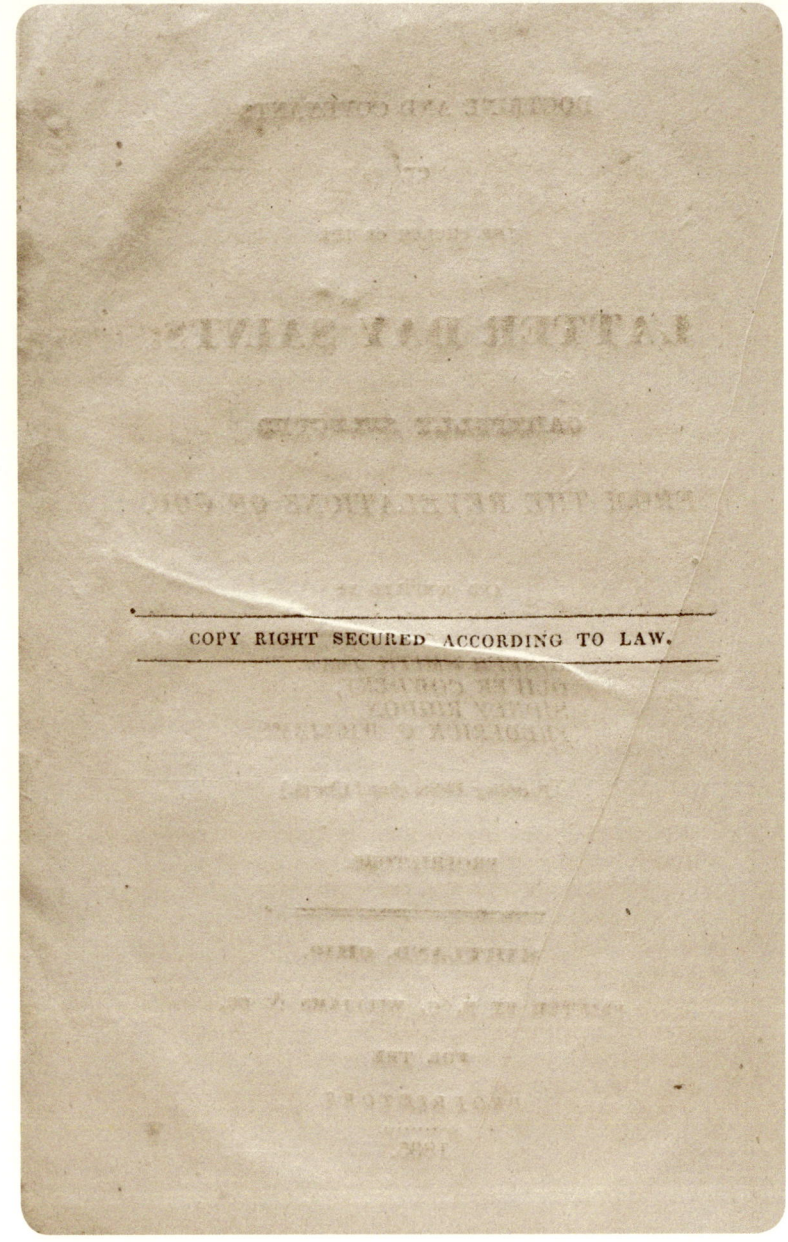

line 1

COPY RIGHT SECURED ACCORDING TO LAW.

PREFACE.

To the members of the church of the Latter Day Saints—

DEAR BRETHREN:

We deem it to be unnecessary te entertain you with a lengthy preface to the following volume, but merely to say, that it contains in short, the leading items of the religion which we have professed to believe.

The first part of the book will be found to contain a series of Lectures as delivered before a Theological class in this place, and in consequence of their embracing the important doctrine of salvation, we have arranged them into the following work.

The second part contains items or principles for the regulation of the church, as taken from the revelations which have been given since its organization, as well as from former ones.

There may be an aversion in the minds of some against receiving any thing purporting to be articles of religious faith, in consequence of there being so many now extant; but if men believe a system, and profess that it was given by inspiration, certainly, the more intelligibly they can present it, the better. It does not make a principle untrue to *print* it, neither does it make it true not to print it.

The church viewing this subject to be of importance, appointed, through their servants and delegates the High Council, your servants to select and compile this work. Several reasons might be adduced in favor of this move of the Council, but we only add a few words. They knew that the church was evil spoken of in many places—its faith and belief misrepresented, and the iv

line 1

way of truth thus subverted.   By some it was represented as disbelieving the bible, by others as being an
enemy to all good order and uprightness, and by others as being injurious to the peace of all governments
civil and political.

   We have, therefore, endeavored to present, though
in few words, *our* belief, and when we say this, humbly trust, the faith and principles of this society as a
body.

   We do not present this little volume with any other
expectation than that we are to be called to answer to
every principle advanced, in that day when the secrets of all hearts will be revealed, and the reward of
every man's labor be given him.

         With sentiments of esteem
             and sincere respect, we subscribe
                 ourselves your brethren in the bonds of
                     the gospel of our Lord Jesus Christ.
                         JOSEPH SMITH jr.
                         OLIVER COWDERY.
                         SIDNEY RIGDON.
                         F. G. WILLIAMS.
Kirtland, Ohio, February 17, 1835.

line 1

THEOLOGY.

LECTURE FIRST

On the doctrine of the church of the

Latter Day Saints.

5

Of Faith.

SECTION I.

1. FAITH being the first principle in revealed religion,
and the foundation of all righteousness, necessarily
claims the first place in a course of lectures which are
10 designed to unfold to the understanding the doctrine
of Jesus Christ.

2 In presenting the subject of faith, we shall observe
the following order:

3 First, Faith itself—what it is:

15 4 Secondly, The object on which it rests; and

5 Thirdly, The effects which flow from it.

6 Agreeably to this order we have first to show what
faith is.

7 The author of the epistle to the Hebrews, in the
20 eleventh chapter of that epistle, and first verse, gives
the following definition of the word faith:

8 Now faith is the substance [assurance] of things
hoped for, the evidence of things not seen.

9 From this we learn, that faith is the assurance
25 which men have of the existence of things which they
have not seen; and the principle of action in all intelligent beings.

10 If men were duly to consider themselves, and
turn their thoughts and reflections to the operations of

30 A2

---

line 1. First lecture on faith, ca. winter 1834–1835. This lecture was printed as a broadside circa February 1835. Identical placement of broken pieces of type in both this version and the broadside indicates that the same typesetting was used for both printings. Corrections and additions to the Doctrine and Covenants version, however, indicate that the broadside version was set in type first. (*Theology. Lecture First,* [Kirtland, OH: ca. Feb. 1835], copy at CHL.)

line 30. "A2" is the first of two signature marks in this gathering; the second is on the recto of the seventh leaf. These marks were used in collating the gatherings after the sheets were folded.

line 1

their own minds, they would readily discover that it is faith, and faith only, which is the moving cause of all action, in them; that without it, both mind and body would be in a state of inactivity, and all their exertions would cease, both physical and mental.

11 Were this class to go back and reflect upon the history of their lives, from the period of their first recollection, and ask themselves, what principle excited them to action, or what gave them energy and activity, in all their lawful avocations, callings and pursuits, what would be the answer? Would it not be that it was the assurance which we had of the existence of things which we had not seen, as yet?— Was it not the hope which you had, in consequence of your belief in the existence of unseen things, which stimulated you to action and exertion, in order to obtain them? Are you not dependant on your faith, or belief, for the acquisition of all knowledge, wisdom and intelligence? Would you exert yourselves to obtain wisdom and intelligence, unless you did believe that you could obtain them? Would you have ever sown if you had not believed that you would reap? Would you have ever planted if you had not believed that you would gather? Would you have ever asked unless you had believed that you would receive? Would you have ever sought unless you had believed that you would have found? Or would you have ever knocked unless you had believed that it would have been opened unto you? In a word, is there any thing that you would have done, either physical or mental, if you had not previously believed? Are not all your exertions, of every kind, dependant on your faith? Or may we not ask, what have you, or what do you possess, which you have not obtained by reason of your faith? Your food, your raiment, your lodgings, are they not all by reason of your faith? Reflect, and ask yourselves, if these things are not so. Turn your thoughts on

7.

line 1
your own minds, and see if faith is not the moving cause of all action in yourselves; and if the moving cause in you, is it not in all other intelligent beings?

12 And as faith is the moving cause of all action in temporal concerns, so it is in spiritual; for the Savior has said, and that truly, that he that *believeth* and is baptized, shall be saved. Mark 16:16.

13 As we receive by faith, all temporal blessings that we do receive, so we, in like manner, receive by faith all spiritual blessings, that we do receive. But faith is not only the principle of action, but of power, also, in all intelligent beings, whether in heaven, or on earth. Thus says the author of the epistle to the Hebrews, 11:3:

14 Through faith we understand that the worlds were framed by the word of God: so that things which are seen were not made of things which do appear.

15 By this we understand that the principle of power, which existed in the bosom of God, by which the worlds were framed, was faith; and that it is by reason of this principle of power, existing in the Deity, that all created things exist—so that all things in heaven, on earth, or under the earth, exist by reason of faith, as it existed in HIM.

16 Had it not been for the principle of faith the worlds would never have been framed, neither would man have been formed of the dust—it is the principle by which Jehovah works, and through which he exercises power over all temporal, as well as eternal things. Take this principle or attribute, (for it is an attribute) from the Deity and he would cease to exist.

17 Who cannot see, that if God framed the worlds by faith, that it is by faith that he exercises power over them, and that faith is the principle of power? And that if the principle of power, it must be so in man as well as in the Deity? This is the testimony of all

8

the sacred writers, and the lesson which they have been endeavoring to teach to man.

18 The Savior says, Matthew 17:19,20, in explaining the reason why the disciples could not cast out the devil, that it was because of their unbelief: "For verily, I say unto you," said he, "if ye have faith as a grain of mustard-seed, ye shall say unto this mountain, Remove hence to yonder place! and it shall remove: and nothing shall be impossible unto you."

19 Moroni, while abridging and compiling the record of his fathers, has given us the following account of faith as the principle of power: He says, page 563, that it was the faith of Alma and Amulek which caused the walls of the prison to be wrent, as recorded on the 264th page; that it was the faith of Nephi and Lehi which caused a change to be wrought upon the hearts of the Lamanites, when they were immersed with the Holy Spirit, and with fire, as seen on the 421st page, and that it was by faith that the mountain Zerin was removed, when the brother of Jared spake in the name of the Lord.   See also 565th page.

20 In addition to this we are told in Hebrews, 11:32, 33,34,35, that Gideon, Barak, Samson, Jephthah, David, Samuel, and the prophets, through faith subdued kingdoms, wrought righteousness, obtained promises, stopped the mouths of lions, quenched the violence of fire, escaped the edge of the sword, out of weakness were made strong, waxed valiant in fight, turned to flight the armies of the aliens; and that women received their dead raised to life again, &c. &c.

21 Also, Joshua, in the sight of all Israel, bade the sun and moon to stand still, and it was done. Josh. 10:12.

22 We here understand, that the sacred writers say, that all these things were done by faith—It was by faith that the worlds were framed—God spake, chaos heard, and worlds came into order, by reason of the faith there was in HIM. So with man also—he spake

9

by faith in the name of God, and the sun stood still, the moon obeyed, mountains removed, prisons fell, lions' mouths were closed, the human heart lost its enmity, fire its violence, armies their power, the sword its terror, and death its dominion; and all this by reason of the faith which was in them.

23 Had it not been for the faith which was in man, they might have spoken to the sun, the moon, the mountains, prisons, lions, the human heart, fire, armies, the sword, or to death in vain!

24 Faith, then, is the first great governing principle which has power, dominion, and authority over all things: by it they exist, by it they are upheld, by it they are changed, or by it they remain, agreeably to the will of God. Without it, there is no power, and without power there could be no creation, nor existence!

OF THEOLOGY.

Question.—What is theology?

Answer:—It is that revealed science which treats of the being and attributes of God—his relations to us—the dispensations of his providence—his will with respect to our actions—and his purposes with respect to our end. [Buck's Theological Dictionary, page 582.]

Q. What is the first principle in this revealed science?

A. Faith. [§ 1. ¶ 1.]

Q. Why is faith the first principle in this revealed science?

A. Because it is the foundation of all righteousness. Heb 11:6. Without faith it is impossible to please God. 1st. John, 3:7. Little children, let no man deceive you: he that doeth righteousness, is righteous, even as he [God] is righteous. [§ 1. ¶ 1.]

Q. What arrangement should be followed in presenting the subject of faith?

A. First, Should be shown what faith is: [§ 1. ¶ 3.] Secondly, The object upon which it rests; and [§ 1. ¶ 4.] Thirdly, The effects which flow from it. [§ 1. ¶ 5.]

Q. What is faith?

A. It is the assurance of things hoped for, the evidence of things not seen: Heb. 11:1. That is, it is the assurance we have of the existence of unseen things. And being the assu-

---

line 18. This catechism, a summary of doctrine in question-and-answer format, is preceded by the topical heading "OF THEOLOGY." Catechisms for the remaining six lectures do not bear headings.

10

line 1
rance which we have of the existence of unseen things, must
be the principle of action in all intelligent beings.   Heb. 11:3.
Through faith we understand the worlds were framed by the
word of God.   [§ 1. ¶ 8,9.]

Q.   How do you prove that faith is the principle of action in
all intelligent beings?

A.   First, By duly considering the operations of my own
mind; and secondly, by the direct declaration of scripture.—
Heb. 11:7.   By faith Noah, being warned of things not seen
as yet, moved with fear, prepared an ark to the saving of his
house; by the which he condemned the world, and became
heir of the righteousness which is by faith.   Heb. 11:8.   By
faith Abraham, when he was called to go out into a place
which he should after receive for an inheritance, obeyed; and
he went out not knowing whither he went.   Heb. 11:9.   By
faith he sojourned in the land of promise, as in a strange country, dwelling in tabernacles with Isaac and Jacob, the heirs
with him of the same promise.   Heb. 11:27.   By faith Moses
forsook Egypt, not fearing the wrath of the king: for he endured as seeing him who is invisible.   [§ 1. ¶ 10,11.]

Q.   Is not faith the principle of action in spiritual things
as well as in temporal?

A.   It is.

Q.   How do you prove it?

A.   Heb. 11:6.   Without faith it is impossible to please
God.   Mark 16:16.   He that believeth and is baptized, shall
be saved.   Rom. 4:16.   Therefore, it is of faith, that it might
be by grace; to the end the promise might be sure to all the
seed: not to that only which is of the law, but to that also
which is of the faith of Abraham, who is the father of us all.—
[§ 1. ¶ 12,13.]

Q.   Is faith any thing else beside the principle of action?

A.   It is.

Q.   What is it?

A.   It is the principle of power, also.   [§ 1. ¶ 13.]

Q.   How do you prove it?

A.   First, It is the principle of power in the Deity, as well
as in man.   Heb. 11:3.   Through faith we understand that
the worlds were framed by the word of God, so that things
which are seen were not made of things which do appear.—
[§ 1. ¶ 14,15,16.]

Secondly, It is the principle of power in man also.   Book of
Mormon, page 264.   Alma and Amulek are delivered from
prison.   Do. page 421.   Nephi and Lehi, with the Lamanites,
are immersed with the Spirit.   Do. page 565.   The mountain
Zerin, by the faith of the brother of Jared, is removed.   Josh.

11

line 1

10:12. Then spake Joshua to the Lord in the day when the Lord delivered up the Amorites before the children of Israel, and he said in the sight of Israel, Sun, stand thou still upon Gibeon, and thou Moon, in the valley of Ajalon. Josh. 10:13.

5

And the sun stood still, and the moon stayed, until the people had avenged themselves of their enemies. Is not this written in the book of Jasher? So the sun stood still in the midst of heaven, and hasted not to go down about a whole day. Mat. 17:19. Then came the disciples to Jesus apart, and said,

10

Why could not we cast him out? Mat. 17:20. And Jesus said unto them, Because of your unbelief: for verily I say unto you, if ye have faith as a grain of mustard-seed, ye shall say unto this mountain, Remove hence to yonder place; and it shall remove; and nothing shall be impossible unto you.—

15

Heb. 11:32. And what shall I say more? for the time would fail me to tell of Gideon, and of Barak, and of Samson, and of Jephthah, of David also, and Samuel, and of the prophets. Heb. 11:33. Who through faith subdued kingdoms, wrought righteousness, obtained promises, stopped the mouths

20

of lions, Heb. 11:34. Quenched the violence of fire, escaped the edge of the sword, out of weakness were made strong, waxed valiant in fight, turned to flight the armies of the aliens. Heb. 11:35. Women received their dead raised to life again: and others were tortured, not accepting deliverance; that they

25

might obtain a better resurrection. [§ 1. ¶ 16,17,18,19,20,21, 22.]

Q. How would you define faith in its most unlimited sense?

A. It is the first great governing principle, which has power, dominion and authority over all things. [§ 1. ¶ 24.]

30

Q. How do you convey to the understanding more clearly, that faith is the first great governing principle, which has power, dominion, and authority over all things?

A. By it they exist, by it they are upheld, by it they are changed, or by it they remain, agreeably to the will of God;

35

and without it there is no power; and without power there could be no creation, nor existence! [§ 1. ¶ 24.]

line 1

LECTURE SECOND.

Of Faith.

SECTION II.

1 Having shown in our previous lecture "faith itself—what it is," we shall proceed to show secondly
the object on which it rests.

2 We here observe that God is the only supreme
governor, and independent being, in whom all fulness
and perfection dwells; who is omnipotent, omnipresent, and omnicient; without beginning of days or end
of life; and that in him every good gift, and every
good principle dwells; and that he is the Father of
lights: In him the principle of faith dwells independently; and he is the object in whom the faith of all
other rational and accountable beings centers, for life
and salvation.

3 In order to present this part of the subject in a
clear and conspicuous point of light, it is necessary
to go back and show the evidences which mankind
have had, and the foundation on which these evidences are, or were based, since the creation, to believe
in the existence of a God.

4 We do not mean those evidences which are manifested by the works of creation, which we daily behold with our natural eyes: we are sensible, that after a revelation of Jesus Christ, the works of creation,
throughout their vast forms and varieties, clearly ex-
hibit his eternal power and Godhead.   Romans 1:20.
For the invisible things of him from the creation of
the world are clearly seen, being understood by the
things that are made: even his eternal power and
Godhead.   But we mean those evidences by which
the first thoughts were suggested to the minds of men
that there was a God who created all things.

5 We shall now proceed to examine the situation of

line 1. Second lecture on faith, ca. winter 1834–1835.

13

man at his first creation. Moses, the historian, has given us the following account of him in the first chapt. of the book of Genesis, beginning with the 20th verse, and closing with the 30th. We copy from the New Translation:

6 And the Lord God said unto the Only Begotten, who was with him from the beginning, Let us make man in our image, after our likeness: and it was done.

7 And the Lord God said, Let them have dominion over the fish of the sea, and over the fowl of the air, and over the cattle, and over all the earth, and over every creeping thing that creaps upon the earth.

8 So God created man in his own image, in the image of the Only Begotten created he him; male and female created he them. And God blessed them, and God said unto them, Be fruitful, and multiply, and replenish the earth, and subdue it: and have dominion over the fish of the sea, and over the fowl of the air, and over every living thing that moves upon the earth.

9 And the Lord God said unto man, Behold, I have given you every herb bearing seed, which is upon the face of all the earth, and every tree in the which is the fruit of a tree yielding seed; to you it shall be for meat.

10 Again, Genesis 2:15,16,17,19,20: And the Lord God took the man, and put him into the garden of Eden, to dress it and to keep it. And the Lord God commanded the man, saying, Of every tree of the garden you may freely eat: but of the tree of the knowledge of good and evil you shall not eat of it, neither shall you touch it; nevertheless, you may choose for yourself, for it is given unto you; but remember that I forbid it: for in the day that you eat thereof you shall surely die.

B

14

11 And out of the ground the Lord God formed every beast of the field, and every fowl of the air, and commanded that they should be brought unto Adam, to see what he would call them. * * * And whatever Adam called every living creature, that was the name thereof. And Adam gave names to all cattle, and to the fowl of the air, and to every beast of the field.

12 From the foregoing we learn man's situation at his first creation; the knowledge with which he was endowed, and the high and exalted station in which he was placed—lord, or governor of all things on earth, and at the same time enjoying communion and intercourse with his Maker, without a vail to separate between. We shall next proceed to examine the account given of his fall, and of his being driven out of the garden of Eden, and from the presence of the Lord.

13 Moses proceeds: And they [Adam and Eve] heard the voice of the Lord God as they were walking in the garden in the cool of the day, and Adam and his wife hid themselves from the presence of the Lord God among the trees of the garden. And the Lord God called unto Adam, and said unto him, Where are you going? And he said, I heard your voice in the garden, and I was afraid, because I beheld that I was naked, and I hid myself.

14 And the Lord God said unto Adam, Who told you that you were naked? Have you eaten of the tree whereof I told you that you should not eat? If so, you should surely die? And the man said, The woman whom you gave me, and commanded that she should remain with me, gave me of the fruit of the tree, and I did eat.

15 And the Lord God said unto the woman, What is this which you have done? And the woman said, The serpent beguiled me, and I did eat.

15

16 And again, the Lord said unto the woman, I will greatly multiply your sorrow, and your conception: in sorrow you shall bring forth children; and your desire shall be to your husband, and he shall rule over you.

17 And the Lord God said unto Adam, because you have hearkened unto the voice of your wife, and have eaten of the fruit of the tree of which I commanded you, saying, You shall not eat of it! cursed shall be the ground for your sake: in sorrow you shall eat of it all the days of your life. Thorns also, and thistles shall it bring forth to you: and you shall eat the herb of the field. By the sweat of your face shall you eat bread, until you shall return unto the ground —for you shall surely die—for out of it you were taken; for dust you were, and unto dust you shall return. This was immediately followed by the fulfillment of what we previously said: Man was driven, or sent out of Eden.

18 Two important items are shown from the former quotations: First, After man was created, he was not left without intelligence, or understanding, to wander in darkness, and spend an existence in ignorance and doubt—on the great and important point which effected his happiness,—as to the real fact by whom he was created, or unto whom he was amenable for his conduct. God conversed with him face to face: in his presence he was permitted to stand, and from his own mouth he was permitted to receive instruction—he heard his voice, walked before him, and gazed upon his glory—while intelligence burst upon his understanding, and enabled him to give names to the vast assemblage of his Maker's works.

19 Secondly, we have seen, that, though man did transgress, his transgression did not deprive him of the previous knowledge with which he was endowed, relative to the existence and glory of his Creator;

16

line 1 for no sooner did he hear his voice, than he sought
to hide himself from his presence.

20 Having shown, then, in the first instance, that
God began to converse with man, immediately after
he "breathed into his nostrils the breath of life," and
that he did not cease to manifest himself to him, even
after his fall, we shall next proceed to show, that,
though he was cast out from the garden of Eden, his
knowledge of the existence of God was not lost, neither did God cease to manifest his will unto him.

21 We next proceed to present the account of the
direct revelation which man received, after he was
cast out of Eden, and further copy from the New
Translation:

22 After Adam had been driven out of the garden,
he began to till the earth, and to have dominion over
all the beasts of the field, and to eat his bread by the
sweat of his brow, as the Lord had commanded him:
and he called upon the name of the Lord, and so did
Eve his wife also. And they heard the voice of the
Lord from the way toward the garden of Eden, speaking unto them; and they saw him not, for they were
shut out from his presence: but he gave unto them commandments that they should worship the Lord their
God, and should offer the firstlings of their flocks for
an offering unto the Lord. And Adam was obedient
unto the commandment.

23 And after many days an angel of the Lord appeared unto Adam, saying, why do you offer sacrifices unto the Lord? And Adam said unto him, I
know not; but the Lord commanded me to offer sacrifices.

24 And the angel said unto him, This thing is a
similitude of the sacrifice of the Only Begotten of the
Father, who is full of grace and truth. And you
shall do all that you do in the name of the Son: and
you shall repent and call upon God in his name for-

17

line 1   ever. In that day the Holy Spirit fell upon Adam, and bore record of the Father and the Son.

25 This last quotation, or summary, shows this important fact, that though our first parents were driven 5 out of the garden of Eden, and were even separated from the presence of God, by a vail, they still retained a knowledge of his existence, and that sufficiently to move them to call upon him. And further, that no sooner was the plan of redemption revealed to man, 10 and he began to call upon God, than the Holy Spirit was given, bearing record of the Father and Son.

26 Moses also gives us an account, in the 4th of Genesis, of the transgression of Cain, and the righteousness of Abel, and of the revelations of God to 15 them. He says: In process of time Cain brought of the fruit of the ground, an offering unto the Lord.— And Abel also brought of the firstlings of his flock, and of the fat thereof. And the Lord had respect unto Abel, and to his offering: but unto Cain and to 20 his offering he had not respect. Now satan knew this, and it pleased him. And Cain was very angry, and his countenance fell. And the Lord said unto Cain, Why are you angry? why is your countenance fallen? If you do well, will you not be accepted?— 25 And if you do not well, sin lies at the door, and satan desires to have you; and except you shall hearken unto my commandments, I will deliver you up: and it shall be unto you according to his desire.

27 And Cain went into the field and talked with his 30 brother Abel. And while they were in the field, Cain rose up against his brother Abel, and slew him. And Cain gloried in what he had done, saying, I am free! surely the flocks of my brother will now fall into my hands.

35 28 But the Lord said unto Cain, Where is Abel, your brother? And he said, I know not: am I my

B

---

line 37. This page begins the second gathering of the book. "B" is the first of two signature marks in this gathering; the second is on the recto of the following leaf. These marks were used in collating the gatherings after the sheets were folded.

18

line 1
brother's keeper? And the Lord said, What have
you done? the voice of your brother's blood cries unto me from the ground. And now, you shall be cursed from the earth which has opened her mouth to receive your brother's blood, from your hand. When
you till the ground, she shall not henceforth yield unto you her strength. A fugitive and a vagabond also,
you shall be in the earth.

29 And Cain said unto the Lord, Satan tempted me
because of my brother's flocks. And I was also angry: for his offering was accepted, and mine was not:
My punishment is greater than I can bear. Behold,
you have driven me out this day from the face of
men, and from your face shall I be hid also; and I
shall be a fugitive and a vagabond in the earth; and
it shall come to pass, every one that finds me will
slay me, because of my oath; for these things are
not hid from the Lord. And the Lord said unto him,
Therefore, whoever slays Cain, vengeance shall be
taken on him seven fold. And the Lord set a mark
upon Cain, lest any finding him should kill him.

30 The object of the foregoing quotations is to show
to this class the way by which mankind were first
made acquainted with the existence of a God: that it
was by a manifestation of God to man, and that God
continued, after man's transgression to manifest himself to him and his posterity: and notwithstanding they
were separated from his immediate presence, that
they could not see his face, they continued to hear his
voice.

31 Adam thus being made acquainted with God,
communicated the knowledge which he had unto his
posterity; and it was through this means that the
thought was first suggested to their minds that there
was a God. Which laid the foundation for the exercise of their faith, through which they could obtain a
knowledge of his character and also of his glory.

19

line 1

32 Not only was there a manifestation made unto Adam of the existence of a God, but Moses informs us, as before quoted, that God condescended to talk with Cain after his great transgression, in slaying his brother, and that Cain knew that it was the Lord that was talking with him: so that when he was driven out from the presence of his brethren, he carried with him the knowledge of the existence of a God: and through this means, doubtless his posterity became acquainted with the fact that such a being existed.

33 From this we can see that the whole human family, in the early age of their existence, in all their different branches, had this knowledge disseminated among them; so that the existence of God became an object of faith, in the early age of the world. And the evidences which these men had of the existence of a God, was the testimony of their fathers in the first instance.

34 The reason why we have been thus particular on this part of our subject, is, that this class may see by what means it was that God became an object of faith among men after the fall; and what it was that stirred up the faith of multitudes to feel after him; to search after a knowledge of his character, perfections and attributes, until they became extensively acquainted with him; and not only commune with him, and behold his glory, but be partakers of his power, and stand in his presence.

35 Let this class mark particularly that the testimony which these men had of the existence of a God, was the testimony of man; for previous to the time that any of Adam's posterity had obtained a manifestation of God to themselves, Adam their common father had testified unto them of the existence of God, and of his eternal power and Godhead.

36 For instance, Abel, before he received the assu-
2*

20

line 1

rance from heaven that his offerings were acceptable
unto God, had received the important information of
his father, that such a being did exist, who had created, and who did uphold all things. Neither can
there be a doubt existing on the mind of any person,
that Adam was the first who did communicate the
knowledge of the existence of a God, to his posterity;
and that the whole faith of the world, from that time
down to the present, is in a certain degree, dependent
on the knowledge first communicated to them by their
common progenitor; and it has been handed down to
the day and generation in which we live, as we shall
show from the face of the sacred records.

37 First, Adam was 130 years old when Seth was
born. Gen. 5:3. And the days of Adam, after he
had begotten Seth, were 800 years; making him
930 years old when he died. Gen. 5:4,5. Seth was
105 when Enos was born. 5:6. Enos was 90 when
Cainan was born. 5:9. Cainan was 70 when Mahalaleel was born. 5:12. Mahalaleel was 65 when Jared
was born. 5:15: Jared was 162 when Enoch was
born. 5:18. Enoch was 65 when Methusaleh was
born. 5:21. Methuseleh was 187 when Lamech was
born. 5:25. Lamech was 182 when Noah was born.
5:28.

38 From this account it appears that Lamech, the
9th from Adam, and the father of Noah, was 56 years
old when Adam died; Methuseleh, 243; Enoch, 308;
Jared 470; Mahalaleel, 535; Cainan, 605; Enos, 695;
and Seth, 800.

39 So that Lamech, the father of Noah; Methusaleh, Enoch, Jared, Mahalaleel, Cainan, Enos, Seth,
and Adam, were all living at the same time, and beyond all controversy, were all preachers of righteousness.

40 Moses further informs us, that Seth lived, after
he begat Enos, 807 years; making him 912 years old

line 1   at his death. Gen. 5:7,8. And Enos lived, after he
begat Cainan, 815 years: making him 905 years old
when he died. 5:10,11. And Cainan lived, after he
begat Mahalaleel, 840 years: making him 910 years
5   old at his death. 5:13,14. And Mahalaleel lived, after he begat Jared, 830 years: making him 895 years
old when he died. 5:16,17. And Jared lived, after he
begat Enoch, 800 years: making him 962 years old
at his death. 5:19,20. And Enoch walked with God,
10   after he begat Methuseleh 300 years: making him
365 years old when he was translated. 5:22,23. And
Methuseleh lived, after he begat Lamech, 782 years:
making him 969 years old when he died. 5:26,27.
Lamech lived, after he begat Noah, 595 years: ma-
15   king him 777 years old when he died. 5:30,31.

41 Agreeably to this account, Adam died in the
930th year of the world, Enoch was translated in the
987th, Seth died in the 1042nd, Enos in the 1140th,
Cainan in the 1235th, Mahalaleel in the 1290th, Ja-
20   red in the 1422nd, Lamech in the 1651st, and Methusaleh in the 1656th, it being the same year in
which the flood came.

42 So that Noah was 84 years old when Enos died,
176 when Cainan died, 234 when Mahalaleel died,
25   366 when Jared died, 595 when Lamech died, and
600 when Methusaleh died.

43 We can see from this that Enos, Cainan, Mahalaleel, Jared, Methusaleh, Lamach, and Noah all lived on the earth at the same time. And that Enos,
30   Cainan, Mahalaleel, Jared Methusaleh, and Lamech,
were all acquainted with both Adam and Noah.

44 From the foregoing it is easily to be seen, not
only how the knowledge of God came into the world,
but upon what principle it was preserved: that from
35   the time it was first communicated, it was retained
in the minds of righteous men, who taught, not only
their own posterity, but the world; so that there was

22

no need of a new revelation to man, after Adam's creation, to Noah, to give them the first idea, or notion
of the existence of a God: and not only of a God, but
of the true and living God.

45 Having traced the chronology of the world from
Adam to Noah, we will now trace it from Noah to
Abraham. Noah was 502 years old when Shem was
born: 98 years afterward the flood came, being the
600th year of Noah's age. And Moses informs us
that Noah lived after the flood, 350 years: making
him 950 years old when he died. Gen. 9:28,29.

46 Shem was 100 years old when Arphaxed was
born. Gen. 11:10, Arphaxed was 35 when Salah
was born 11:12. Salah was 30 when Eber was born.
11:14. Eber was 34 when Peleg was born: in whose
days the earth was divided. 11:16. Peleg was 30
when Reu was born. 11:18. Reu was 32 when Serug was born. 11:20. Serug was 30 when Nahor
was born. 11:22. Nahor was 29 when Terah was
born. 11:24. Terah was 70 when Haran and Abraham were born. 11:26.

47 There is some difficulty in the account given by
Moses, of Abraham's birth. Some have supposed,
that Abraham was not born until Terah was 130
years old. This conclusion is drawn from a variety
of scriptures, which are not to our purpose at present
to quote. Neither is it a matter of any consequence
to us, whether Abraham was born when Terah was
70 years old, or 130. But in order that there may
no doubt exist upon any mind, in relation to the object
lying immediately before us, in presenting the present chronology, we will date the birth of Abraham at
the latest period: that is, when Terah was 130 years
old. It appears from this account, that from the flood
to the birth of Abraham was 352 years.

48 Moses informs us that Shem lived, after he begat
Arphaxed, 500. Gen. 11:11, This added to 100

23

years, which was his age when Arphaxed was born, makes him 600 years old when he died. Arphaxed lived, after he begat Salah, 403 years. 11:13. This added to 35 years, which was his age when Salah was born, makes him 438 years old when he died. Salah lived, after he begat Eber, 403 years. 11:15.— This added to 30 years, which was his age when Eber was born, makes him 433 years old when he died.— Eber lived, after he begat Peleg, 430 years. 11:17. This added to 34 years, which was his age when Peleg was born, makes him 464 years old. Peleg lived, after he begat Reu, 209 years. 11:19. This added to 30 years, which was his age when Reu was born, makes him 239 years old when he died. Reu lived, after he begat Serug, 207 years. Gen. 11:21. This added to 32 years, which was his age when Serug was born, makes him 239 years old when he died. Serug lived, after he begat Nahor, 200 years. Gen. 11:23. This added to 30 years, which was his age when Nahor was born, makes him 230 years old when he died. Nahor lived, after he begat Terah, 119 years. Gen. 11:25. This added to 29 years, which was his age when Terah was born, makes him 148 years old when he died. Terah was 130 years old when Abraham was born, and is supposed to have lived 75 years after his birth: making him 205 years old when he died.

49 Agreeably to this last account, Peleg died in the 1996th year of the world, Nahor in the 1997th, and Noah in the 2006th. So that Peleg, in whose days the earth was divided, and Nahor, the grand-father of Abraham, both died before Noah: the former being 239 years old, and the latter 148. And who cannot but see, that they must have had a long and intimate acquaintance with Noah?

50 Reu died in the 2026th year of the world, Serug in 2049th, Terah in the 2083rd, Arphaxed in the

24

2096th, Selah in the 2126th, Shem in the 2158th, Abraham in the 2183rd, and Eber in the 2187th: which was 4 years after Abraham's death. And Eber was the fourth from Noah.

51 Nahor, Abraham's brother, was 58 years old when Noah died, Terah 128, Serug 187, Reu 219, Eber 283, Salah 313, Arphaxed 344, and Shem 448.

52 It appears from this account, that Nahor, brother of Abraham, Terah, Nahor, Serug, Reu, Peleg, Eber, Salah, Arphaxed, Shem, and Noah, all lived on the earth at the same time. And that Abraham was 18 years old when Reu died, 41 when Serug and his brother Nahor died, 75 when Terah died, 88 when Arphaxed died, 118 when Salah died, 150 when Shem died, and that Eber lived 4 years after Abraham's death. And that Shem, Arphaxed, Salah, Eber, Reu, Serug, Terah, and Nahor, the brother of Abraham, and Abraham, lived at the same time.— And that Nahor, brother of Abraham, Terah, Serug, Reu, Eber, Salah, Arphaxed, and Shem, were all acquainted with both Noah and Abraham.

53 We have now traced the chronology of the world, agreeably to the account given in our present bible, from Adam to Abraham, and have clearly determined, beyond the power of controversy, that there was no difficulty in preserving the knowledge of God in the world, from the creation of Adam, and the manifestation made to his immediate descendants, as set forth in the former part of this lecture, so that the students, in this class need not have any dubiety resting on their minds, on this subject; for they can easily see, that it is impossible for it to be otherwise; but that the knowledge of the existence of a God, must have continued from father to son, as a matter of tradition, at least. For we cannot suppose, that a knowledge of this important fact, could have existed in the mind of any of the before mentioned individ-

25

line 1 uals, without their having made it known to their
posterity.

54 We have now shown how it was that the first
thought ever existed in the mind of any individual,
5 that there was such a being as a God, who had created and did uphold all things: that it was by reason of
the manifestation which he first made to our father
Adam, when he stood in his presence, and conversed
with him face to face, at the time of his creation.

10 55 Let us here observe, that after any portion of the
human family are made acquainted with the important fact that there is a God who has created and does
uphold all things, the extent of their knowledge, respecting his character and glory, will depend upon
15 their diligence and faithfulness in seeking after him,
until like Enoch the brother of Jared, and Moses, they
shall obtain faith in God, and power with him to behold him face to face.

56 We have now clearly set forth how it is, and
20 how it was, that God became an object of faith for
rational beings; and also, upon what foundation the
testimony was based, which excited the enquiry and
diligent search of the ancient saints, to seek after and
obtain a knowledge of the glory of God: and we have
25 seen that it was human testimony, and human testimony only, that excited this enquiry, in the first instance in their minds—it was the credence they gave
to the testimony of their fathers—this testimony having aroused their minds to enquire after the knowl-
30 edge of God, the enquiry frequently terminated, indeed, always terminated, when rightly persued, in
the most glorious discoveries, and eternal certainty.

———◆———

Question.—Is there a being who has faith in himself indepen-
ently?
35 *Answer.*—There is. Q. Who is it? A. It is God.

26

line 1

Q. How do you prove that God has faith in himself independently?

A. Because he is omnipotent, omnipresent, and omnicient: without beginning of days or end of life, and in him all fulness dwells. Eph. 1:23. Which is his body, the fulness of him that filleth all in all. Col. 1:19. For it pleased the Father, that in him should all fulness dwell. [§ 11. ¶ 2.]

Q. Is he the object in whom the faith of all other rational and accountable beings centers, for life and salvation?

A. He is.

Q. How do you prove it?

A. Isa. 45:22. Look unto me, and be ye saved, all the ends of the earth: for I am God, and there is none else. Rom. 11: 34,35,36. For who hath known the mind of the Lord? or who hath been his counsellor? or who hath first given to him, and it shall be recompensed unto him again? For of him, and through him, and to him, are all things: to whom be glory forever. Amen. Isa. 40: from the 8th to the 18th. O Zion that bringest good tidings, [Or, O thou that tellest good tidings to Zion.] get thee up into the high mountain: O Jerusalem, that bringest good tidings, [Or, O thou that tellest good tidings to Jerusalem,] lift up thy voice with strength; lift it up, be not afraid; say unto the cities of Judah, Behold your God! Behold the Lord your God will come with strong hand, [Or, against the strong.] and his arm shall rule for him: behold, his reward is with him, and his work before him. [Or, recompense for his work.] He shall feed his flock like a shepherd: he shall gather his lambs with his arms, and carry them in his bosom, and shall gently lead those that are with young. Who hath measured the waters in the hollow of his hand, and meted out heaven with the span, and comprehended the dust of the earth in a measure, weighed the mountains in scales, and the hills in a ballance? Who hath directed the Spirit of the Lord, or being his counsellor, hath taught him? With whom took he counsel, and who instructed him, and taught him in the path of judgment, and taught him knowledge, and shewed to him the way of understanding? Behold, the nations are as a drop of a bucket, and are counted as the small dust of the ballance: behold he taketh up the isles as a very little thing. And Lebanon is not sufficient to burn, nor the beasts thereof sufficient for a burnt offering. All nations are before him as nothing; and they are counted to him less than nothing, and vanity! Jer. 51:15,16. He [the Lord] hath made the earth by his power, he hath established the world by his wisdom, and hath streached out the heaven by his understanding. When he uttereth his voice there is a multitude of waters in the heavens;

and he causeth the vapors to ascend from the ends of the earth: he maketh lightnings with rain, and bringeth forth the wind out of his treasures. 1st Cor. 8:6. But to us there is but one God, the Father, of whom are all things, and we in him; and one Lord Jesus Christ, by whom are all things, and we by him. [§ II. ¶ 2.]

Q. How did men first come to the knowledge of the existence of a God, so as to exercise faith in him?

A. In order to answer this question, it will be necessary to go back and examine man at his creation; the circumstances in which he was placed, and the knowledge which he had of God. [§ II. ¶ 3,4,5,6,7,8,9,10,11.]

First, When man was created he stood in the presence of God. Gen. 1:27,28. From this we learn that man, at his creation, stood in the presence of his God, and had most perfect knowledge of his existence.

Secondly, God conversed with him after his transgression. Gen. 3: from the 8th to the 22nd. [§ II. ¶ 13,14,15,16,17.]

From this we learn, that, though man did transgress, he was not deprived of the previous knowledge which he had of the existence of God. [§ II. ¶ 19.]

Thirdly, God conversed with man after he cast him out of the garden. [§ II. ¶ 22,23,24,25.]

Fourthly, God also conversed with Cain after he had slain Abel. Gen. 4: from the 4th to the 6th. [§ II. ¶ 26,27,28,29.]

Q. What is the object of the foregoing quotation?

A. It is that it may be clearly seen how it was that the first thoughts were suggested to the minds of men, of the existence of God, and how extensively this knowledge was spread among the immediate descendants of Adam. [§ II. ¶ 30,31,32,33.]

Q. What testimony had the immediate descendants of Adam, in proof of the existence of a God?

A. The testimony of their father. And after they were made acquainted with his existence, by the testimony of their father, they were dependant upon the exercise of their own faith, for a knowledge of his character, perfections and attributes. [§ II. ¶ 23,24,25,26.]

Q. Had any others of the human family, beside Adam, a knowledge of the existence of God, in the first instance, by any other means than human testimony?

A. They had not. For previous to the time that they could have power to obtain a manifestation for themselves, the all-important fact had been communicated to them by their common father: and so, from father to child, the knowledge was communicated as extensively, as the knowledge of his existence was known; for it was by this means, in the first instance, that men had a knowledge of his existence. [§ II. ¶ 35,36.]

28

Q. How do you know that the knowledge of the existence of God was communicated in this manner, throughout the different ages of the world?

A. By the chronology obtained thro' the revelations of God.

Q. How would you divide that chronology in order to convey it to the understanding clearly?

A. Into two parts: Frst, by embracing that period of the world from Adam to Noah; and secondly, from Noah to Abraham: from which period the knowledge of the existence of God has been so general, that it is a matter of no dispute in what manner the idea of his existence has been retained in the world.

Q. How many noted righteous men lived from Adam to Noah?

A. Nine; which includes Abel, who was slain by his brother.

Q. What are their names?

A. Abel, Seth, Enos, Cainan, Mahalaleel, Jared, Enoch, Methusaleh, and Lamech.

Q. How old was Adam when Seth was born?

A. One hundred and thirty years. Gen. 5:3.

Q. How many years did Adam live after Seth was born?

A. Eight hundred. Gen. 5:4.

Q. How old was Adam when he died?

A. Nine hundred and thirty years. Gen. 5:5.

Q. How old was Seth when Enos was born?

A. One hundred and five years. Gen. 5:6.

Q. How old was Enos when Cainan was born?

A. Ninety years. Gen. 5:9.

Q. How old was Cainan when Mahalaleel was born?

A. Seventy years. Gen. 5:12.

Q. How old was Mahalaleel when Jared was born?

A. Sixty five years. Gen. 5:15.

Q. How old was Jared when Enoch was born?

A. One hundred and sixty two years. Gen. 5:18.

Q. How old was Enoch when Methusaleh was born?

A. Sixty five. Gen. 5:21.

Q. How old was Methusaleh when Lamech was born?

A. One hundred and eighty seven years. Gen. 5:25.

Q. Ho w old was Lamech when Noah was born?

A. On e hundred and eighty two years. Gen. 5:28.

For this chronology see § 11. ¶ 37.

Q. How many years, according to this account, was it from Adam to Noah?

A. One thousand and fifty six years.

Q. How old was Lamech when Adam died?

A. Lamech, the ninth from Adam, (including Abel,) and father of Noah, was fifty six years old when Adam died.

Q. How old was Methusaleh?

29

A. Two hundred and forty three years. Q. How old was Enoch?

A. Three hundred nnd eight years.

Q. How old was Jared?

A. Four hundred and seventy years.

Q. How old was Mahalaleel?

A. Five hundred and thirty five.

Q. How old was Cainan?

A. Six hundred and five years.

Q. How old was Enos?

A. Six hundred and ninety five years.

Q. How old was Seth?

A. Eight hundred.

For this item of the account see section second, paragraph 38.

Q. How many of these noted men were cotemporary with Adam?

A. Nine.

Q. What are their names?

A. Abel, Seth, Enos, Cainan, Mahalaleel, Jared, Enoch, Methusaleh, and Lamech. [§ II. ¶ 39.]

Q. How long did Seth live after Enos was born?

A. Eight hundred and seven years. Gen. 5:7.

Q. What was Seth's age when he died?

A. Nine hundred and twelve years. Gen. 5:8.

Q. How long did Enos live after Cainan was born?

A. Eight hundred and fifteen years. Gen. 5:10.

Q. What was Enos's age when he died?

A. Nine hundred and five years. Gen. 5:11.

Q. How long did Cainan live after Mahalaleel was born?

A. Eight hundred and forty years. Gen. 5:13.

Q. What was Cainan's age when he died?

A. Nine hundred and ten years. Gen. 5:14.

Q. How long did Mahaleel live after Jared was born?

A. Eight hundred and thirty years. Gen. 5:16.

Q. What was Mahalaleel's age when he died?

A. Eight hundred and ninety five years. Gen. 5:17.

Q. How long did Jared live after Enoch was born?

A. Eight hundred years. Gen. 5:19.

Q. What was Jared's age when he died?

A. Nine hundred and sixty two years. Gen. 5:20.

Q. How long did Enoch walk with God after Methusaleh was born?

A. Three hundred years. Gen. 5:22.

Q. What was Enoch's age when he was translatedd?

A. Three hundred and sixty five years. Gen. 5:23.

Q. How long did Methusaleh live after Lamech was born?

30

line 1
A. Seven hundred and eighty two years. Gen. 5:26.
Q. What was Methusaleh's age when he died?
A. Nine hundred and sixty nine years. Gen. 5:27.
Q. How long did Lamech live after Noah was born? A. Five
hundred and ninety five years. Gen. 5:30.
Q. What was Lamech's age when he died?
A. Seven hundred and seventy seven years. Gen. 5:31.
For the account of the last item see [§ 11. ¶ 40.]
Q. In what year of the world did Adam die?
A. In the nine hundred and thirtieth.
Q. In what year was Enoch translated?
A. In the nine hundred and eighty seventh.
Q. In what year did Seth die?
A. In the one thousand and forty second.
Q. In what year did Enos die?
A. In the eleven hundred and fortieth.
Q. In what year did Cainan die?
A. In the twelve hundred and thirty fifth.
Q. In what year did Mahalaleel die?
A. In the twelve hundred and ninetieth.
Q. In what year did Jared die?
A. In the fourteen hundred and twenty second.
Q. In what year did Lamech die?
A. In the sixteen hundred and fifty first.
Q. In what year did Methusaleh die?
A. In the sixteen hundred and fifty sixth.
For this account see § 11. ¶ 41.
Q. How old was Noah when Enos died?
A. Eighty four years.
Q. How old when Cainan died?
A. One hundred and seventy nine years.
Q. How old when Mahalaleel died?
A. Two hundred and thirty four years.
Q. How old when Jared died?
A. Three hundred and sixty six years.
Q. How old when Lamech died?
A. Five hundred and ninety five years.
Q. How old when Methusaleh died?
A. Six hundred years.
See § 11. ¶ 42, for the last item.
Q. How many of those men lived in the days of Noah?
A. Six.
Q. What are their names?
A. Seth, Enos, Cainan, Mahalaleel, Jared, Methusaleh, and
Lamech. [§ 11. ¶ 43.
Q. How many of those men were cotemporary with Adam

line 1 and Noah both? A. Six. Q. What are their names?
A. Enos, Cainan, Mahalaleel, Jared, Methusaleh, and La-
mech. [§ II. ¶ 43.]
Q. According to the foregoing account, how was the knowl-
5 edge of the existence of God first suggested to the minds of
men?
A. By the manifestation made to our father Adam, when he
was in the presence of God, both before and while he was in
Eden. [§ II. ¶ 44.]
10 Q. How was the knowledge of the existence of God dissemi-
nated among the inhabitants of the world?
A. By tradition from father to son. [§ II. ¶ 44.]
Q. How old was Noah when Shem was born?
A. Five hundred and two years. Gen. 5:32. 11:10.
15 Q. What was the term of years from the birth of Shem to the
flood?
A. Ninety eight.
Q. What was the term of years that Noah lived after the
flood?
20 A. Three hundred and fifty. Gen. 9:28.
Q. What was Noah's age when he died?
A. Nine hundred and fifty years. Gen. 9:29. [§ II. ¶ 45.]
Q. What was Shem's age when Arphaxed was born?
A. One hundred years. Gen. 11:10.
25 Q. What was Arphaxed's age when Salah was born?
A. Thirty five years. Gen. 11:12.
Q. What was Salah's age when Eber was born?
A. Thirty. Gen. 11:14.
Q. What was Eber's age when Peleg was born?
30 A. Thirty four years. Gen. 11:16.
Q. What was Peleg's age when Reu was born?
A. Thirty years. Gen. 11:18.
Q. What was Reu's age when Serug was born?
A. Thirty two years. Gen. 11:20.
35 Q. What was Serug's age when Nahor was born?
A. Thirty years. Gen. 11:22.
Q. What was Nahor's age when Terah was born?
A. Twenty nine. Gen. 11:24.
Q. What was Terah's age, when Nahor the father of Abra-
40 ham was born?
A. Seventy years. Gen. 11:26.
Q. What was Terah's age when Abraham was born?
A. Some suppose one hundred and thirty years, and others
seventy. Gen. 12:4. 11:26. [§ II. ¶ 46.]
45 Q. What was the number of years from the flood to the birth
of Abraham?

82

A. Supposing Abraham to have been born when Terah was one hundred and thirty years old, it was three hundred and fifty two years: but if he were born when Terah was seventy years old, it was two hundred and ninety two years. [§ 11 ¶ 47.]

Q. How long did Shem live after Arphaxed was born?
A. Five hundred years. Gen. 11:11.
Q. What was Shem's age when he died?
A. Six hundred years. Gen. 11:11.
Q. What number of years did Arphaxed live after Salah was born?
A. Four hundred and three years. Gen. 21:13.
Q. What was Arphaxed's age when he died?
A. Four hundred and thirty eight years.
Q. What number of years did Salah live after Eber was born?
A. Four hundred and three years. Gen. 11:15.
Q. What was Salah's age when he died?
A. Four hundred and thirty three years.
Q. What number of years did Eber live after Peleg was born?
A. Four hundred and thirty years. Gen. 11:17.
Q. What was Eber's age when he died?
A. Four hundred and sixty four years.
Q. What number of years did Peleg live after Reu was born?
A. Two hundred and nine years. Gen. 11:19.
Q. What was Peleg's age when he died?
A. Two hundred and thirty nine years.
Q. What number of years did Reu live after Serug was born?
A. Two hundred and seven years. Gen. 11:21.
Q. What was Reu's age when he died?
A. Two hundred and thirty nine years.
Q. What number of years did Serug live after Nahor was born?
A. Two hundred years. Gen. 11:23.
Q. What was Serug's age when he died?
A. Two hundred and thirty years.
Q. What number of years did Nahor live after Terah was born?
A. One hundred and nineteen years. Gen. 11:25.
Q. What was Nahor's age when he died?
A. One hundred and forty eight years.
Q. What number of years did Terah live after Abraham was born?
A. Supposing Terah to have been one hundred and thirty years old when Abraham was born, he lived seventy five years; but if Abraham was born when Terah was seventy years old, he lived one hundred and thirty five.
Q. What was Terah's age when he died?

33

line 1 A. Two hundred and five years.   Gen. 11:32.
For this account from the birth of Arphaxed, to the death of
Terah, see [§ 11. ¶ 48.]
Q. In what year of the world did Peleg die?
5 A. Agreeably to the foregoing chronology, he died in the
nineteen hundred and ninety sixth year of the world.
Q. In what year of the world did Nahor die?
A. In the nineteen hundred and ninety seventh.
Q. In what year of the world did Noah die?
10 A. In the two thousand and sixth.
Q. In what year of the world did Reu die?
A. In the two thousand and twenty sixth.
Q. In what year of the world did Serug die?
A. In the two thousand and forty ninth.
15 Q. In what year of the world did Terah die?
A. In the two thousand and eighty third.
Q. In what year of the world did Arphaxed die?
A. In the two thousand and ninty sixth.
Q. In what year of the world did Salah die?
20 A. In the twenty one hundred and twenty sixth.
Q. In what year of the world did Abraham die?
A. In the twenty one hundred and eighty third.
Q. In what year of the world did Eber die?
A. In the twenty one hundred and eighty seventh.
25 For this account of the year of the world in which those men
died, see [§11: ¶ 49,50.]
Q. How old was Nahor, Abraham's brother, when Noah died?
A. Fifty eight years.
Q. How old was Terah?
30 A. One hundred and twenty eight.
Q. How old was Serug?
A. One hundred and eighty seven.
Q. How old was Reu?
A. Two hundred and nineteen.
35 Q. How old was Eber?
A. Two hundred and eighty three.
Q. How old was Salah?
A. Three hundred and thirteen.
Q. How old was Arphaxed?
40 A. Three hundred and forty eight.
Q. How old was Shem?
A. Four hundred and forty eight.
For the last account see [§ 11. ¶ 51.]
Q. How old was Abraham when Reu died?
45 A. Eighteen years, if he were born when Terah was one

c

---

line 46. This page begins the third gathering of the book. "C" is the first of two signature marks in this gathering; the second is on the recto of the following leaf. These marks were used in collating the gatherings after the sheets were folded.

34

line 1 hundred and thirty years old. Q. What was his age when Se-
rug, and Nahor, Abraham's brother died?
A. Forty one years.
Q. What was his age when Terah died?
5 A. Seventy five years.
Q. What was his age when Arphaxed died?
A. Eighty eight.
Q. What was his age when Salah died?
A. One hundred and eighteen years.
10 Q. What was his age when Shem died?
A. One hundred and fifty years.
For this see [§ II. ¶ 52.]
Q. How many noted characters lived from Noah to Abraham?
A. Ten.
15 Q. What are their names?
A. Shem, Arphaxed, Salah, Eber, Peleg, Reu, Serug, Na-
hor, Terah, and Nahor, Abraham's brother. [§ II. ¶ 52.]
Q. How many of these were cotemporary with Noah?
A. The whole.
20 Q. How many with Abraham?
A. Eight.
Q. What are their names?
A. Nahor, Abraham's brother, Terah, Serug, Reu, Eber, Se-
lah, Arphaxed, and Shem. [§ II. ¶ 52.]
25 Q. How many were cotemporary with both Noah and Abra-
ham?
A. Eight.
Q. What are their names?
A. Shem, Arphaxed, Salah, Eber, Reu, Serug, Terah, and
30 Nahor, Abraham's brother. [§ II. ¶ 52.]
Q. Did any of these men die before Noah?
A. They did.
Q. Who were they?
A. Peleg, in whose days the earth was divided, and Nahor
35 Abraham's grand-father. [§ II. ¶ 49.]
Q. Did any one of them live longer than Abraham?
A. There was one. [§ II. ¶. 50.]
Q. Who was it?
A. Eber, the fourth from Noah. [§ II. ¶ 50.]
40 Q. In whose days was the earth divided?
A. In the days of Peleg.
Q. Where have we the account given that the earth was divi-
ded in the days of Peleg?
A. Gen. 10:25.
45 Q. Can you repeat the sentence?
A. Unto Eber were born two sons; the name of one was Pe-
leg; for in his days the earth was divided.

35

Q. What testimony have men, in the first instance, that there is a God?

A. Human testimony, and human testimony only. [§ II. ¶ 56.]

Q. What excited the ancient saints to seek diligently after a knowledge of the glory of God, his perfections and attributes?

A. The credence they gave to the testimony of their fathers. [§ II. ¶ 56.]

Q. How do men obtain a knowledge of the glory of God, his perfections and attributes?

A. By devoting themselves to his service, through prayer and supplication incessantly, strengthening their faith in him, until like Enoch, the brother of Jared, and Moses, they obtain a manifestation of God to themselves. [§ II. ¶ 55.]

Q. Is the knowledge of the existence of God a matter of mere tradition, founded upon human testimony alone, until a person receives a manifestation of God to themselves?

A. It is.

Q. How do you prove it?

A. From the whole of the first lecture of the second section.

LECTURE THIRD.

Of Faith.

SECTION III.

1 In the second lecture it was shown, how it was that the knowledge of the existence of God, came into the world, and by what means the first thoughts were suggested to the minds of men, that such a being did actually exist: and that it was by reason of the knowledge of his existence, that there was a foundation laid for the exercise of faith in him, as the only being in whom faith could center for life and salvation. For faith could not center in a being of whose existence we had no idea; because the idea of his existence in the first instance, is essential to the exercise of faith in him. Rom. 10:14: "How

3*

line 1

5

10

15

20

25

30

35

line 21. Third lecture on faith, ca. winter 1834–1835.

36

line 1 then shall they call on him in whom they have not believed? And how shall they believe in him of whom they have not heard? And how shall they hear without a preacher?" (or one sent to tell them?) So then faith comes by hearing the word of God. [New Translation.]

2 Let us here observe, that three things are necessary, in order that any rational and intelligent being may exercise faith in God unto life and salvation.

3 First, The idea that he actually exists.

4 Secondly, A *correct* idea of his character, perfections and attributes.

5 Thirdly, An actual knowledge that the course of life which he is pursuing, is according to his will.— For without an acquaintance with these three important facts, the faith of every rational being must be imperfect and unproductive; but with this understanding, it can become perfect and fruitful, abounding in righteousness unto the praise and glory of God the Father, and the Lord Jesus Christ.

6 Having previously been made acquainted with the way the idea of his existence came into the world, as well as the fact of his existence, we shall proceed to examine his character, perfections and attributes, in order that this class may see, not only the just grounds which they have for the exercise of faith in him, for life and salvation, but the reasons that all the world, also, as far as the idea of his existence extends, may have to exercise faith in him the Father of all living.

7 As we have been indebted to a revelation which God made of himself to his creatures in the first instance, for the idea of his existence, so in like manner we are indebted to the revelations which he has given to us, for a correct understanding of his character, perfections and attributes; because without the revelations which he has given to us, no man by searching could find out God. Job 11:7,8,9. First

line 1 Cor. 2:9,10,11: "But as it is written, eye has not seen, nor ear heard, neither have entered into the heart of man, the things which God has prepared for them that love him; but God has revealed them unto *5* us by his Spirit: for the Spirit searches all things, yea, the deep things of God. For what man knows the things of a man, save the spirit of man which is in him? Even so, the things of God no man knows but by the Spirit of God."

10 8 Having said so much, we proceed to examine the character which the revelations have given of God.

9 Moses gives us the following account in Exodus, 34:6: "And the Lord passed by before him, and proclaimed, The Lord God, the Lord God, merciful and *15* gracious, long suffering, and abundant in goodness and truth." Psalm 103:6,7,8: "The Lord executes righteousness and judgment for all that are oppressed. He made known his ways unto Moses, his acts unto the children of Israel. The Lord is merci- *20* ful and gracious, slow to anger and plenteous in mercy:" Psalm 103:17,18: "But the mercy of the Lord is from everlasting to everlasting upon them that fear him, and his righteousness unto children's children, to such as keep his covenant, and to those that re- *25* member his commandments to do them." Psalm 90: 2: "Before the mountains were brought forth, or ever you had formed the earth and the world, even from everlasting to everlasting, you are God." Heb. 1:10, 11,12: "And you, Lord, in the beginning have laid *30* the foundation of the earth; and the heavens are the works of your hands: they shall perish, but you shall remain; and they shall wax old as a garment; and as a vesture shall you fold them up, and they shall be changed: but you are the same, and your years shall *35* not fail." James 1:17: "Every good gift, and every perfect gift, is from above, and comes down from the Father of lights; with whom is no variableness,

38

neither shadow of turning." Malachi 3:6. "For I am the Lord, I change not; therefore ye sons of Jacob are not consumed."

10 Book of Commandments, chapt. 2nd, commencing in the third line of the first paragraph: "For God does not walk in crooked paths, neither does he turn to the right hand or the left, or vary from that which he has said, therefore his paths are strait, and his course is one eternal round:" Book of Commandments, chapt. 37:1. "Listen to the voice of the Lord your God, even Alpha and Omega, the beginning and the end, whose course is one eternal round, the same yesterday to-day and forever."

11 Numbers, 23:19. "God is not a man, that he should lie; neither the son of man that he should repent." First John, 4:8. "He that loves not, knows not God; for God is love." Acts, 10:34: "Then Peter opened his mouth and said, Of a truth I perceive that God is no respecter of persons, but in every nation he that fears God and works righteousness is accepted with him."

12 From the foregoing testimonies, we learn the following things respecting the character of God.

13 First, That he was God before the world was created, and the same God that he was, after it was created.

14 Secondly, That he is merciful, and gracious, slow to anger, abundant in goodness, and that he was so from everlasting, and will be to everlasting.

15 Thirdly, That he changes not, neither is there variableness with him; but that he is the same from everlasting to everlasting, being the same yesterday to-day and forever; and that his course is one eternal round, without variation.

16 Fourthly, That he is a God of truth and cannot lie.

17 Fifthly, That he is no respecter of persons; but

39

in every nation he that fears God and works righteousness is accepted of him.

18 Sixthly, That he is love.

19 An acquaintance with these attributes in the divine
character, is essentially necessary, in order that the
faith of any rational being can center in him for life
and salvation. For if he did not, in the first instance,
believe him to be God, that is, the creator and upholder
of all things, he could not *center* his faith in him for
life and salvation, for fear there should be a greater
than he, who would thwart all his plans, and he, like
the gods of the heathen, would be unable to fulfil his
promises; but seeing he is God over all, from everlasting to everlasting, the creator and upholder of all
things, no such fear can exist in the minds of those
who put their trust in him, so that in this respect their
faith can be without wavering.

20 But secondly: Unless he was merciful, and gracious, slow to anger, long suffering, and full of goodness, such is the weakness of human nature, and so
great the frailties and imperfections of men, that unless they believed that these excellencies existed in the
divine character, the faith necessary to salvation
could not exist; for doubt would take the place of
faith, and those who know their weakness and lia-
bility to sin, would be in constant doubt of salvation,
if it were not for the idea which they have of the excellency of the character of God, that he is slow to anger, and long suffering, and of a forgiving disposition, and does forgive iniquity, transgression and sin.
An idea of these facts does away doubt, and makes
faith exceedingly strong.

21 But it is equally as necessary that men should
have the idea that he is a God who changes not, in order to have faith in him, as it is to have the idea that
he is gracious and long suffering. For without the
idea of unchangibleness in the character of the Deity,

40

line 1 doubt would take the place of faith. But with the
idea that he changes not, faith lays hold upon the excellencies in his character with unshaken confidence,
believing he is the same yesterday, to-day and forev-
5 er, and that his course is one eternal round.

22 And again, the idea that he is a God of truth and
cannot lie, is equally as necessary to the exercise of
faith in him, as the idea of his unchangeableness. For
without the idea that he was a God of truth and could
10 not lie, the confidence necessary to be placed in his
word in order to the exercise of faith in him, could
not exist. But having the idea that he is not man
that he can lie, it gives power to the minds of men
to exercise faith in him.

15 23 But it is also necessary that men should have an
idea that he is no respecter of persons; for with the
idea of all the other excellencies in his character, and
this one wanting, men could not exercise faith in him,
because if he were a respecter of persons, they could
20 not tell what their privileges were, nor how far they
were authorized to exercise faith in him, or whether
they were authorized to do it at all, but all must be
confusion; but no sooner are the minds of men made
acquainted with the truth on this point, that he is no
25 respecter of persons, than they see that they have authority by faith to lay hold on eternal life the richest
boon of heaven, because God is no respecter of persons, and that every man in every nation has an equal
privilege.

30 24 And lastly, but not less important to the exercise
of faith in God, is the idea that he is love; for with all
the other excellencies in his character, without this
one to influence them, they could not have such powerful dominion over the minds of men; but when the
35 idea is planted in the mind that he is love, who cannot
see the just ground that men of every nation, kindred

41

and tongue, have to exercise faith in God so as to obtain eternal life?

25 From the above description of the character of the Deity which is given him in the revelations, to men, there is a sure foundation for the exercise of faith in him among every people, nation and kindred, from age to age, and from generation to generation.

26 Let us here observe that the foregoing is the character which is given of God in his revelations to the Former Day Saints, and it is also the character which is given of him in his revelations to the Latter Day Saints, so that the saints of former days, and those of latter days, are both alike in this respect; the "Latter Day Saints" having as good grounds to exercise faith in God, as the former day saints had; because the same character is given of him to both.

Q. What was shown in the second lecture?
A. It was shown how the knowledge of the existence of God came into the world—[§ III. ¶ 1.]
Q. What is the effect of the idea of his existence among men?
A. It lays the foundation for the exercise of faith in him.— [§ III. ¶ 1.]
Q. Is the idea of his existence, in the first instance, necessary in order for the exercise of faith in him?
A. It is. [§ III. ¶ 1.]
Q. How do you prove it?
A. By the 16 chapter to Romans and 14 verse. [§ III. ¶ 1.]
Q. How many things are necessary for us to understand, respecting the Deity and our relation to him, in order that we may exercise faith in him for life and salvation?
A. Three. [§ III. ¶ 2.]
Q. What are they?
A. First, that God does actually exist: Secondly, correct ideas of his character, his perfections and attributes; and Thirdly, that the course which we pursue is according to his mind and will. [§ III. ¶ 3,4,5.]
Q. Would the idea of any one or two of the above mentioned things, enable a person to exercise faith in God?

42

line 1

A. It would not, for without the idea of them all, faith would be imperfect and unproductive. [§ III. ¶ 5.]

Q. Would an idea of these three things lay a sure foundation for the exercise of faith in God, so as to obtain life and salvation?

A. It would; for by the idea of these three things, faith could become perfect, and fruitful, abounding in righteousness unto the praise and glory of God. [§ III. ¶ 5.]

Q. How are we to be made acquainted with the before mentioned things respecting the Deity, and respecting ourselves?

A. By revelation. [§ III. ¶ 6.]

Q. Could these things be found out by any other means than by revelation?

A. They could not.

Q. How do you prove it?

A. By the scriptures: Job 11:7,8:9. 1 Corinthians 2:9,10, 11. [§ III. ¶ 7.]

Q. What things do we learn in the revelations of God respecting his character?

A. We learn the six following things. First, that he was God before the world was created, and the same God that he was after it was created. Secondly, that he is merciful and gracious, slow to anger, abundant in goodness, and that he was so from everlasting, and will be so to everlasting. Thirdly, that he changes not, neither is there variableness with him, and that his course is one eternal round. Fourthly, that he is a God of truth and cannot lie. Fifthly, that he is no respecter of persons; and Sixthly, that he is love. [§ III. ¶ 12,13, 14,15,16,17,18.]

Q. Where do you find the revelations which give us this idea of the character of the Deity?

A. In the bible and book of commandments, and they are quoted in the third lecture. [§ III. ¶ 9,10,11.]

Q. What effect would it have on any rational being not to have an idea that the Lord was God, the creator and upholder of all things?

A. It would prevent him from exercising faith in him unto life and salvation.

Q. Why would it prevent him from exercising faith in God?

A. Because he would be as the heathen not knowing but there might be a being greater and more powerful than he, and thereby he be prevented from fulfilling his promises. [§ III. ¶ 19.]

Q. Does this idea prevent this doubt?

A. It does; for persons having this idea are enabled thereby to exercise faith without this doubt. [§ III. ¶ 19.]

Q. Is it not also necessary to have the idea that God is

43

line 1

merciful, and gracious, long suffering and full of goodness?
A. It is. [§ III. ¶ 20.]
Q. Why is it necessary?
A. Because of the weakness and imperfections of human nature, and the great frailties of man; for such is the weakness
of man, and such his frailties, that he is liable to sin continually, and if God were not long suffering, and full of compassion, gracious and merciful and of a forgiving disposition,
man would be cut off from before him in consequence of which,
he would be in continual doubt and could not exercise faith:
for where doubt is, there faith has no power, but by man's believing that God is full of compassion and forgiveness, long suffering and slow to anger, he can exercise faith in him and overcome doubt, so as to be exceedingly strong. [§ III. ¶ 20.]
Q. Is it not equally as necessary that man should have an
idea that God changes not, neither is there variableness with
him, in order to exercise faith in him unto life and salvation?
A. It is; because without this, he would not know how soon
the mercy of God might change into cruelty, his long suffering into rashness, his love into hatred, and in consequence of
which doubt, man would be incapable of exercising faith in him,
but having the idea that he is unchangeable, man can have faith
in him continually, believing that what he was yesterday he is
to day, and will be forever. [§ III. ¶ 21.]
Q. Is it not necessary also, for men to have an idea that God
is a being of truth, before they can have perfect faith in him?
A. It is; for unless men have this idea they cannot place
confidence in his word, and not being able to place confidence
in his word, they could not have faith in him; but believing
that he is a God of truth, and that his word cannot fail, their
faith can rest in him without doubt. [§ III. ¶ 22.]
Q. Could man exercise faith in God so as to obtain eternal
life unless he believed that God was no respecter of persons?
A. He could not; because without this idea he could not
certainly know that it was his privilege so to do, and in consequence of this doubt his faith could not be sufficiently strong
to save him. [§ III. ¶ 23.]
Q. Would it be possible for a man to exercise faith in God,
so as to be saved, unless he had an idea that God was love?
A. He could not; because man could not love God, unless he
had an idea that God was love, and if he did not love God, he
could not have faith in him. [§ III. ¶ 24.]
Q. What is the description which the sacred writers give of
the character of the Deity calculated to do?
A. It is calculated to lay a foundation for the exercise of
faith in him, as far as the knowledge extends among all people,

44

line 1
tongues, languages, kindreds, and nations and that from age to age, and from generation to generation. [§ III. ¶ 25.]

Q. Is the character which God has given of himself uniform?

A. It is, in all his revelations whether to the Former Day Saints, or to the Latter day saints, so that they all have the authority to exercise faith in him, and to expect by the exercise of their faith, to enjoy the same blessings. [§ III. ¶ 26.]

LECTURE FOURTH.

Of Faith.

SECTION IV.

1 Having shown in the third lecture, that correct ideas of the character of God are necessary in order to the exercise of faith in him unto life and salvation, and that without correct ideas of his character, the minds of men could not have sufficient power with God to the exercise of faith necessary to the enjoyment of eternal life, and that correct ideas of his character lay a foundation as far as his character is concerned, for the exercise of faith, so as to enjoy the fulness of the blessing of the gospel of Jesus Christ, even that of eternal glory; we shall now proceed to show the connection there is between correct ideas of the attributes of God, and the exercise of faith in him unto eternal life.

2 Let us here observe, that the real design which the God of heaven had in view in making the human family acquainted with his attributes, was, that they through the ideas of the existence of his attributes, might be enabled to exercise faith in him, and through the exercise of faith in him, might obtain eternal life. For without the idea of the existence of the attributes which belong to God, the minds of men could not have power to exercise faith

---

line 8. Fourth lecture on faith, ca. winter 1834–1835.

on him so as to lay hold upon eternal life. The God of heaven understanding most perfectly the constitution of human nature, and the weakness of man, knew what was necessary to be revealed, and what ideas must be planted in their minds in order that they might be enabled to exercise faith in him unto eternal life.

3 Having said so much we shall proceed to examine the attributes of God, as set forth in his revelations to the human family, and to show how necessary correct ideas of his attributes are, to enable men to exercise faith in him. For without these ideas being planted in the minds of men, it would be out of the power of any person or persons to exercise faith in God so as to obtain eternal life. So that the divine communications made to man in the first instance, were designed to establish in their minds the ideas necessary to enable them to exercise faith in God, and through this means to be partakers of his glory.

4 We have, in the revelations which he has given to the human family, the following account of his attributes.

5 First, Knowledge. Acts 15:18. Known unto God are all his works from the beginning of the world. Isaiah 46:9,10. Remember the former things of old; for I am God and there is none else; I am God, and there is none like me, *declaring the end from the beginning,* and from ancient time the things that are not yet done, saying, My counsel shall stand, and I will do all my pleasure.

6 Secondly, Faith, or power. Heb. 11:3. Through faith we understand that the worlds were framed by the word of God. Gen. 1:1. In the beginning God created the heaven and the earth. Isaiah 14:24,27. The Lord of hosts has sworn, saying, Surely as I have thought so shall it come to pass; and as I have purposed, so shall it stand. For the Lord of hosts

46

has purposed, and who shall disannul it? and his hand is stretched out, and who shall turn it back?

7 Thirdly, Justice. Ps. 89:14. Justice and judgment are the habitation of thy throne. Isaiah 45:21. Tell ye, and bring them near; yea, let them take council together: who has declared this from the ancient time? Have not I the Lord? and there is no God else beside me; a just God and a Savior. Zeph. 5:5. The just Lord is in the midst thereof. Zech. 9:9. Rejoice greatly, O daughter of Zion; shout, O daughter of Jerusalem: behold, thy King comes unto thee: he is just, and having salvation.

8 Fourthly, Judgment. Ps. 89:14. Justice and judgment are the habitation of thy throne. Deut. 32:4. He is the Rock, his work is perfect; for all his ways are judgment: a God of truth, and without iniquity: just and right is he. Ps. 9:7. But the Lord shall endure forever: he has prepared his throne for judgment. Ps. 9:16. The Lord is known by the judgment which he executes.

9 Fifthly, Mercy. Ps. 89:15. Mercy and truth shall go before his face. Exodus 34:6. And the Lord passed by before him, and proclaimed, The Lord, the Lord God, merciful and gracious. Neh. 9:17.— But thou art a God ready to pardon, gracious and merciful.

10 And Sixthly, Truth. Ps. 89:14. Mercy and truth shall go before thy face. Exodus 34:6. Long suffering and abundant in goodness and truth. Deut. 32:4. He is the Rock, his work is perfect; for all his ways are judgment. A God of truth and without iniquity: just and right is he. Ps. 31:5. Into thy hand I commit my spirit: thou hast redeemed me, O Lord God of truth.

11 By a little reflection it will be seen, that the idea of the existence of these attributes in the Deity, is necessary to enable any rational being to exercise faith

line 1 in him. For without the idea of the existence of these
attributes in the Deity, men could not exercise faith in
him for life and salvation; seeing that without the
knowledge of all things, God would not be able to
5 save any portion of his creatures; for it is by reason
of the knowledge which he has of all things, from the
beginning to the end, that enables him to give that
understanding to his creatures, by which they are
made partakers of eternal life; and if it were not for
10 the idea existing in the minds of men, that God had
all knowledge, it would be impossible for them to exercise faith in him.

12 And it is not less necessary that men should have
the idea of the existence of the attribute power in the
15 Deity. For, unless God had power over all things,
and was able, by his power, to control all things, and
thereby deliver his creatures who put their trust in
him, from the power of all beings that might seek
their destruction, whether in heaven, on earth, or in
20 hell, men could not be saved; but with the idea of the
existence of this attribute, planted in the mind, men
feel as though they had nothing to fear, who put their
trust in God, believing that he has power to save all
who come to him, to the very uttermost.

25 13 It is also necessary, in order to the exercise of
faith in God, unto life and salvation, that men should
have the idea of the existence of the attribute justice, in him. For without the idea of the existence
of the attribute Justice, in the Deity, men could not
30 have confidence sufficiently to place themselves under his guidance and direction; for they would be
filled with fear and doubt, lest the Judge of all the
earth would not do right; and thus fear, or doubt, existing in the mind, would preclude the possibility of the
35 exercise of faith in him for life and salvation. But,
when the idea of the existence of the attribute justice,
in the Deity, is fairly planted in the mind, it leaves

48

no room for doubt to get into the heart, and the mind
is enabled to cast itself upon the Almighty without
fear and without doubt, and with most unshaken confidence, believing that the Judge of all the earth will
do right.

14 It is also of equal importance that men should
have the idea of the existence of the attribute judgment, in God, in order that they may exercise faith
in him for lite and salvation; for without the idea of
the existence of this attribute in the Deity, it would
be impossible for men to exercise faith in him for
life and salvation, seeing that it is through the exercise of this attribute that the faithful in Christ Jesus
are delivered out of the hands of those who seek their
destruction; for if God were not to come out in swift
judgment against the workers of iniquity and the powers of darkness, his saints could not be saved; for it
is by judgment that the Lord delivers his saints out
of the hands of all their enemies, and those who reject the gospel of our Lord Jesus Christ. But no
sooner is the idea of the existence of this attribute,
planted in the minds of men, than it gives power to
the mind for the exercise of faith and confidence in
God, and they are enabled, by faith, to lay hold on
the promises which are set before them, and wade
through all the tribulations and afflictions to which
they are subjected by reason of the persecution from
those who know not God, and obey not the gospel of
our Lord Jesus Christ: believing, that in due time the
Lord will come out in swift judgment against their enemies, and they shall be cut off from before him, and
that in his own due time he will bear them off conquerers and more than conquerers in all things.

15 And again, it is equally important that men should
have the idea of the existence of the attribute mercy,
in the Deity, in order to exercise faith in him for life
and salvation. For, without the idea of the existence

49

line 1 of this attribute in the Deity, the spirits of the saints would faint in the midst of the tribulations, afflictions and persecutions which they have to endure for right-eousness' sake; but when the idea of the existence of
5 this attribute is once established in the mind it gives life and energy to the spirits of the saints: believing that the mercy of God will be poured out upon them in the midst of their afflictions, and that he will com-passionate them in their sufferings; and that the mer-
10 cy of God will lay hold of them and secure them in the arms of his love, so that they will receive a full reward for all their sufferings.

16 And lastly, but not less important to the exer-cise of faith in God, is the idea of the existence of
15 the attribute truth, in him. For, without the idea of the existence of this attribute the mind of man could have nothing upon which it could rest with certainty: all would be confusion and doubt; but with the idea of the existence of this attribute in the Deity, in the
20 mind, all the teachings, instructions, promises and blessings become realities, and the mind is enabled to lay hold of them with certainty and confidence: be-lieving that these things, and all that the Lord has said, shall be fulfilled in their time; and that all the
25 cursings, denunciations and judgments, pronounced upon the heads of the unrighteous will also be execu-ted in the due time of the Lord: and by reason of the truth and veracity of him, the mind beholds its deliv-erance and salvation as being certain.

30 17 Let the mind once reflect sincerely and candid-ly upon the ideas of the existence of the before men-tioned attributes in the Deity, and it will be seen, that as far as his attributes are concerned, there is a sure foundation laid for the exercise of faith in him
35 for life and salvation. For in as much as God pos-sesses the attribute knowledge he can make all things

D

---

line 37. This page begins the fourth gathering of the book. "D" is the first of two signature marks in this gathering; the second is on the recto of the following leaf. These marks were used in collating the gather-ings after the sheets were folded.

50

known to his saints necessary for their salvation; and
as he possesses the attribute power he is able thereby to deliver them from the power of all enemies;
and seeing also, that justice is an attribute of the Deity, he will deal with them upon the principles of
righteousness and equity, and a just reward will be
granted unto them for all their afflictions and sufferings for the truth's sake. And as judgment is an
attribute of the Deity also, his saints can have the
most unshaken confidence, that they will, in due time,
obtain a perfect deliverance out of the hands of all
their enemies, and a complete victory over all those
who have sought their hurt and destruction. And as
mercy is also an attribute of the Deity, his saints can
have confidence that it will be exercised toward them;
and through the exercise of that attribute toward
them, comfort and consolation will be administered
unto them abundantly, amid all their afflictions and
tribulations. And lastly, realizing that truth is an attribute of the Deity, the mind is led to rejoice amid
all its trials and temptations, in hope of that glory
which is to be brought at the revelation of Jesus
Christ, and in view of that crown which is to be placed upon the heads of the saints in the day when the
Lord shall distribute rewards unto them, and in
prospect of that eternal weight of glory which the
Lord has promised to bestow upon them when he shall
bring them into the midst of his throne to dwell in
his presence eternally.

18 In view, then, of the existence of these attributes, the faith of the saints can become exceedingly
strong: abounding in righteousness unto the praise
and glory of God, and can exert its mighty influence
in searching after wisdom and understanding, until it
has obtained a knowledge of all things that pertain to
life and salvation.

19 Such, then, is the foundation, which is laid,

51

line 1 through the revelation of the attributes of God, for
the exercise of faith in him for life and salvation;
and seeing that these are attributes of the Deity, they
are unchangeable—being the same yesterday to day
5 and forever—which gives to the minds of the Latter
Day Saints the same power and authority to exercise
faith in God, which the Former Day Saints had: so
that all the saints, in this respect have been, are and
will be alike, until the end of time; for God never
10 changes, therefore his attributes and character remain
forever the same. And as it is through the revelation of these that a foundation is laid for the exercise
of faith in God unto life and salvation, the foundation, therefore, for the exercise of faith, was, is and
15 ever will be the same. So that all men have had,
and will have an equal privilege.

Question. What was shown in the third lecture?

Answer. It was shown that correct ideas of the character of
God are necessary in order to exercise faith in him unto life
20 and salvation; and that without correct ideas of his character,
men could not have power to exercise faith in him unto life
and salvation, but that correct ideas of his character, as far as
his character is concerned in the exercise of faith in him, lay
a sure foundation for the exercise of it. [§ IV. ¶ 1.]

25 Q. What object had the God of heaven in revealing his attributes to men?

A. That through an acquaintance with his attributes they
might be enabled to exercise faith in him so as to obtain eternal life. [§ IV. ¶ 2.]

30 Q. Could men exercise faith in God without an acquaintance
with his attributes, so as to be enabled to lay hold of eternal
life?

A. They could not. [§ IV. ¶ 2,3.]

Q. What account is given of the attributes of God in in his
35 revelations?

A. First, Knowledge, secondly, Faith, or power, thirdly,
Justice, fourthly, Judgment, fifthly, Mercy, and sixthly truth.
§IV. ¶ 4,5,6,7,8,9 and 10.]

4*

52

line 1   Q. Where are the revelations to be found which give this relation of the attributes of God?

A. In the Old and New Testaments, and they are quoted in the fourth lecture, fifth, sixth, seventh, eighth, ninth, and

5   tenth paragraphs.*

Q. Is the idea of the existence of those attributes, in the Deity, necessary in order to enable any rational being to exercise faith in him unto life and salvation?

A. It is.

10   Q. How do you prove it?

A. By the eleventh, twelfth, thirteenth fourteenth, fifteenth and sixteenth paragraphs in this lecture.*

Q. Does the idea of the existence of these attributes in the Deity, as far as his attributes are concerned, enable a rational

15   being to exercise faith in him unto life and salvation?

A. It does.

Q. How do you prove it?

A. By the seventeenth and eighteenth paragraphs.*

Q. Have the Latter Day Saints as much authoity given

20   them, through the revelation of the attributes of God, to exercise faith in him as the Former Day Saints had?

A. They have.

Q. How do you prove it?

A. By the nineteenth paragraph of this lecture.*

25   *Note.* Let the student turn and commit those paragraphs to memory.

LECTURE FIFTH.

Of Faith.

SECTION V.

30   1 In our former lectures we treated of the being, character, perfections and attributes of God. What we mean by perfections, is, the perfections which belong to all the attributes of his nature. We shall, in this lecture speak of the Godhead: we mean the

35   Father, Son and Holy Spirit.

2 There are two personages who constitute the great, matchless, governing and supreme power over

------

line 27. Fifth lecture on faith, ca. winter 1834–1835. This lecture was first set in type for the 1835 Doctrine and Covenants. It was later retypeset and printed in the May 1835 issue of the *LDS Messenger and Advocate*. ("Lecture Fifth," *LDS Messenger and Advocate,* May 1835, 1:122–124.)

53

all things—by whom all things were created and made, that are created and made, whether visible or invisible: whether in heaven, on earth, or in the earth, under the earth, or throughout the immensity of space—They are the Father and the Son: The Father being a personage of spirit, glory and power: possessing all perfection and fulness: The Son, who was in the bosom of the Father, a personage of tabernacle, made, or fashioned like unto man, or being in the form and likeness of man, or, rather, man was formed after his likeness, and in his image;—he is also the express image and likeness of the personage of the Father: possessing all the fulness of the Father, or, the same fulness with the Fathe; being begotten of him, and was ordained from before the foundation of the world to be a propitiation for the sins of all those who should believe on his name, and is called the Son because of the flesh—and descended in suffering below that which man can suffer, or, in other words, suffered greater sufferings, and was exposed to more powerful contradictions than any man can be. But notwithstanding all this, he kept the law of God, and remained without sin: Showing thereby that it is in the power of man to keep the law and remain also without sin. And also, that by him a righteous judgment might come upon all flesh, and that all who walk not in the law of God, may justly be condemned by the law, and have no excuse for their sins. And he being the only begotten of the Father, full of grace and truth, and having overcome, received a fulness of the glory of the Father—possessing the same mind with the Father, which mind is the Holy Spirit, that bears record of the Father and the Son, and these three are one, or in other words, these three constitute the great, matchless, governing and supreme power over all things: by whom all things were created and made, that were created and made: and these three

54

constitute the Godhead, and are one: The Father and
the Son possessing the same mind, the same wisdom,
glory, power and fulness: Filling all in all—the Son
being filled with the fulness of the Mind, glory and
power, or, in other words, the Spirit, glory and power of the Father—possessing all knowledge and glory,
and the same kingdom: sitting at the right hand
of power, in the express image and likeness of the
Father—a Mediator for man—being filled with the fulness of the Mind of the Father, or, in other words,
the Spirit of the Father: which Spirit is shed forth
upon all who believe on his name and keep his
commandments: and all those who keep his commandments shall grow up from grace to grace, and become
heirs of the heavenly kingdom, and joint heirs with
Jesus Christ; possessing the same mind, being trans-
formed into the same image or likeness, even the
express image of him who fills all in all: being filled
with the fulness of his glory, and become one in
him, even as the Father, Son and Holy Spirit are one.

3 From the foregoing account of the Godhead,
which is given in his revelations, the Saints have a
sure foundation laid for the exercise of faith unto life
and salvation, through the atonement and mediation of
Jesus Christ, by whose blood they have a forgiveness
of sins, and also, a sure reward laid up for them in
heaven, even that of partaking of the fulness of the
Father and the Son, through the Spirit. As the Son
partakes of the fulness of the Father through the Spirit, so the saints are, by the same Spirit, to be partakers of the same fulness, to enjoy the same glory; for
as the Father and the Son are one, so in like manner
the saints are to be one in them, through the love of
the Father, the mediation of Jesus Christ, and the gift
of the Holy Spirit; they are to be heirs of God and
joint heirs with Jesus Christ.

55

Question. Of what do the foregoing lectures treat?

Answer. Of the being, perfections and attributes of the Deity. [§5. ¶1.]

Q. What are we to understand by the perfections of the Deity?

A. The perfections which belong to his attributes.

Q. How many personages are there in the Godhead?

A. Two: the Father and the Son. [§5. ¶1.]

Q. How do you prove that there are two personages in the Godhead?

A. By the Scriptures. Gen. 1:26. Also §2. ¶6. And the Lord God said unto the Only Begotten, who was with him from the beginning, Let us make man in our image, after our likeness:—and it was done. Gen. 3: 22. And the Lord God said unto the Only Begotten, Behold, the man is become as one of us: to know good and evil. John, 17: 5. And now, O Father, glorify thou me with thine own self with the glory which I had with thee before the world was [§5. ¶2.]

Q. What is the Father?

A. He is a personage of glory and of power. [§5. ¶2.

Q. How do you prove that the Father is a personage of glory and of power?

A. Isaiah 60: 19. The Sun shall be no more thy light by day, neither for brightness shall the moon give light unto thee: but the Lord shall be unto thee an everlasting light, and thy God thy glory. 1 Chron. 29: 11. Thine, O Lord, is the greatness, and the power, and the glory. Ps. 29: 3. The voice of the Lord is upon the waters: the God of glory thunders. Ps. 79: 9. Help us, O God of our salvation, for the glory of thy name. Romans 1: 23. And changed the glory of the incorruptible God into an image made like to corruptible men.

Secondly, of power. 1 Chron. 29: 4. Thine, O Lord, is the greatness and the power, and the glory. Jer. 32: 17. Ah! Lord God, behold thou hast made the earth and the heavens by thy great power, and stretched-out arm; and there is nothing too hard for thee. Deut 4: 37. And because he loved thy fathers therefore he chose their seed after them, and bro't them out in his sight with his mighty power. 2. Samuel 22: 33. God is my strength and power. Job 26, commencing with the 7 verse, to the end of the chapter. He stretches out the north over the empty place, and hangs the earth upon nothing. He binds up the waters in his thick clouds; and the cloud is not rent under them. He holds back the face of his throne, and spreads his cloud upon it. He has compassed the waters with bounds, until the day and night come to an

56

end. The pillars of heaven tremble, and are astonished at his reproof. He divides the sea with his power, and by his understanding he smites through the proud. By his Spirit he has garnished the heavens; his hand has formed the crooked serpent. Lo, these are parts of his ways: but how little a portion is heard of him? But the thunder of his power who can understand?

Q. What is the Son?

A. First, he is a personage of tabernacle. [§5. ¶2.]

Q. How do you prove it?

A. John 14: 9, 10, 11; Jesus says unto him, Have I been so long time with you, and yet have you not known me, Philip? He that has seen me has seen the Father; and how do you say then, Show us the Father? Do you not believe, that I am in the Father, and the Father in me? The words that I speak unto you, I speak not of myself: but the Father that dwells in me, he does the works. Believe me that I am in the Father, and the Father in me.

Secondly, and being a personage of tabernacle, was made or fashioned like unto man, or being in the form and likeness of man. [§5. ¶2.]

Philip. 2. Let this mind be in you, which was also in Christ Jesus; who being in the form of God, thought it not robbery to be equal with God; but made himself of no reputation, and took upon him the form of a servant, and was made in the likeness of man, and, being found in fashion as a man, he humbled himself, and became obedient unto death, even the death of the cross. Heb. 2: 14, 16. Forasmuch then as the children are partakers of flesh and blood, he also himself likewise took part of the same. For verily he took not on him the nature of angels: but he took on him the seed of Abraham.

Thirdly, he is also in the likeness of the personage of the Father. [§5. ¶2.]

Heb. 1: 1,2,3. God, who at sundry times, and in divers manners, spake in time past to the fathers, by the prophets, has in these last days spoken unto us by his Son, whom he has appointed heir of all things, by whom also he made the worlds; who, being the brightness of his glory, and the express image of his person. Again, Philip. 2: 5,6. Let this mind be in you, which was also in Christ Jesus; who being in the form of God, thought it not robbery to be equal with God.

Q. Was it by the Father and the Son that all things were created and made, that were created and made?

A. It was. Col. 1: 15, 16, 17. Who is the image of the invisible God, the first born of every creature; for by him were all things created that are in heaven, and that are in earth,

line 1 visible and invisible, whether they be thrones or dominions, principalities or powers; all things were created by him and for him; and he is before all things, and by him all things consist. Gen. 1: 1. In the beginning God created the heavens
5 and the earth. Heb. 1: 2. [God] Has in these last days spoken unto us by his Son, whom he has appointed heir of all things, by whom also he made the worlds.
Q. Does he possess the fulness of the Father?
A. He does. Col. 1: 19. 2: 9. For it pleased the Father
10 that in him should all fulness dwell. For in him dwells all the fulness of the Godhead bodily. Eph. 1: 23. Which is his [Christ's] body, the fulness of him that fills all in all.
Q. Why was he called the Son?
A. Because of the flesh. Luke 1: 33. That holy thing
15 which shall be born of thee, shall be called the Son of God.— Math. 3: 16, 17. And Jesus, when he was baptized, went up straitway out of the water: and lo, the heavens were opened unto him, and he [John] saw the Spirit of God descending like a dove and lighting upon him: and lo, a voice from heaven,
20 saying, This is my beloved Son, in whom I am well pleased.
Q. Was he ordained of the Father, from before the foundation of the world, to be a propitiation for the sins of all those who should believe on his name?
A. He was. 1 Peter, 1: 18, 19, 20. For as much as you
25 know that you were not redeemed with corruptible things, as silver and gold, from your vain conversation, received by tradition from your fathers; but with the precious blood of Christ, as of a lamb without blemish and without spot: who verily was foreordained before the foundation of the world, but was
30 manifested in these last times for you. Rev. 13: 8. And all that dwell upon the earth shall worship him, [the beast] whose names are not written in the book of life of the Lamb slain from the foundation of the world. 1 Corin. 2: 7. But we speak the wisdom of God in a mystery, even the hidden mystery, which
35 God ordained before the world unto our glory.
Q. Do the Father and the Son possess the same mind?
A. They do. John 5: 30. I [Christ] can of my own self do nothing: as I hear, I judge, and my judgment is just; because I seek not my own will, but the will of the Father who sent me.
40 John 6: 38. For I [Christ] came down from heaven, not to do my own will, but the will of him that sent me. John 10: 30. I [Christ] and my Father are one.
Q. What is this mind?
A. The Holy Spirit. John 15: 26. But when the Com-
45 forter is come, whom I will send unto you from the Father, even the Spirit of truth, which proceeds from the Father, he

58

shall testify of me. [Christ.] Gal. 4: 6. And because you are sons, God has sent forth the Spirit of his Son into your hearts.

Q. Do the Father, Son and Holy Spirit constitute the Godhead?

A. They do.   [§5. ¶2.]

Let the student commit this paragraph to memory.

Q. Does the believer in Christ Jesus, through the gift of the Spirit, become one with the Father and the Son, as the Father and the Son are one?

A. They do. John 17: 20, 21. Neither pray I for these (the apostles) alone, but for them also who shall believe on me through their word; that they all may be one; as thou, Father, art in me, and I in thee, that they also may be one in us, that the world may believe that thou hast sent me.

Q. Does the foregoing account of the Godhead lay a sure foundation for the exercise of faith in him unto life and salvation?

A. It does.

Q. How do you prove it?

A. By the third paragraph of this lecture.

Let the student commit this also.

LECTURE SIXTH.

Of Faith.

SECTION VI.

1 Having treated, in the preceding lectures, of the ideas of the character, perfections and attributes of God, we next proceed to treat of the knowledge which persons must have, that the course of life which they pursue is according to the will of God, in order that they may be enabled to exercise faith in him unto life and salvation.

2 This knowledge supplies an important place in revealed religion; for it was by reason of it that the ancients were enabled to endure as seeing him who is invisible. An actual knowledge to any person that

---

line 23. Sixth lecture on faith, ca. winter 1834–1835. This lecture was first set in type for the 1835 Doctrine and Covenants. It was later retypeset and printed in the May 1835 issue of the *LDS Messenger and Advocate.* ("Lecture Sixth," *LDS Messenger and Advocate,* May 1835, 1:124–126.)

line 1 the course of life which he pursues is according to
the will of God, is essentially necessary to enable
him to have that confidence in God, without which no
person can obtain eternal life. It was this that ena-
5 bled the ancient saints to endure all their afflictions
and persecutions, and to take joyfully the spoiling of
their goods, knowing, (not believing merely,) that they
had a more enduring substance. Heb. 10:34.

3 Having the assurance that they were pursuing a
10 course which was agreeable to the will of God, they
were enabled to take, not only the spoiling of their
goods, and the wasting of their substance, joyfully,
but also to suffer death in its most horrid forms; knowing, (not merely believing,) that when this earthly house
15 of their tabernacle was dissolved, they had a building
of God, a house not made with hands, eternal in the
heavens. Second Cor. 5:1.

4 Such was and always will be the situation of the
saints of God, that unless they have an actual knowl-
20 edge that the course that they are pursuing is according to the will of God, they will grow weary in their
minds and faint; for such has been and always will be
the opposition in the hearts of unbelievers and those
that know not God, against the pure and unadulterated
25 religion of heaven, (the only thing which ensures
eternal life,) that they will persecute, to the uttermost,
all that worship God according to his revelations, receive the truth in the love of it, and submit themselves
to be guided and directed by his will, and drive them
30 to such extremities that nothing short of an actual
knowledge of their being the favorites of heaven, and
of their having embraced that order of things which
God has established for the redemption of man, will
enable them to exercise that confidence in him neces-
35 sary for them to overcome the world, and obtain that
crown of glory which is laid up for them that fear
God.

60

5 For a man to lay down his all, his character and reputation, his honor and applause, his good name among men, his houses, his lands, his brothers and sisters, his wife and children, and even his own life also, counting all things but filth and dross for the excellency of the knowledge of Jesus Christ, requires more than mere belief, or supposition that he is doing the will of God, but actual knowledge: realizing, that when these sufferings are ended he will enter into eternal rest; and be a partaker of the glory of God

6 For unless a person does know that he is walking according to the will of God, it would be offering an insult to the dignity of the Creator, were he to say that he would be a partaker of his glory when he should be done with the things of this life. But when he has this knowledge, and most assuredly knows that he is doing the will of God, his confidence can be equally strong that he will be a partaker of the glory of God.

7 Let us here observe, that a religion that does not require the sacrifice of all things, never has power sufficient to produce the faith necessary unto life and salvation; for from the first existence of man, the faith necessary unto the enjoyment of life and salvation never could be obtained without the sacrifice of all earthly things: it was through this sacrifice, and this only, that God has ordained that men should enjoy eternal life; and it is through the medium of the sacrifice of all earthly things, that men do actually know that they are doing the things that are well pleasing in the sight of God. When a man has offered in sacrifice all that he has, for the truth's sake, not even withholding his life, and believing before God that he has been called to make this sacrifice, because he seeks to do his will, he does know most assuredly, that God does and will accept his sacrifice & offering, & that he has not nor will not seek his face in

vain. Under these circumstances, then, he can obtain the faith necessary for him to lay hold on eternal life.

8 It is in vain for persons to fancy to themselves that they are heirs with those, or can be heirs with them, who have offered their all in sacrifice, and by this means obtained faith in God and favor with him so as to obtain eternal life, unless they in like manner offer unto him the same sacrifice, and through that offering obtain the knowledge that they are accepted of him.

9 It was in offering sacrifices that Abel, the first martyr, obtained knowledge that he was accepted of God. And from the days of righteous Abel to the present time, the knowledge that men have that they are accepted in the sight of God, is obtained by offering sacrifice: and in the last days, before the Lord comes, he is to gather together his saints who have made a covenant with him by sacrifice. Ps. 50:3,4,5. Our God shall come, and shall not keep silence: a fire shall devour before him, and it shall be very tempestuous round about him. He shall call to the heavens from above, and to the earth, that he may judge his people. Gather my saints together unto me; those that have made a covenant unto me by sacrifice.

10 Those, then, who make the sacrifice will have the testimony that their course is pleasing in the sight of God, and those who have this testimony will have faith to lay hold on eternal life, and will be enabled, through faith, to endure unto the end, and receive the crown that is laid up for them that love the appearing of our Lord Jesus Christ. But those who do not make the sacrifice cannot enjoy this faith, because men are dependent upon this sacrifice in order to obtain this faith; therefore, they cannot lay hold upon eternal life, because the revelations of God do not guarantee unto them the authority so to do; and without this guarantee faith could not exist.

62

11 All the saints of whom we have account in all the revelations of God which are extant, obtained the knowledge which they had of their acceptance in his sight, through the sacrifice which they offered unto him: and through the knowledge thus obtained, their faith became sufficiently strong to lay hold upon the promise of eternal life, and to endure us seeing him who is invisible; and were enabled, through faith, to combat the powers of darkness, contend against the wiles of the adversary, overcome the world, and obtain the end of their faith, even the salvation of their souls.

12 But those who have not made this sacrifice to God, do not know that the course which they pursue is well pleasing in his sight; for whatever may be their belief or their opinion, it is a matter of doubt and uncertainty in their mind; and where doubt and uncertainty is, there faith is not, nor can it be. For doubt and faith do not exist in the same person at the same time. So that persons whose minds are under doubts and fears cannot have unshaken confidence, and where unshaken confidence is not, there faith is weak, and where faith is weak, the persons will not be able to contend against all the opposition, tribulations and afflictions which they will have to encounter in order to be heirs of God, and joint heirs with Christ Jesus; and they will grow weary in their minds, and the adversary will have power over them and destroy them.

Note. This lecture is so plain, and the facts set forth so self-evident, that it is deemed unnecessary to form a catechism upon it: the student is therefore instructed to commit the whole to memory.

LECTURE SEVENTH.

Of Faith.

SECTION VII

1 In the preceding lectures, we treated of what faith was, and of the object on which it rested· agreeably to our plan we now proceed to speak of its effects.

2 As we have seen in our former lectures, that faith was the principle of action and of power in all intelligent beings, both in heaven and on earth, it will not be expected that we will, in a lecture of this description attempt to unfold all its effects; neither is it necessary to our purpose so to do; for it would embrace all things in heaven and on earth, and encompass all the creations of God, with all their endless varieties: for no world has yet been framed that was not framed by faith; neither has there been an intelligent being on any of God's creations who did not get there by reason of faith, as it existed in himself or in some other being; nor has there been a change or a revolution in any of the creations of God but it has been effected by faith: neither will there be a change or a revolution unless it is effected in the same way, in any of the vast creations of the Almighty; for it is by faith that the Deity works.

3 Let us here offer some explanation in relation to faith that our meaning may be clearly comprehended: We ask, then, what are we to understand by a man's working by faith? We answer: We understand that when a man works by faith he works by mental exertion instead of physical force: it is by words instead of exerting his physical powers, with which every being works when he works by faith——

---

line 1. Seventh lecture on faith, ca. winter 1834–1835.

64

God said, Let there be light, and there was light—
Joshua spake and the great lights which God had
created stood still—Elijah commanded and the heavens were stayed for the space of three years and six
months, so that it did not rain: He again commanded,
and the heavens gave forth rain,—all this was done
by faith; and the Savior says, If you have faith as
a grain of mustard seed, say to this mountain, remove, and it will remove; or say to that sycamine
tree, Be ye plucked up and planted in the midst of
the sea, and it shall obey you. Faith, then, works by
words; and with these its mightiest works have been,
and will be performed.

4 It surely will not be required of us to prove, that
this is the principle upon which all eternty has acted
and will act; for every reflecting mind must know,
that it is by reason of this power that all the hosts of
heaven perform their works of wonder, majesty and
glory: Angels move from place to place by virtue of
this power—it is by reason of it that they are enabled
to descend from heaven to earth; and were it not for
the power of faith they never could be ministering
spirits to them who should be heirs of salvation, neither could they act as heavenly messengers; for they
would be destitute of the power necessary to enable
them to do the will of God.

5 It is only necessary for us to say, that the whole
visible creation, as it now exists, is the effect of faith
—It was faith by which it was framed, and it is by
the power of faith that it continues in its organized
form, and by which the planets move round their or-
bits and sparkle forth their glory: So, then, faith is
truly the first principle in the science of THEOLOGY,
and when undrstood, leads the mind back to the beginning and carries it forward to the end; or in other
words, from eternity to eternity.

6 As faith, then, is the principle by which the heav-

65

line 1 enly hosts perform their works, and by which they
enjoy all their felicity, we might expect to find it set
forth in a revelation from God as the principle upon
which his creatures, here below, must act, in order,
5 to obtain the felicities enjoyed by the saints in the
eternal world, and that when God would undertake to
raise up men for the enjoyment of himself, he would
teach them the necessity of living by faith, and the
impossibility there was of their enjoying the blessed-
10 ness of eternity without it, seeing that all the blessings of eternity are the effects of faith.

7 Therefore, it is said, and appropriately too, that
without faith it is impossible to please God. If it should
be asked, Why is it impossible to please God without
15 faith? the answer would be, because, without faith it
is impossible for men to be saved; and as God desires
the salvation of man he must of course desire that
they should have faith, and he could not be pleased
unless they had, or else he could be pleased with their
20 destruction.

8 From this we learn that the many exhortations
which have been given by inspired men to those who
had received the word of the Lord, to have faith in
him, were not mere common-place matters, but were
25 for the best of all reasons, and that was, because,
without it there was no salvation, neither in this world
nor in that which is to come. When men begin to
live by faith they begin to draw near to God; and
when faith is perfected they are like him; and be-
30 cause he is saved they are saved also; for they will
be in the same situation he is in, because they have
come to him; and when he appears they shall be like
him, for they will see him as he is.

9 As all the visible creation is an effect of faith, so is
35 salvation, also. (We mean salvation in its most extensive latitude of interpretation, whether it is tempo-

E

---

line 37. This page begins the fifth gathering of the book. "E" is the first of two signature marks in this gathering; the second is on the recto of the following leaf. These marks were used in collating the gatherings after the sheets were folded.

66

line 1 ral or spiritual.) In order to have this subject clearly set before the mind, let us ask what situation must
a person be in, in order to be saved? or what is the
difference between a saved man and one who is not
5 saved? We answer from what we have before seen
of the heavenly worlds, they must be persons who
can work by faith, and who are able, by faith to be
ministering spirits to them who shall be heirs of salvation. And they must have faith to enable them to
10 act in the presence of the Lord, otherwise they cannot be saved. And what constitutes the real difference between a saved person and one not saved, is
the difference in the degree of their faith: one's faith
has become perfect enough to lay hold upon eternal
15 life, and the other's has not. But to be a little more
particular, let us ask, where shall we find a prototype
into whose likeness we may be assimulated, in order
that we may be made partakers of life and salvation?
or in other words, where shall we find a saved being?
20 for if we can find a saved being, we may ascertain,
without much difficulty, what all others must be, in
order to be saved— they must be like that individual
or they cannot be saved: we think, that it will not be
a matter of dispute, that two beings, who are unlike
25 each other, cannot both be saved; for whatever constitutes the salvation of one, will constitute the salvation of every creature which will be saved: and if
we find one saved being in all existance, we may see
what all others must be, or else not be saved. We
30 ask, then, where is the prototype? or where is the
saved being? We conclude as to the answer of this
question there will be no dispute among those who believe the bible, that it is Christ: all will agree in this
that he is the prototype or standard of salvation, or
35 in other words, that he is a saved being. And if we
should continue our interogation, and ask how it is
that he is saved, the answer would be, because he is

67

a just and holy being; and if he were any thing different from what he is he would not be saved; for his salvation depends on his being precisely what he is and nothing else; for if it were possible for him to change in the least degree, so sure he would fail of salvation and lose all his dominion, power, authority and glory, which constitutes salvation; for salvation consists in the glory, authority, majesty, power and dominion which Jehovah possesses, and in nothing else; and no being can possess it but himself or one like him: Thus says John, in his first epistle, 3:2 and 3: Behold, now we are the sons of God, and it doth not appear what we shall be; but we know, that when he shall appear we shall be like him; for we shall see him as he is. And any man that has this hope in him purifies himself, even as he is pure.— Why purify himself as he is pure? because, if they do not they cannot be like him.

10 The Lord said unto Moses, Leviticus, 19:2:— Speak unto all the congregation of the children of Israel, and say unto them, Ye shall be holy: for I the Lord your God am holy. And Peter says, first epistle, 1:15 and 16: But as he who has called you is holy, so be ye holy in all manner of conversation; because it is written, Be ye holy; for I am holy. And the Savior says, Matthew, 15:48: Be ye perfect, even as your Father who is in heaven is perfect. If any should ask, why all these sayings? the answer is to be found from what is before quoted from John's epistle, that when he (the Lord) shall appear, the saints will be like him: and if they are not holy, as he is holy, and perfect as he is perfect, they cannot be like him; for no being can enjoy his glory without possessing his perfections and holiness, no more than they could reign in his kingdom without his power.

11 This clearly sets forth the propriety of the Sav-
5*

68

line 1
ior's saying, recorded in John's testimony, 4:12: Verily, verily I say unto you, he that believeth on me,
the works that I do shall he do also; and greater
works than these, because I go unto the Father.—

5
This taken in connection with some of the sayings in
the Savior's prayer, recorded in the 17th chapter,
gives great clearness to his expressions: He says, in
the 20,21, 22,23 and 24: Neither pray I for these
alone; but for them also who shall believe on me

10
through their words; that they all may be one, as
thou, Father art in me, and I in thee, that they also
may be one in us: that the world may believe that
thou hast sent me. And the glory which thou gavest
me, I have given them, that they may be one, even

15
as we are one; I in them, and thou in me, that they
may be made perfect in one; and that the world may
know that thou hast sent me, and hast loved them as
thou hast loved me. Father, I will that they also
whom thou hast given me be with me where I am:

20
that they may behold my glory which thou hast given
me; for thou lovedest me before the foundation of the
world.
  12 All these sayings put together, give as clear an account of the state of the glorified saints as language

25
could give—The works that Jesus done they were to
do, and greater works than those which he done
among them should they do, and that because he went
to the Father. He does not say that they should do
these works in time; but they should do greater works

30
because he went to the Father. He says, in the 24th
verse: Father, I will that they also whom thou hast
given me, be with me where I am; that they may
behold my glory. These sayings, taken in connection, make it very plain, that the greater works, which

35
those that believed on his name, were to do, were to
be done in eternity, where he was going, and where
they should behold his glory. He had said, in an-

other part of his prayer, that he desired of his Father, that those who believed on him should be one in him, as he, and the Father were one in each other: Neither pray I for these (the apostles) alone, but for them also who shall believe on me through their words; that they all may be one: that is, they who believe on him through the apostles' words, as well as the apostles themselves: that they all may be one, as thou, Father, art in me and I in thee: that they also may be one in us.

13 What language can be plainer than this? The Savior surely intended to be understood by his disciples: and he so spake that they might understand him; for he declares to his Father, in language not to be easily mistaken, that he wanted his disciples, even all of them, to be as himself and the Father: for as he and the Father were one, so they might be one with them. And what is said in the 22nd verse is calculated to more firmly establish this belief, if it needs any thing to establish it. He says, And the glory which thou gavest me, I have given them, that they may be one, even as we are one. As much as to say, that unless they have the glory which the Father had given him, they could not be one with them: For he says he had given them the glory that the Father had given him, that they might be one; or in other words, to make them one.

14 This fills up the measure of information on this subject, and shows most clearly, that the Savior wished his disciples to understand, that they were to be partakers with him in all things: not even his glory excepted.

15 It is scarcely necessary here to observe what we have previously noticed: That the glory which the Father and the Son have, is because they are just and holy beings; and that if they were lacking in one attribute or perfection which they have,

70

the glory which they have, never could be enjoyed
by them; for it requires them to be precisely what
they are in order to enjoy it: and if the Savior gives
this glory to any others, he must do it in the very
way set forth in his prayer to his Father: by making
them one with him, as he and the Father are one.—
In so doing he would give them the glory which the
Father has given him; and when his disciples are
made one with the Father and the Son, as the Father
and the Son are one, who cannot see the propriety of
the Savior's saying, The works which I do, shall they
do; and greater works than these shall they do, because I go to the Father?

16 These teachings of the Savior most clearly show
unto us the nature of salvation; and what he proposed unto the human family when he proposed to save
them—That he proposed to make them like unto himself; and he was like the Father, the great prototype
of all saved beings: And for any portion of the human family to be assimulated into their likeness is to
be saved; and to be unlike them is to be destroyed:
and on this hinge turns the door of salvation.

17 Who cannot see, then, that salvation is the effect of faith? for as we have previously observed, all
the heavenly beings work by this principle; and it is
because they are able so to do that they are saved:
for nothing but this could save them. And this is the
lesson which the God of heaven, by the mouth of all
his holy prophets, has been endeavoring to teach to
the world. Hence we are told, that without faith it
is impossible to please God; and that salvation is of
faith, that it might be by grace to the end, the promise might be sure to all the seed. Romans 4:16.—
And that Israel, who followed after the law of righteousness, has not attained to the law of righteousness. Wherefore? because they sought it not by
faith, but as it were by the works of the law; for

71

they stumbled at that stumbling stone.   Romans 9:32.
And Jesus said unto the man who brought his son to
him, to get the devil who tormented him, cast out, If
thou canst believe, all things are possible to him that
believeth.   Mark, 9:23. These with a multitude of
other scriptures, which might be quoted, plainly set
forth the light, in which the Savior, as well as the
Former Day Saints, viewed the plan of salvation.—
That it was a system of faith—it begins with faith,
and continues by faith; and every blessing which is
obtained, in relation to it, is the effect of faith, whether it pertains to this life or that which is to come.—
To this, all the revelations of God bear witness.   If
there were children of promise, they were the effects
of faith: not even the Savior of the world excepted:
Blessed is she that believed, said Elizabeth to Mary,
when she went to visit her;—for there shall be a per-
formance of the things which were told her of the
Lord; Luke, 1:45:   Nor was the birth of John the
baptist the less a matter of faith; for in order that his
father Zacharias might believe he was struck dumb.
And through the whole history of the scheme of life
and salvation, it is a matter of faith: every man received according to his faith: according as his faith
was, so were his blessings and privileges; and nothing was withheld from him when his faith was sufficient to receive it.   He could stop the mouths of lions, quench the violence of fire, escape the edge of
the sword, wax valiant in fight, and put to flight the
armies of the aliens; women could, by their faith,
receive the dead children to life again: in a word,
there was nothing impossible with them who had
faith.   All things were in subjection to the Former
Day Saints, according as their faith was—By their
faith they could obtain heavenly visions, the ministering of angels, have knowledge of the spirits of just
men made perfect, of the general assembly and church

72

line 1   of the first born, whose names are written in heaven,
of God the judge of all, of Jesus the Mediator of the
new covenant, and become familiar with the third
heavens, see and hear things which were not only un-
5   utterable, but were unlawful to utter. Peter, in view of
the power of faith, 2nd epistle, 1:1,2 and 3 says, to the
Former Day Saints: grace and peace be multiplied
unto you, through the knowledge of God, and of Jesus our Lord, according as his divine power hath
10   given unto us all things that pertain unto life and
godliness, through the knowledge of him that has cail-
ed us unto glory and virtue. In the first epistle, 1:3,
4 and 5 he says, Blessed be the God and Father of
our Lord Jesus Christ, who according to his abundant
15   mercy, has begotten us again unto a lively hope by
the resurrection of Jesus Christ from the dead, to an
inheritance incorruptible and undefiled, and that
fadeth not away, reserved in heaven for you, who
are kept by the power of God through faith unto sal-
20   vation, ready to be revealed in the last time.

16 These sayings put together, show the Apostle's
views, most clearly, so as to admit of no mistake on
the mind of any individual. He says that all things
that pertain to life and godliness were given unto them
25   through the knowledge of God and our Savior Jesus
Christ. And if the question is asked, how were they
to obtain the knowledge of God? (for there is a great
difference between believing in God and knowing
him: knowledge implies more than faith. And no-
30   tice, that all things that pertain to life and godliness,
were given through the knowledge of God;) the answer is given, through faith they were to obtain this
knowledge; and having power by faith to obtain the
knowledge of God, they could with it obtain all other
35   things which pertain to life and godliness.

17 By these sayings of the Apostle we learn, that it
was by obtaining a knowledge of God, that men got

the all things which pertain to life and godliness; and this knowledge was the effect of faith. So that all things which pertain to life and godliness are the effects of faith.

18 From this we may extend as far as any circumstances may require whether on earth or in heaven, and we will find it the testimony of all inspired men, or heavenly messengers, that all things that pertain to life and godliness are the effects of faith and nothing else: all learning, wisdom, and prudence fail, and every thing else as a means of salvation but faith. This is the reason that the fishermen of Gallilee could teach the world—because they sought by faith and by faith obtained. And this is the reason that Paul counted all things but filth and dross—what he formerly called his gain he called his loss; yea, and he counted all things but loss for the excellency of the knowledge of Christ Jesus the Lord. Philipians 3: 7, 8, 9 & 10. Because, to obtain the faith by which he could enjoy the knowledge of Christ Jesus the Lord, he had to suffer the loss of all things: this is the reason that the Former Day Saints knew more, and understood more of heaven, and of heavenly things than all others beside, because this information is the effect of faith—to be obtained by no other means. And this is the reason, that men, as soon as they lose their faith, run into strifes, contentions, darkness and difficulties; for the knowledge which tends to life disappears with faith, but returns when faith returns; for when faith comes, it brings its train of attendants with it—apostles, prophets, evangelists, pastors, teachers, gifts, wisdom, knowledge, miracles, healings, tongues, interpretation of tongues, &c. All these appear when faith appears on the earth, and disappear when it disappears from the earth. For these are the effects of faith and always have, and always will attend it. For where faith is, there will the knowledge

74

of God be also, with all things which pertain thereto—
revelations, visions, and dreams, as well as every other necessary thing in order that the possessors of faith
may be perfected and obtain salvation; for God must
change, otherwise faith will prevail with him. And
he who possesses it will, through it, obtain all necessary knowledge and wisdom, until he shall know God,
and the Lord Jesus Christ, whom he has sent: whom
to know is eternal life: Amen.

line 1

PART SECOND.

COVENANTS AND COMMANDMENTS

OF THE LORD,

to his servants of the church of the

LATTER DAY SAINTS.

SECTION I.

1 Hearken, O ye people of my church, saith the voice of him who dwells on high, and whose eyes are upon all men; yea, verily I say, hearken ye people from afar, and ye that are upon the islands of the sea, listen together; for verily the voice of the Lord is unto all men, and there is none to escape, and there is no eye that shall not see, neither ear that shall not hear, neither heart that shall not be penetrated: and the rebellious shall be pierced with much sorrow, for their iniquities shall be spoken upon the house-tops, and their secret acts shall be revealed; and the voice of warning shall be unto all people, by the mouths of my disciples, whom I have chosen in these last days, and they shall go forth and none shall stay them, for I the Lord have commanded them.

2 Behold, this is mine authority, and the authority of my servants, and my preface unto the book of my commandments, which I have given them to publish unto you O inhabitants of the earth: wherefore fear and tremble, O ye people, for what I the Lord have decreed, in them, shall be fulfilled. And verily, I say unto you, that they who go forth, bearing these tidings unto the inhabitants of the earth, to them is power given to seal both on earth and in heaven, the unbelieving and rebellious; yea, verily, to seal them up unto the day when the wrath of God shall be poured out upon the wicked without measure: unto the day when the Lord shall come to recompense unto every man according to his work, and measure to every man according to the measure which he has measured to his fellow man.

3 Wherefore the voice of the Lord is unto the ends of the earth, that all that will hear may hear: prepare ye, prepare ye

---

line 6. Revelation, 1 Nov. 1831–B [D&C 1]. Oliver Cowdery's copy of the Book of Commandments bears a notation marking this revelation for inclusion in the 1835 Doctrine and Covenants. This version reflects an editing mark made in the Cowdery volume and closely corresponds to the version in chapter 1 of that book, indicating that the Cowdery volume was used as a source text for this version. (See p. 600 herein.)

76

line 1 for that which is to come, for the Lord is nigh; and the anger
of the Lord is kindled, and his sword is bathed in heaven, and
it shall fall upon the inhabitants of the earth; and the arm of
the Lord shall be revealed; and the day cometh, that they who
5 will not hear the voice of the Lord, neither the voice of his servants, neither give heed to the words of the prophets, and
apostles, shall be cut off from among the people: for they have
strayed from mine ordinances, and have broken mine everlasting covenant; they seek not the Lord to establish his right-
10 eousness, but every man walketh in his own way, and after
the image of his own god, whose image is in the likeness of the
world, and whose substance is that of an idol, which waxeth
old and shall perish in Babylon, even Babylon the great, which
shall fall:

15 4 Wherefore I the Lord, knowing the calamity which should
come upon the inhabitants of the earth, called upon my servant
Joseph Smith jr. and spake unto him from heaven, and gave
him commandments; and also gave commandments to others,
that they should proclaim these things unto the world; and all
20 this that it might be fulfilled, which was written by the prophets: the weak things of the world shall come forth and break
down the mighty and strong ones, that man should not counsel his fellow man, neither trust in the arm of flesh, but that
every man might speak in the name of God, the Lord, even
25 the Savior of the world; that faith also might increase in the
earth; that mine everlasting covenant might be established;
that the fulness of my gospel might be proclaimed by the weak
and the simple, unto the ends of the world, and before kings
and rulers.

30 5 Behold I am God and have spoken it: these commandments
are of me, and were given unto my servants in their weakness,
after the manner of their language, that they might come to
understanding; and inasmuch as they erred it might be made
known: and inasmuch as they sought wisdom, they might be
35 instructed; and inasmuch as they sinned they might be chastened, that they might repent; and inasmuch as they were
humble, they might be made strong, and blessed from on high,
and receive knowledge from time to time: and after having received the record of the Nephites, yea, even my servant Joseph
40 Smith jr. might have power to translate through the mercy of
God, by the power of God, the book of Mormon: and also,
those to whom these commandments were given, might have
power to lay the foundation of this church, and to bring it forth
out of obscurity, and out of darkness, the only true and living
45 church upon the face of the whole earth, with which I the
Lord am well pleased, speaking unto the church collectively

77

line 1 and not individually; for I the Lord cannot look upon sin with
the least degree of allowance: nevertheless, he that repents
and does the commandments of the Lord, shall be forgiven,
and he that repents not, from him shall be taken even the light
5 which he has received, for my Spirit shall not always strive
with man, saith the Lord of hosts.

6 And again, verily I say unto you, O inhabitants of the
earth, I the Lord am willing to make these things known unto all flesh, for I am no respecter of persons, and willeth that
10 all men shall know that the day speedily cometh, the hour is
not yet, but is nigh at hand, when peace shall be taken from
the earth, and the devil shall have power over his own dominion; and also, the Lord shall have power over his saints, and
shall reign in their midst, and shall come down in judgment
15 upon Idumea, or the world.

7 Search these commandments, for they are true and faithful, and the prophecies and promises which are in them shall
all be fulfilled.

8 What I the Lord have spoken, I have spoken, and I excuse
20 not myself, and though the heavens and the earth pass away,
my word shall not pass away, but shall all be fulfilled, whether by mine own voice, or by the voice of my servants, it is the
same: for behold, and lo, the Lord is God, and the Spirit beareth record, and the record is true, and the truth abideth forev-
25 er and ever: Amen.

SECTION II.

1 The rise of the church of Christ in these last days, being
one thousand eight hundred and thirty years since the coming of our Lord and Savior Jesus Christ in the flesh, it being
30 regularly organized and established agreeably to the laws of
our country, by the will and commandments of God in the
fourth month, and on the sixth day of the month which is
called April: which commandments were given to Joseph
Smith jr. who was called of God and ordained an apostle of
35 Jesus Christ, to be the first elder of this church; and to Oliver
Cowdery, who was also called of God an apostle of Jesus
Christ, to be the second elder of this church, and ordained under his hand: and this according to the grace of our Lord and
Savior Jesus Christ, to whom be all glory both now and for-
40 ever. Amen.

2 After it was truly manifested unto this first elder that he
had received a remission of his sins he was entangled again in
the vanities of the world; but after repenting, and humbling
himself, sincerely, through faith God ministered unto him by

---

line 26. Articles and covenants, 10 Apr. 1830 [D&C 20]. Oliver Cowdery's copy of the Book of
Commandments bears a notation marking this revelation for inclusion in the 1835 Doctrine and
Covenants. This version closely corresponds to the version in the June 1832 issue of *Evening and Morning
Star* (printed Jan. 1835), suggesting that the latter was used as a source text for the former.

78

line 1 an holy angel whose countenance was as lightning, and whose
garments were pure and white above all other whiteness, and
gave unto him commandments which inspired him, and gave
him power from on high, by the means which were before pre-
5 pared, to translate the book of Mormon, which contains a record of a fallen people, and the fulness of the gospel of Jesus
Christ to the Gentiles, and to the Jews also, which was given
by inspiration, and is confirmed to others by the ministering
of angels, and is declared unto the world by them, proving to
10 the world that the holy scriptures are true, and that God does
inspire men and call them to his holy work in this age and
generation, as well as in generations of old, thereby showing
that he is the same God yesterday, to-day, and forever.—
Amen.
15 3 Therefore, having so great witnesses, by them shall the
world be judged, even as many as shall hereafter come to a
knowledge of this work; and those who receive it in faith and
work righteousness, shall receive a crown of eternal life; but
those who harden their hearts in unbelief and reject it, it shall
20 turn to their own condemnation, for the Lord God has spoken
it; and we, the elders of the church, have heard and bear witness to the words of the glorious Majesty on high, to whom be
glory forever and ever.   Amen.
4 By these things we know that there is a God in heaven
25 who is infinite and eternal, from everlasting to everlasting the
same unchangeable God, the framer of heaven and earth and all
things which are in them, and that he created man male and
female: after his own image and in his own likeness created
he them, and gave unto them commandments that they should
30 love and serve him the only living and true God, and that he
should be the only being whom they should worship.   But by
the transgression of these holy laws, man became sensual and
devilish, and became fallen man.
5 Wherefore the Almighty God gave his only begotten Son,
35 as it is written in those scriptures which have been given of
him; he suffered temptations but gave no heed unto them; he
was crucified, died, and rose again the third day; and ascended into heaven to sit down on the right hand of the Father, to
reign with almighty power according to the will of the Father,
40 that as many as would believe and be baptized, in his holy
name, and endure in faith to the end should be saved: not only those who believed after he came in the meridian of time in
the flesh, but all those from the beginning, even as many as
were before he came, who believed in the words of the holy
45 prophets, who spake as they were inspired by the gift of the
Holy Ghost, who truly testified of him in all things, should

line 1 have eternal life, as well as those who should come after, who
should believe in the gifts and callings of God by the Holy
Ghost, which beareth record of the Father, and of the Son,
which Father, Son, and Holy Ghost are one God, infinite and
5 eternal, without end. Amen.

6 And we know that all men must repent and believe on the
name of Jesus Christ and worship the Father in his name, and
endure in faith on his name to the end, or they cannot be saved in the kingdom of God. And we know that justification
10 through the grace of our Lord and Savior Jesus Christ, is just
and true: and we know, also, that sanctification through the
grace of our Lord and Savior Jesus Christ, is just and true, to
all those who love and serve God with all their mights, minds,
and strength; but there is a possibility that man may fall from
15 grace and depart from the living God. Therefore let the church
take heed and pray always, lest they fall into temptations;
yea, and even let those who are sanctified, take heed also.—
And we know that these things are true and according to the
revelations of John, neither adding to, nor diminishing from
20 the prophecy of his book, the holy scriptures, or the revelations
of God which shall come hereafter by the gift and power of
the Holy Ghost, the voice of God, or the ministering of angels: and the Lord God has spoken it; and honor, power, and
glory, be rendered to his holy name, both now and ever.—
25 Amen.

7 *And again by way of commandment to the church concerning*
the manner of baptism.

All those who humble themselves before God and desire to
be baptized, and come forth with broken hearts and contrite
30 spirits, and witness before the church that they have truly repented of all their sins and are willing to take upon them the
name of Jesus Christ, having a determination to serve him to
the end, and truly manifest by their works that they have received of the Spirit of Christ unto the remission of their sins,
35 shall be received by baptism into his church.

8 *The duty of the elders, priests, teachers, deacons, and mem-*
bers of the church of Christ.

An elder, and it is his calling to baptize, and
to ordain other elders, priests, teachers, and deacons, and to
40 administer bread and wine—the emblems of the flesh and blood
of Christ—and to confirm those who are baptized into the
church, by the laying on of hands for the baptism of fire and
the Holy Ghost, according to the scriptures; and to teach,
expound exhort, baptize, and watch over the church; and to
45 confirm the church by the laying on of the hands, and the giving of the Holy Ghost—and to take the lead of all meetings.

80

9 The elders are to conduct the meetings as they are led by
the Holy Ghost, according to the commandments and revelations of God.

10 The priest's duty is to preach, teach, expound, exhort,
and baptize, and administer the sacrament, and visit the house
of each member, and exhort them to pray vocally and in secret, and attend to all family duties: and he may also ordain
other priests, teachers, and deacons—and he is to take the
lead of meetings when there is no elder present, but when
there is an elder present he is only to preach, teach, expound,
exhort, and baptize, and visit the house of each member, exhorting them to pray vocally and in secret, and attend to all
family duties. In all these duties the priest is to assist the elder if occasion requires.

11 The teacher's duty is to watch over the church always,
and be with, and strengthen them, and see that there is no iniquity in the church, neither hardness with each other; neither lying, backbiting, nor evil speaking; and see that the
church meet together often, and also see that all the members
do their duty—and he is to take the lead of meetings in the
absence of the elder or priest—and is to be assisted always
in all his duties in the church, by the deacons, if occasion requires: but neither teachers nor deacons have authority to
baptize, administer the sacrament, or lay on hands; they are
however to warn, expound, exhort, and teach, and invite all
to come unto Christ.

12 Every elder, priest, teacher, or deacon, is to be ordained
according to the gifts and callings of God unto him: and he is
to be ordained by the power of the Holy Ghost which is in the
one who ordains him.

13 The several elders composing this church of Christ are to
meet in conference once in three months, or from time to time,
as said conferences shall direct or appoint: and said conferences are to do whatever church business is necessary to be done
at the time.

14 The elders are to receive their licences from other elders
by vote of the church to which they belong, or from the conferences.

15 Each priest, teacher, or deacon, who is ordained by a
priest, may take a certificate from him at the time, which certificate when presented to an elder, shall entitle him to a license, which shall authorize him to perform the duties of his
calling—or he may receive it from a conference.

16 No person is to be ordained to any office in this church,
where there is a regularly organized branch of the same, without the vote of that church; but the presiding elders, travel-

81

line 1 ling bishops, high counsellors, high priests, and elders, may have the privilege of ordaining, where there is no branch of the church, that a vote may be called.

17 Every president of the high priesthood, (or presiding elder,) bishop, high counsellor, and high priest, is to be ordained *5* by the direction of a high counsel, or general conference.

18 *The duty of the members after they are received by baptism:*

19 The elders or priests are to have a sufficient time to expound all things concerning the church of Christ to their understanding, previous to their partaking of the sacrament, and *10* being confirmed by the laying on of the hands of the elders; so that all things may be done in order. And the members shall manifest before the church and also before the elders, by a godly walk and conversation, that they are worthy of it, *15* that there may be works and faith agreeable to the holy scriptures—walking in holiness before the Lord.

20 Every member of the church of Christ having children, is to bring them unto the elders before the church, who are to lay their hands upon them in the name of Jesus Christ, and *20* bless them in his name.

21 No one can be received into the church of Christ unless he has arrived unto the years of accountability before God, and is capable of repentance.

22 Baptism is to be administered in the following manner *25* unto all those who repent: The person who is called of God and has authority from Jesus Christ to baptize, shall go down into the water with the person who has presented him or herself for baptism, and shall say, calling him or her by name: Having been commissioned of Jesus Christ, I baptize you in the name *30* of the Father, and of the Son, and of the Holy Ghost, Amen. Then shall he immerse him or her in the water, and come forth again out of the water.

23 It is expedient that the church meet together often to partake of bread and wine in remembrance of the Lord Jesus: and *35* the elder or priest shall administer it: and after this manner shall he administer it: he shall kneel with the church and call upon the Father in solemn prayer, saying, O God, the eternal Father, we ask thee in the name of thy Son Jesus Christ to bless and sanctify this bread to the souls of all those who par- *40* take of it, that they may eat in remembrance of the body of thy Son, and witness unto thee O God, the eternal Father, that they are willing to take upon them the name of thy Son, and always remember him and keep his commandments which he has given them, that they may always have his Spirit to be *45* with them. Amen.

F

---

line 46. This page begins the sixth gathering of the book. "F" is the first of two signature marks in this gathering; the second is on the recto of the following leaf. These marks were used in collating the gatherings after the sheets were folded.

82

line 1
24 The manner of administering the wine: He shall take the cup also, and say, O God, the eternal Father, we ask thee in the name of thy Son Jesus Christ, to bless and sanctify this wine to the souls of all those who drink of it, that they may do it in remembrance of the blood of thy Son which was shed for them, that they may witness unto thee, O God, the eternal Father, that they do always remember him, that they may have his Spirit to be with them. Amen.

25 Any member of the church of Christ transgressing, or being overtaken in a fault, shall be dealt with as the scriptures direct.

26 It shall be the duty of the several churches composing the church of Christ, to send one or more of their teachers to attend the several conferences, held by the elders of the church, with a list of the names of the several members uniting themselves with the church since the last conference, or send by the hand of some priest, so that a regular list of all the names of the whole church may be kept in a book, by one of the elders, whoever the other elders shall appoint from time to time:— and also, if any have been expelled from the church; so that their names may be blotted out of the general church record of names.

27 All members removing from the church where they reside, if going to a church where they are not known, may take a letter certifying that they are regular members and in good standing; which certificate may be signed by any elder or priest, if the member receiving the letter is personally acquainted with the elder or priest, or it may be signed by the teachers, or deacons of the church.

SECTION III.

ON PRIESTHOOD.

1 There are, in the church, two priesthoods, namely: the Melchizedek, and the Aaronic, including the Levitical priesthood. Why the first is called the Melchizedek priesthood, is because Melchizedek was such a great high priest: before his day it was called *the holy priesthood, after the order of the Son of God;* but out of respect or reverence to the name of the Supreme Being, to avoid the too frequent repetition of his name, they, the church, in ancient days, called that priesthood after Melchizedek, or the Melchizedek priesthood.

2 All other authorities, or offices in the church are appendages to this priesthood; but there are two divisions, or grand heads—one is the Melchizedek priesthood, and the other is the Aaronic, or Levitical priesthood.

---

line 30. Instruction on priesthood, ca. Apr. 1835 [D&C 107]. This text first appeared in the 1835 Doctrine and Covenants. Beginning in verse 31, the text quotes Revelation, 11 November 1831–B. The wording in this quoted portion corresponds to the wording in some early manuscript versions, but the source text for this version is unknown. Some of the content of this item is not found in any extant manuscript text.

line 1   3 The office of an elder comes under the priesthood of Melchizedek. The Melchisedek priesthood holds the right of
presidency, and has power and authority over all the offices in
the church, in all ages of the world, to administer in spiritual
5   things.
4 The presidency of the high priesthood, after the order of
Melchizedek, have a right to officiate in all the offices in the
church.
5 High priests, after the order of the Melchizedek priesthood,
10   have a right to officiate in their own standing, under the direction of the presidency, in administering spiritual things, and
also in the office of an elder, priest, (of the Levitical order,)
teacher, deacon and member.
6 An elder has a right to officiate in his stead when the high
15   priest is not present.
7 The high priest, and elder, are to administer in spiritual
things, agreeably to the covenants and commandments of the
church; and they have a right to officiate in all these offices of
the church when there are no higher authorities present.
20   8 The second priesthood is called the priesthood of Aaron,
because it was conferred upon Aaron and his seed, throughout
all their generations. Why it is called the lesser priesthood,
is because it is an appendage to the greater, or the Melchizedek priesthood, and has power in administering outward ordi-
25   nances. The bishopric is the presidency of this priesthood
and holds the keys, or authority of the same. No man has a
legal right to this office, to hold the keys of this priesthood,
except he be a litteral descendant of Aaron. But as a high
priest, of the Melchizedek priesthood, has authority to officiate
30   in all the lesser offices, he may officiate in the office of bishop
when no literal descendant of Aaron can be found; provided
he is called and set apart and ordained unto this power by the
hands of the presidency of the Melchizedek priesthood.
9 The power and authority of the higher or Melchizedek
35   priesthood, is to hold the keys of all the spiritual blessings of the
church—to have the privilege of receiving the mysteries of the
kingdom of heaven—to have the heavens opened unto them—
to commune with the general assembly and church of the first
born, and to enjoy the communion and presence of God the
40   Father, and Jesus the Mediator of the new covenant.
10 The power and authority of the lesser, or Aaronic priesthood, is, to hold the keys of the ministring of angels, and to
administer in outward ordinances—the letter of the gospel—
the baptism of repentance for the remission of sins, agreeably
45   to the covenants and commandments.
6*

84

11 Of necessity there are presidents, or presiding offices growing out of, or appointed of, or from among those who are ordained to the several offices in these two priesthoods. Of the Melchizedek priesthood, three presiding high priests, chosen by the body, appointed and ordained to that office, and upheld by the confidence, faith and prayer of the church, form a quorum of the presidency of the church. The twelve travelling counsellors are called to be the twelve apostles, or special witnesses of the name of Christ, in all the world: thus differing from other officers in the church in the duties of their calling. And they form a quorum equal in authority and power to the three presidents, previously mentioned. The seventy are also called to preach the gospel, and to be especial witnesses unto the Gentiles and in all the world. Thus differing from other officers in the church in the duties of their calling: and they form a quorum equal in authority to that of the twelve especial witnesses or apostles, just named. And every descision made by either of these quorums, must be by the unanimous voice of the same; that is, every member in each quorum must be agreed to its decisions in order to make their decisions of the same power or validity one with the other. [A majority may form a quorum when circumstances render it impossible to be otherwise.] Unless this is the case, their decisions are not entitled to the same blessings which the decisions of a quorum of three presidents were anciently, who were ordained after the order of Melchizedek, and were righteous and holy men. The decisions of these quorums, or either of them are to be made in all righteousness; in holiness and lowliness of heart; meekness and long suffering; and in faith and virtue and knowledge; temperance, patience, godliness brotherly kindness and charity, because the promise is, if these things abound in them, they shall not be unfruitful in the knowledge of the Lord. And in case that any decision, of these quorums, is made in unrighteousness, it may be brought before a general assembly of the several quorums which constitute the spiritual authorities of the church, otherwise there can be no appeal from their decision.

12 The twelve are a travelling, presiding high council, to officiate in the name of the Lord, under the direction of the presidency of the church, agreeably to the institution of heaven; to build up the church, and regulate all the affairs of the same, in all nations: first unto the Gentiles, and secondly unto the Jews.

13 The seventy are to act in the name of the Lord, under the direction of the twelve, or the travelling high council, in building up the church and regulating all the affairs of the

85

same, in all nations: first unto the Gentiles and then to the Jews:—the twelve being sent out, holding the keys, to open the door by the proclamation of the gospel of Jesus Christ; and first unto the Gentiles and then unto the Jews.

14 The standing high councils, at the stakes of Zion, form a quorum equal in authority, in the affairs of the church, in all their decisions, to the quorum of the presidency, or to the travelling high council.

15 The high council in Zion, forms a quorum equal in authority, in the affairs of the church, in all their decisions, to the councils of the twelve at the stakes of Zion.

16 It is the duty of the travelling high council to call upon the seventy, when they need assistance, to fill the several calls for preaching and administering the gospel, in stead of any others.

17 It is the duty of the twelve in all large branches of the church, to ordain evangelical ministers, as they shall be designated unto them by revelation.

18 The order of this priesthood was confirmed to be handed down from father to son, and rightly belongs to the literal descendants of the chosen seed, to whom the promises were made. This order was instituted in the days of Adam, and came down by lineage in the following manner:

19 From Adam to Seth, who was ordained by Adam at the age of 69 years, and was blessed by him three years previous to his (Adam's) death, and received the promise of God by his father, that his posterity should be the chosen of the Lord, and that they should be preserved unto the end of the earth, because he [Seth] was a perfect man, and his likeness was the express likeness of his father's, insomuch that he seemed to be like unto his father in all things; and could be distinguished from him only by his age.

20 Enos was ordained at the age of 134 years, and four months, by the hand of Adam.

21 God called upon Cainan in the wilderness, in the fortieth year of his age, and he met Adam in journeying to the place Shedolamak: he was eighty seven years old when he received his ordination.

22 Mahalaleel was 496 years and seven days old when he was ordained by the hand of Adam, who also blessed him.

23 Jared was 200 years old when he was ordained under the hand of Adam, who also blessed him.

24 Enoch, was 25 years old when he was ordained under the hand of Adam, and he was 65 and Adam blessed him—and he saw the Lord: and he walked with him, and was before his face continually: and he walked with God 365 years: making him 430 years old when he was translated.

86

line 1

25 Methuselah was 100 years old when he was ordained under the hand of Adam.

26 Lamech was 32 years old when he was ordained under the hand of Seth.

27 Noah was 10 years old when he was ordained under the hand of Methuselah.

28 Three years previous to the death of Adam, he called Seth, Enos, Cainan, Mahalaleel, Jared, Enoch and Methuselah, who were all high priests, with the residue of his posterity, who were righteous, into the valley of Adam-ondi-ahman, and there bestowed upon them his last blessing. And the Lord appeared unto them, and they rose up and blessed Adam, and called him Michael, the Prince, the Archangel. And the Lord administered comfort unto Adam, and said unto him, I have set thee to be at the head: a multitude of nations shall come of thee; and thou art a prince over them for ever.

29 And Adam stood up in the midst of the congregation, and notwithstanding he was bowed down with age, being full of the Holy Ghost, predicted whatsoever should befall his posterity unto the latest generation. These things were all written in the book of Enoch, and are to be testified of in due time.

30 It is the duty of the twelve, also, to ordain and set in order all the other officers of the church, agreeably to the revelation which says:

31 To the church of Christ in the land of Zion, in addition to the church laws, respecting church business: Verily, I say unto you, says the Lord of hosts, There must needs be presiding elders, to preside over those who are of the office of an elder; and also priests, to preside over those who are of the office of a priest; and also teachers to preside over those who are of the office of a teacher, in like manner; and also the deacons: wherefore, from deacon to teacher, and from teacher to priest, and from priest to elder, severally as they are appointed, according to the covenants and commandments of the church; then comes the high priesthood, which is the greatest of all. Wherefore, it must needs be that one be appointed, of the high priesthood, to preside over the priesthood; and he shall be called president of the high priesthood of the church, or, in other words, the presiding high priest over the high priesthood of the church. From the same comes the administering of ordinances and blessings upon the church, by the laying on of the hands.

32 Wherefore the office of a bishop is not equal unto it; for the office of a bishop is in administering all temporal things: nevertheless, a bishop must be chosen from the high priest-

87

line 1 hood, unless he is a literal descendant of Aaron; for unless
he is a literal descendant of Aaron he cannot hold the keys
of that priesthood. Nevertheless, a high priest, that is after
the order of Melchizedek, may be set apart unto the minis-
5 tering of temporal things, having a knowledge of them by the
Spirit of truth, and also to be a judge in Israel, to do the business of the church to sit in judgment upon transgressors, upon
testimony, as it shall be laid before him, according to the laws,
by the assistance of his counsellors, whom he has chosen,
10 or will chose among the elders of the church. This is the
duty of a bishop who is not a literal descendant of Aaron,
but has been ordained to the high priesthood after the order of
Melchizedek.

33 Thus shall he be a judge, even a common judge among the
15 inhabitants of Zion, or in a stake of Zion, or in any branch of
the church where he shall be set apart unto this ministry, until the borders of Zion are enlarged, and it becomes necessary
to have other bishops, or judges in Zion, or elsewhere: and inasmuch as there are other bishops appointed they shall act in
20 the same office.

34 But a literal descendant of Aaron has a legal right to the
presidency of this priesthood, to the keys of this ministry, to
act in the office of bishop independently, without counsellors,
except in a case where a president of the high priesthood, after
25 the order of Melchizedek, is tried; to sit as a judge in Israel.—
And the decision of either of these councils, agreeably to the
commandment which says;

35 Again, verily, I say unto you: The most important business of the church, and the most difficult cases of the church,
30 inasmuch as there is not satisfaction upon the decision of
the bishop, or judges, it shall be handed over and carried up
unto the council of the church, before the presidency of the
high priesthood; and the presidency of the council of the
high priesthood shall have power to call other high priests,
35 even twelve, to assist as counsellors; and thus the presidency
of the high priesthood, and its counsellors shall have power
to decide upon testimony according to the laws of the church.
And after this decision it shall be had in remembrance no
more before the Lord; for this is the highest council of the
40 church of God, and a final decision upon controversies, in
spiritual matters.

36 There is not any person belonging to the church, who is
exempt from this council of the church.

37 And inasmuch as a president of the high priesthood
45 shall transgress, he shall be had in remembrance before the
common council of the church, who shall be assisted by twelve

88

line 1

counsellors of the high priesthood; and their decision upon his
head shall be an end of controversy concerning him. Thus,
none shall be exempted from the justice and the laws of God;
that all things may be done in order and in solemnity, before
him, according to truth and righteousness.

38 And again, verily I say unto you, the duty of a president over the office of a deacon, is to preside over twelve deacons, to sit in council with them, and to teach them their duty—edifying one another, as it is given according to the covenants.

39 And also the duty of the president over the office of the
teachers, is to preside over twenty four of the teachers, and to
sit in council with them—teaching them the duties of their
office, as given in the covenants.

40 Also the duty of the president over the priesthood of Aaron, is to preside over forty eight priests, and sit in council with
them, to teach them the duties of their office, as is given in the
covenants. This president is to be a bishop; for this is one
of the duties of this priesthood.

41 Again, the duty of the president over the office of elders
is to preside over ninety six elders, and to sit in council with
them, and to teach them according to the covenants. This
presidency is a distinct one from that of the seventy, and is
designed for those who do not travel into all the world.

42 And again, the duty of the president of the office of the
high priesthood is to preside over the whole church, and to be
like unto Moses. Behold, here is wisdom—yea, to be a seer,
a revelator, a translator and a prophet—having all the gifts of
God which he bestows upon the head of the church.

43 And it is according to the vision, showing the order of the
seventy, that they should have seven presidents to preside
over them, chosen out of the number of the seventy, and the
seventh president of these presidents is to preside over the six;
and these seven presidents are to choose other seventy besides
the first seventy, to whom they belong, and are to preside over
them; and also other seventy until seven times seventy, if the
labor in the vineyard of necessity requires it. And these seventy are to be travelling ministers unto the Gentiles, first,
and also unto the Jews, whereas other offices of the church
who belong not unto the twelve neither to the seventy, are
not under the responsibility to travel among all nations, but
are to travel as their circumstances shall allow, notwithstanding they may hold as high and responsible offices in the church.

44 Wherefore, now let every man learn his duty, and to act
in the office in which he is appointed, in all diligence. He
that is slothful shall not be counted worthy to stand, and he-

89

line 1

that learns not his duty and shows himself not approved, shall not be counted worthy to stand; even so. Amen.

SECTION IV.

A Revelation given the 22d and 23d of Sept. 1832.

ON PRIESTHOOD.

1 A revelation of Jesus Christ unto his servant Joseph Smith, jr. and six elders, as they united their hearts and lifted their voices on high; yea, the word of the Lord concerning his church, established in the last days for the restoration of his people as he has spoken by the mouth of his prophets, and for the gathering of his saints to stand upon mount Zion, which shall be the city New Jerusalem; which city shall be built, beginning at the Temple Lot, which is appointed by the finger of the Lord, in the western boundaries of the state of Missouri, and dedicated by the hand of Joseph Smith, jr. and others, with whom the Lord was well pleased.

2 Verily, this is the word of the Lord, that the city New Jerusalem shall be built by the gathering of the saints, beginning at this place, even the place of the temple, which temple shall be reared in this generation; for verily, this generation shall not all pass away until an house shall be built unto the Lord and a cloud shall rest upon it, which cloud shall be even the glory of the Lord, which shall fill the house. And the sons of Moses, according to the holy priesthood, which he received under the hand of his father-in-law, Jethro, and Jethro received it under the hand of Caleb, and Caleb received it under the hand of Elihu, and Elihu under the hand of Jeremy, and Jeremy under the hand of Gad and Gad under the hand of Esaias, and Esaias received it under the hand of God; Esaias also lived in the days of Abraham and was blessed of him, which Abraham received the priesthood from Melchizedek, who received it through the lineage of his fathers, even till Noah; and from Noah till Enoch, through the lineage of their fathers, and from Enoch to Abel, who was slain by the conspiracy of his brother, who received the priesthood by the commandments of God by the hand of his father Adam, who was the first man; which priesthood continueth in the church of God in all generations, and is without beginning of days or end of years.

3 And the Lord confirmed a priesthood also upon Aaron and his seed throughout all their generations, which priesthood also continueth and abideth forever, with the priesthood which

---

line 3. Revelation, 22 and 23 Sept. 1832 [D&C 84]. This version reflects editing marks made in Revelation Book 2, indicating that the latter was used as a source text for the former. (See *JSP,* MRB:453–475.)

90

is after the holiest order of God. And this greater priesthood
administereth the gospel and holdeth the key of the mysteries
of the kingdom, even the key of the knowledge of God.—
Therefore, in the ordinances thereof the power of godliness
is manifest; and without the ordinances thereof, and the authority of the priesthood, the power of godliness is not manifest unto men in the flesh; for without this no man can see the
face of God, even the Father, and live.

4 Now this Moses plainly taught to the children of Israel
in the wilderness, and sought diligently to sanctify his people
that they might behold the face of God; but they hardened
their hearts and could not endure his presence, therefore, the
Lord, in his wrath, (for his anger was kindled against them,)
swore that they should not enter into his rest, while in the wilderness, which rest is the fulness of his glory. Therefore he
took Moses out of their midst and the holy priesthood also;
and the lesser priesthood continued, which priesthood holdeth
the key of the ministering of angels and the preparatory gospel,
which gospel is the gospel of repentance and of baptism and
the remission of sins and the law of carnal commandments,
which the Lord, in his wrath, caused to continue with the
house of Aaron among the children of Israel until John, whom
God raised up, being filled with the Holy Ghost from his
mother's womb: for he was baptized while he was yet in his
childhood, and was ordained by the angel of God at the time he
was eight days old unto this power—to overthrow the kingdom of the Jews, and to make straight the way of the Lord before the face of his people, to prepare them for the coming of
the Lord, in whose hand is given all power.

5 And again, the office of elder and bishop are necessary appendages belonging unto the high priesthood. And again, the
offices of teachers and deacons are necessary appendages belonging to the lesser priesthood, which priesthood was confirmed upon Aaron and his sons.

6 Therefore, as I said concerning the Sons of Moses—for the
sons of Moses and also the sons of Aaron shall offer an acceptable offering and sacrifice in the house of the Lord, which house
shall be built unto the Lord in this generation upon the consecrated spot, as I have appointed—and the sons of Moses and of
Aaron shall be filled with the glory of the Lord upon mount
Zion in the Lord's house, whose sons are ye; and also many
whom I have called and sent forth to build up my church; for
whoso is faithful unto the obtaining these two priesthoods of
which I have spoken, and the magnifying their calling, are sanc-
tifyed by the Spirit unto the renewing of their bodies: they
become the sons of Moses and of Aaron and the seed of Abra-

91

line 1 ham, and the church and kingdom and the elect of God; and
also all they who receive this priesthood receiveth me, saith
the Lord, for he that receiveth my servants receiveth me, and
he that receiveth me receiveth my Father, and he that receiv-
5 eth my Father receiveth my Father's kingdom. Therefore, all
that my Father hath shall be given unto him; and this is according to the oath and covenant which belongeth to the
priesthood. Therefore, all those who receive the priesthood
receive this oath and covenant of my Father which he cannot
10 break, neither can it be moved; but whoso breaketh this covenant, after he hath received it, and altogether turneth therefrom, shall not have forgiveness of sins in this world nor in
the world to come. And all those who come not unto this
priesthood, which ye have received, which I now confirm up-
15 on you who are present, this day, by mine own voice out
of the heavens, and even I have given the heavenly hosts and
mine angels charge covcerning you.

7 And I now give unto you a commandment to beware concerning yourselves, to give diligent heed to the words of
20 eternal life; for you shall live by every word that proceedeth
forth from the mouth of God. For the word of the Lord is
truth, and whatsoever is truth is light, and whatsoever is light
is Spirit, even the Spirit of Jesus Christ; and the Spirit giveth
light to every man that cometh into the world: and the Spirit
25 enlighteneth every man through the world, that hearkeneth
to the voice of the Spirit; and every one that hearkeneth to
the voice of the Spirit, cometh unto God, even the Father;
and the Father teacheth him of the covenant which he has
renewed and confirmed upon you, which is confirmed upon
30 you for your sakes, and not for your sakes only, but for the
sake of the whole world: and the whole world lieth in sin, and
groaneth under darkness and under the bondage of sin; and by
this you may know they are under the bondage of sin, because they come not unto me; for whoso cometh not unto
35 me is under the bondage of sin; and whoso receiveth not my
voice is not acquainted with my voice, and is not of me; and
by this you may know the righteous from the wicked, and
that the whole world groaneth under sin and darkness even now.

8 And your minds in times past have been darkened because of
40 unbelief, and because you have treated lightly the things you
have received, which vanity and unbelief hath brought the whole
church under condemnation. And this condemnation resteth
upon the children of Zion, even all; and they shall remain under this condemnation until they repent and remember the
45 new covenant, even the book of Mormon and the former commandments which I have given them, not only to say, but to

92

line 1

do according to that which I have written, that they may
bring forth fruit meet for their Father's kingdom, otherwise
their remaineth a scourge and a judgment to be poured out
upon the children of Zion: for shall the children of the kingdom pollute my holy land? Verily, I say unto you, Nay.

9 Verily, verily, I say you, who now have my words, which
is my voice, blessed are ye inasmuch as you receive these
things: for I will forgive you of your sins with this commandment, that you remain steadfast in your minds in solemnity
and the spirit of prayer, in bearing testimony to all the world
of those things which are communicated unto you.

10 Therefore go ye into all the world, and whatsoever place
ye cannot go into ye shall send, that the testimony may go
from you into all the world, unto every creature. And as I
said unto mine apostles, even so I say unto you; for you are
mine apostles, even God's highpriests: ye are they whom my
Father hath given me: ye are my friends; therefore, as I said
unto mine apostles I say unto you again, that every soul who
believeth on your words, and is baptized by water for the remission of sins, shall receive the Holy Ghost; and these signs
shall follow them that believe:

11 In my name they shall do many wonderful works: in my
name they shall cast out devils: in my name they shall heal
the sick: in my name they shall open the eys of the blind, and
unstop the ears of the deaf; and the tongue of the dumb shall
speak: and if any man shall administer poison unto them it
shall not hurt them: and the poison of a serpent shall not
have power to harm them. But a commandment I give unto
them, that they shall not boast themselves of these things,
neither speak them before the world: for these things are giv-
en unto you for your profit and for salvation.

12 Verily, verily, I say unto you, they who believe not on your
words, and are not baptized by water, in my name, for the remission of their sins, that they may receive the Holy Ghost,
shall be damned. and shall not come into my Father's kingdom, where my Father and I am. And this revelation unto
you, and commandment, is in force from this very hour upon
all the world, and the gospel is unto all who have not received
it. But verily I say unto all those to whom the kingdom has
been given, from you it must be preached unto them that they
shall repent of their former evil works; for they are to be
upbraided for their evil hearts of unbelief: and your brethren
in Zion for their rebellion against you at the time I sent you.

13 And again, I say unto you my friends, (for from henceforth I shall call you friends,) it is expedient that I give unto
you this commandment, that ye become even as my friends in

93

days when I was with them travelling to preach this gospel
in my power; for I suffered them not to have purse or scrip,
neither two coats: behold I send you out to prove the world,
and the laborer is worthy of his hire. And any man that shall
go and preach this gospel of the kingdom, and fail not to continue faithful in all things, shall not be weary in mind, neither
darkened, neither in body, limb or joint; and an hair of his
head shall not fall to the ground unnoticed. And they shall
not go hungry, neither athirst.

14 Therefore, take no thought for the morrow, for what ye
shall eat, or what ye shall drink, or wherewithal ye shall be
clothed; for consider the lillies of the field, how they grow,
they toil not, neither do they spin; and the kingdoms of the
world, in all their glory, are not arrayed like one of these;
for your Father who art in heaven, knoweth that you have
need of all these things. Therefore, let the morrow take
thought for the things of itself. Neither take ye thought be-
forehand what ye shall say, but treasure up in your minds continually the words of life, and it shall be given you in the very
hour that portion that shall be meted unto every man.

15 Therefore let no man among you, (for this commandment
is unto all the faithful who are called of God in the church,
unto the ministry,) from this hour, take purse or scrip, that
goeth forth to proclaim this gospel of the kingdom. Behold
I send you out to reprove the world of all their unrighteous
deeds, and to teach them of a judgment which is to come—
And whoso receiveth you, there I will be also: for I will go
before your face: I will be on your right hand and on your left,
and my Spirit shall be in your hearts, and mine angels round
about you, to bear you up.

16 Whoso receiveth you, receiveth me, and the same will
feed you, and clothe you, and give you money. And he who
feeds you, or clothes you, or gives you money, shall in no wise
lose his reward: and he that doeth not these things is not my
disciple: by this you may know my disciples. He that receiveth you not, go away from him alone by yourselves, and cleanse
your feet, even with water, pure water, whether in heat or in
cold, and bear testimony of it unto your Father which is in
heaven, and return not again unto that man. And in whatsoever village or city ye enter, do likewise. Nevertheless, search
diligently and spare not; and wo unto that house, or that village, or city, that rejecteth you, or your words, or testimony
concerning me. Wo, I say again, unto that house, or that
village, or city, that rejecteth you, or your words, or your testimony of me; for I the Almighty, have laid my hands upon
the nations to scourge them for their wickedness; and plagues

94

shall go forth, & they shall not be taken from the earth until I
have completed my work which shall be cut short in righteousness; until all shall know me, who remain, even from the least
unto the greatest, and shall be filled with the knowledge of the
Lord, and shall see eye to eye, and shall lift up their voice,
and with the voice together sing this new song, saying,

17 The Lord hath brought again Zion:
The Lord hath redeemed his people, Israel,
According to the election of grace,
Which was brought to pass by the faith,
And covenant of their fathers.
The Lord hath redeemed his people,
And satan is bound, and time is no longer:
The Lord hath gathered all things in one:
The Lord hath brought down Zion from above:
The Lord hath brought up Zion from beneath:
The earth hath travailed and brought forth her strength;
And truth is established in her bowels;
And the heavens have smiled upon her;
And she is clothed with the glory of her God:
For he stands in the midst of his people:
Glory, and honor, and power, and might,
Be ascribed to our God, for he is full of mercy,
Justice, grace and truth, and peace,
For ever and ever Amen.

18 And again, verily, verily I say unto you, it is expedient,
that every man who goes forth to proclaim mine everlasting
gospel, that inasmuch as they have families and receive moneys by gift, that they should send it unto them, or make use
of it for their benefit, as the Lord shall direct them, for thus it
seemeth me good. And let all those who have not families,
who receive moneys, send it up unto the bishop in Zion, or
unto the bishop in Ohio, that it may be consecrated for the
bringing forth of the revelations and the printing thereof, and
for establishing Zion.

19 And if any man shall give unto any of you a coat, or a
suit, take the old and cast it unto the poor, and go your way
rejoicing. And if any man among you be strong in the Spirit,
let him take with him he that is weak, that he may be edified
in all meekness, that he may become strong also.

20 Therefore, take with you those who are ordained unto
the lesser priesthood, and send them before you to make appointments, and to prepare the way, and to fill appointments
that you yourselves are not able to fill. Behold this is the
way that mine apostles, in ancient days, built up my church
unto me.

95

21 Therefore let every man stand in his own office, and labor in his own calling: and let not the head say unto the feet, it hath no need of the feet, for without the feet how shall the body be able to stand? also the body hath need of every member, that all may be edified together, that the system may be kept perfect.

22 And behold, the high priests should travel, and also the elders, and also the lesser priests; but the deacons and teachers should be appointed to watch over the church, to be standing ministers unto the church.

23 And the bishop, Newel K. Whitney, also, should travel round about and among all the churches, searching after the poor, to administer to their wants by humbling the rich and the proud: he should also, employ an agent to take charge and to do his secular business, as he shall direct; nevertheless, let the bishop go unto the city of New York, and also to the city of Albany, and also to the city of Boston, and warn the people of those cities with the sound of the gospel, with a loud voice, of the desolation and utter abolishment which awaits them if they do reject these things; for if they do reject these things the hour of their judgment is nigh: and their house shall be left unto them desolate. Let him trust in me and he shall not be confounded; and an hair of his head shall not fall to the ground unnoticed.

24 And verily, I say unto you, the rest of my servants, go ye forth as your circumstances shall permit, in your several callings, unto the great and notable cities and villages, reproving the world in righteousness of all their unrighteous and ungodly deeds, setting forth clearly and understandingly the desolation of abomination in the last days; for with you, saith the Lord Almighty, I will rend their kingdoms: I will not only shake the earth, but the starry heavens shall tremble: for I the Lord have put forth my hand to exert the powers of heaven: ye cannot see it now, yet a little while and ye shall see it, and know that I am, and that I will come and reign with my people. I am Alpha and Omega, the beginning and the end: Amen.

SECTION V.

Minutes of the organization of the High Council of the church of Christ of Latter Day Saints, Kirtland, February 17, 1834.

1 This day a general council of twenty four high priests assembled at the house of Joseph Smith, jr. by revelation, and proceeded to organize the high council of the church of Christ, which was to consist of twelve high priests, and one or three

---

line 38. Minutes, 17 Feb. 1834 [D&C 102]. This version reflects editing marks made in Revelation Book 2, indicating that the latter was used as a source text for the former. (See *JSP*, MRB:639–647.)

96

presidents, as the case might require. This high council was appointed by revelation for the purpose of settling important difficulties, which might arise in the church, which could not be settled by the church, or the bishop's council, to the satisfaction of the parties.

2 Joseph Smith, jr. Sidney Rigdon and Frederick G. Williams, were acknowledged presidents by the voice of the council: and Joseph Smith, sen. John Smith, Joseph Coe, John Johnson, Martin Harris, John S. Carter, Jared Carter, Oliver Cowdery, Samuel H. Smith, Orson Hyde, Sylvester Smith and Luke Johnson, high priests, were chosen to be a standing council for the church, by the unanimous voice of the council. The above named counsellors were then asked whether they accepted their appointments, and whether they would act in that office according to the law of heaven: to which they all answered, that they accepted their appointments, and would fill their offices according to the grace of God bestowed upon them.

3 The number composing the council, who voted in the name and for the church in appointing the above named counsellors, were forty three, as follows: nine high priests, seventeen elders, four priests and thirteen members.

4 Voted, that the high council can not have power to act without seven of the above named counsellors, or their regularly appointed successors, are present. These seven shall have power to appoint other high priests, whom they may consider worthy and capable, to act in the place of absent counsellors.

5 Voted, that whenever any vacancy shall occur by the death, removal from office for transgression, or removal from the bounds of this church government, of any one of the above named counsellors, it shall be filled by the nomination of the president or presidents, and sanctioned by the voice of a general council of high priests, convened for that purpose, to act in the name of the church.

6 The president of the church, who is also the president of the council, is appointed by revelation, and acknowledged, in his administration, by the voice of the church; and it is according to the dignity of his office, that he should preside over the high council of the church; and it is his privilege to be assisted by two other presidents, appointed after the same manner, that he himself was appointed; and in case of the absence of one or both of those who are appointed to assist him, he has power to preside over the council without an assistant; and in case that he himself is absent, the other presidents have power to preside in his stead, both or either of them.

7 Whenever a high council of the church of Christ is regu-

97·

line 1

larly organized, according to the foregoing pattern, it shall be
the duty of the twelve counsellors to cast lots by numbers, and
thereby ascertain who, of the twelve, shall speak first, commencing with number 1; and so in succession to number 12.

5

8 Whenever this council convenes to act upon any case, the
twelve counsellors shall consider whether it is a difficult
one or not; if it is not, two only of the counsellors shall speak
upon it, according to the form above written. But if it is
thought to be difficult, four shall be appointed; and if more

10

difficult, six: but in no case shall more than six be appointed
to speak. The accused, in all cases, has a right to one half of
the council, to prevent insult or injustice; and the counsellors appointed to speak before the council, are to present
the case, after the evidence is examined, in its true light, be-

15

fore the council; and every man is to speak according to equity and justice. Those counsellors who draw even numbers,
that is, 2, 4, 6, 8, 10 and 12, are the individuals who are to
stand up in the behalf of the accused, and prevent insult or injustice.

20

9 In all cases the accuser and the accused shall have a privilege of speaking for themselves, before the council, after the
evidences are heard, and the counsellors who are appointed to
speak on the case, have finished their remarks. After the evidences are heard, the counsellors, accuser and accused have

25

spoken, the president shall give a decision according to the understanding which he shall have of the case, and call upon the
twelve counsellors to sanction the same by their vote. But
should the remaining counsellors, who have not spoken, or
any one of them, after hearing the evidences and pleadings im-

30

partially, discover an error in the decision of the president,
they can manifest it, and the case shall have a re-hearing; and
if, after a careful re-hearing, any additional light is shown
upon the case, the decision shall be altered accordingly: but
in case no additional light is given, the first decision shall

35

stand, the majority of the council having power to determine
the same.

10 In cases of difficulty respecting doctrine, or principle, (if
there is not a sufficiency written to make the case clear to the
minds of the council,) the president may inquire and obtain

40

the mind of the Lord by revelation.

11 The high priests, when abroad, have power to call and
organize a council after the manner of the foregoing, to settle
difficulties when the parties, or either of them, shall request it:
and the said council of high priests shall have power to ap-

45

point one of their own number, to preside over such council

G

---

line 46. This page begins the seventh gathering of the book. "G" is the first of two signature marks in
this gathering; the second is on the recto of the following leaf. These marks were used in collating the
gatherings after the sheets were folded.

98

line 1 for the time being. It shall be the duty of said council to
transmit, immediately, a copy of their proceedings, with a full
statement of the testimony accompanying their decision, to
the high council of the seat of the first presidency of the
5 church. Should the parties, or either of them, be dissatisfied
with the decision of said council, they may appeal to the high
council of the seat of the first presidency of the church, and
have a re-hearing, which case shall there be conducted, according to the former pattern written, as though no such decision
10 had been made.

12 This council of high priests abroad, is only to be called on
the most difficult cases of church matters: and no common or
ordinary case is to be sufficient to call such council. The
travelling or located high priests abroad, have power to say
15 whether it is necessary to call such a council or not.

13 There is a distinction between the high council of travelling high priests abroad, and the travelling high council composed of the twelve apostles, in their decisions: From the decision of the former there can be an appeal, but from the de-
20 cision of the latter there cannot. The latter can only be called in question by the general authorities of the church in case
of transgression.

14 Resolved that the president, or presidents of the seat of
the first presidency of the church, shall have power to deter-
25 mine whether any such case, as may be appealed, is justly entitled to a re-hearing, after examining the appeal and the evidences and statements accompanying it.

15 The twelve counsellors then proceeded to cast lots, or
ballot, to ascertain who should speak first, and the following
30 was the result; namely:—

OLIVER COWDERY, No.	1	JOHN JOHNSON No.	7
JOSEPH COE "	2	ORSON HYDE "	8
SAMUEL H. SMITH "	3	JARED CARTER "	9
LUKE JOHNSON "	4	JOSEPH SMITH sen. "	10
JOHN S. CARTER "	5	JOHN SMITH "	11
SYLVESTER SMITH "	6	MARTIN HARRIS "	12

After prayer the conference adjourned.

OLIVER COWDERY, ⎱ Clerks.
ORSON HYDE, ⎰

99

line 1

SECTION VI.

*Revelation explaining the parable of the wheat and the tares,
December 6, 1832.*

ON PRIESTHOOD.

1 Verily thus saith the Lord unto you, my servants, concerning the parable of the wheat, and of the tares: behold, verily I say, that the field was the world; and the apostles were the sowers of the seed; and after they have fallen asleep, the great persecutor of the church, the apostate, the whore, even Babylon, that maketh all nations to drink of her cup, in whose hearts the enemy, even Satan sitteth to reign: Behold he soweth the tares; wherefore the tares choke the wheat and drive the church into the wilderness.

2 But behold, in the last days, even now while the Lord is beginning to bring forth the word, and the blade is springing up and is yet tender, behold, verily I say unto you, the angels are crying unto the Lord day and night, who are ready and waiting to be sent forth to reap down the fields: but the Lord saith unto them, pluck not up the tares while the blade is yet tender: (for verily your faith is weak,) lest you destroy the wheat also: Therefore let the wheat and the tares grow together until the harvest is fully ripe, then ye shall first gather out the wheat from among the tares, and after the gathering of the wheat, behold and lo! the tares are bound in bundles, and the field remaineth to be burned.

3 Therefore thus saith the Lord unto you, with whom the priesthood hath continued through the lineage of your fathers, for ye are lawful heirs according to the flesh, and have been hid from the world with Christ in God: therefore your life and the priesthood hath remained, and must needs remain, through you and your lineage, until the restoration of all things spoken by the mouths of all the holy prophets since the world began.

4 Therefore, blessed are ye if ye continue in my goodness, a light unto the Gentiles, and through this priesthood, a savor unto my people Israel; The Lord hath said it: Amen.

7*

line 1. Revelation, 6 Dec. 1832 [D&C 86]. Revelation Book 2 bears a notation marking this revelation for inclusion in the 1835 Doctrine and Covenants. The source text for this version is unknown. (See *JSP,* MRB:475–477.)

100

SECTION VII.

Revelation given December 27, 1832.

1 Verily, thus saith the Lord unto you, who have assembled yourselves together to receive his will concerning you. Behold, this is pleasing unto your Lord, and the angels rejoice over you; the alms of your prayers have come up into the ears of the Lord of Sabaoth, and are recorded in the book of the names of the sanctified: even them of the celestial world.— Wherefore, I now send upon you another comforter; even upon you my friends, that it may abide in your hearts, even the Holy Spirit of promise; which other comforter is the same that I promised unto my disciples, as is recorded in the testimony of John.

2 This comforter is the promise which I give unto you of eternal life; even the glory of the celestial kingdom: which glory is that of the church of the first born; even of God the holiest of all, through Jesus Christ his Son: he that ascended up on high; as also he descended below all things; in that he comprehended all things, that he might be in all, and through all things; the light of truth; which truth shineth. This is the light of Christ. As also he is in the sun, and the light of the sun, and the power thereof by which it was made. As also he is in the moon, and is the light of the moon, and the power thereof by which it was made. As also the light of the stars, and the power thereof by which they were made. And the earth also, and the power thereof; even the earth upon which you stand.

3 And the light which now shineth, which giveth you light, is through him who enlighteneth your eyes, which is the same light that quickeneth your understandings; which light proceedeth forth from the presence of God, to fill the immensity of space. The light which is in all things; which giveth life to all things; which is the law by which all things are governed: even the power of God, who sitteth upon his throne, who is in the bosom of eternity, who is in the midst of all things.

4 Now verily, I say unto you, that through the redemption which is made for you, is brought to pass the resurrection from the dead. And the spirit and the body is the soul of man.— And the resurrection from the dead is the redemption of the soul; and the redemption of the soul is through him who quickeneth all things, in whose bosom it is decreed, that the poor and the meek of the earth shall inherit it. Therefore, it must needs be sanctified from all unrighteousness, that it may be prepared for the celestial glory; for after it hath filled the measure of its creation, it shall be crowned with glory, even

---

line 1. Revelations, 27 and 28 Dec. 1832 and 3 Jan. 1833 [D&C 88]. The portion of this text comprising Revelation, 27 and 28 December 1832 (verses 1–38), reflects editing marks made in Revelation Book 2, indicating that the latter was used as a source text for the former. Significant modifications to the portion of this text comprising Revelation, 3 January 1833 (verses 39–46), are not found in any extant manuscript text; the source text for this second portion is unknown. (See *JSP,* MRB:479–509.)

101

with the presence of God the Father; that bodies who are of the celestial kingdom may possess it forever, and ever; for, for this intent was it made, and created; and for this intent are they sanctified.

5 And they who are not sanctified through the law which I have given unto you; even the law of Christ, must inherit another kingdom, even that of a terrestrial kingdom, or that of a telestial kingdom. For he who is not able to abide the law of a celestial kingdom, cannot abide a celestial glory: and he who cannot abide the law of a terrestrial kingdom, cannot abide a terrestrial glory: he who cannot abide the law of a telestial kingdom, cannot abide a telestial glory: therefore, he is not meet for a kingdom of glory. Therefore, he must abide a kingdom which is not a kingdom of glory.

6 And again, verily I say unto you, the earth abideth the law of a celestial kingdom, for it filleth the measure of its creation, and transgresseth not the law. Wherefore, it shall be sanctified; yea, notwithstanding it shall die, it shall be quickened again, and shall abide the power by which it is quickened. and the righteous shall inherit it: for notwithstanding they die, they also shall rise again a spiritual body: they who are of a celestial spirit, shall receive the same body which was a natural body; even ye shall receive your bodies, and your glory shall be that glory by which your bodies are quickened. Ye who are quickened by a portion of the celestial glory, shall then receive of the same, even a fulness: and they who are quickened by a portion of the terrestrial glory, shall then receive of the same, even a fulness: and also, they who are quickened by a portion of the telestial glory, shall then receive of the same, even a fulness: and they who remain, shall also be quickened; nevertheless, they shall return again to their own place, to enjoy that which they are willing to receive, because they were not willing to enjoy that which they might have received.

7 For what doth it profit a man if a gift is bestowed upon him, and he receive not the gift? Behold he rejoices not in that which is given unto him, neither rejoices in him who is the giver of the gift.

8 And again, verily I say unto you, that which is governed by law, is also preserved by law, and perfected and sanctified by the same: that which breaketh a law, and abideth not by law, but seeketh to become a law unto itself, and willeth to abide in sin, and altogether abideth in sin, cannot be sanctified by law, neither by mercy, justice, or judgment. Therefore, they must remain filthy still.

9 All kingdoms have a law given; and there are many kingdoms; for there is no space in the which there is no king-

102

line 1
dom; and there is no kingdom in which there is no space,
either a greater or lesser kingdom. And unto every kingdom
is given a law; and unto every law there are certain bounds,
also, and conditions.

10 All beings who abide not in those conditions, are not justified; for intelligence cleaveth unto intelligence; wisdom receiveth wisdom; truth embraceth truth; virtue loveth virtue;
light cleaveth unto light; mercy hath compassion on mercy,
and claimeth her own; justice continueth its course, and
claimeth its own; judgment goeth before the face of him who
sitteth upon the throne, and governeth and executeth all
things; he comprehendeth all things, and all things are before
him, and all things are round about him; and he is above all
things, and in all things, and is through all things, and is round
about all things: and all things are by him, and of him; even
God, forever, and ever.

11 And again, verily I say unto you, he hath given a law
unto all things by which they move in their times, and their
seasons; and their courses are fixed; even the courses of the
heavens, and the earth; which comprehend the earth and all
the planets; and they give light to each other in their times,
and in their seasons, in their minutes, in their hours, in their
days, in their weeks, in their months, in their years: all these
are one year with God, but not with man.

12 The earth rolls upon her wings; and the sun giveth his
light by day, and the moon giveth her light by night; and the
stars also giveth their light, as they roll upon their wings, in
their glory, in the midst of the power of God. Unto what
shall I liken these kingdoms, that ye may understand? Behold,
all these are kingdoms, and any man who hath seen any or
the least of these, hath seen God moving in his majesty and
power. I say unto you, he hath seen him: nevertheless, he
who came unto his own was not comprehended. The light
shineth in darkness, and the darkness comprehendeth it not;
nevertheless, the day shall come when you shall comprehend
even God; being quickened in him, and by him. Then shall
ye know that ye have seen me, that I am, and that I am the
true light that is in you, and that you are in me, otherwise ye
could not abound.

13 Behold, I will liken these kingdoms unto a man having a
field, and he sent forth his servants into the field, to dig in the
field; and he said unto the first, go ye and labor in the field,
and in the first hour I will come unto you and ye shall behold
the joy of my countenance: and he said unto the second, go ye
also into the field, and in the second hour I will visit you with
the joy of my countenance: and also unto the third, saying, I

line 1 will visit you; and unto the fourth, and so on unto the twelfth.

14 And the lord of the field went unto the first in the first hour, and tarried with him all that hour, and he was made glad with the light of the countenance of his lord; and then he with-
5 drew from the first that he might visit the second also, and the third, and the fourth, and so on unto the twelfth; and thus they all received the light of the countenance of their lord: every man in his hour, and in his time, and in his season; begin-ning at the first, and so on unto the last, and from the last un-
10 to the first, and from the first unto the last; every man in his own order, until his hour was finished, even according as his lord had commanded him, that his lord might be glorified in him, and he in him, that they all might be glorified.

15 Therefore, unto this parable will I liken all these king-
15 doms, and the inhabitants thereof; every kingdom in its hour, and in its time, and in its season; even according to the decree which God hath made.

16 And again, verily I say unto you, my friends, I leave these sayings with you, to ponder in your hearts with this com-
20 mandment which I give unto you, that ye shall call upon me while I am near; draw near unto me, and I will draw near un-to you; seek me dilligently and ye shall find me; ask and ye shall receive; knock and it shall be opened unto you: whatso-ever ye ask the Father in my name it shall be given unto you,
25 that is expedient for you; and if ye ask any thing that is not expedient for you, it shall turn unto your condemnation.

17 Behold, that which you hear is as the voice of one crying in the wilderness; in the wilderness, because you cannot see him: my voice, because my voice is spirit; my spirit is truth;
30 truth abideth and hath no end; and if it be in you it shall abound.

18 And if your eye be single to my glory, your whole bodies shall be filled with light, and there shall be no darkness in you, and that body which is filled with light comprehendeth all
35 things. Therefore, sanctify yourselves that your minds be-come single to God, and the days will come that you shall see him: [for he will unveil his face unto you, and it shall be in his own time, and in his own way, and according to his own will.

40 19 Remember the great and last promise which I have made unto you: cast away your idle thoughts and your excess of laughter far from you; tarry ye, tarry ye in this place, and call a solemn assembly, even of those who are the first laborers in this last kingdom; and let those whom they have warned in
45 their travelling, call on the Lord, and ponder the warning in their hearts which they have received, for a little season,—

104

Behold, and lo, I will take care of your flocks and will raise up elders and send unto them.

20 Behold, I will hasten my work in its time; and I give unto you who are the first laborers in this last kingdom, a commandment, that you assemble yourselves together, and organize yourselves, and prepare yourselves; and sanctify yourselves; yea, purify your hearts, and cleanse your hands and your feet before me, that I may make you clean; that I may testify unto your Father, and your God, and my God, that you are clean from the blood of this wicked generation: that I may fulfil this promise, this great and last promise which I have made unto you, when I will.

21 Also, I give unto you a commandment, that ye shall continue in prayer and fasting from this time forth. And I give unto you a commandment, that you shall teach one another the doctrine of the kingdom; teach ye diligently and my grace shall attend you, that you may be instructed more perfectly in theory, in principle, in doctrine, in the law of the gospel, in all things that pertain unto the kingdom of God, that is expedient for you to understand; of things both in heaven, and in the earth, and under the earth; things which have been; things which are; things which must shortly come to pass; things which are at home; things which are abroad; the wars and the perplexities of the nations; and the judgments which are on the land; and a knowledge also of countries, and of kingoms, that ye may be prepared in all things when I shall send you again, to magnify the calling whereunto I have called you, and the mission with which I have commissioned you.

22 Behold I sent you out to testify and warn the people, and it becometh every man who hath been warned, to warn his neighbor. Therefore, they are left without excuse, and their sins are upon their own heads. He that seeketh me early shall find me, and shall not be forsaken.

23 Therefore, tarry ye, and labor dilligently, that you may be perfected in your ministry, to go forth among the Gentiles for the last time, as many as the mouth of the Lord shall name, to bind up the law, and seal up the testimony, and to prepare the saints for the hour of judgment which is to come; that their souls may escape the wrath of God, the desolation of abomination, which await the wicked, both in this world, and in the world to come. Verily, I say unto you, let those who are not the first elders, continue in the vineyard, until the mouth of the Lord shall call them, for their time is not yet come; their garments are not clean from the blood of this generation.

24 Abide ye in the liberty wherewith ye are made free; entangle not yourselves in sin, but let your hands be clean, un-

line 1
til the Lord come, for not many days hence and the earth shall
tremble, and reel to and fro as a drunken man, and the sun
shall hide his face, and shall refuse to give light, and the moon
shall be bathed in blood, and the stars shall become exceeding
angry, and shall cast themselves down as a fig that falleth from
off a fig-tree.

25 And after your testimony, cometh wrath and indignation
upon the people; for after your testimony cometh the testimony of earthquakes, that shall cause groanings in the midst of
her, and men shall fall upon the ground, and shall not be able
to stand.   And also cometh the testimony of the voice of thun-
drings, and the voice of lightnings, and the voice of tempests,
and the voice of the waves of the sea, heaving themselves beyond their bounds.   And all things shall be in commotion;
and surely, men's hearts shall fail them; for fear shall come
upon all people; and angels shall fly through the midst of heav-
en, crying with a loud voice, sounding the trump of God, saying, prepare ye, prepare ye, O inhabitants of the earth: for
the judgment of our God is come: behold, and lo, the Bridegroom cometh, go ye out to meet him.

26 And immediately there shall appear a great sign in heav-
en, and all people shall see it together.   And another angel
shall sound his trump, saying, that great church, the mother
of abominations, that made all nations drink of the wine of the
wrath of her fornication, that persecuteth the saints of God,
that shed their blood: her who sitteth upon many waters, and
upon the islands of the sea; behold, she is the tares of the earth,
she is bound in bundles, her bands are made strong, no man
can loose them; therefore, she is ready to be burned.   And he
shall sound his trump both long and loud, and all nations shall
hear it.

27 And there shall be silence in heaven for the space of half
an hour, and immediately after shall the curtain of heaven be
unfolded, as a scroll is unfolded after it is rolled up, and the
face of the Lord shall be unveiled; and the saints that are upon the earth, who are alive, shall be quickened, and be caught
up to meet him.   And they who have slept in their graves,
shall come forth; for their graves shall be opened, and they also shall be caught up to meet him in the midst of the pillar of
heaven: they are Christ's, the first fruits: they who shall descend with him first, and they who are on the earth and in
their graves, who are first caught up to meet him: and all this
by the voice of the sounding of the trump of the angel of
God.

28 And after this another angel shall sound, which is the
second trump; and then cometh the redemption of those who

106

are Christ's at his coming; who have received their part in
that prison which is prepared for them, that they might receive the gospel, and be judged according to men in the flesh.

29 And again, another trump shall sound, which is the third
trump: and then cometh the spirits of men who are to be judged, and are found under condemnation: and these are the rest
of the dead, and they live not again until the thousand years
are ended, neither again, until the end of the earth.

30 And another trump shall sound, which is the fourth trump,
saying, these are found among those who are to remain until
that great and last day, even the end, who shall remain filthy
still.

31 And another trump shall sound, which is the fifth trump,
which is the fifth angel who committeth the everlasting gospel, flying through the midst of heaven, unto all nations, kindreds, tongues and people; and this shall be the sound of his
trump, saying to all people, both in heaven, and in earth, and
that are under the earth; for every ear shall hear it, and every
knee shall bow, and every tongue shall confess, while they
hear the sound of the trump, saying, fear God, and give glory to him who sitteth upon the throne, forever, and ever; for
the hour of his judgment is come.

32 And again, another angel shall sound his trump, which is
the sixth angel, saying, she is fallen, who made all nations
drink of the wine of the wrath of her fornication: she is fallen!
is fallen!

33 And again, another angel shall sound his trump, which is
the seventh angel, saying, it is finished! it is finished! the
Lamb of God hath overcome, and trodden the wine-press
alone; even the wine-press of the fierceness of the wrath of
Almighty God: and then shall the angels be crowned with
the glory of his might, and the saints shall be filled with his
glory, and receive their inheritance and be made equal with
him.

34 And then shall the first angel again sound his trump in
the ears of all living, and reveal the secret acts of men, and
the mighty works of God in the first thousandth year.

35 And then shall the second angel sound his trump, and reveal the secret acts of men, and the thoughts and intents of
their hearts, and the mighty works of God in the second thousandth year: and so on, until the seventh angel shall sound
his trump: and he shall stand forth upon the land and upon
the sea, and swear in the name of him who sitteth upon the
throne, that there shall be time no longer, and satan shall be
bound, that old serpent who is called the devil, and shall not
be loosed for the space of a thousand years. And then he shall

line 1 be loosed for a little season, that he may gather together his armies: and Michael the seventh angel, even the archangel, shall gather together his armies, even the hosts of heaven.— And the devil shall gather together his armies; even the hosts
5 of hell, and shall come up to battle against Michael and his armies: and then cometh the battle of the great God! and the devil and his armies shall be cast away into their own place, that they shall not have power over the saints any more at all; for Michael shall fight their battles, and shall overcome
10 him who seeketh the throne of him who sitteth upon the throne, even the Lamb. This is the glory of God, and the sanctified; and they shall not any more see death.

36 Therefore, verily I say unto you, my friends, call your solemn assembly, as I have commanded you; and as all have
15 not faith, seek ye diligently and teach one another words of wisdom; yea, seek ye out of the best books words of wisdom: seek learning even by study, and also by faith. Organize yourselves; prepare every needful thing, and establish a house, even a house of prayer, a house of fasting, a house of faith, a
20 house of learning, a house of glory, a house of order, a house of God; that your incomings may be in the name of the Lord; that your outgoings may be in the name of the Lord; that all your salutations may be in the name of the Lord, with uplifted hands unto the Most High.

25 37 Therefore, cease from all your light speeches; from all laughter; from all your lustful desires: from all your pride and lightmindedness, and from all your wicked doings. Appoint among yourselves a teacher, and let not all be spokesmen at once; but let one speak at a time, and let all listen
30 unto his sayings, that when all have spoken, that all may be edified of all, and that every man may have an equal privilege.

38 See that ye love one another; cease to be covetous, learn to impart one to another as the gospel requires; cease to be idle, cease to be unclean; cease to find fault one with another;
35 cease to sleep longer than is needful; retire to thy bed early, that ye may not be weary; arise early, that your bodies and your minds may be invigorated: and above all things, clothe yourselves with the bonds of charity, as with a mantle, which is the bond of perfectness and peace: pray always, that you
40 may not faint until I come: behold, and lo, I will come quickly, and receive you unto myself: Amen.

39 And again, the order of the house prepared for the presidency of the school of the prophets, established for their instruction in all things that are expedient for them, even for
45 all the officers of the church, or in other words, those who are called to the ministry in the church, beginning at the high-

108

priests, even down to the deacons: and this shall be the order of the house of the presidency of the school: He that is appointed to be president, or teacher, shall be found standing in his place, in the house, which shall be prepared for him. Therefore, he shall be first in the house of God, in a place that the congregation in the house may hear his words carefully and distinctly, not with loud speech. And when he cometh into the house of God, (for he should be first in the house; behold this is beautiful, that he may be an example,)

40 Let him offer himself in prayer upon his knees before God, in token, or remembrance, of the everlasting covenant, and when any shall come in after him let the teacher arise, and with uplifted hands to heaven; yea, even directly, salute his brother or brethren with these words:

41 Art thou a brother or brethren, I salute you in the name of the Lord Jesus Christ, in token, or remembrance of the everlasting covenant, in which covenant I receive you to fellowship in a determination that is fixed, immovable and unchangable, to be your friend and brother through the grace of God, in the bonds of love, to walk in all the commandments of God blameless, in thanksgiving, forever and ever. Amen.

42 And he that is found unworthy of this salutation, shall not have place among you; for ye shall not suffer that mine house shall be polluted by them.

43 And he that cometh in and is faithful before me, and is a brother, or if they be brethren, they shall salute the president or teacher with uplifted hands to heaven with this same prayer and covenant, or by saying, Amen, in token of the same.

44 Behold, verily I say unto you, this is a sample unto you for a salutation to one another in the house of God, in the school of the prophets. And ye are called to do this by prayer and thanksgiving as the Spirit shall give utterance, in all your doings in the house of the Lord, in the school of the prophets, that it may become a sanctuary, a tabernacle, of the Holy Spirit to your edification.

45 And ye shall not receive any among you, into this school save he is clean from the blood of this generation: and he shall be received by the ordinance of the washing of feet; for unto this end was the ordinance of the washing of feet instituted.

46 And again, the ordinance of washing feet is to be administered by the president, or presiding elder of the church. It is to be commenced with prayer: and after partaking of bread and wine he is to gird himself, according to the pattern given in the thirteenth chapter of John's testimony concerning me. Amen.

109

line 1

SECTION VIII.

*Revelation given April, 1829, to Oliver Cowdery, and
Joseph Smith jr.*

1 A great and marvelous work is about to come forth unto
the children of men: behold I am God, and give heed unto
my word, which is quick and powerful, sharper than a two
edged sword, to the dividing asunder of both joints and marrow: Therefore give heed unto my words.

2 Behold the field is white already to harvest, therefore
whoso desireth to reap, let him thrust in his sickle with his
might and reap while the day lasts, that he may treasure up
for his soul everlasting salvation in the kingdom of God: Yea,
whosoever will thrust in his sickle and reap, the same is called of God; therefore, if you will ask of me you shall receive;
if you will knock it shall be opened unto you.

3 Now as you have asked, behold I say unto you, keep my
commandments, and seek to bring forth and establish the
cause of Zion: seek not for riches but for wisdom, and behold
the mysteries of God shall be unfolded unto you, and then
shall you be made rich. Behold he that hath eternal life is
rich.

4 Verily, verily I say unto you, even as you desire of me,
so shall it be unto you; and if you desire, you shall be the
means of doing much good in this generation. Say nothing
but repentance unto this generation: keep my commandments and assist to bring forth my work according to my commandments, and you shall be blessed.

5 Behold thou hast a gift, and blessed art thou because of
thy gift. Remember it is sacred and cometh from above: and
if thou wilt inquire, thou shalt know mysteries which are
great and marvelous: therefore thou shalt exercise thy gift,
that thou mayest find out mysteries, that thou mayest bring
many to the knowledge of the truth; yea, convince them of
the error of their ways. Make not thy gift known unto any,
save it be those who are of thy faith. Trifle not with sacred things. If thou wilt do good, yea and hold out faithful to
the end, thou shalt be saved in the kingdom of God, which is
the greatest of all the gifts of God; for there is no gift greater
than the gift of salvation.

6 Verily, verily I say unto thee, blessed art thou for what
thou hast done, for thou hast inquired of me, and behold as often as thou hast inquired, thou hast received instruction of my
Spirit. If it had not been so, thou wouldst not have come to
the place where thou art at this time.

---

line 1. Revelation, Apr. 1829–A [D&C 6]. This version closely corresponds to the version in chapter 5 of
the Book of Commandments, suggesting that the latter was used as a source text for the former.

110

line 1

7 Behold thou knowest that thou hast inquired of me, and I did enlighten thy mind; and now I tell thee these things, that thou mayest know that thou hast been enlightened by the Spirit of truth; yea, I tell thee, that thou mayest know that there is none else save God, that knowest thy thoughts and the intents of thy heart: I tell thee these things as a witness unto thee, that the words or the work which thou hast been writing is true.

8 Therefore be diligent, stand by my servant Joseph faithfully in whatsoever difficult circumstances he may be, for the word's sake. Admonish him in his faults and also receive admonition of him. Be patient; be sober; be temperate: have patience, faith, hope and charity.

9 Behold thou art Oliver, and I have spoken unto thee because of thy desires; therefore, treasure up these words in thy heart. Be faithful and diligent in keeping the commandments of God, and I will encircle thee in the arms of my love.

10 Behold I am Jesus Christ, the Son of God. I am the same that came unto my own and my own received me not.— I am the light which shineth in darkness, and the darkness comprehendeth it not.

11 Verily, verily I say unto you, if you desire a further witness, cast your mind upon the night that you cried unto me in your heart, that you might know concerning the truth of these things; did I not speak peace to your mind concerning the matter? What greater witness can you have than from God? And now behold, you have received a witness, for if I have told you things which no man knoweth, have you not received a witness? And behold I grant unto you a gift, if you desire of me, to translate even as my servant Joseph.

12 Verily, verily I say unto you, that there are records which contain much of my gospel, which have been kept back because of the wickedness of the people; and now I command you, that if you have good desires, a desire to lay up treasures for yourself in heaven, then shall you assist in bringing to light, with your gift, those parts of my scriptures which have been hidden because of iniquity.

13 And now, behold I give unto you, and also unto my servant Joseph the keys of this gift, which shall bring to light this ministry; and in the mouth of two or three witnesses, shall every word be established.

14 Verily, verily I say unto you, if they reject my words, and this part of my gospel and ministry, blessed are ye, for they can do no more unto you than unto me; and if they do unto you, even as they have done unto me, blessed are ye, for you shall dwell with me in glory: but if they reject not my

111

line 1 words, which shall be established by the testimony which shall
be given, blessed are they; and then shall ye have joy in the
fruit of your labors.

15 Verily, verily I say unto you, as I said unto my disciples, .
5 where two or three are gathered together in my name, as
touching one thing, behold there will I be in the midst of them:
even so am I in the midst of you. Fear not to do good my
sons, for whatsoever ye sow, that shall ye also reap: therefore,
if ye sow good, ye shall also reap good for your reward:

10 16 Therefore fear not little flock, do good, let earth and hell
combine against you, for if ye are built upon my Rock, they
cannot prevail. Behold I do not condemn you, go your ways
and sin no more: perform with soberness the work which I
have commanded you; look unto me in every thought, doubt

15 not, fear not: behold the wounds which pierced my side, and
also the prints of the nails in my hands and feet: be faithful:
keep my commandments, and ye shall inherit the kingdom of
heaven: Amen.

SECTION IX.

20 *Revelation given to Joseph Smith, jr. and Oliver Cowdery,*
July, 1830.

1 Behold thou wast called and chosen to write the book of
Mormon, and to my ministry: and I have lifted thee up out of
thy afflictions, and have counselled thee, that thou hast been

25 delivered from all thine enemies, and thou hast been delivered
from the powers of satan, and from darkness! Nevertheless,
thou art not excusable in thy transgressions; nevertheless go
thy way and sin no more.

2 Magnify thine office; and after thou hast sowed thy fields

30 and secured them, go speedily unto the church which is in
Colesville, Fayette and Manchester, and they shall support
thee; and I will bless them both spiritually and temporally;
but if they receive thee not, I will send upon them a cursing
instead of a blessing.

35 3 And thou shalt continue in calling upon God in my name,
and writing the things which shall be given thee by the Comforter, and expounding all scriptures unto the church, and it
shall be given thee in the very moment, what thou shalt speak
and write; and they shall hear it, or I will send unto them a

40 cursing instead of a blessing:

4 For thou shalt devote all thy service in Zion. And in this
thou shalt have strength. Be patient in afflictions, for thou
shalt have many: but endure them, for lo, I am with you, even

---

line 19. Revelation, July 1830–A [D&C 24]. Oliver Cowdery's copy of the Book of Commandments bears a notation marking this revelation for inclusion in the 1835 Doctrine and Covenants. This version closely corresponds to the version in chapter 25 of the Book of Commandments, indicating that the latter was used as a source text for the former.

112

line 1   unto the end of thy days. And in temporal labors thou shalt not have strength, for this is not thy calling. Attend to thy calling and thou shalt have wherewith to magnify thine office, and to expound all scriptures. And continue in laying on of
5   the hands, and confirming the churches.

  5 And thy brother Oliver shall continue in bearing my name before the world; and also to the church. And he shall not suppose that he can say enough in my cause; and lo I am with him to the end. In me he shall have glory, and not of
10   himself, whether in weakness or in strength, whether in bonds or free: And at all times and in all places, he shall open his mouth and declare my gospel as with the voice of a trump, both day and night. And I will give unto him strength such as is not known among men.

15   6 Require not miracles, except I shall command you; except casting out devils; healing the sick; and against poisonous serpents; and against deadly poisons; and these things ye shall not do, except it be required of you, by them who desire it, that the scriptures might be fulfilled, for ye shall do accor-
20   ding to that which is written. And in whatsoever place ye shall enter, and they receive you not, in my name, ye shall leave a cursing instead of a blessing, by casting off the dust of your feet against them as a testimony, and cleansing your feet by the wayside.

25   7 And it shall come to pass, that whosoever shall lay their hands upon you by violence, ye shall command to be smitten in my name, and behold I will smite them according to your words, in mine own due time. And whosoever shall go to law with thee shall be cursed by the law. And thou shalt take no
30   purse, nor scrip, neither staves, neither two coats, for the church shall give unto thee in the very hour what thou need-est for food, and for raiment, and for shoes, and for money, and for scrip: For thou art called to prune my vineyard with a mighty pruning, yea, even for the last time. Yea, and also,
35   all those whom thou hast ordained. And they shall do even according to this pattern. Amen.

SECTION X.

Revelation given in the presence of six elders, in Fayette, New-York, September, 1830.

40   1 Listen to the voice of Jesus Christ, your Redeemer, the Great I AM, whose arm of mercy hath atoned for your sins; who will gather his people even as a hen gathereth her chick-ens under her wings, even as many as will hearken to my

---

line 37. Revelation, Sept. 1830–A [D&C 29]. Oliver Cowdery's copy of the Book of Commandments bears a notation marking this revelation for inclusion in the 1835 Doctrine and Covenants. This version closely corresponds to the version in chapter 29 of the Book of Commandments, indicating that the latter was used as a source text for the former.

113

line 1 voice, and humble themselves before me, and call upon me in
        mighty prayer. Behold, verily, verily I say unto you, that at
        this time your sins are forgiven you, therefore ye receive these
        things: but remember to sin no more, lest perils shall come
5   upon you.
        2 Verily I say unto you, that ye are chosen out of the world
        to declare my gospel with the sound of rejoicing, as with the
        voice of a trump: lift up your hearts and be glad for I am in
        your midst, and am your advocate with the Father; and it is
10   his good will to give you the kingdom; and as it is written,
        Whatsoever ye shall ask in faith, being united in prayer ac-
        cording to my command, ye shall receive; and ye are called
        to bring to pass the gathering of mine elect, for mine elect
        hear my voice and harden not their hearts: wherefore the de-
15   cree hath gone forth from the Father, that they shall be gath-
        ered in unto one place, upon the face of this land, to prepare
        their hearts, and be prepared in all things, against the day
        when tribulation and desolation are sent forth upon the wicked:
        for the hour is nigh, and the day soon at hand, when the earth
20   is ripe: and all the proud, and they that do wickedly, shall be
        as stubble, and I will burn them up, saith the Lord of hosts,
        that wickedness shall not be upon the earth: for the hour is
        nigh, and that which was spoken by mine apostles must be
        fulfilled; for as they spoke so shall it come to pass; for I will
25   reveal myself from heaven with power and great glory, with
        all the hosts thereof, and dwell in righteousness with men on
        earth a thousand years, and the wicked shall not stand.
        3 And again, verily, verily I say unto you, and it hath gone
        forth in a firm decree, by the will of the Father, that mine
30   apostles, the twelve which were with me in my ministry at
        Jerusalem, shall stand at my right hand at the day of my com-
        ing in a pillar of fire, being clothed with robes of righteousness,
        with crowns upon their heads, in glory even as I am, to judge
        the whole house of Israel, even as many as have loved me and
35   kept my commandments, and none else; for a trump shall
        sound both long and loud, even as upon mount Sinai, and all
        the earth shall quake, and they shall come forth: yea, even
        the dead which died in me, to receive a crown of righteous-
        ness, and to be clothed upon, even as I am, to be with me, that
40   we may be one.
        4 But behold, I say unto you, that before this great day shall
        come, the sun shall be darkened, and the moon shall be turned
        into blood, and the stars shall fall from heaven; and there shall
        be greater signs in heaven above, and in the earth beneath;
45   and there shall be weeping and wailing among the hosts of

H

---

line 46. This page begins the eighth gathering of the book. "H" is the first of two signature marks in this gathering; the second is on the recto of the following leaf. These marks were used in collating the gatherings after the sheets were folded.

114

men; and there shall be a great hailstorm sent forth to destroy the crops of the earth: and it shall come to pass, because of the wickedness of the world, that I will take vengeance upon the wicked, for they will not repent: for the cup of mine indignation is full; for behold, my blood shall not cleanse them if they hear me not.

5 Wherefore I the Lord God will send forth flies upon the face of the earth, which shall take hold of the inhabitants thereof, and shall eat their flesh, and shall cause maggots to come in upon them, and their tongues shall be stayed that they shall not utter against me, and their flesh shall fall from off their bones, and their eyes from their sockets; and it shall come to pass, that the beasts of the forests, and the fowls of the air, shall devour them up: and that great and abominable church, which is the whore of all the earth, shall be cast down by devouring fire, according as it is spoken by the mouth of Ezekiel the prophet, which spoke of these things, which have not come to pass, but surely must, as I live, for abomination shall not reign.

6 And again, verily, verily I say unto you, that when the thousand years are ended, and men again begin to deny their God, then will I spare the earth but for a little season; and the end shall come, and the heaven and the earth shall be consumed, and pass away, and there shall be a new heaven and a new earth; for all old things shall pass away, and all things shall become new, even the heaven and the earth, and all the fulness thereof, both men and beasts: the fowls of the air, and the fishes of the sea, and not one hair, neither mote, shall be lost, for it is the workmanship of mine hand.

7 But behold, verily I say unto you, before the earth shall pass away, Michael mine archangel, shall sound his trump, and then shall all the dead awake, for their graves shall be opened, and they shall come forth; yea, even all; and the righteous shall be gathered on my right hand unto eternal life: and the wicked on my left hand will I be ashamed to own before the Father: wherefore I will say unto them, depart from me ye cursed into everlasting fire, prepared for the devil and his angels.

8 And now behold I say unto you, never at any time, have I declared from mine own mouth, that they should return, for where I am they cannot come, for they have no power; but remember, that all my judgments are not given unto men: and as the words have gone forth out of my mouth, even so shall they be fulfilled, that the first shall be last, and that the last shall be first in all things, whatsoever I have created by the word of my power, which is the power of my Spirit; for

115

by the power of my Spirit, created I them: yea, all things
both spiritual and temporal: firstly spiritual, secondly temporal, which is the beginning of my work: and again, firstly
temporal, and secondly spiritual, which is the last of my
work: speaking unto you, that you may naturally understand.
but unto myself my works have no end, neither beginning; but
it is given unto you, that ye may understand, because ye have
asked it of me and are agreed.

9 Wherefore, verily I say unto you, that all things unto me
are spiritual, and not at any time have I given unto you a
law which was temporal, neither any man, nor the children
of men: neither Adam your father, whom I created: behold
I gave unto him that he should be an agent unto himself; and
I gave unto him commandment, but no temporal commandment gave I unto him; for my commandments are spiritual:
they are not natural, nor temporal, neither carnal nor sensual.

10 And it came to pass, that Adam being tempted of the devil, for behold the devil was before Adam, for he rebelled
against me saying, Give me thine honor, which is my power:
and also a third part of the hosts of heaven turned he away
from me because of their agency: and they were thrust down,
and thus came the devil and his angels; and behold, there is
a place prepared for them from the beginning, which place is
hell: and it must needs be that the devil should tempt the
children of men, or they could not be agents unto themselves,
for if they never should have bitter, they could not know the
sweet.

11 Wherefore, it came to pass, that the devil tempted Adam
and he partook the forbidden fruit, and transgressed the commandment, wherein he became subject to the will of the devil, because he yielded unto temptation. Wherefore, I the
Lord God caused that he should be cast out from the garden
of Eden, from my presence, because of his transgression;
wherein he became spiritually dead: which is the first death,
even that same death, which is the last death, which is spiritual, which shall be pronounced upon the wicked when I shall
say, Depart ye cursed.

12 But behold I say unto you, that I the Lord God gave unto Adam and unto his seed, that they should not die as to the
temporal death, until I the Lord God should send forth angels to declare unto them repentance and redemption, through
faith on the name of mine only begotten Son: and thus did
I the Lord God appoint unto man the days of his probation;
that by his natural death, he might be raised in immortality
unto eternal life, even as many as would believe, and they

116

line 1 that believe not, unto eternal damnation, for they cannot be
redeemed from their spiritual fall, because they repent not,
for they will love darkness rather than light, and their deeds
are evil, and they receive their wages of whom they list to
5 obey.

13 But behold I say unto you, that little children are redeemed from the foundation of the world, through mine Only
begotten: Wherefore they cannot sin, for power is not given
unto satan to tempt little children, until they begin to become
10 accountable before me; for it is given unto them even as I
will, according to mine own pleasure, that great things may
be required at the hand of their fathers.

14 And again I say unto you, that whoso having knowledge,
have I not commanded to repent? and he that hath no under-
15 standing, it remaineth in me to do according as it is written.
And now, I declare no more unto you at this time.   Amen.

SECTION XI.

Revelation to Joseph Smith jr. and Sidney Rigdon,
December, 1830.

20 1 Listen to the voice of the Lord your God, even Alpha and
Omega, the beginning and the end, whose course is one eternal round, the same to-day as yesterday and forever. I am Jesus Christ, the Son of God, who was crucified for the sins of
the world, even as many as will believe on my name, that they
25 may become the sons of God, even one in me as I am in the
Father, as the Father is one in me, that we may be one.

2 Behold, verily, verily I say unto my servant Sidney, I have
looked upon thee and thy works. I have heard thy prayers
and prepared thee for a greater work. Thou art blessed, for
30 thou shalt do great things. Behold thou wast sent forth even
as John, to prepare the way before me, and before Elijah which
should come, and thou knew it not. Thou didst baptize by
water unto repentance, but they received not the Holy Ghost;
but now I give unto thee a commandment, that thou shalt bap-
35 tize by water, and they shall receive the Holy Ghost by the
laying on of the hands, even as the apostles of old.

3 And it shall come to pass, that there shall be a great work
in the land even among the Gentiles, for their folly and their
abominations shall be made manifest, in the eyes of all people:
40 for I am God and mine arm is not shortened and I will show
miracles, signs and wonders, unto all those who believe on my
name. And whoso shall ask it in my name, in faith, they
shall cast out devils; they shall heal the sick; they shall cause

---

line 17. Revelation, 7 Dec. 1830 [D&C 35]. Oliver Cowdery's copy of the Book of Commandments
bears a notation marking this revelation for inclusion in the 1835 Doctrine and Covenants. This version
reflects editing marks made in chapter 37 of the Cowdery volume, indicating that the latter was used as
a source text for the former. (See pp. 610–611 herein.)

117

line 1 the blind to receive their sight, and the deaf to hear, and the dumb to speak, and the lame to walk: and the time speedily cometh that great things are to be shown forth unto the children of men: but without faith shall not any thing be shown forth except desolations upon Babylon, the same which has made all nations drink of the wine of the wrath of her fornication. And there are none that doeth good except those who are ready to receive the fulness of my gospel, which I have sent forth to this generation:

4 Wherefore, I have called upon the weak things of the world, those who are unlearned and despised, to thresh the nations by the power of my Spirit: and their arm shall be my arm, and I will be their shield and their buckler, and I will gird up their loins, and they shall fight manfully for me: and their enemies shall be under their feet; and I will let fall the sword in their behalf; and by the fire of mine indignation will I preserve them. And the poor and the meek shall have the gospel preached unto them, and they shall be looking forth for the time of my coming, for it is nigh at hand: and they shall learn the parable of the fig-tree: for even now already summer is nigh, and I have sent forth the fulness of my gospel by the hand of my servant Joseph: and in weakness have I blessed him, and I have given unto him the keys of the mystery of those things which have been sealed, even things which were from the foundation of the world, and the things which shall come from this time until the time of my coming, if he abide in me, and if not, another will I plant in his stead.

5 Wherefore watch over him that his faith fail not, and it shall be given by the Comforter, the Holy Ghost, that knoweth all things: and a commandment I give unto thee, that thou shalt write for him: and the scriptures shall be given even as they are in mine own bosom, to the salvation of mine own elect: for they will hear my voice, and shall see me, and shall not be asleep, and shall abide the day of my coming, for they shall be purified even as I am pure. And now I say unto you, tarry with him and he shall journey with you; forsake him not and surely these things shall be fulfilled. And inasmuch as ye do not write, behold it shall be given unto him to prophesy: And thou shalt preach my gospel, and call on the holy prophets to prove his words, as they shall be given him.

6 Keep all the commandments and covenants by which ye are bound, and I will cause the heavens to shake for your good: and satan shall tremble; and Zion shall rejoice upon the hills, and flourish; and Israel shall be saved in mine own due time. And by the keys which I have given, shall they be led and no more be confounded at all. Lift up your hearts and be glad:

line 1

118

your redemption draweth nigh. Fear not little flock, the kingdom is yours until I come. Behold I come quickly; even so:
Amen.

SECTION. XII.

Revelation given January, 1831.

5

1 Thus saith the Lord your God, even Jesus Christ, the
Great I AM, Alpha and Omega, the beginning and the end.
the same which looked upon the wide expanse of eternity, and
all the seraphic hosts of heaven, before the world was made:
10 the same which knoweth all things, for all things are present
before mine eyes: I am the same which spake and the world
was made, and all things came by me: I am the same which
have taken the Zion of Enoch into mine own bosom: and verily I say, even as many as have believed on my name, for I
15 am Christ, and in mine own name, by the virtue of the blood
which I have spilt, have I plead before the Father for them:
But behold the residue of the wicked have I kept in chains of
darkness until the judgment of the great day, which shall come
at the end of the earth: and even so will I cause the wicked to
20 be kept, that will not hear my voice but harden their hearts,
and wo, wo, wo is their doom.
2 But behold, verily, verily I say unto you, that mine eyes
are upon you; I am in your midst and ye cannot see me, but
the day soon cometh that ye shall see me and know that I am:
25 for the vail of darkness shall soon be rent, and he that is not
purified shall not abide the day: wherefore gird up your loins
and be prepared. Behold the kingdom is yours and the ene
my shall not overcome.
3 Verily I say unto you, ye are clean but not all; and there is
30 none else with whom I am well pleased, for all flesh is corruptible before me, and the powers of darkness prevail upon the
earth, among the children of men, in the presence of all the
hosts of heaven, which causeth silence to reign, and all eternity is pained, and the angels are waiting the great command to
35 reap down the earth, to gather the tares that they may be
burned: and behold the enemy is combined.
4 And now I show unto you a mystery, a thing which is had
in secret chambers, to bring to pass even your destruction, in
process of time, and ye knew it not, but now I tell it unto
40 you, and ye are blessed, not because of your iniquity, neither
your hearts of unbelief, for verily some of you are guilty before
me; but I will be merciful unto your weakness. Therefore,
be ye strong from henceforth; fear not for the kingdom is

---

line 4. Revelation, 2 Jan. 1831 [D&C 38]. Oliver Cowdery's copy of the Book of Commandments bears
a notation marking this revelation for inclusion in the 1835 Doctrine and Covenants. This version reflects
editing marks made in chapter 40 of the Cowdery volume, indicating that the latter was used as a source
text for the former. (See pp. 612–614 herein.)

line 1
youts: and for your salvation I give unto you a commandment,
for I have heard your prayers, and the poor have complained
before me, and the rich have I made, and all flesh is mine, and
I am no respecter of persons. And I have made the earth rich,
and behold it is my footstool: wherefore, again I will stand upon it: and I hold forth and deign to give unto you greater riches, even a land of promise; a land flowing with milk and honey, upon which there shall be no curse when the Lord cometh:
and I will give it unto you for the land of your inheritance, if
you seek it with all your hearts: and this shall be my covenant
with you, ye shall have it for the land of your inheritance, and
for the inheritance of your children forever, while the earth
shall stand, and ye shall possess it again in eternity, no more
to pass away.

5 But verily I say unto you, that in time ye shall have no
king nor ruler, for I will be your king and watch over you.—
Wherefore, hear my voice and follow me, and you shall be a
free people, and ye shall have no laws but my laws, when I
come, for I am your Lawgiver, and what can stay my hand?
But verily I say unto you, teach one another according to the
office wherewith I have appointed you, and let every man
esteem his brother as himself, and practice virtue and holiness
before me. And again I say unto you, et every man esteem
his brother as himself: for what man among you having twelve
sons, and is no respecter to them, and they serve him obediently, and he saith unto the one, be thou clothed in robes and sit
thou here; and to the other, be thou clothed in rags and sit
thou there, and looketh upon his sons and saith I am just.

6 Behold, this I have given unto you a parable, and it is even
as I am: I say unto you, be one; and if ye are not one, ye are
not mine. And again I say unto you, that the enemy in the
secret chambers seeketh your lives: Ye hear of wars in far
countries, and you say that there will soon be great wars in far
countries, but ye know not the hearts of them in your own
land: I tell you these thing because of your prayers: wherefore, treasure up wisdom in your bosoms, lest the wickedness
of men reveal these things unto you, by their wickedness, in a
manner which shall speak in your ears, with a voice louder
than that which shall shake the earth: but if ye are prepared,
ye shall not fear.

7 And that ye might escape the power of the enemy, and be
gathered unto me a righteous people, without spot and blameless: wherefore, for this cause I gave unto you the commandment, that ye should go to the Ohio: and there I will give unto you my law; and there you shall be endowed with power
from on high, and from thence, whomsoever I will shall go

120

line 1 forth among all nations, and it shall be told them what they shall do: for I have a great work laid up in store: for Israel shall be saved, and I will lead them whithersoever I will, and no power shall stay my hand.

5 8 And now I give unto the church in these parts, a commandment, that certain men among them shall be appointed, and they shall be appointed by the voice of the church: and they shall look to the poor and the needy, and administer to their relief, that they shall not suffer; and send them forth to *10* the place which I have commanded them; and this shall be their work, to govern the affairs of the property of this church. And they that have farms that cannot be sold, let them be left or rented as seemeth them good. See that all things are preserved, and when men are endowed with power from on high, *15* and sent forth, all these things shall be gathered unto the bosom of the church.

9 And if ye seek the riches which it is the will of the Father to give unto you, ye shall be the richest of all people; for ye shall have the riches of eternity: and it must needs be that the *20* riches of the earth is mine to give: but beware of pride, lest ye become as the Nephites of old. And again I say unto you, I give unto you a commandment, that every man, both elder, priest, teacher and also member, go to with his might, with the labor of his hands, to prepare and accomplish the things *25* which I have commanded. And let your preaching be the warning voice, every man to his neighbor, in mildness and in meekness. And go ye out from among the wicked. Save yourselves. Be ye clean that bear the vessels of the Lord; even so: Amen.

30 ### SECTION XIII.

Revelation given February, 1831.

1 Hearken, O ye elders of my church who have assembled yourselves together, in my name, even Jesus Christ, the Son of the living God, the Savior of the world; inasmuch as they *35* believe on my name and keep my commandments; again I say unto you, hearken and hear and obey the law which I shall give unto you: for verily I say, as ye have assembled yourselves together according to the commandment wherewith I commanded you, and are agreed as touching this one thing, *40* and have asked the Father in my name, even so ye shall receive.

2 Behold, verily I say unto you, I give unto you this first commandment, that ye shall go forth in my name, every one

line 30. Revelation, 9 and 23 Feb. 1831 [D&C 42]. The contents of this section were divided into two different chapters in the Book of Commandments (chapters 44 and 47). Oliver Cowdery's copy of the Book of Commandments bears notations marking both chapters for inclusion in the 1835 Doctrine and Covenants. Verses 1–5 of this section reflect editing marks made in chapter 44 of the Cowdery volume, indicating that the latter was used as a source text for the former. The remainder closely corresponds to versions in two issues of *Evening and Morning Star*—July 1832 (printed Feb. 1835) and October 1832 (printed June 1835)—suggesting that those issues were used as source texts for this version. (See pp. 616–617 herein.)

121

line 1

of you, excepting my servants Joseph Smith, jr. and Sidney Rigdon. And I give unto them a commandment that they shall go forth for a little season, and it shall be given by the power of my Spirit when they shall return: and ye shall go forth in the power of my Spirit, preaching my gospel, two by two, in my name, lifting up your voices as with the voice of a trump, declaring my word like unto angels of God: and ye shall go forth baptizing with water, saying, Repent ye, repent ye, for the kingdom of heaven is at hand.

3 And from this place ye shall go forth into the regions westward, and inasmuch as ye shall find them that will receive you, ye shall build up my church in every region, until the time shall come when it shall be revealed unto you, from on high, when the city of the New Jerusalem shall be prepared that ye may be gathered in one, that ye may be my people and I will be your God. And again, I say unto you, that my servant Edward Partridge shall stand in the office wherewith I have appointed him. And it shall come to pass that if he transgress another shall be appointed in his stead; even so: Amen.

4 Again I say unto you, that it shall not be given to any one to go forth to preach my gospel, or to build up my church, except he be ordained by some one who has authority, and it is known to the church that he has authority, and has been regularly ordained by the heads of the church.

5 And again, the elders, priests and teachers of this church, shall teach the principles of my gospel which are in the bible and the book of Mormon, in the which is the fulness of the gospel; and they shall observe the covenants and church articles to do them, and these shall be their teachings, as they shall be directed by the Spirit: and the Spirit shall be given unto you by the prayer of faith, and if ye receive not the Spirit, ye shall not teach. And all this ye shall observe to do as I have commanded, concerning your teaching, until the fulness of my scriptures are given. And as ye shall lift up your voices by the Comforter, ye shall speak and prophesy as seemeth me good; for behold, the Comforter knoweth all things, and beareth record of the Father and of the Son.

6 And now, behold I speak unto the church: Thou shalt not kill; and he that kills shall not have forgiveness, in this world, nor in the world to come.

7 And again, I say, thou shalt not kill: but he that killeth shall die. Thou shalt not steal; and he that stealeth and will not repent, shall be cast out. Thou shalt not lie; he that lieth and will not repent, shall be cast out. Thou shalt love thy wife with all thy heart, and shall cleave unto her and none

122

else; and he that looketh upon a woman to lust after her, shall deny the faith, and shall not have the Spirit, and if he repents not he shall be cast out. Thou shalt not commit adultery; and he that committeth adultery and repenteth not, shall be cast out; but he that has committed adultery and repents with all his heart, and forsaketh it, and doeth it no more, thou shalt forgive; but if he doeth it again, he shall not be forgiven but shall be cast out. Thou shalt not speak evil of thy neighbor, nor do him any harm. Thou knowest my laws concerning these things are given in my scriptures: he that sinneth and repenteth not, shall be cast out.

8 If thou lovest me thou shalt serve me and keep all my commandments. And behold, thou wilt remember the poor, and consecrate of thy properties for their support, that which thou hast to impart unto them, with a covenant and a deed which cannot be broken—and inasmuch as ye impart of your substance unto the poor, ye will do it unto me—and they shall be laid before the bishop of my church and his counsellors, two of the elders, or high priests, such as he shall or has appointed and set apart for that purpose.

9 And it shall come to pass, that after they are laid before the bishop of my church, and after that he has received these testimonies concerning the consecration of the properties of my church, that they cannot be taken from the church, agreeable to my commandments, every man shall be made accountable unto me, a steward over his own property, or that which he has received by consecration, inasmuch as is sufficient for himself and family.

10 And again, if there shall be properties in the hands of the church, or any individuals of it, more than is necessary for their support, after this first consecration, which is a residue, to be consecrated unto the bishop, it shall be kept to administer to those who have not, from time to time, that every man who has need may be amply supplied, and receive according to his wants. Therefore, the residue shall be kept in my store house, to administer to the poor and the needy, as shall be appointed by the high council of the church, and the bishop and his council, and for the purpose of purchasing lands for the public benefit of the church, and building houses of worship, and building up of the New Jerusalem which is hereafter to be revealed, that my covenant people may be gathered in one in that day when I shall come to my temple. And this I do for the salvation of my people.

11 And it shall come to pass, that he that sinneth and repenteth not, shall be cast out of the church, and shall not receive again that which he has consecrated unto the poor and

123

line 1 the needy of my church, or in other words, unto me, for inasmuch as ye do it unto the least of these ye do it unto me—for it shall come to pass, that which I spake by the mouths of my prophets, shall be fulfilled; for I will consecrate of the riches 5 of those who embrace my gospel among the Gentiles, unto the poor of my people who are of the house of Israel.

12 And again, thou shalt not be proud in thy heart, let all thy garments be plain, and their beauty the beauty of the work of thine own hands; and let all things be done in cleanliness 10 before me. Thou shalt not be idle; for he that is idle shall not eat the bread, nor wear the garments of the laborer. And whosoever among you are sick, and have not faith to be healed, but believe, shall be nourished with all tenderness with herbs and mild food, and that not by the hand of an enemy. 15 And the elders of the church, two or more, shall be called, and shall pray for and lay their hands upon them in my name, and if they die they shall die unto me, and if they live they shall live unto me. Thou shalt live together in love, insomuch that thou shalt weep for the loss of them that die, and more 20 especially for those that have not hope of a glorious resurrection. And it shall come to pass, that those that die in me, shall not taste of death, for it shall be sweet unto them, and they that die not in me, wo unto them, for their death is bitter!

13 And again, it shall come to pass, that he that has faith in 25 me to be healed, and is not appointed unto death, shall be healed: he who has faith to see shall see: he who has faith to hear shall hear: the lame who have faith to leap shall leap; and they who have not faith to do these things, but believe in me, have power to become my sons: and inasmuch as they 30 break not my laws, thou shalt bear their infirmities.

14 Thou shalt stand in the place of thy stewardship: thou shalt not take thy brother's garment: thou shalt pay for that which thou shalt receive of thy brother: and if thou obtainest more than that which would be for thy support, thou shalt 35 give it into my store house, that all things may be done according to that which I have said.

15 Thou shalt ask, and my scriptures shall be given as I have appointed, and they shall be preserved in safety: and it is expedient that thou shouldst hold thy peace concerning them, 40 and not teach them until ye have received them in full. And I give unto you a commandment, that then ye shall teach them unto all men: for they shall be taught unto all nations, kindreds, tongues and people.

16 Thou shalt take the things which thou hast received, 45 which have been given unto thee in my scriptures for a law, to be my law, to govern my church; and he that doeth accor-

124

line 1

ding to these things, shall be saved, and he that doeth them not shall be damned, if he continues.

17 If thou shalt ask, thou shalt receive revelation upon revelation; knowledge upon knowledge, that thou mayest know the mysteries, and peaceable things; that which bringeth joy, that which bringeth life eternal. Thou shalt ask, and it shall be revealed unto you in mine own due time, where the New Jerusalem shall be built.

18 And behold, it shall come to pass, that my servants shall be sent forth to the east, and to the west, to the north, and to the south; and even now, let him that goeth to the east, teach them that shall be converted to flee to the west; and this in consequence of that which is coming on the earth, and of secret combinations. Behold thou shalt observe all these things, and great shall be thy reward; for unto you it is given to know the mysteries of the kingdom, but unto the world it is not given to know them. Ye shall observe the laws which ye have received, and be faithful. And ye shall hereafter receive church covenants, such as shall be sufficient to establish you, both here, and in the New Jerusalem. Therefore, he that lacketh wisdom, let him ask of me, and I will give him liberally, and upbraid him not. Lift up your hearts and rejoice, for unto you the kingdom, or in other words, the keys of the church, have been given; even so Amen.

19 The priests and teachers shall have their stewardships, even as the members, and the elders, or high priests who are appointed to assist the bishop as counsellors, in all things are to have their families supported out of the property which is consecrated to the bishop, for the good of the poor, and for other purposes, as before mentioned; or they are to receive a just remuneration for all their services; either a stewardship, or otherwise, as may be thought best, or decided by the counsellors and bishop. And the bishop also, shall receive his support, or a just remuneration for all his services, in the church.

20 Behold, verily I say unto you, that whatever persons among you having put away their companions for the cause of fornication, or in other words, if they shall testify before you in all lowliness of heart that this is the case, ye shall not cast them out from among you; but if ye shall find that any persons have left their companions for the sake of adultery, and they themselves are the offenders, and their companions are living, they shall be cast out from among you. And again I say unto you, that ye shall be watchful and careful, with all inquiry, that ye receive none such among you if they are married, and if they are not married, they shall repent of all their sins, or ye shall not receive them.

125

21 And again, every person who belongeth to this church of Christ shall observe to keep all the commandments and covenants of the church: And it shall come to pass, that if any persons among you shall kill, they shall be delivered up and dealt with according to the laws of the land; For remember, that he hath no forgiveness; and it shall be proven according to the laws of the land.

22 And if any man or woman shall commit adultery, he or she shall be tried before two elders of the church or more, and every word shall be established against him or her by two witnesses of the church, and not of the enemy. But if there are more than two witnesses it is better: but he or she shall be condemned by the mouth of two witnesses, and the elders shall lay the case before the church, and the church shall lift up their hands against him or her, that they may be dealt with according to the law of God. And if it can be, it is necessary that the bishop is present also. And thus ye shall do in all cases which shall come before you. And if a man or woman shall rob, he or she shall be delivered up unto the law of the land. And if he or she shall steal, he or she shall be delivered up unto the law of the land. And if he or she shall lie, he or she shall be delivered up unto the law of the land. If he or she do any manner of iniquity, he or she shall be delivered up unto the law, even that of God.

23 And if thy brother or sister offend thee, thou shalt take him or her between him or her and thee alone; and if he or she confess, thou shalt be reconciled. And if he or she confess not, thou shalt deliver him or her up unto the church, not to the members but to the elders. And it shall be done in a meeting, and that not before the world. And if thy brother or sister offend many, he or she shall be chastened before many. And if any one offend openly, he or she shall be rebuked openly, that he or she may be ashamed. And if he or she confess not, he or she shall be delivered up unto the law of God. If any shall offend in secret, he or she shall be rebuked in secret, that he or she may have opportunity to confess in secret to him or her whom he or she has offended, and to God, that the church may not speak reproachfully of him or her. And thus shall ye conduct in all things.

SECTION XIV.

A Revelation given February, 1831.

1 O hearken, ye elders of my church, and give ear to the words which I shall speak unto you: for behold, verily, verily

---

line 40. Revelation, Feb. 1831–A [D&C 43]. Oliver Cowdery's copy of the Book of Commandments bears a notation marking this revelation for inclusion in the 1835 Doctrine and Covenants. The source text for this version is unknown.

126

I say unto you, that ye have received a commandment for a
law unto my church, through him whom I have appointed unto you, to receive commandments and revelations from my
hand. And this ye shall know assuredly, that there is none
other appointed unto you to receive commandments and revelations until he be taken, if he abide in me.

2 But verily, verily I say unto you, that none else shall be
appointed unto this gift except it be through him, for if it be
taken from him he shall not have power, except to appoint
another in his stead: and this shall be a law unto you, that ye
receive not the teachings of any that shall come before you
as revelations or commandments: and this I give unto you,
that you may not be deceived; that you may know they are
not of me. For verily I say unto you, that he that is ordained of me shall come in at the gate and be ordained as I have
told you before, to teach those revelations which you have
received, and shall receive through him whom I have appointed.

3 And now behold I give unto you a commandment, that
when ye are assembled together, ye shall instruct and edify
each other, that ye may know how to act and direct my
church how to act upon the points of my law and commandments, which I have given: and thus ye shall become instructed in the law of my church, and be sanctified by that which
ye have received, and ye shall bind yourselves to act in all holiness before me, that inasmuch as ye do this, glory shall
be added to the kingdom which ye have received. Inasmuch
as ye do it not, it shall be taken even that which ye have received. Purge ye out the iniquity which is among you: sanctify yourselves before me and if ye desire the glories of the
kingdom, appoint ye my servant Joseph Smith, jr. and uphold
him before me by the prayer of faith. And again, I say unto
you, that if ye desire the mysteries of the kingdom, provide
for him food and raiment and whatsoever thing he needeth to
accomplish the work, wherewith I have commanded him: and
if ye do it not, he shall remain unto them that have received
him, that I may reserve unto myself a pure people before me.

4 Again I say, hearken ye elders of my church, whom I have
appointed: ye are not sent forth to be taught, but to teach
the children of men the things which I have put into your
hands by the power of my Spirit: and ye are to be taught
from on high. Sanctify yourselves and ye shall be endowed
with power, that ye may give even as I have spoken.

5 Hearken ye, for behold the great day of the Lord is nigh
at hand. For the day cometh that the Lord shall utter his
voice out of heaven; the heavens shall shake and the earth

127

shall tremble, and the trump of God shall sound both long and loud, and shall say to the sleeping nations: Ye saints arise and live: Ye sinners stay and sleep until I shall call again: wherefore gird up your loins, least ye be found among the wicked. Lift up your voices and spare not. Call upon the nations to repent, both old and young, both bond and free; saying, Prepare yourselves for the great day of the Lord: for if I, who am a man, do lift up my voice and call upon you to repent, and ye hate me, what will ye say when the day cometh when the thunders shall utter their voices from the ends of the earth, speaking to the ears of all that live, saying: Repent, and prepare for the great day of the Lord? yea, and again, when the lightnings shall streak forth from the east unto the west, and shall utter forth their voices unto all that live, and make the ears of all tingle, that hear, saying these words: Repent ye, for the great day of the Lord is come?

6 And again, the Lord shall utter his voice out of heaven, saying: Hearken, O ye nations of the earth, and hear the words of that God who made you. O ye nations of the earth, how often would I have gathered you together as a hen gathereth her chickens under her wings, but ye would not? How oft have I called upon you by the mouth of my servants; and by the ministering of angels; and by mine own voice; and by the voice of thunderings; and by the voice of lightnings; and by the voice of tempests; and by the voice of earthquakes; and great hailstorms; and by the voice of famines, and pestilences of every kind; and by the great sound of a tramp; and by the voice of judgment; and by the voice of mercy all the day long; and by the voice of glory, and honor, and the riches of eternal life; and would have saved you with an everlasting salvation, but ye would not? Behold the day has come, when the cup of the wrath of mine indignation is full.

7 Behold, verily I say unto you, that these are the words of the Lord your God: wherefore, labor ye, labor ye, in my vineyard for the last time: for the last time call upon the inhabitants of the earth, for in mine own due time will I come upon the earth in judgment: and my people shall be redeemed and shall reign with me on earth: for the great Millennial, which I have spoken by the mouth of my servants, shall come; for satan shall be bound; and when he is loosed again, he shall only reign for a little season, and then cometh the end of the earth: and he that liveth in righteousness, shall be changed in the twinkling of an eye; and the earth shall pass away so as by fire; and the wicked shall go away into unquenchable fire; and their end no man knoweth, on earth, nor ever shall know, until they come before me in judgment.

128

line 1

8 Hearken ye to these words; behold I am Jesus Christ the Savior of the world. Treasure these things up in your hearts, and let the solemnities of eternity rest upon your minds. Be sober. Keep all my commandments; even so: Amen.

SECTION XV.

Revelation given March 7, 1831.

1 Hearken, O ye people of my church to whom the kingdom has been given: hearken ye and give ear to him who laid the foundation of the earth; who made the heavens and all the host thereof, and by whom all things were made which live and move and have a being. And again I say, hearken unto my voice, lest death shall overtake you: in an hour when ye think not the summer shall be past, and the harvest ended, and your souls not saved. Listen to him who is the Advocate with the Father, who is pleading your cause before him; saying, Father behold the sufferings and death of him who did no sin, in whom thou wast well pleased: behold the blood of thy Son which was shed, the blood of him whom thou gavest that thyself might be glorified: wherefore, Father spare these my brethren that believe on my name, that they may come unto me and have everlasting life.

2 Hearken O ye people of my church, and ye elders listen together, and hear my voice while it is called to-day and harden not your hearts; for verily I say unto you that I am Alpha and Omega, the beginning and the end, the light and the life of the world; a light that shineth in darkness and the darkness comprehendeth it not: I came unto my own and my own received me not; but unto as many as received me gave I power to do many miracles, and to become the sons of God, and even unto them that believed on my name, gave I power to obtain eternal life. And even so I have sent mine everlasting covenant into the world; to be a light to the world, and to be a standard for my people and for the Gentiles to seek to it: and to be a messenger before my face to prepare the way before me. Wherefore come ye unto it, and with him that cometh I will reason as with men in days of old, and I will show unto you my strong reasoning; wherefore hearken ye together and let me show it unto you, even my wisdom, the wisdom of him whom ye say is the God of Enoch, and his brethren, who were separated from the earth, and were received unto myself—a city reserved until a day of righteousness shall come—a day which was sought for by all holy men, and they found

---

line 6. Revelation, ca. 7 Mar. 1831 [D&C 45]. Oliver Cowdery's copy of the Book of Commandments bears a notation marking this revelation for inclusion in the 1835 Doctrine and Covenants. This version reflects editing marks made in chapter 48 of the Cowdery volume, indicating that the latter was used as a source text for the former. (See pp. 618–621 herein.)

129

line 1 it not because of wickedness and abominations: and confessed
that they were strangers and pilgrims on the earth: but obtained a promise that they should find it, and see it in their flesh.
Wherefore hearken and I will reason with you, and I will
5 speak unto you and prophesy as unto men in days of old and
I will show it plainly as I showed it unto my disciples, as I
stood before them in the flesh, and spake unto them saying:
As ye have asked of me concerning the signs of my coming,
in the day when I shall come in my glory in the clouds of
10 heaven, to fulfil the promises that I have made unto your fathers: for as ye have looked upon the long absence of your
spirits from your bodies to be a bondage, I will show unto you
how the day of redemption shall come, and also the restoration of the scattered Israel.
15 3 And now ye behold this temple which is in Jerusalem,
which ye call the house of God, and your enemies say that
this house shall never fall. But verily I say unto you, that
desolation shall come upon this generation as a thief in the
night, and this people shall be destroyed and scattered among
20 all nations. And this temple which ye now see, shall be
thrown down that there shall not be left one stone upon another. And it shall come to pass, that this generation of Jews
shall not pass away, until every desolation which I have told
you concerning them, shall come to pass. Ye say that ye
25 know that the end of the world cometh; ye say also that ye
know that the heavens and the earth shall pass away; and in
this ye say truly, for so it is; but these things which I have
told you, shall not pass away until all shall be fulfilled. And
this I have told you concerning Jerusalem, and when that day
30 shall come, shall a remnant be scattered among all nations,
but they shall be gathered again; but they shall remain until
the times of the Gentiles be fulfilled.
4 And in that day shall be heard of wars and rumors of wars,
and the whole earth shall be in commotion, and men's hearts
35 shall fail them, and they shall say that Christ delayeth his
coming until the end of the earth. And the love of men shall
wax cold, and iniquity shall abound; and when the time of the
Gentiles is come in, a light shall break forth among them that
sit in darkness, and it shall be the fulness of my gospel; but
40 they receive it not, for they perceive not the light, and they
turn their hearts from me because of the precepts of men; and
in that generation shall the times of the Gentiles be fulfilled:
and there shall be men standing in that generation, that shall
not pass, until they shall see an overflowing scourge; for a
45 desolating sickness shall cover the land: but my disciples shall

I

line 46. This page begins the ninth gathering of the book. "I" is the first of two signature marks in this gathering; the second is on the recto of the following leaf. These marks were used in collating the gatherings after the sheets were folded.

130

stand in holy places, and shall not be moved; but among the wicked, men shall lift up their voices and curse God and die. And there shall be earthquakes, also, in divers places, and many desolations, yet men will harden their hearts against me; and they will take up the sword one against another, and they will kill one another.

5 And now, when I the Lord had spoken these words unto my disciples, they were troubled; and I said unto them, be not troubled, for when all these things shall come to pass, ye may know that the promises which have been made unto you, shall be fulfilled: and when the light shall begin to break forth, it shall be with them like unto a parable which I will show you: ye look and behold the fig-trees, and ye see them with your eyes, and ye say when they begin to shoot forth and their leaves are yet tender, that summer is now nigh at hand: even so it shall be in that day, when they shall see all these things, then shall they know that the hour is nigh.

6 And it shall come to pass that he that feareth me shall be looking forth for the great day of the Lord to come, even for the signs of the coming of the Son of man; and they shall see signs and wonders, for they shall be shown forth in the heavens above, and in the earth beneath; and they shall behold blood and fire, and vapors of smoke; and before the day of the Lord shall come, the sun shall be darkened, and the moon be turned into blood, and stars fall from heaven; and the remnant shall be gathered unto this place; and then they shall look for me, and behold I will come: and they shall see me in the clouds of heaven, clothed with power and great glory, with all the holy angels; and he that watches not for me shall be cut off.

7 But before the arm of the Lord shall fall, an angel shall sound his trump, and the saints that have slept, shall come forth to meet me in the cloud. Wherefore if ye have slept in peace, blessed are you, for as you now behold me and know that I am, even so shall ye come unto me and your souls shall live, and your redemption shall be perfected, and the saints shall come forth from the four quarters of the earth.

8 Then shall the arm of the Lord fall upon the nations, and then shall the Lord set his foot upon this mount, and it shall cleave in twain, and the earth shall tremble and reel to and fro, and the heavens also shall shake, and the Lord shall utter his voice and all the ends of the earth shall hear it, and the nations of the earth shall mourn, and they that have laughed shall see their folly, and calamity shall cover the mocker, and the scorner shall be consumed, and they that have watched for iniquity, shall be hewn down and cast into the fire.

9 And then shall the Jews look upon me and say, What are

131

line 1 these wounds in thine hands, and in thy feet? Then shall
they know that I am the Lord; for I will say unto them, These
wounds are the wounds with which I was wounded in the
house of my friends. I am he who was lifted up. I am Jesus
5 that was crucified. I am the Son of God. And then shall
they weep because of their iniquities; then shall they lament
because they persecuted their King.

10 And then shall the heathen nations be redeemed, and they
that knew no law shall have part in the first resurrection;
10 and it shall be tolerable for them: and satan shall be bound
that he shall have no place in the hearts of the children of
men. And at that day when I shall come in my glory, shall
the parable be fulfilled which I spake concerning the ten virgins: for they that are wise and have received the truth, and
15 have taken the Holy Spirit for their guide, and have not been
deceived, verily I say unto you, they shall not be hewn down
and cast into the fire, but shall abide the day, and the earth
shall be given unto them for an inheritance: and they shall
multiply and wax strong, and their children shall grow up
20 without sin unto salvation, for the Lord shall be in their midst,
and his glory shall be upon them, and he will be their King
and their Lawgiver.

11 And now, behold I say unto you, it shall not be given unto you to know any farther concerning this chapter, until the
25 new testament be translated, and in it all these things shall be
made known:wherefore I give unto you that ye may now translate it, that ye may be prepared for the things to come: for
verily I say unto you, that great things await you; ye hear of
wars in foreign lands, but behold I say unto you, they are nigh
30 even at your doors and not many years hence ye shall hear of
wars in your own lands.

12 Wherefore I the Lord have said gather ye out from the
eastern lands, assemble ye yourselves together ye elders of my
church; go ye forth into the western countries, call upon the
35 inhabitants to repent, and inasmuch as they do repent, build
up churches unto me; and with one heart and with one mind,
gather up your riches that ye may purchase an inheritance
which shall hereafter be appointed unto you, and it shall be
called the New Jerusalem, a land of peace, a city of refuge, a
40 place of safety for the saints of the most high God; and the
glory of the Lord shall be there, and the terror of the Lord also shall be there, insomuch that the wicked will not come unto it: and it shall be called Zion.

13 And it shall come to pass, among the wicked, that every
45 man that will not take his sword against his neighbor, must
10*

---

line 46. This signature mark should read "9*".

132

needs flee unto Zion for safety. And there shall be gathered unto it out of every nation under heaven: and it shall be the only people that shall not be at war one with another. And it shall be said among the wicked, Let us not go up to battle
against Zion, for the inhabitants of Zion are terrible. Wherefore we cannot stand.

14 And it shall come to pass that the righteous shall be gathered out from among all nations, and shall come to Zion singing, with songs of everlasting joy.

15 And now I say unto you, keep these things from going abroad unto the world, until it is expedient in me, that ye may accomplish this work in the eyes of the people, and in the eyes of your enemies, that they may not know your works un-til ye have accomplished the thing which I have commanded
you: that when they shall know it, that they may consider these things, for when the Lord shall appear he shall be terri-ble unto them, that fear may seize upon them, and they shall stand afar off and tremble: and all nations shall be afraid because of the terror of the Lord, and the power of his might; even so:
Amen.

SECTION XVI.

Revelation given March, 1831.

1 Hearken, O ye people of my church, for verily I say unto you, that these things were spoken unto you for your profit
and learning; but notwithstanding those things which are written, it always has been given to the elders of my church, from the beginning, and ever shall be, to conduct all meetings as they are directed and guided by the Holy Spirit: neverthe-less ye are commanded never to cast any one out from your
public meetings, which are held before the world: ye are also commanded not to cast any one, who belongeth to the church, out of your sacrament meetings: nevertheless, if any have trespassed, let him not partake until he makes reconciliation.

2 And again I say unto you, ye shall not cast any one out of
your sacrament meetings, who is earnestly seeking the king-dom: I speak this concerning those who are not of the church.

3 And again I say unto you, concerning your confirmation meetings, that if there be any that is not of the church, that is earnestly seeking after the kingdom, ye shall not cast them
out; but ye are commanded in all things to ask of God who giveth liberally, and that which the Sprit testifies unto you, even so I would that ye should do in all holiness of heart, walking uprightly before me, considering the end of your sal-

---

133

vation, doing all things with prayer and thanksgiving, that ye may not be seduced by evil spirits, or doctrines of devils, or the commandments of men, for some are of men, and others of devils.

4 Wherefore, beware lest ye are deceived! and that ye may not be deceived, seek ye earnestly the best gifts, always remembering for what they are given; for verily I say unto you, they are given for the benefit of those who love me and keep all my commandments, and him that seeketh so to do, that all may be benefited, that seeketh or that asketh of me, that asketh and not for a sign that he may consume it upon his lusts.

5 And again, verily I say unto you, I would that ye should always remember, and always retain in your minds what those gifts are, that are given unto the church, for all have not every gift given unto them: for there are many gifts, and to every man is given a gift by the Spirit of God: to some it is given one, and to some is given another, that all may be profited thereby; to some it is given by the Holy Ghost to know that Jesus Christ is the Son of God, and that he was crucified for the sins of the world; to others it is given to believe on their words, that they also might have eternal life, if they continue faithful.

6 And again, to some it is given by the Holy Ghost to know the differences of administration, as it will be pleasing unto the same Lord, according as the Lord will, suiting his mercies according to the conditions of the children of men. And again it is given by the Holy Ghost to some to know the diversities of operations, whether it be of God, that the manifestations of the Spirit may be given to every man to profit withal.

7 And again, verily I say unto you, to some it is given, by the Spirit of God, the word of wisdom; to another it is given the word of knowledge, that all may be taught to be wise and to have knowledge. And again, to some it is given to have faith to be healed, and to others it is given to have faith to heal. And again, to some it is given the working of miracles; and to others it is given to prophesy, and to others the discerning of spirits. And again, it is given to some to speak with tongues, and to another it is given the interpretation of tongues: and all these gifts cometh from God, for the benefit of the children of God. And unto the bishop of the church, and unto such as God shall appoint and ordain to watch over the church, and to be elders unto the church, are to have it given unto them to discern all those gifts, lest there shall be any among you professing and yet be not of God.

8 And it shall come to pass that he that asketh in spirit shall receive in spirit; that unto some it may be given to have all

134

line 1 those gifts, that there may be a head, in order that every member may be profited thereby: he that asketh in the spirit, asketh according to the will of God, wherefore it is done even as
he asketh.

5 9 And again I say unto you, all things must be done in the
name of Christ, whatsoever you do in the spirit; and ye must
give thanks unto God in the spirit for whatsoever blessing ye
are blessed with: and ye must practice virtue and holiness before me continually; even so: Amen.

10 SECTION XVII.

A Revelation given May, 1831.

1 Hearken, O ye elders of my church, and give ear to the
voice of the living God; and attend to the words of wisdom
which shall be given unto you, according as ye have asked and
15 are agreed as touching the church, and the spirits which have
gone abroad in the earth. Behold verily I say unto you, that
there are many spirits which are false spirits, which have gone
forth in the earth, deceiving the world: and also satan hath
sought to deceive you, that he might overthrow you.

20 2 Behold I the Lord have looked upon you, and have seen
abominations in the church, that profess my name; but blessed are they who are faithful and endure, whether in life or
in death, for they shall inherit eternal life. But wo unto them
that are deceivers, and hypocrites, for thus saith the Lord, I
25 will bring them to judgment.

3 Behold verily I say unto you, there are hypocrites among
you, and have deceived some, which has given the adversary
power, but behold such shall be reclaimed; but the hypocrites
shall be detected and shall be cut off, either in life or in death,
30 even as I will, and wo unto them who are cut off from my
church, for the same are overcome of the world: wherefore,
let every man beware lest he do that which is not in truth and
righteousness before me.

4 And now come, saith the Lord, by the Spirit, unto the el-
35 ders of his church, and let us reason together, that ye may understand: let us reason even as a man reasoneth one with another face to face: now when a man reasoneth, he is understood
of man, because he reasoneth as a man; even so will I the
Lord reason with you that you may understand: wherefore I
40 the Lord asketh you this question, unto what were ye ordained? To preach my gospel by the Spirit, even the Comforter
which was sent forth to teach the truth; and then received ye
spirits which ye could not understand, and received them to

---

line 10. Revelation, 9 May 1831 [D&C 50]. Oliver Cowdery's copy of the Book of Commandments bears
a notation marking this revelation for inclusion in the 1835 Doctrine and Covenants. This version corresponds to the version in chapter 53 of the Book of Commandments, indicating that the latter was used as
a source text for the former.

135

be of God, and in this are ye justified? Behold ye shall answer this question yourselves; nevertheless I will be merciful
unto you: he that is weak among you hereafter shall be made
strong.

5 5 Verily I say unto you, he that is ordained of me and sent
forth to preach the word of truth by the Comforter, in the spirit of truth, doth he preach it by the spirit of truth, or some other way? and if it be by some other way, it be not of God. And
again, he that receiveth the word of truth, doth he receive it
10 by the spirit of truth, or some other way? if it be some other
way, it be not of God: therefore, why is it that ye cannot understand and know that he that receiveth the word by the spirit of truth, receiveth it as it is preached by the spirit of truth?

6 Wherefore, he that preacheth and he that receiveth, un-
15 derstandeth one another, and both are edified and rejoice together; and that which doth not edify, is not of God, and is
darkness: that which is of God is light, and he that receiveth
light and continueth in God, receiveth more light, and that
light groweth brighter and brighter, until the perfect day. And
20 again, verily I say unto you, and I say it that you may know
the truth, that you may chase darkness from among you, for
he that is ordained of God and sent forth, the same is appointed to be the greatest, notwithstanding he is least, and the servant of all: wherefore he is possessor of all things, for all
25 things are subject unto him, both in heaven and on the earth,
the life, and the light, the spirit, and the power, sent forth by
the will of the Father, through Jesus Christ, his Son; but no
man is possessor of all things, except he be purified and
cleansed from all sin; and if ye are purified and cleansed from
30 all sin, ye shall ask whatsoever you will in the name of Jesus,
and it shall be done: but know this, it shall be given you what
you shall ask, and as ye are appointed to the head, the spirits
shall be subject unto you:

7 Wherefore it shall come to pass, that if you behold a spirit
35 manifested that you cannot understand, and you receive not
that spirit, ye shall ask of the Father in the name of Jesus,
and if he give not unto you that spirit, that you may know
that it is not of God: and it shall be given unto you power over
that spirit, and you shall proclaim against that spirit with a
40 loud voice, that it is not of God: not with railing accusation,
that ye be not overcome; neither with boasting, nor rejoicing,
lest you be seized therewith: he that receiveth of God, let him
account it of God, and let him rejoice that he is accounted of
God worthy to receive, and by giving heed and doing these
45 things which ye have received, and which ye shall hereafter
receive: and the kingdom is given you of the Father, and pow-

136

line 1 er to overcome all things, which is not ordained of him: and
behold, verily I say unto you, blessed are you who are now
hearing these words of mine from the mouth of my servant,
for your sins are forgiven you.

5 8 Let my servant Joseph Wakefield, in whom I am well
pleased, and my servant Parley P. Pratt, go forth among the
churches and strengthen them by the word of exhortation; and
also my servant John Corrill, or as many of my servants as
are ordained unto this office, and let them labor in the vine-

10 yard; and let no man hinder them of doing that which I have
appointed unto them: wherefore in this thing my servant Edward Partridge, is not justified, nevertheless let him repent
and he shall be forgiven. Behold ye are little children, and
ye cannot bear all things now; ye must grow in grace and in

15 the knowledge of the truth. Fear not, little children, for you
are mine, and I have overcome the world, and you are of them
that my Father hath given me; and none of them that my
Father hath given me shall be lost: and the Father and I are
one: I am in the Father and the Father in me: and inasmuch

20 as ye have received me, ye are in me, and I in you: wherefore
I am in your midst; and I am the good Shepherd, (and the
stone of Israel: He that buildeth upon this rock shall never
fall.) And the day cometh that you shall hear my voice and
see me, and know that I am. Watch, therefore, that ye may

25 be ready; even so: Amen.

SECTION XVIII.

Revelation given in Zion, August, 1831.

1 Hearken O ye elders of my church, and give ear to my
word, and learn of me what I will concerning you, and also

30 concerning this land unto which I have sent you: for verily I
say unto you, blessed is he that keepeth my commandments,
whether in life or in death; and he that is faithful in tribulation
the reward of the same is greater in the kingdom of heaven.

2 Ye cannot behold with your natural eyes, for the present

35 time, the design of your God concerning those things which
shall come hereafter, and the glory which shall follow, after
much tribulation. For after much tribulation cometh the blessings. Wherefore, the day cometh that ye shall be crowned
with much glory, the hour is not yet but is nigh at hand.

40 3 Remember this which I tell you before, that you may lay
it to heart, and receive that which shall follow. Behold, verily I say unto you, for this cause I have sent you that you
might be obedient, and that your hearts might be prepared to

---

line 26. Revelation, 1 Aug. 1831 [D&C 58]. Oliver Cowdery's copy of the Book of Commandments bears
a notation marking this revelation for inclusion in the 1835 Doctrine and Covenants. This version reflects
editing marks made in Revelation Book 1 and in chapter 59 of the Cowdery volume, indicating that both
were used as source texts for this version. (See *JSP,* MRB:161–169; and pp. 627–630 herein.)

137

bear testimony of the things which are to come; and also that you might be honored of laying the foundation, and of bearing record of the land upon which the Zion of God shall stand; and also, that a feast of fat things might be prepared for the poor; yea a feast of fat things, of wine on the lees well refined, that the earth may know that the mouths of the prophets shall not fail; yea, a supper of the house of the Lord, well prepared unto which all nations shall be invited. Firstly the rich, and the learned, the wise and the noble; and after that cometh the day of my power: then shall the poor, the lame and the blind, and the deaf, come in unto the marriage of the Lamb, and partake of the supper of the Lord, prepared for the great day to come. Behold I the Lord have spoken it.

4 And that the testimony might go forth from Zion; yea from the mouth of the city of the heritage of God: yea, for this cause I have sent you hither; and have selected my servant Edward Partridge and have appointed unto him his mission in this land: but if he repent not of his sins, which are unbelief and blindness of heart, let him take heed lest he fall. Behold his mission is given unto him and it shall not be given again. And whoso standeth in this mission, is appointed to be a judge in Israel, like as it was in ancient days, to divide the lands of the heritage of God unto his children; and to judge his people by the testimony of the just, and by the assistance of his counsellors, according to the laws of the kingdom which are given by the prophets of God: for verily I say unto you, my laws shall be kept on this land.

5 Let no man think that he is ruler, but let God rule him that judgeth, according to the counsel of his own will: or in other words, him that counselleth, or sitteth upon the judgment seat. Let no man break the laws of the land, for he that keepeth the laws of God, hath no need to break the laws of the land: wherefore be subject to the powers that be, until He reigns whose right it is to reign, and subdues all enemies under his feet. Behold the laws which ye have received from my hand, are the laws of the church; and in this light ye shall hold them forth. Behold here is wisdom.

6 And now as I spake concerning my servant Edward Partridge: this land is the land of his residence, and those whom he has appointed for his counsellors. And also the land of the residence of him whom I have appointed to keep my storehouse: wherefore let them bring their families to this land, as they shall counsel between themselves and me: for behold it is not meet that I should command in all things, for he that is compelled in all things, the same is a slothful and not a wise servant; wherefore he receiveth no reward. Verily I say, men

138

should be anxiously engaged in a good cause, and do many
things of their own free will, and bring to pass much righteousness: for the power is in them, wherein they are agents unto
themselves. And inasmuch as men do good they shall in no
wise lose their reward. But he that doeth not any thing until he is commanded, and receiveth a commandment with
doubtful heart, and keepeth it with slothfulness, the same is
damned. Who am I that made man, saith the Lord, that will
hold him guiltless that obeys not my commandments? Who
am I, saith the Lord, that have promised and have not fulfilled? I command and a man obeys not, I revoke and they receive not the blessing: then they say in their hearts, this is
not the work of the Lord, for his promises are not fulfilled.—
But wo unto such, for their reward lurketh beneath, and not
from above.

7 And now I give unto you further directions concerning this
land. It is wisdom in me, that my servant Martin Harris
should be an example unto the church, in laying his moneys
before the bishop of the church. And also, this is a law unto
every man that cometh unto this land, to receive an inheritance; and he shall do with his moneys according as the law
directs. And it is wisdom also, that there should be lands
purchased in Independence, for the place of the storehouse:
and also for the house of the printing.

8 And other directions, concerning my servant Martin Harris,
shall be given him of the Spirit, that he may receive his inheritance as seemeth him good. And let him repent of his sins,
for he seeketh the praise of the world.

9 And also let my servant William W. Phelps stand in the
office which I have appointed him, and receive his inheritance
in the land. And also, he hath need to repent, for I the Lord
am not well pleased with him, for he seeketh to excell and
he is not sufficiently meek before me. Behold he who has
repented of his sins the same is forgiven, and I the Lord remembereth them no more. By this ye may know if a man
repenteth of his sins. Behold he will confess them and forsake them. And now verily I say, concerning the residue of
the elders of my church, the time has not yet come for many
years, for them to receive their inheritance in this land; except they desire it through the prayer of faith, only as it shall
be appointed unto them of the Lord. For behold they shall
push the people together from the ends of the earth: wherefore assemble yourselves together, and they who are not appointed to stay in this land, let them preach the gospel in the
regions round about; and after that, let them return to their
homes. Let them preach by the way, and bear testimony of

139

the truth in all places, and call upon the rich, the high, and the low, and the poor, to repent; and let them build up churches inasmuch as the inhabitants of the earth will repent.

10 And let there be an agent appointed by the voice of the church, unto the church in Ohio, to receive moneys to purchase lands in Zion.

11 And I give unto my servant Sidney Rigdon, a commandment, that he shall write a description of the land of Zion, and a statement of the will of God, as it shall be made known by the Spirit, unto him; and an epistle and subscription, to be presented unto all the churches, to obtain moneys, to be put into the hands of the bishop, to purchase lands for an inheritance for the children of God, of himself or the agent, as seemeth him good, or as he shall direct. For behold, verily I say unto you, the Lord willeth that the disciples, and the children of men, should open their hearts even to purchase this whole region of country, as soon as time will permit. Behold here is wisdom; let them do this lest they receive none inheritance, save it be by the shedding of blood.

12 And again, inasmuch as there is land obtained, let there be workmen sent forth, of all kinds, unto this land, to labor for the saints of God. Let all these things be done in order. And let the privileges of the lands be made known from time to time, by the bishop, or the agent of the church. And let the work of the gathering be not in haste, nor by flight, but let it be done as it shall be counselled by the elders of the church at the conferences, according to the knowledge which they receive from time to time.

13 And let my servant Sidney Rigdon consecrate and dedicate this land, and the spot of the temple, unto the Lord. And let a conference meeting be called, and after that, let my servant Sidney Rigdon and Joseph Smith, jr. return, and also Oliver Cowdery with them, to accomplish the residue of the work, which I have appointed unto them in their own land: and the residue as shall be ruled by the conferences.

14 And let no man return from this land, except he bear record by the way, of that which he knows and most assuredly believes. Let that which has been bestowed upon Ziba Peterson, be taken from him: and let him stand as a member in the church, and labor with his own hands, with the brethren, until he is sufficiently chastened for all his sins, for he confesseth them not, and he thinketh to hide them.

15 Let the residue of the elders of this church, who are coming to this land, some of whom are exceedingly blessed even above measure, also, hold a conference upon this land. And let my servant Edward Partridge direct the conference, which

line 1

shall be held by them. And let them also return, preaching the gospel by the way, bearing record of the things which are revealed unto them: for verily the sound must go forth from this place into all the world; and unto the uttermost parts of the earth, the gospel must be preached unto every creature, with signs following them that believe. And behold the Son of man cometh: Amen.

SECTION XIX.

Revelation given in Zion, August, 1831.

1 Behold, blessed, saith the Lord, are they who have come up unto this land with an eye single to my glory, according to my commandments: for them that live shall inherit the earth, and them that die shall rest from all their labors, and their works shall follow them, and they shall receive a crown in the mansions of my Father, which I have prepared for them; yea, blessed are they whose feet stand upon the land of Zion, who have obeyed my gospel, for they shall receive for their reward the good things of the earth; and it shall bring forth in its strength: and they shall also be crowned with blessings from above; yea and with commandments not a few; and with revelations in their time: they that are faithful and diligent before me:

2 Wherefore I give unto them a commandment, saying thus: Thou shalt love the Lord thy God, with all thy heart, with all thy might, mind, and strength: and in the name of Jesus Christ thou shalt serve him. Thou shalt love thy neighbor as thyself. Thou shalt not steal. Neither commit adultery, nor kill, nor do any thing like unto it. Thou shalt thank the Lord thy God in all things. Thou shalt offer a sacrifice unto the Lord thy God in righteousness: even that of a broken heart and a contrite spirit. And that thou mayest more fully keep thyself unspotted from the world, thou shalt go to the house of prayer and offer up thy sacraments upon my holy day; for verily this is a day appointed unto you to rest from your labors, and to pay thy devotions unto the Most High; nevertheless thy vows shall be offered up in righteousness on all days, and at all times; but remember that on this, the Lord's day, thou shalt offer thine oblations, and thy sacraments, unto the Most High, confessing thy sins unto thy brethren, and before the Lord.

3 And on this day thou shalt do none other thing, only let thy food be prepared with singleness of heart, that thy fasting may be perfect, or in other words, that thy joy may be full.—

---

line 8. Revelation, 7 Aug. 1831 [D&C 59]. Oliver Cowdery's copy of the Book of Commandments bears a notation marking this revelation for inclusion in the 1835 Doctrine and Covenants. This version closely corresponds to the version in chapter 60 of the Book of Commandments, indicating that the latter was used as a source text for the former.

141

line 1
Verily this is fasting and prayer; or, in other words, rejoicing and prayer.

4 And inasmuch as ye do these things, with thanksgiving, with cheerful hearts, and countenances; not with much laughter, for this is sin, but with a glad heart and a cheerful countenance; verily I say, that inasmuch as ye do this the fulness of the earth is yours: the beasts of the fields, and the fowls of the air, and that which climbeth upon the trees, and walketh upon the earth: yea, and the herb, and the good things which cometh of the earth, whether for food or for raiment, or for houses or for barns, or for orchards, or for gardens, or for vineyards: yea, all things which cometh of the earth, in the season thereof, is made for the benefit and the use of man, both to please the eye, and to gladden the heart: yea, for food and for raiment, for taste, and for smell, to strengthen the body, and to enliven the soul.

5 And it pleaseth God that he hath given all these things unto man: for unto this end were they made, to be used with judgment, not to excess, neither by extortion: and in nothing doth man offend God, or against none is his wrath kindled, save those who confess not his hand in all things, and obey not his commandments. Behold this is according to the law and the prophets: wherefore trouble me no more concerning this matter, but learn that he who doeth the works of righteousness, shall receive his reward, even peace in this world, and eternal life in the world to come. I the Lord have spoken it and the Spirit beareth record. Amen.

SECTION XX.

Revelation given in Kirtland, August, 1831.

1 Hearken, O ye people, and open your hearts, and give ear from afar: and listen, you that call yourselves. the people of the Lord, and hear the word of the Lord, and his will concerning you: yea, verily, I say, hear the word of him whose anger is kindled against the wicked, and rebellious; who willeth to take even them whom he will take, and preserveth in life them whom he will preserve: who buildeth up at his own will and pleasure; and destroyeth when he please; and is able to cast the soul down to hell.

2 Behold I the Lord utter my voice, and it shall be obeyed. Wherefore verily I say, let the wicked take heed, and let the rebellious fear, and tremble. And let the unbelieving hold their lips, for the day of wrath shall come upon them as a whirlwind, and all flesh shall know that I am God. And he that seeketh signs shall see signs, but not unto salvation.

---

line 28. Revelation, 30 Aug. 1831 [D&C 63]. Oliver Cowdery's copy of the Book of Commandments bears a notation marking this revelation for inclusion in the 1835 Doctrine and Covenants. This version reflects editing marks made in Revelation Book 1 and in chapter 64 of the Cowdery volume, indicating that both were used as source texts for this version. (See *JSP,* MRB:181–189; and p. 635 herein.)

142

line 1

3 Verily I say unto you, there are those among you who seek signs: and there have been such even from the beginning. But behold, faith cometh not by signs, but signs follow those that believe. Yea, signs cometh by faith, not by the will of men, nor as they please, but by the will of God. Yea, signs cometh by faith, unto mighty works, for without faith, no man pleaseth God: and with whom God is angry, he is not well pleased: wherefore, unto such he showeth no signs, only in wrath unto their condemnation.

4 Wherefore I the Lord am not pleased with those among you, who have sought after signs and wonders for faith, and not for the good of men unto my glory: nevertheless, I gave commandments and many have turned away from my commandments, and have not kept them. There were among you adulterers and adulteresses; some of whom have turned away from you, and others remain with you: that hereafter shall be revealed. Let such beware and repent speedily, lest judgments shall come upon them as a snare, and their folly shall be made manifest, and their works shall follow them in the eyes of the people.

5 And verily I say unto you, as I have said before, he that looketh on a woman to lust after her, or if any shall commit adultery in their hearts, they shall not have the Spirit, but shall deny the faith and shall fear: wherefore I the Lord have said that the fearful, and the unbelieving, and all liars, and whosoever loveth and maketh a lie, and the whoremonger, and the sorcerer, shall have their part in that lake which burneth with fire and brimstone, which is the second death. Verily I say, that they shall not have part in the first resurrection.

6 And now behold, I the Lord saith unto you, that ye are not justified because these things are among you, nevertheless he that endureth in faith and doeth my will, the same shall overcome, and shall receive an inheritance upon the earth, when the day of transfiguration shall come; when the earth shall be transfigured, even according to the pattern which was shown unto mine apostles upon the mount: of which account the fulness ye have not yet received.

7 And now, verily I say unto you, that as I said that I would make known my will unto you, behold I will make it known unto you, not by the way of commandment, for there are many who observe not to keep my commandments, but unto him that keepeth my commandments, I will give the mysteries of my kingdom, and the same shall be in him a well of living water, springing up unto everlasting life.

8 And now, behold this is the will of the Lord your God concerning his saints, that they should assemble themselves to-

143

gether unto the land of Zion, not in haste, lest there should
be confusion, which bringeth pestilence. Behold the land of
Zion, I the Lord holdeth it in mine own hands: nevertheless,
I the Lord renderth unto Cæsar the things which are Cæsar's:
wherefore I the Lord willeth, that you should purchase the
lands, that you may have advantage of the world, that you
may have claim on the world, that they may not be stirred up
unto anger: for satan putteth it into their hearts to anger
against you, and to the shedding of blood: wherefore the land
of Zion shall not be obtained but by purchase, or by blood,
otherwise there is none inheritance for you. And if by purchase behold you are blessed; and if by blood, as you are forbidden to shed blood, lo, your enemies are upon you, and ye
shall be scourged from city to city, and from synagogue to
synagogue, and but few shall stand to receive an inheritance.
9 I the Lord am angry with the wicked; I am holding my
Spirit from the inhabitants of the earth. I have sworn in my
wrath and decreed wars upon the face of the earth, and the
wicked shall slay the wicked, and fear shall come upon every
man and the saints also shall hardly escape: nevertheless, I
the Lord am with them, and will come down in heaven from
the presence of my Father, and consume the wicked with unquenchable fire. And behold this is not yet, but by and by:
wherefore seeing that I the Lord have decreed all these things
upon the face of the earth, I willeth that my saints should be
assembled upon the land of Zion; and that every man should
take righteousness in his hands, and faithfulness upon his loins,
and lift a warning voice unto the inhabitants of the earth; and
declare both by word and by flight. that desolation shall come
upon the wicked. Wherefore let my disciples in Kirtland, arrange their temporal concerns, which dwell upon this farm.
10 Let my servant Titus Billings, who has the care thereof dispose of the land, that he may be prepared in the coming spring,
to take his journey up unto the land of Zion, with those that
dwell upon the face thereof, excepting those whom I shall reserve unto myself, that shall not go until I shall command them.
And let all the moneys which can be spared, it mattereth not
unto me whether it be little or much, sent up unto the land of
Zion, unto them whom I have appointed to receive.
11 Behold I the Lord will give unto my servants Joseph Smith,
Jr. power, that he shall be enabled to discern by the Spirit
those who shall go up unto the land of Zion, and those of my
disciples who shall tarry.
12 Let my servant Newel K. Whitney retain his store, or in
other words, the store yet for a little season. Nevertheless let
him impart all the money which he can impart, to be sent up un-

144

line 1
to the land of Zion. Behold these things are in his own hands, let him do according to wisdom. Verily I say, let him be ordained as an agent unto the disciples that shall tarry, and let him be ordained unto this power; and now speedily visit the churches, expounding these things unto them, with my servant Oliver Cowdery. Behold this is my will, obtaining moneys even as I have directed.

13 He that is faithful and endureth shall overcome the world. He that sendeth up treasures unto the land of Zion, shall receive an inheritance in this world, and his works shall follow him; and also, a reward in the world to come; yea, and blessed are the dead that die in the Lord from henceforth, when the Lord shall come and old things shall pass away, and all things become new, they shall rise from the dead and shall not die after, and shall receive an inheritance before the Lord, in the holy city, and he that liveth when the Lord shall come, and have kept the faith, blessed is he; nevertheless it is appointed to him to die at the age of man: wherefore children shall grow up until they become old, old men shall die; but they shall not sleep in the dust, but they shall be changed in the twinkling of an eye: wherefore, for this cause preached the apostles unto the world, the resurrection of the dead: these things are the things that ye must look for, and speaking after the manner of the Lord, they are now nigh at hand; and in a time to come, even in the day of the coming of the Son of man, and until that hour, there will be foolish virgins among the wise, and at that hour cometh an entire separation of the righteous and the wicked; and in that day will I send mine angels, to pluck out the wicked, and cast them into unquenchable fire.

14 And now behold, verily I say unto you, I the Lord am not pleased with my servant Sidney Rigdon, he exalted himself in his heart, and received not counsel, but grieved the Spirit: wherefore his writing is not acceptable unto the Lord, and he shall make another; and if the Lord receive it not, behold he standeth no longer in the office which I have appointed him.

15 And again, verily I say unto you, those who desire in their hearts, in meekness, to warn sinners to repentance, let them be ordained unto this power: for this is a day of warning, and not a day of many words. For I the Lord am not to be mocked in the last days. Behold I am from above, and my power lieth beneath. I am over all, and in all, and through all, and searcheth all things: and the day cometh that all things shall be subject unto me. Behold I am Alpha and Omega, even Jesus Christ. Wherefore let all men be-

145

line 1 ware, how they take my name in their lips: for behold verily I
say, that many there be who are under this condemnation;
who useth the name of the Lord, and useth it in vain, having
not authority. Wherefore let the church repent of their sins,
5 and I the Lord will own them, otherwise they shall be cut off.
16 Remember, that that which cometh from above is sacred,
and must be spoken with care, and by constraint of the Spirit,
and in this there is no condemnation; and ye receive the Spirit through prayer: wherefore without this, there remaineth
10 condemnation: Let my servant Joseph Smith, jr. and Sidney
Rigdon, seek them a home as they are taught through prayer,
by the Spirit. These things remain to overcome, through patience, that such may receive a more exceeding and eternal
weight of glory; otherwise, a greater condemnation: Amen.

15 ## SECTION XXI.

A Revelation given in Kirtland, September, 1831.

1 Behold, thus saith the Lord your God unto you, O ye elders
of my church, hearken ye, and hear, and receive my will concerning you: for verily I say unto you, I will that ye should
20 overcome the world: wherefore I will have compassion upon
you. There are those among you who have sinned; but verily
I say, for this once, for mine own glory, and for the salvation
of souls, I have forgiven you your sins.
2 I will be merciful unto you, for I have given unto you the
25 kingdom: and the keys of the mysteries of the kingdom, shall
not be taken from my servant Joseph Smith, jr. through the
means I have appointed, while he liveth, inasmuch as he
obeyeth mine ordinances. There are those who have sought
occasion against him without cause; nevertheless he has sin-
30 ned, but verily I say unto you, I the Lord forgiveth sins unto
those who confess their sins before me, and ask forgiveness,
who have not sinned unto death. My disciples, in days of
old, sought occasion against one another, and forgave not one
another in their hearts, and for this evil they were afflicted,
35 and sorely chastened: wherefore I say unto you, that ye ought
to forgive one another, for he that forgiveth not his brother
his trespasses, standeth condemned before the Lord, for there
remaineth in him the greater sin. I the Lord will forgive
whom I will forgive, but of you it is required to forgive all
40 men; and ye ought to say in your hearts, let God judge between me and thee, and reward thee according to thy deeds.
And he that repenteth not of his sins, and confesseth them

J

---

line 15. Revelation, 11 Sept. 1831 [D&C 64]. Oliver Cowdery's copy of the Book of Commandments bears a notation marking this revelation for inclusion in the 1835 Doctrine and Covenants. This version reflects editing marks made in Revelation Book 1, indicating that the latter was used as a source text for the former. (See *JSP,* MRB:189–195.)

line 43. This page begins the tenth gathering of the book. "J" is the first of two signature marks in this gathering; the second is on the recto of the following leaf. These marks were used in collating the gatherings after the sheets were folded.

146

line 1
not, then ye shall bring him before the church, and do, with him as the Scriptures saith unto you, either by commandment, or by revelation. And this ye shall do that God might be glorified, not because ye forgive not, having not compassion, but that ye may be justified in the eyes of the law, that ye may not offend him who is your Lawgiver.

3 Verily I say, for this cause ye shall do these things. Behold I the Lord was angry with him who was my servant Ezra Booth; and also, my servant Isaac Morley; for they kept not the law, neither the commandment; they sought evil in their hearts, and I the Lord withheld my Spirit. They condemned for evil, that thing in which there was no evil; nevertheless I have forgiven my servant Isaac Morley. And also my servant Edward Partridge, behold he hath sinned, and satan seeketh to destroy his soul; but when these things are made known unto them, they repent of the evil, and they shall be forgiven.

4 And now verily I say, that it is expedient in me that my servant Sidney Gilbert, after a few weeks, should return upon his business, and to his agency in the land of Zion; and that which he hath seen and heard may be made known unto my disciples, that they perish not. And for this cause have I spoken these things. And again, I say unto you, that my servant Isaac Morley may not be tempted above that which he is able to bear, and counsel wrongfully to your hurt, I gave commandment that this farm should be sold. I willeth not that my servant Frederick G. Williams should sell his farm, for I the Lord willeth to retain a strong hold in the land of Kirtland, for the space of five years, in the which I will not overthrow the wicked, that thereby I may save some; and after that day, I the Lord will not hold any guilty, that shall go, with an open heart. up to the land of Zion: for I the Lord requireth the hearts of the children of men.

5 Behold now it is called to-day, (until the coming of the Son of man) and verily it is a day of sacrifice, and a day for the tithing of my people; for he that is tithed shall not be burned (at his coming;) for after to-day cometh the burning: this is speaking after the manner of the Lord; for verily I say, to-morrow all the proud and they that do wickedly shall be as stubble: and I will burn them up, for I am the Lord of hosts; and I will not spare any that remaineth in Babylon. Wherefore, if ye believe me, ye will labor while it is called to-day.— And it is not meet that my servants, Newel K. Whitney and Sidney Gilbert should sell their store, and their possessions here, for this is not wisdom until the residue of the church, which remaineth in this place, shall go up unto the land of Zion.

147

6 Behold it is said in my laws, or forbidden to get in debt to thine enemies; but behold it is not said at any time, that the Lord should not take when he please, and pay as seemeth him good: wherefore as ye are agents, and ye are on the Lord's errand; and whatever ye do according to the will of the Lord, is the Lord's business, and he hath set you to provide for his saints in these last days, that they may obtain an inheritance in the land of Zion; and behold I the Lord declare unto you, and my words are sure and shall not fail, that they shall obtain it; but all things must come to pass in their time; wherefore be not weary in well doing, for ye are laying the foundation of a great work. And out of small things proceedeth that which is great.

7 Behold the Lord requireth the heart and a willing mind; and the willing and obedient shall eat the good of the land of Zion in these last days; and the rebellious shall be cut off out of the land of Zion, and shall be sent away and shall not inherit the land: for verily I say that the rebellious are not of the blood of Ephraim, wherefore they shall be plucked out. Behold I the Lord have made my church in these last days, like unto a judge sitting on an hill, or in an high place, to judge the nations: for it shall come to pass, that the inhabitants of Zion shall judge all things pertaining to Zion: and liars, and hypocrites shall be proved by them, and they who are not apostles and prophets shall be known.

8 And even the bishop, who is a judge, and his counsellors, if they are not faithful in their stewardships, shall be condemned, and others shall be planted in their stead: for behold I say unto you that Zion shall flourish, and the glory of the Lord shall be upon her, and she shall be an ensign unto the people: and there shall come unto her out of every nation under heaven. And the day shall come, when the nations of the earth shall tremble because of her, and shall fear because of her terrible ones: the Lord hath spoken it: Amen.

SECTION XXII.

A Revelation, given November, 1831, to Orson Hyde, Luke Johnson, Lyman Johnson and William E. McLellin. The mind and will of the Lord, as made known by the voice of the Spirit to a conference concerning certain elders; and also certain items, as made known, in addition to the covenants and commandments.

1 My servant, Orson Hyde, was called, by his ordinance, to proclaim the everlasting gospel, by the Spirit of the living God,

10*

---

line 35. Revelation, 1 Nov. 1831–A [D&C 68]. Revelation Book 1 bears a notation marking this revelation for inclusion in the 1835 Doctrine and Covenants. This version closely corresponds to the version in the October 1832 issue of *Evening and Morning Star* (printed June 1835), suggesting that the latter was used as a source text for the former. (See *JSP,* MRB:199.)

148

from people to people, and from land to land, in the congregations of the wicked, in their synagogues, reasoning with and
expounding all scriptures unto them: and behold and lo, this
is an ensample unto all those who were ordained unto this
priesthood, whose mission is appointed unto them to go forth:
and this is the ensample unto them, that they shall speak as
they are moved upon by the Holy Ghost; and whatsoever they
shall speak when moved upon by the Holy Ghost, shall be
scripture; shall be the will of the Lord; shall be the mind of
the Lord; shall be the word of the Lord; shall be the voice of
the Lord, and the power of God unto salvation; behold this
is the promise of the Lord unto you, O ye my servants: wherefore, be of good cheer, and do not fear, for I the Lord am with
you, and will stand by you; and ye shall bear record of me
even Jesus Christ, that I am the Son of the living God; that
I was; that I am; and that I am to come. This is the word of
the Lord unto you my servant, Orson Hyde; and also unto
my servant, Luke Johnson, and unto my servant, Lyman
Johnson, and unto my servant, William E. McLellin; and unto all the faithful elders of my church: Go ye into all the
world; preach the gospel to every creature; acting in the authority which I have given you; baptizing in the name of the
Father, and of the Son, and of the Holy Ghost, and he that
believeth, and is baptized, shall be saved, and he that believeth
not shall be damned; and he that believeth shall be blessed
with signs following, even as it is written: and unto you it
shall be given to know the signs of the times, and the signs of
the coming of the Son of man; and of as many as the Father
shall bear record, to you it shall be given power to seal them
up unto eternal life: Amen.

2 And now concerning the items in addition to the covenants
and commandments, they are these: There remaineth hereafter
in the due time of the Lord, other bishops to be set apart unto the church to minister even according to the first: wherefore they shall be high priests who are worthy, and they shall
be appointed by the first presidency of the Melchizedek priesthood, except they be literal descendants of Aaron; and if they
be literal descendants of Aaron, they have a legal right to the
bishopric, if they are the first born among the sons of Aaron:
for the first born holds the right of presidency over this priesthood, and the keys or authority of the same. No man has a
legal right to this office, to hold the keys of this priesthood,
except he be a literal descendant and the first born of Aaron:
but as a high priest of the Melchizedek priesthood, has authority to officiate in all the lesser offices, he may officiate in the
office of bishop when no literal descendant of Aaron can be

149

found; provided he is called and set apart, and ordained unto this power under the hands of the first presidency of the Melchizedek priesthood. And a literal descendant of Aaron, also, must be designated by this presidency, and found worthy, and anointed, and ordained under the hands of this presidency, otherwise they are not legally authorized to officiate in their priesthood: but by virtue of the decree concerning their right of the priesthood descending from father to son, they may claim their annointing, if at any time they can prove their lineage, or do ascertain it by revelation from the Lord under the hands of the above named presidency.

3 And again, no bishop or high priest, who shall be set apart for this ministry, shall be tried or condemned for any crime save it be before the first presidency of the church; and inasmuch as he is found guilty before this presidency, by testimony that cannot be impeached, he shall be condemned, and if he repents he shall be forgiven, according to the covenants and commandments of the church.

4 And again, inasmuch as parents have children in Zion, or in any of her stakes which are organized, that teach them not to understand the doctrine of repentance; faith in Christ the Son of the living God; and of baptism and the gift of the Holy Ghost by the laying on of the hands, when eight years old, the sin be upon the head of the parents, for this shall be a law unto the inhabitants of Zion, or in any of her stakes which are organized: and their children shall be baptized for the remission of their sins when eight years old, and receive the laying on of the hands: and they shall also teach their children to pray, and to walk uprightly before the Lord. And the inhabitants of Zion shall also observe the Sabbath day to keep it holy. And the inhabitants of Zion, also, shall remember their labors, inasmuch as they are appointed to labor, in all faithfulness, for the idler shall be had in remembrance before the Lord. Now I the Lord am not well pleased with the inhabitants of Zion, for there are idlers among them; and their children are also growing up in wickedness: They also seek not earnestly the riches of eternity, but their eyes are full of greediness. These things ought not to be, and must be done away from among them: wherefore let my servant Oliver Cowdery, carry these sayings unto the land of Zion. And a commandment I give unto them, that he that observeth not his prayers before the Lord in the season thereof, let him be had in remembrance before the judge of my people. These sayings are true and faithful: wherefore transgress them not, neither take therefrom. Behold I am Alpha and Omega, and I come quickly: Amen.

150

line 1

SECTION XXIII.

Revelation given May, 1831.

1 Hearken unto me, saith the Lord your God, and I will speak unto my servant Edward Partridge, and give unto him directions: for it must needs be that he receive directions how to organize this people: for it must needs be that they are organized according to my laws, if otherwise they will be cut off: wherefore let my servant Edward Partridge, and those whom he has chosen, in whom I am well pleased, appoint unto this people their portion, every man equal according to their families, according to their circumstances, and their wants and needs; and let my servant Edward Partridge, when he shall appoint a man his portion, give unto him a writing that shall secure unto him his portion, that he shall hold it, even this right and this inheritance in the church, until he transgresses and is not accounted worthy by the voice of the church, according to the laws and covenants of the church, to belong to the church: and if he shall transgress, and is not accounted worthy to belong in the church, he shall not have power to claim that portion which he has consecrated unto the bishop for the poor and the needy of my church: therefore, he shall not retain the gift, but shall only have claim on that portion that is deeded unto him. And thus, all things shall be made sure according to the laws of the land.

2 And let that which belongs to this people, be appointed unto this people; and the money which is left unto this people, let there be an agent appointed unto this people, to take the money to provide food and raiment, according to the wants of this people. And let every man deal honestly, and be alike among this people, and receive alike, that ye may be one, even as I have commanded you.

3 And let that which belongeth to this people not be taken and given unto that of another church; wherefore if another church would receive money of this church, let them pay unto this church again according as they shall agree; and this shall be done through the bishop or the agent, which shall be appointed by the voice of the church.

4 And again, let the bishop appoint a storehouse unto this church, and let all things, both in money and in meat, which is more than is needful for the want of this people, be kept in the hands of the bishop. And let him also reserve unto himself, for his own wants, and for the wants of his family, as he shall be employed in doing this business. And thus I grant unto this people a privilege of organizing themselves according

---

line 1. Revelation, 20 May 1831 [D&C 51]. This version reflects editing marks made in Revelation Book 1, indicating that the latter was used as a source text for the former. (See *JSP*, MRB:145–147.)

151

line 1

to my laws; and I consecrate unto them this land for a little season, until I the Lord shall provide for them otherwise, and command them to go hence; and the hour and the day is not given unto them: wherefore let them act upon this land as for

5 years; and this shall turn unto them for their good.

5 Behold, this shall be an example unto my servant Edward Partridge, in other places, in all churches. And whoso is found a faithful, a just and a wise steward, shall enter into the joy of his Lord, and shall inherit eternal life. Verily I say unto

10 you, I am Jesus Christ, who cometh quickly, in an hour you think not: even so. Amen.

SECTION XXIV.

Revelation on prayer, given October, 1831.

1 Hearken, and lo, a voice as of one sent down from on high,

15 who is mighty and powerful, whose going forth is unto the ends of the earth; yea, whose voice is unto men, Prepare ye the way of the Lord make his paths straight. The keys of the kingdom of God are committed unto man on the earth, and from thence shall the gospel roll forth unto the ends of

20 the earth, as the stone which is cut out of the mountain without hands shall roll forth, until it has filled the whole earth; yea, a voice crying, Prepare ye the way of the Lord, prepare ye the supper of the Lamb, make ready for the bridegroom; pray unto the Lord; call upon his holy name; make known his

25 wonderful works among the people, call upon the Lord, that his kingdom may go forth upon the earth; that the inhabitants thereof may receive it, and be prepared for the days to come, in the which the Son of man shall come down in heaven, clothed in the brightness of his glory, to meet the kingdom of

30 God which is set up on the earth: wherefore, may the kingdom of God go forth, that the kingdom of heaven may come, that thou O God may be glorified in heaven, so on earth, that thy enemies may be subdued; for thine is the honor, power and glory, forever and ever: Amen.

35 ### SECTION XXV.

Revelation given November, 1831.

1 Behold, and hearken, O ye elders of my church, who have assembled yourselves together, whose prayers I have heard, and whose hearts I know, and whose desires have come up be-

40 ... mine eyes are upon you: and the

---

line 12. Revelation, 30 Oct. 1831 [D&C 65]. Revelation Book 1 bears notations marking both revelations that begin on this page (sections 24 and 25) for inclusion in the 1835 Doctrine and Covenants. Section 24 reflects editing marks made in Revelation Book 1 and closely corresponds to the version in the September 1832 issue of *Evening and Morning Star* (printed Apr. 1835), suggesting that both were used as source texts for the version printed here. (See *JSP,* MRB:197.)

line 35. Revelation, 2 Nov. 1831 [D&C 67]. This version reflects editing marks made in Revelation Book 1, indicating that the latter was used as a source text for the former. (See *JSP,* MRB:201–203.)

line 40. The last lines on this page and on page 154—adjacent pages on the unfolded sheet—were incompletely inked, resulting in missing text. The text of the last line, as transcribed from a different copy of the volume, reads: "fore me. Behold and lo, mine eyes are upon you; and the".

152

line 1 heavens and the earth are in mine hands, and the riches of
eternity are mine to give. Ye endeavored to believe that ye
should receive the blessing which was offered unto you, but
behold, verily I say unto you, there were fears in your hearts;
5 and verily this is the reason that ye did not receive.

2 And now I the Lord give unto you a testimony of the truth
of these commandments which are lying before you: your eyes
have been upon my servant Joseph Smith, jr.: and his language you have known; and his imperfections you have known;
10 and you have sought in your hearts knowledge, that you might
express beyond his language: this you also know: now seek
ye out of the book of commandments, even the least that is
among them, and appoint him that is the most wise among
you; or if there be any among you, that shall make one like
15 unto it, then ye are justified in saying that ye do not know
that they are true: but if ye cannot make one like unto it, ye
are under condemnation if ye do not bear record that they are
true: for ye know that there is no unrighteousness in them;
and that which is righteous cometh down from above, from the
20 Father of lights.

3 And again, verily I say unto you, that it is your privilege,
and a promise I give unto you that have been ordained unto
this ministry, that inasmuch as you strip yourselves from
jealousies and fears, and humble yourselves before me, for ye
25 are not sufficiently humble, the vail shall be rent and you shall
see me and know that I am; not with the carnal, neither natural mind, but with the spiritual; for no man has seen God
at any time in the flesh, except quickened by the Spirit of
God: neither can any natural man abide the presence of God;
30 neither after the carnal mind; ye are not able to abide the presence of God now, neither the ministering of angels: wherefore continue in patience until ye are perfected.

4 Let not your minds turn back; and when ye are worthy,
in mine own due time, ye shall see and know that which was
35 conferred upon you by the hands of my servant Joseph Smith,
jr. Amen.

SECTION XXVI.

Revelation given November, 1831.

1 Behold and hearken, O ye inhabitants of Zion, and all ye
40 people of my church, who are far off, and hear the word of the
Lord which I give unto my servant Joseph Smith, jr. ; and
also unto my servant Martin Harris; and also unto my servant Oliver Cowdery; and also unto my servant John Whit-

---

line 37. Revelation, 12 Nov. 1831 [D&C 70]. Revelation Book 1 bears a notation marking this revelation
for inclusion in the 1835 Doctrine and Covenants. This version reflects editing marks made in Revelation
Book 1, indicating that the latter was used as a source text for the former. (See *JSP,* MRB:221–223.)

153

line 1   , and also unto my servant Sidney Rigdon; and also unto my servant Wm. W. Phelps: by the way of commandment unto them, for I give unto them a commandment: wherefore hearken and hear, for thus saith the Lord unto them, I the

5   Lord have appointed them, and ordained them to be stewards over the revelations, and commandments which I have given unto them, and which I shall hereafter give unto them; and an account of this stewardship will I require of them in the day of judgment: wherefore I have appointed unto them, and

10   this is their business in the church of God, to manage them and the concerns thereof, yea, the benefits thereof:

2 Wherefore a commandment I give unto them, that they shall not give these things unto the church, neither unto the world, nevertheless, inasmuch as they receive more than is

15   needful for their necessities, and their wants, it shall be given into my storehouse, and the benefits shall be consecrated unto the inhabitants of Zion, and unto their generations, inasmuch as they become heirs according to the laws of the kingdom.

20   3 Behold this is what the Lord requires of every man in his stewardship; even as I the Lord have appointed, or shall hereafter appoint unto any man. And behold none are exempt from this law who belong to the church of the living God; yea, neither the bishop, neither the agent, who keepeth the

25   Lord's storehouse; neither he who is appointed in a stewardship over temporal things: He who is appointed to administer spiritual things, the same is worthy of his hire, even as those who are appointed to a stewardship, to administer temporal things; yea, even more abundantly, which abund-

30   ance is multiplied unto them through the manifestations of the Spirit: nevertheless, in your temporal things you shall be equal, and this not grudgingly, otherwise the abundance of the manifestations of the Spirit, shall be withheld.

4 Now this commandment I give unto my servants for their

35   benefit while they remain, for a manifestation of my blessings upon their heads, and for a reward of their diligence; and for their security for food and for raiment, for an inheritance; for houses and for lands, in whatsoever circumstances I the Lord shall place them, and whithersoever I the Lord shall send

40   them: for they have been faithful over many things, and have done well inasmuch as they have not sinned. Behold I the Lord am merciful and will bless them, and they shall enter into the joy of these things: even so. Amen.

---

line 1. The missing text, as transcribed from a different copy of the volume, reads "mer;" (a continuation of the name "Whitmer" from the previous page).

154

line 1

SECTION XXVII.

Revelation given in Zion, July, 1831.

1 Hearken, O ye elders of my church, saith the Lord your God, who have assembled yourselves together, according to my commandments, in this land which is the land of Missouri, which is the land which I have appointed and consecrated for the gathering of the saints: wherefore this is the land of promise, and the place for the city of Zion. And thus saith the Lord your God, if you will receive wisdom here is wisdom.— Behold the place which is now called Independence, is the center place, and the spot for the temple is lying westward upon a lot which is not far from the court house: wherefore it is wisdom that the land should be purchased by the saints; and also every tract lying westward, even unto the line running directly between Jew and Gentile. And also every tract bordering by the prairies, inasmuch as my disciples are enabled to buy lands. Behold this is wisdom, that they may obtain it for an everlasting inheritance.

2 And let my servant Sidney Gilbert, stand in the office which I have appointed him, to receive moneys, to be an agent unto the church, to buy land in all the regions round about, inasmuch as can be in righteousness, and as wisdom shall direct.

3 And let my servant Edward Partridge, stand in the office which I have appointed him, to divide the saints their inheritance, even as I have commanded: and also those whom he has appointed to assist him.

4 And again, verily I say unto you, let my servant Sidney Gilbert plant himself in this place, and establish a store, that he may sell goods without fraud, that he may obtain money to buy lands for the good of the saints; and that he may obtain whatsoever things the disciples may need to plant them in their inheritance. And also let my servant Sidney Gilbert obtain a licence, (behold here is wisdom, and whoso readeth let him understand,) that he may send goods also unto the people, even by whom he will as clerks, employed in his service, and thus provide for my saints, that my gospel may be preached unto those who sit in darkness and in the region and shadow of death.

5 And again, verily I say unto you, let my servant William W. Phelps be planted in this place, and be established as a printer unto the church: and lo, if the world receiveth his writings, (behold here is wisdom,) let him obtain whatsoever he can obtain in righteousness, for the good of the ....

line 1
5
10
15
20
25
30
35
40

---

line 1. Revelation, 20 July 1831 [D&C 57]. Revelation Book 1 bears a notation marking this revelation for inclusion in the 1835 Doctrine and Covenants. This version reflects editing marks made in Revelation Book 1, indicating that the latter was used as a source text for the former. (See *JSP,* MRB:159–161.)

line 44. The last lines on this page and on page 151—adjacent pages on the unfolded sheet—were incompletely inked, resulting in missing text. The text of the last line, as transcribed from a different copy of the volume, reads: "can obtain in righteousness, for the good of the saints. And".

155

line 1　let my servant Oliver Cowdery assist him, even as I have commanded, in whatsoever place I shall appoint unto him, to copy, and to correct, and select, that all things may be right before me, as it shall be proved by the Spirit through him.—

5　And thus let those of whom I have spoken, be planted in the land of Zion, as speedily as can be, with their families, to do those things even as I have spoken.

6 And now concerning the gathering, let the bishop and the agent make preparations for those families which have been

10　commanded to come to this land, as soon as possible, and plant them in their inheritance. And unto the residue of both elders and members, further directions shall be given hereafter: even so. Amen.

SECTION XXVIII.

15　*Revelation given November, 1831.*

1 Hearken unto me, saith the Lord your God, for my servant Oliver Cowdery's sake, it is not wisdom in me that he should be entrusted with the commandments and the moneys which he shall carry unto the land of Zion, except one go with him

20　who will be true and faithful: wherefore I the Lord willeth that my servant John Whitmer, should go with my servant Oliver Cowdery. And also that he shall continue in writing and making a history of all the important things which he shall observe and know. concerning my church, and also that

25　he receive counsel and assistance from my servant Oliver Cowdery, and others.

2 And also, my servants who are abroad in the earth, should send forth the accounts of their stewardships to the land of Zion; for the land of Zion shall be a seat and a place to re-

30　ceive and do all these things; nevertheless, let my servant John Whitmer travel many times from place to place, and from church to church, that he may the more easily obtain knowledge: preaching and expounding, writing, copying, se-lecting and obtaining all things which shall be for the good of

35　the church, and for the rising generations, that shall grow up on the land of Zion, to possess it from generation to gen-eration, forever and ever. Amen.

---

line 14. Revelation, 11 Nov. 1831–A [D&C 69]. Revelation Book 1 bears a notation marking this revela-tion for inclusion in the 1835 Doctrine and Covenants. This version reflects editing marks made in Revelation Book 1, indicating that the latter was used as a source text for the former. (See *JSP,* MRB:217.)

156

line 1

SECTION XXIX.

A Revelation to Joseph Smith, jr. and Sidney Rigdon, January, 1832. The word of the Lord unto them concerning the elders of the church of the living God, established in the last days, making known the will of the Lord unto the elders, what they shall do until conference.

1 For verily thus saith the Lord, it is expedient in me, that they should continue preaching the gospel, and in exhortation to the churches, in the regions round about, until conference: and then behold it shall be made known unto them, by the voice of the conference, their several missions.

2 Now verily I say unto you, my servants Joseph Smith, jr. and Sidney Rigdon, saith the Lord, it is expedient to translate again, and inasmuch as it is practicable, to preach in the regions round about until conference, and after that it is expedient to continue the work of translation, until it be finished. And let this be a pattern unto the elders until further knowledge, even as it is written. Now I give no more unto you at this time. Gird up your loins and be sober: even so. Amen.

ON PRIESTHOOD AND CALLING.

SECTION XXX.

Revelation to Joseph Smith, jr. given July, 1828, concerning certain manuscripts on the first part of the book of Mormon, which had been taken from the possession of Martin Harris.

1 The works, and the designs, and the purposes of God, cannot be frustrated, neither can they come to nought, for God doth not walk in crooked paths: neither doth he turn to the right hand nor to the left; neither doth he vary from that which he hath said: therefore his paths are strait and his course is one eternal round.

2 Remember, remember, that it is not the work of God that is frustrated, but the work of men: for although a man may have many revelations, and have power to do many mighty works, yet, if he boasts in his own strength, and sets at nought the counsels of God, and follows after the dictates of his own will, and carnal desires, he must fall and incur the vengeance of a just God upon him.

3 Behold, you have been intrusted with these things, but how strict were your commandments; and remember, also, the promises which were made to you, if you did not transgress

line markers: 1, 5, 10, 15, 20, 25, 30, 35, 40

---

line 1. Revelation, 10 Jan. 1832 [D&C 73]. Revelation Book 1 bears a notation marking this revelation for inclusion in the 1835 Doctrine and Covenants. The source text for this version is unknown. (See *JSP*, MRB:269.)

line 21. Revelation, July 1828 [D&C 3]. This version reflects editing marks made in chapter 2 of Oliver Cowdery's copy of the Book of Commandments, indicating that the latter was used as a source text for the former. (See p. 601 herein.)

157

line 1

them; and behold, how oft you have transgressed the commandments and the laws of God, and have gone on in the persuasions of men: for behold, you should not have feared man more than God, although men set at nought the counsels of God, and despise his words, yet you should have been faithful and he would have extended his arm, and supported you against all the fiery darts of the adversary; and he would have been with you in every time of trouble.

4 Behold thou art Joseph, and thou wast chosen to do the work of the Lord, but because of transgression, if thou art not aware thou wilt fall, but remember God is merciful: therefore, repent of that which thou hast done, which is contrary to the commandment which I gave you, and thou art still chosen, and art again called to the work; except thou do this, thou shalt be delivered up and become as other men, and have no more gift.

5 And when thou deliveredst up that which God had given thee sght and power to translate, thou deliveredst up that which was sacred, into the hands of a wicked man, who has set at nought the counsels of God, and has broken the most sacred promises, which were made before God, and has depended upon his own judgment, and boasted in his own wisdom, and this is the reason that thou hast lost thy privileges for a season, for thou hast suffered the counsel of thy director to be trampled upon from the beginning.

6 Nevertheless my work shall go forth, for, inasmuch as the knowledge of a Savior has come unto the world, through the testimony of the Jews, even so shall the knowledge of a Savior come unto my people; and to the Nephites, and the Jacobites, and the Josephites, and the Zoramites, through the testimony of their fathers; and this testimony shall come to the knowledge of the Lamanites, and the Lemuelites, and the Ishmaelites, who dwindled in unbelief because of the iniquity of their fathers, whom the Lord has suffered to destroy their brethren the Nephites, because of their iniquities and their abominations: and for this very purpose are these plates preserved which contain these records, that the promises of the Lord might be fulfilled, which he made to his people: and that the Lamanites might come to the knowledge of their fathers, and that they might know the promises of the Lord, and that they may believe the gospel and rely upon the merits of Jesus Christ, and be glorified through faith in his name; and that through their repentance they might be saved: Amen.

158

line 1

SECTION XXXI.

Revelation to Joseph Smith, Sen., given February, 1829.

1 Now, behold, a marvellous work is about to come forth
among the children of men, therefore, O ye that embark in
the service of God, see that ye serve him with all your heart,
might, mind and strength, that ye may stand blameless before
God at the last day: therefore, if ye have desires to serve God,
ye are called to the work, for behold the field is white already
to harvest, and lo, he that thrusteth in his sickle with his
might, the same layeth up in store that he perish not, but
bringeth salvation to his soul, and faith, hope, charity, and
love, with an eye single to the glory of God, qualifies him for
the work.
2 Remember faith, virtue, knowledge, temperance, patience,
brotherly kindness, godliness, charity, humility, diligence.—
Ask and ye shall receive, knock and it shall be opened unto
you. Amen.

SECTION XXXII.

Revelation given March, 1829.

1 Behold I say unto you, that as my servant Martin Harris
has desired a witness at my hand, that you, my servant Joseph
Smith, jr. have got the plates of which you have testified and
borne record that you have received of me: and now behold,
this shall you say unto him, He who spake unto you said unto
you, I the Lord am God, and have given these things unto
you, my servant Joseph Smith, jr. and have commanded you
that you shall stand as a witness of these things, and I have
caused you that you should enter into a covenant with me
that you should not show them except to those persons to
whom I command you; and you have no power over them except I grant it unto you. And you have a gift to translate the
plates; and this is the first gift that I bestowed upon you, and
I have commanded that you should pretend to no other gift
until my purpose is fulfilled in this; for I will grant unto you
no other gift until it is finished.
2. Verily I say unto you, that wo shall come unto the inhabitants of the earth if they will not hearken unto my words: for
hereafter you shall be ordained and go forth and deliver my
words unto the children of men. Behold if they will not believe my words, they would not believe you, my servant Joseph, if it were possible that you could show them all these

---

line 1. Revelation, Feb. 1829 [D&C 4]. This version reflects editing marks made in chapter 3 of Oliver Cowdery's copy of the Book of Commandments, indicating that the latter was used as a source text for the former. (See p. 601 herein.)

line 18. Revelation, Mar. 1829 [D&C 5]. This version reflects editing marks made in chapter 4 of Oliver Cowdery's copy of the Book of Commandments, indicating that the latter was used as a source text for the former. (See pp. 602–603 herein.)

159

line 1

things which I have committed unto you. O this unbelieving
and stiffnecked generation, mine anger is kindled against them.

3 Behold verily, I say unto you, I have reserved those things
which I have entrusted unto you, my servant Joseph, for a
wise purpose in me, and it shall be made known unto future
generations; but this generation shall have my word through
you; and in addition to your testimony the testimony of three
of my servants, whom I shall call and ordain, unto whom I
will show these things: and they shall go forth with my words
that are given through you, yea, they shall know of a surety
that these things are true: for from heaven will I declare it
unto them: I will give them power that they may behold and
view these things as they are; and to none else will I grant
this power, to receive this same testimony, among this generation, in this, the beginning of the rising up, and the coming
forth of my church out of the wilderness—clear as the moon
and fair as the sun, and terrible as an army with banners. And
the testimony of three witnesses will I send forth of my word;
and behold whosoever believeth on my words them will I visit
with the manifestation of my Spirit and they shall be born of
me, even of water and of the Spirit. And you must wait yet
a little while; for ye are not yet ordained—and their testimony shall also go forth unto the condemnation of this generation if they harden their hearts against them: for a desolating
scourge shall go forth among the inhabitants of the earth, and
shall continue to be poured out, from time to time, if they repent not, until the earth is empty, and the inhabitants thereof
are consumed away, and utterly destroyed by the brightness of
my coming. Behold, I tell you these things even as I also
told the people of the destruction of Jerusalem, and my word
shall be verified at this time as it hath hitherto been verified.

4 And now I command you, my servant Joseph, to repent
and walk more uprightly before me, and yield to the persuasions of men no more; and that you be firm in keeping the
commandments wherewith I have commanded you, and if you
do this, behold I grant unto you eternal life, even if you should
be slain.

5 And now again I speak unto you, my servant Joseph, concerning the man that desires the witness: Behold I say unto
him he exalts himself and does not humble himself sufficiently
before me: but if he will bow down before me, and humble
himself in mighty prayer and faith, in the sincerity of his
heart, then will I grant unto him a view of the things which
he desires to see. And then he shall say unto the people of
this generation, behold I have seen the things which the Lord
has shown unto Joseph Smith, jr. and I know of a surety that

160

line 1 they are true, for I have seen them: for they have been shown
unto me by the power of God and not of man. And I the
Lord command him, my servant Martin Harris, that he shall
say no more unto them concerning these things, except he
5 shall say I have seen them, and they have been shown unto
me by the power of God: and these are the words which he
shall say. But if he deny this he will break the covenant
which he has before covenanted with me, and behold he is
condemned. And now except he humble himself and ac-
10 knowledge unto me the things that he has done which are
wrong, and covenant with me that he will keep my commandments, and exercise faith in' me, behold, I say unto him, he
shall have no such views; for I will grant unto him no views
of the things of which I have spoken. And if this be the
15 case I command you, my servant Joseph, that you shall say
unto him, that he shall do no more, nor trouble me any more
concerning this matter.
6 And if this be the case, behold I say unto thee Joseph,
when thou hast translated a few more pages thou shalt stop
20 for a season, even until I command thee again: then thou
mayest translate again. And except thou do this, behold
thou shalt have no more gift, and I will take away the things
which I have intrusted with thee. And now because I foresee
the lying in wait to destroy thee: yea, I foresee that if my
25 servant Martin Harris humbleth not himself, and receive a
witness from my hand, that he will fall into transgression; and
there are many that lie in wait to destroy thee from off the
face of the earth: and for this cause, that thy days may be
prolonged, I have given unto thee these commandments:
30 yea, for this cause I have said, stop and stand still until I
command thee, and I will provide means whereby thou mayest accomplish the thing which I have commanded thee; and
if thou art faithful in keeping my commandments, thou shalt
be lifted up at the last day. Amen.

35 ## SECTION XXXIII.

*A Revelation given to Joseph Smith, jr. and Oliver Cowdery, in
Harmony, Pennsylvania, April, 1829, when they desired to
know whether John, the beloved disciple, tarried on earth.—
Translated from parchment, written and hid up by himself.*

40 1 And the Lord said unto me, John, my beloved, what desirest thou? For if ye shall ask, what you will, it shall be
granted unto you. And I said unto him, Lord, give unto me
power over death, that I may live and bring souls unto thee.

---

line 35. Account of John, Apr. 1829–C [D&C 7]. This version reflects editing marks made in chapter 6
of Oliver Cowdery's copy of the Book of Commandments, indicating that the latter was used as a source
text for the former. (See p. 604 herein.)

161

line 1 {And the Lord said unto me, Verily, verily, I say unto thee,
because thou desiredst this thou shalt tarry until I come in my
glory, and shall prophesy before nations, kindreds, tongues
and people.

5 2 And for this cause the Lord said unto Peter, If I will that
he tarry till I come, what is that to thee? For he desiredst of
me that he might bring souls unto me; but thou desiredst that
thou might speedily come unto me in my kingdom. I say unto thee, Peter, this was a good desire, but my beloved has de-

10 sired that he might do more, or a greater work, yet among
men than what he has before done; yea, he has undertaken a
greater work; therefore, I will make him as flaming fire and a
ministering angel: he shall minister for those who shall be
heirs of salvation who dwell on the earth; and I will make

15 thee to minister for him and for thy brother James: and unto
you three I will give this power and the keys of this ministry
until I come.

3 Verily I say unto you, ye shall both have according to your
desires, for ye both joy in that which ye have desired.

20 **SECTION XXXIV.**

Revelation given April, 1829.

1 Oliver Cowdery, verily, verily I say unto you, that assuredly as the Lord liveth, who is your God and your Redeemer,
even so sure shall you receive a knowledge of whatsoever

25 things you shall ask in faith, with an honest heart, believing
that you shall receive a knowledge concerning the engravings
of old records, which are ancient, which contain those parts of
my scripture of which have been spoken, by the manifestation
of my Spirit; yea, behold I will tell you in your mind and in

30 your heart by the Holy Ghost, which shall come upon you
and which shall dwell in your heart

2 Now, behold this is the Spirit of Revelation: behold this
is the Spirit by which Moses brought the children of Israel
through the Red sea on dry ground: therefore this is thy gift;

35 apply unto it and blessed art thou, for it shall deliver you out
of the hands of your enemies, when, if it were not so, they
would slay you and bring your soul to destruction.

3 O remember these words, and keep my commandments.—
Remember this is your gift. Now this is not all thy gift; for

40 you have another gift, which is the gift of Aaron: behold it
has told you many things: behold there is no other power save
the power of God that can cause this gift of Aaron to be with

K

---

line 20. Revelation, Apr. 1829–B [D&C 8]. This version reflects editing marks made in chapter 7 of Oliver Cowdery's copy of the Book of Commandments, indicating that the latter was used as a source text for the former. (See pp. 604–605 herein.)

line 43. This page begins the eleventh gathering of the book. "K" is the first of two signature marks in this gathering; the second is on the recto of the following leaf. These marks were used in collating the gatherings after the sheets were folded.

162

you; therefore, doubt not, for it is the gift of God, and you
shall hold it in your hands, and do marvelous works; and no
power shall be able to take it away out of your hands; for it is
the work of God.   And therefore, whatsoever you shall ask
me to tell you by that means, that will I grant unto you and
you shall have knowledge concerning it: remember, that without faith you can do nothing.   Therefore, ask in faith.   Trifle
not with these things: do not ask for that which you ought
not: ask that you may know the mysteries of God, and that
you may translate and receive knowledge from all those ancient records which have been hid up, that are sacred, and according to your faith shall it be done unto you.   Behold, it is
I that have spoken it: and I am the same who spake unto you
from the beginning.   Amen.

SECTION XXXV.

Revelation given to Oliver Cowdery, April, 1829.

1 Behold I say unto you, my son, that because you did not
translate according to that which you desired of me, and did
commence again to write for my servant Joseph Smith, jr.
even so I would that you should continue until you have finished this record, which I have intrusted unto him: and then
behold, other records have I, that I will give unto you power
that you may assist to translate.

2 Be patient my son, for it is wisdom in me, and it is not
expedient that you should translate at this present time.   Behold the work which you are called to do, is to write for my
servant Joseph; and behold it is because that you did not continue as you commenced, when you began to translate, that I
have taken away this privilege from you.   Do not murmur my
son, for it is wisdom in me that I have dealt with you after
this manner.

3 Behold you have not understood, you have supposed that I
would give it unto you, when you took no thought, save it
was to ask me; but behold I say unto you, that you must study
it out in your mind; then you must ask me if it be right, and
if it is right, I will cause that your bosom shall burn within
you: therefore, you shall feel that it is right; but if it be not
right, you shall have no such feelings, but you shall have a
stupor of thought, that shall cause you to forget the thing
which is wrong: therefore, you cannot write that which is sacred, save it be given you from me.

4 Now if you had known this, you could have translated;
nevertheless, it is not expedient that you should translate now.

---

line 15. Revelation, Apr. 1829–D [D&C 9]. This version reflects editing marks made in chapter 8 of
Oliver Cowdery's copy of the Book of Commandments, indicating that the latter was used as a source
text for the former. (See p. 605 herein.)

168

line 1 Behold it was expedient when you commenced, but you feared and the time is past, and it is not expedient now: for, do you not behold that I have given unto my servant Joseph sufficient strength, whereby it is made up? and neither of you have I condemned.

5 Do this thing which I have commanded you, and you shall prosper. Be faithful, and yield to no temptation. Stand fast in the work wherewith I have called you, and a hair of your head shall not be lost, and you shall be lifted up at the last day. Amen.

SECTION XXXVI.

Revelation given to Joseph Smith, jr. May, 1829, informing him of the alteration of the Manuscript of the fore part of the book of Mormon.

1 Now, behold I say unto you, that because you delivered up those writings which you had power given unto you to translate, by the means of the Urim and Thummim, into the hands of a wicked man, you have lost them; and you also lost your gift at the same time, and your mind became darkened; nevertheless, it is now restored unto you again, therefore see that you are faithful and continue on unto the finishing of the remainder of the work of translation as you have begun: do not run faster, or labor more than you have strength and means provided to enable you to translate; but be diligent unto the end: pray always, that you may come off conqueror; yea, that you may conquer satan and that you may escape the hands of the servants of satan, that do uphold his work. Behold, they have sought to destroy you; yea, even the man in whom you have trusted, has sought to destroy you. And for this cause I said, that he is a wicked man, for he has sought to take away the things wherewith you have been intrusted; and he has also sought to destroy your gift, and because you have delivered the writings into his hands, behold wicked men have taken them from you: therefore, you have delivered them up; yea, that which was sacred unto wickedness. And behold satan has put it into their hearts to alter the words which you have caused to be written, or which you have translated, which have gone out of your hands; and behold I say unto you, that because they have altered the words, they read contrary from that which you translated and caused to be written; and on this wise the devil has sought to lay a cunning plan, that he may destroy this work; for he has put it into their

11*

---

line 11. Revelation, ca. Apr. 1829 [D&C 10]. This version reflects editing marks made in chapter 9 of Oliver Cowdery's copy of the Book of Commandments, indicating that the latter was used as a source text for the former. This revelation should be dated circa April 1829. For more information on this dating, see the discussion of this revelation in the Documents series. (See pp. 606–607 herein.)

164

hearts to do this, that by lying they may say they have caught
you in the words which you have pretended to translate.

2 Verily I say unto you, that I will not suffer that satan shall
accomplish his evil design in this thing, for behold he has put
it into their hearts to get thee to tempt the Lord thy God, in
asking to translate it over again; and then behold they say
and think in their hearts, we will see if God has given him
power to translate, if so, he will also give him power again;
and if God giveth him power again, or if he translate again, or
in other words, if he bringeth forth the same words, behold we
have the same with us, and we have altered them: therefore,
they will not agree, and we will say that he has lied in his
words, and that he has no gift, and that he has no power:
therefore, we will destroy him, and also the work, and we will
do this that we may not be ashamed in the end, and that we
may get glory of the world.

3 Verily, verily I say unto you, that satan has great hold
upon their hearts; he stirreth them up to iniquity against that
which is good, and their hearts are corrupt, and full of wickedness and abominations, and they love darkness rather than
light, because their deeds are evil: therefore they will not ask
of me. Satan stirreth them up, that he may lead their souls
to destruction. And thus he has laid a cunning plan, thinking
to destroy the work of God, but I will require this at their
hands, and it shall turn to their shame and condemnation in
the day of judgment; yea, he stirreth up their hearts to anger
against this work; yea, he saith unto them, Deceive and lie in
wait to catch, that ye may destroy: behold this is no harm,
and thus he flattereth them and telleth them that it is no sin
to lie, that they may catch a man in a lie, that they may destroy him, and thus he flattereth them, and leadeth them along
until he draggeth their souls down to hell; and thus he causeth
them to catch themselves in their own snare; and thus he goeth up and down, to and fro in the earth, seeking to destroy
the souls of men.

4 Verily, verily I say unto you, wo be unto him that lieth to
deceive, because he supposes that another lieth to deceive, for
such are not exempt from the justice of God.

5 Now, behold they have altered those words, because satan
saith unto them, He hath deceived you: and thus he flattereth
them away to do iniquity, to get thee to tempt the Lord thy
God.

6 Behold I say unto you, that you shall not translate again
those words which have gone forth out of your hands; for behold they shall not accomplish their evil designs in lying
against those words. For, behold, if you should bring forth

165

the same words they will say that you have lied; that you have
pretended to translate, but that you have contradicted yourself: and behold they will publish this, and satan will harden
the hearts of the people to stir them up to anger against you,
that they will not believe my words. Thus satan thinketh to
overpower your testimony in this generation, that the work
may not come forth in this generation: but behold here is wisdom, and because I show unto you wisdom, and give you commandments concerning these things, what you shall do, show
it not unto the world until you have accomplished the work of
translation.

7 Marvel not that I said unto you, here is wisdom, show it
not unto the world, for I said, show it not unto the world, that
you may be preserved. Behold I do not say that you shall
not show it unto the righteous; but as you cannot always
judge the righteous, or as you cannot always tell the wicked
from the righteous: therefore, I say unto you, hold your peace
until I shall see fit to make all things known unto the world
concerning the matter.

8 And now, verily I say unto you, that an account of those
things that you have written, which have gone out of your
hands, are engraven upon the plates of Nephi; yea, and you
remember, it was said in those writings, that a more particular account was given of these things upon the plates of Nephi.

9 And now, because the account which is engraven upon
the plates of Nephi, is more particular concerning the things,
which in my wisdom I would bring to the knowledge of the
people in this account: therefore, you shall translate the engravings which are on the plates of Nephi, down even till you
come to the reign of king Benjamin, or until you come to that
which you have translated, which you have retained; and behold, you shall publish it as the record of Nephi, and thus I
will confound those who have altered my words. I will not
suffer that they shall destroy my work; yea, I will show unto
them that my wisdom is greater than the cunning of the devil.

10 Behold they have only got a part, or an abridgment of the
account of Nephi. Behold there are many things engraven
on the plates of Nephi, which do throw greater views upon my
gospel: therefore, it is wisdom in me, that you should translate this first part of the engravings of Nephi, and send forth
in this work. And behold, all the remainder of this work,
does contain all those parts of my gospel which my holy prophets, yea, and also my disciples desired in their prayers,
should come forth unto this people. And I said unto them,
that it should be granted unto them according to their faith in
their prayers; yea, and this was their faith, that my gospel

166

which I gave unto them, that they might preach in their days, might come unto their brethren, the Lamanites, and also, all that had become Lamanites, because of their dissensions.

11 Now this is not all, their faith in their prayers were, that this gospel should be made known also, if it were possible that other nations should possess this land; and thus they did leave a blessing upon this land in their prayers, that whosoever should believe in this gospel, in this land, might have eternal life; yea, that it might be free unto all of whatsoever nation, kindred, tongue, or people, they may be.

12 And now, behold, according to their faith in their prayers, will I bring this part of my gospel to the knowledge of my people. Behold, I do not bring it to destroy that which they have received, but to build it up.

13 And for this cause have I said, if this generation harden not their hearts, I will establish my church among them. Now I do not say this to destroy my church, but I say this to build up my church: therefore, whosoever belongeth to my church need not fear, for such shall inherit the kingdom of heaven: but it is they who do not fear me, neither keep my commandments, but buildeth up churches unto themselves, to get gain; yea, and all those that do wickedly, and buildeth up the kingdom of the devil; yea, verily, verily I say unto you, that it is they that I will disturb, and cause to tremble and shake to the centre.

14 Behold, I am Jesus Christ, the Son of God: I came unto my own, and my own received me not. I am the light which shineth in darkness, and the darkness comprehendeth it not. I am he who said other sheep have I which are not of this fold, unto my disciples, and many there were that understood me not.

15 And I will show unto this people, that I had other sheep, and that they were a branch of the house of Jacob: and I will bring to light their marvelous works, which they did in my name: yea, and I will also bring to light my gospel, which was ministered unto them, and behold they shall not deny that which you have received, but they shall build it up, and shall bring to light the true points of my doctrine: yea, and the only doctrine which is in me; and this I do, that I may establish my gospel, that there may not be so much contention: yea, satan doth stir up the hearts of the people to contention, concerning the points of my doctrine; and in these things they do err, for they do wrest the scriptures, and do not understand them: therefore, I will unfold unto them this great mystery, for behold, I will gather them as a hen gathereth her chickens under her wings, if they will not harden their hearts: yea, if

line 1 they will come, they may, and partake of the waters of life freely.

16 Behold this is my doctrine: whosoever repenteth and cometh unto me, the same is my church: whosoever declareth more or less than this, the same is not of me, but is against me: therefore, he is not of my church.

17 And now, behold whosoever is of my church, and endureth of my church to the end, him will I establish upon my Rock, and the gates of hell shall not prevail against them.

18 And now, remember the words of him who is the life and the light of the world, your Redeemer, your Lord and your God. Amen.

SECTION XXXVII.

Revelation given to Hyrum Smith, May, 1829.

1 A great and marvelous work is about to come forth among the children of men: behold I am God and give heed to my word, which is quick and powerful, sharper than a two-edged sword, to the dividing asunder of both joints and marrow: therefore, give heed unto my word.

2 Behold the field is white already to harvest, therefore, whoso desireth to reap, let him thrust in his sickle with his might, and reap while the day lasts, that he may treasure up for his soul everlasting salvation in the kingdom of God; yea, whosoever will thrust in his sickle and reap, the same is called of God: therefore, if you will ask of me, you shall receive; if you will knock, it shall be opened unto you.

3 Now as you have asked, behold I say unto you, keep my commandments, and seek to bring forth and establish the cause of Zion. Seek not for riches but for wisdom, and behold the mysteries of God shall be unfolded unto you, and then shall you be made rich; behold he that hath eternal life is rich.

4 Verily, verily I say unto you, even as you desire of me, so shall it be done unto you: and, if you desire you shall be the means of doing much good in this generation. Say nothing but repentance unto this generation. Keep my commandments, and assist to bring forth my work according to my commandments, and you shall be blessed.

5 Behold thou hast a gift, or thou shalt have a gift if thou wilt desire of me in faith, with an honest heart, believing in the power of Jesus Christ, or in my power which speaketh unto thee: for behold it is I that speaketh: behold I am the light which shineth in darkness, and by my power I give these words unto thee.

---

line 13. Revelation, May 1829–A [D&C 11]. This version closely corresponds to the version in chapter 10 of the Book of Commandments, suggesting that the latter was used as a source text for the former.

168

6 And now, verily, verily I say unto thee, put your trust in that Spirit which leadeth to do good: yea, to do justly; to walk humbly; to judge righteously; and this is my Spirit.

7 Verily, verily I say unto you, I will impart unto you of my Spirit, which shall enlighten your mind, which shall fill your soul with joy, and then shall ye know, or by this shall you know, all things whatsoever you desire of me, which is pertaining unto things of righteousness, in faith believing in me that you shall receive.

8 Behold I command you, that you need not suppose that you are called to preach until you are called: wait a little longer, until you shall have my word, my rock, my church, and my gospel, that you may know of a surety my doctrine; and then behold, according to your desires, yea, even according to your faith, shall it be done unto you.

9 Keep my commandments; hold your peace; appeal unto my Spirit: yea, cleave unto me with all your heart, that you may assist in bringing to light those things of which have been spoken: yea, the translation of my work: be patient until you shall accomplish it.

10 Behold this is your work, to keep my commandments: yea, with all your might, mind, and strength: seek not to declare my word, but first seek to obtain my word, and then shall your tongue be loosed; then, if you desire, you shall have my Spirit, and my word: yea, the power of God unto the convincing of men: but now hold your peace; study my word which hath gone forth among the children of men; and also study my word which shall come forth among the children of men; or that which is now translating: yea, until you have obtained all which I shall grant unto the children of men in this generation; and then shall all things be added thereunto.

11 Behold thou art Hyrum, my son; seek the kingdom of God and all things shall be added according to that which is just. Build upon my rock, which is my gospel; deny not the Spirit of revelation, nor the Spirit of prophecy, for wo unto him that denieth these things: therefore, treasure up in your hearts until the time which is in my wisdom, that you shall go forth: behold I speak unto all who have good desires, and have thrust in their sickles to reap.

12 Behold I am Jesus Christ, the Son of God: I am the life and the light of the world: I am the same who came unto my own, and my own received me not: but verily, verily I say unto you, that as many as receiveth me, them will I give power to become the sons of God, even to them that believe on my name. Amen.

169

SECTION XXXVIII.

Revelation given to Joseph Knight, Sen. May, 1829.

1 A great and marvelous work is about to come forth among the children of men: behold I am God, and give heed to my word, which is quick and powerful, sharper than a two-edged sword, to the dividing asunder of both joints and marrow: therefore, give heed unto my word.

2 Behold the field is white already to harvest, therefore whoso desireth to reap, let him thrust in his sickle with his might, and reap while the day lasts, that he may treasure up for his soul everlasting salvation in the kingdom of God: yea, whosoever will thrust in his sickle and reap, the same is called of God: therefore if you will ask of me you shall receive; if you will knock it shall be opened unto you.

3 Now as you have asked, behold I say unto you, keep my commandments, and seek to bring forth and establish the cause of Zion.

4 Behold I speak unto you, and also to all those who have desires to bring forth and establish this work, and no one can assist in this work, except he shall be humble and full of love, having faith, hope and charity, being temperate in all things, whatsoever shall be intrusted to his care.

5 Behold I am the light and the life of the world, that speaketh these words: therefore, give heed with your might, and then you are called. Amen.

SECTION XXXIX.

Revelation given to David Whitmer, June, 1829.

1 A great and marvelous work is about to come forth unto the children of men: behold I am God, and give heed to my word; which is quick and powerful, sharper than a two-edged sword, to the dividing asunder of both joints and marrow: therefore, give heed unto my word.

2 Behold the field is white already to harvest, therefore, whoso desireth to reap, let him thrust in his sickle with his might, and reap while the day lasts, that he may treasure up for his soul everlasting salvation in the kingdom of God: yea, whosoever will thrust in his sickle and reap, the same is called of God: therefore, if you will ask of me you shall receive; if you will knock it shall be opened unto you.

3 Seek to bring forth and establish my Zion. Keep my commandments in all things, and if you keep my commandments

---

line 1. Revelation, May 1829–B [D&C 12]. This version closely corresponds to the version in chapter 11 of the Book of Commandments, suggesting that the latter was used as a source text for the former.

line 26. Revelation, June 1829–A [D&C 14]. This version closely corresponds to the version in chapter 12 of the Book of Commandments, suggesting that the latter was used as a source text for the former.

170

line 1
and endure to the end, you shall have eternal life; which gift is the greatest of all the gifts of God.

4 And it shall come to pass, that if you shall ask the Father in my name, in faith believing, you shall receive the Holy Ghost, which giveth utterance, that you may stand as a witness of the things of which you shall both hear and see; and also, that you may declare repentance unto this generation.

5 Behold I am Jesus Christ the Son of the living God, who created the heavens and the earth; a light which cannot be hid in darkness: wherefore, I must bring forth the fulness of my gospel from the Gentiles unto the house of Israel. And behold thou art David, and thou art called to assist: which thing if ye do, and are faithful, ye shall be blessed both spiritually and temporally, and great shall be your reward. Amen.

SECTION XL.

Revelation given to John Whitmer, jr. June, 1829.

1 Hearken my servant John, and listen to the words of Jesus Christ, your Lord and your Redeemer, for behold I speak unto you with sharpness and with power, for mine arm is over all the earth, and I will tell you that which no man knoweth save me and thee alone: for many times you have desired of me to know that which would be of the most worth unto you.

2 Behold, blessed are you for this thing, and for speaking my words which I have given you, according to my commandments:

3 And now behold I say unto you, that the thing which will be of the most worth unto you, will be to declare repentance unto this people, that you may bring souls unto me, that you may rest with them in the kingdom of my Father. Amen.

SECTION XLI.

Revelation given to Peter Whitmer, June, 1829.

1 Hearken my servant Peter, and listen to the words of Jesus Christ, your Lord and your Redeemer, for behold I speak unto you with sharpness and with power, for mine arm is over all the earth, and I will tell you that which no man knoweth save me and thee alone: for many times you have desired of me to know that which would be of the most worth unto you.

2 Behold, blessed are you for this thing, and for speaking my words which I have given you according to my commandments:

---

line 15. Revelation, June 1829–C [D&C 15]. This version closely corresponds to the version in chapter 13 of the Book of Commandments, suggesting that the latter was used as a source text for the former.

line 30. Revelation, June 1829–D [D&C 16]. This version closely corresponds to the version in chapter 14 of the Book of Commandments, suggesting that the latter was used as a source text for the former.

171

line 1 3 And now behold I say unto you, that the thing which will
be of the most worth unto you, will be to declare repentance
unto this people, that you may bring souls unto me, that you
may rest with them in the kingdom of my Father. Amen.

5 SECTION XLII.

Revelation to Oliver Cowdery, David Whitmer and Martin Harris, June, 1829, given previous to their viewing the plates containing the book of Mormon:

1 Behold I say unto you, that you must rely upon my word,
10 which if you do, with full purpose of heart, you shall have a
view of the plates, and also the breastplate, the sword of La-
ban, the Urim and Thummim, which were given to the brother
of Jared upon the mount, when he talked with the Lord face to
face, and the miraculous directors which were given to Lehi
15 while in the wilderness, on the borders of the red sea; and it
is by your faith that you shall obtain a view of them, even by
that faith which was had by the prophets of old.
2 And after that you have obtained faith, and have seen
them with your eyes, you shall testify of them, by the power
20 of God; and this you shall do that my servant Joseph Smith,
jr. may not be destroyed, that I may bring about my righteous
purposes unto the children of men, in this work. And ye
shall testify that you have seen them, even as my servant
Joseph Smith, jr. has seen them, for it is by my power that
25 he has seen them, and it is because he had faith: and he has
translated the book, even that part which I have commanded
him, and as your Lord and your God liveth it is true.
3 Wherefore you have received the same power, and the
same faith, and the same gift like unto him; and if you do these
30 last commandments of mine, which I have given you, the
gates of hell shall not prevail against you; for my grace is sufficient for you: and you shall be lifted up at the last day.—
And I, Jesus Christ, your Lord and your God, have spoken
it unto you, that I might bring about my righteous purposes
35 unto the children of men. Amen.

---

line 5. Revelation, June 1829–E [D&C 17]. This version reflects editing marks made in Revelation Book 2, indicating that the latter was used as a source text for the former. (See *JSP,* MRB:655–657.)

172

SECTION XLIII.

Revelation to Joseph Smith, jr. Oliver Cowdery and David Whitmer, making known the calling of twelve apostles in these last days, and also, instructions relative to building up the church of Christ, according to the fulness of the gospel: Given in Fayette, New York, June, 1829.

1 Now behold, because of the thing which you, my servant Oliver Cowdery, have desired to know of me, I give unto you these words: behold I have manifested unto you, by my Spirit in many instances, that the things which you have written are true: wherefore you know that they are true; and if you know that they are true, behold I give unto you a commandment, that you rely upon the things which are written; for in them are all things written concerning the foundation of my church, my gospel and my rock; wherefore, if you shall build up my church upon the foundation of my gospel and my rock, the gates of hell shall not prevail against you.

2 Behold the world is ripening in iniquity, and it must needs be, that the children of men are stirred up unto repentance, both the Gentiles, and also the house of Israel: wherefore as thou hast been baptized by the hand of my servant, Joseph Smith, jr. according to that which I have commanded him, he hath fulfilled the thing which I commanded him. And now marvel not that I have called him unto mine own purpose, which purpose is known in me: wherefore if he shall be diligent in keeping my commandments, he shall be blessed unto eternal life, and his name is Joseph.

3 And now Oliver Cowdery, I speak unto you, and also unto David Whitmer, by the way of commandment: for behold I command all men every where to repent, and I speak unto you, even as unto Paul mine apostle, for you are called even with that same calling with which he was called. Remember the worth of souls is great in the sight of God: for behold the Lord your Redeemer suffered death in the flesh: wherefore he suffered the pain of all men, that all men might repent and come unto him. And he hath risen again from the dead, that he might bring all men unto him on conditions of repentance. And how great is his joy in the soul that repenteth.— Wherefore you are called to cry repentance unto this people. And if it so be that you should labor all your days, in crying repentance unto this people, and bring save it be one soul unto me, how great shall be your joy with him in the kingdom of my Father?

4 And now if your joy will be great with one soul, that you

line 1. Revelation, June 1829–B [D&C 18]. This version corresponds to the version in chapter 15 of the Book of Commandments, suggesting that the latter was used as a source text for the former.

173

line 1

have brought unto me into the kingdom of my Father, how
great will be your joy, if you should bring many souls unto me?
Behold you have my gospel before you, and my rock, and my
salvation: ask the Father in my name in faith believing that
you shall receive, and you shall have the Holy Ghost which
manifesteth all things, which is expedient unto the children of
men. And if you have not faith, hope and charity, you can
do nothing. Contend against no church, save it be the church
of the devil. Take upon you the name of Christ, and speak
the truth in soberness, and as many as repent, and are baptized in my name, which is Jesus Christ, and endure to the end,
the same shall be saved. Behold Jesus Christ is the name
which is given of the Father, and there is none other name
given whereby man can be saved: wherefore all men must
take upon them the name which is given of the Father, for in
that name shall they be called at the last day: wherefore if
they know not the name by which they are called, they cannot
have place in the kingdom of my Father.

5 And now behold, there are others who are called to declare my gospel, both unto Gentile and unto Jew: yea, even
twelve: and the twelve shall be my disciples, and they
shall take upon them my name: and the twelve are they who
shall desire to take upon them my name, with full purpose of
heart: and if they desire to take upon them my name, with
full purpose of heart, they are called to go into all the world
to preach my gospel unto every creature: and they are they
who are ordained of me to baptize in my name, according to
that which is written; and you have that which is written before you: wherefore you must perform it according to the
words which are written. And now I speak unto the twelve:
Behold my grace is sufficient for you: you must walk uprightly
before me and sin not. And behold you are they who are ordained of me to ordain priests and teachers to declare my gospel, according to the power of the Holy Ghost which is in
you, and according to the callings and gifts of God unto men:
and I Jesus Christ, your Lord and your God, have spoken it.
These words are not of men, nor of man, but of me: wherefore you shall testify they are of me, and not of man; for it is
my voice which speaketh them unto you: for they are given
by my Spirit unto you: and by my power you can read them
one to another; and save it were by my power, you could not
have them: wherefore you can testify that you have heard my
voice, and know my words.

6 And now behold I give unto you, Oliver Cowdery, and also
unto David Whitmer, that you shall search out the twelve
who shall have the desires of which I have spoken; and by

174

line 1 their desires and their works, you shall know them: and when
you have found them you shall show these things unto them.
And you shall fall down and worship the Father in my name:
and you must preach unto the world, saying, you must repent
5 and be baptized in the name of Jesus Christ: for all men must
repent and be baptized; and not only men, but women and
children, who have arriven to the years of accountability.

7 And now, after that you have received this, you must
keep my commandments in all things: and by your hands I
10 will work a marvelous work among the children of men, unto
the convincing of many of their sins, that they may come unto
repentance; and that they may come unto the kingdom of my
Father: wherefore the blessings which I give unto you, are
above all things.   And after that you have received this, if
15 you keep not my commandments, you cannot be saved in the
kingdom of my Father.   Behold I Jesus Christ, your Lord and
your God, and your Redeemer, by the power of my Spirit,
have spoken it. Amen.

SECTION XLIV.

20 *A commandment of God and not of man to Martin Harris, given*
  (Manchester, New York, March. 1830,) by him who is eternal:

1 I am Alpha and Omega, Christ the Lord; yea, even I am
He, the beginning and the end, the Redeemer of the world: I
having accomplished and finished the will of him whose I am,
25 even the Father concerning me: having done this, that I
might subdue all things unto myself: retaining all power, even
to the destroying of satan and his works at the end of the
world, and the last great day of judgment, which I shall pass
upon the inhabitants thereof, judging every man according to
30 his works, and the deeds which he hath done.   And surely
every man must repent or suffer, for I God am endless: wherefore, I revoke not the judgments which I shall pass, but woes
shall go forth, weeping, wailing and gnashing of teeth: yea, to
those who are found on my left hand; nevertheless it is not
35 written, that there shall be no end to this torment; but it is
written endless torment.

2 Again, it is written eternal damnation: wherefore it is more
express than other scriptures, that it might work upon the
hearts of the children of men, altogether for my name's glory:
40 wherefore, I will explain unto you, this mystery, for it is meet
unto you, to know even as mine apostles. I speak unto you
that are chosen in this thing, even as one, that you may enter
into my rest. For behold, the mystery of Godliness, how

---

line 19. Revelation, Mar. 1830 [D&C 19]. This version corresponds to the version in chapter 16 of the
Book of Commandments, suggesting that the latter was used as a source text for the former.

175

line 1

great is it? for behold I am endless, and the punishment which is given from my hand, is endless punishment, for endless is my name; wherefore—

Eternal punishment   } Endless punishment
is God's punishment: } is God's punishment:
wherefore, I command you to repent, and keep the commandments which you have received by the hand of my servant Joseph Smith, jr. in my name: and it is by my almighty power that you have received them: therefore I command you to repent, repent, lest I smite you by the rod of my mouth, and by my wrath, and by my anger, and your sufferings be sore: how sore you know not! how exquisite you know not! yea, how hard to bear you know not! For behold, I God have suffered these things for all, that they might not suffer, if they would repent, but if they would not repent, they must suffer even as I: which suffering caused myself, even God, the greatest of all to tremble because of pain, and to bleed at every pore, and to suffer both body and spirit: and would that I might not drink the bitter cup and shrink: nevertheless, glory be to the Father, and I partook and finished my preparations unto the children of men: wherefore, I command you again to repent lest I humble you by my almighty power, and that you confess your sins lest you suffer these punishments of which I have spoken, of which in the smallest, yea, even in the least degree you have tasted at the time I withdrew my Spirit. And I command you, that you preach nought but repentance; and show not these things unto the world until it is wisdom in me; for they cannot bear meat now, but milk they must receive: wherefore, they must not know these things lest they perish: learn of me, and listen to my words; walk in the meekness of my Spirit and you shall have peace in me: I am Jesus Christ: I came by the will of the Father, and I do his will.

3 And again: I command thee, that thou shalt not covet thy neighbor's wife. Nor seek thy neighbor's life. And again: I command thee, that thou shalt not covet thine own property, but impart it freely to the printing of the book of Mormon, which contains the truth and the word of God, which is my word to the Gentile, that soon it may go to the Jew, of whom the Lamanites are a remnant: that they may believe the gospel, and look not for a Messiah to come who has already come.

4 And again. I command thee, that thou shalt pray vocally as well as in thy heart: yea, before the world as well as in secret; in public as well as in private. And thou shalt declare glad tidings: yea, publish it upon the mountains, and upon every high place, and among every people that thou shalt

176

line 1 be permitted to see. And thou shalt do it with all humility,
trusting in me, reviling not against revilers. And of tenets
thou shalt not talk, but thou shalt declare repentance and faith
on the Savior, and remission of sins by baptism and by fire; yea,
5 even the Holy Ghost.

5 Behold, this is a great, and the last commandment which I
shall give unto you concerning this matter: for this shall suffice for thy daily walk even unto the end of thy life. And
misery thou shalt receive, if thou wilt slight these counsels;
10 yea, even destruction of thyself and property. Impart a portion of thy property; yea, even part of thy lands and all save
the support of thy family. Pay the debt thou hast contracted
with the printer. Release thyself from bondage. Leave thy
house and home, except when thou shalt desire to see thy
15 family. And speak freely to all: yea, preach, exhort, declare
the truth, even with a loud voice; with a sound of rejoicing,
crying hosanna! hosanna! blessed be the name of the Lord
God.

6 Pray always and I will pour out my Spirit upon you, and
20 great shall be your blessing: yea, even more than if you should
obtain treasures of earth, and corruptibleness to the extent
thereof. Behold, canst thou read this without rejoicing and
lifting up thy heart for gladness; or canst thou run about longer as a blind guide; or canst thou be humble and meek and
25 conduct thyself wisely before me: yea, come unto me thy Savior. Amen.

SECTION XLV.

*Revelation to Oliver Cowdery, Hyrum Smith, Samuel H. Smith,
Joseph Smith Sen. and Joseph Knight, Sen. given April, 1830.*

30 1 Behold I speak unto you, Oliver, a few words. Behold
thou art blessed, and art under no condemnation. But be
ware of pride, lest thou shouldst enter into temptation. Make
known thy calling unto the church, and also before the world;
and thy heart shall be opened to preach the truth from hence-
35 forth and forever. Amen.

2 Behold I speak unto you, Hyrum, a few words: for thou
also art under no condemnation, and thy heart is opened, and
thy tongue loosed; and thy calling is to exhortation, and to
strengthen the church continually. Wherefore thy duty is
40 unto the church forever; and this because of thy family. Amen.

3 Behold I speak a few words unto you, Samuel: for thou
also art under no condemnation, and thy calling is to exhortation, and to strengthen the church. And thou art not as yet
called to preach before the world. Amen.

---

line 27. Revelations, Apr. 1830–A through E [D&C 23]. This version, which combines five revelations
that had previously been published separately, closely corresponds to the versions in chapters 17–21 of the
Book of Commandments, suggesting that the Book of Commandments was used as a source text for this
version.

177

4 Behold I speak a few words unto you, Joseph: for thou also art under no condemnation, and thy calling also is to exhortation, and to strengthen the church. And this is thy duty from henceforth and forever. Amen.

5 Behold I manifest unto you, Joseph Knight, by these words, that you must take up your cross, in the which you must pray vocally before the world, as well as in secret, and in your family, and among your friends, and in all places.— And behold it is your duty to unite with the true church, and give your language to exhortation continually, that you may receive the reward of the laborer. Amen.

SECTION XLVI.

Revelation to Joseph Smith, jr. given April 6, 1830.

1 Behold there shall be a record kept among you, and in it thou shalt be called a seer, a translator, a prophet, an apostle of Jesus Christ, an elder of the church through the will of God the Father, and the grace of your Lord Jesus Christ; being inspired of the Holy Ghost to lay the foundation thereof, and to build it up unto the most holy faith; which church was organized and established, in the year of your Lord eighteen hundred and thirty, in the fourth month, and on the sixth day of the month, which is called April.

2 Wherefore, meaning the church, thou shalt give heed unto all his words, and commandments, which he shall give unto you, as he receiveth them, walking in all holiness before me: for his word ye shall receive, as if from mine own mouth, in all patience and faith; for by doing these things, the gates of hell shall not prevail against you: yea, and the Lord God will disperse the powers of darkness from before you; and cause the heavens to shake for your good, and his name's glory.— For thus saith the Lord God, him have I inspired to move the cause of Zion in mighty power for good; and his diligence I know, and his prayers I have heard: yea, his weeping for Zion I have seen, and I will cause that he shall mourn for her no longer, for his days of rejoicing are come unto the remission of his sins, and the manifestations of my blessings upon his works.

3 For behold, I will bless all those who labor in my vineyard, with a mighty blessing, and they shall believe on his words, which are given him through me, by the Comforter, which manifesteth that Jesus was crucified by sinful men for the sins of the world; yea, for the remission of sins unto the contrite heart. Wherefore, it behooveth me, that he should be ordain-

L

---

line 1

5

10

15

20

25

30

35

40

---

line 12. Revelation, 6 Apr. 1830 [D&C 21]. This version reflects editing marks made in chapter 22 of Oliver Cowdery's copy of the Book of Commandments, indicating that the latter was used as a source text for the former. (See p. 608 herein.)

line 43. This page begins the twelfth gathering of the book. "L" is the first of two signature marks in this gathering; the second is on the recto of the following leaf. These marks were used in collating the gatherings after the sheets were folded.

178

line 1

ed by you, Oliver Cowdery, mine apostle; this being an ordinance unto you, that you are an elder under his hand, he
being the first unto you, that you might be an elder unto this
church of Christ, bearing my name; and the first preacher of
this church, unto the church, and before the world; yea, before the Gentiles: yea, and thus saith the Lord God, lo, lo, to
the Jews, also. Amen.

SECTION XLVII.

*Revelation to the church of Christ, which was established in these
last days, in the year of our Lord one thousand eight hundred
and thirty: Given April, 1830, in consequence of some desiring to unite with the church without re-baptism, who had previously been baptized.*

1 Behold I say unto you, that all old covenants have I caused
to be done away in this thing, and this is a new and an everlasting covenant; even that which was from the beginning.—
Wherefore, although a man should be baptized an hundred
times, it availeth him nothing; for you cannot enter in at the
straight gate by the law of Moses, neither by your dead works;
for it is because of your dead works, that I have caused this
last covenant, and this church to be built up unto me; even as
in days of old. Wherefore enter ye in at the gate, as I have
commanded, and seek not to counsel your God. Amen.

SECTION XLVIII.

Revelation given July, 1830.

1 Hearken unto the voice of the Lord your God, while I
speak unto you, Emma Smith, my daughter, for verily I say
unto you, all those who receive my gospel are sons and daughters in my kingdom. A revelation I give unto you concerning
my will, and if thou art faithful and walk in the paths of virtue before me, I will preserve thy life, and thou shalt receive
an inheritance in Zion. Behold thy sins are forgiven thee,
and thou art an elect lady, whom I have called. Murmur not
because of the things which thou hast not seen, for they are
withheld from thee, and from the world, which is wisdom in
me in a time to come.
2 And the office of thy calling shall be for a comfort unto my
servant Joseph Smith, jr. thy husband, in his afflictions with
consoling words, in the spirit of meekness. And thou shalt go
with him at the time of his going, and be unto him for a scribe,

---

line 8. Revelation, 16 Apr. 1830 [D&C 22]. This version closely corresponds to the version in chapter 23 of the Book of Commandments, suggesting that the latter was used as a source text for the former.

line 24. Revelation, July 1830–C [D&C 25]. This version corresponds to the version in chapter 26 of the Book of Commandments, suggesting that the latter was used as a source text for the former.

179

line 1 while there is no one to be a scribe for him, that I may send
my servant Oliver Cowdery, whithersoever I will. And thou
shalt be ordained under his hand to expound scriptures, and to
exhort the church, according as it shall be given thee by my
5 Spirit: for he shall lay his hands upon thee, and thou shalt receive the Holy Ghost, and thy time shall be given to writing,
and to learning much. And thou needst not fear, for thy husband shall support thee in the church: for unto them is his
calling, that all things might be revealed unto them, whatso-
10 ever I will, according to their faith.

3 And verily I say unto thee, that thou shalt lay aside the
things of this world, and seek for the things of a better. And
it shall be given thee, also, to make a selection of sacred
Hymns, as it shall be given thee, which is pleasing unto me,
15 to be had in my church: for my soul delighteth in the song of
the heart: yea, the song of the righteous is a prayer unto me.
And it shall be answered with a blessing upon their heads.—
Wherefore lift up thy heart and rejoice, and cleave unto the
covenants which thou hast made.

20 4 Continue in the spirit of meekness, and beware of pride.
Let thy soul delight in thy husband, and the glory which shall
come upon him. Keep my commandments continually, and
a crown of righteousness thou shalt receive. And except thou
do this, where I am you cannot come. And verily, verily I
25 say unto you, that this is my voice unto all. Amen.

SECTION XLIX.

*Revelation to Joseph Smith, jr. Oliver Cowdery and John Whit-
mer, given July,* 1830.

1 Behold, I say unto you, that you shall let your time be de-
30 voted to the studying of the scriptures, and to preaching, and
to confirming the church at Colesville; and to performing your
labors on the land, such as is required, until after you shall go
to the west, to hold the next conference; and then it shall be
made known what you shall do. And all things shall be done
35 by common consent in the church, by much prayer and faith;
for all things you shall receive by faith. Amen.

SECTION L.

Revelation given September, 1830.

1 Listen to the voice of Jesus Christ, your Lord, your God
40 and your Redeemer, whose word is quick and powerful. For
12*

---

line 26. Revelation, July 1830–B [D&C 26]. This version closely corresponds to the version in chapter 27 of the Book of Commandments, suggesting that the latter was used as a source text for the former.

line 37. Revelation, ca. Aug. 1830 [D&C 27]. This version corresponds to the version in chapter 28 of the Book of Commandments, suggesting that the latter was used as a source text for the former. This revelation should be dated circa August 1830. For more information on this dating, see the discussion of this revelation in the Documents series.

180

behold I say unto you, that it mattereth not what ye shall eat,
or what ye shall drink, when ye partake of the sacrament, if it
so be that ye do it with an eye single to my glory; remembering unto the Father my body which was laid down for you,
and my blood which was shed for the remission of your sins:
wherefore a commandment I give unto you, that you shall not
purchase wine, neither strong drink of your enemies: wherefore you shall partake of none, except it is made new among
you, yea, in this my Father's kingdom which shall be built up
on the earth.

2 Behold this is wisdom in me: wherefore marvel not for the
hour cometh that I will drink of the fruit of the vine with you
on the earth, and with Moroni, whom I have sent unto you to
reveal the book of Mormon, containing the fulness of my everlasting gospel; to whom I have committed the keys of the record of the stick of Ephraim; and also with Elias, to whom I
have committed the keys of bringing to pass the restoration
of all things, or the restorer of all things spoken by the mouth
of all the holy prophets since the world began, concerning the
last days: and also John the son of Zacharias, which Zacharias he (Elias) visited and gave promise that he should have a
son, and his name should be John, and he should be filled with
the spirit of Elias; which John I have sent unto you, my servants, Joseph Smith, jr. and Oliver Cowdery, to ordain you
unto this first priesthood which you have received, that you
might be called and ordained even as Aaron: and also Elijah,
unto whom I have committed the keys of the power of turning the hearts of the fathers to the children and the hearts of
the children to the fathers, that the whole earth may not be
smitten with a curse: and also, with Joseph, and Jacob, and
Isaac, and Abraham your fathers; by whom the promises remain; and also with Michael, or Adam, the father of all, the
prince of all, the ancient of days:

3 And also with Peter, and James, and John, whom I have
sent unto you, by whom I have ordained you and confirmed
you to be apostles and especial witnesses of my name, and bear
the keys of your ministry: and of the same things which I revealed unto them: unto whom I have committed the keys of
my kingdom, and a dispensation of the gospel for the last
times; and for the fulness of times, in the which I will gather
together in one all things both which are in heaven and which
are on earth: and also with all those whom my Father hath
given me out of the world: wherefore lift up your hearts and
rejoice, and gird up your loins, and take upon you my whole
armor, that ye may be able to withstand the evil day; having
done all ye may be able to stand. Stand, therefore, having

181

your loins girt about with truth; having on the breastplate of
righteousness; and your feet shod with the preparation of the
gospel of peace which I have sent mine angels to commit unto you, taking the shield of faith wherewith ye shall be able
to quench all the fiery darts of the wicked; and take the helmet of salvation, and the sword of my Spirit, which I will
pour out upon you, and my word which I reveal unto you,
and be agreed as touching all things whatsoever ye ask of me,
and be faithful until I come, and ye shall be caught up that
where I am ye shall be also. Amen.

SECTION LI.

Revelation given to Oliver Cowdery, September, 1830.

1 Behold I say unto thee, Oliver, that it shall be given unto
thee, that thou shalt be heard by the church, in all things
whatsoever thou shalt teach them by the Comforter, concerning the revelations and commandments which I have given.

2 But behold, verily, verily I say unto thee, no one shall be
appointed to receive commandments and revelations in this
church, excepting my servant Joseph Smith, jr. for he receiveth them even as Moses; and thou shalt be obedient unto the
things which I shall give unto him, even as Aaron, to declare
faithfully the commandments and the revelations, with power
and authority unto the church. And if thou art led at any time
by the Comforter to speak or teach, or at all times by the way
of commandment unto the church, thou mayest do it. But
thou shalt not write by way of commandment, but by wisdom:
And thou shalt not command him who is at thy head, and at
the head of the church; for I have given him the keys of the
mysteries and the revelations which are sealed, until I shall
appoint unto them another in his stead.

3 And now, behold I say unto you, that you shall go unto the
Lamanites and preach my gospel unto them; and inasmuch
as they receive thy teachings, thou shalt cause my church to
be established among them, and thou shalt have revelations
but write them not by way of commandment. And now behold I say unto you, that it is not revealed, and no man knoweth where the city shall be built, but it shall be given hereafter. Behold I say unto you, that it shall be on the borders by
the Lamanites.

4 Thou shalt not leave this place until after the conference
and my servant Joseph shall be appointed to preside over the
conference by the voice of it, and what he saith to thee thou
shalt tell. And again, thou shalt take thy brother Hiram

---

line 11. Revelation, Sept. 1830–B [D&C 28]. This version reflects editing marks made in chapter 30 of Oliver Cowdery's copy of the Book of Commandments, indicating that the latter was used as a source text for the former. (See p. 609 herein.)

182

line 1 Page between him and thee alone, and tell him that those things which he hath written from that stone are not of me, and that satan deceiveth him: for behold these things have not been appointed unto him: neither shall any thing be ap-
5 pointed unto any of this church contrary to the church covenants, for all things must be done in order and by common consent in the church, by the prayer of faith.

5 And thou shalt assist to settle all these things according to the covenants of the church before thou shalt take thy jour-
10 ney among the Lamanites. And it shall be given thee from the time that thou shalt go, until the time that thou shalt return, what thou shalt do. And thou must open thy mouth at all times declaring my gospel with the sound of rejoicing.— Amen.

15   SECTION LII.

Revelation to David Whitmer, Peter Whitmer, jr. and John Whitmer, given September, 1830.

1 Behold I say unto you, David, that you have feared man and have not relied on me for strength, as you ought: but
20 your mind has been on the things of the earth more than on the things of me, your Maker, and the ministry whereunto you have been called; and you have not given heed unto my Spirit, and to those who were set over you, but have been per-suaded by those whom I have not commanded: wherefore you
25 are left to inquire for yourself, at my hand, and ponder upon the things which you have received. And your home shall be at your father's house, until I give unto you further commandments. And you shall attend to the ministry in the church, and before the world, and in the regions round about. Amen.
30 2 Behold I say unto you, Peter, that you shall take your journey with your brother Oliver, for the time has come, that it is expedient in me, that you shall open your mouth to declare my gospel: therefore, fear not but give heed unto the words and advice of your brother, which he shall give you.—
35 And be you afflicted in all his afflictions, ever lifting up your heart unto me in prayer, and faith, for his and your deliverance: for I have given unto him power to build up my church among the Lamanites: and none have I appointed to be his counsellor, over him, in the church, concerning church mat-
40 ters, except it is his brother Joseph Smith, jr. Wherefore give heed unto these things and be diligent in keeping my commandments, and you shall be blessed unto eternal life. Amen.
3 Behold I say unto you, my servant John, that thou shalt

---

line 15. Revelations, Sept. 1830–C through E [D&C 30]. The contents of this section were divided into three different chapters in the Book of Commandments (chapters 31–33). Verse 2 of this section reflects editing marks made in chapter 32 of Oliver Cowdery's copy of the Book of Commandments, and verses 1 and 3 closely correspond to the versions in chapters 31 and 33 of that book, indicating that the Cowdery volume was used as a source text for this version. (See p. 610 herein.)

183

line 1 commence from this time forth to proclaim my gospel, as with the voice of a trump. And your labor shall be at your brother Philip Burroughs', and in that region round about: yea, wherever you can be heard, until I command you to go *5* from hence. And your whole labor shall be in Zion, with all your soul, from henceforth; yea, you shall ever open your mouth in my cause not fearing what man can do, for I am with you. Amen.

SECTION LIII.

10 *Revelation to Thomas B. Marsh, given September, 1830.*

1 Thomas, my son, blessed are you because of your faith in my work. Behold you have had many afflictions because of your family: nevertheless I will bless you, and your family: yea, your little ones, and the day cometh that they will believe *15* and know the truth and be one with you in my church.

2 Lift up your heart and rejoice for the hour of your mission is come; and your tongue shall be loosed; and you shall declare glad tidings of great joy unto this generation. You shall declare the things which have been revealed to my servant Jo- *20* seph Smith, jr. You shall begin to preach from this time forth; yea, to reap in the field which is white already to be burned: therefore thrust in your sickle with all your soul; and your sins are forgiven you; and you shall be laden with sheaves upon your back, for the laborer is worthy of his hire. Wherefore *25* your family shall live.

3 Behold, verily I say unto you, go from them only for a little time, and declare my word, and I will prepare a place for them; yea, I will open the hearts of the people and they will receive you. And I will establish a church by your hand; *30* and you shall strengthen them and prepare them against the time when they shall be gathered. Be patient in afflictions, revile not against those that revile. Govern your house in meekness, and be steadfast.

4 Behold I say unto you, that you shall be a physician unto *35* the church, but not unto the world, for they will not receive you. Go your way whithersoever I will, and it shall be given you by the Comforter what you shall do, and whither you shall go. Pray always, lest you enter into temptation, and lose your reward. Be faithful unto the end and, lo, I am with *40* you. These words are not of man nor of men, but of me, even Jesus Christ, your Redeemer, by the will of the Father. Amen.

---

line 9. Revelation, Sept. 1830–F [D&C 31]. This version closely corresponds to the version in chapter 34 of the Book of Commandments, suggesting that the latter was used as a source text for the former.

184

line 1

SECTION LIV.

Revelation to Parley P. Pratt and Ziba Peterson, given October, 1830.

1 And now concerning my servant Parley P. Pratt, behold I
say unto him, that as I live I will that he shall declare my
gospel and learn of me, and be meek and lowly of heart; and
that which I have appointed unto him, is, that he shall go with
my servants Oliver Cowdery and Peter Whitmer, jr. into the
wilderness, among the Lamanites; and Ziba Peterson, also,
shall go with them, and I myself will go with them and be in
their midst: and I am their Advocate with the Father, and nothing shall prevail. And they shall give heed to that which
is written and pretend to no other revelation, and they shall
pray always that I may unfold them to their understanding;
and they shall give heed unto these words and trifle not, and
I will bless them. Amen.

SECTION LV.

*Revelation to Ezra Thayre and Northrop Sweet, given October,
1830.*

1 Behold I say unto you, my servants Ezra and Northrop,
open ye your ears and hearken to the voice of the Lord your
God, whose word is quick and powerful, sharper than a two
edged sword, to the dividing asunder of the joints and marrow,
soul and spirit: and is a discerner of the thoughts and intents
of the heart. For verily, verily I say unto you, that ye are
called to lift up your voices as with the sound of a trump, to
declare my gospel unto a crooked and a perverse generation:
for behold the field is white already to harvest; and it is the
eleventh hour, and for the last time that I shall call laborers
into my vineyard. And my vineyard has become corrupted
every whit: and there is none which doeth good save it be a
few; and they err in many instances, because of priestcrafts,
all having corrupt minds.

2 And verily, verily I say unto you, that this church have I
established and called forth out of the wilderness: and even so
will I gather mine elect from the four quarters of the earth,
even as many as will believe in me, and hearken unto my
voice: yea, verily, verily I say unto you, that the field is white
already to harvest: wherefore thrust in your sickles, and reap
with all your might, mind and strength. Open your mouths
and they shall be filled; and you shall become even as Nephi

line 1. Revelation, Oct. 1830–A [D&C 32]. A version of this revelation appears in Revelation Book 2,
but the source text for the version printed here is unknown.

line 17. Revelation, Oct. 1830–B [D&C 33]. This version closely corresponds to the version in chapter 35
of the Book of Commandments, suggesting that the latter was used as a source text for the former.

185

line 1   of old, who journeyed from Jerusalem in the wilderness: yea,
          open your mouths and spare not, and you shall be laden with
          sheaves upon your backs, for lo I am with you: yea, open your
          mouths and they shall be filled, saying, Repent, repent and
5   prepare ye the way of the Lord, and make his paths straight:
          for the kingdom of heaven is at hand: yea, repent and be bap-
          tized every one of you; for a remission of your sins; yea, be
          baptized even by water, and then cometh the baptism of fire
          and of the Holy Ghost.
10   3 Behold, verily, verily I say unto you, this is my gospel,
          and remember that they shall have faith in me, or they can in
          no wise be saved: and upon this Rock I will build my church;
          yea, upon this rock ye are built, and if ye continue, the gates
          of hell shall not prevail against you; and ye shall remember
15   the church articles and covenants to keep them: and whoso
          having faith you shall confirm in my church, by the laying on
          of the hands, and I will bestow the gift of the Holy Ghost
          upon them. And the book of Mormon, and the holy scriptures,
          are given of me for your instruction; and the power of my
20   Spirit quickeneth all things: wherefore be faithful, praying al-
          ways, having your lamps trimmed and burning, and oil with
          you, that you may be ready at the coming of the Bridegroom;
          for behold, verily, verily I say unto you, that I come quickly;
          even so: Amen.

25   SECTION LVI.

                  Revelation to Orson Pratt, given November, 1830.

          1 My son Orson, hearken and hear and behold what I the Lord
          God shall say unto you, even Jesus Christ your Redeemer,
          the light and the life of the world: a light which shineth in
30   darkness and the darkness comprehendeth it not: who so loved
          the world that he gave his own life, that as many as would
          believe might become the sons of God: wherefore you are my
          son, and blessed are you because you have believed, and more
          blessed are you because you are called of me to preach my
35   gospel; to lift up your voice as with the sound of a trump, both
          long and loud, and cry repentance unto a crooked and perverse
          generation; preparing the way of the Lord for his second com-
          ing; for behold, verily, verily I say unto you, the time is
          soon at hand, that I shall come in a cloud with power and
40   great glory, and it shall be a great day at the time of my com-
          ing, for all nations shall tremble.
          2 But before that great day shall come, the sun shall be
          darkened, and the moon be turned into blood, and the stars

---

line 25. Revelation, 4 Nov. 1830 [D&C 34]. This version closely corresponds to the version in chapter 36 of the Book of Commandments, suggesting that the latter was used as a source text for the former.

186

shall refuse their shining, and some shall fall, and great destructions await the wicked: wherefore lift up your voice and spare not, for the Lord God hath spoken. Therefore prophesy and it shall be given by the power of the Holy Ghost; and if you are faithful behold I am with you until I come: and verily, verily I say unto you. I come quickly. I am your Lord and your Redeemer; even so. Amen.

SECTION LVII.

Revelation to Edward Partrige, given December, 1830.

1 Thus saith the Lord God, the mighty One of Israel, behold I say unto you, my servant Edward, that you are blessed, and your sins are forgiven you, and you are called to preach my gospel as with the voice of a trump; and I will lay my hand upon you by the hand of my servant Sidney Rigdon, and you shall receive my Spirit, the Holy Ghost, even the Comforter, which shall teach you the peaceable things of the kingdom: and you shall declare it with a loud voice, saying, Hosanna, blessed be the name of the most high God.

2 And now this calling and commandment give I unto you concerning all men, that as many as shall come before my servants Sidney Rigdon and Joseph Smith, jr. embracing this calling and commandment, shall be ordained and sent forth to preach the everlasting gospel among the nations, crying repentance, saying, Save yourselves from this untoward generation, and come forth out of the fire, hating even the garments spotted with the flesh.

3 And this commandment shall be given unto the elders of my church, that every man which will embrace it with singleness of heart, may be ordained and sent forth, even as I have spoken. I am Jesus Christ, the Son of God: wherefore gird up your loins and I will suddenly come to my temple; even so. Amen.

SECTION LVIII.

Revelation to Joseph Smith, jr. and Sidney Rigdon, given December, 1830.

1 Behold I say unto you, that it is not expedient in me that ye should translate any more until ye shall go to the Ohio; and this because of the enemy and for your sakes. And again, I say unto you, that ye shall not go until ye have preached my gospel in those parts, and have strengthened up the church

---

line 8. Revelation, 9 Dec. 1830 [D&C 36]. This version closely corresponds to the version in chapter 38 of the Book of Commandments, suggesting that the latter was used as a source text for the former.

line 33. Revelation, 30 Dec. 1830 [D&C 37]. This version reflects editing marks made in chapter 39 of Oliver Cowdery's copy of the Book of Commandments, indicating that the latter was used as a source text for the former. (See p. 612 herein.)

187

line 1 whithersoever it is found, and more especially in Colesville: for behold they pray unto me in much faith.

2 And again a commandment I give unto the church, that it is expedient in me that they should assemble together at the Ohio, against the time that my servant Oliver Cowdery shall return unto them. Behold here is wisdom, and let every man choose for himself until I come; even so. Amen.

SECTION LIX.

Revelation to James Covill, given January, 1831.

1 Hearken and listen to the voice of him who is from all eternity to all eternity, the Great I AM, even Jesus Christ, the light and the life of the world; a light which shineth in darkness and the darkness comprehendeth it not: the same which came in the meridian of time unto my own, and my own received me not; but to as many as received me, gave I power to become my sons, and even so will I give unto as many as will receive me, power to become my sons.

2 And verily, verily I say unto you, he that receiveth my gospel, receiveth me; and he that receiveth not my gospel, receiveth not me. And this is my gospel: repentance and baptism by water, and then cometh the baptism of fire and the Holy Ghost, even the Comforter, which showeth all things, and teacheth the peaceable things of the kingdom.

3 And now behold I say unto you, my servant James, I have looked upon thy works and I know thee: and verily I say unto thee, thine heart is now right before me at this time, and behold I have bestowed great blessings upon thy head:— nevertheless thou hast seen great sorrow for thou hast rejected me many times because of pride, and the cares of the world: but behold the days of thy deliverance are come, if thou wilt hearken to my voice, which saith unto thee, Arise and be baptized, and wash away your sins, calling on my name and you shall receive my Spirit, and a blessing so great as you never have known. And if thou do this, I have prepared thee for a greater work. Thou shalt preach the fulness of my gospel which I have sent forth in these last days; the covenant which I have sent forth to recover my people, which are of the house of Israel.

4 And it shall come to pass that power shall rest upon thee; thou shalt have great faith and I will be with thee and go before thy face. Thou art called to labor in my vineyard, and to build up my church, and to bring forth Zion, that it may rejoice upon the hills and flourish. Behold, verily, verily I

line numbers: *5*, *10*, *15*, *20*, *25*, *30*, *35*, *40*

---

line 8. Revelation, 5 Jan. 1831 [D&C 39]. This version reflects editing marks made in chapter 41 of Oliver Cowdery's copy of the Book of Commandments, indicating that the latter was used as a source text for the former. (See pp. 615–616 herein.)

188

line 1
say unto thee, thou art not called to go into the eastern countries, but thou art called to go to the Ohio. And inasmuch
as my people shall assemble themselves to the Ohio, I have
kept in store a blessing such as is not known among the children of men, and it shall be poured forth upon their heads.—
And from thence men shall go forth into all nations.

5 Behold, verily, verily I say unto you, that the people in
Ohio call upon me in much faith, thinking I will stay my hand
in judgment upon the nations, but I cannot deny my word:
wherefore lay to with your might and call faithful laborers into my vineyard, that it may be pruned for the last time. And
inasmuch as they do repent and receive the fulness of my gospel, and become sanctified, I will stay mine hand in judgment:
wherefore go forth, crying with a loud voice, saying, The
kingdom of heaven is at hand; crying Hosanna! blessed be
the name of the most high God. Go forth baptizing with water, preparing the way before my face, for the time of my
coming; for the time is at hand: the day nor the hour no man
knoweth, but it surely shall come, and he that receiveth these
things receiveth me; and they shall be gathered unto me in
time and in eternity.

6 And again, it shall come to pass, that on as many as ye
shall baptize with water, ye shall lay your hands, and they
shall receive the gift of the Holy Ghost, and shall be looking
forth for the signs of my coming, and shall know me. Behold
I come quickly; even so. Amen.

SECTION LX.

Revelation to Joseph Smith, jr. and Sidney Rigdon, given Jan-
uary, 1831, explaining why James Covill, obeyed not the reve-
elation which was given unto him.

1 Behold, verily I say unto you, that the heart of my servant James Covill was right before me, for he covenanted
with me, that he would obey my word. And he received the
word with gladness, but straightway satan tempted him; and
the fear of persecution, and the cares of the world, caused him
to reject the word; wherefore he broke my covenant, and it
remaineth in me to do with him as seemeth me good. Amen.

SECTION LXI.

Revelation given February, 1831.

1 Hearken and hear, O ye my people, saith the Lord and
your God, ye whom I delight to bless with the greatest bles-

---

line 27. Revelation, 6 Jan. 1831 [D&C 40]. This version reflects editing marks made in chapter 42 of Oliver Cowdery's copy of the Book of Commandments, indicating that the latter was used as a source text for the former. (See p. 616 herein.)

line 38. Revelation, 4 Feb. 1831 [D&C 41]. This version closely corresponds to the version in chapter 43 of the Book of Commandments, suggesting that the latter was used as a source text for the former.

189

sings; ye that hear me: and ye that hear me not will I curse, that have professed my name, with the heaviest of all cursings. Hearken, O ye elders of my church whom I have called: behold I give unto you a commandment, that ye shall assemble yourselves together to agree upon my word, and by the prayer of your faith ye shall receive my law, that ye may know how to govern my church, and have all things right before me.

2 And I will be your Ruler when I come: and behold, I come quickly: and ye shall see that my law is kept. He that receiveth my law and doeth it the same is my disciple; and he that saith he receiveth it and doeth it not, the same is not my disciple, and shall be cast out from among you: for it is not meet that the things which belong to the children of the kingdom, should be given to them that are not worthy, or to dogs, or the pearls to be cast before swine.

3 And again, it is meet that my servant Joseph Smith, jr. should have a house built, in which to live and translate. And again it is meet that my servant Sidney Rigdon should live as seemeth him good, inasmuch as he keepeth my commandments. And again, I have called my servant Edward Partridge, and give a commandment, that he should be appointed by the voice of the church, and ordained a bishop unto the church, to leave his merchandise and to spend all his time in the labors of the church; to see to all things as it shall be appointed unto him, in my laws in the day that I shall give them. And this because his heart is pure before me, for he is like unto Nathaniel of old, in whom there is no guile. These words are given unto you, and they are pure before me: wherefore beware how you hold them, for they are to be answered upon your souls in the day of judgment; even so. Amen.

SECTION LXII.

Revelation to Joseph Smith, jr. and Sidney Rigdon, given February, 1831.

1 Behold thus saith the Lord unto you my servants, it is expedient in me that the elders of my church should be called together, from the east and from the west, and from the north and from the south, by letter or some other way.

2 And it shall come to pass, that inasmuch as they are faithful, and exercise faith in me, I will pour out my Spirit upon them in the day that they assemble themselves together. And it shall come to pass that they shall go forth into the regions round about, and preach repentance unto the people; and many shall be converted, insomuch that ye shall obtain power to

---

line 31. Revelation, Feb. 1831–B [D&C 44]. This version closely corresponds to the version in chapter 46 of the Book of Commandments, suggesting that the latter was used as a source text for the former.

190

line 1
organize yourselves, according to the laws of man; that your
enemies may not have power over you, that you may be preserved in all things; that you may be enabled to keep my laws,
that every band may be broken wherewith the enemy seeketh

5　to destroy my people.

3 Behold I say unto you, that ye must visit the poor and the
needy and administer to their relief, that they may be kept until all things may be done according to my law which ye have
received. Amen.

10
SECTION LXIII.

*Revelation to Joseph Smith, jr. and John Whitmer, given March,
1831.*

1 Behold it is expedient in me that my servant John should
write and keep a regular history, and assist you, my servant
Joseph, in transcribing all things which shall be given you,

15　until he is called to further duties. Again, verily I say unto
you, that he can also lift up his voice in meetings, whenever it
shall be expedient.

2 And again, I say unto you, that it shall be appointed unto
him to keep the church record and history continually, for Ol-

20　iver Cowdery I have appointed to another office. Wherefore
it shall be given him, inasmuch as he is faithful, by the Comforter, to write these things; even so. Amen.

SECTION LXIV.

25
Revelation given March, 1831.

1 It is necessary that ye should remain, for the present time,
in your places of abode, as it shall be suitable to your circumstances; and inasmuch as ye have lands, ye shall impart to the
eastern brethren; and inasmuch as ye have not lands, let them

30　buy for the present time in those regions round about as seemeth them good, for it must needs be necessary that they have
places to live for the present time.

2 It must needs be necessary, that ye save all the money
that ye can, and that ye obtain all that ye can in righteous-

35　ness, that in time ye may be enabled to purchase lands for an
inheritance, even the city. The place is not yet to be revealed, but after your brethren come from the east, there are to be
certain men appointed, and to them it shall be given to know
the place, or to them it shall be revealed; and they shall be ap-

40　pointed to purchase the lands, and to make a commencement,
to lay the foundation of the city; and then ye shall begin to be

---

line 10. Revelation, ca. 8 Mar. 1831–B [D&C 47]. This version corresponds to the version in chapter 50
of the Book of Commandments, suggesting that the latter was used as a source text for the former.

line 24. Revelation, 10 Mar. 1831 [D&C 48]. This version closely corresponds to the version in chapter 51
of the Book of Commandments, suggesting that the latter was used as a source text for the former.

191

gathered with your families, every man according to his family, according to his circumstances, and as is appointed to him
by the presidency and the bishop of the church, according to
the laws and commandments, which ye have received, and
which ye shall hereafter receive; even so. Amen.

SECTION LXV.

*Revelation to Sidney Rigdon, Parley P. Pratt, and Lemon Cop-
ley, given March, 1831.*

1 Hearken unto my word, my servant Sidney, and Parley,
and Lemon, for behold, verily I say unto you, that I give unto you a commandment, that you shall go and preach my gospel, which ye have received, even as ye have received it, unto
the shakers. Behold I say unto you, that they desire to know
the truth in part, but not all, for they are not right before me,
and must needs repent: wherefore I send you, my servants
Sidney and Parley, to preach the gospel unto them; and my
servant Lemon shall be ordained unto this work, that he may
reason with them, not according to that which he has received
of them, but according to that which shall be taught him by
you, my servants, and by so doing I will bless him, otherwise
he shall not prosper: thus saith the Lord, for I am God and
have sent mine only begotten Son into the world, for the redemption of the world, and have decreed that he that receiveth him
shall be saved, and he that receiveth him not, shall be damned.
2 And they have done unto the Son of man even as they listed; and he has taken his power on the right hand of his glory, and now reigneth in the heavens, and will reign till he descends on the earth to put all enemies under his feet: which
time is nigh at hand: I the Lord God have spoken it: but the
hour and the day no man knoweth, neither the angels in heav-
en, nor shall they know until he comes: wherefore I will that
all men shall repent, for all are under sin, except them which
I have reserved unto myself, holy men that ye know not of:
wherefore I say unto you, that I have sent unto you mine everlasting covenant, even that which was from the beginning,
and that which I have promised I have so fulfilled, and the nations of the earth shall bow to it; and, if not of themselves,
they shall come down, for that which is now exalted of itself,
shall be laid low of power: wherefore I give unto you a commandment, that ye go among this people and say unto them,
like unto mine apostle of old, whose name was Peter: Believe
on the name of the Lord Jesus, who was on the earth, and is
to come, the beginning and the end; repent and be baptized in

---

line 6. Revelation, 7 May 1831 [D&C 49]. This version closely corresponds to the version in chapter 52 of the Book of Commandments, suggesting that the latter was used as a source text for the former. This revelation should be dated 7 May 1831. For more information on this dating, see the discussion of this revelation in the Documents series.

192

line 1

the name of Jesus Christ, according to the holy commandment, for the remission of sins; and whoso doeth this, shall receive the gift of the Holy Ghost, by the laying on of the hands of the elders of this church.

5   3 And again, I say unto you, that whoso forbiddeth to marry, is not ordained of God, for marriage is ordained of God unto man: wherefore it is lawful that he should have one wife, and they twain shall be one flesh, and all this that the earth might answer the end of its creation; and that it might be filled with the measure of man, according to his creation before *10* the world was made. And whoso forbiddeth to abstain from meats, that man should not eat the same, is not ordained of God; for behold the beasts of the field, and the fowls of the air, and that which cometh of the earth, is ordained for the *15* use of man, for food, and for raiment, and that he might have in abundance, but it is not given that one man should possess that which is above another: wherefore the world lieth in sin; and wo be unto man that sheddeth blood or that wasteth flesh and hath no need.

20   4 And again, verily I say unto you, that the Son of man cometh not in the form of a woman, neither of a man travelling on the earth: wherefore be not deceived, but continue in steadfastness, looking forth for the heavens to be shaken; and the earth to tremble, and to reel to and fro as a drunken man; and for *25* the valleys to be exalted; and for the mountains to be made low; and for the rough places to become smooth: and all this when the angel shall sound his trumpet.

   5 But before the great day of the Lord shall come, Jacob shall flourish in the wilderness; and the Lamanites shall blossom as *30* the rose: Zion shall flourish upon the hills, and rejoice upon the mountains, and shall be assembled together unto the place which I have appointed. Behold I say unto you, go forth as I have [s]commanded you; repent of all your sins; ask and ye shall receive; knock and it shall be opened unto you: behold I *35* will go before you, and be your rereward; and I will be in your midst, and you shall not be confounded: behold I am Jesus Christ, and I come quickly; even so. Amen.

SECTION LXVI.

Revelation given June, 1831.

40   1 Behold, thus saith the Lord unto the elders whom he hath called and chosen, in these last days, by the voice of his Spirit, saying, I the Lord will make known unto you what I will that ye shall do from this time until the next conference, which

---

line 38. Revelation, 6 June 1831 [D&C 52]. This version reflects editing marks made in chapter 54 of Oliver Cowdery's copy of the Book of Commandments, indicating that the latter was used as a source text for the former. (See pp. 622–624 herein.)

193

line 1 shall be held in Missouri, upon the land which I will consecrate unto my people, which are a remnant of Jacob, and them
who are heirs according to the covenant.

2 Wherefore, verily I say unto you, let my servant Joseph
line 5 Smith, jr. and Sidney Rigdon take their journey as soon as
preparations can be made to leave their homes, and journey to
the land of Missouri.   And inasmuch as they are faithful unto
me, it shall be made known unto them what they shall do: and
it shall also, inasmuch as they are faithful, be made known un-
line 10 to them the land of your inheritance.   And inasmuch as they
are not faithful, they shall be cut off, even as I will, as seemeth me good.

3 And again, verily I say unto you, let my servant Lyman
Wight, and my servant John Corrill take their journey speedi-
line 15 ly: and also my servant John Murdock, and my servant Hyrum Smith, take their journey unto the same place by the way
of Detroit.   And let them journey from thence preaching the
word by the way, saying none other things than that which
the prophets and apostles have written, and that which is
line 20 taught them by the Comforter, through the prayer of faith.—
Let them go two by two, and thus let them preach by the way
in every congregation, baptizing by water, and the laying on
of the hands by the water side: for thus saith the Lord, I will
cut my work short in righteousness: for the days cometh that
line 25 I will send forth judgment unto victory.   And let my servant
Lyman Wight beware, for satan desireth to sift him as chaff.

4 And behold, he that is faithful shall be made ruler over many things.   And again, I will give unto you a pattern in all
things, that ye may not be deceived, for satan is abroad in the
line 30 land, and he goeth forth deceiving the nations: wherefore he
that prayeth whose spirit is contrite, the same is accepted of
me, if he obey mine ordinances: he that speaketh, whose spirit is contrite, whose language is meek, and edifieth, the same
is of God, if he obey mine ordinances.   And again, he that
line 35 trembleth under my power, shall be made strong, and shall
bring forth fruits of praise, and wisdom, according to the revelations, and truths which I have given you.

5 And again, he that is overcome and bringeth not forth
fruits, even according to this pattern, is not of me: wherefore
line 40 by this pattern ye shall know the spirits in all cases, under the
whole heavens.   And the days have come, according to men's
faith it shall be done unto them.   Behold this commandment
is given unto all the elders whom I have chosen.   And again,
verily I say unto you, let my servant Thomas Marsh, and my
line 45 servant Ezra Thayre, take their journey also, preaching the

M

line 46. This page begins the thirteenth gathering of the book. "M" is the first of two signature marks in this gathering; the second is on the recto of the following leaf. These marks were used in collating the gatherings after the sheets were folded.

194

line 1 word by the way, unto this same land. And again, let my servant Isaac Morley, and my servant Ezra Booth, take their journey, also preaching the word by the way unto the same land.

6 And again, let my servants Edward Partridge and Martin Harris, take their journey with my servants Sidney Rigdon and Joseph Smith, jr. Let my servants David Whitmer and Harvy Whitlock also take their journey, and preach by the way unto this same land. Let my servants Parley P. Pratt and Orson Pratt take their journey, and preach by the way, even unto this same land. And let my servants Solomon Hancock and Simeon Carter also take their journey unto this same land, and preach by the way. Let my servants Edson Fuller and Jacob Scott also take their journey. Let my servants Levi Hancock and Zebedee Coltrin also take their journey. Let my servants Reynolds Cahoon and Samuel H. Smith also take their journey. Let my servants Wheeler Baldwin and William Carter also take their journey.

7 And let my servants Newel Knight and Selah J. Griffin, both be ordained and also take their journey: yea, verily I say, let all these take their journey unto one place, in their several courses, and one man shall not build upon another's foundation, neither journey in another's track. He that is faithful, the same shall be kept and blessed with much fruit.

8 And again, I say unto you, let my servants Joseph Wakefield and Solomon Humphrey take their journey into the eastern lands. Let them labor with their families, declaring none other things than the prophets and apostles, that which they have seen, and heard, and most assuredly believe, that the prophecies may be fulfilled. In consequence of transgression, let that which was bestowed upon Heman Basset, be taken from him, and placed upon the head of Simonds Rider.

9 And again, verily I say unto you, let Jared Carter be ordained a priest, and also George James be ordained a priest.— Let the residue of the elders watch over the churches, and declare the word in the regions among them. And let them labor with their own hands, that there be no idolatry nor wickedness practiced. And remember in all things, the poor and the needy, the sick and the afflicted, for he that doeth not these things, the same is not my disciple. And again, let my servants Joseph Smith, jr. and Sidney Rigdon and Edward Partridge, take with them a recommend from the church.— And let there be one obtained for my servant Oliver Cowdery also: and thus, even as I have said, if ye are faithful, ye shall assemble yourselves together to rejoice upon the land of Missouri, which is the land of your inheritance, which is now the

195

line 1 land of your enemies. But behold I the Lord will hasten the city in its time, and will crown the faithful with joy and with rejoicing. Behold I am Jesus Christ the Son of God, and I will lift them up at the last day; even so. Amen.

SECTION LXVI.

Revelation to Sidney Gilbert, given June, 1831.

1 Behold I say unto you, my servant Sidney Gilbert, that I have heard your prayers, and you have called upon me, that it should be made known unto you, of the Lord your God, concerning your calling, and election in this church, which I the Lord have raised up in these last days.

2 Behold I the Lord, who was crucified for the sins of the world, giveth unto you a commandment, that you shall forsake the world. Take upon you mine ordinances, even that of an elder, to preach faith and repentance, and remission of sins, according to my word, and the reception of the Holy Spirit by the laying on of hands. And also to be an agent unto this church in the place which shall be appointed by the bishop, according to commandments which shall be given hereafter.

3 And again, verily I say unto you, you shall take your journey with my servants Joseph Smith, jr. and Sidney Rigdon. Behold these are the first ordinances which you shall receive: and the residue shall be made known in a time to come, according to your labor in my vineyard. And again, I would that ye should learn that it is he only who is saved, that endureth unto the end; even so. Amen.

SECTION LXVII.

Revelation to Newel Knight, given June, 1831.

1 Behold, thus saith the Lord, even Alpha and Omega, the beginning and the end, even he who was crucified for the sins of the world. Behold, verily, verily I say unto you, my servant Newel Knight, you shall stand fast in the office wherewith I have appointed you: and if your brethren desire to escape their enemies let them repent of all their sins; and become truly humble before me and contrite: and as the covenant which they made unto me, has been broken, even so it has become void and of none effect; and wo to him by whom this offence cometh, for it had been better for him that he had been drowned in the depth of the sea; but blessed are they who have

13*

---

line 5. Revelation, 8 June 1831 [D&C 53]. Sections 66 and 67 (on this page) reflect editing marks made in chapters 55 and 56 of Oliver Cowdery's copy of the Book of Commandments, indicating that the Cowdery volume was used as a source text for the versions printed here. (See pp. 624–625 herein.)

line 5. The printers of the 1835 Doctrine and Covenants mistakenly numbered two sections as 66. Section numbering remains one off for all subsequent sections within the 1835 edition.

line 27. Revelation, 10 June 1831 [D&C 54]. See first note on this page.

196

line 1 kept the covenant, and observed the commandment, for they shall obtain mercy.

2 Wherefore, go to now and flee the land, lest your enemies come upon you: and take your journey, and appoint whom you

5 will to be your leader, and to pay moneys for you. And thus you shall take your journey into the regions westward, unto the land of Missouri, unto the borders of the Lamanites. And after you have done journeying, behold I say unto you, seek ye a living like unto men, until I prepare a place for you.

10 3 And again, be patient in tribulation until I come: and behold I come quickly, and my reward is with me, and they who have sought me early, shall find rest to their souls; even so. Amen.

SECTION LXVIII.

15 *Revelation to William W. Phelps, given June, 1831.*

1 Behold thus saith the Lord unto you, my servant William; yea, even the Lord of the whole earth, thou art called and chosen and after thou hast been baptized by water, which if you do with an eye single to my glory, you shall have a remission

20 of your sins, and a reception of the Holy Spirit, by the laying on of hands. And then thou shalt be ordained by the hand of my servant Joseph Smith, jr. to be an elder unto this church, to preach repentance and remission of sins by way of baptism in the name of Jesus Christ, the Son of the living God; and

25 on whomsoever you shall lay your hands, if they are contrite before me, you shall have power to give the Holy Spirit.

2 And again, you shall be ordained to assist my servant Oliver Cowdery to do the work of printing, and of selecting, and writing books for schools, in this church, that little children

30 also may receive instruction before me as is pleasing unto me. And again verily I say unto you, for this cause you shall take your journey with my servants Joseph Smith, jr. and Sidney Rigdon, that you may be planted in the land of your inheritance, to do this work.

35 3 And again let my servant Joseph Coe also take his journey with them. The residue shall be made known hereafter; even as I will: Amen.

---

line 14. Revelation, 14 June 1831 [D&C 55]. This version reflects editing marks made in chapter 57 of Oliver Cowdery's copy of the Book of Commandments, indicating that the latter was used as a source text for the former. (See pp. 625–626 herein.)

197

line 1

SECTION LXIX.

Revelation given June, 1831

1 Hearken O ye people which profess my name, saith the Lord your God, for behold mine anger is kindled against the rebellious, and they shall know mine arm and mine indignation in the day of visitation and of wrath upon the nations.— And he that will not take up his cross and follow me, and keep my commandments, the same shall not be saved.

2 Behold I the Lord commandeth, and he that will not obey shall be cut off in mine own due time: and after that I have commanded and the commandment is broken, wherefore I the Lord command and revoke, as it seemeth me good; and all this to be answered upon the heads of the rebellious saith the Lord: wherefore I revoke the commandment which was given unto my servants Thomas B. Marsh and Ezra Thayer, and give a new commandment unto my servant Thomas, that he shall take up his journey speedily to the land of Missouri; and my servant Selah J. Griffin shall also go with him: for behold I revoke the commandment which was given unto my servants Selah J. Griffin and Newel Knight, in consequence of the stiffneckedness of my people which are in Thompson; and their rebellions: wherefore let my servant Newel Knight remain with them, and as many as will go may go, that are contrite before me, and be led by him to the land which I have appointed.

3 And again, verily I say unto you, that my servant Ezra Thayer must repent of his pride, and of his selfishness, and obey the former commandment which I have given him concerning the place upon which he lives; and if he will do this, as there shall be no divisions made upon the land, he shall be appointed still to go to the land of Missouri; otherwise he shall receive the money which he has paid, and shall leave the place, and shall be cut off out of my church, saith the Lord God of hosts: and though the heaven and the earth pass away, these words shall not pass away, but shall be fulfilled.

4 And if my servant Joseph Smith, jr. must needs pay the money, behold I the Lord will pay it unto him again in the land of Missouri, that those of whom he shall receive may be reward d again, according to that which they do. For according to that which they do, they shall receive; even in lands for their inheritance. Behold thus saith the Lord unto my people, you have many things to do, and to repent of: for behold your sins have come up unto me, and are not pardoned, because you seek to counsel in your own ways. And your

line 5 *line 10* *line 15* *line 20* *line 25* *line 30* *line 35* *line 40*

---

line 1. Revelation, 15 June 1831 [D&C 56]. This version reflects editing marks made in chapter 58 of Oliver Cowdery's copy of the Book of Commandments, indicating that the latter was used as a source text for the former. (See pp. 626–627 herein.)

198

line 1

hearts are not satisfied.   And ye obey not the truth, but have
pleasure in unrighteousness.

5 Wo unto you rich men, that will not give your substance
to the poor, for your riches will canker your souls! and this
shall be your lamentation in the day of visitation, and of judgment, and of indignation: The harvest is past, the summer is
ended, and my soul is not saved! Wo unto you poor men,
whose hearts are not broken, whose spirits are not contrite,
and whose bellies are not satisfied, and whose hands are not
stayed from laying hold upon other men's goods, whose eyes
are full of greediness, who will not labor with their own
hands!

6 But blessed are the poor, who are pure in heart, whose
hearts are broken, and whose spirits are contrite, for they shall
see the kingdom of God coming in power and great glory unto
their deliverance: for the fatness of the earth shall be theirs:
for behold the Lord shall come, and his recompense shall be
with him, and he shall reward every man, and the poor shall
rejoice: and their generations shall inherit the earth from generation to generation, forever and ever.   And now I make an
end of speaking unto you; even so. Amen.

SECTION LXX.

Revelation given August, 1831.

1 Behold, thus saith the Lord unto the elders of his church,
who are to return speedily to the land from whence they came.
Behold it pleaseth me, that you have come up hither; but with
some I am not well pleased, for they will not open their mouths,
but hide the talent which I have given unto them, because of
the fear of man.   Wo unto such, for mine anger is kindled
against them.

2 And it shall come to pass, if they are not more faithful unto me, it shall be taken away, even that which they have, for
I the Lord ruleth in the heavens above, and among the armies
of the earth; and in the day when I shall make up my jewels,
all men shall know what it is that bespeaketh the power of
God.   But verily I will speak unto you concerning your journey unto the land from whence you came.   Let there be a
craft made, or bought, as seemeth you good, it mattereth not
unto me, and take your journey speedily for the place which
is called St. Louis.   And from thence let my servants Sidney
Rigdon, and Joseph Smith, jr. and Oliver Cowdery, take their
journey for Cincinnati: and in this place let them lift up their
voice, and declare my word with loud voices, without wrath

---

line 22. Revelation, 8 Aug. 1831 [D&C 60]. This version reflects editing marks made in chapter 61 of
Oliver Cowdery's copy of the Book of Commandments, indicating that the latter was used as a source
text for the former. (See pp. 631–632 herein.)

199

line 1

'or doubting, lifting up holy hands upon them. For I am able to make you holy, and your sins are forgiven you.

3 And let the residue take their journey from St. Louis, two by two, and preach the word, not in haste, among the congregations of the wicked, until they return to the churches from whence they came. And all this for the good of the churches; for this intent have I sent them. And let my servant Edward Partridge impart of the money which I have given him, a portion unto mine elders, who are commanded to return; and he that is able, let him return it by the way of the agent, and he that is not, of him it is not required. And now I speak of the residue who are to come unto this land. Behold they have been sent to preach my gospel among the congregations of the wicked: wherefore, I give unto them a commandment thus: Thou shalt not idle away thy time: neither shalt thou bury thy talent that it may not be known.

4 And after thou hast come up unto the land of Zion, and hast proclaimed my word, thou shalt speedily return proclaiming my word among the congregations of the wicked. Not in haste, neither in wrath nor with strife: and shake off the dust of thy feet against those who receive thee not, not in their presence, lest thou provoke them, but in secret, and wash thy feet as a testimony against them in the day of judgment.— Behold this is sufficient for you, and the will of him who hath sent you. And by the mouth of my servant Joseph Smith, jr. it shall be made known concerning Sidney Rigdon and Oliver Cowdery, the residue hereafter; even so. Amen.

SECTION LXXI.

Revelation given August, 1831.

1 Behold, and hearken unto the voice of him who has all power, who is from everlasting to everlasting, even Alpha and Omega, the beginning and the end. Behold, verily thus saith the Lord unto you O ye elders of my church, who are assembled upon this spot, whose sins are now forgiven you, for I the Lord forgiveth sins, and am merciful unto those who confess their sins with humble hearts: but verily I say unto you, that it is not needful for this whole company of mine elders, to be moving swiftly upon the waters, whilst the inhabitants on either side are perishing in unbelief: nevertheless, I suffered it that ye might bear record: behold there are many dangers upon the waters and more especially hereafter, for I the Lord have decreed, in mine anger, many destructions upon the waters; yea, and especially upon these waters; neverthe-

line 5, 10, 15, 20, 25, 30, 35, 40

---

line 28. Revelation, 12 Aug. 1831 [D&C 61]. This version reflects editing marks made in chapter 62 of Oliver Cowdery's copy of the Book of Commandments, indicating that the latter was used as a source text for the former. (See pp. 632–634 herein.)

200

less, all flesh is in mine hand, and he that is faithful among
you, shall not perish by the waters.

2 Wherefore it is expedient that my servant Sidney Gilbert,
and my servant William W. Phelps, be in haste upon their
errand and mission: nevertheless I would not suffer that ye
should part until you are chastened for all your sins, that you
might be one; that you might not perish in wickedness; but now
verily I say, it behoveth me that ye should part: wherefore let
my servants Sidney Gilbert and William W. Phelps, take
their former company, and let them take their journey in haste
that they may fill their mission, and through faith they shall
overcome; and inasmuch as they are faithful, they shall be
preserved, and I the Lord will be with them. And let the residue take that which is needful for clothing. Let my servant
Sidney Gilbert take that which is not needful with him, as
you shall agree. And now behold, for your good I gave unto
you a commandment concerning these things; and I the Lord
will reason with you as with men in days of old.

3 Behold I the Lord in the beginning, blessed the waters, but
in the last days by the mouth of my servant John, I cursed
the waters: wherefore, the days will come that no flesh shall
be safe upon the waters, and it shall be said in days to come,
that none is able to go up to the land of Zion, upon the waters, but he that is upright in heart. And, as I the Lord in
the beginning cursed the land, even so in the last days have I
blessed it, in its time, for the use of my saints, that they may
partake the fatness thereof. And now I give unto you a commandment, and what I say unto one I say unto all, that you
shall forewarn your brethren concerning these waters, that
they come not in journeying upon them, lest their faith fail
and they are caught in her snares: I the Lord have decreed,
and the destroyer rideth upon the face thereof, and I revoke
not the decree: I the Lord was angry with you yesterday, but
to-day mine anger is turned away. Wherefore let those concerning whom I have spoken, that should take their journey
in haste, again I say unto you, let them take their journey in
haste, and it mattereth not unto me, after a little, if it so be
that they fill their mission, whether they go by water or by
land: let this be as it is made known unto them according to
their judgments, hereafter.

4 And now, concerning my servants Sidney Rigdon, and
Joseph Smith, jr. and Oliver Cowdery, let them come not
again upon the waters, save it be upon the canal, while journeying unto their homes, or in other words, they shall not
come upon the waters to journey, save upon the canal. Behold I the Lord have appointed a way for the journeying of

line 1 my saints, and behold this is the way: that after they leave
the canal, they shall journey by land, inasmuch as they are
commanded to journey and go up unto the land of Zion; and
they shall do like unto the children of Israel, pitching their
5 tents by the way.

5 And behold this commandment you shall give unto all your
brethren: nevertheless unto whom it is given power to command the waters, unto him it is given by the Spirit to know
all his ways: wherefore let him do as the Spirit of the living
10 God commandeth him, whether upon the land or upon the
waters, as it remaineth with me to do hereafter; and unto you
it is given the course for the saints, or the way for the saints
of the camp of the Lord, to journey. And again, verily I say
unto you, my servants Sidney Rigdon, and Joseph Smith, jr.
15 and Oliver Cowdery, shall not open their mouths in the congregations of the wicked, until they arrive at Cincinnati; and
in that place they shall lift up their voices unto God against
that people: yea, unto him whose anger is kindled against
their wickedness; a people who is well nigh ripened for des-
20 truction; and from thence let them journey for the congregations of their brethren, for their labors, even now, are wanted
more abundantly among them, than among the congregations
of the wicked.

6 And now concerning the residue, let them journey and de-
25 clare the word among the congregations of the wicked, inasmuch as it is given, and inasmuch as they do this they shall
rid their garments, and they shall be spotless before me; and
let them journey together, or two by two, as seemeth them
good, only let my servant Reynolds Cahoon, and my servant
30 Samuel H. Smith, with whom I am well pleased, be not separated until they return to their homes, and this for a wise
purpose in me. And now verily I say unto you, and what I
say unto one I say unto all, be of good cheer little children,
for I am in your midst, and I have not forsaken you, and in-
35 asmuch as you have humbled yourselves before me, the blessings of the kingdom are yours. Gird up your loins and be
watchful, and be sober, looking forth for the coming of the
Son of man, for he cometh in an hour you think not. Pray
always that you enter not into temptation, that you may abide
40 the day of his coming, whether in life or in death; even so,—
Amen.

202

SECTION LXXII.

Revelation given August, 1831.

1 Behold and hearken, O ye elders of my church, saith the Lord your God; even Jesus Christ, your advocate who knoweth the weakness of man and how to succor them who are tempted: and verily mine eyes are upon those who have not as yet gone up unto the land of Zion: wherefore your mission is not yet full: nevertheless ye are blessed, for the testimony which ye have borne is recorded in heaven for the angels to look upon, and they rejoice over you; and your sins are forgiven you.

2 And now continue your journey. Assemble yourselves upon the land of Zion, and hold a meeting and rejoice together, and offer a sacrament unto the Most High; and then you may return to bear record; yea, even all together, or two by two, as seemeth you good; it mattereth not unto me, only be faithful, and declare glad tidings unto the inhabitants of the earth, or among the congregations of the wicked. Behold I the Lord have brought you together that the promise might be fulfilled, that the faithful among you should be preserved and rejoice together in the land of Missouri. I the Lord promised the faithful and cannot lie.

3 I the Lord am willing, if any among you desireth to ride upon horses, or upon mules, or in chariots, he shall receive this blessing, if he receive it from the hand of the Lord, with a thankful heart in all things. These things remain with you to do according to judgment and the directions of the Spirit— Behold the kingdom is yours. And behold, and lo I am with the faithful always; even so. Amen.

SECTION LXXIII.

An explanation of the epistle to the first Corinthians, 7th chapter, 14th verse.

1 For the unbelieving husband is sanctified by the wife, and the unbelieving wife is sanctified by the husband, else were your children unclean, but now are they holy.

2 Now in the days of the apostles the law of circumcision was had among all the Jews, who believed not the gospel of Jesus Christ. And it came to pass that there arose a great contention among the people concerning the law of circumcision, for the unbelieving husband was desirous that his children should be circumcised and become subject to the law of Moses, which law was fulfilled.

---

line 1. Revelation, 13 Aug. 1831 [D&C 62]. This version reflects editing marks made in chapter 63 of Oliver Cowdery's copy of the Book of Commandments, indicating that the latter was used as a source text for the former. (See p. 634 herein.)

line 30. Explanation of scripture, ca. Dec. 1830 [D&C 74]. Revelation Book 1 bears a notation marking this item for inclusion in the 1835 Doctrine and Covenants. This version reflects editing marks made in Revelation Book 1, indicating that the latter was used as a source text for the former. (See *JSP*, MRB:91–93.)

203

line 1 2 And it came to pass that the children being brought up in subjection to the law of Moses, and give heed to the traditions of their fathers, and believed not the gospel of Christ, wherein they become unholy: wherefore, for this cause the apostle

5 wrote unto the church, giving unto them a commandment, not of the Lord but of himself, that a believer should not be united to an unbeliever except the law of Moses should be done away among them, that their children might remain without circumcision; and that the tradition might be done away,

10 which saith, that little children are unholy: for it was had among the Jews: but little children are holy being sanctified through the atonement of Jesus Christ: and this is what the scriptures mean.

SECTION LXXIV.

15 *Revelation given October, 1830.*

1 Behold, thus saith the Lord, unto you my servant, William E. McLelin, blessed are you, inasmuch as you have turned away from your iniquities, and have received my truths, saith the Lord your Redeemer, the Savior of the world, even of as

20 many as believe on my name. Verily I say unto you, blessed are you for receiving mine everlasting covenant, even the fulness of my gospel, sent forth unto the children of men, that they might have life, and be made partakers of the glories, which are to be revealed in the last days, as it was written by

25 the prophets and apostles in days of old.

2 Verily I say unto you, my servant William, that you are clean, but not all; repent therefore of those things which are not pleasing in my sight, saith the Lord, for the Lord will show them unto you. And now verily I the Lord will show

30 unto you what I will concerning you, or what is my will concerning you, behold, verily I say unto you, that it is my will that you should proclaim my gospel from land to land, and from city to city, yea, in those regions round about where it has not been proclaimed.

35 3 Tarry not many days in this place: go not up unto the land of Zion, as yet; but inasmuch as you can send, send; otherwise think not of thy property. Go unto the eastern lands; bear testimony in every place, unto every people, and in their synagogues; reasoning with the people.

40 4 Let my servant, Samuel H. Smith go with you, and forsake him not, and give him thine instructions: and he that is faithful shall be made strong in every place, and I the Lord will go with you.

---

line 1. The verse that begins on this line should be numbered "3".

line 14. Revelation, 29 Oct. 1831 [D&C 66]. This version reflects editing marks made in Revelation Book 1, indicating that the latter was used as a source text for the former. This revelation should be dated 29 October 1831. For more information on this dating, see the discussion of this revelation in the Documents series. (See *JSP,* MRB:195–197.)

line 1

5

10

15

20

25

30

35

40

204

5 Lay your hands upon the sick and they shall recover. Return not till I the Lord shall send you. Be patient in affliction. Ask and ye shall receive. Knock and it shall be opened unto you. Seek not to be cumbered. Forsake all unrighteousness. Commit not adultery, a temptation with which thou hast been troubled. Keep these sayings true and faithful, and thou shalt magnify thine office, and push many people to Zion, with songs of everlasting joy upon their heads. Continue in these things, even unto the end, and you shall have a crown of eternal life at the right hand of my Father, who is full of grace and truth. Verily thus saith the Lord your God, your Redeemer, even Jesus Christ. Amen.

SECTION LXXV.

Revelation given March, 1832. The order given of the Lord to Enoch, for the purpose of establishing the poor.

1 The Lord spake unto Enoch, saying, Hearken unto me saith the Lord your God, who are ordained unto the high priesthood of my church, who have assembled yourselves together, and listen to the counsel of him who has ordained you from on high, who shall speak in your ears the words of wisdom, that salvation may be unto you in that thing which you have presented before me, saith the Lord God: for verily I say unto you, the time has come, and is now at hand, and behold, and lo, it must needs be that there be an organization of my people, in regulating and establishing the affairs of the storehouse for the poor of my people, both in this place and in the land of Zion, or in other words, the city of Enoch, for a permanent and everlasting establishment and order unto my church, to advance the cause which ye have espoused, to the salvation of man, and to the glory of your Father who is in heaven, that you may be equal in the bands of heavenly things, yea and earthly things also, for the obtaining of heavenly things; for if ye are not equal in earthly things, ye cannot be equal in obtaining heavenly things: for if you will that I give unto you a place in the celestial world, you must prepare yourselves by doing the things which I have commanded you and required of you.

2 And now, verily thus saith the Lord, it is expedient that all things be done unto my glory, that ye should, who are joined together in this order; or in other words, let my servant Ahasdah, and my servant Gazelam, or Enoch, and my servant Pelagoram, sit in council with the saints which are in Zion; otherwise satan seeketh to turn their hearts away from the

---

line 13. Revelation, 1 Mar. 1832 [D&C 78]. This version reflects editing marks made in Revelation Book 1, indicating that the latter was used as a source text for the former. This revelation uses substitute words. (See *JSP,* MRB:267–269; and pp. 708–711 herein.)

205

line 1   truth, that they become blinded, and understand not the things which are prepared for them: wherefore a commandment I give unto you, to prepare and organize yourselves by a bond or everlasting covenant that cannot be broken.

5   3 And he who breaketh it shall lose his office and standing in the church, and shall be delivered over to the buffetings of satan until the day of redemption. Behold this is the preparation wherewith I prepare you, and the foundation, and the ensample, which I give unto you whereby you may accom-

10   plish the commandments which are given you, that through my providence, notwithstanding the tribulation which shall descend upon you, that the church may stand independent above all other creatures beneath the celestial world, that you may come up unto the crown prepared for you, and be made

15   rulers over many kingdoms, saith the Lord God, the Holy One of Zion, who hath established the foundations of Adam-ondi-Ahman; who hath appointed Michael, your prince, and established his feet, and set him upon high; and given unto him the keys of salvation under the counsel and direction of the Holy

20   One, who is without beginning of days or end of life.

4 Verily, verily I say unto you, ye are little children, and ye have not as yet understood how great blessings the Father has in his own hands, and prepared for you; and ye cannot bear all things now, nevertheless be of good cheer, for I will

25   lead you along: the kingdom is yours and the blessings thereof are yours; and the riches of eternity are yours: and he who receiveth all things, with thankfulness, shall be made glorious, and the things of this earth shall be added unto him, even an hundred fold, yea more: wherefore do the things which I have

30   commanded you, saith your Redeemer, even the Son Ahman, who prepareth all things before he taketh you; for ye are the church of the first born, and he will take you up in the cloud, and appoint every man his portion. And he that is a faithful and wise steward shall inherit all things. Amen.

35   ## SECTION LXXVI.

Revelation given March, 1832.

1 Verily I say unto you, that it is my will that my servant Jared Carter should go again into the eastern countries, from place to place, and from city to city, in the power of the ordi-

40   nation wherewith he has been ordained, proclaiming glad tidings of great joy, even the everlasting gospel, and I will send upon him the Comforter which shall teach him the truth and the way whither he shall go; and inasmuch as he is faithful I

---

line 35. Revelation, 12 Mar. 1832 [D&C 79]. This version reflects editing marks made in Revelation Book 1, indicating that the latter was used as a source text for the former. (See *JSP,* MRB:271.)

206

will crown him again with sheaves: wherefore let your heart be glad my servant Jared Carter, and fear not saith your Lord, even Jesus Christ. Amen.

SECTION LXXVII.

Revelation given March, 1832.

1 Verily, thus saith the Lord, unto you my servant Stephen Burnett, go ye, go ye, into the world, and preach the gospel to every creature that cometh under the sound of your voice, and inasmuch as you desire a companion I will give unto you my servant Eden Smith: wherefore go ye and preach my gospel, whether to the north, or to the south; to the east, or to the west, it mattereth not, for ye cannot go amiss: therefore declare the things which ye have heard and verily believe, and know to be true. Behold this is the will of him who hath called you, your Redeemer, even Jesus Christ. Amen.

SECTION LXXVIII.

Revelation given August, 1832.

1 Behold thus saith the Lord unto my servant John Murdock, thou art called to go into the eastern countries from house to house, from village to village, and from city to city, to proclaim mine everlasting gospel unto the inhabitants thereof, in the midst of persecution and wickedness; and whoso receiveth you receiveth me, and you shall have power to declare my word in the demonstration of my Holy Spirit; and whoso receiveth you as a little child, receiveth my kingdom and blessed are they, for they shall obtain mercy; and whoso rejecteth you shall be rejected of my Father, and his house: and you shall cleanse your feet in the secret places by the way for a testimony against them.

2 And behold, and lo, I come quickly to judgment, to convince all of their ungodly deeds which they have committed against me, as it is written of me in the volume of the book.— And now verily I say unto you, that it is not expedient that you should go until your children are provided for, and kindly sent up unto the bishop in Zion, and after a few years, if thou desirest of me thou mayest go up also unto the goodly land, to possess thine inheritance; otherwise thou shalt continue proclaiming my gospel until thou be taken. Amen.

---

line 4. Revelation, 7 Mar. 1832 [D&C 80]. This version reflects editing marks made in Revelation Book 1, indicating that the latter was used as a source text for the former. (See *JSP,* MRB:271.)

line 16. Revelation, 29 Aug. 1832 [D&C 99]. Versions of this revelation appear in Revelation Books 1 and 2, but the source text for the version printed here is unknown.

207

line 1

SECTION LXXIX.

Revelation given March, 1832.

1 Verily, verily I say unto you my servant Frederick G.
Williams, listen to the voice of him who speaketh, to the
line 5
word of the Lord your God, and hearken to the calling wherewith you are called, even to be a high priest in my church,
and a counsellor unto my servant Joseph Smith, jr. unto whom
I have given the keys of the kingdom, which belongeth always
unto the presidency of the high priesthood: therefore, verily I
line 10
acknowledge him and will bless him, and also thee, inasmuch
as thou art faithful in council, in the office which I have appointed unto you, in prayer always vocally, and in thy heart,
in public and in private; also in thy ministry in proclaiming
the gospel in the land of the living, and among thy brethren;
line 15
and in doing these things thou wilt do the greatest good unto
thy fellow-beings, and will promote the glory of him who is
your Lord: wherefore, be faithful, stand in the office which I
have appointed unto you, succor the weak, lift up the hands
which hang down, and strengthen the feeble knees: and if thou
line 20
art faithful unto the end thou shalt have a crown of immortality and eternal life in the mansions which I have prepared in
the house of my Father. Behold, and lo, these are the words
of Alpha and Omega, even Jesus Christ. Amen.

SECTION LXXX.

line 25
A word of wisdom for the benefit of the council of high priests, as-
sembled in Kirtland, and church; and also, the saints in Zion:
to be sent greeting: not by commandment, or constraint: but
by revelation and the word of wisdom: showing forth the order
and will of God in the temporal salvation of all saints in the
line 30
last days. Given for a principle with promise, adapted to the
capacity of the weak, and the weakest of all saints, who are or
can be called saints.

1 Behold, verily thus saith the Lord unto you, in consequence of evils and designs which do, and will exist in the
line 35
hearts of conspiring men in the last days, I have warned you,
and forewarn you, by giving unto you this word of wisdom by
revelation, that inasmuch as any man drinketh wine or strong
drink among you, behold it is not good, neither meet in the
sight of your Father, only in assembling yourselves together,
line 40
to offer up your sacraments before him. And behold, this
should be wine, yea, pure wine of the grape of the vine, of

---

line 1. Revelation, 15 Mar. 1832 [D&C 81]. Versions of this revelation appear in Revelation Books 1 and 2,
but the source text for the version printed here is unknown.

line 24. Revelation, 27 Feb. 1833 [D&C 89]. This version closely corresponds to a broadside printed
January 1834, suggesting that the latter was used as a source text for the former. (See *Verily, thus saith the
Lord unto you, who have assembled,* [Kirtland, OH: ca. Jan. 1834], copy at BYU [D&C 88, 89].)

line 1 your own make. And again, strong drinks are not for the belly, but for the washing of your bodies. And again, tobacco is not for the body, neither for the belly; and is not good for man; but is an herb for bruises, and all sick cattle, to be

5 used with judgment and skill. And again, hot drinks are not for the body, or belly.

2 And again, verily I say unto you, all wholesome herbs God hath ordained for the constitution, nature, and use of man.— Every herb in the season thereof, and every fruit in the season

10 thereof. All these to be used with prudence and thanksgiving. Yea, flesh also of beasts and of the fowls of the air, I the Lord hath ordained for the use of man with thanksgiving. Nevertheless, they are to be used sparingly; and it is pleasing unto me, that they should not be used only in times of winter or of

15 cold, or famine. All grain is ordained for the use of man, and of beasts, to be the staff of life, not only for man, but for the beasts of the field, and the fowls of heaven, and all wild animals that run or creep on the earth: and these hath God made for the use of man only in times of famine, and excess of hun-

20 ger.

3 All grain is good for the food of man, as also the fruit of the vine, that which yieldeth fruit, whether in the ground or above the ground. Nevertheless wheat for man, and corn for the ox, and oats for the horse, and rye for the fowls, and for

25 swine, and for all beasts of the field, and barley for all useful animals, and for mild drinks; as also other grain. And all saints who remember to keep and do these sayings, walking in obedience to the commandments, shall receive health in their navel, and marrow to their bones and shall find wisdom,

30 and great treasures of knowledge, even hidden treasures; and shall run and not be weary, and shall walk and not faint: and I the Lord give unto them a promise, that the destroying angel shall pass by them, as the children of Israel, and not slay them. Amen.

SECTION LXXXI.

35
Revelation given August, 1833.

1 Verily I say unto you my friends, I speak unto you with my voice, even the voice of my Spirit, that I may show unto you my will concerning your brethren in the land of Zion,

40 many of whom are truly humble, and are seeking diligently to learn wisdom and to find truth: verily, verily I say unto you, blessed are all such for they shall obtain, for I the Lord showeth mercy unto all the meek, and upon all whomsoever I will,

---

line 35. Revelation, 2 Aug. 1833–A [D&C 97]. This version reflects editing marks made in Revelation Book 2, indicating that the latter was used as a source text for the former. (See *JSP,* MRB:537–543.)

209

line 1 that I may be justified, when I shall bring them into judgment.

2 Behold I say unto you, concerning the school in Zion, I the Lord am well pleased that there should be a school in Zi- *5* on: and also with my servant Parley P. Pratt, for he abideth in me: and inasmuch as he continueth to abide in me, he shall continue to preside over the school, in the land of Zion, until I shall give unto him other commandments; and I will bless him with a multiplicity of blessings, in expounding all scrip- *10* tures and mysteries to the edification of the school, and of the church in Zion: and to the residue of the school, I the Lord am willing to show mercy, nevertheless there are those that must needs be chastened, and their works shall be made known: The axe is laid at the root of the trees, and every tree that *15* bringeth not forth good fruit, shall be hewn down and cast into the fire; I the Lord have spoken it. Verily I say unto you, all among them who know their hearts are honest, and are broken, and their spirits contrite, and are willing to observe their covenants by sacrifice; yea, every sacrifice which I the *20* Lord shall command, they are all accepted of me, for I the Lord will cause them to bring forth as a very fruitful tree which is planted in a goodly land, by a pure stream, that yieldeth much precious fruit.

3 Verily I say unto you, that it is my will that an house *25* should be built unto me in the land of Zion, like unto the pattern which I have given you; yea, let it be built speedily by the tithing of my people: behold this is the tithing and the sacrifice which I the Lord require at their hands, that there may be an house built unto me for the salvation of Zion: for *30* a place of thanksgiving, for all saints, and for a place of instruction for all those who are called to the work of the ministry, in all their several callings, and offices: that they may be perfected in the understanding of their ministry: in theory, in principle, and in doctrine, in all things pertaining to the *35* kingdom of God on the earth, the keys of which kingdom have been conferred upon you.

4 And inasmuch as my people build an house unto me, in the name of the Lord, and do not suffer any unclean thing to come into it, that it be not defiled, my glory shall rest upon it; *40* yea, and my presence shall be there, for I will come into it, and all the pure in heart that shall come into it, shall see God: but if it be defiled I will not come into it, and my glory shall not be there, for I will not come into unholy temples.

5 And now behold if Zion do these things, she shall prosper *45* and spread herself and become very glorious, very great, and

N

---

line 46. This page begins the fourteenth gathering of the book. "N" is the first of two signature marks in this gathering; the second is on the recto of the following leaf. These marks were used in collating the gatherings after the sheets were folded.

210

line 1 very terrible; and the nations of the earth shall honor her, and shall say, surely Zion is the city of our God; and surely Zion cannot fall, neither be moved out of her place, for God is there, and the hand of the Lord is there, and he hath sworn by the power of his might to be her salvation, and her high tower:

5 therefore verily thus saith the Lord let Zion rejoice, for this is Zion, THE PURE IN HEART: therefore let Zion rejoice, while all the wicked shall mourn: for behold and lo, vengeance cometh speedily upon the ungodly, as the whirlwind, and who shall

10 escape it: the Lord's scourge shall pass over by night and by day; and the report thereof shall vex all people; yet, it shall not be stayed until the Lord come: for the indignation of the Lord is kindled against their abominations, and all their wicked works: nevertheless Zion shall escape if she observe to do

15 all things whatsoever I have commanded her, but if she observe not to do whatsoever I have commanded her, I will visit her according to all her works: with sore affliction; with pestilence; with plague; with sword; with vengeance, with devouring fire: nevertheless, let it be read this once in their

20 ears, that I the Lord have accepted of their offering; and if she sin no more, none of these things shall come upon her, and I will bless her with blessings, and multiply a multiplicity of blessings upon her, and upon her generations, forever and ever, saith the Lord your God. Amen.

25
SECTION LXXXII.

Revelation given May, 1833.

1 Verily thus saith the Lord, it shall come to pass that every soul who forsaketh their sins and cometh unto me, and calleth on my name, and obeyeth my voice, and keepeth my com-

30 mandments, shall see my face, and know that I am, and that I am the true light that lighteth every man that cometh into the world: and that I am in the Father and the Father in me, and the Father and I are one: the Father because he gave me of his fulness; and the Son because I was in the world and made

35 flesh my tabernacle, and dwelt among the sons of men: I was in the world and received of my Father, and the works of him were plainly manifest; and John saw and bore record of the fulness of my glory; and the fulness of John's record is hereafter to be revealed: And he bore record, saying, I saw his

40 glory that he was in the beginning before the world was: therefore, in the beginning the Word was; for he was the Word, even the messenger of salvation, the light and the Redeemer of the world; the Spirit of truth, who came into the world

---

line 25. Revelation, 6 May 1833 [D&C 93]. Versions of this revelation appear in Revelation Books 1 and 2, but the source text for the version printed here is unknown.

line 1

because the world was made by him; and in him was the life
of men and the light of men.   The worlds were made by him.
Men were made by him.   All things were made by him, and
through him, and of him: And I John bare record that I beheld his glory, as the glory of the Only Begotten of the Father, full of grace and truth; even the Spirit of truth which came
and dwelt in the flesh, and dwelt among us.

  2 And I John saw that he received not of the fulness at the
first, but received grace for grace: and he received not of the
fulness at first, but continued from grace to grace, until he received a fulness: and thus he was called the Son of God, because he received not of the fulness at the first.   And I John
bare record, and lo, the heavens were opened and the Holy
Ghost descended upon him in the form of a dove, and sat upon
him, and there came a voice out of heaven saying, this is my
beloved Son.   And I John bare record that he received a fulness of the glory of the Father; and he received all power,
both in heaven and on earth; and the glory of the Father was
with him, for he dwelt in him.

  3 And it shall come to pass that if you are faithful, you shall
receive the fulness of the record of John.   I give unto you
those sayings that you may understand and know how to worship, and know what you worship, that you may come unto
the Father in my name, and in due time receive of his fulness
for if you keep my commandments you shall receive of his fulness and be glorified in me as I am in the Father: therefore,
I say unto you, you shall receive grace for grace.

  4 And now verily I say unto you, I was in the beginning with
the Father, and am the first born; and all those who are begotten through me, are partakers of the glory of the same, and
are the church of the first born.   Ye were also in the beginning with the Father: that which is Spirit, even the Spirit
of truth; and truth is knowledge of things as they are, and
as they were, and as they are to come; and whatsoever is
more or less than this, is the spirit of that wicked one, who
was a liar from the beginning.   The Spirit of truth is of God:
I am the Spirit of truth.   And John bore record of me, saying,
he received a fulness of truth; yea, even of all truth, and no
man receiveth a fulness unless he keepeth his commandments.
He that keepeth his commandments, receiveth truth and light,
until he is glorified in truth, and knoweth all things.

  5 Man was also in the beginning with God.   Intelligence,
or the light of truth was not created or made, neither indeed
can be.   All truth is independent in that sphere in which God
has placed it, to act for itself, as all intelligence also, other-

14*

212

wise there is no existence. Behold here is the agency of man,
and here is the condemnation of man because that which was
from the beginning is plainly manifest unto them, and they receive not the light. And every man whose spirit receiveth not
the light, is under condemnation, for man is spirit. The elements are eternal, and spirit and element, inseparably connect-
ed, receiveth a fulness of joy; and when separated, man connot
receive a fulness of joy. The elements are the tabernacle of
God; yea, man is the tabernacle of God, even temples; and
whatsoever temple is defiled, God shall destroy that temple.

6 The glory of God is intelligence, or, in other words, light
and truth: light and truth forsaketh that evil one. Every
spirit of man was innocent in the beginning, and God having
redeemed man from the fall, men became again in their infant
state, innocent before God. And that wicked one cometh
and taketh away light and truth, through disobedience, from
the children of men, and because of the tradition of their fathers. But I have commanded you, to bring up your children
in light and truth: but verily I say unto you, my servant Frederick G. Williams, you have continued under this condemnation; you have not taught your children light and truth, according to the commandments, and that wicked one hath power, as yet, over you, and this is the cause of your affliction.—
And now a commandment I give unto you, if you will be delivered, you shall set in order your own house, for there are
many things that are not right in your house.

7 Verily I say unto my servant Sidney Rigdon, that in some
things he hath not kept the commandments, concerning his
children: therefore, firstly set in order thy house.

8 Verily I say unto my servant Joseph Smith, jr. or, in other words, I will call you friends, for you are my friends, and
ye shall have an inheritance with me. I called you servants
for the world's sake, and ye are their servants for my sake,
and now verily I say unto Joseph Smith jr. you have not
kept the commandments, and must needs stand rebuked before the Lord. Your family must needs repent and forsake
some things, and give more earnest heed unto your sayings,
or be removed out of their place. What I say unto one I say
unto all: pray always lest that wicked one have power in you,
and remove you out of your place.

9 My servant Newel K. Whitney, also a bishop of my church,
hath need to be chastened and set in order his family, and see
that they are more diligent and concerned at home, and pray
always or they shall be removed out of their place.

10 Now I say unto you, my friends, let my servant Sidney
Rigdon go his journey, and make haste, and also proclaim the

213

line 1 acceptable year of the Lord, and the gospel of salvation, as I shall give him utterance, and by your prayer of faith with one consent, I will uphold him.

11 And let my servants Joseph Smith, jr. and Frederick G.

5 Williams, make haste also, and it shall be given them even according to the prayer of faith, and inasmuch you keep my sayings, you shall not be confounded in this world, nor in the world to come.

12 And verily I say unto you, that it is my will that you should

10 hasten to translate my scriptures, and to obtain a knowledge of history, and of countries, and of kingdoms, of laws of God and man, and all this for the salvation of Zion. Amen.

SECTION LXXXIII.

Revelation given same date.

15 1 And again, verily I say unto you, my friends, a commandment I give unto you, that ye shall commence a work of laying out and preparing a beginning and foundation of the city of the stake of Zion, here in the land of Kirtland, beginning at my house: and behold it must be done according to the pat-

20 tern which I have given unto you. And let the first lot on the south, be consecrated unto me for the building of an house for the presidency, for the work of the presidency, in obtaining revelations; and for the work of the ministry of the presidency, in all things pertaining to the church and kingdom.

25 2 Verily I say unto you, that it shall be built fifty-five by sixty-five feet in the width thereof, and in the length thereof, in the inner court; and there shall be a lower court, and an higher court, according to the pattern which shall be given unto you hereafter: and it shall be dedicated unto the Lord

30 from the foundation thereof, according to the order of the priesthood, according to the pattern which shall be given unto you hereafter: and it shall be wholly dedicated unto the Lord for the work of the presidency. And ye shall not suffer any unclean thing to come in unto it; and my glory shall be

35 there, and my presence shall be there: but if there shall come into it any unclean thing my glory shall not be there; and my presence shall not come into it.

3 And again, verily I say unto you, the second lot on the south shall be dedicated unto me for the building of an house

40 unto me, for the work of the printing of the translation of my scriptures, and all things, whatsoever I shall command you; and it shall be fifty five by sixty five feet in the width thereof, and the length thereof in the inner court; and there shall be

---

line 13. Revelation, 2 Aug. 1833–B [D&C 94]. This version reflects editing marks made in Revelation Book 2, indicating that the latter was used as a source text for the former. (See *JSP*, MRB:543–547.)

line 14. The date of the revelation in this section is 2 August 1833, which is the same date of the revelation appearing two sections earlier (section 81). The immediately preceding section (section 82) is dated 6 May 1833.

214

line 1
a lower and a higher court; and this house shall be wholly
dedicated unto the Lord from the foundation thereof, for the
work of the printing, in all things whatsoever I shall command you, to be holy, undefiled, according to the pattern in
all things, as it shall be given unto you.

4 And on the third lot shall my servant Hyrum Smith receive his inheritance. And on the first and second lots on the
north shall my servants Reynolds Cahoon and Jared Carter
receive their inheritance, that they may do the work which I
have appointed unto them, to be a committee to build mine
houses, according to the commandment, which I the Lord
God have given unto you. These two houses are not to be
built until I give unto you a commandment concerning them.

5 And now I give unto you no more at this time. Amen.

SECTION LXXXIV.

Revelation to Joseph Smith, jr. given March, 1833.

1 Thus saith the Lord, verily, verily I say unto you, my son,
thy sins are forgiven thee, according to thy petition, for thy
prayers and the prayers of thy brethren, have come up into
my ears: therefore thou art blessed from henceforth that bear
the keys of the kingdom given unto you; which kingdom is
coming forth for the last time.

2 Verily I say unto you, the keys of this kingdom shall never be taken from you, while thou art in the world, neither in
the world to come: nevertheless, through you shall the oracles be given to another; yea, even unto the church. And all
they who receive the oracles of God, let them beware how
they hold them, lest they are accounted as a light thing, and
are brought under condemnation thereby, and stumble and fall,
when the storms descend, and the winds blow, and the rains
descend, and beat upon their house.

3 And again, verily I say unto thy brethren Sidney Rigdon,
and Frederick G. Williams, their sins are forgiven them also,
and they are accounted as equal with thee in holding the keys
of this last kingdom: as also through your administration the
keys of the school of the prophets, which I have commanded
to be organized, that thereby they may be perfected in their
ministry for the salvation of Zion, and of the nations of Israel,
and of the Gentiles, as many as will believe, that through your
administration, they may receive the word, and through their
administration, the word may go forth unto the ends of the
earth, unto the Gentiles first, and then behold, and lo, they
shall turn unto the Jews: and then cometh the day when the

---

line 15. Revelation, 8 Mar. 1833 [D&C 90]. This version reflects editing marks made in Revelation Book 1, indicating that the latter was used as a source text for the former. (See *JSP,* MRB:313–317.)

line 1   arm of the Lord shall be revealed in power in convincing the
nations, the heathen nations, the house of Joseph of the gospel of their salvation.

    4 For it shall come to pass in that day, that every man shall
5   hear the fulness of the gospel in his own tongue, and in his
own language, through those who are ordained unto this power, by the administration of the Comforter, shed forth upon
them, for the revelation of Jesus Christ.

    5 And now verily I say unto you, I give unto you a com-
10   mandment, that you continue in the ministry and presidency,
and when you have finished the translation of the prophets,
you shall from thenceforth preside over the affairs of the church
and the school; and from time to time, as shall be manifest by
the Comforter, receive revelations to unfold the mysteries of
15   the kingdom, and set in order the churches, and study and
learn, and become acquainted with all good books, and with
languages, tongues and people. And this shall be your business and mission in all your lives to preside in counsel and set
in order all the affairs of this church and kingdom. Be not
20   ashamed neither confounded; but be admonished in all your
highmindedness and pride, for it bringeth a snare upon your
souls. Set in order your houses; keep slothfulness and un-
cleanness far from you.

    6 Now verily, I say unto you, let there be a place provided
25   as soon as it is possible, for the family of thy counsellor and
scribe, even Frederick G. Williams: and let mine aged servant
Joseph Smith, sen. continue with his family upon the place
where he now lives, and let it not be sold until the mouth of
the Lord shall name. And let thy counsellor, even Sidney
30   Rigdon, remain where he now resides, until the mouth of the
Lord shall name. And let the bishop search diligently, to obtain an agent; and let it be a man who has got riches in store;
a man of God and of strong faith: that thereby he may be enabled to discharge every debt; that the storehouse of the Lord
35   may not be brought into disrepute before the eyes of the people. Search diligently, pray always, and be believing, and all
things shall work together for your good, if ye walk uprightly,
and remember the covenant wherewith ye have covenanted
one with another. Let your families be small, especially mine
40   aged servant Joseph Smith, sen. as pertaining to those who
do not belong to your families: that those things that are provided for you, to bring to pass my work, are not taken from
you and given to those that are not worthy, and thereby you
are hindred in accomplishing those things which I have com-
45   manded you.

    7 And again, verily I say unto you, it is my will that my

216

line 1

handmaid, Vienna Jaques, should receive money to bear her
expenses, and go up unto the land of Zion; and the residue of
the money may be consecrated unto me, and she be rewarded
in mine own due time. Verily I say unto you, that it is meet
in mine eyes, that she should go up unto the land of Zion, and
receive an inheritance from the hand of the bishop, that she
may settle down in peace inasmuch as she is faithful, and not
be idle in her days from thenceforth.

8 And behold, verily I say unto you, that ye shall write this
commandment, and say unto your brethren in Zion, in love
greeting, that I have called you also to preside over Zion in
mine own due time: therefore let them cease wearying me
concerning this matter. Behold, I say unto you, that your
brethren in Zion begin to repent, and the angels rejoice over
them; nevertheless, I am not well pleased with many things:
and I am not well pleased with my servant William E. McLelin, neither with my servant Sidney Gilbert; and the bishop also: and others have many things to repent of: but verily I say
unto you, that I the Lord will contend with Zion and plead
with her strong ones, and chasten her, until she overcomes
and is clean before me: for she shall not be removed out of her
place: I the Lord have spoken it. Amen.

SECTION LXXXV.

Revelation given August, 1833.

1 Verily I say unto you, my friends, fear not, let your hearts
be comforted; yea, rejoice evermore, and in every thing give
thanks, waiting patiently on the Lord: for your prayers have
entered into the ears of the Lord of Sabaoth, and are recorded with this seal and testament: the Lord hath sworn and
decreed that they shall be granted: therefore he giveth this
promise unto you, with an immutable covenant, that they shall
be fulfilled, and all things wherewith you have been afflicted,
shall work together for your good, and to my name's glory
saith the Lord.

2 And now verily I say unto you, concerning the laws of the
land, it is my will that my people should observe to do all
things whatsoever I command them, and that law of the
land, which is constitutional, supporting that principle of freedom, in maintaining rights and privileges belongs to all mankind and is justifiable before me: therefore I the Lord justifi-
eth you, and your brethren of my church, in befriending that
law which is the constitutional law of the land: and as pertaining to law of man, whatsoever is more or less than these,

---

line 23. Revelation, 6 Aug. 1833 [D&C 98]. Versions of this revelation appear in Revelation Books 1 and 2, but the source text for the version printed here is unknown.

cometh of evil. I the Lord God maketh you free: therefore
ye are free indeed: and the law also maketh you free: nevertheless when the wicked rule the people mourn: wherefore
honest men and wise men should be sought for, diligently,
and good men and wise men, ye should observe to uphold;
otherwise whatsoever is less than these, cometh of evil.

3 And I give unto you a commandment, that ye shall forsake
all evil and cleave unto all good, that ye shall live by every
word which proceedeth forth out of the mouth of God: for he
will give unto the faithful, line upon line; precept upon precept: and I will try you, and prove you herewith: and whoso layeth down his life in my cause, for my name's sake, shall
find it again; even life eternal: therefore be not afraid of your
enemies, for I have decreed in my heart, saith the Lord, that I
will prove you in all things, whether you will abide in my covenant, even unto death, that you may be found worthy: for
if ye will not abide in my covenant, ye are not worthy of me:
therefore renounce war and proclaim peace, and seek diligently to turn the hearts of their children to their fathers, and the
hearts of the fathers to the children. And again the hearts of
the Jews unto the prophets; and the prophets unto the Jews,
lest I come and smite the whole earth with a curse, and all
flesh be consumed before me. Let not your hearts be troubled,
for in my Father's house are many mansions, and I have prepared a place for you, and where my Father and I am, there ye
shall be also.

4 Behold I the Lord am not well pleased with many who
are in the church at Kirtland, for they do not forsake their
sins, and their wicked ways, the pride of their hearts, and
their covetousness, and all their detestable things, and observe the words of wisdom and eternal life which I have given
unto them. Verily I say unto you, that I the Lord will chasten them and will do whatsoever I list, if they do not repent
and observe all things whatsoever I have said unto them.—
And again I say unto you, if ye observe to do whatsoever I
command you, I the Lord will turn away all wrath and indignation from you, and the gates of hell shall not prevail against
you.

5 Now I speak unto you, concerning your families: if men
will smite you, or your families, once and ye bear it patiently and revile not against them, neither seek revenge, ye shall
be rewarded; but if ye bear it not patiently, it shall be accounted unto you as being meeted out a just measure unto you.—
And again if your enemy shall smite you the second time, and
you revile not against your enemy, and bear it patiently, your
reward shall be an hundred fold. And again if he shall smite

218

line 1 you the third time, and ye bear it patiently, your reward shall be doubled unto you four fold: and these three testimonies shall stand against your enemy, if he repent not, and shall not be blotted out. And now verily I say unto you if that enemy
5 shall escape my vengeance that he be not brought into judgment before me, then ye shall see to it, that ye warn him in my name that he come no more upon you, neither upon your family, even your children's children unto the third and fourth generation: and then if he shall come upon you, or your chil-
10 dren, or your children's children, unto the third and fourth generation: I have delivered thine enemy into thine hands, and then if thou wilt spare him thou shalt be rewarded for thy righteousness; and also thy children and thy children's children unto the third and fourth generation: nevertheless thine
15 enemy is in thine hands, and if thou reward him according to his works, thou art justified, if he has sought thy life, and thy life is endangered by him; thine enemy is in thine hands, and thou art justified.
6 Behold this is the law I gave unto my servant Nephi; and
20 thy father Joseph, and Jacob, and Isaac, and Abraham, and all mine ancient prophets and apostles. And again this is the law that I gave unto mine ancients, that they should not go out unto battle against any nation, kindred, tongue, or people, save I the Lord commanded them. And if any nation,
25 tongue, or people should proclaim war against them, they should first lift a standard of peace unto that people, nation, or tongue, and if that people did not accept the offering of peace, neither the second nor the third time, they should bring these testimonies before the Lord; then I the Lord would give unto
30 them a commandment, and justify them in going out to battle against that nation, tongue, or people, and I the Lord would fight their battles, and their children's battles and their children's children until they had avenged themselves on all their enemies, to the third and fourth generation, behold this is an
35 ensample unto all people, saith the Lord your God, for justification before me.
7 And again verily I say unto you, if, after thine enemy has come upon thee the first time, he repent and come unto thee praying thy forgiveness thou shalt forgive him and shall hold
40 it no more as a testimony against thine enemy, and so on unto the second and the third time; and as oft as thine enemy repenteth of the trespass wherewith he has trespassed against thee, thou shalt forgive him, until seventy times seven; and if he trespass against thee and repent not the first time, never-
45 theless thou shalt forgive him; and if he trespass against thee the second time, and repent not, nevertheless thou shalt for-

219

line 1 give him; and if he trespass against thee the third time and
repent not thou shalt also forgive him; but if he trespass
against thee the fourth time, thou shalt not forgive him but
shall bring these testimonies before the Lord, and they shall
5 not be blotted out until he repent and reward the four fold in
all things wherewith he has tresspassed against you; and if he
do this thou shalt forgive him with all thine heart, and if he do
not this, I the Lord will avenge thee of thine enemy and hundred fold; and upon his children, and upon his children's chil-
10 dren, of all them that hate me, unto the third and fourth generation: but if the children shall repent, or the children's children and turn unto the Lord their God with all their hearts,
and with all their might, mind, and strength, and restore four
fold for all their trespasses, wherewith they have trespassed,
15 or wherewith their fathers have trespassed or their father's
fathers then thine indignation shall be turned away and vengeance shall no more come upon them, saith the Lord your
God, andtheir trespasses shall never be brought any more as a
testimony before the Lord against them. Amen.

20 ## SECTION LXXXVI.

*Revelation given April, 1832, showing the order given to Enoch
and the church in his day.*

1 Verily, verily I say unto you, my servants, that inasmuch
as you have forgiven one another your trespasses, even so I
25 the Lord forgive you; nevertheless there are those among you
who have sinned exceedingly; yea, even all of you have sinned,
but verily I say unto you, beware from henceforth and refrain
from sin lest sore judgments fall upon your heads: for unto
whom much is given much is required; and he who sins
30 against the greater light shall receive the greater condemnation. Ye call upon my name for revelations, and I give them
unto you; and inasmuch as ye keep not my sayings which I
give unto you, ye become transgressors, and justice and judgment is the penalty which is affixed unto my law: therefore,
35 what I say unto one I say unto all, watch, for the adversary
spreadeth his dominions and darkness reigneth; and the anger
of God kindleth against the inhabitants of the earth: and none
doeth good, for all have gone out of the way.
2 And now verily I say unto you, I the Lord will not lay
40 any sin to your charge: go your ways and sin no more: but
unto that soul who sinneth shall the former sins return, saith
the Lord your God.
3 And again, I say unto you, I give unto you a new com-

---

line 20. Revelation, 26 Apr. 1832 [D&C 82]. This version reflects editing marks made in Revelation
Book 1, indicating that the latter was used as a source text for the former. This revelation uses substitute
words. (See *JSP*, MRB:229–231; and pp. 708–711 herein.)

220

mandment, that you may understand my will concerning you;
or, in other words, I give unto you directions how you may act
before me, that it may turn to you for your salvation. I the
Lord am bound when ye do what I say, but when ye do not
what I say, ye have no promise.

4 Therefore, verily I say unto you, that it is expedient for
my servant Alam and Ahashdah, Mahalaleel and Pelagoram,
and my servant Gazelam, and Horah, and Olihah, and Shale-
manasseh, and Mehemson, be bound together by a bond and
covenant that cannot be broken by transgression except judgment shall immediately follow, in your several stewardships,
to manage the affairs of the poor, and all things pertaining to
the bishopric both in the land of Zion, and in the land of
Shinehah, for I have consecrated the land of Shinehah in mine
own due time for the benefit of the saints of the Most High,
and for a stake to Zion: for Zion must increase in beauty, and
in holiness: her borders must be enlarged; her stakes must be
strengthened: yea, verily I say unto you, Zion must arise and
put on her beautiful garments: therefore I give unto you this
commandment, that ye bind yourselves by this covenant, and
it shall be done according to the laws of the Lord. Behold
here is wisdom, also, in me, for your good. And you are to
be equal, or in other words, you are to have equal claims on
the properties, for the benefit of managing the concerns of
your stewardships, every man according to his wants and his
needs, inasmuch as his wants are just: and all this for the
benefit of the church of the living God, that every man may
improve upon his talent, that every man may gain other talents; yea, even an hundred fold, to be cast into the Lord's
storehouse, to become the common property of the whole
church, every man seeking the interest of his neighbor, and
doing all things with an eye single to the glory of God.

5 This order I have appointed to be an everlasting order unto
you and unto your successors, inasmuch as you sin not: and
the soul that sins against this covenant, and hardeneth his
heart against it, shall be dealt with according to the laws of
my church, and shall be delivered over to the buffitings of satan until the day of redemption.

6 And now verily I say unto you, and this is wisdom, make
unto yourselves friends with the mammon of unrighteousness,
and they will not destroy you. Leave judgment alone with
me, for it is mine and I will repay. Peace be with you; my
blessings continue with you, for even yet the kingdom is yours,
and shall be forever if you fall not from your steadfastness;
even so. Amen.

line 1

221

SECTION LXXXVII.

Revelation given January, 1832.

1 Verily, verily I say unto you, I who speak even by the voice of my Spirit; even Alpha and Omega, your Lord and your God: hearken, O ye who have given your names to go forth to proclaim my gospel, and to prune my vineyard. Behold I say unto you, that it is my will that you should go forth and not tarry, neither be idle, but labor with your mights lifting up your voices as with the sound of a trump proclaiming the truth according to the revelations and commandments which I have given you, and thus if ye are faithful ye shall be laden with many sheaves, and crowned with honor, and glory, and immortality, and eternal life.

2 Therefore verily I say unto my servant William E. McLelin I revoke the commission which I gave unto him, to go unto the eastern countries, and I give unto him a new commission and a new commandment, in the which I the Lord chasteneth him for the murmurings of his heart; and he sinned, nevertheless I forgive him and say unto him again, go ye into the south countries; and let my servant Luke Johnson go with him and proclaim the things which I have commanded them, calling on the name of the Lord for the comforter, which shall teach them all things that are expedient for them, praying always that they faint not; and inasmuch as they do this, I will be with them even unto the end. Behold this is the will of the Lord your God concerning you; even so. Amen.

3 And again, verily thus saith the Lord, let my servant Orson Hyde and my servant Samuel H. Smith take their journey into the eastern countries, and proclaim the things which I have commanded them: and inasmuch as they are faithful, lo I will be with them even unto the end. And again, verily I say unto my servant Lyman Johnson, and unto my servant Orson Pratt, they shall also take their journey into the eastern countries: and behold and lo, I am with them also even unto the end. And again I say unto my servant Asa Dodds and unto my servant Calves Wilson, that they also shall take their journey unto the western countries, and proclaim my gospel even as I have commanded them. And he who is faithful shall overcome all things, and shall be lifted up at the last day. And again, I say unto my servant Major N. Ashley and my servant Burr Riggs, let them take their journey also unto the south country: yea, let all those take their journey as I have commanded them, going from house to house, and from village to village, and from city to city; and in whatsoever

---

line 1. Revelation, 25 Jan. 1832 [D&C 75]. This version reflects editing marks made in Revelation Book 1, indicating that the latter was used as a source text for the former. (See *JSP,* MRB:231–237.)

222

line 1 house ye enter, and they receive you, leave your blessings upon that house; and in whatsoever house ye enter, and they receive you not, ye shall depart speedily from that house, and
shake off the dust of your feet as a testimony against them;
5 and you shall be filled with joy and gladness and know this,
that in the day of judgement you shall be judges of that house,
and condemn them; and it shall be more tolerable for the heathen in the day of judgment, than for that house: therefore
gird up your loins and be faithful and ye shall overcome all
10 things and be lifted up at the last day; even so. Amen.

4 And again thus saith the Lord unto you, O ye elders of my
church, who have given your names that you might know his
will concerning you: behold I say unto you that it is the duty
of the church to assist in supporting the families of those, and
15 also to supprt the families of those who are called and must
needs be sent unto the world to proclaim the gospel unto the
world: wherefore I the Lord give unto you this commandment,
that ye obtain places for your families, inasmuch as your
brethren are willing to open their hearts; and let all such as
20 can, obtain places for their families, and support of the
church for them, not fail to go into the world; whether to the
east, or to the west, or to the north, or to the south, let them
ask and they shall receive; knock and it shall be opened unto
them, and made known from on high, even by the Comforter,
25 whither they shall go.

5 And again verily I say unto you that every man who is
obliged to provide for his own family, let him provide and he
shall in no wise lose his crown; and let him labor in the church.
Let every man be diligent in all things. And the idler shall
30 not have place in the church, except he repents and mends his
ways. Wherefore let my servant Simeon Carter and my servant Emer Harris be united in the ministry. And also my
servant Ezra Thayre and my servant Thomas B. Marsh. Also
my servant Hyrum Smith and my servant Reynolds Cahoon;
35 and also my servant Daniel Stanton and my servant Seymour
Brunson; and also my servant Silvester Smith and my servant
Gideon Carter; and also my servant Ruggles Eames and my
servant Stephen Burnett; and also my servant Micah B. Wel-
ton and also my servant Eden Smith; even so. Amen.

40 ## SECTION LXXXVIII.

Revelation given April, 1832.

1 Verily thus saith the Lord, in addition to the laws of the
church concerning women and children, those who belong to

---

line 40. Revelation, 30 Apr. 1832 [D&C 83]. This version reflects editing marks made in Revelation
Book 2, indicating that the latter was used as a source text for the former. (See *JSP,* MRB:237.)

223

line 1 the church, who have lost their husbands or fathers: women have claim on their husbands for their maintenance until their husbands are taken; and if they are not found transgressors they shall have fellowship in the church, and if they are not 5 faithful, they shall not have fellowship in the church; yet they may remain upon their inheritances according to the laws of the land.

2 All children have claim upon their parents for their main-tainance until they are of age; and after that, they have claim 10 upon the church; or, in other words upon the Lord's store-house, if their parents have not wherewith to give them inher-itances. And the storehouse shall be kept by the consecra-tions of the church, that widows and orphans shall be provided for, as also the poor. Amen.

15 ### SECTION LXXXIX.

Revelation given December, 1831.

1 Hearken and listen to the voice of the Lord, O ye who have assembled yourselves together, who are the high priests of my church, to whom the kingdom and power has been given. For 20 verily thus saith the Lord, it is expedient in me, for a bishop to be appointed unto you, or of you unto the church in this part of the Lord's vineyard: and verily in this thing ye have done wisely, for it is required of the Lord, at the hand of ev-ery steward, to render an account of his stewardship, both in 25 time and in eternity. For he who is faithful and wise in time, is accounted worthy to inherit the mansions prepared for them of my Father. Verily I say unto you, the elders of the church in this part of my vineyard, shall render an account of their stewardship, unto the bishop which shall be appointed of me, 30 in this part of my vineyard. These things shall be had on re-cord to be handed over unto the bishop in Zion; and the duty of the bishop shall be made known by the commandments which have been given, and the voice of the conference.

2 And now, verily I say unto you, my servant Newel K. 35 Whitney is the man who shall be appointed, and ordained un-to this power: this is the will of the Lord your God, your Re-deemer; even so. Amen.

3 The word of the Lord, in addition to the law which has been given, making known the duty of the bishop, which has 40 been ordained unto the church in this part of the vineyard; which is verily this: to keep the Lord's storehouse; to receive the funds of the church in this part of the vineyard; to take an account of the elders as before has been commanded, and

---

line 15. Revelation, 4 Dec. 1831 [D&C 72]. This version closely corresponds to the version in the December 1832 issue of *The Evening and the Morning Star,* suggesting that the latter was used as a source text for the former.

224

line 1
to administer to their wants, who shall pay for that which
they receive, inasmuch as they have wherewith to pay; that
this also may be consecrated to the good of the church, to the
poor and needy: and he who hath not wherewith to pay, an
account shall be taken and handed over to the bishop of Zion,
who shall pay the debt out of that which the Lord shall put
into his hands: and the labors of the faithful who labor in
spiritual things, in administering the gospel and the things
of the kingdom, unto the church, and unto the world, shall
answer the debt unto the bishop in Zion: thus it cometh out
of the church, for according to the law every man that cometh up to Zion, must lay all things before the bishop in Zion.

4 And now, verily I say unto you, that as every elder in this
part of the vineyard, must give an account of his stewardship
unto the bishop in this part of the vineyard, a certificate from
the judge or bishop in this part of the vineyard, unto the bishop
in Zion, rendereth every man acceptable, and answereth all
things, for an inheritance, and to be received as a wise steward, and as a faithful laborer; otherwise he shall not be accepted of the bishop in Zion. And now, verily I say unto you, let
every elder who shall give an account unto the bishop of the
church, in this part of the vineyard, be recommended by the
church or churches, in which he labors, that he may render
himself and his accounts approved in all things. And again,
let my servants who are appointed as stewards over the literary concerns of my church, have claim for assistance upon the
bishop or bishops, in all things, that the revelations may be
published, and go forth unto the ends of the earth, that they
also may obtain funds which shall benefit the church, in all
things; that they also may render themselves approved in all
things and be accounted as wise stewards. And now, behold
this shall be an ensample for all the extensive branches of my
church, in whatsoever land they shall be established. And
now I make an end of my sayings. Amen.

5 A few words in addition to the laws of the kingdom, respecting the members of the church; they that are appointed
by the Holy Spirit to go up unto Zion; and they who are privileged to go up unto Zion. Let them carry up unto the bishop
a certificate from three elders of the church, or a certificate
from the bishop, otherwise he who shall go up unto the land
of Zion, shall not be accounted as a wise steward. This is
also an ensample. Amen.

line 1

SECTION XC.

Revelation given December, 1831.

1 Behold, thus saith the Lord unto you my servants, Joseph Smith, jr. aad Sidney Rigdon, that the time has verily come, that it is necessary and expedient in me that you should open your mouths in proclaiming my gospel, the things of the kingdom, expounding the mysteries thereof out of the scriptures, according to that portion of spirit and power, which shall be given unto you, even as I will.

2 Verily I say unto you, proclaim unto the world in the regions round about, and in the church also, for the space of a season, even until it shall be made known unto you. Verily this is a mission for a season, which I give unto you, wherefore, labor ye in my vineyard. Call upon the inhabitants of the earth, and bear record, and prepare the way for the commandments and revelations which are to come. Now, behold this is wisdom; whoso readeth let him understand and receive also; for unto him that receiveth it shall be given more abundantly, even power: wherefore, confound your enemies; call upon them to meet you, both in public and in private; and inasmuch as ye are faithful their shame shall be made manifest. Wherefore, let them bring forth their strong reasons against the Lord. Verily thus saith the Lord unto you, there is no weapon that is formed against you shall prosper; and if any man lift his voice against you, he shall be confounded in mine own due time: wherefore, keep these commandments: they are true and faithful, even so. Amen.

SECTION XCI.

A Vision.

1 Hear, O ye heavens, and give ear, O earth, and rejoice ye inhabitants thereof, for the Lord is God, and beside him there is no Savior; great is his wisdom; marvellous are his ways; and the extent of his doings, none can find out; his purposes fail not, neither are there any who can stay his hand: from eternity to eternity, he is the same and his years never fail.

2 For thus saith the Lord, I the Lord am merciful and gracious unto those who fear me, and delight to honor those who serve me in righteousness, and in truth unto the end; great shall be their reward, and eternal shall be their glory; and to them will I reveal all mysteries; yea, all the hidden mysteries

o

5

10

15

20

25

30

35

40

---

line 1. Revelation, 1 Dec. 1831 [D&C 71]. Versions of this revelation appear in Revelation Books 1 and 2, but the source text for the version printed here is unknown.

line 28. Vision, 16 Feb. 1832 [D&C 76]. This version closely corresponds to the version in the July 1832 issue of *Evening and Morning Star* (printed Feb. 1835), suggesting that the latter was used as a source text for the former.

line 41. This page begins the fifteenth gathering of the book. "O" is the first of two signature marks in this gathering; the second is on the recto of the following leaf. These marks were used in collating the gatherings after the sheets were folded.

226

line 1

of my kingdom from days of old; and for ages to come will I make known unto them the good pleasure of my will concerning all things pertaining to my kingdom; yea, even the wonders of eternity shall they know, and things to come will I show them, even the things of many generations; their wisdom shall be great, and their understanding reach to heaven: and before them the wisdom of the wise shall perish, and the understanding of the prudent shall come to nought; for by my Spirit will I enlighten them, and by my power will I make known unto them the secrets of my will; yea, even those things which eye has not seen, nor ear heard, nor yet entered into the heart of man.

3 We, Joseph Smith, jr. and Sidney Rigdon, being in the Spirit on the sixteenth of February, in the year of our Lord, one thousand eight hundred and thirty two, by the power of the Spirit our eyes were opened, and our understandings were enlightened, so as to see and understand the things of God; even those things which were from the beginning before the world was, which were ordained of the Father, through his only begotten Son, who was in the bosom of the Father, even from the beginning, of whom we bear record, and the record which we bear is the fulness of the gospel of Jesus Christ, who is the Son, whom we saw and with whom we conversed in the heavenly vision; for while we were doing the work of translation, which the Lord had appointed, unto us, we came to the twenty ninth verse of the fifth chapter of John, which was given unto us as follows:—speaking of the resurrection of the dead, concerning those who shall hear the voice of the Son of man—and shall come forth; they who have done good in the resurrection of the just, and they who have done evil in the resurrection of the unjust. Now this caused us to marvel, for it was given unto us of the Spirit: and while we meditated upon these things, the Lord touched the eyes of our understandings, and they were opened, and the glory of the Lord shone round about: and we beheld the glory of the Son, on the right hand of the Father, and received of his fulness; and saw the holy angels, and they who are sanctified before his throne, worshiping God and the Lamb, who worship him forever and ever. And now, after the many testimonies which have been given of him, this is the testimony, last of all, which we give of him, that he lives; for we saw him, even on the right hand of God; and we heard the voice bearing record that he is the only begotten of the Father; that by him, and through him, and of him, the worlds are and were created; and the inhabitants thereof are begotten sons and daughters unto God. And this we saw also, and bear record, that an angel of God,

line 1

who was in authority in the presence of God, who rebelled
against the only begotten Son—whom the Father loved, and
who was in the bosom of the Father—and was thrust down
from the presence of God and the Son, and was called Perdition: for the heavens wept over him; he was Lucifer, a son
of the morning; and we beheld and lo, he is fallen! is fallen!
even a son of the morning. And while we were yet in the
Spirit, the Lord commanded us that we should write the vision: for we beheld satan, that old serpent, even the devil, who
rebelled against God, and sought to take the kingdom of our
God, and his Christ; wherefore he maketh war with the saints
of God, and encompasses them round about. And we saw a
vision of the sufferings of those with whom he made war and
overcame, for thus came the voice of the Lord unto us.

4 Thus saith the Lord, concerning all those who know my
power, and have been made partakers thereof, and suffered
themselves, through the power of the devil, to be overcome,
and to deny the truth, and defy my power: they are they who
are the sons of perdition, of whom I say it had been better for
them never to have been born; for they are vessels of wrath
doomed to suffer the wrath of God, with the devil and his angels, in eternity: concerning whom I have said there is no forgiveness in this world nor in the world to come: having denied the Holy Spirit, after having received it, and having denied
the only begotten Son of the Father, having crucified him unto themselves, and put him to an open shame: these are they
who shall go away into the lake of fire and brimstone, with
the devil and his angels, and the only ones on whom the second death shall have any power: yea, verily the only ones who
shall not be redeemed in the due time of the Lord, after the
sufferings of his wrath; for all the rest shall be brought forth
by the resurrection of the dead, through the triumph and the
glory of the Lamb, who was slain, who was in the bosom of
the Father before the worlds were made. And this is the gospel, the glad tidings which the voice out of the heavens bore
record unto us, that he came into the world, even Jesus to be
crucified for the world, and to bear the sins of the world, and
to sanctify the world, and to cleanse it from all unrighteousness; that through him all might be saved, whom the Father
had put into his power, and made by him; who glorifies the
Father, and saves all the works of his hands, except those sons
of perdition, who deny the Son after the Father has revealed
him: wherefore he saves all except them; they shall go away
into everlasting punishment, which is endless punishment,
which is eternal punishment, to reign with the devil and his

15*

228

line 1

angels in eternity, where their worm dieth not and the fire is
not quenched, which is their torment, and the end thereof, neither the place thereof, nor their torment, no man knows, neither was it revealed, neither is, neither will be revealed unto
man, except to them who are made partakers thereof: nevertheless I the Lord show it by vision unto many, but straightway
shut it up again: wherefore the end, the width, the height,
the depth, and the misery thereof, they understand not, neither any man except them who are ordained unto this condemnation. And we heard the voice saying, Write the vision
for lo! this is the end of the vision of the sufferings of the ungodly!

5 And again, we bear record for we saw and heard, and this,
is the testimony of the gospel of Christ, concerning them who
come forth in the resurrection of the just: they are they who
received the testimony of Jesus, and believed on his name,
and were baptized after the manner of his burial, being buried
in the water in his name, and this according to the commandment which he has given, that, by keeping the commandments,
they might be washed and cleansed from all their sins, and receive the Holy Spirit by the laying on of the hands of him who
is ordained and sealed unto this power; and who overcome by
faith, and are sealed by that Holy Spirit of promise, which the
Father sheds forth upon all those who are just and true: they
are they who are the church of the first-born: they are they
into whose hands the Father has given all things: they are
they who are priests and kings, who have received of his fulness, and of his glory, and are priests of the Most High after
the order of Melchizedek, which was after the order of Enoch,
which was after the order of the only begotten Son: wherefore, as it is written, they are gods, even the sons of God:
wherefore all things are theirs, whether life or death, or things
present, or things to come, all are theirs, and they are Christ's,
and Christ is God's; and they shall overcome all things: wherefore let no man glory in man, but rather let him glory in God,
who shall subdue all enemies under his feet: these shall dwell
in the presence of God and his Christ forever and ever: these
are they whom he shall bring with him, when he shall come
in the clouds of heaven, to reign on the earth over his people:
these are they who shall have part in the first resurrection:
these are they who shall come forth in the resurrection of the
just: these are they who are come unto mount Zion, and unto
the city of the living God, the heavenly place, the holiest of
all: these are they who have come to an innumerable company of angels; to the general assembly and church of Enoch,
and of the first born: these are they whose names are written

in heaven, where God and Christ are the judge of all: these
are they who are just men made perfect through Jesus the mediator of the new covenant, who wrought out this perfect
atonement through the shedding of his own blood: these are
they whose bodies are celestial, whose glory is that of the sun,
even the glory of God the highest of all; whose glory the sun
of the firmament is written of as being typical.

6 And again, we saw the terrestrial world, and behold and lo!
these are they who are of the terrestrial, whose glory differs
from that of the church of the first born, who have received
the fulness of the Father, even as that of the moon differs
from the sun of the firmament. Behold, these are they who
died without law; and also they who are the spirits of men
kept in prison, whom the Son visited, and preached the gospel unto them, that they might be judged according to men in
the flesh, who received not the testimony of Jesus in the flesh,
but afterwards received it: these are they who are honorable
men of the earth, who were blinded by the craftiness of men:
these are they who receive of his glory, but not of his fulness;
these are they who receive of the presence of the Son, but not
of the fulness of the Father: wherefore they are bodies terrestrial, and not bodies celestial, and differ in glory as the moon
differs from the sun: these are they who are not valiant in the
testimony of Jesus: wherefore they obtained not the crown
over the kingdom of our God. And now this is the end of the
vision which we saw of the terrestrial, that the Lord commanded us to write while we were yet in the Spirit.

7 And again, we saw the glory of the telestial, which glory
is that of the lesser, even as the glory of the stars differ from
that of the glory of the moon in the firmament; these are they
who received not the gospel of Christ, neither the testimony
of Jesus: these are they who deny not the Holy Spirit: these
are they who are thrust down to hell: these are they who shall
not be redeemed from the devil, until the last resurrection, until the Lord, even Christ the Lamb, shall have finished his
work: these are they who receive not of his fulness in the eternal world, but of the Holy Spirit through the ministration of
the terrestrial; and the terrestrial through the ministration of
the celestial; and also the telestial receive it of the administering of angels, who are appointed to minister for them, or who
are appointed to be ministering spirits for them, for they shall
be heirs of salvation. And thus we saw in the heavenly vision, the glory of the telestial which surpasses all understanding; and no man knows it except him to whom God has revealed it. And thus we saw the glory of the terrestrial, which
excels in all things the glory of the telestial, even in glory,

230

line 1 and in power, and in might, and in dominion. And thus we
saw the glory of the celestial, which excels in all things;
where God, even the Father, reigns upon his throne forever
and ever: before whose throne all things bow in humble rever-
5 ence and give him glory forever and ever. They who dwell
in his presence are the church of the first born; and they see
as they are seen, and know as they are known, having received of his fulness and of his grace; and he makes them equal in
power, and in might, and in dominion. And the glory of the
10 celestial is one, even as the glory of the sun is one. And the
glory of the terrestrial is one, even as the glory of the moon is
one. And the glory of the telestial is one, even as the glory
of the stars is one for as one star differs from another star in
glory, even so differs one from another in glory in the teles-
15 tial world: for these are they who are of Paul, and of Apollos,
and of Cephas: these are they who say they are some of one
and some of another; some of Christ; and some of John; and
some of Moses; and some of Elias; and some of Esaias; and
some of Isaiah; and some of Enoch, but received not the gos-
20 pel; neither the testimony of Jesus; neither the prophets; neither the everlasting covenant; last of all, these all are they
who will not be gathered with the saints, to be caught up unto the church of the first born, and received into the cloud:
these are they who are liars, and sorcerers, and adulterers, and
25 whoremongers, and whosoever loves and makes a lie: these are
they who suffer the wrath of God on the earth: these are they
who suffer the vengeance of eternal fire: these are they who
are cast down to hell and suffer the wrath of Almighty God until
the fulness of times, when Christ shall have subdued all ene-
30 mies under his feet, and shall have perfected his work, when
he shall deliver up the kingdom and present it unto the Father
spotless, saying: I have overcome and have trodden the wine-
press alone, even the wine-press of the fierceness of the wrath
of Almighty God: then shall he be crowned with the crown
35 of his glory, to sit on the throne of his power to reign forever
and ever. But behold and lo, we saw the glory and the inhabitants of the telestial world, that they were as innumerable as
the stars in the firmament of heaven, or as the sand upon the
sea shore, and heard the voice of the Lord saying: These all
40 shall bow the knee, and every tongue shall confess to him who
sits upon the throne forever and ever: for they shall be judged
according to their works; and every man shall receive according to his own works, and his own dominion, in the mansions
which are prepared, and they shall be servants of the Most
45 High, but where God and Christ dwell they cannot come,
worlds without end. This is the end of the vision which we

231

line 1   saw, which we were commanded to write while we were yet
in the Spirit.

8 But great and marvellous are the works of the Lord and the
mysteries of his kingdom which he showed unto us, which
5   surpasses all understanding in glory, and in might, and in dominion, which he commanded us we should not write, while
we were yet in the Spirit, and are not lawful for man to utter:
neither is man capable to make them known, for they are only
to be seen and understood by the power of the Holy Spirit,
10   which God bestows on those who love him and purify themselves before him: to whom he grants this privilege of seeing
and knowing for themselves: that through the power and manifestation of the Spirit, while in the flesh, they may be able to
bear his presence in the world of glory. And to God and the
15   Lamb be glory, and honor, and dominion forever and ever.—
Amen.

SECTION. XCII.

Revelation given March, 1833.

1 Verily, thus saith the Lord unto you, concerning the Apoc-
20   rypha, there are many things contained therein that are true,
and it is mostly translated correct: there are many things contained therein that are not true, which are interpolations by
the hands of men. Verily I say unto you, that it is not needful that the Apocrypha should be translated. Therefore,
25   whoso readeth it let him understand, for the Spirit manifesteth
truth: and whoso is enlightened by the Spirit shall obtain benefit therefrom; and whoso receiveth not by the Spirit, cannot be
benefitted: therefore, it is not needful that it should be translated. Amen.

30   ### SECTION XCIII.

*Revelation to Enoch, on the order of the Church for the benefit of
the poor, given to the saints in Kirtland, March, 1833.*

1 Verily, thus saith the Lord, I give unto the united order,
organized agreeable to the commandment previously given, a
35   revelation and commandment concerning my servant Shederlaomach, that ye shall receive him into the order. What I say
unto one I say unto all.

2 And again, I say unto you, my servant Shederlaomach,
you shall be a lively member in this order; and inasmuch as
40   you are faithful in keeping all former commandments, you
shall be blessed forever. Amen.

---

line 17. Revelation, 9 Mar. 1833 [D&C 91]. Revelation Book 2 bears a notation possibly marking this revelation for inclusion in the 1835 Doctrine and Covenants, but the source text for this version is unknown. (See *JSP*, MRB:523).

line 30. Revelation, 15 Mar. 1833 [D&C 92]. This version reflects editing marks made in Revelation Book 2, indicating that the latter was used as a source text for the former. This revelation uses substitute words. (See *JSP*, MRB:523; and pp. 708–711 herein.)

232

SECTION XCIV.

Revelation given in Perrysburgh, N. Y. to Joseph Smith jr.
and Sidney Rigdon, October, 1833.

1 Verily, thus saith the Lord unto you my friends, Sidney,
and Joseph, your families are well: they are in mine hands,
and I will do with them as seemeth me good; for in me there
is all power: therefore, follow me, and listen to the council
which I shall give unto you: Behold, and lo, I have much people in this place, in the regions round about, and an effectual
door shall be opened in the regions round about in this eastern
land: Therefore, I the Lord have suffered you to come unto
this place; for thus it was expedient in me for the salvation of
souls: therefore, verily I say unto you, lift up your voices unto this people; speak the thoughts that I shall put into your
hearts, and ye shall not be confounded before men; for it shall
be given you in the very hour, yea, in the very moment, what
ye shall say.

2 But a commandment I give unto you, that ye shall declare
whatsoever things ye declare in my name, in solemnity of
heart, in the spirit of meekness, in all things. And I give unto you this promise, that inasmuch as ye do this, the Holy
Ghost shall be shed forth in bearing record unto all things whatsoever ye shall say.

3 And it is expedient in me that you, my servant Sidney,
should be a spokesman unto this people; yea, verily, I will
ordain you unto this calling, even to be a spokesman unto my
servant Joseph; and I will give unto him power to be mighty
in testimony; and I will give unto thee power to be mighty in
expounding all scriptures, that thou mayest be a spokesman
unto him, and he shall be a revelator unto thee, that thou
mayest know the certainty of all things pertaining to the things
of my kingdom on the earth. Therefore, continue your journey and let your hearts rejoice; for, behold, and lo, I am with
you even unto the end.

4 And now I give unto you a word concerning Zion: Zion
shall be redeemed, although she is chastened for a little season.
Thy brethren, my servants, Orson Hyde and John Gould, are
in my hands, and inasmuch as they keep my commandments
they shall be saved. Therefore, let your hearts be comforted,
for all things shall work together for good to them that walk
uprightly, and to the sanctification of the church; for I will
raise up unto myself a pure people, that will serve me in righteousness; and all that call on the name of the Lord and keep
his commandments, shall be saved; even so. Amen.

---

line 1. Revelation, 12 Oct. 1833 [D&C 100]. This version reflects editing marks made in Revelation Book 2,
indicating that the latter was used as a source text for the former. (See *JSP*, MRB:559–561.)

233

SECTION XCV.

Revelation given June, 1833.

1 Verily thus saith the Lord unto you, whom I love, and whom I love I also chasten, that their sins may be forgiven, for with the chastisement I prepare a way for their deliverance, in all things out of temptation: and I have loved you: Wherefore ye must needs be chastened, and stand rebuked before my face, for ye have sinned against me a very grievous sin, in that ye have not considered the great commandment in all things, that I have given unto you, concerning the building of mine house, for the preparation wherewith I design to prepare mine apostles to prune my vineyard for the last time, that I may bring to pass my strange act, that I may pour out my Spirit upon all flesh. But behold, verily I say unto you, there are many who have been ordained among you, whom I have called, but few of them are chosen: they who are not chosen have sinned a very grievous sin, in that they are walking in darkness at noon-day; and for this cause, I gave unto you a commandment, that you should call your solemn assembly; that your fastings and your mourning might come up into the ears of the Lord of Sabaoth, which is, by interpretation, the Creator of the first day; the beginning and the end.

2 Yea, verily I say unto you, I gave unto you a commandment, that you should build an house, in the which house I design to endow those whom I have chosen with power from on high: for this is the promise of the Father unto you: therefore I commanded you to tarry, even as mine apostles at Jerusalem: nevertheless my servants sinned a very grievous sin; and contentions arose in the school of the prophets, which was very grievous unto me, saith your Lord: therefore I sent them forth to be chastened.

3 Verily I say unto you, it is my will that you should build an house: if you keep my commandments, you shall have power to build it; if you keep not my commandments the love of the Father, shall not continue with you: therefore you shall walk in darkness. Now here is wisdom and the mind of the Lord: let the house be built, not after the manner of the world, for I give not unto you, that ye shall live after the manner of the world: therefore let it be built after the manner which I shall show unto three of you, whom ye shall appoint and ordain unto this power. And the size thereof shall be fifty and five feet in width, and let it be sixty-five feet in length, in the inner court thereof; and let the lower part of the inner court

---

line 1. Revelation, 1 June 1833 [D&C 95]. Versions of this revelation appear in Revelation Books 1 and 2, but the source text for the version printed here is unknown.

234

line 1

be dedicated unto me for your sacrament offering, and for your preaching: and your fasting; and your praying, and the offering up your most holy desires unto me, saith your Lord.— And let the higher part of the inner court, be dedicated unto me for the school of mine apostles, saith Son Ahman; or, in other words, Alphus; or, in other words, Omegus; even Jesus Christ your Lord. Amen.

SECTION XCVI.

A Revelation to Enoch, showing the order of the city or stake of Zion, Shinehah, given for a sample to the saints in Kirtland, June, 1833.

1 Behold, I say unto you, here is wisdom whereby ye may know how to act concerning this matter: for it is expedient in me that this stake that I have set for the strength of Zion, should be made strong: therefore, let my servant Ahashdah take charge of the place which is named among you, upon which I design to build mine holy house: and again let it be divided into lots according to wisdom, for the benefit of those who seek inheritances, as it shall be determined in council among you. Therefore, take heed that ye see to this matter, and that portion that is necessary to benefit mine order, for the purpose of bringing forth my word to the children of men, for behold verily I say unto you, this is the most expedient in me, that my word should go forth unto the children of men, for the purpose of subduing the hearts of the children of men, for your good; even so. Amen.

2 And again, verily I say unto you, it is wisdom and expedient in me, that my servant Zombre, whose offering I have accepted, and whose prayers I have heard: unto whom I give a promise of eternal life inasmuch as he keepeth my commandments from henceforth: for he is a descendant of Seth, and a partaker of the blessings of the promise made unto his fathers. Verily I say unto you, it is expedient in me that he should become a member of the order, that he may assist in bringing forth my word unto the children of men: therefore ye shall ordain him unto this blessing: and he shall seek diligently to take away incumbrances, that are upon the house named among you, that he may dwell therein; even so. Amen.

---

line 8. Revelation, 4 June 1833 [D&C 96]. This version reflects editing marks made in Revelation Book 2, indicating that the latter was used as a source text for the former. This revelation uses substitute words. (See *JSP,* MRB:533–535; and pp. 708–711 herein.)

235

SECTION XCVII.

Revelation given December, 1833.

line 1

1 Verily, I say unto you, concerning your brethren who have been afflicted, and persecuted, and cast out from the land of their inheritance, I the Lord have suffered the affliction to come upon them, wherewith they have been afflicted in consequence of their transgressions; yet, I will own them, and they shall be mine in that day when I shall come to make up my jewels.

2 Therefore, they must needs be chastened, and tried, even as Abraham, who was commanded to offer up his only son; for all those who will not endure chastening, but deny me, cannot be sanctified.

3 Behold, I say unto you, there were jarrings, and contentions, and envyings, and strifes, and lustful and covetous desires among them; therefore by these things they polluted their inheritances. They were slow to hearken unto the voice of the Lord their God; therefore, the Lord their God is slow to hearken unto their prayers, to answer them in the day of their trouble. In the day of their peace they esteemed lightly my counsel; but in the day of their trouble, of necessity they feel after me.

4 Verily, I say unto you, notwithstanding their sins my bowels are filled with compassion toward them: I will not utterly cast them off; and in the day of wrath I will remember mercy. I have sworn, and the decree hath gone forth by a former commandment which I have given unto you, that I would let fall the sword of mine indignation in the behalf of my people; and even as I have said, it shall come to pass. Mine indignation is soon to be poured out without measure upon all nations, and this will I do when the cup of their iniquity is full. And in that day, all who are found upon the watch tower, or in other words, all mine Israel shall be saved. And they that have been scattered shall be gathered: and all they who have mourned shall be comforted; and all they who have given their lives for my name shall be crowned. Therefore, let your hearts be comforted concerning Zion; for all flesh is in mine hands: be still, and know that I am God. Zion shall not be moved out of her place, notwithstanding her children are scattered, they that remain and are pure in heart shall return and come to their inheritances; they and their children, with songs of everlasting joy; to build up the waste places of Zion. And all these things, that the prophets might be fulfilled.— And behold, there is none other place appointed than that

---

line 1. Revelation, 16 and 17 Dec. 1833 [D&C 101]. This version closely corresponds to a broadside printed circa January 1834, suggesting that the latter was used as a source text for the former. (See *Verily, I say unto you, concerning your brethren who have been afflicted,* [Kirtland, OH: ca. Jan. 1834], copy at CHL [D&C 101].)

236

which I have appointed; neither shall there be any other place appointed than that which I have appointed for the work of the gathering of my saints, until the day cometh when there is found no more room for them; and then I have other places which I will appoint unto them, and they shall be called stakes, for the curtains, or the strength of Zion.

5 Behold it is my will, that all they who call on my name, and worship me according to mine everlasting gospel, should gather together and stand in holy places, and prepare for the revelation which is to come when the veil of the covering of my temple, in my tabernacle, which hideth the earth, shall be taken off, and all flesh shall see me together. And every corruptible thing, both of man, or of the beasts of the field, or of the fowls of heaven, or of the fish of the sea, that dwell upon all the face of the earth, shall be consumed; and also, that of element shall melt with fervent heat; and all things shall become new, that my knowledge and glory may dwell upon all the earth. And in that day the enmity of man, and the enmity of beasts; yea, the enmity of all flesh shall cease from before my face. And in that day whatsoever any man shall ask it shall be given unto him. And in that day satan shall not have power to tempt any man. And there shall be no sorrow because there is no death. In that day an infant shall not die until he is old, and his life shall be as the age of a tree, and when he dies he shall not sleep, (that is to say in the earth,) but shall be changed in the twinkling of an eye, and shall be caught up, and his rest shall be glorious. Yea, verily I say unto you, in that day when the Lord shall come he shall reveal all things; things which have passed, and hidden things which no man knew; things of the earth by which it was made, and the purpose and the end thereof; things most precious; things that are above, and things that are beneath; things that are in the earth, and upon the earth, and in heaven. And all they who suffer persecution for my name, and endure in faith, though they are called to lay down their lives for my sake, yet shall they partake of all this glory. Wherefore, fear not even unto death; for in this world your joy is not full, but in me your joy is full. Therefore, care not for the body, neither the life of the body; but care for the soul, and for the life of the soul: and seek the face of the Lord always, that in patience ye may possess your souls, and ye shall have eternal life. When men are called unto mine everlasting gospel, and covenant with an everlasting covenant, they are accounted as the salt of the earth, and the savor of men.— They are called to be the savor of men. Therefore, if that salt of the earth lose its savor, behold it is thenceforth good

line 1
for nothing, only to be cast out and trodden under the feet of men. Behold, here is wisdom concerning the children of Zion; even many, but not all: they were found transgressors, therefore, they must needs be chastened. He that exalteth himself shall be abased, and he that abaseth himself shall be exalted.

6 And now, I will show unto you a parable that you may know my will concerning the redemption of Zion: a certain nobleman had a spot of land, very choice; and he said unto his servants, go ye into my vineyard, even upon this very choice piece of land, and plant twelve olive trees; and set watchmen round about them and build a tower, that one may overlook the land round about, to be a watchman upon the tower; that mine olive trees may not be broken down, when the enemy shall come to spoil, and take unto themselves the fruit of my vineyard. Now the servants of the nobleman went and did as their lord commanded them; and planted the olive trees, and built a hedge round about, and set watchmen, and began to build the tower. And while they were yet laying the foundation thereof, they began to say among themselves, and what need hath my lord of this tower? and consulted for a long time, saying among themselves, what need hath my lord of this tower, seeing this is a time of peace? Might not this money be given to the exchangers? for there is no need of these things! And while they were at variance one with another, they became very slothful, and they hearkened not unto the commandments of their lord: and the enemy came by night, and broke down the hedge, and the servants of the nobleman arose, and were affrighted, and fled: and the enemy destroyed their works, and broke down the olive trees.

7 Now behold, the nobleman, the lord of the vineyard, called upon his servants, and said unto them, Why! what is the cause of this great evil? ought ye not to have done even as I commanded you? and after ye had planted the vineyard, and built the hedge round about, and set watchmen upon the walls thereof, built the tower also, and set a watchman upon the tower, and watched for my vineyard, and not have fallen asleep, lest the enemy should come upon you? and behold, the watchman upon the tower would have seen the enemy while he was yet afar off: and then ye could have made ready and kept the enemy from breaking down the hedge thereof, and saved my vineyard from the hands of the destroyer. And the lord of the vineyard said unto one of his servants, Go and gather together the residue of my servants; and take all the strength of mine house, which are my warriors, my young men, and they that are of middle age also, among all my ser-

233

line 1 vants, who are the strength of mine house, save those only
whom I have appointed to tarry; and go ye straightway unto
the land of my vineyard, and redeem my vineyard, for it is
mine, I have bought it with money. Therefore get ye straightway unto my land; break down the walls of mine enemies;
throw down their tower, and scatter their watchmen: and inasmuch as they gather together against you, avenge me of
mine enemies; that by and by, I may come with the residue
of mine house and possess the land.

8 And the servant said unto his lord, when shall these things
be? And he said unto his servant, when I will: go ye straightway, and do all things whatsoever I have commanded you;
and this shall be my seal and blessing upon you; a faithful
and wise steward in the midst of mine house: a ruler in my
kingdom. And his servant went straightway; and done all
things whatsoever his lord commanded him, and after many
days all things were fulfilled.

9 Again, verily I say unto you, I will show unto you wisdom
in me concerning all the churches, inasmuch as they are willing to be guided in a right and proper way for their salvation,
that the work of the gathering together of my saints may continue, that I may build them up unto my name upon holy
places; for the time of harvest is come, and my word must
needs be fulfilled. Therefore, I must gather together my people according to the parable of the wheat and the tares, that
the wheat may be secured in the garners to possess eternal
life, and be crowned with celestial glory when I shall come in
the kingdom of my Father, to reward every man according as
his work shall be, while the tares shall be bound in bundles,
and their bands made strong, that they may be burned with unquenchable fire. Therefore, a commandment I give unto all
the churches, that they shall continue to gather together unto
the places which I have appointed; nevertheless, as I have
said unto you in a former commandment, let not your gathering be in haste, nor by flight; but let all things, be prepared
before you, and in order that all things be prepared before you,
observe the commandments which I have given concerning
these things, which saith, or teacheth, to purchase all the
lands by money, which can be purchased for money, in the
region round about the land which I have appointed to be the
land of Zion, for the beginning of the gathering of my saints;
all the land which can be purchased in Jackson county, and
the counties round about, and leave the residue in mine hand.

10 Now verily I say unto you, let all the churches gather
together all their moneys; let these things be done in their
time, be not in haste; and observe to have all things prepared

239

before you. And let honorable men be appointed, even wise men, and send them to purchase these lands; and every church in the eastern countries when they are built up, if they will hearken unto this counsel, they may buy lands and gather together upon them, and in this way they may establish Zion. There is even now already in store a sufficient; yea, even abundance to redeem Zion, and establish her waste places no more to be thrown down, were the churches, who call themselves after my name willing to hearken to my voice. And, again I say unto you, those who have been scattered by their enemies, it is my will that they should continue to importune for redress, and redemption, by the hands of those who are placed as rulers, and are in authority over you, according to the laws and constitution of the people which I have suffered to be established, and should be maintained for the rights and protection of all flesh, according to just and holy principles, that every man may act in doctrine, and principle pertaining to futurity, according to the moral agency which I have given unto them that every man may be accountable for his own sins in the day of judgment. Therefore it is not right that any man should be in bondage one to another. And for this purpose have I established the Constitution of this land, by the hands of wise men whom I raised up unto this very purpose, and redeemed the land by the shedding of blood.

11 Now, unto what shall I liken the children of Zion? I will liken them unto the parable of the woman and the unjust judge, (for men ought always to pray and not faint,) which saith, There was in a city a judge which feared not God, neither regarded man. And there was a widow in that city, and she came unto him, saying, avenge me of mine adversary.— And he would not for a while, but afterward he said within himself, though I fear not God, nor regard man, yet because this widow troubleth me I will avenge her, lest by her continual coming, she weary me. Thus will I liken the children of Zion.

12 Let them importune at the feet of the Judge; and if he heed them not, let them importune at the feet of the governor; and if the governor heed them not, let them importune at the feet of the President; and if the President heed them not, then will the Lord arise and come forth out of his hiding place, and in his fury vex the nation, and in his hot displeasure, and in his fierce anger, in his time, will cut off these wicked, unfaithful, and unjust stewards, and appoint them their portion among hypocrites and unbelievers; even in outer darkness, where there is weeping, and wailing, and gnashing of teeth.— Pray ye therefore, that their ears may be opened unto your

240

line 1

cries, that I may be merciful unto them, that these things may not come upon them. What I have said unto you, must needs be, that all men may be left without excuse; that wise men and rulers may hear and know that which they have never considered; that I may proceed to bring to pass my act, my strange act, and perform my work, my strange work. That men may discern between the righteous and the wicked, saith your God.

13 And, again I say unto you, it is contrary to my commandment, and my will, that my servant Sidney Gilbert should sell my store house, which I have appointed unto my people, into the hands of mine enemies. Let not that which I have appointed, be polluted by mine enemies, by the consent of those who call themselves after my name: for this is a very sore and grievous sin against me, and against my people, in consequence of those things which I have decreed, and are soon to befall the nations. Therefore, it is my will that my people should claim, and hold claim, upon that which I have appointed unto them, though they should not be permitted to dwell thereon; nevertheless, I do not say they shall not dwell thereon; for inasmuch as they bring forth fruit and works meet for my kingdom, they shall dwell thereon; they shall build, and another shall not inherit it: they shall plant vineyards, and they shall eat the fruit thereof; even so. Amen.

SECTION XCVIII.

Revelation given to Enoch, concerning the order of the church for the benefit of the poor.

1 Verily I say unto you my friends, I give unto you counsel and a commandment, concerning all the properties which belong to the order, which I commanded to be organized and established, to be an united order, and an everlasting order for the benefit of my church, and for the salvation of men until I come, with promise immutable and unchangeable, that inasmuch as those whom I commanded were faithful, they should be blessed with a multiplicity of blessings; but inasmuch as they were not faithful, they were nigh unto cursing. Therefore inasmuch as some of my servants have not kept the commandment, but have broken the covenant, by covetousness and with feigned words, I have cursed them with a very sore and grievous curse: for I the Lord have decreed in my heart, that inasmuch as any man, belonging to the order, shall be found a transgressor; or, in other words, shall break the covenant with which ye are bound, he shall be cursed in his life, and

---

line 25. Revelation, 23 Apr. 1834 [D&C 104]. This version reflects editing marks made in Revelation Book 1, indicating that the latter was used as a source text for the former. This revelation uses substitute words. (See *JSP,* MRB:361–373; and pp. 708–711 herein.)

241

shall be trodden down by whom I will, for I the Lord am not to
be mocked in these things: and all this that the innocent among
you, may not be condemned with the unjust; and that the
guilty among you may not escape, because I the Lord have
promised unto you a crown of glory at my right hand. Therefore inasmuch as you are found transgressors, ye cannot escape
my wrath in your lives: inasmuch as ye are cut off by transgression, ye cannot escape the buffetings of satan until the
day of redemption.

2 And I now give unto you power from this very hour, that
if any man among you, of the order, is found a transgressor,
and repenteth not of the evil, that ye shall deliver him over
unto the buffetings of satan; and he shall not have power to
bring evil upon you. It is wisdom in me: therefore a commandment I give unto you, that ye shall organize yourselves,
and appoint every man his stewardship, that every man may
give an account unto me of the stewardship which is appointed unto him: for it is expedient that I the Lord should make
every man accountable, as stewards over earthly blessings,
which I have made and prepared for my creatures. I the Lord
stretched out the heavens, and builded the earth as a very han-
dy work; and all things therein are mine; and it is my purpose
to provide for my saints, for all things are mine; but it must
needs be done in mine own way: and behold this is the way,
that I the Lord have decreed to provide for my saints: that
the poor shall be exalted, in that the rich are made low; for
the earth is full, and there is enough and to spare, yea, I prepared all things, and have given unto the children of men to
be agents unto themselves. Therefore if any man shall take
of the abundance which I have made, and impart not his portion, according to the law of my gospel, unto the poor, and
the needy, he shall, with the wicked, lift up his eyes in hell,
being in torment.

3 And now, verily I say unto you, concerning the properties
of the order: let my servant Pelagoram have appointed unto
him the place where he now resides, and the lot of Tahhanes,
for his stewardship, for his support while he is laboring in my
vineyard, even as I will when I shall command him; and let
all things be done according to counsel of the order, and united consent, or voice of the order which dwell in the land of
Shinehah. And this stewardship and blessing, I the Lord
confer upon my servant Pelagoram, for a blessing upon him,
and his seed after him; and I will multiply blessings upon him,
inasmuch as he shall be humble before me.

4 And again, let my servant Mahemson have appointed unto

P

---

line 46. This page begins the sixteenth gathering of the book. "P" is the first of two signature marks in this gathering; the second is on the recto of the following leaf. These marks were used in collating the gatherings after the sheets were folded.

242

line 1

him, for his stewardship, the lot of land which my servant
Zombre obtained in exchange for his former inheritance, for
him and his seed after him; and inasmuch as he is faithful I
will multiply blessings upon him and his seed after him. And
let my servant Mahemson devote his moneys for the proclaiming of my words, according as my servant Gazelam shall direct.

5 And again, let my servant Shederlaomach have the place
upon which he now dwells. And let my servant Olihah have
the lot which is set off joining the house which is to be for the
Lane-shine-house, which is lot number one: and also the lot
upon which his father resides. And let my servant Shederlaomach and Olihah have the Lane-shine-house and all things
that pertain unto it; and this shall be their stewardship which
shall be appointed unto them; and inasmuch as they are faithful, behold I will bless, and multiply blessings upon them: and
this is the beginning of the stewardship which I have appointed them, for them and their seed after them; and inasmuch as
they are faithful, I will multiply blessings upon them and
their seed after them; even a multiplicity of blessings.

6 And again, let my servant Zombre have the house in which
he lives, and the inheritance, all save the ground which has
been reserved for the building of my houses, which pertains to
that inheritance; and those lots which have been named for
my servant Olihah. And inasmuch as he is faithful, I will
multiply blessings upon him. And it is my will that he should
sell the lots that are laid off for the building up of the city of
my saints, inasmuch as it shall be made known to him by the
voice of the Spirit, and according to the counsel of the order;
and by the voice of the order. And this is the beginning of
the stewardship which I have appointed unto him, for a blessing unto him, and his seed after him; and inasmuch as he is
faithful, I will multiply a multiplicity of blessings upon him.

7 And again, let my servant Ahashdah have appointed unto
him, the houses and lot where he now resides, and the lot and
building on which the Ozondah stands; and also the lot which
is on the corner south of the Ozondah; and also the lot on
which the Shule is situated: And all this I have appointed unto my servant Ahashdah, for his stewardship, for a blessing
upon him and his seed after him, for the benefit of the Ozondah of my order, which I have established for my stake in the
land of Shinehah; yea, verily this is the stewardship which
I have appointed unto my servant Ahashdah; even this whole
Ozondah establishment, him and his agent, and his seed after
him, and inasmuch as he is faithful in keeping my commandments , which I have given unto him, I will multiply blessings
upon him, and his seed after him, even a multiplicity of blessings.

line 1

8 And again, let my servant Gazelam have appointed unto him, the lot which is laid off for the building of my house, which is forty rods long, and twelve wide, and also the inheritance upon which his father now resides; and this is the beginning of the stewardship which I have appointed unto him, for a blessing upon him, and upon his father, for behold, I have reserved an inheritance for his father, for his support: therefore he shall be reckoned in the house of my servant Gazelam; and I will multiply blessings upon the house of my servant Gazelam, inasmuch as he is faithful, even a multiplicity of blessings.

9 And now a commandment I give unto you concerning Zion, that you shall no longer be bound as an united order to your brethren of Zion, only on this wise: after you are organized you shall be called the united order of the stake of Zion, the city of Shinehah. And your brethren, after they are organized, shall be called the united order of the city of Zion: and they shall be organized in their own names, and in their own name; and they shall do their business in their own name, and in their own names: and you shall do your business in your own name, and in your own names. And this I have commanded to be done for your salvation and also for their salvation in consequence of their being driven out and that which is to come. The covenants being broken through transgression, by covetousness and feigned words: therefore, you are desolved as a united order with your brethren, that you are not bound only up to this hour, unto them, only on this wise, as I said, by loan, as shall be agreed by this order, in council, as your circumstances will admit, and the voice of the council direct.

10 And again, a commandment I give unto you concerning your stewardship which I have appointed unto you: behold all these properties are mine, or else your faith is vain, and ye are found hypocrites, and the covenants which ye have made unto me are broken: and if the properties are mine then ye are stewards, otherwise ye are no stewards. But verily I say unto you, I have appointed unto you to be stewards over mine house, even stewards indeed: and for this purpose I have commanded you to organize yourselves, even to shinelah my words, the fulness of my scriptures, the revelations which I have given unto you, and which I shall hereafter, from time to time, give unto you, for the purpose of building up my church and kingdom on the earth, and to prepare my people for the time when I shall dwell with them, which is nigh at hand.

11 And ye shall prepare for yourselves a place for a treasury, and consecrate it unto my name; and ye shall appoint one

16*

244

among you to keep the treasury, and he shall be ordained unto this blessing; and there shall be a seal upon the treasury,
and all the sacred things shall be delivered into the treasury,
and no man among you shall call it his own, or any part of it,
for it shall belong to you all with one accord; and I give it unto you from this very hour: and now see to it, that ye go to
and make use of the stewardship which I have appointed unto
you, exclusive of the sacred things, for the purpose of shine-
lane these sacred things, as I have said: and the avails of the
sacred things shall be had in the treasury, and a seal shall be
upon it, and it shall not be used or taken out of the treasury
by any one, neither shall the seal be loosed which shall be
placed upon it, only by the voice of the order, or by commandment. And thus shall ye preserve all the avails of the sacred
things in the treasury, for sacred and holy purposes: and this
shall be called the sacred treasury of the Lord: and a seal shall
be kept upon it that it may be holy and consecrated unto the
Lord.

12 And again, there shall be another treasury prepared and a
treasurer appointed to keep the treasury, and a seal shall be
placed upon it; and all moneys that you receive in your stewardships, by improving upon the properties which I have appointed unto you, in houses or in lands, or in cattle, or in all
things save it be the holy and sacred writings, which I have
reserved unto myself for holy and sacred purposes, shall be
cast into the treasury as fast as you receive moneys by hundreds or by fifties, or by twenties, or by tens, or by fives, or in
other words, if any man among you obtain five talents let him
cast them into the treasury; or if he obtain ten, or twenty, or
fifty, or an hundred, let him do likewise; and let not any man
among you say that it is his own, for it shall not be called his,
nor any part of it; and there shall not any part of it be used,
or taken out of the treasury, only by the voice and common
consent of the order. And this shall be the voice and common consent of the order: that any man among you, say unto
the treasurer, I have need of this to help me in my stewardship: if it be five talents, or if it be ten talents, or twenty, or
fifty, or an hundred, the treasurer shall give unto him the sum
which he requires, to help him in his stewardship, until he be
found a transgressor, and it is manifest before the council of
the order plainly, that he is an unfaithful, and an unwise steward; but so long as he is in full fellowship, and is faithful, and
wise in his stewardship, this shall be his token unto the treasurer that the treasurer shall not withhold. But in case of
transgression the treasurer shall be subject unto the council
and voice of the order. And in case the treasurer is found an

245

line 1
unfaithful, and an unwise steward, he shall be subject to the counsel and voice of the order, and shall be removed out of his place, and another shall he appointed in his stead.

13 And again, verily I say unto you, concerning your debts, behold it is my will that you should pay all your debts; and it is my will that you should humble yourselves before me, and obtain this blessing by your diligence and humility, and the prayer of faith: and inasmuch as you are diligent and humble, and exercise the prayer of faith, behold I will soften the hearts of those to whom you are in debt, until I shall send means unto you for your deliverance. Therefore write speedily unto Cainhannoch, and write according to that which shall be dictated by my Spirit, and I will soften the hearts of those to whom you are in debt, that it shall be taken away out of their minds to bring affliction upon you. And inasmuch as ye are humble and faithful and call on my name, behold I will give you the victory: I give unto you a promise, that you shall be delivered this once, out of your bondage: inasmuch as you obtain a chance to loan money by hundreds, or thousands, even until you shall loan enough to deliver yourselves from bondage, it is your privilege, and pledge the properties which I have put into your hands, this once, by giving your names, by common consent, or otherwise, as it shall seem good unto you: I give unto you this privilege, this once, and behold, if you proceed to do the things which I have laid before you, according to my commandments, all these things are mine, and ye are my stewards, and the master will not suffer his house to be broken up: even so. Amen.

SECTION XCIX.

Revelation given November, 1834.

1 It is my will that my servant Warren A. Cowdery should be appointed and ordained a presiding high priest over my church in the land of Freedom and the regions round about, and should preach my everlasting gospel and lift up his voice and warn the people, not only in his own place, but in the adjoining countries, and devote his whole time in this high and holy calling which I now give unto him, seeking diligently the kingdom of heaven and its righteousness, and all things necessary shall be added thereunto; for the laborer is worthy of his hire.

2 And again, verily I say unto you, the coming of the Lord draweth nigh, and it overtaketh the world as a thief in the night: therefore, gird up your loins that you may be the chil-

---

line 29. Revelation, 25 Nov. 1834 [D&C 106]. This version reflects editing marks made in Revelation Book 2, indicating that the latter was used as a source text for the former. (See *JSP*, MRB:649.)

246

line 1

dren of the light, and that day shall not overtake you as a thief.

3 And again, verily I say unto you, there was joy in heaven when my servant Warren bowed to my scepter, and separated himself from the crafts of men: therefore, blessed is my servant Warren, for I will have mercy on him, and notwithstanding the vanity of his heart I will lift him up inasmuch as he will humble himself before me; and I will give him grace and assurance wherewith he may stand; and if he continues to be a faithful witness and a light unto the church, I have prepared a crown for him in the mansions of my Father: even so.— Amen.

247

line 1

SECTION C.

APPENDIX.

1 Hearken, O ye people of my church, saith the Lord your God, and hear the word of the Lord concerning you; the Lord who shall suddenly come to his temple: the Lord who shall come down upon the world with a curse to judgment; yea, upon all the nations that forget God, and upon all the ungodly among you. For he shall make bare his holy arm in the eyes of all the nations, and all the ends of the earth shall see the salvation of their God. Wherefore, prepare ye, prepare ye, O my people; sanctify yourselves; gather ye together, O ye people of my church, upon the land of Zion, all you that have not been commanded to tarry. Go ye out from Babylon. Be ye clean that bear the vessels of the Lord. Call your solemn assemblies, and speak often one to another. And let every man call upon the name of the Lord; yea, verily I say unto you, again, the time has come when the voice of the Lord is unto you, Go ye out of Babylon; gather ye out from among the nations, from the four winds, from one end of heaven to the other.

2 Send forth the elders of my church unto the nations which are afar off; unto the islands of the sea; send forth unto foreign lands; call upon all nations, firstly, upon the Gentiles, and then upon the Jews. And behold and lo, this shall be their cry, and the voice of the Lord unto all people: Go ye forth unto the land of Zion, that the borders of my people may be enlarged, and that her stakes may be strengthened, and that Zion may go forth unto the regions round about: yea, let the cry go forth among all people; Awake and arise and go forth to meet the Bridegroom: behold and lo the Bridegroom cometh, go ye out to meet him. Prepare yourselves for the great day of the Lord. Watch, therefore, for ye know neither the day nor the hour. Let them, therefore, who are among the Gentiles, flee unto Zion. And let them who be of Judah, flee unto Jerusalem, unto the mountains of the Lord's house. Go ye out from among the nations, even from Babylon, from the midst of wickedness, which is spiritual Babylon. But verily thus saith the Lord, let not your flight be in haste, but let all things be prepared before you: and he that goeth, let him not look back, lest sudden destruction shall come upon him.

3 Hearken and hear O ye inhabitants of the earth. Listen ye elders of my church together, and hear the voice of the Lord, for he calleth upon all men and he commandeth all men every where to repent: for behold the Lord God hath sent

---

line 1. Revelation, 3 Nov. 1831 [D&C 133]. This version closely corresponds to the version in the May 1833 issue of *The Evening and the Morning Star,* suggesting that the latter was used as a source text for the former.

line 2. As early as May 1833, this revelation was referred to as an "appendix." (See 174n3 herein.)

248.

line 1 forth the angel, crying through the midst of heaven, saying:
Prepare ye the way of the Lord, and make his paths strait,
for the hour of his coming is nigh, when the Lamb shall stand
upon mount Zion, and with him a hundred and forty four
5 thousand, having his Father's name written in their foreheads:
wherefore, prepare ye for the coming of the Bridegroom: go
ye, go ye out to meet him, for behold he shall stand upon the
mount of Olivet, and upon the mighty ocean, even the great
deep, and upon the islands of the sea, and upon the land of
10 Zion; and he shall utter his voice out of Zion, and he shall
speak from Jerusalem, and his voice shall be heard among all
people, and it shall be a voice as the voice of many waters,
and as the voice of a great thunder, which shall break down
the mountains, and the vallies shall not be found: he shall
15 command the great deep and it shall be driven back into the
north countries, and the islands shall become one land, and
the land of Jerusalem and the land of Zion, shall be turned
back into their own place, and the earth shall be like as it was
in the days before it was divided. And the Lord even the Sav-
20 ior shall stand in the midst of his people, and shall reign over
all flesh. And they who are in the north countries shall come
in remembrance before the Lord, and their prophets shall hear
his voice, and shall no longer stay themselves, and they shall
smite the rocks, and the ice shall flow down at their presence.
25 And an high way shall be cast up in the midst of the great
deep. Their enemies shall become a prey unto them, and in
the barren deserts there shall come forth pools of living water;
and the parched ground shall no longer be a thirsty land.—
And they shall bring forth their rich treasures unto the chil-
30 dren of Ephraim my servants. And the boundaries of the everlasting hills shall tremble at their presence. And then shall
they fall down and be crowned with glory, even in Zion, by
the hands of the servants of the Lord, even the children of
Ephraim; and they shall be filled with songs of everlasting joy.
35 Behold this is the blessing of the everlasting God upon the
tribes of Israel, and the richer blessing upon the head of
Ephraim and his fellows. And they also of the tribe of Judah,
after their pain, shall be sanctified in holiness before the Lord
to dwell in his presence day and night forever and ever.
40   4 And now verily saith the Lord, that these things might be
known among you, O inhabitants of the earth, I have sent
forth mine angel, flying through the midst of heaven, having
the everlasting gospel, who hath appeared unto some, and
hath committed it unto man, who shall appear unto many that
45 dwell on the earth: and this gospel shall be preached unto every nation, and kindred, and tongue, and people, and the sea-

249

line 1 vants of God shall go forth, saying, with a loud voice: Fear God and give glory to him: for the hour of his judgment is come: and worship him that made heaven, and earth, and sea, and the fountain of waters, calling upon the name of the Lord
5 day and night, saying: O that thou wouldst rend the heavens, that thou wouldst come down, that the mountains might flow down at thy presence. And it shall be answered upon their heads, for the presence of the Lord shall be as the melting fire that burneth, and as the fire which causeth the waters to boil.
10 O Lord, thou shalt come down to make thy name known to thine adversaries, and all nations shall tremble at thy presence. When thou doeth terrible things, things they look not for; yea, when thou comest down and the mountains flow down at thy presence, thou shalt meet him who rejoiceth and worketh
15 righteousness, who remember thee in thy ways: for since the beginning of the world have not men heard nor perceived by the ear, neither hath any eye seen, O God, besides thee, how great things thou hast prepared for him that waiteth for thee.
5 And it shall be said, Who is this that cometh down from
20 God in heaven whith died garments: yea, from the regions which are not known, clothed in his glorious apparel, travelling in the greatness of his strength? And he shall say I am he who spake in righteousness, mighty to save. And the Lord shall be red in his apparel, and his garments like him
25 that treaddeth in the wine vat, and so great shall be the glory of his presence, that the sun shall hide his face in shame; and the moon shall withhold its light; and the stars shall be hurled from their places: and his voice shall be heard, I have trodden the wine-press alone, and have brought judgment upon all peo-
30 ple; and none was with me; and I have trampled them in my fury, and I did tread upon them in mine anger, and their blood have I sprinkled upon my garments, and stained all my raiment: for this was the day of vengeance which was in my heart. And now the year of my redeemed is come, and they
35 shall mention the loving kindness of their Lord, and all that he has bestowed upon them, according to his goodness, and according to his loving kindness, forever and ever. In all their afflictions he was afflicted. And the angel of his presence saved them; and in his love, and in his pity, he redeemed
40 them, and bare them, and carried them all the days of old; yea, and Enoch also, and they who were with him, the prophets who were before him, and Noah also, and they who were before him, and Moses also, and they who were before him, and from Moses to Elijah, and from Elijah to John, who were
45 with Christ in his resurrection, and the holy apostles, with Abraham, Isaac and Jacob, shall be in the presence of the

250

line 1

Lamb. And the graves of the saints shall be opened, and they shall come forth and stand on the right hand of the Lamb, when he shall stand upon mount Zion, and upon the holy city, the New Jerusalem, and they shall sing the song of the Lamb day and night forever and ever.

6 And for this cause, that men might be made partakers of the glories which were to be revealed, the Lord sent forth the fulness of his gospel, his everlasting covenant, reasoning in plainness, and simplicity, to prepare the weak for those things which are coming on the earth; and for the Lord's errand in the day when the weak should confound the wise, and the little one become a strong nation, and two should put their tens of thousands to flight; and by the weak things of the earth, the Lord should thresh the nations by the power of his Spirit. And for this cause these commandments were given; they were commanded to be kept from the world in the day that they were given, but now are to go forth unto all flesh. And this according to the mind and will of the Lord, who ruleth over all flesh; and unto him that repenteth and sanctifieth himself before the Lord, shall be given eternal life. And upon them that hearken not to the voice of the Lord, shall be fulfilled that which was written by the prophet Moses, that they should be cut off from among the people.

7 And also that which was written by the prophet Malachi: For behold the day cometh that shall burn as an oven, and all the proud: yea, and all that do wickedly, shall be stubble: and the day that cometh shall burn them up saith the Lord of hosts, that it shall leave them neither root nor branch. Wherefore this shall be the answer of the Lord unto them: In that day when I came unto my own, no man among you received me, and you were driven out. When I called again, there was none of you to answer, yet my arm was not shortened at all, that I could not redeem, neither my power to deliver.— Behold at my rebuke I dry up the sea. I make the rivers a wilderness: their fish stinketh, and dieth for thirst. I clothe the heavens with blackness, and make sackcloth their covering. And this shall ye have of my hand, ye shall lay down in sorrow.

8 Behold and lo there are none to deliver you, for ye obeyed not my voice when I called to you out of the heavens, ye believed not my servants; and when they were sent unto you ye received them not: wherefore they sealed up the testimony and bound up the law, and ye were delivered over unto darkness: these shall go away into outer darkness, where there is weeping, and wailing, and gnashing of teeth. Behold the Lord your God hath spoken it. Amen.

251

SECTION CI.

MARRIAGE.

1 According to the custom of all civilized nations, marriage is regulated by laws and ceremonies: therefore we believe, that all marriages in this church of Christ of Latter Day Saints, should be solemnized in a public meeting, or feast, prepared for that purpose: and that the solemnization should be performed by a presiding high priest, high priest, bishop, elder, or priest, not even prohibiting those persons who are desirous to get married, of being married by other authority. We believe that it is not right to prohibit members of this church from marrying out of the church, if it be their determination so to do, but such persons will be considered weak in the faith of our Lord and Savior Jesus Christ.

2 Marriage should be celebrated with prayer and thanksgiving; and at the solemnization, the persons to be married, standing together, the man on the right, and the woman on the left, shall be addressed, by the person officiating, as he shall be directed by the holy Spirit; and if there be no legal objections, he shall say, calling each by their names: "You both mutually agree to be each other's companion, husband and wife, observing the legal rights belonging to this condition; that is, keeping yourselves wholly for each other, and from all others, during your lives." And when they have answered "Yes," he shall pronounce them "husband and wife" in the name of the Lord Jesus Christ, and by virtue of the laws of the country and authority vested in him: "may God add his blessings and keep you to fulfill your covenants from henceforth and forever. Amen."

3 The clerk of every church should keep a record of all marriages, solemnized in his branch.

4 All legal contracts of marriage made before a person is baptized into this church, should be held sacred and fulfilled. Inasmuch as this church of Christ has been reproached with the crime of fornication, and polygamy: we declare that we believe, that one man should have one wife; and one woman, but one husband, except in case of death, when either is at liberty to marry again. It is not right to persuade a woman to be baptized contrary to the will of her husband, neither is it lawful to influence her to leave her husband. All children are bound by law to obey their parents; and to influence them to embrace any religious faith, or be baptized, or leave their parents without their consent, is unlawful and unjust. We believe that all persons who exercise control over their fellow

line margins: 1, 5, 10, 15, 20, 25, 30, 35, 40

---

line 1. "Marriage," ca. Aug. 1835. This statement had not yet been published as of 17 August 1835, the date when a church assembly approved this text and voted to include it in the 1835 Doctrine and Covenants. (See p. 567 herein.)

lines 43 and 44. The errata found at the back of the 1835 Doctrine and Covenants calls for corrections to be made to these two lines. (See p. 593 herein.)

252

line 1 beings, and prevent them from embracing the truth, will have
to answer for that sin.

SECTION CII.

Of Governments and Laws in General.

5 *That our belief, with regard to earthly governments and laws in*
general, may not be misinterpreted nor misunderstood, we
have thought proper to present, at the close of this volume, our
opinion concerning the same.

1 We believe that Governments were instituted of God for
10 the benefit of man, and that he holds men accountable for their
acts in relation to them, either in making laws or administering them, for the good and safety of society.

2 We believe that no Government can exist, in peace, except such laws are framed and held inviolate as will secure to
15 each individual the free exercise of concience, the right and
control of property and the protection of life.

3 We believe that all Governments necessarily require civil
officers and magistrates to enforce the laws of the same, and
that such as will administer the law in equity and justice
20 should be sought for and upheld by the voice of the people,
(if a Republic,) or the will of the Sovereign.

4 We believe that religion is instituted of God, and that
men are amenable to him and to him only for the exercise of
it, unless their religious opinion prompts them to infringe up-
25 on the rights and liberties of others; but we do not believe that
human law has a right to interfere in prescribing rules of worship to bind the consciences of men, nor dictate forms for public or private devotion; that the civil magistrate should re-
strain crime, but never control conscience; should punish
30 guilt, but never surpress the freedom of the soul.

5 We believe that all men are bound to sustain and uphold
the respective Governments in which they reside, while protected in their inherent and unalienable rights by the laws of
such Governments, and that sedition and rebellion are unbe-
35 coming every citizen thus protected, and should be punished
accordingly; and that all Governments have a right to enact
such laws as in their own judgments are best calculated to secure the public interest, at the same time, however, holding sacred the freedom of conscience.

6 We believe that every man should be honored in his sta-
40 tion: rulers and magistrates as such—being placed for the protection of the innocent and the punishment of the guilty; and
that to the laws all men owe respect and deference, as without

---

lines 1 and 2. The errata found at the back of the 1835 Doctrine and Covenants calls for corrections to be
made to these two lines. (See p. 593 herein.)

line 3. "Of Governments and Laws in General," ca. Aug. 1835 [D&C 134]. This statement had not yet
been published as of 17 August 1835, the date when a church assembly approved this text and voted to
include it in the 1835 Doctrine and Covenants. (See p. 567 herein.)

line 1 them peace and harmony would be supplanted by anarchy and terror: human laws being instituted for the express purpose of regulating our interests as individuals and nations, between man and man, and divine laws, given of heaven, prescribing

5 rules on spiritual concerns, for faith and worship, both to be answered by man to his Maker.

7 We believe that Rulers, States and Governments have a right, and are bound to enact laws for the protection of all citizens in the free exercise of their religious belief; but we do

10 not believe that they have a right, in justice, to deprive citizens of this privilege, or proscribe them in their opinions, so long as a regard and reverence is shown to the laws, and such religious opinions do not justify sedition nor conspiracy.

8 We believe that the commission of crime should be punish-

15 ed according to the nature of the offence: that murder, treason, robbery, theft and the breach of the general peace, in all respects, should be punished according to their criminality and their tendency to evil among men, by the laws of that Government in which the offence is committed: and for the public

20 peace and tranquility, all men should step forward and use their ability in bringing offenders, against good laws, to punishment.

9 We do not believe it just to mingle religious influence with civil Government, whereby one religious society is foster-

25 ed and another proscribed in its spiritual privileges, and the individual rights of its members, as citizens, denied.

10 We believe that all religious societies have a right to deal with their members for disorderly conduct according to the rules and regulations of such societies, provided that such

30 dealing be for fellowship and good standing; but we do not believe that any religious society has authority to try men on the right of property or life, to take from them this world's goods, or put them in jeopardy either life or limb, neither to inflict any physical punishment upon them,—they can only

35 excommunicate them from their society and withdraw from their fellowship.

11 We believe that men should appeal to the civil law for redress of all wrongs and grievances, where personal abuse is inflicted, or the right of property or character infringed, where

40 such laws exist as will protect the same; but we believe that all men are justified in defending themselves, their friends and property, and the Government, from the unlawful assaults and encroachments of all persons, in times of exigencies, where immediate appeal cannot be made to the laws, and re-

45 lief afforded.

12 We believe it just to preach the gospel to the nations of

254

line 1

the earth, and warn the righteous to save themselves from the
corruption of the world; but we do not believe it right to interfere with bond-servants, neither preach the gospel to, nor baptize them, contrary to the will and wish of their masters, nor
to meddle with, or influence them in the least to cause them
to be dissatisfied with their situations in this life, thereby jeop-
ardizing the lives of men: such interference we believe to be
unlawful and unjust, and dangerous to the peace of every Government allowing human beings to be held in servitude.

255

GENERAL ASSEMBLY.

At a General Assembly of the Church of the LATTER DAY SAINTS, *according to previous notice, held on the 17th of August, 1835, to take into consideration the labors of a certain committee which had been appointed by a General Assembly of September 24, 1834, as follows:*

"The Assembly being duly organized, and after transacting certain business of the church, proceeded to appoint a committee to arrange the items of doctrine of Jesus Christ, for the government of his church of the Latter Day Saints, which church was organized and commenced its rise on the 6th day of April, 1830. These items are to be taken from the bible, book of Mormon, and the revelations which have been given to said church up to this date, or shall be until such arrangement is made.

"Elder Samuel H. Smith, for the assembly, moved that presiding elders, Joseph Smith, jr. Oliver Cowdery, Sidney Rigdon and Frederick G. Williams compose said committee. The nomination was seconded by elder Hyrum Smith, whereupon it received the unanimous vote of the assembly.

(SIGNED.) OLIVER COWDERY, } *Clerks.*"
ORSON HYDE.

Wherefore Presidents O. Cowdery and S. Rigdon, proceeded and organized the high council of the church at Kirtland, and Presidents W. W. Phelps and J. Whitmer proceeded and organized the high council of the church in Missouri. Bishop Newel K. Whitney proceeded and organized his counsellors of the church in Kirtland, and acting Bishop John Corrill, organized the counsellors of the church in Missouri: and also Presidents Leonard Rich, Levi W. Hancock, Sylvester Smith and Lyman Sherman, organized the council of the seventy; and also, Elder John Gould, acting President, organized the travelling Elders; and also Ira Ames, acting President, organized the Priests; and also Erastus Babbit, acting President, organized the Teachers; and also William Burgess, acting President, organized the Deacons; and also Thomas Gates, assisted by John Young, William Cowdery, Andrew H. Aldrich, Job S. Lewis and Oliver Higley, as Presidents of the day, organized the whole assembly. Elder Levi W. Hancock appointed chorister: a hymn was then sung and the services of the day opened by the prayer of President O. Cowdery, and the solemnities of eternity rested upon the audience. Another hymn was sung: after transacting some business for the church the audience adjourned for one hour.

---

line *1*. These minutes of a general assembly of the church are a condensed version of the minutes found in Minute Book 1, 17 Aug. 1835. The same version of the minutes printed here appeared in *LDS Messenger and Advocate,* Aug. 1835, 1:161–164, except that the newspaper version made the corrections called for in the errata and included the statements on marriage and government.

line *23*. The errata found at the back of the 1835 Doctrine and Covenants calls for corrections to be made to the last paragraph on this page. (See p. 593 herein.)

256

line 1

AFTERNOON.—After a hymn was sung, President Cowdery arose and introduced the "Book of doctrine and covenants of the church of the Latter Day Saints," in behalf of the committee: he was followed by President Rigdon, who explained the manner by which they intended to obtain the voice of the assembly for or against said book: the other two committee, named above, were absent. According to said arrangement W. W. Phelps bore record that the book presented to the assembly, was true. President John Whitmer, also arose, and testified that it was true. Elder John Smith, taking the lead of the high council in Kirtland, bore record that the revelations in said book were true, and that the lectures were judiciously arranged and compiled, and were profitable for doctrine; whereupon the high council of Kirtland accepted and acknowledged them as the doctrine and covenants of their faith, by a unanimous vote. Elder Levi Jackman, taking the lead of the high council of the church in Missouri, bore testimony that the revelations in said book were true, and the said high council of Missouri accepted and acknowledged them as the doctrine and covenants of their faith, by a unanimous vote.

President W. W. Phelps then read the written testimony of the Twelve, as follows. "The testimony of the witnesses to the book of the Lord's commandments, which he gave to his church through Joseph Smith, jr. who was appointed by the voice of the church for this purpose: we therefore feel willing to bear testimony to all the world of mankind, to every creature upon the face of all the earth, and upon the islands of the sea, that the Lord has borne record to our souls, through the Holy Ghost shed forth upon us, that these commandments were given by inspiration of God, and are profitable for all men, and are verily true. We give this testimony unto the world, the Lord being our helper: and it is through the grace of God, the Father, and his Son Jesus Christ, that we are permitted to have this privilege of bearing this testimony unto the world, in the which we rejoice exceedingly, praying the Lord always, that the children of men may be profited thereby." Elder Leonard Rich bore record of the truth of the book and the council of the Seventy accepted and acknowledged it as the doctrine and covenants of their faith, by a unanimous vote.

Bishop N. K. Whitney bore record of the truth of the book, and with his counsellors, accepted and acknowledged it as the doctrine and covenants of their faith, by a unanimous vote.

Acting Bishop, John Corrill, bore record of the truth of the book, and with his counsellors, accepted and acknowledged it as the doctrine and covenants of their faith, by a unanimous

257

line 1   vote. Acting President, John Gould, gave his testimony in favor of the book, and with the travelling Elders, accepted and acknowledged it as the doctrine and covenants of their faith, by a unanimous vote.

5   Ira Ames, acting President of the Priests, gave his testimony in favor of the book, and with the Priests, accepted and acknowledged it as the doctrine and covenants of their faith, by a unanimous vote.

    Erastus Babbit, acting President of the Teachers, gave his *10* testimony in favor of the book, and they accepted and acknowledged it as the doctrine and covenants of their faith, by a unanimous vote.

    Wm. Burges acting President of the Deacons, bore record of the truth of the book, and they accepted and acknowledged *15* it as the doctrine and covenants of their faith, by a unanimous vote.

    The venerable President, Thomas Gates, then bore record of the truth of the book, and with his five silver-headed assistants, and the whole congregation, accepted and acknowl-*20* edged it as the doctrine and covenants of their faith, by a unanimous vote. The several authorities, and the general assembly, by a unanimous vote, accepted of the labors of the committee.

    President W. W. Phelps then read an article on Marriage, *25* which was accepted and adopted, and ordered to be printed in said book, by a unanimous vote.

    President O. Cowdery then read an article on "governments and laws in general," which was accepted and adopted, and ordered to be printed in said book, by a unanimous vote.

30   A hymn was then sung. President S. Rigdon returned thanks, after which the assembly was blessed by the Presidency, with uplifted hands, and dismissed.

THOMAS BURDICK,
WARREN PARRISH,   } CLERKS.
35 SYLVESTER SMITH,

Q

---

lines 17 and 33. The errata found at the back of the 1835 Doctrine and Covenants calls for corrections to be made to the fourth full paragraph and the list of signatories on this page. (See p. 593 herein.)

line 36. This page begins the seventeenth gathering of the book. "Q" is the first of two signature marks in this gathering; the second is on the recto of the following leaf. These marks were used in collating the gatherings after the sheets were folded.

i

17*

---

line 1. This "Index" functions as a table of contents, in modern terms.

line 20. "do" is a common nineteenth-century abbreviation for "ditto."

line 26. The page number on this line should be "125" rather than "126".

line 31. The page number on this line should be "140" rather than "149".

line 38. "ib" is an abbreviation for "ibidem," Latin for "in the same place." A more common abbreviation is "ibid."

ii

---

line 22. The year on this line should be "1830" rather than "1829".
line 34. The year on this line should be "1830" rather than "1839".

iii

---

line 2. The index reflects the same numbering error made in the body of the volume. (See p. 505 herein.)
line 14. The month on this line should be "August" rather than "March".
line 34. The page number on this line should be "240" rather than "340".

line 1. This list of "Contents" functions as an index, in modern terms. With a few apparently uninten-
tional exceptions, the entries grouped under each letter of the alphabet are arranged in the order of the
section and paragraph (or verse) numbers listed in the second and third columns.

line 10. The section number on this line should be "3" instead of "5".

line 30. The section and verse locator provided do not obviously correspond to this reference. It is possible the reference should read "example" and that the locator should be section 23, verse 5. Or the locator
could be section 22, verse 1, which uses the word "ensample".

vi

line 4. The section and verse locator provided do not correspond to this reference. Section 89, verse 3, may have been intended.

line 17. Section 17 does not have a verse 9, but verse 8 of that section corresponds to this reference.

vii

---

line 3. Verse 3 of section 84 does not correspond to this reference, but verse 8 does.

---

line 1. The section referenced in the second column is the first of two sections in the volume numbered 66.

lines 34–37. Verse 24 of section 4 does not correspond to this reference, but verse 22 does. In other copies of the 1835 Doctrine and Covenants, the verse numbers in section 4 are out of order (21, 24, 22, 23), though the text is the same as in this copy. Compilers of the index were likely using proof sheets of a copy that contained this erroneous versification.

---

line 4. The words "day of redemption" are found at the end of verse 2 of section 15. Verse 3, though not using the words "day of redemption", could also correspond to this reference.

X

Elders to go forth,	13	2
——— to be called,	13	12
Edify each other,	14	3
Everlasting covenant sent into the world,	15	2
Earth shall hear the voice of the Lord,	15	8
Elders to conduct meetings &c.	16	1
Every man take righteousness, &c.	20	9
——————— deal honestly,	23	2
——————— in his stewardship,	26	3
Engravings of Nephi,	36	10
Establish the cause of Zion,	37	3
Eternal damnation,	44	2
——— punishment,	44	2
Expound scriptures,	48	2
Elders called together,	62	1
Election in this church,	66	1
Ezra Thayre must repent,	69	3
Every man shall hear the fulness of the gospel,	84	4
Eastern countries,	87	2
Expounding scriptures,	90	1
End of the vision,	91	7
Endow those whom I have chosen,	95	2
Enmity of man shall cease,	97	5

F

Fulness preached by the weak and the simple,	1	4
Fulness of the gospel to the Gentiles and Jews,	2	3
Form of baptism,	2	22
——— of administering bread,	2	23
——————— wine	2	24
Further duty of the twelve,	3	30
Face of the Lord unveiled,	7	27
First angel again sound his trump,	7	34
Faithful salute	7	43
Field is white,	8	2
Faithful and diligent,	8	9
Fear not to do good,	8	15
Flies sent forth,	10	5
First last, &c.	10	8
Faith to be healed and not to be healed,	13	13
Fulness of the scriptures given,	16	16
Faith comes not by signs,	20	3
Forbidden to get in debt,	21	6
Faith, virtue, &c.	31	2

line 16. The section referenced in the second column is the second of two sections in the volume numbered 66.

line 26. Verse 3 of section 2 does not correspond to this reference, but verse 2 does.

line 40. The section and verse locator provided do not correspond to this reference. Section 13, verse 5, may have been intended.

xi

line 1	Fear not but give heed, &c.	52	2
	Field ready to be burned,	53	2
	—— is white for harvest,	55	1
	Father and I are one,	82	1
5	Family must needs repent,	82	8
	Forgiving 70 times 7	85	7
	Feigned words,	98	1
	Flee to Zion,	100	2
	—— Jerusalem,	100	2
10	Free exercise of conscience,	102	2

G

	God is infinite and eternal,	2	4
	Godly walk and conversation required,	2	19
	Gathering of the saints to the place of the city—		
15	Zion,	4	1
	God's servants to live by every word that proceedeth		
	from his mouth,	11	4
	Gifts come from God,	16	7
	God is light,	17	6
20	Go with my servant,	28	1
	God is merciful,	30	4
	Gift of Aaron,	34	4
	Give heed,	38	5
	———— unto all his words,	46	2
25	Go unto the Lamanites,	61	3
	—— with my servant Oliver,	54	1
	Great day shall come,	56	2
	Go to the Ohio,	58	1
	Great I Am,	50	1
30	Gift of the Holy Ghost,	59	6
	Go forth and preach,	62	2
	Give a new commandment to Thomas,	69	2
	Go to certain countries,	76	1
	— ye, go ye into the world,	77	1
35	Glory of the Father was with him,	82	2
	Grace for grace,	82	2
	Go to battle,	85	6
	Go from house to house,	87	3
	Great is his wisdom,	91	1
40	Glory of the Moon,	91	7
	Grants this privilege,	91	8
	Go and gather together, &c.	97	7
	Gird up your loins,	99	2

---

lines 14 and 15. Several section and verse locators on this page do not correspond to the references provided. For this entry, section 4, verse 7, may have been intended.

line 22. Section 34 does not have a verse 4, but verse 3 of that section corresponds to this reference.

line 25. See first note on this page. Section 51, verse 3, may have been intended.

line 29. See first note on this page. Several passages in the 1835 Doctrine and Covenants use "Great I Am" or similar wording, but based on the order of the references, section 59, verse 1, was likely intended.

---

line 20. Verse 2 of section 101 better corresponds to this reference than does verse 1.

line 6. The section referenced in the second column is the first of two sections in the volume numbered 66.

xiv

M

---

line 26. The section referenced in the second column is the first of two sections in the volume numbered 66.

line 27. The section referenced in the second column is the second of two sections in the volume numbered 66.

line 31. Section 73 has three verses, but the last two are both numbered "2". This index entry is correct in pointing to the third and final verse.

---

line 22. Section 35 has only 5 verses. Section 36 was likely intended: verse 7 of that section begins "Marvel not".

line 43. This page begins the eighteenth gathering of the book. "R" is the first of two signature marks in this gathering; the second is on the recto of the following leaf. These marks were used in collating the gatherings after the sheets were folded.

xvii

18*

---

line 1. Verse 30 of section 3 does not correspond to this reference, but verse 31 does.

line 1

5

10

15

20

25

30

35

40

---

line 38. Verse 1 of section 39 does not correspond to this reference, but verse 2 does.

XIX

line 1	Reap with all your might,	55	2
	Ruler when I come,	61	2
	Reason with them,	65	1
	Recorded in heaven for the angels to look upon,	72	1
5	Ride upon Mules or in chariots,	72	3
	Restore four fold,	85	7
	Render account of stewardship,	89	1
	Recommended by church,	89	4
	Received of his fulness,	91	3
10	Ruler in my kingdom,	97	8
	Red in his apparel,	100	5
	Record all marriages,	101	3
	Religious belief,	102	7

S

15	Secret things shall be revealed,	1	1
	Sword of the Lord bathed in heaven,	1	3
	Spirit will not always strive with man,	1	5
	Search these commandments,	1	7
	Son of God given,	2	5
20	Seventy directed by the twelve,	3	13
	Seth ordained and blessed by Adam,	3	19
	Seven Presidents called to preside of the number of seventy,	3	43
	Sons of Moses and of Aaron to offer an acceptable sacrifice in this generation,	4	6
25	Song of the redeemed,	4	17
	Seven counsellors necessary for a council,	5	4
	Sanctify yourselves,	7	18
	Seek knowledge,	7	21
30	Signs in the heavens,	7	24
	Sounding of the trump,	7	26
	Second angel again sound, &c.	7	35
	Satan bound,	7	35
	Salvation, &c.	7	41
35	————— a sample for, &c.	7	44
	Stand faithfully,	8	8
	Sinners shall be cast out,	13	11
	Scriptures for church government,	13	16
	Sent forth to teach, &c.	14	4
40	Solemnities of eternity,	14	8
	Signs of his coming,	15	6
	Sacrament meetings,	16	2
	Seek the best gifts,	16	4
	Sound must go forth from this place,	18	15

---

lines 34 and 35. The reference for these two lines should likely be "salutation", rather than "salvation".

XX

line 1	Shall make another,	20	14
	Spirit received through prayer,	20	16
	Sought evil in their hearts,	21	3
	Sell goods without fraud,	27	4
5	Stop and stand still,	32	6
	Spirit by which Moses, &c.	34	2
	Satan stirs them up,	36	3
	Sharper than a two-edged sword,	37	1
	Seek to bring forth Zion,	38	3
10	Shall build up, &c.	43	1
	Save one soul,	43	3
	Straight gate, &c.	47	1
	Selection of sacred hymns,	48	3
	Settle all things according to the covenants,	51	5
15	Singleness of heart,	57	3
	Satan tempted him,	60	1
	Shall be damned,	65	1
	Son of man comes not in the form of a woman,	65	4
	Satan abroad in the land,	66	4
20	Shake off the dust of thy feet,	70	4
	Savior of the world,	74	1
	Saints who are at Zion,	75	2
	Son Ahman,	75	4
	Salvation of Zion,	81	3
25	See God,	81	4
	Stake of Zion,	83	1
	School of the prophets,	84	3
	Smite you or your families,	85	5
	Sin no more,	86	2
30	Soul that sins, &c.	86	5
	Sons of perdition,	91	4
	Suffering of the ungodly,	91	4
	Sun of the firmament, &c.	91	5
	Shederlaomach a member,	93	2
35	Spokesman unto my servant,	94	3
	Strange act,	95	1
	Stake set for the strength of Zion,	96	1
	Salt of the earth,	97	5
	See the salvation of God,	99	3
40	Sedition and rebellion,	102	5
	Spiritual privileges,	102	9

T

Two first elders,	2	1
Transgression of his holy laws,	2	4

---

line 39. The section and verse locator provided do not obviously correspond to this reference. Section 100, verse 1, was likely intended.

xxi

U

---

line 1. The section and verse locator provided do not obviously correspond to this reference.
lines 9–14. The section number for all these references to "trump" should be "7".

---

line 25. Section 67 has only three verses. Verse 5 of section 69, which begins "Wo unto you rich men", was likely intended.

xxix

line 1

Y

Years of accountability before baptism,	3	21
———— the redeemed is come,	100	5
You were driven out,	100	7

5

Z

Zion shall rejoice,	11	6
—— a place of safety,	15	13
—— shall flourish,	21	8
—— shall be a seat,	28	2
———— flourish upon the hills,	65	6
—— do these things, shall prosper,	81	5
—— shall be redeemed,	93	4
———— turned back, &c.	100	3

10

———————

line 2. Verse 21 of section 3 does not correspond to this reference, but verse 21 of section 2 does.
line 10. Section 65 does not have a verse 6, but verse 5 of that section corresponds to this reference.
line 12. Section 93 has only two verses. Section 94, verse 4, was likely intended.

XXV

NOTES TO THE READER.

Several errors have escaped the eye of the proof reader: They will be carefully sought, and, in the next edition, *correc ted*:lest, however, that any should be mislead, the last paragraph of the article on Marriage, page 251, should read: "We believe that husbands, parents and masters who exercise control over their wives, children and servants, and prevent them from embracing the truth, will have to answer for that sin."

In the proceedings of the General Assembly, page 255, it should read: "Wherefore O. Cowdery and S. Rigdon, Presidents of the first presidency, appointed Thomas Burdick, Warren Parrish and Silvester Smith, Clerks, and proceeded to organize the whole assembly, as follows: "They organized," &c. And it should read at the 9th line from the bottom, "And they also, as the assembly was large, appointed Thomas Gates, John Young, William Cowdery, Andrew H. Aldrich, Job S. Lewis, and Oliver Higley, as assistant presidents of the day, to assist in preserving order, &c. in the whole assembly." And on the 257th page, 5th paragraph, it should read: "The venerable assistant President," &c. And the whole proceedings should be signed,

OLIVER COWDERY, } *Pres'ts.*
SIDNEY RIGDON,

THOMAS BURDICK,
WARREN PARRISH, } *Clerks.*
SILVESTER SMITH,

A source text for the Doctrine and Covenants. Editors of the first edition of the Doctrine and Covenants (bottom) used Oliver Cowdery's copy of the Book of Commandments (top), along with several other source texts, to select and prepare Joseph Smith's revelations for publication. Church History Library, Salt Lake City.

APPENDIX 2:
SELECTIONS FROM OLIVER COWDERY'S COPY OF THE BOOK OF COMMANDMENTS

Source Note

A Book of Commandments, for the Government of the Church of Christ, Organized according to Law, on the 6th of April, 1830; *Zion [Independence], MO: W. W. Phelps & Co., 1833; incomplete (printing interrupted); [1]–160 pp.; includes typeset signature marks and copyright notice. The copy excerpted herein is held at CHL; includes early marginalia and editorial marks.*

This volume, which was owned by Oliver Cowdery, measures 4¼ × 3 inches (11 × 8 cm) and is bound in vertically striated, salmon-colored calfskin. The text block edges are stained yellow. The recto of the front flyleaf has "Joseph Smith Jr" written in JS's handwriting upside down along the bottom of the page. On the verso of the front flyleaf is inscribed "Joseph Smith J[r] | & Oliver Cowdery | Book for the | printing office". The recto of the back flyleaf bears a similar inscription: "Joseph Smith J[r] | Oliver Cowdery | for the off[ic]e". In both cases, JS's name is in JS's handwriting and the remainder of the notation is in Cowdery's handwriting.

This copy was acquired by The Church of Jesus Christ of Latter-day Saints from a grandson of Warren Cowdery, the brother of Oliver. The church acquired from the same man a copy of the first edition of the Doctrine and Covenants (1835) that belonged to Warren Cowdery. It is possible that Warren Cowdery obtained this copy of the Book of Commandments when he began editing the Kirtland, Ohio, newspaper *Latter Day Saints' Messenger and Advocate* in February 1837. It is clear from the notations on the flyleaves and numerous marks throughout the volume that this copy of the Book of Commandments was used in the Kirtland printing office.

Introduction

This appendix presents all data and images needed for readers to access and use Oliver Cowdery's copy of the Book of Commandments as a resource for understanding the printing history of the 1835 Doctrine and Covenants.

Oliver Cowdery's copy of the Book of Commandments was used, along with several other source texts, by the editors of the 1835 Doctrine and Covenants as they were preparing JS's revelations for publication in that volume.[1] Cowdery and William W. Phelps made

---

1. See pp. 305–306 herein.

editorial marks throughout this copy of the Book of Commandments, and it is possible that other unknown individuals also made marks. The editors marked and edited within this copy some of the revelations that were to be included in the new publication and then used this copy to set type for some portions of the 1835 Doctrine and Covenants.

Each image in this appendix is accompanied by a note indicating to which chapter of the Book of Commandments the pictured page belongs. The note also references the page number(s) in this volume where the corresponding portion of the 1835 Doctrine and Covenants is reproduced. Because this appendix does not present the full Cowdery copy of the Book of Commandments, no other textual notes are provided. Readers should consult the full Book of Commandments printed in this volume (beginning on page 3 herein) for an analysis of the printing of the Book of Commandments.

Explanation of Editing Marks

Because limited space on the following image pages does not allow for explanation of the editing marks seen on the images, a brief explanation of each type of editing mark is provided here.

Oliver Cowdery wrote "Covenants" in graphite at the head of sixteen revelations in his copy of the Book of Commandments, all of which appear in the first 21 sections of the 1835 Doctrine and Covenants.[2] Various pages throughout the book are marked with a capital "S" in red grease pencil.[3] All texts published in both the Book of Commandments and the 1835 Doctrine and Covenants bear this "S" mark in Cowdery's Book of Commandments except chapter 28 and those chapters that correspond to sections 68 through 72 of the 1835 Doctrine and Covenants (chapters 57, 58, 61, 62, and 63).[4] Though the precise meaning of the letter is unknown, this notation suggests a systematic survey of the contents of the volume to ensure that all the revelations in the Book of Commandments were included in the 1835 Doctrine and Covenants. Because the "Covenants" mark and the "S" mark appear frequently in the volume and have a uniform appearance, the pages on which they appear will not be reproduced herein unless the page also bears one of the editorial marks described in the following paragraph.

---

2. In one case (chapter 1), the penciled notation reads "Covenants 1" rather than "Covenants." Except section 8, all of the sections from 1 through 21 of the 1835 Doctrine and Covenants that were also published in the Book of Commandments are marked with the "Covenants" notation in the Cowdery copy. The sixteen chapters Cowdery marked with the "Covenants" notation correspond to Doctrine and Covenants 1, 2, 9–21, 1835 ed. [D&C 1, 20, 24, 29, 35, 38, 42–43, 45–46, 50, 58–59, 63–64]. Two chapters in the Book of Commandments (44 and 47) were combined into section 13 of the 1835 publication. The texts in Doctrine and Covenants 3–7, 1835 ed. [D&C 107, 84, 102, 86, 88], were not published in the Book of Commandments.

3. Editors also used red grease pencil to mark up other sources for publication in the 1835 Doctrine and Covenants. In two cases in the Book of Commandments, the "S" is not in red grease pencil but in graphite: chapter 39 (page 80) and chapter 41 (page 86) [D&C 37 and 39]. (See "Table 3: Relationship between Items in Revelation Books 1 and 2 and the 1835 Doctrine and Covenants," in *JSP*, MRB:701.)

4. Doctrine and Covenants 68–72, 1835 ed. [D&C 55–56, 60–62], are the last sections of the 1835 Doctrine and Covenants to have used the Book of Commandments as a source text.

Several other editing marks were inscribed in Cowdery's copy of the Book of Commandments. Editors added paragraph marks and numerals on many pages to denote versification for the 1835 publication. A bracket or parenthesis in Cowdery's Book of Commandments at times corresponds to a line ending in the 1835 Doctrine and Covenants.[5] To denote deletions, editors usually struck through words and phrases or marked them with an "X." To denote additions, editors usually inserted individual words or phrases. When revisions were too lengthy or complex to indicate on the small pages of the Book of Commandments, editors sometimes referred the copyist or typesetter to some other source by marking passages with a caret or similar mark, which was sometimes accompanied by a notation such as "see" in the margin.[6] In other cases where revisions were complex, editors circled passages that were to be ignored in the Book of Commandments in favor of some other source text.[7] Thus, typesetters or copyists worked directly from the Book of Commandments until they reached a caret or a passage that had been circled, at which point they presumably turned to an additional source now no longer extant. Where a passage in the Book of Commandments referred to a person by first name or first name and initial, surnames were sometimes written in by hand and other times a caret was inscribed after the name, indicating that the copyist or typesetter should add the surname.[8] The Cowdery copy of the Book of Commandments also contains three additional editing marks whose purpose is unknown.[9]

The following table provides a comprehensive list of the editing marks found in the Cowdery volume. The first column of the table lists the number of each chapter of the Book of Commandments. The second column provides the standard date for the item included in each chapter and a bracketed "D&C" reference to the section number in which the item appears in the 1981 Latter-day Saint edition of the Doctrine and Covenants.[10] The third column identifies the editing marks found in each chapter of the Cowdery Book of Commandments. In this column, "Covenants" and "'S' mark" refer to the commonly appearing marks described above (in cases when "S" marks are found on pages other than the first page of a chapter, the numbers of those pages are identified in parentheses). The term "editing marks" as used in this column refers to all other types of editing marks made by editors, as described in the immediately preceding paragraph. The fourth column lists the number of the section in which each item was published in the 1835 Doctrine and Covenants.

---

5. See, for example, p. 607 herein.

6. See, for example, p. 601 herein.

7. See, for example, p. 602 herein.

8. See, for example, p. 624 herein.

9. The marks, which are similar to one another, appear in Book of Commandments 39 (page 79), 41 (page 85), and 42 (page 87), which correspond to Doctrine and Covenants 58, 59, and 60, 1835 ed. [D&C 37, 39, 40].

10. For more information on these dates, see p. 719 herein.

Key to column titles

1833:	Book of Commandments
Date:	Date of item, followed by section number in Doctrine and Covenants, 1981 edition, The Church of Jesus Christ of Latter-day Saints
Editing Marks:	Editing marks in the Oliver Cowdery copy of the Book of Commandments
1835:	Doctrine and Covenants, 1835 edition, part 2

1833	DATE	EDITING MARKS	1835
1	1 Nov. 1831–B [D&C 1]	"Covenants 1"; "S" mark; editing marks	1
2	July 1828 [D&C 3]	"S" mark; editing marks	30
3	Feb. 1829 [D&C 4]	"S" mark; editing marks	31
4	Mar. 1829 [D&C 5]	"S" mark; editing marks	32
5	Apr. 1829–A [D&C 6]	"S" mark	8
6	Apr. 1829–C [D&C 7]	"S" mark; editing marks	33
7	Apr. 1829–B [D&C 8]	"S" mark; editing marks	34
8	Apr. 1829–D [D&C 9]	"S" mark; editing marks	35
9	ca. Apr. 1829 [D&C 10]	"S" mark; editing marks	36
10	May 1829–A [D&C 11]	"S" mark	37
11	May 1829–B [D&C 12]	"S" mark	38
12	June 1829–A [D&C 14]	"S" mark	39
13	June 1829–C [D&C 15]	"S" mark	40
14	June 1829–D [D&C 16]	"S" mark	41
15	June 1829–B [D&C 18]	"S" marks (pp. 34, 35)	43
16	Mar. 1830 [D&C 19]	"S" mark	44
17	Apr. 1830–A [D&C 23:1–2]	"S" mark	45:1
18	Apr. 1830–B [D&C 23:3]	"S" mark	45:2
19	Apr. 1830–C [D&C 23:4]	"S" mark	45:3
20	Apr. 1830–D [D&C 23:5]	"S" mark	45:4
21	Apr. 1830–E [D&C 23:6–7]	"S" mark	45:5
22	6 Apr. 1830 [D&C 21]	"S" mark; editing marks	46
23	16 Apr. 1830 [D&C 22]	"S" mark	47
24	10 Apr. 1830 [D&C 20]	"Covenants"; "S" mark	2
25	July 1830–A [D&C 24]	"Covenants"; "S" mark	9
26	July 1830–C [D&C 25]	"S" mark	48
27	July 1830–B [D&C 26]	"S" mark	49
28	ca. Aug. 1830 [D&C 27]		50
29	Sept. 1830–A [D&C 29]	"Covenants"; "S" mark	10
30	Sept. 1830–B [D&C 28]	"S" mark; editing marks	51

1833	Date	Editing Marks	1835
31	Sept. 1830–C [D&C 30:1–4]	"S" mark	52:1
32	Sept. 1830–D [D&C 30:5–8]	"S" marks (pp. 69, 70); editing marks	52:2
33	Sept. 1830–E [D&C 30:9–11]	"S" mark	52:3
34	Sept. 1830–F [D&C 31]	"S" mark	53
35	Oct. 1830–B [D&C 33]	"S" marks (pp. 72, 73)	55
36	4 Nov. 1830 [D&C 34]	"S" mark	56
37	7 Dec. 1830 [D&C 35]	"Covenants"; "S" mark; editing marks	11
38	9 Dec. 1830 [D&C 36]	"S" marks (pp. 78, 79)	57
39	30 Dec. 1830 [D&C 37]	"S" mark (p. 80); editing marks	58
40	2 Jan. 1831 [D&C 38]	"Covenants"; "S" mark; editing marks	12
41	5 Jan. 1831 [D&C 39]	"S" mark (p. 85, 86); editing marks	59
42	6 Jan. 1831 [D&C 40]	"S" mark; editing marks	60
43	4 Feb. 1831 [D&C 41]	"S" mark	61
44	9 Feb. 1831 [D&C 42:1–72]	"Covenants"; "S" mark; editing marks	13:1–19
45	Feb. 1831–A [D&C 43]	"Covnants" "S" mark;	14
46	Feb. 1831–B [D&C 44]	"S" mark	62
47	23 Feb. 1831 [D&C 42:73–93]	"Covenants"; "S" mark	13:20–23
48	ca. 7 Mar. 1831 [D&C 45]	"Covenants"; "S" mark; editing marks	15
49	ca. 8 Mar. 1831–A [D&C 46]	"Covenants"; "S" mark; editing marks	16
50	ca. 8 Mar. 1831–B [D&C 47]	"S" mark	63
51	10 Mar. 1831 [D&C 48]	"S" mark	64
52	7 May 1831 [D&C 49]	"S" marks (pp. 116, 117)	65
53	9 May 1831 [D&C 50]	"Covenants"; "S" mark	17
54	6 June 1831 [D&C 52]	"S" mark; editing marks	66
55	8 June 1831 [D&C 53]	"S" mark; editing marks	66[11]
56	10 June 1831 [D&C 54]	"S" mark; editing marks	67
57	14 June 1831 [D&C 55]	editing marks	68
58	15 June 1831 [D&C 56]	editing marks	69
59	1 Aug. 1831 [D&C 58]	"Covenants"; "S" mark; editing marks	18
60	7 Aug. 1831 [D&C 59]	"Covenants"; "S" mark	19
61	8 Aug. 1831 [D&C 60]	editing marks	70
62	12 Aug. 1831 [D&C 61]	editing marks	71
63	13 Aug. 1831 [D&C 62]	editing marks	72
64	30 Aug. 1831 [D&C 63]	"Covenants"; "S" mark; editing mark	20
65[12]	11 Sept. 1831 [D&C 64]	"Covenants"; "S" mark	21

11. The second of the two sections numbered 66.

12. Because the printing office was destroyed, this revelation was not printed in full.

should proclaim these things unto the world, and all this that it might be fulfilled, which was written by the prophets: The weak things of the world should come forth and break down the mighty and strong ones; that man should not counsel his fellow man, neither trust in the arm of flesh, but that every man might speak in the name of God, the Lord, even the Savior of the world; that f ith also might increase in the earth; that mine everlasting covenant might be established; that the fulness of my gospel might be proclaimed by the weak and the simple, unto the ends of the world; and before kings and rulers.

5 Behold I am God and have spoken it: these commandments are of me, and were given unto my servants in their weakness, after the manner of their language, that they might come to understanding; and inasmuch as they erred, it might be made known: and inasmuch as they sought wisdom, they might be instructed; and inasmuch as they sinned, they might be chastened, that they might repent; and inasmuch as they were humble, they might be made strong, and blessed from on high, and receive knowledge from time to time: after they, having received the record of the Nephites; yea, even my servant Joseph might have power to translate through the mercy of God, by the power of God, the book of Mormon: And also, those to whom these commandments were given, might have power to lay the foundation of this church, and to bring it forth out of obscurity, and out of darkness, the only true and living church upon the face of the whole earth, with which I the Lord am well pleased, speaking unto the church collectively and not individually, for I the Lord can not look upon sin

A
BOOK
OF
COMMANDMENTS,
FOR THE GOVERNMENT OF THE
Church of Christ,
ORGANIZED ACCORDING TO LAW, ON THE
6th of April, 1830.

ZION:
PUBLISHED BY W. W. PHELPS & CO.
....
1833.

Left: Title page. *Right:* Excerpt of chapter 1 of the Book of Commandments. (See pp. 386–387 herein.)

9

that they might know the promises of the Lord, and that they may believe the gospel and rely upon the merits of Jesus Christ, and be glorified through faith in his name; and that through their repentance they might be saved: Amen.

CHAPTER III.

1. *A Revelation given to Joseph, the father of Joseph, in Harmony, Pennsylvania, February, 1829, saying:*

NOW, behold, a marvelous work is about to come forth among the children of men, therefore, O ye that embark in the service of God, see, that ye serve him with all your heart, might, mind and strength, that ye may stand blameless before God at the last day: Therefore, if ye have desires to serve God, ye are called to the work, for behold, the field is white already to harvest, and lo, he that thrusteth in his sickle with his might, the same layeth up in store that he perish not, but bringeth salvation to his soul, and faith, hope, charity, and love, with an eye single to the glory of God, qualifies him for the work.

2. Remember temperance, patience, humility, diligence, &c., ask and ye shall receive, knock and it shall be opened unto you: Amen.

8

4. Behold thou art Joseph, and thou wast chosen to do the work of the Lord, but because of transgression, if thou art not aware thou wilt fall, but remember God is merciful: Therefore, repent of that which thou hast done, and he will only cause thee to be afflicted for a season, and thou art still chosen, and wilt again be called to the work; and except thou do this, thou shalt be delivered up and become as other men, and have no more gift.

5. And when thou deliveredst up that which God had given thee sight and power to translate, thou deliveredst up that which was sacred, into the hands of a wicked man, who has set at nought the counsels of God, and has broken the most sacred promises, which were made before God, and has depended upon his own judgment, and boasted in his own wisdom, and this is the reason that thou hast lost thy privileges for a season, for thou hast suffered the counsel of thy director to be trampled upon from the beginning.

6. Nevertheless, my work shall go forth and accomplish my purposes, for as the knowledge of a Savior has come into the world, even so shall the knowledge of my people, the Nephites, and the Jacobites, and the Josephites, and the Zoramites, come to the knowledge of the Lamanites, and the Lemuelites and the Ishmaelites, which dwindled in unbelief, because of the iniquities of their fathers, who have been suffered to destroy their brethren, because of their iniquities, and their abominations: and for this very purpose are these plates preserved which contain these records, that the promises of the Lord might be fulfilled, which he made to his people; and that the Lamanites might come to the knowledge of their fathers, and

Left: Excerpt of chapter 2 of the Book of Commandments. (See p. 467 herein.) *Right:* Excerpt of chapter 2 and entirety of chapter 3 of the Book of Commandments. (See pp. 467–468 herein.)

CHAPTER IV.

1 *A Revelation given to Joseph and Martin, in Harmony, Pennsylvania, March, 1829, when Martin desired of the Lord to know whether Joseph had, in his possession, the record of the Nephites.*

BEHOLD, I say unto you, that my servant Martin has desired a witness from my hand, that my servant Joseph has got the things of which he has testified, and borne record that he has received of me.

2 And now, behold, this shall you say unto him:—I the Lord am God, and I have given these things unto my servant Joseph, and I have commanded him that he should stand as a witness of these things, nevertheless I have caused him that he should enter into a covenant with me, that he should not show them except I command him, and he has no power over them except I grant it unto him; and he has a gift to translate the book, and I have commanded him that he shall pretend to no other gift, for I will grant him no other gift.

3 And verily I say unto you, that wo shall come unto the inhabitants of the earth, if they will not hearken unto my words, for, behold, if they will not believe my words, they would not believe my servant Joseph, if it were possible that he could show them all things. O ye unbelieving, ye stiffnecked generation, mine anger is kindled against you!

4 Behold, verily I say, I have reserved the things of which I have spoken, which I have intrusted to my servant, for a wise purpose in me, and it shall be made known unto future generations: But this generation shall have my words, yea and the testi-

many of three of my servants shall go forth with the words unto this generation; yea, three shall know of a surety that these things are true, for I will give them power, that they may behold and view these things as they are, and to none else will I grant this power, to receive this same testimony among this generation. And the testimony of three witnesses will I send forth and my word, and behold, whosoever believeth in my word, then will I visit with the manifestation of my Spirit, and they shall be born of me, and their testimony shall also go forth.

5 And thus, if the people of this generation harden not their hearts, I will work a reformation among them, and I will put down all lyings, and deceivings, and priestcrafts, and envyings, and strifes, and idolatries, and sorceries, and all manner of iniquities, and I will establish my church, like unto the church which was taught by my disciples in the days of old.

6 And now if this generation do harden their hearts against my word, behold I will deliver them up unto satan, for he reigneth and hath much power at this time, for he hath got great hold upon the hearts of the people of this generation: and not far from the iniquities of Solom and Gomorah, do they come at this time; and behold the sword of justice hangeth over their heads, and if they persist in the hardiness of their hearts, the time cometh that it must fall upon them. Behold I tell you these things even as I also told the people of the destruction of Jerusalem, and my word shall be verified at this time as it hath hitherto been verified.

7 And now I command my servant Joseph to repent, and walk more uprightly before me, and yield to the persuasions of men no more; and that he be

Both pages: Excerpt of chapter 4 of the Book of Commandments. (See pp. 468–469 herein.)

13

thou shalt stop for a season, even until I command thee again: then thou mayest translate again. And except thou do this, behold thou shalt have no more gift, and I will take away the things which I have intrusted with thee.

7. And now, because I foresee the lying in wait to destroy thee: Yea, I foresee that if my servant humbleth not himself, and receive a witness from my hand, that he will fall into transgression; and there are many that lie in wait to destroy thee from off the face of the earth: And for this cause, that thy days may be prolonged, I have given unto thee these commandments; yea, for this cause I have said, stop and stand still until I command thee, and I will provide means whereby thou mayest accomplish the thing which I have commanded thee; and if thou art faithful in keeping my commandments, thou shalt be lifted up at the last day. Amen.

12

from in keeping the commandments wherewith I have commanded him; and if he doeth this, behold I grant unto him eternal life; even if he should be slain.

8 And now I speak again concerning the man that desireth a witness: behold I say unto him, he exalteth himself and doth not humble himself sufficiently before me, but if he will go out and bow down before me, and humble himself in mighty prayer and faith, in the sincerity of his heart, then will I grant unto him a view of the things which he desireth to know: and then he shall say unto the people of this generation, behold I have seen the things and I know of a surety that they are true, for I have seen them, and they have been shown unto me by the power of God and not of man. And I command him that he shall say no more unto them, concerning these things, except he shall say, I have seen them, and they have been shown unto me by the power of God.

9 And these are the words which he shall say:— But if he deny this, he will break the covenant which he has before covenanted with me, and behold he is condemned. And now except he humble himself and acknowledge unto me the things that he has done, which are wrong, and covenant with me that he will keep my commandments, and exercise faith in me, behold I say unto him, he shall have no such views, for I will grant unto him no views of the things of which I have spoken. And if this be the case, I command him that he shall do no more, nor trouble me any more concerning this matter.

10 And if this be the case, behold I say unto you, Joseph, when thou hast translated a few more pages;

Both pages: Excerpt of chapter 4 of the Book of Commandments. (See pp. 469–470 herein.)

19

CHAPTER VII.

1 *A Revelation given to Oliver, in Harmony, Pennsylvania, April, 1829.*

OLIVER, verily, verily I say unto you, that as surely as the Lord liveth, which is your God and your Redeemer, even so sure shall you receive a knowledge of whatsoever things you shall ask in faith, with an honest heart, believing that you shall receive a knowledge concerning the engravings of old records, which are ancient, which contain those parts of my scripture of which have been spoken, by the manifestation of my Spirit; yea, behold I will tell you in your mind and in your heart by the Holy Ghost, which shall come upon you and which shall dwell in your heart.

2 Now, behold this is the Spirit of revelation:—behold this is the Spirit by which Moses brought the children of Israel through the Red sea on dry ground; therefore, this is thy gift; apply unto it and blessed art thou, for it shall deliver you out of the hands of your enemies, when, if it were not so, they would slay you and bring your soul to destruction.

3 O remember, these words and keep my commandments. Remember this is your gift. Now this is not all, for you have another gift, which is the gift of working with the rod: behold it has told you things: behold there is no other power save God, that can cause this rod of nature, to work in your hands, for it is the work of God; and therefore whatsoever you shall ask me to tell you by that means, that will I grant unto you, that you shall know.

4 Remember that without faith you can do noth-

18

CHAPTER VI.

1 *A Revelation given to Joseph and Oliver, in Harmony, Pennsylvania, April, 1829, when they desired to know whether John, the beloved disciple, tarried on earth. Translated from parchment, written and hid up by himself.*

AND the Lord said unto me, John my beloved, what desirest thou? and I said Lord, give unto me power that I may bring souls unto thee. And the Lord said unto me Verily, verily I say unto thee, because thou desiredst this, thou shalt tarry till I come in my glory:

2 And for this cause, the Lord said unto Peter:—If I will that he tarry till I come, what is that to thee? for he desiredst of me that he might bring souls fly come unto me in my kingdom: I say unto thee, Peter, this was a good desire, but my beloved has undertaken a greater work.

3 Verily I say unto you, ye shall both have according to your desires, for ye both joy in that which ye have desired.

Left: Chapter 6 of the Book of Commandments. (See pp. 470–471 herein.) *Right:* Excerpt of chapter 7 of the Book of Commandments. (See pp. 471–472 herein.)

20

ing. Trifle not with these things. Do not ask for that which you ought not. Ask that you may know the mysteries of God, and that you may translate all those ancient records, which have been hid up, which are sacred, and according to your faith shall it be done unto you.

5 Behold it is I that have spoken it, and I am the same which spake unto you from the beginning:—Amen.

CHAPTER VIII.

1 *A Revelation given to Oliver, in Harmony, Pennsylvania, April, 1829.*

BEHOLD I say unto you, my son, that, because you did not translate according to that which you desired of me, and did commence again to write for my servant Joseph, even so I would that you should continue until you have finished this record, which I have intrusted unto you: and then behold, other records have I, that I will give unto you power that you may assist to translate.

2 Be patient my son, for it is wisdom in me, and it is not expedient that you should translate at this present time. Behold the work which you are called to do, is to write for my servant Joseph; and behold it is because that you did not continue as you commenced, when you began to translate, that I have taken away this privilege from you. Do not murmur my son, for it is wisdom in me that I have dealt with you after this manner.

3 Behold you have not understood, you have supposed that I would give it unto you, when you took

21

no thought, save it was to ask me; but behold I say unto you, that you must study it out in your mind; then you must ask me if it be right, and if it is right, I will cause that your bosom shall burn within you: therefore, you shall feel that it is right; but if it be not right, you shall have no such feelings, but you shall have a stupor of though, that shall cause you to forget the thing which is wrong; therefore, you cannot write that which is sacred, save it be given you from me.

4 Now if you had known this, you could have translated: nevertheless, it is not expedient that you should translate now. Behold it was expedient when you commenced, but you feared and the time is past, and it is not expedient now: for, do you not behold that I have given unto my servant Joseph sufficient strength, whereby it is made up? and neither of you have I condemned.

5 Do this thing which I have commanded you, and you shall prosper. Be faithful, and yield to no temptation. Stand fast in the work wherewith I have called you, and a hair of your head shall not be lost, and you shall be lifted up at the last day: Amen.

Left: Excerpts of chapters 7–8 of the Book of Commandments. (See p. 472 herein.) *Right:* Excerpt of chapter 8 of the Book of Commandments. (See pp. 472–473 herein.)

23

plan, that he may destroy this work: for he has put it into their hearts to do this, that by lying they may say they have caught you in the words which you have pretended to translate.

2 Verily I say unto you, that I will not suffer that satan shall accomplish his evil design in this thing; for behold he has put it into their hearts to tempt the Lord their God: for behold they say in their hearts, We will see if God has given him power to translate, if so, he will also give him power again; and if God giveth him power again, or if he translate again, or in other words, if he bringeth forth the same words, behold we have the same with us, and we have altered them: Therefore, they will not agree, and we will say that he has lied in his words, and that he has no gift, and that he has no power: therefore, we will destroy him, and also the work, and we will do this that we may not be ashamed in the end, and that we may get glory of the world.

4 Verily, verily I say unto you, that satan has great hold upon their hearts; he stirreth them up to do iniquity against that which is good; that he may lead their souls to destruction, and thus he has laid a cunning plan to destroy the work of God; yea, he stirreth up their hearts to anger against this work; yea, he saith unto them, Deceive and lie in wait to catch, that ye may destroy: behold this is no harm, and thus he flattereth them and telleth them that it is no sin to lie, that they may catch a man in a lie, that they may destroy him, and thus he flattereth them, and leadeth them along until he draggeth their souls down to hell; and thus he causeth them to catch themselves in their own snare; and thus he goeth up and down, to and fro in the earth, seeking to destroy the souls of men.

22

CHAPTER IX.

1 *A Revelation given to Joseph, in Harmony, Pennsylvania, May, 1829, informing him of the alteration of the Manuscript of the fore part of the book of Mormon.*

NOW, behold I say unto you, that because you delivered up so many writings, which you had power to translate, into the hands of a wicked man, you have lost them, and you also lost your gift at the same time, nevertheless it has been restored unto you again: therefore see that you are faithful and go on unto the finishing of the remainder of the work as you have begun. Do not run faster than you have strength and means provided to translate, but be diligent unto the end, that you may come off conqueror; yea, that you may conquer satan, and those that do uphold his work.

2 Behold they have sought to destroy you; yea, even the man in whom you have trusted; and for this cause I said, that he is a wicked man, for he has sought to take away the things wherewith you have been intrusted: and he has also sought to destroy your gift, and because you have delivered the wri- ting into his hands, behold they have taken them from you: therefore, you have delivered them up; yea, that which was sacred unto wickedness. And behold, satan has put it into their hearts to alter the words which you have caused to be written, or which you have translated, which have gone out of your hands; and behold I say unto you, that because they have altered the words, they read contrary from that which you translated and caused to be written; and on this wise the devil has sought to lay a cunning

Both pages: Excerpt of chapter 9 of the Book of Commandments. (See pp. 473–474 herein.)

27

other sheep, and that they were a branch of the house of Jacob; and I will bring to light their marvelous works, which they did in my name; yea, and I will also bring to light my gospel, which was ministered unto them, and behold they shall not deny that which you have received, but they shall build it up, and shall bring to light the true points of my doctrine: Yea, and the only doctrine which is in me; and this I do, that I may establish my gospel, that there may not be so much contention: Yea, satan doth stir up the hearts of the people to contention, concerning the points of my doctrine; and in these things they do err, for they do wrest the scriptures, and do not understand them: therefore, I will unfold unto them this great mystery, for behold, I will gather them as a hen gathereth her chickens under her wings, if they will not harden their hearts: Yea, if they will come, they may, and partake of the waters of life freely.

17 Behold this is my doctrine: whosoever repenteth, and cometh unto me, the same is my church: whosoever declareth more or less than this, the same is not of me, but is against me: therefore, he is not of my church.

18 And now, behold whosoever is of my church, and endureth of my church to the end, him will I establish upon my Rock, and the gates of hell shall not prevail against them.

19 And now, remember the words of him who is the life and the light of the world, your Redeemer, your Lord and your God: Amen.

25

3 Verily, verily I say unto you, wo be unto him that lieth to decieve, because he supposeth that another lieth to decieve, for such are not exempt from the justice of God.

6 Now, behold they have altered those words, because satan saith unto them, He hath decieved you, and thus he flattereth them away to do iniquity, to tempt the Lord their God.

7 Behold I say unto you, that you shall not translate again those words which have gone forth out of your hands; for behold, they shall not lie any more against those words; for behold, if you should bring forth the same words, they would say that you have lied; that you have pretended to translate, but that you have contradicted your words; and behold they would publish this, and satan would harden the hearts of the people, to stir them up to anger against you, that they might not believe my words: thus satan would overpower this generation, that the work might not come forth in this generation: but behold here is wisdom, and because I show unto you wisdom, and give you commandments concerning these things, what you shall do, show it not unto the world until you have accomplished the work.

8 Marvel not that I said unto you, here is wisdom, show it not unto the world, for I said, show it not unto the world, that you may be preserved. Behold I do not say that you shall not show it unto the righteous; but as you cannot always judge the righteous, or as you cannot always tell the wicked from the righteous: therefore, I say unto you, hold your peace until I shall see fit to make all things known unto the world concerning the matter.

9 And now, verily I say unto you, that an account of these things that you have written, which have

Both pages: Excerpts of chapter 9 of the Book of Commandments. (See pp. 474–477 herein.)

46

heavens to shake for your good, and his name's glory.

8 For thus saith the Lord God, him have I inspired to move the cause of Zion in mighty power for good; and his diligence I know, and his prayers I have heard:

9 Yea, his weeping for Zion I have seen, and I will cause that he shall mourn for her no longer, for his days of rejoicing are come unto the remission of his sins, and the manifestations of my blessings upon his works.

10 For behold, I will bless all those who labor in my vineyard, with a mighty blessing, and they shall believe on his words, which are given him through me, by the Comforter:

11 Which manifesteth that Jesus was crucified by sinful men for the sins of the world:

12 Yea, for the remission of sins unto the contrite heart.

13 Wherefore, it behooveth me, that he should be ordained by you, Oliver, mine apostle;

14 This being an ordinance unto you, that you are an elder under his hand, he being the first unto you, that you might be an elder unto this church of Christ, bearing my name;

15 And the first preacher of this church, unto the church, and before the world; yea, before the Gentiles:

16 Yea, and thus saith the Lord God, lo, lo, to the Jews, also. Amen.

45

in secret, and in your family, and among your friends, and in all places.

2 And behold it is your duty to unite with the true church, and give your language to exhortation continually, that you may receive the reward of the laborer. Amen.

CHAPTER XXII.

1 *A Revelation to Joseph, given in Manchester, New-York, April 6, 1830.*

BEHOLD there shall be a record kept among you, and in it thou shalt be called a seer, a translator, a prophet, an apostle of Jesus Christ, an elder of the church through the will of God the Father, and the grace of our Lord Jesus Christ;

2 Being inspired of the Holy Ghost to lay the foundation thereof, and to build it up unto the most holy faith;

3 Which church was organized and established, in the year of our Lord eighteen hundred and thirty, in the fourth month, and on the sixth day of the month, which is called April.

4 Wherefore, meaning the church, thou shalt give heed unto all his words, and commandments, which he shall give unto you, as he receiveth them, walking in all holiness before me:

5 For this word ye shall receive, as if from mine own mouth, in all patience and faith;

6 For by doing these things, the gates of hell shall not prevail against you:

7 Yea, and the Lord God will disperse the powers of darkness from before you; and cause the

B7

Left: Excerpts of chapters 21–22 of the Book of Commandments. (See p. 487 herein.) *Right:* Excerpt of chapter 22 of the Book of Commandments. (See pp. 487–488 herein.)

them. And thou shalt have revelations but write them not by way of commandment.

8 And now behold I say unto you, that it is not revealed, and no man knoweth where the city shall be built, but it shall be given hereafter.

9 Behold I say unto you, that it shall be on the borders by the Lamanites.

10 Thou shalt not leave this place until after the conference, and my servant Joseph shall be appointed to rule the conference by the voice of it, and what he saith to thee, that thou shalt tell.

11 And again, thou shalt take thy brother Hiram between him and thee alone, and tell him that those things which he hath written from that stone are not of me, and that satan deceiveth him:

12 For behold these things have not been appointed unto him:

13 Neither shall any thing be appointed unto any of this church contrary to the church covenants, for all things must be done in order and by common consent in the church, by the prayer of faith.

14 And thou shalt settle all these things according to the covenants of the church before thou shalt take thy journey among the Lamanites.

15 And it shall be given thee from the time that thou shalt go, until the time that thou shalt return, what thou shalt do.

16 And thou must open thy mouth at all times declaring my gospel with the sound of rejoicing.—Amen.

do according as it is written. And now, I declare no more unto you at this time. Amen.

CHAPTER XXX.

1 *A Revelation to Oliver, given in Fayette, New York, September, 1830.*

BEHOLD I say unto you, Oliver, that it shall be given unto thee, that thou shalt be heard by the church, in all things whatsoever thou shalt teach them by the Comforter, concerning the revelations and commandments which I have given.

2 But behold, verily, verily I say unto you, no one shall be appointed to receive commandments and revelations in this church, excepting my servant Joseph, for he receiveth them even as Moses:

3 And thou shalt be obedient unto the things which I shall give unto him, even as Aaron, to declare faithfully the commandments and the revelations, with power and authority unto the church.

4 And if thou art led at any time by the Comforter to speak or teach, or at all times by the way of commandment unto the church, thou mayest do it.

5 But thou shalt not write by way of commandment, but by wisdom:

6 And thou shalt not command him who is at thy head, and at the head of the church, for I have given him the keys of the mysteries and the revelations which are sealed, until I shall appoint unto them another in his stead.

7 And now, behold I say unto you, that you shall go unto the Lamanites and preach my gospel unto them, and cause my church to be established among

Left: Excerpts of chapters 29–30 of the Book of Commandments. (See pp. 426 and 491 herein.) *Right:* Excerpt of chapter 30 of the Book of Commandments. (See pp. 491–492 herein.)

76

3 Behold, verily, verily I say unto my servant Sidney, I have looked upon thee and thy works.

4 I have heard thy prayers and prepared thee for a greater work.

5 Thou art blessed for thou shalt do great things.

6 Behold thou wast sent forth, even as John, to prepare the way before me, and before Elijah which should come, and thou knew it not.

7 Thou didst baptize by water unto repentance, but they received not the Holy Ghost; but now I give unto thee a commandment, that thou shalt baptize by water, and they shall receive the Holy Ghost by the laying on of hands, even as the apostles of old.

8 And it shall come to pass, that there shall be a great work in the land even among the Gentiles, for their folly and their abominations shall be made manifest, in the eyes of all people:

9 For I am God and mine arm is not shortened and I will show miracles, signs and wonders, unto all those who believe on my name.

10 And whoso shall ask it in my name, in faith, they shall cast out devils; they shall heal the sick; they shall cause the blind to receive their sight, and the deaf to hear, and the dumb to speak, and the lame to walk:

11 And the time speedily cometh, that great things are to be shown forth unto the children of men:

12 But without faith shall not any thing be shown forth except desolations upon Babylon, the same which has made all nations drink of the wine of the wrath of her fornication.

13 And there are none that doeth good except those who are ready to receive the fullness of my gospel, which I have sent forth to this generation:

70

3 And be you afflicted in all his afflictions, ever lifting up your heart unto me in prayer, and faith, for his and your deliverance:

4 For I have given unto him to build up my church among your brethren, the Lamanites.

5 And none have I appointed to be over him in the church, except it is his brother Joseph.

6 Wherefore give heed unto these things and be diligent in keeping my commandments, and you shall be blessed unto eternal life. Amen.

CHAPTER XXXIII.

A Revelation to John, given in Fayette, New-York, September, 1830.

BEHOLD I say unto you my servant, John, that thou shalt commence from this time forth to proclaim my gospel, as with the voice of a trump.

2 And your labor shall be at your brother Philip's, and in that region round about:

3 Yea, wherever you can be heard, until I command you to go from hence.

4 And your whole labor shall be in my Zion, with all your soul, from henceforth; yea, you shall ever open your mouth in my cause not fearing what man can do, for I am with you. Amen.

Left: Excerpt of chapter 32 and entirety of chapter 33 of the Book of Commandments. (See pp. 492–493 herein.) *Right:* Excerpt of chapter 37 of the Book of Commandments. (See pp. 426–427 herein.)

78

pure. And now I say unto you, tarry with him and he shall journey with you; forsake him not and surely these things shall be fulfilled.

24 And inasmuch as ye do not write, behold it shall be given unto him to prophesy.

25 And thou shalt preach my gospel, and call on the holy prophets to prove his words, as they shall be given him.

26 Keep all the commandments and covenants by which ye are bound, and I will cause the heavens to shake for your good:

27 And satan shall tremble; and Zion shall rejoice upon the hills, and flourish; and Israel shall be saved in mine own due time.

28 And by the keys which I have given, shall they be led and no more be confounded at all.

29 Lift up your hearts and be glad: your redemption draweth nigh.

30 Fear not little flock, the kingdom is yours until I come.

31 Behold I come quickly; even so: Amen.

CHAPTER XXXVIII.

A Revelation to Edward, given in Fayette, New York, December, 1830.

THUS saith the Lord God, the mighty One of Israel, behold I say unto you, my servant Edward, that you are blessed, and your sins are forgiven you, and you are called to preach my gospel as with the voice of a trump; and I will lay my hand upon you by the hand of my servant Sidney, and you shall receive my Spirit, the Holy Ghost.

77

14 Wherefore, I have called upon the weak things of the world, those who are unlearned and despised, to thresh the nations by the power of my Spirit:

15 And their arm shall be mine arm, and I will be their shield and their buckler, and I will gird up their loins, and they shall fight manfully for me:

16 And their enemies shall be under their feet; and I will let fall the sword in their behalf; and by the fire of mine indignation will I preserve them.

17 And the poor and the meek shall have the gospel preached unto them, and they shall be looking forth for the time of my coming, for it is nigh at hand:

18 And they shall learn the parable of the fig-tree: for even now already summer is nigh, and I have sent forth the fulness of my gospel by the hand of my servant Joseph:

19 And in weakness have I blessed him, and I have given unto him the keys of the mystery of those things which have been sealed, even things which were from the foundation of the world, and the things which shall come from this time until the time of my coming, if he abide in me, and if not, another will I plant in his stead.

20 Wherefore watch over him that his faith fail not, and it shall be given by the Comforter, the Holy Ghost, that knoweth all things:

21 And a commandment I give unto thee, that thou shalt write for him:

22 And the scriptures shall be given even as they are in mine own bosom, to the salvation of mine own elect:

23 For they will hear my voice, and shall see me, and shall not be asleep, and shall abide the day of my coming, for they shall be purified even as I am

Left: Excerpt of chapter 37 of the Book of Commandments. (See p. 427 herein.) *Right:* Excerpts of chapters 37–38 of the Book of Commandments. (See pp. 427–428 and 496 herein.)

80

it is found, and more especially in Colesville.

3 For behold they pray unto me in much faith.

4 And again a commandment I give unto the church, that it is expedient in me that they should assemble together at the Ohio, against the time that my servant Oliver shall return unto them.

5 Behold here is wisdom, and let every man choose for himself until I come; even so: Amen.

CHAPTER XL.

A Revelation to the churches in New-York, commanding them to remove to Ohio, given in Fayette, New-York, January, 1831.

THUS saith the Lord your God, even Jesus Christ, the Great I AM, Alpha and Omega, the beginning and the end, the same which looked upon the wide expanse of eternity, and all the seraphic hosts of heaven, before the world was made, the same which knoweth all things, for all things are present before mine eyes:

2 I am the same which spake and the world was made, and all things came by me.

3 I am the same which hath taken the Zion of Enoch into mine own bosom:

4 And verily I say, even as many as have believed on my name, for I am Christ, and in mine own name, by the virtue of the blood which I have spilt, have I pleard before the Father for them:

5 But behold the residue of the wicked have I kept in chains of darkness until the judgment of the great day, which shall come at the end of the earth, and even so will I cause the wicked to be kept, that

39

ven the Comforter which shall teach you the peaceable things of the kingdom:

2 And you shall declare it with a loud voice saying, Hosanna, blessed be the name of the most high God.

3 And now this calling and commandment give I unto all men, that as many as shall come before my servant Sidney and Joseph, embracing this calling and commandment, shall be ordained and sent forth to preach the everlasting gospel among the nations, crying repentance, saying, Save yourselves from this untoward generation, and come forth out of the fire, hating even the garment spotted with the flesh.

4 And this commandment shall be given unto the elders of my church, that every man which will embrace it with singleness of heart, may be ordained and sent forth, even as I have spoken.

5 I am Jesus Christ, the Son of God:

6 Wherefore gird up your loins and I will suddenly come to my temple; even so: Amen.

CHAPTER XXXIX.

A Revelation to Joseph and Sidney, given in Canandaigua, New-York, December, 1830.

BEHOLD I say unto you, that it is not expedient in me that ye should translate any more until ye shall go to the Ohio; and this because of the enemy and for your sakes.

2 And again, I say unto you, that ye shall not go until ye have preached my gospel in those parts, and have strengthened up the church whithersoever

Left: Excerpts of chapters 38–39 of the Book of Commandments. (See pp. 496–497 herein.) *Right:* Excerpts of chapters 39–40 of the Book of Commandments. (See pp. 497 and 428 herein.)

51

will not hear my voice but harden their hearts, and wo, wo, wo is their doom.

6 But behold, verily, verily I say unto you, that mine eyes are upon you; I am in your midst and ye cannot see me, but the day soon cometh that ye shall see me and know that I am:

7 For the vail of darkness shall soon be rent, and he that is not purified shall not abide the day:

8 Wherefore gird up your loins and be prepared.

9 Behold the kingdom is yours and the enemy shall not overcome.

10 Verily I say unto you, ye are clean but not all; and there is none else with whom I am well pleased, for all flesh is corruptible before me, and the powers of darkness prevail upon the earth, among the children of men, in the presence of all the hosts of heaven, which causeth silence to reign; and all eternity is pained, and the angels are waiting the great command, to reap down the earth, to gather the tares that they may be burned:

11 And behold the enemy is combined.

12 And now I show unto you a mystery, a thing which is had in secret chambers, to bring to pass even your destruction, in process of time, and ye knew it not, but now I tell it unto you, and ye are blessed, not because of your iniquity, neither your hearts of unbelief, for verily some of you are guilty before me; but I will be merciful unto your weakness.

13 Therefore, be ye strong from henceforth; fear not for the kingdom is yours:

14 And for your salvation I give unto you a commandment, for I have heard your prayers, and the poor have complained before me, and the rich have I made, and all flesh is mine, and I am no respect-

52

er to persons. And I have made the earth rich, and behold it is my footstool: wherefore, again I will stand upon it:

15 And I hold forth and deign to give unto you greater riches, even a land of promise; a land flowing with milk and honey, upon which there shall be no curse when the Lord cometh, and I will give it unto you for the land of your inheritance, if you seek it with all your hearts:

16 And this shall be my covenant with you, ye shall have it for the land of your inheritance, and for the inheritance of your children forever; while the earth shall stand, and ye shall possess it again in eternity, no more to pass away?

17 But verily I say unto you, that in time ye shall have no king nor ruler, for I will be your King and watch over you.

18 Wherefore, hear my voice and follow me, and you shall be a free people, and ye shall have no laws but my laws, when I come; for I am your Lawgiver, and what can stay my hand.

19 But verily I say unto you, teach one another according to the office wherewith I have appointed you, and let every man esteem his brother as himself, and practice virtue and holiness before me.

20 And again I say unto you, let every man esteem his brother as himself:

21 For what man among you, having twelve sons, and is no respecter to them, and they serve him obediently, and he saith unto the one, be thou clothed in robes and sit thou here; and to the other, be thou clothed in rags and sit thou there, and looketh upon his sons and saith I am just.

22 Behold, this I have given unto you a parable; and it is even as I am, I say unto you, be one:

Both pages: Excerpt of chapter 40 of the Book of Commandments. (See pp. 428–429 herein.)

84

property of this church. And they that have farms, that can not be sold, let them be left or rented as seemeth them good.

31 See that all things are preserved, and when men are endowed with power from on high, and are sent forth, all these things shall be gathered unto the bosom of the church.

32 And if ye seek the riches which it is the will of the Father to give unto you, ye shall be the richest of all people, for ye shall have the riches of eternity:

33 And it must needs be that the riches of the earth is mine to give:

34 But beware of pride, lest ye become as the Nephites of old.

35 And again: I say unto you, I give unto you a commandment, that every man both elder, priest, teacher and also member, go to with his might, with the labor of his hands, to prepare and accomplish the things which I have commanded.

36 And let your preaching be the warning voice, every man to his neighbor, in mildness and in meekness.

37 And go ye out from among the wicked. Save yourselves.

38 Be ye clean that bear the vessels of the Lord, even so: Amen.

83

and if ye are not one, ye are not mine. And again I say unto you, that the enemy in the secret chambers, seeketh your lives:

23 Ye hear of wars in far countries, and you say in your hearts there will soon be great wars in far countries, but ye know not the hearts of them in your own land:

24 I tell you these things because of your prayers:

25 Wherefore, treasure up wisdom in your bosoms, lest the wickedness of men reveal these things unto you, by their wickedness, in a manner which shall speak in your ears, with a voice louder than that which shall shake the earth:

26 But if ye are prepared, ye shall not fear.

27 And that ye might escape the power of the enemy, and be gathered unto me a righteous people, without spot and blameless:

28 Wherefore, for this cause I gave unto you the commandment, that ye should go to the Ohio: and there I will give unto you my law, and there you shall be endowed with power from on high, and from thence, whomsoever I will shall go forth among all nations, and it shall be told them what they shall do, for I have a great work laid up in store:

29 For Israel shall be saved, and I will lead them whithersoever I will, and no power shall stay my hand.

30 And now I give unto the church in these parts, a commandment, that certain men among them shall be appointed, and they shall be appointed by the voice of the church; and they shall look to the poor and the needy, and administer to their relief, that they shall not suffer: and send them forth to the place which I have commanded them; and this shall be their work, to govern the affairs of the

Both pages: Excerpt of chapter 40 of the Book of Commandments. (See pp. 429–430 herein.)

CHAPTER XLI.

A Revelation to James (C.) given in Fayette, New-York, January, 1831.

HEARKEN and listen to the voice of him who is from all eternity to all eternity, the Great I AM, even Jesus Christ, the light and the life of the world; a light which shineth in darkness and the darkness comprehendeth it not:

2 The same which came in the meridian of time unto my own, and my own received me not; but to as many as received me, gave I power to become my sons, and even so will I give unto as many as will receive me, power to become my sons.

3 And verily, verily I say unto you, he that receiveth my gospel, receiveth me; and he that receiveth not my gospel, receiveth not me.

4 And this is my gospel: Repentance and baptism by water, and then cometh the baptism of fire and the Holy Ghost, even the Comforter, which showeth all things, and teacheth the peaceable things of the kingdom.

5 And now behold I say unto you, my servant James, I have looked upon thy works and I know thee:

6 And verily I say unto thee, thine heart is now right before me at this time, and behold I have bestowed great blessings upon thy head:

7 Nevertheless thou hast seen great sorrow, for thou hast rejected me many times because of pride, and the cares of the world:

8 But behold the days of thy deliverance are come,

9 Arise and be baptized, and wash away your sins, calling on my name and you shall receive my Spirit, and a blessing so great as you never have

known. And if thou do this, I have prepared thee for a greater work.

10 Thou shalt preach the fulness of my gospel which I have sent forth in these last days; the covenant which I have sent forth to recover my people, which are of the house of Israel.

11 And it shall come to pass that power shall rest upon thee; thou shalt have great faith and I will be with thee and go before thy face.

12 Thou art called to labor in my vineyard, and to build up my church, and to bring forth Zion, that it may rejoice upon the hills and flourish.

13 Behold, verily, verily I say unto thee, thou art not called to go into the eastern countries, but thou art called to go to the Ohio.

14 And inasmuch as my people shall assemble themselves to the Ohio, I have kept in store a blessing such as is not known among the children of men, and it shall be poured forth upon their heads.

15 And from thence men shall go forth into all nations.

16 Behold, verily, verily I say unto you, that the people in Ohio call upon me in much faith, thinking I will stay my hand in judgment upon the nations, but I can not deny my word:

17 Wherefore I say to with your might and call faithful laborers into my vineyard, that it may be pruned for the last time.

18 And inasmuch as they do repent and receive the fulness of my gospel, and become sanctified, I will stay mine hand in judgment:

19 Wherefore go forth, crying with a loud voice, saying, The kingdom of heaven is at hand; crying Hosanna! blessed be the name of the most high God.

Both pages: Excerpt of chapter 41 of the Book of Commandments. (See pp. 497–498 herein.)

87

20 Go forth baptizing with water, preparing the way before my face, for the time of my coming; for the time is at hand:

21 The day nor the hour no man knoweth, but it surely shall come, and he that receiveth these things receiveth me; and they shall be gathered unto me in time and in eternity.

22 And again, it shall come to pass, that on as many as ye shall baptize with water, ye shall lay your hands, and they shall receive the gift of the Holy Ghost, and shall be looking forth for the signs of my coming, and shall know me.

23 Behold I come quickly; even so: Amen.

CHAPTER XLII.

Revelation to Joseph, and Sidney, given in Fayette, New-York, January, 1831, explaining why James (C.,) obeyed not the revelation which was given unto him.

BEHOLD, verily I say unto you, that his heart was right before me, for he covenanted with me, that he would obey my word.

2 And he received the word with gladness, but straitway satan tempted him; and the fear of persecution, and the cares of the world, caused him to reject the word;

3 Wherefore he broke my covenant, and it remaineth in me to do with him as seemeth me good. Amen.

90

ing this one thing, and have asked the Father in my name, even so ye shall receive.

5 Behold, verily I say unto you, I give unto you this first commandment, that ye shall go forth in my name, every one of you, excepting my servants Joseph and Sidney.

6 And I give unto them a commandment that they shall go forth for a little season, and it shall be given by the power of my Spirit when they shall return:

7 And ye shall go forth in the power of my Spirit, preaching my gospel, two by two, in my name, lifting up your voices as with the voice of a trump, declaring my word like unto angels of God:

8 And ye shall go forth baptizing with water, saying, Repent ye, repent ye, for the kingdom of heaven is at hand.

9 And from this place ye shall go forth into the regions westward, and inasmuch as ye shall find them that will receive you, ye shall build up my church in every region, until the time shall come when it shall be revealed unto you, from on high, when the city of the New Jerusalem shall be prepared that ye may be gathered in one, that ye may be my people and I will be your God.

10 And again, I say unto you, that my servant Edward shall stand in the office wherewith I have appointed him.

11 And it shall come to pass that if he transgress another shall be appointed in his stead; even so: Amen.

12 Again I say unto you, that it shall not be given to any one to go forth to preach my gospel, or to build up my church, except he be ordained by some one who has authority, and it is known to the church

Left: Excerpt of chapter 41 and entirety of chapter 42 of the Book of Commandments. (See p. 498 herein.) *Right:* Excerpt of chapter 44 of the Book of Commandments. (See pp. 430–431 herein.)

31

that he has authority, and has been regularly ordained by the heads of the church.

13 And again, the elders, priests, and teachers of
this church, shall teach the scriptures which are in
the bible, and the book of Mormon, in the which is
the fulness of the gospel; and they shall observe the
covenants and church articles to do them; and
these shall be their teachings.

14 And they shall be directed by the Spirit, which
shall be given them by the prayer of faith; and if
they receive not the Spirit, they shall not teach.

15 And all this they shall observe to do, as I have
commanded concerning their teaching, until the fulness of my scriptures are given.

16 And as they shall lift up their voices by the
Comforter, they shall speak and prophesy as seemeth me good; for behold the Comforter knoweth all
things, and beareth record of the Father, and of the
Son.

17 And now behold I speak unto the church:

18 Thou shalt not kill; and he that killeth, shall
not have forgiveness, neither in this world, nor in
the world to come.

19 And again, thou shalt not kill; he that killeth
shall die.

20 Thou shalt not steal; and he that stealeth and
will not repent, shall be cast out.

21 Thou shalt not lie; he that lieth and will not
repent, shall be cast out.

22 Thou shalt love thy wife with all thy heart,
and shall cleave unto her and none else; and he
that looketh upon a woman to lust after her, shall
deny the faith, and shall not have the Spirit, and if
he repent not, he shall be cast out.

23 Thou shalt not commit adultery; and he that

32

committeth adultery and repenteth not, shall be
cast out; and he that committeth adultery and repenteth with all his heart, and forsaketh and doeth
it no more, thou shalt forgive him; but if he doeth
it again, he shall not be forgiven, but shall be cast
out.

24 Thou shalt not speak evil of thy neighbor, or
do him any harm.

25 Thou knowest my laws, they are given in my
scriptures, he that sinneth and repenteth not, shall
be cast out.

26 If thou lovest me, thou shalt serve me and keep
all my commandments; and behold, thou shalt consecrate all thy properties, that which thou hast unto me, with a covenant and a deed which can not
be broken; and they shall be laid before the bishop
of my church, and two of the elders, such as he shall
appoint and set apart for that purpose.

27 And it shall come to pass, that the bishop of
my church, after that he has received the properties
of my church, that it can not be taken from the
church, he shall appoint every man a steward over
his own property, or that which he has received, inasmuch as is sufficient for himself and family:

28 And the residue shall be kept to administer to
him who has not, that every man may receive according as he stands in need:

29 And the residue shall be kept in my storehouse,
to administer to the poor and needy, as shall be appointed by the elders of the church and the bishop;
and for the purpose of purchasing lands, and the
building up of the New Jerusalem, which is hereafter to be revealed; that my covenant people may
be gathered in one, in the day that I shall come to
my temple:

Both pages: Excerpt of chapter 44 of the Book of Commandments. (See pp. 431–432 herein.)

103

15 But obtained a promise that they should find it, and see it in their flesh.

16 Wherefore hearken and I will reason with you, and I will speak unto you and prophesy as unto men in days of old, and I will show it plainly as I showed it unto my disciples, as I stood before them in the flesh and spake unto them saying:

17 As ye have asked of me concerning the signs of my coming, in the day when I shall come in my glory, in the clouds of heaven, to fulfil the promises that I have made unto your fathers;

18 For as ye have looked upon the long absence of your spirits from your bodies to be a bondage, I will show unto you how the day of redemption shall come and also the restoration of the scattered Israel.

19 And now ye behold this temple which is in Jerusalem, which ye call the house of God, and your enemies say that this house shall never fall.

20 But verily I say unto you, that desolation shall come upon this generation as a thief in the night, and this people shall be destroyed and scattered among all nations.

21 And this temple which ye now see, shall be thrown down that there shall not be left one stone upon another.

22 And it shall come to pass, that this generation of Jews shall not pass away, until every desolation which I have told you concerning them, shall come to pass.

23 Ye say that ye know, that the end of the world cometh; ye say also that ye know, that the heavens and the earth shall pass away; and in this ye say truly, for so it is;

24 But these things which I have told you, shall not pass away until all shall be fulfilled.

104

self might be glorified: wherefore Father spare these my brethren that believe on my name, that they may come unto me and have everlasting life.

7 Hearken O ye people of my church, and ye elders listen together, and hear my voice while it is called today, and harden not your hearts;

8 For verily I say unto you that I am Alpha and Omega, the beginning and the end, the light and the life of the world, a light that shineth in darkness and the darkness comprehendeth it not:

9 I came unto my own and my own received me not:

10 But unto as many as received me, gave I power to do many miracles, and to become the sons of God, and even unto them that believed on my name gave I power to obtain eternal life.

11 And even so I have sent mine everlasting covenant into the world, to be a light to the world, and to be a standard for my people, and for the Gentiles to seek to it;

12 And to be a messenger before my face to prepare the way before me.

13 Wherefore come ye unto it, and with him that cometh I will reason as with men in days of old, and I will show unto you my strong reasoning;

14 Wherefore hearken ye together and let me show it unto you, even my wisdom, the wisdom of him whom ye say is the God of Enoch, and his brethren, who were separated from the earth, and were reserved unto myself, a city reserved until a day of righteousness shall come, a day which was sought for by all holy men, and they found it not because of wickedness and abominations, and confessed that they were strangers and pilgrims on the earth;

Both pages: Excerpt of chapter 48 of the Book of Commandments. (See pp. 438–439 herein.)

106

25 And this I have told you concerning Jerusalem, and when that day shall come, shall a remnant be scattered among all nations, but they shall be gathered again; but they shall remain until the times of the Gentiles be fulfilled.

26 And in that day shall be heard of wars and rumors of wars, and the whole earth shall be in commotion, and men's hearts shall fail them, and they shall say that Christ delayeth his coming until the end of the earth.

27 And the love of men shall wax cold, and iniquity shall abound; and when the time of the Gentiles is come in, a light shall break forth among them that sit in darkness, and it shall be the fulness of my gospel; but they receive it not, for they perceive not the light, and they turn their hearts from me because of the precepts of men; and in that generation shall the times of the Gentiles be fulfilled:

28 And there shall be men standing in that generation, that shall not pass, until they shall see an overflowing scourge; for a desolating sickness shall cover the land:

29 But my disciples shall stand in holy places, and shall not be moved; but among the wicked, men shall lift up their voices and curse God and die.

30 And there shall be earthquakes, also, in divers places, and many desolations, yet men will harden their hearts against me; and they will take up the sword one against another, and they will kill one another.

31 And now, when I the Lord had spoken these words unto my disciples, they were troubled; and I said unto them, be not troubled, for when all these

107

things shall come to pass, ye may know that the promises which have been made unto you, shall be fulfilled:

32 And when the light shall begin to break forth, it shall be with them like unto a parable which I will show you:

33 Ye look and behold the fig-trees, and ye see them with your eyes, and ye say when they begin to shoot forth and their leaves are yet tender, ye say that summer is now nigh at hand;

34 Even so it shall be in that day, when they shall see all these things, then shall they know that the hour is nigh.

35 And it shall come to pass that he that feareth me shall be looking for the great day of the Lord to come, even for the signs of the coming of the Son of man; and they shall see signs and wonders, for they shall be shown forth in the heavens above, and in the earth beneath; and they shall behold blood and fire, and vapors of smoke:

36 And before the day of the Lord shall come, the sun shall be darkened, and the moon be turned into blood, and stars fall from heaven;

37 And the remnant shall be gathered unto this place; and then they shall look for me, and behold I will come; and they shall see me in the clouds of heaven, clothed with power and great glory, with all the holy angels;

38 And he that watches not for me shall be cut off.

39 But before the arm of the Lord shall fall, an angel shall sound his trump, and the saints that have slept, shall come forth to meet me in the cloud.

40 Wherefore if ye have slept in peace, blessed

Both pages: Excerpt of chapter 48 of the Book of Commandments. (See pp. 439–440 herein.)

109

50 And at that day when I shall come in my glory, shall the parable be fulfilled which I spake concerning the ten virgins:

51 For they that are wise and have received the truth, and have taken the Holy Spirit for their guide, and have not been deceived;

52 Verily I say unto you, they shall not be hewn down and cast into the fire, but shall abide the day, and the earth shall be given unto them for an inheritance:

53 And they shall multiply and wax strong, and their children shall grow up without sin unto salvation, for the Lord shall be in their midst, and his glory shall be upon them, and he will be their King and their Lawgiver.

54 And now, behold I say unto you, it shall not be given unto you to know any farther than this, until the new testament be translated, and in it all these things shall be made known;

55 Wherefore I give unto you that ye may now translate it, that ye may be prepared for the things to come;

56 For verily I say unto you, that great things await you;

57 Ye hear of wars in foreign lands, but behold I say unto you they are nigh even unto your doors, and not many years hence ye shall hear of wars in your own lands.

58 Wherefore I the Lord have said gather ye out from the eastern lands, assemble ye yourselves together ye elders of my church;

59 Go ye forth into the western countries, call upon the inhabitants to repent, and inasmuch as they do repent, build up churches unto me; and with one heart and with one mind, gather up your riches

D7

108

are you, for as you now behold me and know that I am, even so shall ye come unto me and your souls shall live, and your redemption shall be perfected, and the saints shall come forth from the four quarters of the earth.

41 Then shall the arm of the Lord fall upon the nations, and then shall the Lord set his foot upon this mount, and it shall cleave in twain, and the earth shall tremble and reel to and fro, and the heavens also shall shake, and the Lord shall utter his voice and all the ends of the earth shall hear it, and the nations of the earth shall mourn, and they that have laughed shall see their folly, and calamity shall cover the mocker, and the scorner shall be consumed; and they that have watched for iniquity, shall be hewn down and cast into the fire.

42 And then shall the Jews look upon me, and say, What are these wounds in thine hands, and in thy feet?

43 Then shall they know that I am the Lord; for I will say unto them, These wounds, are the wounds with which I was wounded in the house of my friends.

44 I am he who was lifted up.

45 I am Jesus that was crucified.

46 I am the Son of God.

47 And then shall they weep because of their iniquities; then shall they lament because they persecuted their King.

48 And then shall the heathen nations be redeemed, and they which knew no law shall have part in the first resurrection;

49 And it shall be tolerable for them; and satan shall be bound that he shall have no place in the hearts of the children of man.

Both pages: Excerpt of chapter 48 of the Book of Commandments. (See pp. 440–441 herein.)

111

tremble: and all nations shall be afraid because of the terror of the Lord, and the power of his might; even so: Amen.

CHAPTER XLIX.

A Revelation to the church, given in Kirtland, Ohio, March, 1831.

HEARKEN, O ye people of my church, for verily I say unto you, that these things were spoken unto you for your profit and learning;

2 But notwithstanding those things which are written, it always has been given to the elders of my church, from the beginning, and ever shall be, to conduct all meetings as they are directed and guided by the Holy Spirit;

3 Nevertheless ye are commanded never to cast any one out from your public meetings, which are held before the world:

4 Ye are also commanded not to cast any one, who belongeth to the church, out of your sacrament meetings:

5 Nevertheless, if any have trespassed, let him not partake until he makes reconciliation.

6 And again I say unto you, ye shall not cast any one out of your sacrament meetings, who is earnestly seeking the kingdom;

7 I speak this concerning those who are not of the church.

8 And again I say unto you, concerning your confirmation meetings, that if there be any that is not of the church, that is earnestly seeking after the kingdom, ye shall not cast them out;

110

that ye may purchase an inheritance which shall hereafter be appointed unto you, and it shall be called the New Jerusalem, a land of peace, a city of refuge, a place of safety for the saints of the most high God;

60 And the glory of the Lord shall be there, and the terror of the Lord also shall be there, insomuch that the wicked will not come unto it:

61 And it shall be called Zion:

62 And it shall come to pass, among the wicked, that every man that will not take his sword against his neighbor, must needs flee unto Zion for safety.

63 And there shall be gathered unto it out of every nation under heaven:

64 And it shall be the only people that shall not be at war one with another.

65 And it shall be said among the wicked, let us not go up to battle against Zion, for the inhabitants of Zion are terrible:

66 Wherefore we can not stand.

67 And it shall come to pass that the righteous shall be gathered out from among all nations, and shall come to Zion singing, with songs of everlasting joy.

68 And now I say unto you, keep these things from going abroad unto the world, until it is expedient in me, that ye may accomplish this work in the eyes of the people, and in the eyes of your enemies, that they may not know your works until ye have accomplished the thing which I have commanded you;

69 That when they shall know it, that they may consider these things, for when the Lord shall appear he shall be terrible unto them; that fear may seize upon them, and they shall stand afar off and

Left: Excerpt of chapter 48 of the Book of Commandments. (See pp. 441–442 herein.) *Right:* Excerpts of chapters 48–49 of the Book of Commandments. (See p. 442 herein.)

112

9 But ye are commanded in all things to ask of God who giveth liberally, and that which the Spirit testifies unto you, even so I would that ye should do in all holiness of heart, walking uprightly before me, considering the end of your salvation, doing all things with prayer and thanksgiving, that ye may not be seduced by evil spirits, or doctrines of devils, or the commandments of men, for some are of men, and others of devils.

10 Wherefore, beware lest ye are deceived! and that ye may not be deceived, seek ye earnestly the best gifts, always remembering for what they are given;

11 For verily I say unto you, they are given for the benefit of those who love me and keep all my commandments, and him that seeketh so to do, that all may be benefitted, that seeketh or that asketh of me, that asketh and not for a sign that he may consume it upon his lusts.

12 And again, verily I say unto you, I would that ye should always remember, and always retain in your minds what those gifts are, that are given unto the church, for all have not every gift given unto them: for there are many gifts, and to every man is given a gift by the Spirit of God.

13 To some it is given one, and to some is given another, that all may be profited thereby;

14 To some it is given by the Holy Ghost to know that Jesus Christ is the Son of God, and that he was crucified for the sins of the world; to others it is given to believe on their words, that they also might have eternal life, if they continue faithful.

15 And again, to some it is given by the Holy Ghost to know the differences of administration, as it will be pleasing unto the same Lord, according

123

38 Fear not, little children, for you are mine, and I have overcome the world, and you are of them that my Father hath given me;

39 And none of them which my Father hath given me shall be lost:

40 And the Father and I are one; I am in the Father and the Father in me:

41 And inasmuch as ye have received me, ye are in me, and I in you; wherefore I am in your midst; and I am the good Shepherd;

42 And the day cometh that you shall hear my voice and see me, and know that I am.

43 Watch, therefore, that ye may be ready; even so: Amen.

CHAPTER LIV.

A Revelation to the elders of the church, assembled in Kirtland, Ohio, given Jun., 1831.

BEHOLD, thus saith the Lord unto the elders whom he hath called and chosen, in these last days, by the voice of his Spirit, saying, I the Lord will make known unto you what I will that ye shall do from this time until the next conference, which shall be held in Missouri, upon the land which I will consecrate unto my people, which are a remnant of Jacob, and them who are heirs according to the covenant.

2 Wherefore, verily I say unto you, let my servants Joseph and Sidney take their journey as soon as preparations can be made to leave their homes, and journey to the land of Missouri.

3 And inasmuch as they are faithful unto me, it

Left: Excerpt of chapter 49 of the Book of Commandments. (See pp. 442–443 herein.) *Right:* Excerpts of chapters 53–54 of the Book of Commandments. (See pp. 446 and 502–503 herein.)

125

trite, the same is accepted of me, if he obey mine ordinances:

16 He that speaketh, whose spirit is contrite, whose language is meek, and edifieth, the same is of God, if he obey mine ordinances.

17 And again, he that trembleth under my power, shall be made strong, and shall bring forth fruits of praise, and wisdom, according to the revelations, and truths which I have given you.

18 And again, he that is overcome and bringeth not forth fruits, even according to this pattern, is not of me:

19 Wherefore by this pattern ye shall know the spirits in all cases, under the whole heavens.

20 And the days have come, according to men's faith it shall be done unto them.

21 Behold this commandment is given unto all the elders whom I have chosen.

22 And again, verily I say unto you, let my servant Thomas, and my servant Ezra, take their journey also, preaching the word by the way, unto this same land.

23 And again, let my servant Isaac and my servant Ezra (B.,) take their journey, also preaching the word by the way unto the same land.

24 And again, let my servant Edward and Martin take their journey with my servants Sidney and Joseph.

25 Let my servant David and Harvey also take their journey, and preach by the way unto this same land.

26 Let my servants Parley and Orson (P.) take their journey, and preach by the way, even unto this same land.

27 And let my servants Solomon and Simeon

124

shall be made known unto them what they shall do:

4 And it shall also, inasmuch as they are faithful, be made known unto them the land of your inheritance.

5 And inasmuch as they are not faithful, they shall be cut off, even as I will, as seemeth me good.

6 And again, verily I say unto you, let my servant Lyman (W.,) and my servant John (C.,) take their journey speedily:

7 And also my servant John (M.) and my servant Hyrum, take their journey unto the same place by the way of Detroit.

8 And let then journey from thence preaching the word by the way, saying none other things than that which the prophets and apostles have written, and that which is taught them by the Comforter, through the prayer of faith.

9 Let them go two by two, and thus let them preach by the way in every congregation, baptizing by water, and the laying on of the hands by the water side:

10 For thus saith the Lord, I will cut my work short in righteousness:

11 For the days cometh that I will send forth judgment unto victory.

12 And let my servant Lyman beware, for satan desireth to sift him as chaff.

13 And behold, he that is faithful shall be made ruler over many things.

14 And again, I will give unto you a pattern in all things, that ye may not be deceived, for satan is abroad in the land, and he goeth forth deceiving the nations:

15 Wherefore he that prayeth whose spirit is con-

Both pages: Excerpt of chapter 54 of the Book of Commandments. (See pp. 503–504 herein.)

126

also take their journey unto this same land, and preach by the way.

29 Let my servants Edson and Jacob (S.,) also take their journey.

30 Let my servants Levi and Zebidee also take their journey.

31 Let my servants Reynolds and Samuel, also take their journey.

31 Let my servants Wheeler and William (C.,) also take their journey.

32 And let my servants Newel (K.) and Selah, both be ordained and also take their journey:

33 Yea, verily I say, let all these take their journey, unto one place, in their several courses, and one man shall not build upon another's foundation, neither journey in another's track.

34 He that is faithful, the same shall be kept and blessed with much fruit.

35 And again, I say unto you, let my servant Joseph (W.,) and Solomon (H.,) take their journey into the eastern lands.

36 Let them labor with their families, declaring none other things than the prophets and apostles, that which they have seen, and heard, and most assuredly believe, that the prophecies may be fulfilled.

37 In consequence of transgression, let that which was bestowed upon Heman, be taken from him, and placed upon the head of Simonds.

38 And again, verily I say unto you, let Jared be ordained a priest, and also George be ordained a priest.

39 Let the residue of the elders watch over the churches, and declare the word in the regions among them.

40 And let them labor with their own hands, that

127

there be no idolatry nor wickedness practiced. And remember in all things, the poor and the needy, the sick and the afflicted, for he that doeth not these things, the same is not my disciple.

41 And again, let my servants Joseph and Sidney and Edward, take with them a recommend from the church.

42 And let there be one obtained for my servant Oliver also:

43 And thus, even as I have said, if ye are faithful, ye shall assemble yourselves together to rejoice upon the land of Missouri, which is the land of your inheritance, which is now the land of your enemies.

44 But behold I the Lord will hasten the city in its time;

45 And will crown the faithful with joy and with rejoicing.

46 Behold I am Jesus Christ, the Son of God, and I will lift them up at the last day; even so: Amen.

CHAPTER LV.

Revelation to Sidney (G.,) given in Kirtland, Ohio, June, 1831.

BEHOLD I say unto you, my servant Sidney, that I have heard your prayers, and you have called upon me, that I should be made known unto you, of the Lord your God, concerning your calling, and election in this church, which I the Lord have raised up in these last days.

2 Behold I the Lord, who was crucified for the sins of the world, giveth unto you a commandment, that you shall forsake the world.

Left: Excerpt of chapter 54 of the Book of Commandments. (See p. 504 herein.) *Right:* Excerpts of chapters 54–55 of the Book of Commandments. (See pp. 504–505 herein.)

128

Take upon you mine ordinances, even that of an elder, to preach faith and repentance, and remission of sins, according to my word, and the reception of the Holy Spirit by the laying on of hands.

4 And also to be an agent unto this church in the place which shall be appointed by the bishop, according to commandments which shall be given hereafter.

5 And again, verily I say unto you, you shall take your journey with my servants Joseph and Sidney.

6 Behold these are the first ordinances which you shall receive:

7 And the residue shall be made known unto you in a time to come, according to your labor in my vineyard.

8 And again, I would that ye should learn that it is he only who is saved, that endureth unto the end, even so: Amen.

CHAPTER LVI.

A Revelation to Newel (K.,) and the church in Thompson, given in Kirtland, Ohio, June, 1831.

BEHOLD, thus saith the Lord, even Alpha and Omega, the beginning and the end, even he who was crucified for the sins of the world.

2 Behold, verily, verily I say unto you, my servant Newel, you shall stand fast in the office wherewith I have appointed you:

3 And if your brethren desire to escape their enemies let them repent of all their sins, and become truly humble before me and contrite;

129

4 And as the covenant which they made unto me, has been broken, even so it has become void and of none effect;

5 And wo to him by whom this offence cometh, for it had been better for him that he had been drowned in the depth of the sea;

6 But blessed are they who have kept the covenant, and observed the commandment, for they shall obtain mercy:

7 Wherefore, go to now and flee the land, lest your enemies come upon you:

8 And take your journey, and appoint whom you will to be your leader, and to pay moneys for you.

9 And thus you shall take your journey into the regions westward, unto the land of Missouri, unto the borders of the Lamanites.

10 And after you have done journeying, behold I say unto you, seek ye a living like unto men, until I prepare a place for you.

11 And again, be patient in tribulation until I come:

12 And behold I come quickly, and my reward is with me, and they who have sought me early, shall find rest to their souls; even so: Amen.

CHAPTER LVII.

A Revelation to William, given in Kirtland, Ohio, June, 1831.

BEHOLD thus saith the Lord unto you, my servant William; yea, even the Lord of the whole earth,

2 Thou art called and chosen and after thou hast

F1

Left: Excerpts of chapters 55–56 of the Book of Commandments. (See p. 505 herein.) *Right:* Excerpts of chapters 56–57 of the Book of Commandments. (See pp. 505–506 herein.)

131

shall know mine arm and mine indignation in the day of visitation and of wrath upon the nations.

2 And he that will not take up his cross and follow me, and keep my commandments, the same shall not be saved.

3 Behold I the Lord commandeth, and he that will not obey shall be cut off in mine own due time:

4 And after that I have commanded and the commandment is broken, wherefore I the Lord command and revoke, as it seemeth me good; and all this to be answered upon the heads of the rebellious saith the Lord;

5 Wherefore I revoke the commandment which was given unto my servants Thomas and Ezra, and give a new commandment unto my servant Thomas, that he shall take up his journey speedily to the land of Missouri;

6 And my servant Selah shall also go with him:

7 For behold I revoke the commandment which was given unto my servants Selah and Newel, in consequence of the stiffneckedness of my people which are in Thompson; and their rebellions:

8 Wherefore let my servant Newel remain with them, and as many as will go may go, that are contrite before me, and be led by him to the land which I have appointed.

9 And again, verily I say unto you, that my servant Ezra must repent of his pride, and of his selfishness, and obey the former commandment which I have given him concerning the place upon which he lives;

10 And if he will do this, as there shall be no divisions made upon the land, he shall be appointed still to go to the land of Missouri;

11 Otherwise he shall rece'v the money which he

E2

130

been baptized by water, which if you do with an eye single to my glory, you shall have a remission of your sins; and a reception of the Holy Spirit, by the laying on of hands:

3 And then thou shalt be ordained by the hand of my servant Joseph, to be an elder unto this church, to preach repentance and remission of sins by way of baptism in the name of Jesus Christ, the Son of the living God;

4 And on whomsoever you shall lay your hands, if they are contrite before me, you shall have power to give the Holy Spirit.

5 And again, you shall be ordained to assist my servant Oliver to do the work of printing, and of selecting, and writing books for schools, in this church, that little children also may receive instruction before me as is pleasing unto me.

6 And again verily I say unto you, for this cause you shall take your journey with my servants Joseph and Sidney, that you may be planted in the land of your inheritance, to do this work.

7 And again let my servant Joseph (C.) also take his journey with them.

8 The residue shall be made known hereafter; even as I will: Amen.

CHAPTER LVIII.

Revelation to the church, and certain elders, given in Kirtland, Ohio, June, 1831.

HEARKEN O ye people which profess my name, saith the Lord your God, for behold mine anger is kindled against the rebellious, and they

---

Left: Excerpts of chapters 57–58 of the Book of Commandments. (See pp. 506–507 herein.) *Right:* Excerpt of chapter 58 of the Book of Commandments. (See p. 507 herein.)

133

tize, for they shall see the kingdom of God coming in power and great glory unto their deliverance:

23 For the fatness of the earth shall be theirs:

24 For behold the Lord shall come, and his recompense shall be with him, and he shall reward every man, and the poor shall rejoice: and their generations shall inherit the earth from generation to generation, for ever and ever.

25 And now I make an end of speaking unto you: even so: Amen.

CHAPTER LIX.

A Revelation to the elders of the church, assembled on the land of Zion, given August, 1831.

HEARKEN O ye elders of my church, and give ear to my word, and learn of me what I will concerning you, and also concerning this land unto which I have sent you:

2 For verily I say unto you, blessed is he that keepeth my commandments, whether in life or in death:

3 And he that is faithful in tribulation the reward of the same is greater in the kingdom of heaven.

4 Ye can not behold with your natural eyes, for the present time, the design of your God concerning those things which shall come hereafter, and the glory which shall follow, after much tribulation.

5 For after much tribulation cometh the blessings.

6 Wherefore, the day cometh that ye shall be crowned with much glory, the hour is not yet but is nigh at hand.

7 Remember this which I tell you before, that you may lay it to heart, and receive that which shall—

132

has paid, and shall leave the place, and shall be cut off out of my church, saith the Lord God of hosts:

12 And though the heaven and the earth pass away, these words shall not pass away, but shall be fulfilled.

13 And if my servant Joseph must needs pay the money, behold I the Lord will pay it unto him again in the land of Missouri, that those of whom he shall receive may be rewarded again, according to that which they do.

14 For according to that which they do, they shall receive; even in lands for their inheritance.

15 Behold thus saith the Lord unto my people, you have many things to do, and to repent of:

16 For behold your sins have come up unto me, and are not pardoned, because you seek to counsel in your own ways.

17 And your hearts are not satisfied.

18 And ye obey not the truth, but have pleasure in unrighteousness.

19 Wo unto you rich men, that will not give your substance to the poor, for your riches will canker your souls; and this shall be your lamentation in the day of visitation, and of judgment, and of indignation:

20 The harvest is past, the summer is ended, and my soul is not saved!

21 Wo unto you poor men, whose hearts are not broken, whose spirits are not contrite, and whose bellies are not satisfied, and whose hands are not stayed from laying hold upon other men's goods, whose eyes are full of greediness, who will not labor with their own hands!

22 But blessed are the poor, who are pure in heart, whose hearts are broken, and whose spirits are con-

Left: Excerpt of chapter 58 of the Book of Commandments. (See pp. 507–508 herein.) *Right:* Excerpts of chapters 58–59 of the Book of Commandments. (See pp. 508 and 446 herein.)

135

days, to divide the lands of the heritage of God unto his children; and to judge his people by the testimony of the just, and by the assistance of his counsellors, according to the laws of the kingdom which are given by the prophets of God:

22 For verily I say unto you, my laws shall be kept on this land.

23 Let no man think that he is ruler, but let God rule him that judgeth, according to the counsel of his own will:

24 Or in other words, him that counselleth, or sitteth upon the judgment seat.

25 Let no man break the laws of the land, for he that keepeth the laws of God, hath no need to break the laws of the land:

26 Wherefore be subject to the powers that be, until He reigns whose right it is to reign, and subdues all enemies under his feet.

27 Behold the laws which ye have received from my hand, are the laws of the church;

28 And in this light ye shall hold them forth.

29 Behold here is wisdom.

30 And now as I spake concerning my servant Edward: this land is the land of his residence, and those whom he has appointed for his counsellors.

31 And also the land of the residence of him whom I have appointed to keep my storehouse:

32 Wherefore let them bring their families to this land, as they shall counsel between themselves and me:

33 For behold it is not meet that I should command in all things, for he that is compelled in all things, the same is a slothful and not a wise servant:

34 Wherefore he receiveth no reward.

35 Verily I say, men should be anxiously engaged

134

follow. Behold, verily I say unto you, for this cause I have sent you that you might be obedient, and that your hearts might be prepared to bear testimony of the things which are to come;

8 And also, that you might be honored of laying the foundation, and of bearing record of the land upon which the Zion of God shall stand;

9 And also, that a feast of fat things might be prepared for the poor;

10 Yea a feast of fat things, of wine on the lees well refined, that the earth may know that the mouths of the prophets shall not fall;

11 Yea, a supper of the house of the Lord, well prepared, unto which all nations shall be invited.

12 Firstly the rich, and the learned, the wise and the noble;

13 And after that cometh the day of my power:

14 Then shall the poor, the lame and the blind, and the deaf, come in unto the marriage of the Lamb, and partake of the supper of the Lord, prepared for the great day to come.

15 Behold I the Lord have spoken it.

16 And that the testimony might go forth from Zion; yea from the mouth of the city of the heritage of God:

17 Yea, for this cause I have sent you hither:

18 And have selected my servant Edward and appointed unto him his mission in this land:

19 But if he repent not of his sins, which are unbelief and blindness of heart, let him take heed lest he fall.

20 Behold his mission is given unto him and it shall not be given again.

21 And whoso standeth in this mission, is appointed to be a judge in Israel, like as it was in ancien

Both pages: Excerpt of chapter 59 of the Book of Commandments. (See pp. 446–448 herein.)

137

50 And other directions, concerning my servant Martin, shall be given him of the Spirit, that he may receive his inheritance as seemeth him good. And let him repent of his sins, for he seeketh the praise of the world.

51 And also let my servant William stand in the office which I have appointed him, and receive his inheritance in the land.

52 And also, he hath need to repent; for I the Lord am not pleased with him, for he seeketh to excell, and he is not sufficiently meek before me.

53 Behold he who has repented of his sins the same is forgiven, and I the Lord remembereth them no more.

54 By this ye may know if a man repenteth of his sins.

55 Behold he will confess them and forsake them.

56 And now verily I say, concerning the residue of the elders of my church, the time has not yet come for many years, for them to receive their inheritance in this land; except they desire it through prayer, only as it shall be appointed unto them of the Lord.

57 For behold they shall push the people together from the ends of the earth:

58 Wherefore assemble yourselves together, and they who are not appointed to stay in this land, let them preach the gospel in the regions round about;

59 And after that, let them return to their homes.

60 Let them preach by the way, and bear testimony of the truth in all places, and call upon the rich, the high, and the low, and the poor, to repent;

61 And let them build up churches inasmuch as the inhabitants of the earth will repent.

62 And let there be an agent appointed by the

136

in a good cause, and do many things of their own free will, and bring to pass much righteousness:

36 For the power is in them, wherein they are agents unto themselves.

37 And inasmuch as men do good, they shall in no wise lose their reward.

38 But he that doeth not any thing until he is commanded, and receiveth a commandment with doubtful heart, and keepeth it with slothfulness, the same is damned.

39 Who am I that made man, saith the Lord, that will hold him guiltless, that obey not my commandments?

40 Who am I, saith the Lord, that have promised and have not fulfilled?

41 I command and a man obeys not, I revoke and they receive not the blessing:

42 Then they say in their hearts, this is not the work of the Lord, for his promises are not fulfilled.

43 But wo unto such, for their reward lurketh beneath, and not from above.

44 And now I give unto you further directions concerning this land.

45 It is wisdom in me, that my servant Martin should be an example unto the church, in laying his moneys before the bishop of the church.

46 And also, this is a law unto every man that cometh unto this land, to receive an inheritance;

47 And he shall do with his moneys according as the law directs.

48 And it is wisdom also, that there should be lands purchased in Independence, for the place of the storehouse:

49 And also for the house of the printing.

Both pages: Excerpt of chapter 59 of the Book of Commandments. (See pp. 448–449 herein.)

138

voice of the church, unto the church in Ohio, to receive moneys to purchase lands in Zion.

63 And I give unto my servant Sidney a commandment, that he shall write a description of the
land of Zion, and a statement of the will of God,
as it shall be made known by the Spirit, unto him;
and an epistle and subscription, to be presented unto all the churches, to obtain moneys, to be put into
the hands of the bishop, to purchase lands for an inheritance for the children of God, of himself or the
agent, as seemeth him good, or as he shall direct.

64 For behold, verily I say unto you, the Lord
willeth that the disciples, and the children of men,
should open their hearts, even to purchase this whole
region of country, as soon as time will permit.

65 Behold here is wisdom; let them do this lest
they receive none inheritance, save it be by the shedding of blood.

66 And again, inasmuch as there is land obtained, let there be workmen sent forth, of all kinds, unto this land, to labor for the saints of God.

67 Let all these things be done in order.

68 And let the privileges of the lands be made
known from time to time, by the bishop, or the agent
of the church.

69 And let the work of the gathering be not in
haste, nor by flight, but let it be done as it shall be
counselled by the elders of the church at the conferences, according to the knowledge which they receive from time to time.

70 And let my servant Sidney consecrate and dedicate this land, and the spot of the temple, unto the
Lord.

71 And let a conference meeting be called, and
after that, let my servant Sidney and Joseph return,

139

and also Oliver with them, to accomplish the residue of the work, which I have appointed unto them
in their own land:

72 And the residue as shall be ruled by the conferences.

73 And let no man return from this land, except
he bear record by the way, of that which he knows
and most assuredly believes.

74 Let that which has been bestowed upon Ziba,
be taken from him;

75 And let him stand as a member in the church,
and labor with his own hands, with the brethren,
until he is sufficiently chastened for all his sins, for
he confesseth them not, and he thinketh to hide
them.

76 Let the residue of the elders of this church,
which are coming to this land, some of whom are
exceedingly blessed even above measure, also, hold
a conference upon this land.

77 And let my servant Edward direct the conference, which shall be held by them.

78 And let them also return, preaching the gospel
by the way, bearing record of the things which are
revealed unto them:

79 For verily the sound must go forth from this
place into all the world;

80 And unto the uttermost parts of the earth,
the gospel must be preached unto every creature,
with signs following them that believe.

81 And behold the Son of man cometh: Amen.

Both pages: Excerpt of chapter 59 of the Book of Commandments. (See pp. 449–450 herein.)

143

will not open their mouths, but hide the [ ] which I have given unto them, because of the fear of man.

4 Wo unto such, for mine anger is kindled against them.

5 And it shall come to pass, if they are not more faithful unto me, it shall be taken away, even that which they have, for I the Lord ruleth in the heavens above, and among the armies of the earth;

6 And in the day when I shall make up my jewels, all men shall know what it is that bespeaketh the power of God.

7 But verily I will speak unto you concerning your journey unto the land from whence you came.

8 Let there be a craft made, or bought, as seemeth you good, it mattereth not unto me, and take your journey speedily for the place which is called St. Louis.

9 And from thence let my servants Sidney and Joseph and Oliver, take their journey for Cincinnati:

10 And in this place let them lift up their voice, and declare my word with loud voices, without wrath or doubting, lifting up holy hands upon them.

11 For I am able to make you holy, and your sins are forgiven you.

12 And let the residue take their journey from St. Louis, two by two, and preach the word, not in haste, among the congregations of the wicked, until they return to the churches from whence they came.

13 And all this for the good of the churches; for this intent have I sent them.

14 And let my servant Edward impart of the moneys which I have given him, a portion unto mine el-

---

142

the season thereof, is made for the benefit and the use of man, both to please the eye, and to gladden the heart:

29 Yea, for food and for raiment, for taste, and for smell, to strengthen the body, and to enliven the soul.

30 And it pleaseth God that he hath given all these things unto man:

31 For unto this end were they made, to be used with judgment, not to excess, neither by extortion:

32 And in nothing doth man offend God, or against none is his wrath kindled, save those who confess not his hand in all things, and obey not his commandments.

33 Behold this is according to the law and the prophets:

34 Wherefore trouble me no more concerning this matter, but learn that he who doeth the works of righteousness, shall receive his reward, even peace in this world, and eternal life in the world to come.

35 I the Lord have spoken it and the spirit beareth record. Amen.

CHAPTER LXI.

Revelation [ ] tions of the church given [ ] August, 1831.

BEHOLD, thus saith the Lord unto the elders of his church, who are to return speedily to the land from whence they came.

2 Behold it pleaseth me, that you have come up hither:

3 But with some I am not well pleased, for they

Left: Excerpts of chapters 60–61 of the Book of Commandments. (See pp. 451 and 508 herein.) *Right:* Excerpt of chapter 61 of the Book of Commandments. (See pp. 508–509 herein.)

145

CHAPTER LXII.

Revelation .... , given .... , August, 1831.

BEHOLD, and hearken unto the voice of him who has all power, who is from everlasting to everlasting, even Alpha and Omega, the beginning and the end.

2 Behold, verily thus saith the Lord unto you O ye elders of my church, who are assembled upon this spot, whose sins are now forgiven you, for I the Lord forgiveth sins, and am merciful unto those who confess their sins with humble hearts:

3 But verily I say unto you, that it is not needful for this whole company of mine elders, to be moving swiftly upon the waters, whilst the inhabitants on either side are perishing in unbelief:

4 Nevertheless, I suffered it that ye might bear record:

5 Behold there are many dangers upon the waters and more especially hereafter, for I the Lord have decreed, in mine anger, many destructions upon the waters;

6 Yea, and especially upon these waters;

7 Nevertheless, all flesh is in mine hand, and he that is faithful among you, shall not perish by the waters,

8 Wherefore it is expedient that my servant Sidney (G.) and my servant William be in haste upon their errand and mission:

9 Nevertheless I would not suffer that ye should part until you are chastened for all your sins, that you might be one;

10 That you might not perish in wickedness;

11 But now verily I say, it behooveth me that ye

141

ders, ... are commanded to return; and he that is able, let him return it by the way of the agent, and he that is not, of him it is not required.

15 And now I speak of the residue which are to come unto this land.

16 Behold they have been sent to preach my gospel among the congregations of the wicked:

17 Wherefore, I give unto them a commandment thus:

18 Thou shalt not idle away thy time:

19 Neither shalt thou bury thy talent that it may not be known.

20 And after thou hast come up unto the land of Zion, and hast proclaimed my word, thou shalt speedily return proclaiming the word among the congregations of the wicked.

21 Not in haste, neither in wrath, nor with strife:

22 And shake off the dust of thy feet against those who receive thee not, not in their presence, lest thou provoke them, but in secret, and wash thy feet as a testimony against them in the day of judgment.

23 Behold this is sufficient for you, and the will of him who hath sent you.

24 And by the mouth of my servant Joseph, it shall be made known concerning Sidney and Oliver.

25 The residue hereafter; even so: Amen.

Left: Excerpt of chapter 61 of the Book of Commandments. (See p. 509 herein.) *Right:* Excerpt of chapter 62 of the Book of Commandments. (See pp. 509–510 herein.)

146

should part: wherefore let my servants Sidney and William, take their former company, and let them take their journey in haste that they may fill their mission, and through faith they shall overcome;

12 And inasmuch as they are faithful, they shall be preserved, and I the Lord will be with them.

13 And let the residue take that which is needful for clothing,

14 Let my servant Sidney take that which is not needful with him, as you shall agree.

15 And now behold, for your good I gave unto you a commandment concerning these things; and I the Lord will reason with you as with men in days of old.

16 Behold I the Lord in the beginning, blessed the waters, but in the last days by the mouth of my servant John, I cursed the waters.

17 Wherefore, the days will come that no flesh shall be safe upon the waters, and it shall be said in days to come, that none is able to go up to the land of Zion, upon the waters, but he that is upright in heart.

18 And, as I the Lord in the beginning cursed the land, even so in the last days have I blessed it, in its time, for the use of my saints, that they may partake the fatness thereof.

19 And now I give unto you a commandment, and what I say unto one I say unto all, that you shall forewarn your brethren concerning these waters, that they come not in journeying upon them, lest their faith fail and they are caught in her snares:

20 I the Lord have decreed, and the destroyer rideth upon the face thereof, and I revoke not the decree;

147

21 I the Lord was angry with you yesterday, but to-day mine anger is turned away:

22 Wherefore let those concerning whom I have spoken, that should take their journey in haste:

23 Again I say unto you, let them take their journey in haste, and it mattereth not unto me, after a little, if it so be that they fill their mission, whether they go by water or by land:

24 Let this be as it is made known unto them according to their judgments, hereafter.

25 And now, concerning my servants Sidney, and Joseph, and Oliver, let them come not again upon the waters, save it be upon the canal, while journeying unto their homes, or in other words they shall not come upon the waters to journey, save upon the canal.

26 Behold I the Lord have appointed a way for the journeying of my saints, and behold this is the way:

27 That after they leave the canal, they shall journey by land, inasmuch as they are commanded to journey and go up unto the land of Zion; and they shall do like unto the children of Israel, pitching their tents by the way.

28 And behold this commandment, you shall give unto all your brethren: nevertheless unto whom it is given power to command the waters, unto him it is given by the Spirit to know all his ways:

29 Wherefore let him do as the Spirit of the living God commandeth him, whether upon the land or upon the waters, as it remaineth with me to do hereafter;

30 And unto you it is given the course for the saints, or the way for the saints of the camp of the Lord, to journey.

Both pages: Excerpt of chapter 62 of the Book of Commandments. (See pp. 510–511 herein.)

148

31 And again, verily I say unto you, my servants Sidney, and Joseph, and Oliver, shall not open their mouths in the congregations of the wicked, until they arrive at Cincinnati;

32 And in that place they shall lift up their voices unto God against that people.

33 Yea, unto him whose anger is kindled against their wickedness; a people which is well nigh ripened for destruction;

34 And from thence let them journey for the congregations of their brethren, for their labors, even now, are wanted more abundantly among them, than among the congregations of the wicked.

35 And now concerning the residue, let them journey and declare the word among the congregations of the wicked, inasmuch as it is given, and inasmuch as they do this they shall rid their garments, and they shall be spotless before me;

36 And let them journey together, or two by two, as seemeth them good, only let my servant Reynolds, and my servant Samuel, with whom I am well pleased, be not separated until they return to their homes, and this for a wise purpose in me.

37 And now verily I say unto you, and what I say unto one I say unto all, be of good cheer little children; for I am in your midst, and I have not forsaken you, and inasmuch as you have humbled yourselves before me, the blessings of the kingdom are yours:

38 Gird up your loins and be watchful, and be sober, looking forth for the coming of the Son of man, for he cometh in an hour you think not.

39 Pray always that you enter not into temptation, that you may abide the day of his coming, whether in life or in death; even so: Amen.

149

CHAPTER LXIII.

Revelation to certain elders . . . given . . . August, 1831.

BEHOLD and hearken, O ye elders of my church, saith the Lord your God; even Jesus Christ, your advocate who knoweth the weakness of man and how to succor them who are tempted:

2 And verily mine eyes are upon those who have not as yet gone up unto the land of Zion:

3 Wherefore your mission is not yet full:

4 Nevertheless, ye are blessed, for the testimony which ye have borne, is recorded in heaven for the angels to look upon; and they rejoice over you; and your sins are forgiven you.

5 And now continue your journey.

6 Assemble yourselves upon the land of Zion, and hold a meeting and rejoice together, and offer a sacrament unto the Most High:

7 And then you may return to bear record;

8 Yea, even all together, or two by two, as seemeth you good;

9 It mattereth not unto me, only be faithful, and declare glad tidings unto the inhabitants of the earth, or among the congregations of the wicked.

10 Behold I the Lord have brought you together that the promise might be fulfilled, that the faithful among you should be preserved and rejoice together in the land of Missouri.

11 I the Lord promised the faithful, and cannot lie.

12 I the Lord am willing, if any among you desireth to ride upon horses, or upon mules, or in chariots, shall receive this blessing, if he receive it

Left: Excerpt of chapter 62 of the Book of Commandments. (See p. 511 herein.) *Right:* Excerpt of chapter 63 of the Book of Commandments. (See p. 512 herein.)

133

purchase the lands, that you may have advantage of the world, that you may have claim on the world, that they may not be stirred up unto anger:

29 For satan putteth it into their hearts to anger against you, and to the shedding of blood:

30 Wherefore the land of Zion shall not be obtained but by purchase, or by blood, otherwise there is none inheritance for you.

31 And if by purchase behold you are blessed;

32 And if by blood, as you are forbidden to shed blood, lo, your enemies are upon you, and ye shall be scourged from city to city, and from synagogue to synagogue, and but few shall stand to receive an inheritance.

33 I the Lord am angry with the wicked;

34 I am holding my Spirit from the inhabitants of the earth.

35 I have sworn in my wrath and decreed wars upon the face of the earth, and the wicked shall slay the wicked, and fear shall come upon every man and the saints also shall hardly escape:

36 Nevertheless, I the Lord am with them, and will come down in heaven from the presence of God, and consume the wicked with unquenchable fire;

37 And behold this is not yet, but by and by:

38 Wherefore seeing that I the Lord have decreed all these things upon the face of the earth, I willeth that my saints should be assembled upon the land of Zion;

39 And that every man should take righteousness in his hands, and faithfulness upon his loins, and lift a warning voice unto the inhabitants of the earth;

40 And declare both by word and by flight, that desolation shall come upon the wicked.

Left: Excerpt of chapter 64 of the Book of Commandments. (See p. 453 herein.)

Second edition of the Doctrine and Covenants. Church printer Ebenezer Robinson began stereotyping the second edition of the Doctrine and Covenants in spring 1841, using the first edition of the volume as his primary source text. The following year, Robinson sold his printing business to Joseph Smith, and apostles Wilford Woodruff and John Taylor were placed in charge of the project. The publication was completed in late summer 1844, after the death of Joseph Smith. The copy shown here and excerpted in this volume was presented to Jane Glenn. Church History Library, Salt Lake City.

DOCTRINE AND COVENANTS, 1844 (SECTIONS 101–107)

Source Note

The *Doctrine and Covenants of the Church of Jesus Christ of Latter Day Saints; Carefully Selected from the Revelations of God.* By Joseph Smith, President of Said Church. *2nd ed. Nauvoo, IL: John Taylor, 1844; 3–448; includes typeset signature marks and copyright notice. The copy excerpted herein is held at CHL; includes marginalia and archival markings. Presented herein: sections 101–107 of part 2, pp. 385–431.*

All but the final gathering of this book was printed in octodecimo format on thirteen sheets that were cut and folded into thirteen gatherings of eighteen leaves (thirty-six pages) each. The final gathering comprises eight leaves (sixteen pages). The text block measures 5⅞ × 3⅝ inches (15 × 9 cm).

The copy of the book excerpted herein is in a presentation binding of red sheepskin with gilt edges. The volume measures 6 × 3⅞ × 1 inches (15 × 10 × 3 cm). The spine is stamped with gilt ornamental panels and "Doctrine | and | Covenants" and "J. Glenn." in gilt. The front and back pastedowns, the front flyleaf, and the back flyleaf are single-sided marbled leaves featuring a shell pattern with brown body and veins of red and white. In this copy, the first leaf of the first gathering, which is blank in other extant copies, is missing. The verso of the front flyleaf has two inscriptions, the first in graphite and the second in ink: "RN 69025 | Vault | Book Area | M223.1 | D632 | 1844" and "Jane Glenn | from her friend | Leonora Taylor | Nauvoo Oct 27th | 1844". The handwriting of the first inscription is unknown; Leonora Taylor inscribed the second.

As the aforementioned ink inscription indicates, Leonora Taylor, wife of early church leader and printer John Taylor, presented this book to Jane Glenn. The book came into the possession of the Historical Department of The Church of Jesus Christ of Latter-day Saints circa 1983.

Historical Introduction

The late 1830s and early 1840s were a period of rapid growth for the young church. As converts continued to join in large numbers, the need for a new edition of the Doctrine and Covenants became increasingly evident. In 1839, apostle Parley P. Pratt, who had stopped in New York on his way to serve a mission in England, wrote to JS describing the growth of the church and missionary work in the eastern United States. In his letter he stated that there was "a great call for our Books" and proposed plans to begin printing the Book of Mormon and other church publications.[1] Requests for church publications continued to

---

1. Parley P. Pratt, New York City, NY, to JS, [Nauvoo, IL], 22 Nov. 1839, in JS Letterbook 2, p. 77. Pratt did not specifically propose to publish the revelations.

come from other branches of the church during the early 1840s.[2] Church leaders in Nauvoo, Illinois, expressed a concern about scriptures being published in the United States without the "immediate inspection" of the First Presidency of the church.[3] Though careful about the authority under which scripture such as the Doctrine and Covenants would be published, the leadership in Nauvoo made it clear that the publication of scripture was a top priority. Published minutes of a conference held in October 1840 indicated that another edition of the Book of Mormon was nearly completed and that arrangements had been made for printing the Doctrine and Covenants and the church hymnal.[4]

In the spring of 1841, Ebenezer Robinson turned his attention to stereotyping what would become the second edition of the Doctrine and Covenants,[5] using the first edition of the volume as the primary source text. Robinson, an experienced editor and printer, had recently assisted with printing the third edition of the Book of Mormon (1840).[6] At the time Robinson began stereotyping the Doctrine and Covenants, the Nauvoo printing establishment was housed in a frame building at the corner of Water and Bain streets, near

---

2. See, for example, Charles Thompson, Batavia, NY, 2 Feb. 1841, Letter to the editor, *Times and Seasons*, 15 Mar. 1841, 2:349: "I would say further, there is a great call for Books of Mormon here: had I one hundred I could dispose of them all in a short time, and also the Book of Doctrine and Covenants, and Hymn Books."

3. Hyrum Smith, Nauvoo, IL, to Parley P. Pratt, New York City, NY, 22 Dec. 1839, in JS Letterbook 2, pp. 80–81; Hyrum Smith, Nauvoo, IL, to Lucian Foster, Jan. 1840, in JS Letterbook 2, pp. 83–84; Hyrum Smith, Nauvoo, IL, to JS and Elias Higbee, Washington DC, 2 Jan. 1840, in JS Letterbook 2, pp. 92–93. This restriction did not apply in the mission in England, perhaps because of the cost of shipping books overseas from the United States. JS told the Quorum of the Twelve that he had no objection to the Doctrine and Covenants being published in England and that "if there is a great demand for them," he "would rather encourage it." (JS, Nauvoo, IL, to "Beloved Brethren," [England], 15 Dec. 1840, JS Collection, CHL; see also H. Smith to P. Pratt, 22 Dec. 1839, in JS Letterbook 2, p. 81.)

4. "Minutes of the General Conference," *Times and Seasons*, Oct. 1840, 1:186. The original minutes from which the published version came did not mention the Doctrine and Covenants. A First Presidency report published in the same issue of *Times and Seasons* stated that arrangements were being made for printing the Doctrine and Covenants. (General Church Minutes, 3 Oct. 1840; "Report from the Presidency," *Times and Seasons*, Oct. 1840, 1:187–188.)

5. Ebenezer Robinson, "Items of Personal History of the Editor," *The Return*, July 1890, 302. Robinson acquired stereotyping equipment at least by early January 1841. Stereotyping, a common nineteenth-century printing practice, was intended to speed up the process of mass printing. After setting type for a page, the printer created a mold of the type, into which he poured hot lead, thereby creating a plate from which to print each page. This allowed the individual pieces of type to be reused to set additional pages. The plates could be reused for later printings. (Advertisement, *Times and Seasons*, 1 Jan. 1841, 2:272; Gaskell, *New Introduction to Bibliography*, 201–204.)

6. Ebenezer Robinson, "Items of Personal History of the Editor," *The Return*, May 1890, 259; see also "Minutes of the General Conference," *Times and Seasons*, Oct. 1840, 1:186. Robinson was also coeditor and copublisher of the Nauvoo newspaper *Times and Seasons* through December 1840. Robinson and Don Carlos Smith began publishing that newspaper in 1839 as partners, but their partnership dissolved in "mutual consent" in mid-December 1840, with Smith taking charge of the newspaper and Robinson of the "Books, or Book & fancy printing." Robinson began editing and publishing the newspaper again in August 1841, following the death of Don Carlos Smith. ("Dissolution," *Times and Seasons*, 15 Dec. 1840, 2:256; "To the Patrons of the Times and Seasons," *Times and Seasons*, 16 Aug. 1841, 2:511.)

the river. Before the end of 1841, it moved into a larger building, located across the street from the earlier building at the same intersection.[7]

In early 1842, while the stereotyping work was still ongoing, control of the printing establishment was transferred from Robinson to the Quorum of the Twelve Apostles. A January 1842 revelation dictated by JS commanded the Twelve to "take in hand the Editorial department of the *Times and Seasons*," ratifying a decision that had already been discussed in earlier meetings of the Quorum of the Twelve.[8] According to Wilford Woodruff, a member of that quorum, the Twelve were to "govern the printing of the Times & Seasons & all the church publications as they are directed by my Holy Spirit in the midst of their councils."[9] Ebenezer Robinson recalled telling JS and the other leaders "that they could have the *Times and Seasons,* but they must [also] take the *whole establishment,* including the stereotype foundery, book-bindery, and the whole book concern."[10] This request was accepted, and Robinson sold the entire business to JS for the sum of $6,600 on 4 February 1842.[11] Wilford Woodruff and fellow apostle John Taylor were placed in charge of the printing office.[12]

The Doctrine and Covenants had likely been stereotyped through page 109 when Robinson left.[13] It is unknown who else assisted in the initial stereotyping, but Robinson's departure delayed the project's completion. Robinson recalled working with JS, comparing the 1830 and 1837 editions of the Book of Mormon in preparation for the publication of the 1840 edition.[14] If similar preliminary work was done before the stereotyping of the Doctrine and Covenants commenced, JS likely would have had some input in the format of the newer edition.[15] Whatever the preparatory process, the 1844 Doctrine and Covenants is— in content, arrangement, basic format, and section and verse numbering—largely a reprint

---

7. Bray, "Times and Seasons: An Archaeological Perspective," 67–73; Notice, *Times and Seasons,* 1 Dec. 1841, 3:615. Besides the two structures mentioned, Bray identifies two additional buildings in Nauvoo that housed the printing establishment for a time, but those other buildings were not being used for printing at the time the 1844 Doctrine and Covenants was printed.

8. JS, Journal, 28 Jan. 1842, p. 67, JS Collection, CHL; Quorum of the Twelve Apostles, Minutes, 31 Nov. 1841 and 17 Jan. 1842.

9. Woodruff, Journal, 3 Feb. 1842. The Twelve had already enjoyed success with printing a number of publications in England, such as the 1840 hymnal, printed in Manchester; the *Latter-day Saints' Millennial Star,* begun in May 1840; and the 1841 edition of the Book of Mormon, printed in Liverpool.

10. Ebenezer Robinson, "Items of Personal History of the Editor," *The Return,* Sept. 1890, 325; emphasis in original.

11. Contract, Ebenezer Robinson to Willard Richards, Nauvoo, IL, 4 Feb. 1844, Newel K. Whitney, Papers, BYU; Ebenezer Robinson, "Items of Personal History of the Editor," *The Return,* Oct. 1890, 346; Woodruff, Journal, 4 Feb. 1842.

12. See Ebenezer Robinson, "Valedictory," *Times and Seasons,* 15 Feb. 1842, 3:695–696; and Woodruff, Journal, 3 and 19 Feb. 1842.

13. "No 4 Joseph Smith a/c Dr as pr Printing Office Books," ca. Jan. 1846, Newel K. Whitney, Papers, BYU.

14. Ebenezer Robinson, "Items of Personal History of the Editor," *The Return,* May 1890, 259.

15. JS's involvement is hinted at in a notice printed in two issues of *Times and Seasons* in early 1842. After announcing that the office of the recorder (Willard Richards) would be open to receive tithing donations only on Saturdays, the notice explained: "This regulation is necessary, to give the Trustee [JS] and Recorder time to arrange the Book of Mormon, New Translation of the Bible, Hymn Book, and

of the 1835 edition. The 1844 edition matches the 1835 edition almost word for word and character for character, except for minor corrections and stylistic changes and a few substantive changes.[16]

Work on printing the Doctrine and Covenants did not resume until a year after the printing establishment had changed hands. According to Woodruff, stereotyping recommenced on 30 January 1843.[17] JS and William W. Phelps read proofs of this work a few weeks later.[18] By the end of 1843, the printers had stereotyped to page 409 (partway into the twelfth gathering), leaving a modest amount of stereotyping to be completed the following year.[19] It appears that the printing may have been delayed for want of paper and other materials. On 7 November 1843, the Quorum of the Twelve appointed Woodruff, Brigham Young, Parley P. Pratt, Willard Richards, and John Taylor, all members of that quorum, as a committee to raise five hundred dollars "to get paper &c to print the Doctrine and covenants."[20] A month later, on 5 December, JS advised the Twelve "to raise money to send Elder [Orson] Hyde east to get paper to print Doctrine & Covenants— get new type & metal for stereotyping."[21]

By the following summer, the work was nearly complete. A notice dated 11 June 1844 and published the next day in the *Nauvoo Neighbor* announced optimistically: "The Book of *Doctrine and Covenants* will be published in about one month from this time. Those wishing for an early supply had better make immediate application."[22] A little over two weeks later, however, JS and Hyrum Smith were killed by a mob at Carthage, Illinois, and printer John Taylor was seriously wounded, delaying the printing of the volume yet again.[23] The above-mentioned notice continued to run in the *Nauvoo Neighbor* from 26 June

---

Doctrine and Covenants for the press; all of which the brethren are anxious to see, in their most perfect form." ("Tithings and Consecrations," *Times and Seasons,* 15 Jan. 1842, 3:667; 1 Feb. 1842, 3:677.)

16. The 1844 edition made light changes in spelling, capitalization, punctuation, grammar, and versification. These changes included employing British spelling for some words, such as "Savior" (Saviour). Aside from adding eight new sections (as discussed later in this introduction), the 1844 edition made only a small number of substantive changes. For example, the phrase "and we beheld and lo, he is fallen! is fallen! even a son of the morning," which appears in verse 3 of section 91 of the 1835 edition, was deleted in verse 3 of section 92 in the 1844 edition (Vision, 16 Feb. 1832 [D&C 76:27]). The deletion could have been accidental, since there is another phrase ending "son of the morning" earlier in the same sentence. A comprehensive study of the variants between the two editions is beyond the scope of this volume.

17. Woodruff, Journal, 1–4 Feb. 1843.

18. JS, Journal, 3 and 14 Feb. 1843, JS Collection, CHL.

19. In what appears to be an end-of-year account, the work of stereotyping to page 409 was recorded on 30 December 1843. ("No 4 Joseph Smith a/c Dr as pr Printing Office Books," ca. Jan. 1846, Newel K. Whitney, Papers, BYU.)

20. Quorum of the Twelve Apostles, Minutes, 7 Nov. 1843; see also Woodruff, Journal, 7 Nov. 1843. A few weeks earlier, a newspaper notice called for donations to support the church's printing establishment. ("End of the Third Volume," *Times and Seasons,* 15 Oct. 1842, 3:958.)

21. JS, Journal, 5 Dec. 1843, JS Collection, CHL.

22. "Notice," *Nauvoo Neighbor,* 12 June 1844, [3].

23. Taylor later recalled that before going to Carthage with JS and Hyrum Smith, he removed the "Type, Stereotype plates and most of the valuable things . . . from the printing office" for fear the office would be burned by enemies. (John Taylor, Statement, 23 Aug. 1856, p. 26, Historian's Office, JS History Draft Notes, [ca. 1840–1880], CHL.)

through 30 October 1844, though copies of the volume were available well before the 30 October issue.

In a letter to his wife written from Carthage two days before the killings, John Taylor stated that "1000 copies of the Book of Doctrine & Covenants" should be printed "as quick as possible."[24] At a 28 July 1844 church meeting, William W. Phelps announced that names would be taken of those desiring to purchase the volume at one dollar and twenty-five cents. Two weeks later, Phelps stated in another meeting that the "1000 copies [of the Doctrine and Covenants] are not all yet taken up," suggesting that the books were sold by subscription.[25] The date on which the new edition was first available to the public is unknown, but the volume was in use soon after its release: it was cited in the 2 September 1844 issue of *Times and Seasons,* and Parley P. Pratt quoted from it at a meeting on 8 September 1844.[26] Because the book had been stereotyped, keeping it in print was practical. A second printing of the book was authorized the following year and a third in 1846, presumably indicating a short supply of the books and a growing demand.[27]

Besides the individuals identified above as having assisted with or overseen work on the publication, others may have contributed as compilers, editors, typesetters, or printers. A number of people worked in the Nauvoo printing office at the time the volume was being produced, but records do not identify which of them had a hand in this project.[28]

The 1844 edition of the Doctrine and Covenants is essentially a reprint of the 1835 edition, with the addition of eight new items. The second edition reprinted the seven "Lectures on Faith" and all 103 numbered sections included in the "Covenants and Commandments" part of the 1835 Doctrine and Covenants. The 1835 edition included two sections numbered 66 (here referred to as 66a and 66b). This mistake was corrected in the 1844 edition. As a result, sections 1 through 66a of the 1835 edition correspond with sections 1 through 66 of the 1844 edition, and sections 66b through 99 in the 1835 edition correspond with sections 67 through 100 in the 1844 edition. The final three sections of the 1835 edition, sections 100 through 102, were numbered as sections 108 through 110 in the 1844 edition.

The eight new items added to the 1844 edition became sections 101 through 107 and section 111. Sections 101 and 102—both revelations regarding the redemption of Zion— were available for use in the 1835 publication but were not printed therein. Sections 103 (which was printed without a section number), 104, and 107 are JS revelations dictated after 1835. Sections 105 and 106 are JS letters written in the 1840s. Section 111, a tribute to the slain JS and Hyrum Smith, is believed to have been written by John Taylor, the publisher

---

24. John Taylor, Carthage, IL, to Leonora Taylor, Nauvoo, IL, 25 June 1844, John Taylor Collection, CHL.

25. General Church Minutes, 28 July and 8 Aug. 1844.

26. "Ten Virgins," *Times and Seasons,* 2 Sept. 1844, 5:636; "Trial of Elder Rigdon," *Times and Seasons,* 15 Sept. 1844, 5:647–655.

27. *The Doctrine and Covenants of the Church of Jesus Christ of Latter Day Saints; Carefully Selected from the Revelations of God,* comp. Joseph Smith, 3rd ed. (Nauvoo, IL: John Taylor, 1845); *The Doctrine and Covenants of the Church of Jesus Christ of Latter Day Saints; Carefully Selected from the Reve[l]ations of God,* comp. Joseph Smith, 4th ed. (Nauvoo, IL: John Taylor, 1846).

28. For more information about individuals who worked in the Nauvoo printing shop, see the Directory of Printers, p. 699 herein.

of the 1844 Doctrine and Covenants and an eyewitness to the murders. It was composed after most of the work on the volume had been completed. Only by using a smaller type-face than what appears in the rest of the volume were the printers able to fit this last section into the available space following section 110 and preceding a brief three-page "index." The editors of the 1844 edition used a variety of sources to set type for these eight items.[29] The sources used by the editors contained other revelations and letters that would have been candidates for publication in the Doctrine and Covenants, and the reasons for selecting the particular revelations and letters that were included are unknown.

Rather than presenting the entire 1844 edition of the Doctrine and Covenants, this volume of *The Joseph Smith Papers* presents only sections 101 through 107, which are texts created during JS's lifetime but not included in the 1835 edition.

---

29. Sources used by editors of the 1844 Doctrine and Covenants for the newly added items include Revelation Book 2, *Times and Seasons,* JS's journal, and various loose manuscripts. (See pp. 645, 649, 674, and 678 herein.)

line 1

5

10

THE

DOCTRINE AND COVENANTS

OF

THE CHURCH OF JESUS CHRIST

OF

LATTER DAY SAINTS;

CAREFULLY SELECTED FROM THE REVELATIONS OF GOD.

BY JOSEPH SMITH,
PRESIDENT OF SAID CHURCH.

SECOND EDITION.

NAUVOO, ILL:
PRINTED BY JOHN TAYLOR.
1844.

line 1 Entered according to the act of Congress, in the year 1835,
By Joseph Smith,
In the clerk's office of the district court of Ohio.

line 1

my servant Warren, for I will have mercy on him, and notwithstanding the vanity of his heart, I will lift him up inasmuch as he will humble himself before me; and I will give him grace and assurance wherewith he may stand; and if he continue to be a faithful witness and a light unto the church, I have prepared a crown for him in the mansions of my Father: even so; Amen.

line 10

SECTION CI.

Revelation given February, 1834.

1 Verily I say unto you, my friends, behold I will give unto you a revelation and commandment, that you may know how to act in the discharge of your duties concerning the salvation and redemption of your brethren, who have been scattered on the land of Zion, being driven and smitten by the hands of mine enemies; on whom I will pour out my wrath without measure in mine own time: for I have suffered them thus far, that they might fill up the measure of their iniquities, that their cup might be full; and that those who call themselves after my name might be chastened for a little season, with a sore and greivous chastisement, because they did not hearken altogether unto the precepts and commandments which I gave unto them.

2 But verily I say unto you, that I have decreed a decree which my people shall realize, inasmuch as they hearken from this very

line 15

line 20

line 25

line 30

33

---

line 1. This is the conclusion of section 100, which is not reproduced in full here because it also appears in the 1835 edition. (Revelation, 25 Nov. 1834, in Doctrine and Covenants 99, 1835 ed. [D&C 106].)

line 10. Revelation, 24 Feb. 1834 [D&C 103]. A loose revelation manuscript in the handwriting of Willard Richards, only a fragment of which is extant, bears editing marks that are reflected in portions of this version, indicating that the full manuscript was used as a source text for this version. (See Revelation, 24 Feb. 1834, in JS History, vol. B-1, miscellaneous papers [D&C 103:8–18].)

line 32. "33" is the fifth signature mark in the eleventh gathering of the 1844 Doctrine and Covenants. Six signature marks appear in each gathering; the sixth in this gathering appears on the recto of the leaf after the next. These marks were used in collating the gatherings after the sheets were folded.

hour, unto the counsel which 1 the Lord their
God shall give unto them.   Behold they shall,
for I have decreed it, begin to prevail against
mine enemies from this very hour, and by
hearkening to observe all the words whlch I,
the Lord their God, shall speak unto them,
they shall never cease to prevail until the
kingdoms of the world are subdued under my
feet; and the earth is given unto the saints, to
possess it forever and ever.   But inasmuch
as they keep not my commandments, and
hearken not to observe all my words, the kingdoms of the world shall prevail against them,
for they were set to be a light unto the world,
and to be the saviors of men; and inasmuch
as they are not the saviors of men, they are
as salt that has lost its sovor, and is thenceforth good for nothing but to be cast out and
trodden under foot of men.

3 But verily I say unto you, I have decreed
that your brethren, which have been scattered,
shall return to the land of their inheritances
and build up the waste places of Zion; fo after
much tribulation, as I have said unto you in a
former commandment, cometh the blessing.—
Behold, this is the blessing which I have promised after your tribulations, and the tribulations of your brethren; your redemption, and
the redemption of your brethren; even their
restoration to the land o Zion, to be established, no more to be thrown down; nevertheless, if they pollute their inheritances, they
shall be thrown down; for I will not spare
them if they pollute their inheritances.   Be
hold I say unto you, the redemption of Zion

line 1

must needs come by power; therefore, I will
raise up unto my people a man, who shall lead
them like as Moses led the children of Israel,
for ye are the children of Israel, and of the
seed of Abraham; and ye must needs be led
out of bondage by power, and with a stretched out arm: and as your fathers were led at
the first, even so shall the redemption of Zion
be. Therefore, let not your hearts faint, for
I say not unto you as I said unto your fathers,
mine angel shall go up before you, but not my
presence; but I say unto you, mine angels
shall go before you, and also my presence,
and in time ye shall possess the goodly land.

4 Verily, verily I say unto you, that my servant Baurak Ale is the man to whom I liken-
ed the servant to whom the Lord of the vine-
yark spoke in the parable which I have given
unto you.

5 Therefore, let my servant Baurak Ale say
unto the strength of my house, my young men
and the middle aged, Gather yourselves together unto the land of Zion, upon the land
whith I have bought with moneys that have
been consecrated unto me; and let all the
churches send up wise men, with their moneys, and purchase lands even as I have commanded them; and inasmuch as mine enemies
come against you to drive you from my goodly land, which I have consecrated to be the
land of Zion; even from your own lands after
these testimonies, which ye have brought before me, against them, ye shall curse them;
and whomsoever ye curse, I will curse; and
ye shall avenge me of mine enemies: and my

---

line 16. This is the first of two revelations first published in the 1844 Doctrine and Covenants that uses substitute words. The majority of names in this revelation, however, were printed as they appear in the early manuscript sources. (See pp. 708–711 herein.)

line 1 presence shall be with you, even in avenging
me of mine enemies, unto the third and fourth
generation of them that hate me.

6 Let no man be afraid to lay down his life
5 for my sake; for whoso layeth down his life
for my sake, shall find it again. And whoso
is not willing to lay down his life for my sake,
is not my disciple. It is my will, that my
servant Sidney Rigdon shall lift up his voice
10 in the congregations, in the eastern countries,
in preparing the churches to keep the commandments which I have given unto them,
concerning the restoration and redemption of
Zion. It is my will that my servant Parley
15 P. Pratt, and my servant Lyman Wight should
not return to the land of their brethren, until
they have obtained companies to go up unto
the land of Zion, by tens, or by twenties, or
by fifties, or by an hundred, until they have
20 obtained to the number of five hundred of the
strength of my house. Behold, this is my
will; ask and you shall receive, but men do
not always do my will: therefore, if you cannot obtain five hundred, seek diligently that
25 peradventure you may obtain three hundred;
and if ye cannot obtain three hundred, seek
diligently that peradventure ye may obtain
one hundred. But verily I say unto you, a
commandment I give unto you, that ye shall
30 not go up unto the land of Zion, until you
have obtained one hundred of the strength of
my house, to go up with you unto the land of
Zion. Therefore, as I said unto you, ask and
ye shall receive: pray earnestly that perad-
35 venture my servant Baurak Ale may go with

line 1   you and preside in the midst of my people, and organize my kingdom upon the consecrated land; and establish the children of Zion, upon the laws and commandments, which

5   have been, and which shall be given, unto you.

7 All victory and glory is brought to pass unto you through your diligence, faithfulness, and prayers of faith. Let my servant Parley P. Pratt, journey with my servant Joseph

10   Smith, jr. Let my servant Lyman Wight, journey with my servant Sidney Rigdon.— Let my servant Hyrum Smith, journey with my servant Frederic G. Williams. Let my servant Orson Hyde, journey with my servant Orson Pratt; whithersoever my servant Joseph

15   Smith, jr., shall counsel them in obtaining the fulfilment of these commandments, which I have given unto you, and leave the residue in my hands: even so; Amen.

SECTION CII.

20

Revelation given on Fishing River, Missouri, June 22, 1834.

1 Verily I say unto you, who have assembled yourselves together that you may learn

25   my will concerning the redemption of mine afflicted people:

2 Behold, I say unto you, were it not for the transgressions of my people, speaking concerning the church and not individuals, they

30   might have been redeemed even now: but behold, they have not learned to be obedient

33*

---

line 20. Revelation, 22 June 1834 [D&C 105]. This version reflects editing marks made in Revelation Book 2, indicating that the latter was used as a source text for the former. This is the second of two revelations first published in the 1844 Doctrine and Covenants that uses substitute words. (See *JSP*, MRB:611–617; and pp. 708–711 herein.)

390 COVENANTS AND

line 1 to the things which I require at their hands,
but are full of all manner of evil, and do not
impart of their substance, as becometh saints,
to the poor and afflicted among them, and are
5 not united according to the union required by
the law of the celestial kingdom; and Zion
cannot be built up unless it is by the principles of the law of the celestial kingdom, otherwise I cannot receive her unto myself; and
10 my people must needs be chastened until they
learn obedience, if it must needs be, by the
things which they suffer.

3 I speak not concerning those who are appointed to lead my people, who are the first
15 elders of my church, for they are not all under
this condemnation; but I speak concerning
my churches abroad: there are many who will
say, Where is their God? Behold, he will deliver in time of trouble; otherwise we will not
20 go up unto Zion, and will keep our moneys.
Therefore, in consequence of the trangres-
sion of my people, it is expedient in me that
mine elders should wait for a little season for
the redemption of Zion, that they themselves
25 may be prepared, and that my people may be
taught more perfectly, and have experience,
and know more perfectly, concerning their
duty, and the things which I require at their
hands; and this cannot be brought to pass un-
30 til mine elders are endowed with power from
on high: for behold, I have prepared a great
endowment and blessing to be poured out upon
them, inasmuch as they are faithful, and continue in humility before me; therefore, it is
35 expedient in me that mine elders should wait

line 1

for a little season, for the redemption of Zion:
for behold, I do not require at their hands to
fight the battles of Zion; for, as I said in a
former commandment, even so will I fulfil, I
will fight your battles.

4 Behold, the destroyer I have sent forth
to destroy and lay waste mine enemies; and not
many years hence, they shall not be left to pollute mine heritage, and to blaspheme my name
upon the lands which I have consecrated for
the gathering together of my saints.

5 Behold, I have commanded my servant
Baurak Ale to say unto the strength of my
house, even my warriors, my young men and
middle-aged, to gather together for the redemption of my people, and throw down the
towers of mine enemies, and scatter their
watchmen; but the strength of mine house
have not hearkened unto my words; but inasmuch as there are those who have hearkened
unto my words, I have prepared a blessing
and an endowment for them, if they continue
faithful. I have heard their prayers, and will
accept their offering; and it is expedient in
me, that they should be brought thus far, for a
trial of their faith.

6 And now, verily I say unto you, a commandment I give unto you, that as many as
have come up hither, that can stay in the region round about, let them stay; and those
that cannot stay, who have families in the
east, let them tarry for a little season, inasmuch as my servant Joseph shall appoint unto
them, for I will counsel him concerning this

line 1 matter; and all things whatsoever he shall appoint unto them shall be fulfilled.

7 And let all my people who dwell in the regions round about, be very faithful, and *5* prayerful, and humble before me, and reveal not the things which I have revealed unto them, until it is wisdom in me that they should be revealed. Talk not judgment, neither boast of faith, nor of mighty works; but care-*10* fully gather together, as much in one region as can be consistently with the feelings of the people: and behold, I will give unto you favor and grace in their eyes, that you may rest in peace and safety, while you are saying unto *15* the people, execute judgment and justice for us according to law, and redress us of our wrongs.

8 Now, behold, I say unto you, my friends, in this way you may find favor in the eyes of *20* the people, until the army of Israel becomes very great: and I will soften the hearts of the people, as I did the heart of Pharaoh, from time to time, until my servant Baurak Ale, and Baneemy, whom I have appointed, shall *25* have time to gather up the strength of my house, and to have sent wise men, to fulfil that which I have commanded concerning the purchasing of all the lands in Jackson county, that can be purchased, and in the adjoining *30* counties round about; for it is my will that these lands should be purchased, and after they are purchased that my saints should pos-sess them according to the laws of consecra-tion which I have given; and after these

line 1 lands are purchased, I will hold the armies of Israel guiltless in taking possession of their own lands, which they have previously purchased with their moneys, and of throwing down the towers of mine enemies, that may be upon them, and scattering their watchmen, and avenging me of mine enemies, unto the third and fourth generation of them that hate me.

9 But firstly, let my army become very great, and let it be sanctified before me, that it may become fair as the sun, and clear as the moon, and that her banners may be terrible unto all nations; that the kingdoms of this world may be constrained to acknowledge that the kingdom of Zion is in very deed the kingdom of our God and his Christ: therefore, let us become subject unto her laws.

10 Verily I say unto you, it is expedient in me that the first elders of my church should receive their endowment from on high, in my house, which I have commanded to be built unto my name in the land of Kirtland: and let those commandments which I have given concerning Zion and her law, be executed and fulfilled, after her redemption. There has been a day of calling, but the time has come for a day of choosing; and let those be chosen that are worthy: and it shall be manifest unto my servant, by the voice of the Spirit, those that are chosen, and they shall be sanctified: and inasmuch as they follow the counsel which they receive, they shall have power after many days to accomplish all things pertaining to Zion.

line 1

11 And again I say unto you, sue for peace, not only the people that have smitten you, but also to all people; and lift up an ensign of peace, and make a proclamation for peace unto the ends of the earth; and make proposals for peace, unto those who have smitten you, according to the voice of the Spirit which is in you, and all things shall work together for your good: therefore be faithful, and behold, and lo! I am with you even unto the end, even so; Amen.

Revelation given to Joseph Smith, January 19, 1841.

1 Verily, thus saith the Lord unto you, my servant Joseph Smith, I am well pleased with your offering and acknowledgements, which you have made, for unto this end have I raised you up, that I might shew forth my wisdom through the weak things of the earth. Your prayers are acceptable before me, and in answer to them I say unto you, that you are now called, immediately to make a solemn proclamation of my gospel, and of this stake which I have planted to be a corner-stone of Zion, which shall be polished with that refinement which is after the similitude of a palace. This proclamation shall be made to all the kings of the world, to the four corners thereof —To the honorable President elect, and the high-minded governors of the nation in which you live, and to all the nations of the earth, scattered abroad. Let it be written in the Spirit of meekness, and by the power of

---

line 12. Revelation, 19 Jan. 1841 [D&C 124]. The source text for this version is unknown. Though this section bears no number, the sequence of the surrounding section numbers indicates it should be numbered 103.

line 1
the Holy Gnost, which shall be in you at the
time of the writing of the same; for it shall be
given you by the Holy Ghost to know my
will concerning those kings and authorities,
even what shall befal them in a time to come.
For, behold! I am about to call upon them to
give heed to the light and glory of Zion, for
the set time has come to favor her.

2. Call ye, therefore, upon them with loud
proclamation, and with your testimony, fearing them not, for they are as grass, and all
their glory as the flower thereof, which soon
falleth, that they may be left also without excuse, and that I may visit them in the day of
visiation, when I shall unveil the face of my
covering, to appoint the portion of the oppres-
sor among hypocrites, where there is gnashing of teeth; if they reject my servants and
my testimony which I have revealed unto
them.   And again, I will visit and soften their
hearts, many of them, for your good, that ye
may find grace in their eyes, that they may
come to the light of truth, and the Gentiles to
the exaltation or lifting up of Zion.   For the
day of my visitation come h speedily, in an
hour when ye think not of, and where shall
be the safety of my people? and refuge for
those who shall be left of them?

3 Awake! O kings of the earth! Come
ye, O! come ye, with your gold and your silver, to the help of my people, to the house
of the daughters of Zion.

4 And agan, verily I say unto you, let my
servant Robert B. Thompson help you to
write this proclamation; for I am well pleased

line 1
with him, and that he should be with you; let
him, therefore, hearken to your counsel, and
I will bless him with a multiplicity of blessings;
let him be faithful and true in all things from
5henceforth, and he shall be great in mine eyes;
but let him remember that his stewardship
will I require at his hands.

5 And again, verily I say unto you, blessed
is my servant Hyrum Smith, for I the Lord
10loveth him, because of the integrity of his
heart, and because he loveth that which is
right before me, saith the Lord.

6 Again, let my servant John C. Bennett,
help you in your labor in sending my word to
15the kings and people of the earth, and stand
by you, even you my servant Joseph Smith,
in the hour of affliction, and his reward shall
not fail, if he receive counsel; and for his love
he shall be great; for he shall be mine if he
20do this, saith the Lord. I have seen the
work which he hath done, which I accept, if
he continue, and will crown him with blessings and great glory.

7 And again, I say unto you, that it is my
25will that my servant Lyman Wight should
continue in preaching for Zion, in the spirit
of meekness, confessing me before the world,
and I will bear him up as on eagle's wings,
and he shall beget glory and honor to himself,
30and unto my name, that when he shall finish
his work, that I may receive him unto myself,
even as I did my servant David Patten, who
is with me at this time, and also my servant
Edward Partridge, and also my aged servant
35Joseph Smith, sen., who sitteth with Abra-

COMMANDMENTS.   397

line 1 ham, at his right hand, and blessed and holy
is he, for he is mine.

8 And again, verily I say unto you, my servant George Miller is without guile; he may
5 be trusted because of the integrity of his
heart; and for the love which he has to my
testimony, I the Lord loveth him; I therefore
say unto you, I seal upon his head the office
of a bishoprick, like unto my servant Edward
10 Partridge, that he may receive the consecra-
tions of mine house, that he may administer
blessings upon the heads of the poor of my
people, saith the Lord. Let no man despise
my servant George, for he shall honor me.

15 9 Let my servant George, and my servant
Lyman, and my servant John Snider, and
others, build a house unto my name, such an
one, as my servant Joseph shall show unto
them; upon the place which he shall show
20 unto them also. And it shall be for a house
for boarding, a house that strangers may come
from afar to lodge therein: therefore, let it be
a good house, worthy of all acceptation, that
the weary traveller may find health and safety
25 while he shall contemplate the word of the
Lord, and the corner-stone have I appointed
for Zion. This house shall be a healthy habitation, if it be built unto my name, and if the
governor, which shall be appointed unto it
30 shall not suffer any pollution to come upon it.
It shall be holy, or the Lord your God will not
dwell therein.

10 And again, verily I say unto you, let all
my saints from afar; and send ye swift mes-
35 34

---

line 35. This page begins the twelfth gathering of the book. "34" is the first of six signature marks in this gathering; the second through sixth are found on the rectos of the third, seventh, ninth, thirteenth, and fifteenth leaves. These marks were used in collating the gatherings after the sheets were folded.

line 1 sengers, yea, chosen messengers, and say unto them, Come ye, with all your gold, and your silver, and your precious stones, and with all your antiquities; and with all who have know-
5 ledge of antiquities, that will come may come, and bring the box tree, and the fir tree, and the pine tree, together with all the precious trees of the earth; and with iron, with copper, and with brass, and with zinc, and with all
10 your precious things of the earth, and build a house to my name, for the Most High to dwell therein; for there is not a place found on earth that he may come and restore again that which was lost unto you, or, which he hath ta-
15 ken away, even the fulness of the priesthood; for a baptismal font there is not upon the earth; that they, my saints, may be baptized for those who are dead: for this ordinance belongeth to my house, and cannot be accep-
20 table to me, only in the days of your poverty, wherein ye are not able to build a house unto me. But I command you, all ye my saints, to build a house unto me; and I grant unto you a sufficient time to build a house unto me,
25 and during this time your baptisms shall be acceptable unto me.

11 But, behold, at the end of this appoint-
ment, your baptisms for your dead shall not be acceptable unto me; and if you do not
30 these things at the end of the appointment, ye shall be rejected as a church with your dead, saith the Lord your God. For, verily I say unto you, that after you have had sufficient time to build a house to me, wherein
35 the ordinance of baptizing for the dead be-

line 1 longeth, and for which the same was instituted
from before the foundation of the world, your
baptisms for your dead cannot be acceptable
unto me; for therein are the keys of the holy
5 priesthood, ordained, that you may receive
honor and glory. And after this time, your
baptisms for the dead, by those who are scattered abroad, are not acceptable unto me, saith
the Lord; for it is ordained that in Zion and
10 in her stakes, and in Jerusalem, those places
which I have appointed for refuge, shall be
the places for your baptisms for your dead.

12 And again, verily I say unto you, how
shall your washings be acceptable unto me,
15 except ye perform them in a house which you
have built to my name? For, for this cause
I commanded Moses that he should build a
tabernacle, that they should bear it with them
in the wilderness, and to build a house in the
20 land of promise, that those ordinances might
be revealed, which had been hid from before
the world was; therefore, verily I say unto
you, that your anointings and your washings,
and your baptisms for the dead, and your sol-
25 emn assemblies, and your memorials for your
sacrifices, by the sons of Levi, and for your
oracles in your most holy places, wherein you
receive conversations, and your statutes and
judgments, for the beginning of the revelations
30 and foundation of Zion, and for the glory,
honor and endowment of all her municipals,
are ordained by the ordinance of my holy
house which my people are always commanded to build unto my holy name.

35 13 And verily I say unto you, let this house

400 COVENANTS AND

line 1 be built unto my name, that I may reveal
mine ordinances therein, unto my people; for
I deign to reveal unto my church, things
which have been kept hid from before the
5 foundation of the world; things that pertain
to the dispensation of the fulness of times; and
I will show unto my servant Joseph all things
pertaining to this house, and the priesthood
thereof; and the place whereon it shall be
10 built: and ye shall build it on the place where
you have contemplated building it; for that is
the spot which I have chosen for you to build
it. If ye labor with all your mights, I will
consecrate that spot, that it shall be made
15 holy; and if my people will hearken unto my
voice, and unto the voice of my servants whom
I have appointed to lead my people, behold,
verily I say unto you, they shall not be moved
out of their place. But if they will not hear-
20 ken to my voice, nor unto the voice of these
men whom I have appointed, they shall not be
blest, because they pollute mine holy grounds,
and mine holy ordinances, and charters, and
my holy words, which I give unto them.
25 14 And it shall come to pass, that if you
build a house unto my name, and do not do the
things that I say, I will not perform the oath
which I make unto you, neither fulfil the promises which ye expect at my hands, saith the
30 Lord; for instead of blessings, ye, by your
own works, bring cursings, wrath, indignation, and judgments, upon your own heads, by
your follies, and by all your abominations,
which you practice before me, saith the Lord.
35 15 Verily, verily I say unto you, that when

line 1   I give a commandment to any of the sons of
men, to do a work unto my name, and those
sons of men go with all their mights, and with
all they have, to perform that work, and cease
5   not their diligence, and their enemies come
upon them, and hinder them from performing
that work; behold, it behoveth me to require
that work no more at the hands of those sons
of men, but to accept of their offerings; and
10   the iniquity and transgression of my holy laws
and commandments, I will visit upon the
heads of those who hindered my work, unto
the third and fourth generation, so long as they
repent not, and hate me, saith the Lord God.
15   Therefore for this cause have I accepted the
offerings of those whom I commanded to build
up a city and a house unto my name, in Jackson county, Missouri, and were hindered by
their enemies, saith the Lord your God: and
20   I will answer judgment, wrath, and indignation, wailing, and anguish, and gnashing of
teeth, upon their heads, unto the third and
fourth generation, so long as they repent not,
and hate me, saith the Lord your God.

25   16. And this I make an example unto you,
for your consolation, concerning all those who
have been commanded to do a work, and have
been hindered by the hands of their enemies,
and by oppression, saith the Lord your God;
30   for I am the Lord your God, and will save all
those of your brethren, who have been pure
in heart, and have been slain in the land of
Missouri, saith the Lord.

    17 And again, verily I say unto you, I com-
35   34*

line 1 mand you again to build a house to my name,
even in this place that you may prove yourselves unto me, that ye are faithful in all things
whatsoever I command you, that I may bless
5 you, and crown you with honor, immortality,
and eternal life.

18 And now, I say unto you, as pertaining
to my boarding-house, which I have commanded you to build, for the boarding of strangers,
10 let it be built unto my name, and let my name
be named upon it, and let my servant Joseph
and his house have place therein, from generation to generation: for this annointing have
I put upon his head, that his blessing shall
15 also be put upon the head of his posterity
after him; and as I said unto Abrahm, concerning the kindreds of the earth; even so I
say unto my servant Joseph, in thee, and in
thy seed, shall the kindred of the earth be
20 blessed. Therefore, let my servant Joseph
and his seed after him have place in that house,
from generation to generation, forever and
ever, saith the Lord, and let the name of that
house be called the Nauvoo House; and let it
25 be a delightful habitation for man, and a resting place for the weary traveler, that he may
contemplate the glory of Zion, and the glory
of this the corner-stone thereof; that he may
receive, also, the counsel from those whom I
30 have set to be as plants of renown, and as
watchmen upon her walls.

19 Behold! verily I say unto you, let my
servant George Miller, and my servant Lyman Wight, and my servant John Snider, and
35 my servant Peter Haws, organize themselves,

and appoint one of them to be a president
over their quorum for the purpose of building
that house.   And they shall form a constitution whereby they may receive stock for the
building of that house.   And they shall not
receive less than fifty dollars for a share of
stock in that house, and they shall be permitted to receive fifteen thousand dollars from
any one man for stock in that house; but
they shall not be permitted to receive over
fifteen thousand dollars stock, from any one
man; and they shall not be permitted to receive under fifty dollars for a share of stock
from any one man, in that house; and they
shall not be permitted to receive any man as
a stockholder in this house, except the same
shall pay his stock into their hands at the time
he receives stock; and in proportion to the
amount of stock he pays into their hands, he
shall receive stock in that house; but if he
pay nothing into their hands, he shall not receive any stock in that house.   And if any
pay stock into their hands, it shall be for
stock in that house, for himself, and for his
generation after him, from generation to generation, so long as he and his heirs shall hold
that stock, and do not sell or convey the stock
away out of their hands by their own free will
and act: if you will do my will, saith the
Lord your God.

20 And again, verily I say unto you, if my
servant George Miller, and my servant Lyman Wight, and my servant John Snider, and
my servant Peter Haws, receive any stock
into their hands, in moneys, or in properties,

line 1 wherein they receive the real value of moneys, they shall not appropriate any portion
of that stock to any other purpose, only in
that house; and if they do appropriate any
5 portion of that stock any where else, only in
that house, without the consent of the stockholder, and do not repay fourfold, for the
stock which they appropriate any where else,
only in that house, they shall be accursed,
10 and shall be moved out of their place, saith
the Lord God, for I the Lord am God, and
cannot be mocked in any of these things.

21 Verily I say unto you, let my servant
Joseph pay stock into their hands for the
15 building of that house, as seemeth him good;
but my servant Joseph cannot pay over fifteen
thousand dollars stock in that house, nor under
fifty dollars; neither can any other man, saith
the Lord.

20 22 And there are others also, who wish
to know my will concerning them; for they
have asked it at my hands: Therefore I say
unto you, concerning my servant Vinson
Knight, if he will do my will, let him put
25 stock into that house for himself and for his
generation after him, from generation to generation, and let him lift up his voice, long and
loud, in the midst of the people, to plead the
cause of the poor and the needy, and let him
30 not fail, neither let his heart faint, and I will
accept of his offerings; for they shall not be
unto me as the offerings of Cain, for he shall
be mine, saith the Lord. Let his family rejoice, and turn away their hearts from afflic-
35 tion, for I have chosen him and anointed him,

line 1   and he shall be honored in the midst of his
house, for I will forgive all his sins, saith the
Lord; Amen.

23 Verily I say unto you, let my servant
Hyrum put stock into that house, as seemeth
him good, for himself and his generation after
after him, from generation to generation.

24 Let my servant Isaac Galland put stock
into that house, for I the Lord loveth him for
the work he hath done, and will forgive all
his sins; therefore, let him be remembered for
an interest in that house, from generation to
generation. Let my servant Isaac Galland
be appointed among you, and be ordained by
my servant William Marks, and be blessed of
him, to go with my servant Hyrum, to accomplish the work that my servant Joseph shall
point out to them, and they shall be greatly
blessed.

25 Let my servant William Marks pay
stock into that house, as seemeth him good,
for himself and his generation, from generation to generation.

26 Let my servant Henry G. Sherwood
pay stock into that house, as seemeth him
good, for himself and his seed after him, from
generation to generation.

27 Let my servant William Law pay stock
into that house, for himself and his seed after
him, from generation to generation. If he
will do my will, let him not take his family
unto the eastern lands, even unto Kirtland;
nevertheless I the Lord will build up Kirtland,
but I the Lord have a scourge prepared for
the inhabitants thereof. And with my servant

line 1 Almon Babbitt there are many things with
which I am not well pleased; behold, he aspi-
reth to establish his council instead of the council which I have ordained, even the presiden-
5 cy of my church, and he setteth up a golden
calf for the worship of my people. Let no
man go from this place who has come here es-
saying to keep my commandments. If they
live here let them live unto me; and if they
10 die let them die unto me; for they shall rest
from all their labors here, and shall continue
their works. Therefore, let my servant William put his trust in me, and cease to fear concerning his family, because of the sickness of
15 the land. If ye love me, keep my commandments, and the sickness of the land shall re-
dound to your glory.

28 Let my servant William go and proclaim
my everlasting gospel, with a loud voice, and
20 with great joy, as he shall be moved upon by
my spirit, unto the inhabitants of Warsaw, and
also unto the inhabitants of Carthage, and also
unto the inhabitants of Burlington, and also
unto the inhabitants of Madison, and await
25 patiently and diligently for further instructions at my general conference, saith the Lord.
If he will do my will, let him from henceforth
hearken to the counsel of my servant Joseph,
and with his interest support the cause of the
30 poor, and publish the new translation of my
holy word unto the inhabitants of the earth;
and if he will do this, I will bless him with a
multiplicity of blessings, that he shall not be
forsaken, nor his seed be found begging bread.
35 29 And again, verily I say unto you, let my

line 1

servant William be appointed, ordained, and anointed, as a councillor unto my servant Joseph, in the room of my servant Hyrum; that my servant Hyrum may take the office of priesthood and patriarch, which was appointed unto him by his father, by blessing and also by right, that from henceforth he shall hold the keys of the patriarchal blessings upon the heads of all my people, that whoever he blesses shall be blessed, and whoever he curseth shall be cursed; that whatsoever he shall bind on earth shall be bound in heaven; and whatsoever he shall loose on earth shall be loosed in heaven; and from this time forth, I appoint unto him that he may be a prophet and a seer and a revelator unto my church, as well as my servant Joseph, that he may act in concert also with my servant Joseph, and that he shall receive counsel from my servant Joseph, who shall shew unto him the keys whereby he may ask and receive, and be crowned with the same blessing, and glory, and honor, and priesthood, and gifts of the priesthood, that once were put upon him that was my servant Oliver Cowdery; that my servant Hyrum may bear record of the things which I shall shew unto him, that his name may be had in honorable remembrance from generation to generation, forever and ever.

30 Let my servant William Law also receive the keys by which he may ask and receive blessings; let him be humble before me, and be without guile, and he shall receive of my spirit, even the comforter, which shall manifest unto him the truth of all things, and

408   COVENANTS AND

line 1 shall give him in the very hour, what he shall
say, and these signs shall follow him: he shall
heal the sick, he shall cast out devils, and shall
be delivered from those who would administer
5 unto him deadly poison; and he shall be led
in paths where the poisonous serpent cannot
lay hold upon his heel, and he shall mount up
in the imagination of his thoughts as upon
eagle's wings; and what if I will that he should
10 raise the dead, let him not withhold his voice.
Therefore let my servant William cry aloud
and spare not, with joy and rejoicing, and
with hosannas to him that sitteth upon the
throne forever and ever, saith the Lord your
15 God.

31 Behold I say unto you, I have a mission
in store for my servant William and my servant Hyrum, and for them alone; and let my
servant Joseph tarry at home, for he is needed;
20 the remainder I will shew unto you hereafter:
even so; Amen.

32 And again, verily I say unto you, if my
servant Sidney will serve me and be councillor unto my servant Joseph, let him arise and
25 come up and stand in the office of his calling,
and humble himself before me; and if he will
offer unto me an acceptable offering, and acknowledgements, and remain with my people,
behold, I the Lord your God will heal him
30 that he shall be healed; and he shall lift up his
voice again on the mountains, and be a spokesman before my face. Let him come and locate his family in the neighborhood in which
my servant Joseph resides, and in all his jour-
35 neyings let him lift up his voice as with the

line 1 sound of a trump, and warn the inhabitants of the earth to flee the wrath to come; let him assist my servant Joseph; and also let my servant William Law assist my servant Jo-

5 seph, in making a solemn proclamation unto the kings of the earth, even as I have before said unto you. If my servant Sidney will do my will, let him not remove his family unto the eastern lands, but let him change their

10 habitation, even as I have said. Behold, it is not my will that he shall seek to find safety and refuge out of the city which I have appointed unto you, even the city of Nauvoo.— Verily I say unto you, even now, if he will

15 hearken to my voice, it shall be well with him: even so; Amen.

33 And again, verily I say unto you, let my servant Amos Davis pay stock into the hands of those whom I have appointed to

20 build a house for boarding, even the Nauvoo House; this let him do if he will have an interest, and let him hearken unto the counsel of my servant Joseph, and labor with his own hands that he may obtain the confidence of

25 men; and when he shall prove himself faithful in all things that shall be entrusted unto his care; yea, even a few things, he shall be made ruler over many; let him therefore abase himself that he may be exalted: even

30 so; Amen.

34 And again, verily I say unto you, if my servant Robert D. Foster will obey my voice, let him build a house for my servant Joseph, according to the contract which he has made

35   35

410   COVENANTS AND

line 1 with him, as the door shall be open to him
from time to time; and let him repent of all
his folly, and clothe himself with charity, and
cease to do evil, and lay aside all his hard
5 speeches, and pay stock also into the hands
of the quorum of the Nauvoo House, for himself and for his generation after him, from generation to generation, and hearken unto the
counsel of my servants Joseph and Hyrum
10 and William Law, and unto the authorities
which I have called to lay the foundation of
Zion, and it shall be well with him forever
and ever: even so; Amen.

35 And again, verily I say unto you, let no
15 man pay stock to the quorum of the Nauvoo
House, unless he shall be a believer in the
Book of Mormon, and the revelations I have
given unto you, saith the Lord your God: for
that which is more or less than this cometh of
20 evil, and shall be attended with cursings and
not blessings, saith the Lord your God: even
so; Amen.

36 And again, verily I say unto you, let
the quorum of the Nauvoo House have a just
25 recompense of wages for all their labors which
they do in building the Nauvoo House, and
let their wages be as shall be agreed among
themselves, as pertaining to the price thereof;
and let every man who pays stock bear his
30 proportion of their wages, if it must needs be,
for their support, saith the Lord; otherwise
their labors shall be accounted unto them for
stock in that house: even so; Amen.

37 Verily I say unto you, I now give unto
35 you the officers belonging to my Priesthood,

line 1

that ye may hold the keys thereof, even the priesthood which is after the order of Melchisedek, which is after the order of my only begotten Son.

38 First, I give unto you Hyrum Smith to to be a patriarch unto you to hold the sealing blessings of my church, even the Holy Spirit of promise, whereby ye are sealed up unto the day of redemption, that ye may not fall; notwithstanding the hour of temptation that may come upon you.

39 I give unto you my servant Joseph, to be a Presiding Elder over all my church, to be a translator, a revelator, a seer and prophet. I give unto him for councillors my servant Sidney Rigdon, and my servant William Law, that these may constitute a quorum and first presidency, to receive the oracles for the whole church.

40 I give unto you my servant Brigham Young, to be a president over the twelve travelling council, which twelve hold the keys to open up the authority of my kingdom upon the four corners of the earth, and after that to send my word to every creature; they are: Heber C. Kimball, Parley P. Pratt, Orson Pratt, Orson Hyde, William Smith, John Taylor, John E. Page, Wilford Woodruff, Willard Richards, George A. Smith; David Patten I have taken unto myself, behold his priesthood no man taketh from him; but verily I say unto you, another may be appointed unto the same calling.

41 And again, I say unto you, I give unto you a High Council, for the corner stone of

412   COVENANTS AND

line 1 Zion; viz: Samuel Bent, H. G. Sherwood,
George W. Harris, Charles C. Rich, Thomas
Grover, Newel Night, David Dort, Dunbar
Wilson; Seymour Brunson I have taken unto
5 myself, no man taketh his priesthood, but another may be appointed unto the same priesthood in his stead, (and verily I say unto you,
let my servant Aaron Johnson be ordained
unto this calling in his stead,) David Fulmer,
10 Alpheus Cutler, William Huntington.

42 And again, I give unto you Don C.
Smith to be a president over a Quorum of
High-priests: which ordinance is instituted
for the purpose of qualifying those who shall
15 be appointed standing presidents or servants
over different stakes scattered abroad, and
they may travel also if they choose, but rather
be ordained for standing presidents, this is the
office of their calling saith the Lord your God.
20 I give unto him Amasa Lyman and Noah
Packard for councillors that they made presid
over the quorum of high-priests of my church
saith the Lord.

43 And again I say unto you, I give unto
25 you John A. Hicks, Samuel Williams, and
Jesse Baker which priesthood is to preside
over the quorum of Elders which quorum is
instituted for standing ministers, nevertheless
they may travel, yet they are ordained to be
30 standing ministers to my church, saith the
Lord.

44 And, again, I give unto you Joseph
Young, Josiah Butterfield, Daniel Miles, Henry Herriman, Zera Pulsipher, Levi Hancock,
35 James Foster, to preside over the quorum

line 1

of seventies, which quorum is instituted for travelling elders to bear record of my name in all the world, wherever the travelling high council, my apostles, shall send them to prepare a way before my face. The difference between this quorum and the quorum of elders is, that one is to travel continually, and the other is to preside over the churches from time to time, the one has the responsibility of presiding from time to time and the other has no responsibility of presiding, saith the Lord your God.

45 And again I say unto you, I give unto you Vinson Knight, Samuel H. Smith, and Shadrach Roundy if he will receive it to preside over the Bishopric, a knowledge of said Bishopric is given unto you, in the Book of Doctrine and Covenants.

46 And, again, I say unto you Samuel Rolfe and his councillors for Priests, and the president of the Teachers and his councillors and also the president of the Deacons and his councillors, and also the president of the Stake and his councillors: the above offices I have given unto you, and the keys thereof for helps and for governments, for the work of the ministry, and the perfecting of my saints, and a commandment I give unto you that you should fill all these offices and approve of those names which I have mentioned or else disapprove of, them at my general conference, and that ye should prepare rooms for all these offices in my house when you build it unto my name saith the Lord your God: even so: Amen.

85*

line 35. This signature mark should read "35*".

414   COVENANTS AND

SECTION CIV.

The word of the Lord, given unto Thomas B. Marsh, at Kirtland July 23, 1837, concerning the twelve apostles of the Lamb.

1 Verily thus saith the Lord unto you my servant Thomas, I have heard thy prayers, and thine alms have come up as a memorial before me, in behalf of those thy brethren who were chosen to bear testimony of my name, and to send it abroad among all nations, kindreds, tongues, and people; and ordained through the instrumentality of my servants.

2 Verily I say unto you, there have been some few things in thine heart and with thee, with which I the Lord was not well pleased; nevertheless inasmuch as thou hast abased thyself thou shalt be exalted: therefore all thy sins are forgiven thee. Let thy heart be of good cheer before my face, and thou shalt bear record of my name, not only unto the Gentiles, but also unto the Jews; and thou shalt send forth my word unto the ends of the earth.

3 Contend thou therefore morning by morning, and day after day let thy warning voice go forth; and when the night cometh, let not the inhabitants of the earth slumber because of thy speech.

4 Let thy habitation be known in Zion, and remove not thy house, for I the Lord have a great work for thee to do, in publishing my name among the children of men: therefore gird up thy loins for the work. Let thy feet be shod also for thou art chosen and thy path

line 1. Revelation, 23 July 1837 [D&C 112]. This version reflects editing marks made both in the version copied into JS's journal and in a manuscript in the handwriting of William W. Phelps, indicating that both were used as source texts for this version. (See Revelation, 23 July 1837, in JS, Journal, Mar.–Sept. 1838, in *JSP,* J1:306–309 [D&C 112]; and Revelation, 23 July 1837, in Revelations Collection, CHL [D&C 112].)

line 1 lieth among the mountains, and among many
nations; and by thy word many high ones
shall be brought low; and by thy word many
low ones shall be exalted. Thy voice shall be
5 a rebuke unto the transgressor; and at thy
rebuke let the tongue of the slanderer cease
its perverseness.

5 Be thou humble and the Lord thy God
shall lead thee by thy hand, and give the an-
10 swer to thy prayers. I know thy heart and
have heard thy prayers concerning thy brethren. Be not partial towards them in love
above many others, but let thy love be for
them as for thyself; and let thy love abound
15 unto all men, and unto all who love my name.
And pray for thy brethren of the twelve.—
Admonish them sharply for my name's sake,
and let them be admonished for all their sins
and be ye faithful before me unto my name.
20 And after their temptations, and much tribulations, behold I the Lord will feel after them,
and if they harden not their hearts, and stiffen
not their necks against me, they shall be converted, and I will heal them.

25 6 Now I say unto you, and what I say unto
you, I say unto all the twelve, arise and gird
up your loins, take up your cross, follow me,
and feed my sheep. Exalt not yourselves;
rebel not against my servant Joseph, for verily
30 I say unto you I am with him, and my hand
shall be over him; and the keys which I have
given unto him, and also to youward, shall not
be taken from him till I come.

35 7 Verily I say unto you, my servant Thomas thou art the man whom I have chosen to

hold the keys of my kingdom (as pertaining to the twelve) abroad among all nations, that thou mayest be my servant to unlock the door of the kingdom in all places where my servant Joseph, and my servant Sidney, and my servant Hyrum, cannot come: for on them have I laid the burden of all the churches for a little season: wherefore, whithersoever they shall send you, go ye, and I will be with you, and in whatsoever place ye shall proclaim my name, an effectual door shall be opened unto you, that they may receive my word; whosoever receiveth my word receiveth me, and whosoever receiveth me, receiveth those (the first presidency) whom I have sent, whom I have made counsellors for my names sake unto you.

8. And again I say unto you, that whosoever ye shall send in my name, by the voice of your brethren, the twelve, duly recommended and authorized by you, shall have power to open the door of my kingdom unto any nation whithersoever ye shall send them, inasmuch as they shall humble themselves before me, and abide in my word, and hearken to the voice of my spirit.

9 Verily, Verily, I say unto you, darkness covereth the earth and gross darkness the minds of the people, and all flesh has become corrupt before my face! Behold vengeance cometh speedily upon the inhabitants of the earth; a day of wrath; a day of burning; a day of desolation; of weeping; of mourning and of lamentation; and as a whirlwind it shall come upon all the face of the earth, saith the Lord

line 1

10 And upon my house shall it begin; and from my house shall it go forth saith the Lord. First among those among you saith the Lord; who have professed to know my name and have not known me, and have blasphemed against me in the midst of my house saith the Lord.

11 Therefore see to it that ye trouble not yourselves concerning the affairs of my church in this place, saith the Lord: but purify your hearts before me, and then go ye into all the world and preach my gospel unto every creature, who have not received it, and he that believeth and is baptized shall be saved, and he that believeth not, and is not baptised shall be damned.

12 For unto you (the twelve) and those (the first presidency) who are appointed with you to be your counsellors and your leaders, is the power of this priesthood given for the last days and for the last time, in the which is the dispensation of the fulness of times, which power you hold in connection with all those who have received a dispensation at any time from the beginning of the creation: for verily I say unto you the keys of the dispensation which ye have received, have came down from the fathers: and last of all, being sent down from heaven unto you.

13. Verily I say unto you, behold how great is your calling. Cleanse your hearts and your garments, lest the blood of this generation be required at your hands. Be faithful until I come for I come quickly, and my reward is with me to recompense every man according as his work shall be. I am Alpha and Omega: Amen.

418   COVENANTS AND

SECTION CV.

Nauvoo, September 1, 1842.

TO ALL THE SAINTS IN NAUVOO:—

1 Forasmuch as the Lord has revealed unto me that my enemies, both of Missouri and
this State, were again on the pursuit of me;
and inasmuch as they pursue me without cause,
and have not the least shadow, or coloring of
justice or right on their side, in the getting up
of their prosecutions against me: and inasmuch as their pretensions are all founded in
falsehood, of the blackest die, I have thought
it expedient, and wisdom in me to leave the
place for a short season, for my own safety
and the safety of this people. I would say to
all those with whom I have business, that I
have left my affairs with agents and clerks,
who will transact all business in a prompt and
proper manner; and will see that all my debts
are cancelled in due time, by turning out
property, or otherwise as the case may require, or as the circumstances may admit of.
When I learn that the storm is fully blown
over, then I will return to you again.

2 And as for the perils which I am called
to pass through, they seem but a small thing
to me, as the envy and wrath of man have
been my common lot all the days of my life;
and for what cause it seems mysterious, unless I was ordained from before the foundation of the world, for some good end, or bad
as you may choose to call it. Judge ye for
yourselves. God knoweth all these things,

---

line 1. JS to the Saints in Nauvoo, 1 Sept. 1842 [D&C 127]. This version closely corresponds to the version in the 15 September 1842 issue of *Times and Seasons,* suggesting that the latter was used as a source
text for the former. (See JS, "Tidings," *Times and Seasons,* 15 Sept. 1842, 3:919–920.)

line 1

whether it be good or bad.   But nevertheless,
deep water is what I am wont to swim in; it
all has become a second nature to me.   And
I feel like Paul, to glory in tribulation, for to
this day has the God of my Fathers delivered
me out of them all, and will deliver me from
henceforth; for behold, and lo, I shall triumph
over all my enemies, for the Lord God hath
spoken it.

3 Let all the saints rejoice, therefore, and
be exceeding glad, for Israel's God is their
God: and he will mete out a just recompense of
reward upon the heads of all your oppressors.

4 And again, verily thus saith the Lord,
let the work of my temple, and all the works
which I have appointed unto you, be continued on and not cease; and let your diligence
and your perseverance, and patience, and
your works be redoubled; and you shall in no
wise lose your reward saith the Lord of Hosts.
And if they persecute you, so persecuted they
the prophets, and righteous men that were before you. For all this there is a reward in heaven

5 And again, I give unto you a word in relation to the baptism for your dead.   Verily,
thus saith the Lord unto you concerning your
dead: When any of you are baptised for your
dead, let there be a recorder; and let him be
eye witness of your baptisms; let him hear
with his ears, that he may testify of a truth,
saith the Lord; that in all your recordings, it
may be recorded in heaven; that whatsoever
you bind on earth, may be bound in heaven:
whatsoever you loose on earth may be loosed
in heaven; for I am about to restore many

420   COVENANTS AND

line 1   things to the earth, pertaining to the priesthood, saith the Lord of Hosts.

6 And again, let all the records be had in
order, that they may be put in the archives
5   of my Holy Temple, to be held in remembrance from generation to generation, saith
the Lord of Hosts.

7 I will say to all the saints, that I desired,
with exceeding great desire, to have address-
10   ed them from the stand, on the subject of baptism for the dead, on the following Sabbath.—
But inasmuch as it is out of my power to do
so, I will write the word of the Lord from
time to time, on that subject, and send
15   it you by mail, as well as many other things.

8 I now close my letter for the present, for
the want of more time: for the enemy is on
the alert, and, as the Saviour said, the prince
of this world cometh, but he hath nothing in
20   me.

9 Behold, my prayer to God is, that you
all may be saved. And I subscribe myself
your servant in the Lord, prophet and seer of
the Church of Jesus Christ of Latter Day
25   Saints.   JOSEPH SMITH.

SECTION CVI.

Nauvoo, September 6, 1842.

To the Church of Jesus Chrsst of Latter
Day Saints, sendeth greeting:
30   1 As I stated to you in my letter before I
left my place, that I would write to you from
time to time, and give you information in re-

---

line 26. JS to "the Church of Jesus Christ of Latter Day Saints," 7 Sept. 1842 [D&C 128]. This version
closely corresponds to the version in the 1 October 1842 issue of *Times and Seasons,* suggesting that the
latter was used as a source text for the former. This letter should be dated 7 September 1842. For more
information on this dating, see the discussion of this item in the Documents series. (See JS, "Letter from
Joseph Smith," *Times and Seasons,* 1 Oct. 1842, 3:934–936.)

line 1 lation to many subjects, I now resume the subject of the baptism for the dead; as that subject seems to occupy my mind, and press itself upon my feelings the strongest, since I

5 have been pursued by my enemies.

2 I wrote a few words of revelation to you concerning a recorder. I have had a few additional views in relation to this matter, which I now certify. That is, it was declared in my

10 former letter that there should be a recorder, who should be eye-witness, and also to hear with his ears, that he might make a record of a truth before the Lord.

3 Now, in relation to this matter, it would

15 be very difficult for one recorder to be present at all times, and to do all the business. To obviate this difficulty, there can be a recorder appointed in each ward of the city, who is well qualified for taking accurate minutes;

20 and let him be very particular and precise in taking the whole proceedings : certifying in his record that he saw with his eyes, and heard with his ears; giving the date, and names, &c., and the history of the whole

25 transaction; naming also, some three individuals that are present, if there be any present, who can at any time when called upon, certify to the same, that in the mouth of two or three witnesses every word may be estab-

30 lished.

4 Then let there be a general recorder, to whom these other records can be handed, being attended with certificates over their own signatures; certifying that the record which

35 36

line 1 they have made is true. Then the general
church Recorder can enter the record on the
general church book, with the certificates and
all the attending witnesses, with his own state-
5 ment that he verily believes the above statement and records to be true, from his knowledge of the general character and appointment of those men by the church. And when
this is done on the general church book, the
10 record shall be just as holy, and shall answer
the ordinance just the same as if he had seen
with his eyes, and heard with his ears, and
made a record of the same on the general
church book.

15 5 You may think this order of things to be
very particular, but let me tell you that they
are only to answer the will of God, by conforming to the ordinance and preparation
that the Lord ordained and prepared before
20 the foundation of the world, for the salvation
of the dead, who should die without a knowledge of the gospel.

6 And further, I want you to remember
that John the Revelator was contemplating
25 this very subject in relation to the dead, when
he declared, as you will find recorded in Revelations, xx: 12. "And I saw the dead, small
and great, stand before God; and the books
were opened; and another book was opened,
30 which was the book of life; and the dead
were judged out of those things which were
written in the books, according to their
works."

7 You will discover in this quotation, that
35 the books were opened; and another book

line 1 was opened, which was the book of life; but
the dead were judged out of those things
which were written in the books, according
to their works: consequently the books spo-
5 ken of must be the books which contained
the record of their works; and refer to the
records which are kept on the earth. And
the book which was the book of life, is the
record which is kept in heaven; the principle
10 agreeing precisely with the doctrine which is
commanded you in the revelation contained
in the letter which I wrote to you previous to
my leaving my place, " that in all your recordings it may be recorded in heaven."

15   8 Now the nature of this ordinance consists in the power of the priesthood, by the
revelation of Jesus Christ; wherein it is
granted, that whatsoever you bind on earth,
shall be bound in heaven, and whatsoever you
20 loose on earth, shall be loosed in heaven. Or
in other words, taking a different view of the
translation, whatsoever you record on earth,
shall be recorded in heaven; and whatsoever
you do not record on earth, shall not be re-
25 corded in heaven: for out of the books shall
your dead be judged, according to their
works, whether they themselves have attended to the ordinances in their own propria per-
sona, or by the means of their own agents,
30 according to the ordinance which God has
prepared for their salvation from before the
foundation of the world, according to the records which they have kept concerning their
dead.

35   9 It may seem to some to be a very bold

line 1 doctrine that we talk of: a power which records, or binds on earth, and binds in heaven:
nevertheless, in all ages of the world, whenever the Lord has given a dispensation of the
5 priesthood to any man by actual revelation,
or any set of men, this power has always been
given. Hence whatsoever those men did in
authority, in the name of the Lord, and did it
truly and faithfully, and kept a proper and
10 faithful record of the same, it became a law
on earth and in heaven, and could not be an-
nulled, according to the decrees of the great
Jehovah. This is a faithful saying! Who
can hear it?

15 10 And again, for a precedent, Matthew,
xvi: 18,19. "And I say also unto thee, that
thou art Peter: and upon this rock I will build
my church; and the gates of hell shall not
prevail against it: and I will give unto thee
20 the keys of the kingdom of heaven, and whatsoever thou shalt bind on earth shall be bound
in heaven: and whatsoever thou shalt loose
on earth shall be loosed in heaven."

11 Now the great and grand secret of the
25 whole matter, and the sum and bonum of the
whole subject that is lying before us, consists
in obtaining the powers of the Holy Priesthood. For him to whom these keys are giv-
en, there is no difficulty in obtaining a knowl-
30 edge of facts in relation to the salvation of
the children of men, both as well for the dead
as for the living.

12 Herein is glory and honor, and immortality and eternal life. The ordinance of
35 baptism by water, to be immersed therein in

line 1

order to answer to the likeness of the dead, that one principle might accord with the other. To be immersed in the water and come forth out of the water is in the likeness of the resurrection of the dead in coming forth out of their graves; hence, this ordinance was instituted to form a relationship with the ordinance of baptism for the dead, being in likeness of the dead.

13 Consequently the baptismal font was instituted as a simile of the grave, and was commanded to be in a place underneath where the living are wont to assemble, to shew forth the living and the dead: and that all things may have their likeness, and that they may accord one with another; that which is earthly, conforming to that which is heavenly, as Paul, hath declared, 1 Corinthians, xv:46,47, and 48.

14 "Howbeit that was not first which is spiritual, but that which is natural, and afterwards that which is spiritual. The first man is of the earth, earthy; the second man is the Lord, from heaven. As is the earthy, such are they also that are earthy; and as is the heavenly, such are they also that are heavenly." And as are the records on the earth in relation to your dead, which are truly made out, so also are the records in heaven. This therefore is the sealing and binding power, and in one sense of the word the keys of the kingdom, which consists in the key of knowledge.

15 And now my dearly and beloved brethren and sisters, let me assure you that these

35*

---

line 36. This signature mark should read "36*".

line 1 are principles, in relation to the dead and the living, that cannot be lightly passed over, as pertaining to our salvation.   For their salvation is necessary and essential to our salvation, as Paul says concerning the fathers, 'that they without us cannot be made perfect;' neither can we without our dead, be made perfect.

16 And now in relation to the baptism for the dead, I will give you another quotation of Paul 1 Corinthians, xv:29. "Else what shall they do which are baptised for the dead if the dead rise not at all; why are they then baptised for the dead.

17 And again, in connexion with this quotation, I will give you a quotation from one of the prophets, who had his eye fixed on the restoration of the priesthood, the glories to be revealed in the last days, and in an especial manner this most glorious of all subjects belonging to the everlasting gospel, viz: the baptism for the dead; for Malachi says, last chapter, verses 5th and 6th, "Behold I will send you Elijah the prophet, before the coming of the great and dreadful day of the Lord: and he shall turn the heart of the fathers to the children, and the heart of the children to their fathers, lest I come and smite the earth with a curse.

18 I might have rendered a plainer translation to this, but it is sufficiently plain to suit my purpose as it stands.   It is sufficient to know in this case, that the earth will be smitten with a curse, unless there is a welding link of some kind or other, between the fath-

line 1 ers and the children, upon some subject or other, and behold, what is that subject? It is the baptism for the dead. For we without them cannot be made perfect; neither can

5 they without us be made perfect. Neither can they or us, be made perfect without those who have died in the gospel also; for it is necessary in the ushering in of tne dispensation of the fulness of times; which dispensation is

10 now beginning to usher in, that a whole, and complete, and perfect union, and welding together of dispensations, and keys, and powers, and glories should take place, and be revealed, from the days of Adam even to the

15 present time; and not only this, but those things which never have been revealed from the foundation of the world, but have been kept hid from the wise and prudent, shall be revealed unto babes and sucklings in this the

20 dispensation of the fulness of times.

19 Now what do we hear in the gospel which we have received? "A voice of gladness! A voice of mercy from Heaven; and a voice of truth out of the earth, glad tidings for

25 the dead: a voice of gladness for the living and the dead; glad tidings of great joy; how beautiful upon the mountains are the feet of those that bring glad tidings of good things; and that say unto Zion, behold! thy God reign-

30 eth. As the dews of Carmel, so shall the knowledge of God descend upon them."

20 And again, what do we hear? Glad tidings from Cumorah! Moroni, an angel from heaven, declaring the fulfilment of the proph-

35 ets—the book to be revealed. A voice of the

428   COVENANTS AND

Lord in the wilderness of Fayette, Seneca
county, declaring the three witnesses to bear
record of the book.   The voice of Michael on
the banks of the Susquehanna, detecting the
devil when he appeared as an angel of light.
The voice of Peter, James, and John, in the
wilderness between Harmony, Susquehanna
county, and Colesville, Broome county, on
the Susquehanna river, declaring themselves
as possessing the keys of the kingdom, and of
the dispensation of the fulness of times.

21 And again, the voice of God in the
chamber of old father Whitmer, in Fayette,
Seneca county, and at sundry times, and in
divers places, through all the travels and tribulations of this Church of Jesus Christ of Latter day Saints.   And the voice of Michael,
the archangel; the voice of Gabriel, and of
Raphael, and of divers angels, from Michael
or Adam, down to the present time, all declaring each one their dispensation, their rights,
their keys, their honors, their majesty and
glory, and the power of their priesthood; giving line upon line, precept upon precept;
here a little, and there a little—giving us consolation by holding forth that which is to
come, confirming our hope.

22 Brethren shall we not go on in so great
a cause? Go forward and not backward.—
Courage, brethren; and on, on to the victory!
Let your hearts rejoice, and be exceeding glad.
Let the earth break forth into singing. Let
the dead speak forth anthems of eternal praise
to the King Immanuel, who hath ordained
before the world was, that which would ena-

line 1   ble us to redeem them out of their prisons; for the prisoners shall go free.

23 Let the mountains shout for joy, and all ye valleys cry aloud; and all ye seas and dry lands tell the wonders of your eternal King. And ye rivers, and brooks, and rills, flow down with gladness. Let the woods, and all the trees of the field praise the Lord; and ye solid rocks weep for joy. And let the sun, moon, and the morning stars sing together, and let all the sons of God shout for joy.— And let the eternal creations declare his name for ever and ever. And again I say, how glorious is the voice we hear from heaven, proclaiming in our ears, glory, and salvation, and honor, and immortality, and eternal life: kingdoms, principalities, and powers.

24 Behold the great day of the Lord is at hand, and who can abide the day of his coming, and who can stand when he appeareth, for he is like a refiners fire and like fullers soap; and he shall sit as a refiner and purifier of silver, and he shall purify the sons of Levi, and purge them as gold and silver, that they may offer unto the Lord an offering in righteousness. Let us therefore, as a church and a people, and as Latter day Saints, offer unto the Lord an offering in righteousness, and let us present in his holy temple when it is finished, a book containing the records of our dead, which shall be worthy of all acceptation.

25 Brethren, I have many things to say to you on the subject; but shall now close for the present, and continue the subject another time.

430   COVENANTS AND

line 1   I am, as ever, your humble servant an1
never deviating friend,

JOSEPH SMITH.

SECTION CVII.

5   *Revelation, given at Far West, Missouri, Ju-*
ly 8, 1838,

In answer to the question: O Lord shew
unto thy servants how much thou requirest of
the properties of thy people for a tithing?
10   1 Verily thus saith the Lord, I require all
their surplus property to be put into the
hands of the bishop of my church of Zion, for
the building of mine house, and for the laying
the foundation of Zion, and for the priesthood,
15   and for the debts of the presidency of my
church; and this shall be the beginning of the
tithing of my people: and after that, those
who have thus been tithed, shall pay one
tenth of all their interest annually, and this
20   shall be a standing law unto them forever, for
my holy priesthood, saith the Lord.
2 Verily I say unto you, it shall come to
pass, that all those who gather unto the land
of Zion shall be tithed of their surplus proper-
25   ties, and shall observe this law, or they shall
not be found worthy to abide among you.—
And I say unto you, if my people observe
snot this law, to keep it holy, and by this law
sanctify the land of Zion unto me, that my
30   statutes and my judgments, may be kept
thereon, that it may be most holy, behold,
verily I say unto you, it shall not be a land of

---

line 4. Revelation, 8 July 1838–C [D&C 119]. Editing marks made in JS's journal are reflected in both
this version and the version in the 15 August 1844 issue of *Times and Seasons*. Because the newspaper version and the version printed here appeared within a month of each other, it is difficult to determine which
was set in type first. (See Revelation, 8 July 1838–C, in JS, Journal, 8 July 1838, in *JSP,* J1:288 [D&C
119]; and "A Word to the Wise," *Times and Seasons,* 15 Aug. 1844, 5:618.)

line 1 Zion unto you: and this shall be an ensample unto all the stakes of Zion: even so, Amen.

SECTION CVIII.

APPENDIX.

5 1 Hearken, O ye people of my church, saith the Lord your God, and hear the word of the Lord concerning you; the Lord who shall suddenly come to his temple: the Lord who shall come down upon the world with a *10* curse to judgment; yea, upon all the nations that forget God, and upon all the ungodly among you. For he shall make bare his holy arm in the eyes of all the nations, and all the ends of the earth shall see the salvation of *15* their God.

2 Wherefore prepare ye, prepare ye, O my people; sanctify yourselves; gather ye together, O ye people of my church, upon the land of Zion, all you that have not been com-*20* manded to tarry. Go ye out from Babylon. Be ye clean that bear the vessels of the Lord. Call your solemn assemblies, and speak often one to another. And let every man call upon the name of the Lord; yea, verily I say unto *25* you again, the time has come when the voice of the Lord is unto you, go ye out of Baby-lon; gather ye out from among the nations, from the four winds, from one end of heaven to the other.

30 3 Send forth the elders of my church unto the nations which are afar off; unto the isl-ands of the sea; send forth unto foreign lands;

---

line 3. Revelation, 3 Nov. 1831 [D&C 133]. This section and three others were included at the end of the 1844 Doctrine and Covenants but are not reproduced here. (See pp. 641–642 herein.)

REFERENCE
MATERIAL

Chronology for the Years 1831–1835, 1844

This brief chronology emphasizes events related to Mormon record keeping and publication efforts, particularly the recording and publishing of revelations. The chronology begins in 1831, when scribes began recording revelations in Revelation Book 1, and ends in 1844, the year the second edition of the Doctrine and Covenants was published. For broader historical context, see the Journals series and the Documents series of *The Joseph Smith Papers*. Readers wishing to conduct further research may also consult the documented chronology posted on the Joseph Smith Papers website.

1831

ca. March		John Whitmer began copying existing revelations and other items into Revelation Book 1, Ohio.
July	20	Revelation appointing William W. Phelps as church printer, Independence, Jackson County, Missouri.
ca. September		William W. Phelps instructed at Hiram, Ohio, to purchase press and type for Jackson County printing operation.
October	mid	William W. Phelps departed Kirtland, Ohio, for move to Independence.
November	1	Revelation designated as preface to forthcoming Book of Commandments; church conference resolved to publish ten thousand copies of volume, Hiram.
	3	Revelation designated as appendix to Book of Commandments.
	8	Sidney Rigdon commented on errors in revelations at church conference, Hiram. JS appointed to "correct those errors or mistakes which he may discover by the holy Spirit."
	11	Revelation at Hiram directing John Whitmer to continue writing history and to carry revelations to Missouri on journey with Oliver Cowdery.
	12	JS, Martin Harris, Oliver Cowdery, John Whitmer, and Sidney Rigdon appointed at Hiram as stewards over JS revelations. (These five and William W. Phelps later formed Literary Firm.) JS blessed Oliver Cowdery and John Whitmer and dedicated revelations to be carried to Missouri.
	20	Oliver Cowdery and John Whitmer departed Kirtland for journey to Missouri, carrying revelations with them.

1832

January	5	Oliver Cowdery and John Whitmer arrived in Independence.
	by 23	William W. Phelps arrived in Independence, bringing the printing press he had been instructed to purchase in Cincinnati, Ohio.
	25	JS appointed "President of the High Priesthood," Amherst, Ohio.
February	16	JS and Sidney Rigdon's vision of degrees of heavenly glory, Hiram.
	23	Prospectus for *The Evening and the Morning Star* published, Independence.
ca. February		Frederick G. Williams and JS began copying existing revelations and other items into Revelation Book 2, Ohio.
March	8	JS selected Sidney Rigdon and Jesse Gause as counselors in presidency of the high priesthood, Hiram.
April	early	JS, Sidney Rigdon, and others purchased paper in Wheeling, Virginia, for printing press in Independence. They continued on to Missouri.
	30	Literary Firm decided to print only three thousand copies of Book of Commandments, Independence. At same meeting, William W. Phelps, Oliver Cowdery, and John Whitmer appointed to select revelations for publication and to "make all necessary verbal corrections."
May	29	Edward Partridge dedicated printing office in Independence.
June		First issues of *The Evening and the Morning Star* and *Upper Missouri Advertiser* published on Mormon press, Independence.
ca. Summer		JS 1832 history written, Hiram.
November	27	JS began first Ohio journal, a record kept intermittently over next two years.
ca. November		JS and Frederick G. Williams began copying letters, largely sent by JS, into JS Letterbook 1, Kirtland.
December		Book of Commandments in press by this time, Independence.
ca. December		Frederick G. Williams began copying minutes of meetings into Minute Book 1, Kirtland.

1833

January	by 22	Frederick G. Williams selected as counselor to JS in presidency of the high priesthood, Kirtland.
February	13	Copyright for Book of Commandments secured, Missouri.
May	ca. late	Three gatherings of the Book of Commandments printed by this time.
June	6	Latter-day Saints began construction on temple, Kirtland.
	25	From Kirtland, JS sent plat for city of Zion with temple plan to Missouri Latter-day Saints.
July	2	JS concluded work on Bible revision, Kirtland.
	20	Vigilantes, demanding removal of Latter-day Saints from Jackson County, destroyed printing office and tarred and feathered

		Edward Partridge and Charles Allen, Independence. Few copies of unfinished Book of Commandments are known to have survived.
August	2	Revelation commanding Saints to build printing establishment in Kirtland to publish Bible revision and other works, Kirtland.
	9	Oliver Cowdery arrived in Kirtland with news of Jackson County citizens' demands for expulsion of Latter-day Saints.
September	11	Kirtland members of Literary Firm established press under name "F. G. Williams & Co.," Kirtland.
October	1	Oliver Cowdery departed Kirtland for New York with eight hundred dollars to purchase printing press.
	5	JS departed Kirtland on journey to Mount Pleasant, Upper Canada, to proselytize.
	ca. 26	Oliver Cowdery returned to Kirtland from journey to New York.
November	4	JS returned to Kirtland from journey to Mount Pleasant.
	25	JS notified by Orson Hyde and John Gould that Latter-day Saints had been expelled from Jackson County earlier in month, Kirtland.
December	18	JS and others gathered in printing office to dedicate press and view proof sheet of fifteenth issue of *The Evening and the Morning Star,* marking first issue published following destruction of Missouri printing office, Kirtland.

1834

ca. January		Four revelations printed as broadsides, Kirtland.
February	17	JS organized first high council, Kirtland.
April	19	JS and others blessed Oliver Cowdery and Sidney Rigdon to continue selecting and arranging revelations for publication, Norton, Ohio.
	23	Revelation appointing Oliver Cowdery and Frederick G. Williams to oversee printing office, directing that copyrights be secured for Bible revision and future publication of revelations, and mandating establishment of treasury to house sacred writings before publication, Kirtland.
May	5	JS departed Kirtland for Missouri at head of Camp of Israel expedition (later known as Zion's Camp) to restore Mormons to Missouri land. Oliver Cowdery and Sidney Rigdon remained in Kirtland.
June	22	Revelation in Washington Township, Clay County, Missouri, indicating that redemption of Zion must "wait for a little season" until elders were "endowed with power from on high" in Kirtland temple.
July	3	Church high council organized in Missouri with David Whitmer appointed president and William W. Phelps and John Whitmer appointed assistants, Liberty, Clay County.
August	ca. 1	JS returned to Kirtland from expedition to Missouri.
September	24	Kirtland high council appointed JS, Oliver Cowdery, Sidney Rigdon, and Frederick G. Williams to arrange and publish revelations.

October		First issue of *LDS Messenger and Advocate* published, Kirtland; Oliver Cowdery appointed editor.
December	5	JS ordained Oliver Cowdery an assistant president of the high priesthood, Kirtland.

1835

January		First issue of *Evening and Morning Star* (edited reprint of *The Evening and the Morning Star*) published, Kirtland.
	14	Copyright for Doctrine and Covenants secured, Ohio.
February		First issue of political newspaper *Northern Times* published on Mormon press, Kirtland.
	14	Three Witnesses to the Book of Mormon selected Quorum of the Twelve Apostles, Kirtland.
	17	JS and counselors wrote preface to Doctrine and Covenants, Kirtland.
	28	JS organized Quorum of the Seventy, Kirtland.
May	16	John Whitmer and William W. Phelps arrived in Kirtland from Clay County to participate in dedication of Kirtland temple.
	late	First six gatherings of Doctrine and Covenants set in type by this time.
		John Whitmer replaced Oliver Cowdery as editor of *LDS Messenger and Advocate,* Kirtland; William W. Phelps began assisting with editorial duties.
July	early	JS purchased Egyptian mummies and papyri associated with later book of Abraham translation, Kirtland.
August	17	Church conference approved publication of Doctrine and Covenants, Kirtland.
September	mid	First copies of Doctrine and Covenants arrived from Cleveland bindery by this time and available for purchase at one dollar per copy, Kirtland.
	16	Samuel Smith and David Whitmer assigned "to act in the name of and for the literary firm," Kirtland.

Editorial Note

The effort to publish a second edition of the Doctrine and Covenants began after the Saints were driven from Missouri in 1838 and 1839 and after they established a settlement near the Mississippi River. Ebenezer Robinson began to set the type for a new edition in the early part of 1841. However, Robinson's work at the Nauvoo, Illinois, printing establishment ended after the Quorum of the Twelve assumed control of the operation in accordance with a revelation of January 1842. Other priorities delayed publication of the Doctrine and Covenants. In February 1843, Wilford Woodruff resumed the stereotyping work. Later that year, the Twelve were appointed to raise money to buy paper for the second edition of the Doctrine and Covenants, suggesting that the work was nearing completion.

1844

January	29	JS nominated as candidate for president of United States, Nauvoo.
February		John Taylor published fifteen hundred copies of a twelve-page pamphlet titled *General Smith's Views of the Powers and Policy of the Government of the United States,* Nauvoo. Demand for pamphlet prompted two subsequent 1844 reprintings by Taylor in Nauvoo.
April	7	At church conference, JS delivered funeral sermon for King Follett, Nauvoo.
June	7	First issue of *Nauvoo Expositor* urged repeal of Nauvoo charter and accused JS of unfairly limiting economic competition, perverting church doctrines, and practicing "abominations and whoredoms," Nauvoo.
	10	Nauvoo City Council declared *Nauvoo Expositor* a public nuisance and ordered city marshal to destroy the press.
	by 11	John Taylor published third edition of Parley P. Pratt's *A Voice of Warning,* Nauvoo.
	25	JS surrendered with brother Hyrum Smith to authorities in Carthage, Illinois; justice of the peace Robert Smith ordered them held without bail until 29 June, when a material witness could appear. John Taylor and Willard Richards remained with Smiths in jail.
	27	While in custody at Carthage jail, JS and Hyrum Smith killed by armed mob just after 5:00 p.m.; John Taylor severely wounded.
	30	*Nauvoo Neighbor* published first official Mormon statement on deaths of JS and Hyrum Smith. Several subsequent articles and tracts offered accounts of the tragedy.
August		Second edition of Doctrine and Covenants printed and available for purchase by this time.

Directory of Printers

This directory provides information about individuals who assisted, or who may have assisted, in preparing, typesetting, or printing the publications that are reproduced in this volume. The directory is divided into two parts: Part 1 identifies individuals who worked in church printing offices and members of two groups tasked with supporting publishing efforts. Part 2 comprises biographical sketches of ten individuals known to have been directly involved in the publication of the revelations.

The first table in part 1 identifies all individuals known to have worked in church printing offices when the revelations reproduced in this volume were being printed. Individuals are included even if it is not known that they worked specifically on printing the revelations. The second table in part 1 identifies members of the Literary Firm and the United Firm, organizations responsible for overseeing and providing monetary support for the publication of the revelations.

Part 2 of this directory provides biographical sketches for those individuals known to have assisted specifically in printing the revelations or preparing them for publication, even if they did not work directly in the church's printing offices. While these individuals may have assisted in typesetting and printing the revelations, they may also have compiled and edited the revelations or performed other intellectual work that preceded printing.

The difference in the criteria for inclusion between parts 1 and 2 can be illustrated by the cases of Elias Smith and Frederick G. Williams. Elias Smith's journal indicates that he worked in the church printing office in Nauvoo, Illinois, from 1843 to 1846 as a manager of two newspapers. Because the 1844 edition of the Doctrine and Covenants was being printed at this time in Nauvoo, it is possible Smith assisted in printing that volume. He is therefore listed in the first table in part 1. However, since known evidence does not confirm that he actually assisted with printing the Doctrine and Covenants, he does not have a biographical sketch in part 2. A biographical sketch for Frederick G. Williams, on the other hand, appears in part 2 because Williams was a member of the committee assigned to publish the 1835 Doctrine and Covenants and because he was an owner of F. G. Williams & Co., which published that book. Though he was a major player in publishing the revelations, he does not appear in the first table of part 1 because known evidence does not indicate that he worked directly in a church printing office.

Many people who were involved in printing efforts for the church between 1832 and 1844 are not included in this directory because evidence clearly indicates they did not assist with printing the publications featured in this volume. For example, this directory does not give information about Thomas B. Marsh, publisher of the issues of *Elders' Journal of the Church of Jesus Christ of Latter Day Saints* printed in Far West, Missouri, in 1838.

Documentation for the information in this directory is available on the Joseph Smith Papers website, josephsmithpapers.org.

Part 1: Likely Contributors to Publication of the Revelations

The first table below lists in alphabetical order all named individuals known to have worked in the church's printing offices in Independence, Missouri; Kirtland, Ohio; and Nauvoo, Illinois, when the publications reproduced in this volume were being printed. Individuals are included even if it is not known that they worked specifically on printing the revelations. The first column identifies individuals who worked in the Independence printing office. The second column lists individuals who worked in the Kirtland printing office. The third column identifies those who worked in the printing office in Nauvoo.

The second table lists in alphabetical order the members of the Literary Firm and the United Firm, two organizations that were closely involved with publishing the revelations in the early 1830s. The first column identifies the members of the Literary Firm, and the second column lists members of the United Firm.

Short overviews of the activities of each printing office or organization precede the relevant tables.

Table 1: Individuals Working in Church Printing Offices

INDEPENDENCE, MISSOURI

Fourteen issues of *The Evening and the Morning Star* were published in the church printing office in Independence, Missouri, between June 1832 and July 1833. Of those issues, twelve included one or more revelation texts. The Book of Commandments was typeset and printed in the same office, beginning probably in late 1832 and continuing to July 1833, when the office was destroyed. The Independence printing office also published a community newspaper and one or more miscellaneous publications.

KIRTLAND, OHIO

Following the destruction of the printing office in Missouri, the church resumed printing *The Evening and the Morning Star* in Kirtland, Ohio. No revelations, however, were included in the ten issues published in Ohio. Beginning in January 1835, all twenty-four issues of the *Star* were edited and reprinted in Kirtland under the title *Evening and Morning Star*. The twelve issues of the original newspaper that contained revelations were reprinted in the following months: January to April 1835, June 1835, September 1835, and April to June 1836 (see table on page 201 herein). Issues of *Evening and Morning Star* did not state who edited the publication, but Oliver Cowdery, the editor of the Kirtland *Latter Day Saints' Messenger and Advocate* (the successor newspaper to *The Evening and the Morning Star*), is known to have been responsible for printing *Evening and Morning Star* as well. The first edition of the Doctrine and Covenants was typeset and printed in the Kirtland office, beginning likely in February 1835 and continuing until the volume was completed circa September 1835. The Kirtland printing office also published a second edition of the Book of Mormon, two issues of *Elders' Journal of the Church of Latter Day Saints,* a hymnal, a community newspaper, and a number of broadsides and other items.

NAUVOO, ILLINOIS

Work on the second edition of the Doctrine and Covenants began in spring 1841 in the church printing office in Nauvoo, Illinois, and continued, with interruptions, until the volume was published circa August 1844. Reprints of the volume were authorized in 1845 and 1846. The Nauvoo printing office also published the church newspaper *Times and Seasons,* a third edition of the Book of Mormon, a hymnal, a community newspaper named *The Wasp* (later renamed *Nauvoo Neighbor*), many broadsides and books, and other items.

INDEPENDENCE	KIRTLAND	NAUVOO
Oliver Cowdery	Samuel Brannan	Ariah Brower
Solomon Wilbur Denton	James Carrell	Joseph Cain
William Hobert	Oliver Cowdery	George Q. Cannon
William W. Phelps	Warren Cowdery	William Conner
John Whitmer	Solomon Wilbur Denton	Matthias Cowley
	William W. Phelps	Lyman Gaylord
	Ebenezer Robinson	John Greenhow
	Don Carlos Smith	George Hales
	John Whitmer	Hartley
	Phineas Young	Ann Hatfield
		Reuben Hedlock
		Francis Higbee
		Gustavus Hills
		Chauncey Jennings
		Lyman Littlefield
		William W. Phelps
		John Regan
		Willard Richards
		Ebenezer Robinson
		Gilbert H. Rolfe
		William Rowley
		Alfred Smith
		Don Carlos Smith
		Elias Smith
		Joseph Smith Jr.
		William Smith
		John Taylor
		William Taylor
		Robert B. Thompson
		Horace Whitney
		Wilford Woodruff

Table 2: Members of the Literary Firm and the United Firm

LITERARY FIRM

In November 1831, a revelation charged a group of men, later called the Literary Firm, to oversee publication of JS's revelations. The firm's primary focus and accomplishment was printing the Book of Commandments. After the Mormons were driven out of Jackson County, Missouri, in 1833, responsibility for printing the revelations was transferred to F. G. Williams & Co. in Kirtland, Ohio, a company that was largely made up of Literary Firm members. Thereafter, the activity of the Literary Firm slowly decreased, though the firm continued to exist through the mid-1830s.

UNITED FIRM

Acting in accordance with revelation, JS established a company called the United Firm in April 1832. Its role was, among other things, to provide monetary support to the Literary Firm to assist with publishing the Book of Commandments. After the Mormons were driven out of Jackson County, Missouri, in 1833, the United Firm established a new press in Kirtland, Ohio, that was operated by F. G. Williams & Co. Many of the responsibilities of the United Firm were gradually assumed by church high councils in Missouri and Ohio. The firm was terminated in 1834.

LITERARY FIRM	UNITED FIRM
Oliver Cowdery	Oliver Cowdery
Martin Harris	Jesse Gause
William W. Phelps	Sidney Gilbert
Sidney Rigdon	Martin Harris
Joseph Smith Jr.	John Johnson Sr.
John Whitmer	Edward Partridge
	William W. Phelps
	Sidney Rigdon
	Joseph Smith Jr.
	John Whitmer
	Newel K. Whitney
	Frederick G. Williams

PART 2: BIOGRAPHICAL SKETCHES

The following biographical sketches provide information about the individuals who are known to have assisted in preparing, typesetting, or printing the revelations in the publications featured in this volume. Evidence clearly supports that these individuals were directly involved in publishing the revelations, though they may not have worked in the church's printing offices. While some of the individuals listed below were, in fact, involved in the printing of revelation texts, others edited, compiled, or otherwise prepared the revelations for publication but may not have been involved in the actual printing of them.

These entries identify individuals by complete name (correctly spelled), birth and death dates, and additional information, such as parentage and birthplace, migrations and places of residence, dates of marriage and names of spouses, occupation and denominational affiliations, religious and civic positions, and place of death. The entries emphasize scribal assignments and activities related to printing and publishing. Because unverified and sometimes incorrect data has been recirculated for decades, professional genealogists on the staff of the Joseph Smith Papers Project have utilized original sources to ensure accuracy.

In these sketches, "LDS church" refers to the church established by JS in 1830 and later known as the Church of Jesus Christ of Latter-day Saints. Locations that are noted include city or town, county, and state, when identified, for the first mention of a locale in each sketch. Each entry in this directory provides, of necessity, only a bare skeleton of a person's life. Readers wishing to conduct further research may consult the documented biographical directory posted on the Joseph Smith Papers website.

Cowdery, Oliver (3 Oct. 1806–3 Mar. 1850); clerk, teacher, justice of the peace, lawyer, newspaper editor; born at Wells, Rutland Co., Vermont. Son of William Cowdery and Rebecca Fuller. Taught term as local schoolmaster at Manchester, Ontario Co., New York, 1828–1829. Assisted JS as principal scribe in translation of Book of Mormon, 1829. With JS, received Aaronic and Melchizedek priesthoods and baptized, 1829. Moved to Fayette, Seneca Co., New York, and was one of the Three Witnesses of the Book of Mormon, June 1829. Helped oversee printing of Book of Mormon by E. B. Grandin, 1829–1830. Among six original members of church, 6 Apr. 1830. Assisted JS as scribe in revision of Bible, 1830. Led missionaries through Ohio and to Missouri, 1830–1831. With John Whitmer, left Ohio to take revelations to Missouri for publication, Nov. 1831. Assisted William W. Phelps in conducting church's printing operations, which included printing revelations in *The Evening and the Morning Star* and Book of Commandments, at Jackson Co., Missouri, 1832–1833. Married Elizabeth Ann Whitmer, 1832, in Jackson Co. Moved to Kirtland, Geauga Co., Ohio, ca. 1833. Member of United Firm, Literary Firm, and Kirtland high council. Appointed assistant president of church, 5 Dec. 1834. Edited Kirtland continuation of *The Evening and the Morning Star,* 1833, and edited reprint under modified title *Evening and Morning Star,* 1835–1836. Edited *LDS Messenger and Advocate,* 1834–1835, 1836–1837, and *Northern Times,* 1835. Served as church recorder, 1830–1831, 1835–1837. Member of publications committee that printed Doctrine and Covenants, 1834–1835. Assisted in publishing second edition of Book of Mormon, 1837. Moved to Far West, Caldwell Co., Missouri, 1837. Excommunicated, 1838. Returned to Kirtland, 1838, and briefly practiced law. Moved to Tiffin, Seneca Co., Ohio, where he continued law practice and held political offices, 1840–1847. Moved to Elkhorn, Walworth Co., Wisconsin Territory, 1847. Coeditor of *Walworth County Democrat,* 1848. Requested and received readmission to LDS church, Kanesville, Pottawattamie Co., Iowa, 1848. Died at Richmond, Ray Co., Missouri.

Phelps, William Wines (17 Feb. 1792–7 Mar. 1872); writer, teacher, printer, newspaper editor, publisher, postmaster, lawyer; born at Hanover, Morris Co., New Jersey. Son of Enon Phelps and Mehitabel Goldsmith. Married Sally Waterman, 28 Apr. 1815, in Smyrna, Chenango Co., New York. Editor of *Western Courier.* Edited Anti-Masonic newspaper *Lake Light* at Trumansburg, Tompkins Co., New York. Published Anti-Masonic newspaper *Ontario Phoenix* at Canandaigua, Ontario Co., New York. Obtained copy of Book of Mormon, 1830. Met JS, 21 Dec. 1830. Migrated to Kirtland, Geauga Co., Ohio, 1831. Baptized at Kirtland, 10 June 1831. Ordained an elder by JS, June 1831, at Kirtland. Appointed church printer, 20 July 1831. Ordained a high priest, 1831. Moved to Jackson Co., Missouri, Oct. 1831. Member of Literary Firm and United Firm, 1831–1836. Became editor of *The Evening and the Morning Star* and *Upper Missouri Advertiser,* published 1832–1833 at Independence, Jackson Co. Published Book of Commandments, but most copies destroyed by mob action when printing office razed, 20 July 1833. Exiled from Jackson Co. to Clay Co., Missouri, Nov. 1833. Appointed counselor/assistant president to David Whitmer, president of chuch in Missouri, 3 July 1834. Returned to Kirtland and served as JS's scribe. Helped compile Doctrine and Covenants and first Latter-day Saint hymnal, 1835, at Kirtland. Prolific writer of hymns. Appointed to draft rules and regulations for Kirtland temple, 14 Jan. 1836. Returned from Kirtland to Clay Co., where he resumed duties with Missouri presidency, 1836. Appointed postmaster, 27 May 1837, at Far West, Caldwell Co., Missouri. Excommunicated, 17 Mar. 1838. Moved to Dayton, Montgomery Co., Ohio, before Mar. 1840. Reconciled with church, July 1840; rebaptized, 1841. Returned to Kirtland, by May 1841. Appointed to serve mission to eastern U.S., 23 May 1841. Appointed assistant church historian, 27 Aug. 1841. Appointed recorder of church licenses, 3 Oct. 1841, in Kirtland. Moved to Nauvoo, Hancock Co., Illinois, by Dec. 1841. Acted as clerk to JS and assisted John Taylor in editing *Times and Seasons* and *Nauvoo Neighbor.* Assisted with publishing of 1844 Doctrine and Covenants, 1843. Elected to Nauvoo City Council, early 1844. Member of Council of Fifty, by 11 Mar. 1844. Migrated to Salt Lake Valley, 1848. Died at Salt Lake City.

Richards, Willard (24 June 1804–11 Mar. 1854); teacher, lecturer, doctor, clerk, printer, editor, postmaster; born at Hopkinton, Middlesex Co., Massachusetts. Son of Joseph Richards and Rhoda Howe. Moved to Kirtland, Geauga Co., Ohio, by Dec. 1836. Baptized by Brigham Young, 31 Dec. 1836, in Kirtland. Appointed to serve mission to eastern U.S., 13 Mar. 1837. Served mission to England, 1837–1841. Married Jennetta Richards, 24 Sept. 1838, in Walker Ford, Chaigley, Lancashire, England. Ordained member of Quorum of the Twelve, 14 Apr. 1840, at Preston, Lancashire, England. Moved to Nauvoo, Hancock Co., Illinois. Moved to Warsaw, Hancock Co., 31 Aug. 1841; returned to Nauvoo, 1841. Before death of JS, completed personal history of JS up to Aug. 1838. Elected to Nauvoo City Council, 1841. Appointed recorder for Nauvoo temple, private secretary to JS, and church clerk, 13 Dec. 1841. Joined Nauvoo Masonic Lodge, 7 Apr. 1842. Appointed church historian, Dec. 1842; church recorder, 30 July 1843; and Nauvoo city recorder, Aug. 1843. Served as major in Nauvoo Legion. Participated in plural marriage during JS's lifetime. Copied revelations for and read proofs of the 1844 Doctrine and Covenants, 1843. With JS in jail in Carthage, Hancock Co., when JS and Hyrum Smith were murdered, 27 June 1844. Moved to Winter Quarters, unorganized U.S. territory (now in Omaha, Douglas Co., Nebraska), 1846. Migrated to Salt Lake Valley and returned to Winter Quarters, 1847. Appointed second counselor to Brigham Young in church presidency, 27 Dec. 1847, at Council Point (later Council Bluffs), Pottawattamie Co., Iowa. Returned to Salt Lake Valley. Editor of *Deseret News.* Died at Salt Lake City.

Rigdon, Sidney (19 Feb. 1793–14 July 1876); tanner, farmer, minister; born at St. Clair, Allegheny Co., Pennsylvania. Son of William Rigdon and Nancy Gallaher. Married Phebe Brook, 12 June 1820, at Warren, Trumbull Co., Ohio. Joined Reformed Baptist (later Disciples of Christ or Campbellite) movement and was influential preacher. Introduced to Mormonism by his former proselyte to Reformed Baptist faith, Parley P. Pratt, who was en route with Oliver Cowdery and others on mission to unorganized Indian Territory. Baptized into LDS church by Oliver Cowdery, Nov. 1830. Scribe for JS, 1830. Member of Literary Firm and United Firm, 1831–1838. Ordained a high priest by Lyman Wight, 4 June 1831, in Kirtland, Geauga Co., Ohio. Counselor/assistant president in church presidency, 1832–1844. Accompanied JS to Upper Canada on proselytizing mission and helped keep JS's diary during trip, 1833. Member of publications committee that printed Doctrine and Covenants, 1834–1835. Arrived at Far West, Caldwell Co., Missouri, from Kirtland, 4 Apr. 1838. With JS in jail at Liberty, Clay Co., Missouri, Nov. 1838–Feb. 1839. After release, found refuge at Quincy, Adams Co., Illinois. Accompanied JS to Washington DC to seek redress for Missouri grievances, 1839–1840. Member of city council in Nauvoo, Hancock Co., Illinois. Claimed right to lead church after death of JS; excommunicated, 1844. Moved to Pittsburgh to lead schismatic Church of Jesus Christ of Latter Day Saints, 1844; name of church changed to Church of Christ, 1845. Removed to Friendship, Allegany Co., New York, where he died.

Robinson, Ebenezer (25 May 1816–11 Mar. 1891); printer, editor, publisher; born at Floyd (near Rome), Oneida Co., New York. Son of Nathan Robinson and Mary Brown. Moved to Utica, Oneida Co., ca. 1831, and learned printing trade at *Utica Observer.* Moved to Ravenna, Portage Co., Ohio, Aug. 1833, and worked as compositor on *The Ohio Star.* Moved to Kirtland, Geauga Co., Ohio, May 1835, and worked in printing office, 1835–1837. Baptized by JS, 16 Oct. 1835. Married first Angelina (Angeline) Eliza Works, 13 Dec. 1835, at Kirtland. Ordained an elder, 29 Apr. 1836, and a seventy, 20 Dec. 1836. Served mission to Richland Co., Ohio, June–July 1836, and shortly after served mission to New York. Moved to Far West, Caldwell Co., Missouri, spring 1837. Assisted with publication of *Elders' Journal,* summer 1838. Church clerk and recorder and clerk of Missouri high council, 1838. Member of Far West high council, Dec. 1838. When driven from Missouri, moved to Quincy, Adams Co., Illinois, and worked on *Quincy Whig,* 1839. Became publisher, co-editor, and editor of *Times and Seasons,* 1839–1842, at Commerce (later Nauvoo), Hancock Co., Illinois. Oversaw publication of 1840 edition of Book of Mormon, 1840. Began stereotyping 1844 Doctrine and Covenants, 1841. Served mission to New York, 1843. Affiliated with Sidney Rigdon and served as his counselor. Moved to Pittsburgh, June 1844. Moved to Greencastle, Franklin Co., Pennsylvania, May 1846, where he edited Rigdonite *Messenger and Advocate of the Church of Christ.* Baptized into RLDS church by William W. Blair, 29 Apr. 1863, at Pleasanton, Hamilton Township, Decatur Co., Iowa. Wife died, 1880. Married second Martha A. Cunningham, 5 Feb. 1885. Affiliated with David Whitmer's Church of Christ, 1888. Edited Whitmerite periodical *The Return,* 1889–1891. Died at Davis City, Decatur Co.

Smith, Joseph (23 Dec. 1805–27 June 1844); for biographical information, see General Introduction: Joseph Smith and His Papers, in *JSP*, J1:xv–xli, and Timeline of Joseph Smith's Life, p. xvii herein.

Taylor, John (1 Nov. 1808–25 July 1887); preacher, editor, publisher, politician; born at Milnthorpe, Westmoreland Co., England. Son of James Taylor and Agnes Taylor. Married Leonora Cannon, 28 Jan. 1833, at York, York Township, York Co., Home District, Upper Canada. Baptized by Parley P. Pratt, 9 May 1836, and ordained an elder shortly after. Appointed to preside over churches in Upper Canada. Ordained a high priest by JS and others, 21 Aug. 1837. Moved to Kirtland, Geauga Co., Ohio. Moved to Far West, Caldwell Co., Missouri, 1838. Ordained member of Quorum of the Twelve by Brigham Young and Heber C. Kimball, 19 Dec. 1838, at Far West. Served mission to England, 1839–1841. In Nauvoo, Hancock Co., Illinois, served as member of city council and judge advocate of Nauvoo Legion. Editor and copublisher of *The Wasp,* 1842–1843. Editor of *Times and Seasons* and *Nauvoo Neighbor,* 1842–1846. Assisted with publishing 1844 Doctrine and Covenants, 1843. Participated in plural marriage during JS's lifetime. With JS in jail in Carthage, Hancock Co., when JS and Hyrum Smith were murdered, 27 June 1844. Served mission to England, 1846–1847. Arrived in Salt Lake Valley, 1847. Served mission to France and Germany, 1849–1852; arranged for translation of Book of Mormon into French and published *L'Etoile du Deseret* (The Star of Deseret). In Germany, supervised translation of Book of Mormon into German and published *Zions Panier* (Zion's Banner). Editor of *The Mormon,* New York City, 1855–1857. Following death of Brigham Young, presided over church from 1877 to 1887. Ordained president of church, 10 Oct. 1880. Died at Kaysville, Davis Co., Utah Territory. Buried in Salt Lake City.

Whitmer, John (27 Aug. 1802–11 July 1878); farmer, stock raiser, newspaper editor; born in Pennsylvania. Son of Peter Whitmer Sr. and Mary Musselman. Evidently baptized by Oliver Cowdery, June 1829, in Seneca Lake, Seneca Co., New York. Acted as scribe during translation of Book of Mormon at Whitmer home. One of the Eight Witnesses of the Book of Mormon, June 1829. Ordained an elder by 9 June 1830. Copied revelations as scribe to JS, July 1830. Acted as scribe for JS during revision of Bible. Sent by JS to Kirtland, Geauga Co., Ohio, ca. Dec. 1830. Appointed church historian, ca. 8 Mar. 1831. Worked on a church history, 1831–ca. 1847. Ordained a high priest, 4 June 1831, at Kirtland. Member of Literary Firm and United Firm, 1831–1836. With Oliver Cowdery, left Ohio to take revelations to Missouri for publication, Nov. 1831. Assisted in church's printing operations at Jackson Co., Missouri, 1832–1833. Married to Sarah Maria Jackson by William W. Phelps, 10 Feb. 1833, at Kaw Township, Jackson Co. Forced to remove from Jackson Co. to Clay Co., Missouri, Nov. 1833. Appointed an assistant to his brother David Whitmer in Missouri church presidency, July 1834. Editor of *LDS Messenger and Advocate,* Kirtland, 1835–1836. Lived in Clay Co., 1836. Helped establish Latter-day Saints at Far West, Caldwell Co., Missouri. Excommunicated, 10 Mar. 1838, at Far West. Left Far West for Richmond, Ray Co., Missouri, June 1838. Returned to Far West after departure of Latter-day Saints. In Sept. 1847, met with his brother David Whitmer and William E. McLellin at Far West in an attempt to reconstitute Church of Christ under presidency of David Whitmer. Died at the site of Far West.

Williams, Frederick Granger (28 Oct. 1787–10 Oct. 1842); ship's pilot, teacher, physician, justice of the peace; born at Suffield, Hartford Co., Connecticut. Son of William Wheeler Williams and Ruth Granger. Married Rebecca Swain, Dec. 1815. Worshipped with Sidney Rigdon's Reformed Baptist (later Disciples of Christ or Campbellite) congregation. Moved to Chardon, Geauga Co., Ohio, by 1828. Moved to Kirtland, Geauga Co., 1830. Baptized into LDS church and ordained an elder, Oct./Nov. 1830, by missionaries under leadership of Oliver Cowdery who were en route to Missouri and unorganized Indian Territory. Accompanied Cowdery to Missouri frontier on mission. Appointed clerk and scribe to JS, 20 July 1832, though acted as scribe for JS as early as Feb.–Mar. 1832. Inscribed Revelation Book 2; parts of JS History, ca. summer 1832; and JS's journal, 1832–1834. Assistant president/counselor in presidency of church, 1833–1837. Became member of United Firm, Mar. 1833. Consecrated by deed to JS roughly 142 prime acres in Kirtland, 1834. Participated in Zion's Camp expedition to Missouri, 1834. Inscribed JS Letterbook 1, Minute Book 1, and numerous revelations; also inscribed JS History, 1834–1836. Editor of *Northern Times* and member of publications committee that printed Doctrine and Covenants and Emma Smith's *A Collection of Sacred Hymns, for the Church of the Latter Day Saints* under auspices of firm F. G. Williams & Co., 1834–1836. Helped organize and was a trustee of School of the Prophets. Removed from church presidency, 7 Nov. 1837. Moved to Far West, Caldwell Co., Missouri, late 1837. Rebaptized into LDS church, before 5 July 1838. An 8 July 1838 JS revelation directed Williams to be ordained an elder and preach abroad. Excommunicated, 17 Mar. 1839, at Quincy, Adams Co., Illinois. Restored to fellowship at Nauvoo, Hancock Co., Illinois, Apr. 1840. Died at Quincy.

Woodruff, Wilford (1 Mar. 1807–2 Sept. 1898); farmer, miller; born at Farmington, Hartford Co., Connecticut. Son of Aphek Woodruff and Beulah Thompson. Baptized by Zera Pulsipher, 31 Dec. 1833, near Richland, Oswego Co., New York. Ordained a teacher, 2 Jan. 1834, at Richland. Moved to Kirtland, Geauga Co., Ohio, Apr. 1834. Participated in Zion's Camp expedition to Missouri, 1834. Ordained a priest, 5 Nov. 1834. Served mission to Arkansas, Tennessee, and Kentucky, 1834–1836. Ordained an elder, 1835. Appointed member of the Seventy, 31 May 1836. Married to Phoebe Carter by Frederick G. Williams, 13 Apr. 1837, at Kirtland. Served missions to New England and Fox Islands off coast of Maine, 1837–1838. Ordained member of Quorum of the Twelve by Brigham Young, 26 Apr. 1839, at Far West, Caldwell Co., Missouri. Served mission to Great Britain, 1839–1841. With John Taylor, published *The Wasp,* 1842–1843. Copublisher of *Times and Seasons* and *Nauvoo Neighbor,* 1842–1844. Assisted in publishing 1844 Doctrine and Covenants, 1843. Served mission to eastern states to raise funds for building Nauvoo temple, 1843. Served mission to eastern states to campaign for JS as candidate for U.S. president, 1844. Presided over British mission, Aug. 1844–Apr. 1846. Member of Brigham Young pioneer company that journeyed to Salt Lake Valley, 1847. Appointed assistant church historian, 7 Apr. 1856. President of Quorum of the Twelve, 1880. Sustained as church historian and general church recorder, 1883. President of church, 7 Apr. 1889–2 Sept. 1898. Died at San Francisco.

Substitute Words in the 1835 and 1844 Editions of the Doctrine and Covenants

In preparation for the publication of the 1835 edition of the Doctrine and Covenants, editors replaced some personal names, place names, and other words with substitute words, in order to obscure certain information from the public. Five revelations in the 1835 edition were revised in this way.[1] Two revelations published in the 1844 edition of the Doctrine and Covenants but not previously included in the 1835 edition also contain substitute words.[2] Using Revelation Books 1 and 2, which often contain the earliest extant manuscript versions of revelations, it is possible to identify the original words that were replaced in the Doctrine and Covenants. In some cases, Revelation Books 1 and 2 also served as the immediate source texts for the typesetting of these revelations and bear the actual editing marks that instructed the typesetter, or the copyist who made clean copy for the typesetter, to insert the substitute words.

According to reminiscences of those close to JS, editors of the 1835 Doctrine and Covenants wished to protect specific individuals and the church's business affairs—specifically the United Firm and the Literary Firm—from those antagonistic toward the church. Orson Pratt recalled that because of the great desire to print certain revelations notwithstanding the sensitive information they included, "it was concluded, through the suggestions of the Spirit, that by altering the *real* names given in the manuscripts, and substituting fictitious ones in their stead, they might thus safely appear in print without endangering the welfare of the individuals whose real names were contained therein."[3] At the time the Doctrine and Covenants was being prepared for publication, church leaders in Kirtland were deeply interested in ancient languages, including Hebrew. Some authors have seen a

---

1. Revelation, 1 Mar. 1832, in Doctrine and Covenants 75, 1835 ed. [D&C 78]; Revelation, 26 Apr. 1832, in Doctrine and Covenants 86, 1835 ed. [D&C 82]; Revelation, 15 Mar. 1833, in Doctrine and Covenants 93, 1835 ed. [D&C 92]; Revelation, 4 June 1833, in Doctrine and Covenants 96, 1835 ed. [D&C 96]; Revelation, 23 Apr. 1834, in Doctrine and Covenants 98, 1835 ed. [D&C 104]. These five revelations were reprinted (with the same substitute words used in the 1835 edition) in the 1844 edition of the Doctrine and Covenants.

2. Revelation, 24 Feb. 1834, in Doctrine and Covenants 101, 1844 ed. [D&C 103]; Revelation, 22 June 1834, in Doctrine and Covenants 102, 1844 ed. [D&C 105]. In contrast to the approach used for the 1835 Doctrine and Covenants, editors of these two sections in the 1844 edition replaced only some of the personal names contained in the texts, leaving other personal names in their original form.

3. Orson Pratt, "Explanation of Substituted Names in the Covenants," *The Seer,* Mar. 1854, 228; emphasis in original. Concerns about divulging sensitive information persisted into the 1840s and in at least one case were manifest outside of the context of publishing the revelations. Willard Richards, while copying a letter dated 25 June 1833 into the JS manuscript history in May 1843, replaced some names with substitute words. That portion of the history was printed with the substitute terms in the 15 February 1845 issue of *Times and Seasons.* (Richards, Journal, 20 May 1843; JS History, vol. A-1, 310–315; "History of Joseph Smith," *Times and Seasons,* 15 Feb. 1845, 6:800–803.)

correlation between some of the substitute words and Hebrew; other scholars have pointed to the Mormons' experimentation with and expectation of the restoration of the pure language of Adam, suggesting some of the substitute words may have arisen from that pursuit.[4] Though several early members later recalled interpretations or translations of many of the substitute words, an analysis of the meaning or origin of the words is beyond the scope of this volume.[5]

The two tables below identify all of the substitute words used in the 1835 and 1844 editions of the Doctrine and Covenants and the original antecedents to those substitute words. The first column of each table lists substitute words in alphabetical order. This column includes not only words that replaced personal or place names but also words (sometimes in English) that replaced common nouns. The second column of each table provides the name or other term that was replaced (that is, the antecedent), based on manuscript evidence. The third column gives the location of the substitute term in the 1835 or 1844 edition of the Doctrine and Covenants. Each section from the 1835 Doctrine and Covenants that is listed below is preceded by a section heading that contains at least one substitute word. Identical substitute words found in the headings and the main text are assumed to have the same antecedents. The fourth and fifth columns, which appear in the first table only, list the page number(s) in Revelation Book 1 or 2 where the antecedent appears. At times editors wrote the substitute words directly on the manuscript; other times, they marked with numerals or asterisks the words that should be replaced. The numerals and asterisks corresponded to now nonextant manuscripts that either listed substitute words or provided a copy of a revelation with the substitute words already incorporated. In cases where a substitute word actually appears on the manuscript page, an asterisk has been placed next to the page number(s) in the fourth or fifth column.

4. See Zucker, "Joseph Smith as a Student of Hebrew," 48–50; Whittaker, "Substituted Names in the Published Revelations of Joseph Smith," 103–112; and Brown, "Joseph (Smith) in Egypt," 26–65.

5. See William W. Phelps, Great Salt Lake City, Utah Territory, to Brigham Young, Great Salt Lake City, Utah Territory, 10 Apr. 1854, Brigham Young, Office Files, CHL; George A. Smith, Discourse, 14 Nov. 1864, George D. Watt, Papers, CHL, as transcribed in Staker, *Hearken, O Ye People,* 581–582; and Orson Pratt, in *Journal of Discourses,* 16 Aug. 1873, 16:156. For a contemporary, non-Mormon perspective on the substitute names, see West, *Few Interesting Facts,* 6–14.

Key to column titles

Substitute Word: Word or phrase used in the 1835 or 1844 edition of the Doctrine and Covenants that replaced a word or phrase found in manuscript versions of the revelation

Antecedent: Word or phrase found in manuscript versions that was replaced in the 1835 or 1844 edition of the Doctrine and Covenants with a substitute word or phrase

1835: Section and verse number(s) where the substitute word or phrase appears in Doctrine and Covenants, 1835 edition, part 2. If the substitute word appears in a section heading rather than a numbered verse, this is noted.

1844: Section and verse number(s) where the substitute word or phrase appears in Doctrine and Covenants, 1844 edition, part 2

RB1: Pages in Revelation Book 1 where the antecedent term appears and where an editorially inserted substitute word may also appear

RB2: Pages in Revelation Book 2 where the antecedent term appears and where an editorially inserted substitute word may also appear

Substitute Word	Antecedent	1835	RB1	RB2
Ahashdah	Newel K. Whitney	75:2 86:4 96:1 98:7	145* 128 195	 60
Alam	Edward Partridge	86:4	128	
Cainhannoch	New York	98:13	198	
Enoch	Joseph Smith	75:section heading, 1–2 93:section heading 96:section heading 98:section heading	145*	 Slip of paper between 60 and 61[6]
Gazelam	Joseph Smith	75:2 86:4 98:4, 8	145* 128 194–195	
Horah	John Whitmer	86:4	128	
inheritance	"farm"	98:4, 6, 8	194*–195	
Lane-shine-house	"printing office"	98:5	194	
Mahalaleel	Sidney Gilbert	86:4	128	
Mehemson	Martin Harris	86:4 98:4	128 194	

---

6. The text on this slip of paper uses substitute words but does not contain any antecedents.

Substitute Word	Antecedent	1835	RB1	RB2
Olihah	Oliver Cowdery	86:4	128	
		98:5–6	194	
order	"firm"	75:2	145*	
		93:1–2		55
		96:1–2		61*
		98:1–3, 6–7, 9, 11–12	192–198	
Ozondah	"store," "mercantile establishment"	98:7	195	
Pelagoram	Sidney Rigdon	75:2	145*	
		86:4	128	
		98:3	193–194	
proclaiming	printing	98:4	194*	
Seth	Joseph[7]	96:2		61*
Shalemanasseh	William W. Phelps	86:4	128	
Shederlaomach	Frederick G. Williams	93:1–2		55
		98:5	194	
Shinehah	Kirtland	86:4	128	
		96:section heading		Slip of paper between 60 and 61[8]
		98:3, 7, 9	194–195	
shinelah	"print"	98:10	196	
shinelane (possibly shine-lane)	"printing"	98:11	197	
Shule	"ashery"	98:7	195	
Son Ahman, the	Jesus Christ	75:4	146*	
Tahhanes	"Tanery"	98:3	193	
talents	"dollars"	98:12	197	
Zion	Israel	75:3	146*	
Zombre	John Johnson	96:2		61*
		98:4, 6	194	

Substitute Word	Antecedent	1844
Baneemy	"mine elders"	102:8
Baurak Ale	Joseph Smith	101:4–6
		102:5, 8

7. This is not JS, but Joseph of the Old Testament.

8. The text on this slip of paper uses substitute words but does not contain any antecedents.

Works Cited

This list of sources serves as a comprehensive guide to all sources cited in this volume (documentation supporting the reference material in the back of this volume may be found at the Joseph Smith Papers website, josephsmithpapers.org). Annotation has been documented with original sources where possible and practical. In entries for manuscript sources, dates identify when the manuscript was created, which is not necessarily the time period the manuscript covers.

Some sources cited in this volume are referred to on first and subsequent occurrences by a conventional shortened citation. For convenience, some documents are referred to by editorial titles rather than by their original titles or by the titles given in the catalogs of their current repositories, in which case the list of works cited provides the editorial title followed by full bibliographic information.

Scriptural References

The annotation within volumes of *The Joseph Smith Papers* includes numerous references to works accepted as scripture by The Church of Jesus Christ of Latter-day Saints. The principal citations of Mormon scripture appearing in annotation are to JS-era published or manuscript versions. However, for reader convenience, these citations also include a bracketed reference to the current and widely available Latter-day Saint scriptural canon. All versions of scripture cited in this volume, early or modern, are identified in the list of works cited.

The church's current scriptural canon consists of the King James (or Authorized) Version of the Bible (KJV), plus three other volumes: the Book of Mormon, the Doctrine and Covenants, and the Pearl of Great Price. The following paragraphs provide more detailed information about uniquely Mormon scriptures and how they are cited in the *Papers*.

Book of Mormon. The first edition of the Book of Mormon was printed for JS in 1830. He oversaw the publication of subsequent editions in 1837 and 1840. The Book of Mormon, like the Bible, consists of a number of shorter books. However, *Papers* volumes cite early editions of the Book of Mormon by page numbers because these editions were not divided into numbered verses. The bracketed references to the modern (1981) Latter-day Saint edition of this work identify the book name with modern chapter and verse.

Doctrine and Covenants. JS authorized publication of early revelations beginning in 1832 in *The Evening and the Morning Star,* the church's first newspaper, and initiated the publication of a compilation of revelations, which first appeared in 1833 under the title Book of Commandments. Revised and expanded versions of this compilation were published in 1835 and 1844 under the title Doctrine and Covenants. Since JS's time, The Church of Jesus Christ of Latter-day Saints has continued to issue revised and expanded versions of the Doctrine and Covenants, as has the Community of Christ (formerly the

Reorganized Church of Jesus Christ of Latter Day Saints). The bracketed references to the modern (1981) Latter-day Saint edition of the Doctrine and Covenants, which cite by section and verse number, use the abbreviation D&C in the place of Doctrine and Covenants. A table titled Corresponding Published Versions of Revelations, which appears after the list of works cited (page 719 herein), can help readers refer from the featured or cited version of a revelation or other item to certain other versions of that same item. For more information about the format of Doctrine and Covenants citations, see the Editorial Method (pages xli–xlii herein).

Joseph Smith Bible revision. Beginning in June 1830, JS systematically reviewed the text of the KJV and made revisions and additions to it. JS largely completed the work in 1833, but only a few excerpts were published in his lifetime. The Reorganized Church of Jesus Christ of Latter Day Saints published the entire work in 1867 under the title Holy Scriptures and included excerpts from the writings of Moses in two sections of its Doctrine and Covenants. The Church of Jesus Christ of Latter-day Saints, which today officially refers to JS's Bible revisions as the Joseph Smith Translation, has never published the entire work, but two excerpts are canonized in the Pearl of Great Price and many other excerpts are included in the footnotes and appendix of the modern (1979) Latter-day Saint edition of the KJV. In the *Papers,* references to JS's Bible revision are cited to the original manuscripts, with a bracketed reference given where possible to the relevant book, chapter, and verse of the Joseph Smith Translation.

Pearl of Great Price. The Pearl of Great Price, a collection of miscellaneous shorter writings that originated with JS, was first published in 1851 and was canonized by The Church of Jesus Christ of Latter-day Saints in 1880. The modern (1981) edition of this work consists of the following: selections from the book of Moses, an extract from JS's Bible revision manuscripts; the book of Abraham, writings translated from papyri JS and others acquired in 1835 and first published in the *Times and Seasons* in 1842; Joseph Smith—Matthew, another extract from JS's Bible revision manuscripts; Joseph Smith—History, a selection from the history JS began working on in 1838; and the Articles of Faith, a statement of beliefs included in a JS letter to Chicago newspaper editor John Wentworth and published in the *Times and Seasons* in 1842. Except in the case of Joseph Smith—History, citations in the *Papers* to early versions of each of these works also include a bracketed reference to the corresponding chapter and verse in the modern Latter-day Saint canon. The Pearl of Great Price is not part of the canon of the Community of Christ. References to the history JS began work on in 1838 are cited to the original manuscript of that history (see entry on "JS History" in the list of works cited).

Abbreviations for Frequently Cited Repositories

BYU   L. Tom Perry Special Collections, Harold B. Lee Library, Brigham Young University, Provo, Utah

CHL   Church History Library, The Church of Jesus Christ of Latter-day Saints, Salt Lake City

FHL   Family History Library, The Church of Jesus Christ of Latter-day Saints, Salt Lake City

Allen, James B. "Emergence of a Fundamental: The Expanding Role of Joseph Smith's First Vision in Mormon Religious Thought." *Journal of Mormon History* 7 (1980): 43–61.

Behold, blessed saith the Lord, are they who have come up unto this land [D&C 59]. [Kirtland, OH: ca. Jan. 1834]. Copy at CHL.

Berrett, LaMar C., ed. *Sacred Places: A Comprehensive Guide to Early LDS Historical Sites.* 6 vols. Salt Lake City: Deseret Book, 1999–2007.

Book of Doctrine and Covenants: Carefully Selected from the Revelations of God, and Given in the Order of Their Dates. Independence, MO: Herald Publishing House, 2004.

Bray, Robert T. "Times and Seasons: An Archaeological Perspective on Early Latter Day Saints Printing." *Historical Archaeology* 13 (1979): 53–119.

Brown, Samuel. "Joseph (Smith) in Egypt: Babel, Hieroglyphs, and the Pure Language of Eden." *Church History: Studies in Christianity and Culture* 78, no. 1 (Mar. 2009): 26–65.

Bushman, Richard Lyman. *Joseph Smith: Rough Stone Rolling.* With the assistance of Jed Woodworth. New York: Knopf, 2005.

———. "Joseph Smith's Many Histories." In "The Worlds of Joseph Smith: A Bicentennial Conference at the Library of Congress," special issue, *BYU Studies* 44, no. 4 (2005): 3–20.

Cannon, M. Hamlin. "Migration of English Mormons to America." *American Historical Review* 52, no. 3 (Apr. 1947): 436–455.

Cook, Lyndon W. *Joseph Smith and the Law of Consecration.* Provo, UT: Grandin Book, 1985.

Copyright for first edition of Doctrine and Covenants, 14 Jan. 1835. Copyright Records, Ohio, 1831–1848 (Department of State). Unnumbered vol. Rare Book and Special Collections Division, Library of Congress, Washington DC.

Cowdery, Oliver. Letterbook, 1833–1838. Henry E. Huntington Library, San Marino, CA.

———. Letter with Joseph Smith postscript, Kirtland Mills, OH, to William W. Phelps, John Whitmer, Edward Partridge, Isaac Morley, John Corrill, and Sidney Gilbert, [Independence, MO], 10 Aug. 1833. CHL.

Crawley, Peter. *A Descriptive Bibliography of the Mormon Church. Vol. 1, 1830–1847.* Provo, UT: Religious Studies Center, Brigham Young University, 1997.

Dahl, Larry E. "Authorship and History of the Lectures on Faith." In *The Lectures on Faith in Historical Perspective,* edited by Larry E. Dahl and Charles D. Tate Jr., 1–21. Provo, UT: Religious Studies Center, Brigham Young University, 1990.

D&C. See *Doctrine and Covenants of the Church of Jesus Christ of Latter-day Saints* (1981).

Deseret News. Salt Lake City. 1850–.

De Vinne, Theodore Low. *The Practice of Typography: A Treatise on the Processes of Type-Making, the Point System, the Names, Sizes, Styles, and Prices of Plain Printing Types.* New York: Century, 1900.

———. *The Printer's Price List: A Manual for the Use of Clerks and Book-Keepers in Job Printing Offices.* New York: Francis Hart, 1871. As excerpted in Richard-Gabriel Rummonds, *Nineteenth-Century Printing Practices and the Iron Handpress,* 2 vols. (New Castle, DE: Oak Knoll Press, 2004).

Doctrine and Covenants, 2004 Community of Christ edition. See *Book of Doctrine and Covenants.*

The Doctrine and Covenants, of the Church of Jesus Christ of Latter-day Saints, Containing the Revelations Given to Joseph Smith, Jun., the Prophet, for the Building Up of the Kingdom of God in the Last Days. Salt Lake City: Deseret News, 1876.

The Doctrine and Covenants of the Church of Jesus Christ of Latter-day Saints: Containing Revelations Given to Joseph Smith, the Prophet, with Some Additions by His Successors in the Presidency of the Church. Salt Lake City: The Church of Jesus Christ of Latter-day Saints, 1981.

Elders' Journal of the Church of Latter Day Saints. Kirtland, OH, Oct.–Nov. 1837; Far West, MO, July–Aug. 1838.

F. G. Williams and Company. Account Book, 1833–1835. CHL.

Gaskell, Philip. *A New Introduction to Bibliography.* New Castle, DE: Oak Knoll Press, 2009.

General Church Minutes, 1839–1877. CHL.

Gilbert, Algernon Sidney. Notebook of Revelations, 1831–ca. 1833. Revelations Collection, 1831–ca. 1844, 1847, 1861, ca. 1876. CHL.

Gladden, Sanford C. "An Early Printing Press Used in Colorado." Unpublished paper. Boulder, CO, 1977. Copy at CHL.

Hartley, William G. "Letters and Mail between Kirtland and Independence: A Mormon Postal History, 1831–33." *Journal of Mormon History* 35, no. 3 (Summer 2009): 163–189.

Historian's Office. Joseph Smith History Documents, ca. 1839–1856. CHL.

Historian's Office. Joseph Smith History Draft Notes, ca. 1840–1880. CHL.

History of the Church / Smith, Joseph, et al. *History of the Church of Jesus Christ of Latter-day Saints.* Edited by B. H. Roberts. Salt Lake City: Deseret News, 1902–1912 (vols. 1–6), 1932 (vol. 7).

Hyde, Orson. Journal, Feb. 1832–Mar. 1833. CHL.

Jensen, Robin Scott. "'Rely upon the Things Which Are Written': Text, Context, and the Creation of Mormon Revelatory Records." Master's thesis, University of Wisconsin-Milwaukee, 2009.

Johnson, Benjamin Franklin. "A Life Review," after 1893. Benjamin Franklin Johnson, Papers, 1852–1911. CHL.

Journal of Discourses. 26 vols. Liverpool: F. D. Richards, 1855–1886.

JS. In addition to the entries that immediately follow, see entry under "Smith, Joseph."

JS History / Smith, Joseph, et al. History, 1839–1856. Vols. A-1–F-1 (originals), A-2–E-2 (early security copies). CHL. The history for the period after 5 Aug. 1838 was composed after the death of Joseph Smith. Also available as *History of the Church of Jesus Christ of Latter-day Saints, Period 1: History of Joseph Smith, the Prophet, by Himself,* edited by B. H. Roberts, 6 vols. (Salt Lake City: Deseret News, 1902–1912).

JS Letterbook 1 / Smith, Joseph. "Letter Book A," 1832–1835. Joseph Smith Collection. CHL.

JS Letterbook 2 / Smith, Joseph. "Copies of Letters, &c. &c.," 1839–1843. Joseph Smith Collection. CHL.

JSP, J1 / Jessee, Dean C., Mark Ashurst-McGee, and Richard L. Jensen, eds. *Journals, Volume 1: 1832–1839.* Vol. 1 of the Journals series of *The Joseph Smith Papers,* edited by

Dean C. Jessee, Ronald K. Esplin, and Richard Lyman Bushman. Salt Lake City: Church Historian's Press, 2008.

JSP, MRB / Jensen, Robin Scott, Robert J. Woodford, and Steven C. Harper, eds. *Manuscript Revelation Books.* Facsimile edition. First volume of the Revelations and Translations series of *The Joseph Smith Papers,* edited by Dean C. Jessee, Ronald K. Esplin, and Richard Lyman Bushman. Salt Lake City: Church Historian's Press, 2009.

Latter Day Saints' Messenger and Advocate. Kirtland, OH. Oct. 1834–Sept. 1837.

Latter-day Saints' Millennial Star. Manchester, England, 1840–1842; Liverpool, 1842–1932; London, 1932–1970.

"Library Record for the Listing or Cataloguing of Books." In Historian's Office, Library Accession Records, ca. 1890–ca. 1930. CHL.

Mackellar, Thomas. *The American Printer: A Manual of Typography, Containing Complete Instructions for Beginners, as Well as Practical Directions for Managing All Departments of a Printing Office.* Philadelphia: L. Johnson, 1866. As excerpted in Richard-Gabriel Rummonds, *Nineteenth-Century Printing Practices and the Iron Handpress,* 2 vols. (New Castle, DE: Oak Knoll Press, 2004).

May, Dean L. "A Demographic Portrait of the Mormons, 1830–1980." In *After 150 Years: The Latter-day Saints in Sesquicentennial Perspective,* edited by Thomas G. Alexander and Jessie L. Embry, 38–69. [Provo, UT]: Charles Redd Center for Western Studies, 1983.

McLellin, William E. Letter, Independence, MO, to Joseph Smith III, [Plano, IL], July 1872. Letters and Documents Copied from Originals in the Office of the Church Historian, Reorganized Church, no date. Typescript. CHL. Original at Community of Christ Library-Archives, Independence, MO.

Messenger and Advocate of the Church of Christ. Pittsburgh. Apr. 1845–Sept. 1846.

Minute Book 1 / "Conference A," 1832–1837. CHL. Also available as Fred C. Collier and William S. Harwell, eds., *Kirtland Council Minute Book* (Salt Lake City: Collier's Publishing, 1996).

Minute Book 2 / "The Conference Minutes and Record Book of Christ's Church of Latter Day Saints," 1838–ca. 1839, 1842, 1844. CHL. Also available as Donald Q. Cannon and Lyndon W. Cook, eds., *Far West Record: Minutes of the Church of Jesus Christ of Latter-day Saints, 1830–1844* (Salt Lake City: Deseret Book, 1983).

Missouri Circuit Court (5th Circuit). Feb. 1834 term. *William W. Phelps and Oliver Cowdery v. Nathaniel K. Olmstead et al.* Jackson County Records Center, Independence, MO.

Missouri Intelligencer and Boon's Lick Advertiser. Franklin, MO, 1819–1827; Fayette, MO, 1827–1830; Columbia, MO, 1830–1835.

Missouri Writers' Project, Works Progress Administration, comp. *Missouri: A Guide to the "Show Me" State.* American Guide Series. New York: Duell, Sloan and Pearce, 1941.

Nauvoo Neighbor. Nauvoo, IL. 1843–1845.

New York Weekly Herald. New York City, NY. 1836–ca. 1896.

Ohio Star. Ravenna, OH. 1830–1854.

Painesville Telegraph. Painesville, OH. 1831–1838.

Parkin, Max H. "Joseph Smith and the United Firm: The Growth and Decline of the Church's First Master Plan of Business and Finance, Ohio and Missouri, 1832–1834." *BYU Studies* 46, no. 3 (2007): 5–66.

Partridge, Elinore H. *Characteristics of Joseph Smith's Style and Notes on the Authorship of the Lectures on Faith.* Task Papers in LDS History 14. Salt Lake City: History Division, Historical Department, The Church of Jesus Christ of Latter-day Saints, 1976.

Phelps, William W. Diary and Notebook, ca. 1835–1836, 1843, 1864. CHL.

———. Letter, Great Salt Lake City, Utah Territory, to Brigham Young, Great Salt Lake City, Utah Territory, 10 Apr. 1854. In Brigham Young, Office Files, 1832–1878. CHL.

———. Letter, Kirtland Mills, OH, to Sally Phelps, Liberty, MO, 16–18 Sept. 1835. Private possession. Copy in CHL.

———. Letter, Kirtland, OH, to Sally Phelps, Liberty, MO, 14 Nov. 1835. In Historical Department, Journal History of the Church, 1896–. CHL.

———. Papers, 1835–1865. BYU.

———. "A Short History of W. W. Phelps' Stay in Missouri," 1864. CHL.

Phipps, Alan J. "The Lectures on Faith: An Authorship Study." Master's thesis, Brigham Young University, 1977.

Pratt, Orson. Diaries, 1833–1837. CHL.

The Prophet. New York City, NY. May 1844–Dec. 1845.

Quorum of the Twelve Apostles. Minutes, 1840–1844. CHL.

The Return. Davis City, IA, 1889–1891; Richmond, MO, 1892–1893; Davis City, 1895–1896; Denver, CO, 1898; Independence, MO, 1899–1900.

Revelation Book 1 / "A Book of Commandments and Revelations of the Lord Given to Joseph the Seer and Others by the Inspiration of God and Gift and Power of the Holy Ghost Which Beareth Re[c]ord of the Father and Son and Holy Ghost Which Is One God Infinite and Eternal World without End Amen," 1831–1835. CHL. Also available in Robin Scott Jensen, Robert J. Woodford, and Steven C. Harper, eds., *Manuscript Revelation Books,* facsimile edition, first volume of the Revelations and Translations series of *The Joseph Smith Papers,* edited by Dean C. Jessee, Ronald K. Esplin, and Richard Lyman Bushman (Salt Lake City: Church Historian's Press, 2009).

Revelation Book 2 / "Book of Revelations," 1832–1834. Revelations Collection, 1831–ca. 1844, 1847, 1861, ca. 1876. CHL. Also available in Robin Scott Jensen, Robert J. Woodford, and Steven C. Harper, eds., *Manuscript Revelation Books,* facsimile edition, first volume of the Revelations and Translations series of *The Joseph Smith Papers,* edited by Dean C. Jessee, Ronald K. Esplin, and Richard Lyman Bushman (Salt Lake City: Church Historian's Press, 2009).

Revelations Collection, 1831–ca. 1844, 1847, 1861, ca. 1876. CHL.

Reynolds, Noel B. "The Authorship Debate concerning *Lectures on Faith:* Exhumation and Reburial." In *The Disciple as Witness: Essays on Latter-day Saint History and Doctrine in Honor of Richard Lloyd Anderson,* edited by Stephen D. Ricks, Donald W. Parry, and Andrew H. Hedges, 355–382. Provo, UT: Foundation for Ancient Research and Mormon Studies, 2000.

———. "The Case for Sidney Rigdon as Author of the *Lectures on Faith.*" *Journal of Mormon History* 32 (Fall 2005): 1–41.

Richards, Willard. Journal, 1836–1853. CHL.

The Seer. Washington DC, Jan. 1853–June 1854; Liverpool. Jan. 1853–Aug. 1854.

Smith, George Albert. Papers, 1834–1877. CHL.

Smith, Joseph. In addition to the entry that follows, see entries under "JS."

Smith, Joseph. Collection, 1827–1846. CHL.

Smith, Lucy Mack. History, 1844–1845. 18 books. CHL. Also available in Lavina Fielding Anderson, ed., *Lucy's Book: A Critical Edition of Lucy Mack Smith's Family Memoir* (Salt Lake City: Signature Books, 2001).

Staker, Mark Lyman. *Hearken, O Ye People: The Historical Setting of Joseph Smith's Ohio Revelations.* Salt Lake City: Greg Kofford Books, 2009.

Stower, Caleb. *The Printer's Grammar; or, Introduction to the Art of Printing: Containing a Concise History of the Art, with the Improvements in the Practice of Printing, for the Last Fifty Years.* London: Caleb Stower, 1808. As excerpted in Richard-Gabriel Rummonds, *Nineteenth-Century Printing Practices and the Iron Handpress,* 2 vols. (New Castle, DE: Oak Knoll Press, 2004).

Taylor, John. Collection, 1829–1894. CHL.

Theology. Lecture First. [Kirtland, OH: ca. Feb. 1835]. Copy at CHL.

Times and Seasons. Commerce/Nauvoo, IL. Nov. 1839–Feb. 1846.

Underwood, Grant. "Revelation, Text, and Revision: Insight from the Book of Commandments and Revelations." *BYU Studies* 48, no. 3 (2009): 67–84.

United States Circuit Court (8th Circuit). *Reorganized Church of Jesus Christ of Latter Day Saints v. Church of Christ of Independence, Missouri, et al.,* Testimonies and Depositions, 1892. Typescript. CHL.

U.S. and Canada Record Collection. FHL.

Verily, I say unto you, concerning your brethren who have been afflicted [D&C 101]. [Kirtland, OH: ca. Jan. 1834]. Copy at CHL.

Verily, thus saith the Lord unto you, who have assembled yourselves together [D&C 88–89]. [Kirtland, OH: ca. Jan. 1834]. Copy at BYU.

Voree Herald. Voree, Wisconsin Territory. Jan.–Oct. 1846.

Watt, George D. Papers, ca. 1846–1865. CHL.

West, William S. *A Few Interesting Facts, Respecting the Rise Progress and Pretensions of the Mormons.* No publisher, 1837.

Wheaton, Clarence L., and Angela Wheaton. *The Book of Commandments Controversy Reviewed.* Independence, MO: Church of Christ (Temple Lot), 1950.

Whitmer, David. *An Address to Believers in the Book of Mormon.* Richmond, MO: no publisher, 1887.

Whitmer, John. Daybook, 1832–1878. CHL.

Whitney, Newel K. Papers, 1825–1906. BYU.

Whittaker, David J. "Substituted Names in the Published Revelations of Joseph Smith." *BYU Studies* 23 (Winter 1983): 103–112.

Woodford, Robert J. "The Historical Development of the Doctrine and Covenants." 3 vols. PhD diss., Brigham Young University, 1974.

Woodruff, Wilford. Journals, 1833–1844. Wilford Woodruff, Journals and Papers, 1828–1898. CHL. Also available as *Wilford Woodruff's Journals, 1833–1898,* edited by Scott G. Kenney, 9 vols. (Midvale, UT: Signature Books, 1983–1985).

Zucker, Louis C. "Joseph Smith as a Student of Hebrew." *Dialogue: A Journal of Mormon Thought* 3 (Summer 1968): 41–55.

Corresponding Published Versions
of Revelations

The following table is designed to help readers refer from one published version of a revelation or similar item to other published versions of that same item. This table includes revelations announced by JS—plus letters, records of visions, articles, minutes, and other items, some of which were authored by other individuals—that were published in the Book of Commandments or Doctrine and Covenants in or before 1844, the year of JS's death. The 1835 and 1844 editions of the Doctrine and Covenants included a series of lectures on the subject of faith, which constituted part 1 of the volume. Only part 2, the compilation of revelations and other items, is represented in the table.

The first column in the table gives the standard date of each item, based on careful study of original sources. The "standard date" is the date a revelation was originally dictated or recorded. If that date is ambiguous or unknown, the standard date is the best approximation of the date, based on existing evidence. The standard date provides a way to identify each item and situate it chronologically with other documents, but it cannot be assumed that every date corresponds to the day an item was first dictated or recorded. In some cases, an item was recorded without a date notation. It is also possible that a few items were first dictated on a date other than the date surviving manuscripts bear. The dates found in this table were assigned based on all available evidence, including later attempts by JS and his contemporaries to recover date, place, and circumstances.

Where surviving sources provide conflicting information about dating, editorial judgment has been exercised to select the most likely date (occasionally only an approximate month), based on the most reliable sources. In cases in which two or more items bear the same date, they have been listed in the order in which they most likely originated, and a letter of the alphabet has been appended, providing each item a unique editorial title (for example, Oct. 1830–A or Oct. 1830–B). Information on dating issues will accompany publication of these items in the Documents series.

The remaining six columns of the table provide the issue date (in the case of *The Evening and the Morning Star*), chapter number (in the case of the Book of Commandments), or section number (in the case of editions of the Doctrine and Covenants) of each item.

Key to column titles

Star: *The Evening and the Morning Star*
1833:   Book of Commandments
1835:   Doctrine and Covenants, 1835 edition, part 2
1844:   Doctrine and Covenants, 1844 edition, part 2[1]
1981:   Doctrine and Covenants, 1981 edition, The Church of Jesus Christ of
            Latter-day Saints
2004:   Doctrine and Covenants, 2004 edition, Community of Christ

| Date | *Star* | JS-Era Canon | | | | |
		1833	1835	1844	1981	2004
July 1828		2	30	30	3	2
Feb. 1829		3	31	31	4	4
Mar. 1829		4	32	32	5	5
Apr. 1829–A		5	8	8	6	6
ca. Apr. 1829		9	36	36	10	3
Apr. 1829–B		7	34	34	8	8
Apr. 1829–C		6	33	33	7	7
Apr. 1829–D		8	35	35	9	9
May 1829–A		10	37	37	11	10
May 1829–B		11	38	38	12	11
June 1829–A		12	39	39	14	12
June 1829–B		15	43	43	18	16
June 1829–C		13	40	40	15	13
June 1829–D		14	41	41	16	14
June 1829–E			42	42	17	15
Mar. 1830		16	44	44	19	18
6 Apr. 1830		22	46	46	21	19
Apr. 1830–A		17	45:1	45:1	23:1–2	21:1
Apr. 1830–B		18	45:2	45:2	23:3	21:2
Apr. 1830–C		19	45:3	45:3	23:4	21:3
Apr. 1830–D		20	45:4	45:4	23:5	21:4
Apr. 1830–E		21	45:5	45:5	23:6–7	21:5
10 Apr. 1830	June 1832, June 1833	24	2	2	20	17
16 Apr. 1830	June 1832	23	47	47	22	20
July 1830–A		25	9	9	24	23

---

1. The 1844 edition of the Doctrine and Covenants included one item written after the death of JS (section 111). That item is not included in this table.

Date	*Star*	JS-Era Canon				
		1833	1835	1844	1981	2004
July 1830–B		27	49	49	26	25
July 1830–C		26	48	48	25	24
ca. Aug. 1830	Mar. 1833	28	50	50	27	26
Sept. 1830–A	Sept. 1832	29	10	10	29	28
Sept. 1830–B		30	51	51	28	27
Sept. 1830–C		31	52:1	52:1	30:1–4	29:1
Sept. 1830–D		32	52:2	52:2	30:5–8	29:2
Sept. 1830–E		33	52:3	52:3	30:9–11	29:3
Sept. 1830–F		34	53	53	31	30
Oct. 1830–A			54	54	32	31
Oct. 1830–B		35	55	55	33	32
4 Nov. 1830		36	56	56	34	33
ca. Dec. 1830			73	74	74	74
7 Dec. 1830		37	11	11	35	34
9 Dec. 1830		38	57	57	36	35
30 Dec. 1830		39	58	58	37	37
2 Jan. 1831	Jan. 1833	40	12	12	38	38
5 Jan. 1831		41	59	59	39	39
6 Jan. 1831		42	60	60	40	40
4 Feb. 1831		43	61	61	41	41
9 Feb. 1831[2]	July 1832	44	13:1–19	13:1–19	42:1–73	42:1–19
Feb. 1831–A	Oct. 1832	45	14	14	43	43
Feb. 1831–B		46	62	62	44	44
23 Feb. 1831	July 1832	47	13:21–23, 20	13:21–23, 20	42:78–93, 74–77	42:21–23, 20
ca. 7 Mar. 1831	June 1832	48	15	15	45	45
ca. 8 Mar. 1831–A	Aug. 1832	49	16	16	46	46
ca. 8 Mar. 1831–B		50	63	63	47	47
10 Mar. 1831		51	64	64	48	48
7 May 1831	Nov. 1832	52	65	65	49	49
9 May 1831	Aug. 1832	53	17	17	50	50
20 May 1831			23	23	51	51
6 June 1831		54	66	66	52	52
8 June 1831		55	66[3]	67	53	53

---

2. See also the following entry for 23 Feb. 1831.

3. The second of two sections numbered 66. Numbering remains one off for subsequent sections within the 1835 edition.

			JS-Era Canon			
Date	*Star*	1833	1835	1844	1981	2004
10 June 1831		56	67	68	54	54
14 June 1831		57	68	69	55	55
15 June 1831		58	69	70	56	56
20 July 1831			27	27	57	57
1 Aug. 1831		59	18	18	58	58
7 Aug. 1831	July 1832	60	19	19	59	59
8 Aug. 1831		61	70	71	60	60
12 Aug. 1831	Dec. 1832	62	71	72	61	61
13 Aug. 1831		63	72	73	62	62
30 Aug. 1831	Feb. 1833	64	20	20	63	63
11 Sept. 1831		65	21	21	64	64
29 Oct. 1831			74	75	66	66
30 Oct. 1831	Sept. 1832		24	24	65	65
1 Nov. 1831–A	Oct. 1832		22	22	68	68
1 Nov. 1831–B	Mar. 1833	1	1	1	1	1
2 Nov. 1831			25	25	67	67
3 Nov. 1831	May 1833		100	108	133	108
11 Nov. 1831–A			28	28	69	69
11 Nov. 1831–B[4]			3 (partial[5])	3 (partial[6])	107 (partial[7])	104 (partial[8])
12 Nov. 1831			26	26	70	70
1 Dec. 1831			90	91	71	71
4 Dec. 1831	Dec. 1832		89	90	72	72
10 Jan. 1832			29	29	73	73
25 Jan. 1832			87	88	75	75
16 Feb. 1832	July 1832		91	92	76	76
1 Mar. 1832			75	76	78	77
7 Mar. 1832			77	78	80	79
12 Mar. 1832			76	77	79	78
15 Mar. 1832			79	80	81	80
26 Apr. 1832			86	87	82	81
30 Apr. 1832	Jan. 1833		88	89	83	82

---

4. See also the following entry for ca. Apr. 1835.

5. Verses 31–33, 35–42, 44.

6. Verses 31–33, 35–42, 44.

7. Verses 59–69, 71–72, 74–75, 78–87, 89, 91–92, 99–100.

8. Verses 31–33, 35–42, 44.

DATE	STAR	JS-ERA CANON				
		1833	1835	1844	1981	2004
29 Aug. 1832			78	79	99	96
22 and 23 Sept. 1832			4	4	84	83
6 Dec. 1832			6	6	86	84
27 and 28 Dec. 1832	Feb. 1833		7:1–38	7:1–38	88:1–126	85:1–38
3 Jan. 1833	Mar. 1833		7:39–46	7:39–46	88:127–141	85:39–46
27 Feb. 1833			80	81	89	86
8 Mar. 1833			84	85	90	87
9 Mar. 1833			92	93	91	88
15 Mar. 1833			93	94	92	89
6 May 1833			82	83	93	90
1 June 1833			95	96	95	92
4 June 1833			96	97	96	93
2 Aug. 1833–A			81	82	97	94
2 Aug. 1833–B			83	84	94	91
6 Aug. 1833			85	86	98	95
12 Oct. 1833			94	95	100	97
16 and 17 Dec. 1833			97	98	101	98
17 Feb. 1834			5	5	102	99
24 Feb. 1834				101	103	100
23 Apr. 1834			98	99	104	101
22 June 1834				102	105	102
25 Nov. 1834			99	100	106	103
ca. Apr. 1835[9]			3	3	107	104
ca. Aug. 1835 ("Marriage")			101	109		111
ca. Aug. 1835 ("Of Governments and Laws in General")			102	110	134	112
23 July 1837				104	112	105
8 July 1838–C				107	119	106
19 Jan. 1841				[103]	124	107[10]

---

9. See also the preceding entry for 11 Nov. 1831–B.

10. The 2004 Community of Christ edition provides the following note regarding this section: "Placed in the Appendix by action of the 1970 World Conference: the Appendix was subsequently removed by the 1990 World Conference."

		JS-Era Canon				
Date	Star	1833	1835	1844	1981	2004
1 Sept. 1842				105	127	109[11]
7 Sept. 1842				106	128	110[12]

---

11. The 2004 Community of Christ edition provides the following note regarding this section: "Placed in the Appendix by action of the 1970 World Conference: the Appendix was subsequently removed by the 1990 World Conference."

12. The 2004 Community of Christ edition provides the following note regarding this section: "Placed in the Appendix by action of the 1970 World Conference: the Appendix was subsequently removed by the 1990 World Conference."

Acknowledgments

The Joseph Smith Papers Project is made possible by the help and cooperation of hundreds of people. Though we here primarily identify the individuals and institutions who have contributed to this volume, we are mindful of our ever-increasing debt to our many colleagues and friends who are assisting with later volumes, the Joseph Smith Papers Project website, or more general undertakings. Their work informs ours, and we are grateful for their support and collegiality. Administrators and officials of The Church of Jesus Christ of Latter-day Saints, Salt Lake City, and Brigham Young University, Provo, Utah, have provided support and resources that have facilitated this work. We give special acknowledgment to management and staff at the Church History Library, Salt Lake City, where the bulk of the Joseph Smith papers are housed. The project is also blessed by continued, generous funding by the Larry H. Miller and Gail Miller Family Foundation. The support of the Miller family has allowed us to expand our staff and move forward at an ambitious pace. We strive always to produce scholarship that is worthy of the trust and confidence they have placed in us.

We wish to express special thanks to several individuals whose efforts were integral to the success of this volume. In addition to arranging for us to have access to the valuable documents reproduced in this volume, Glenn N. Rowe of the Church History Department, The Church of Jesus Christ of Latter-day Saints, shared with us his encyclopedic knowledge of the documents' provenance. The work of Peter Crawley, a retired professor at Brigham Young University and an eminent collector of Mormon imprints, was essential to our research on early Mormon printing. He also provided thorough and thoughtful feedback on drafts of the material in this volume. Steven C. Harper, of the Department of Church History and Doctrine at Brigham Young University, and Robert J. Woodford, a retired instructor at the Latter-day Saint Institute of Religion at the University of Utah, also carefully reviewed draft material and provided valuable feedback.

The Joseph Smith Papers Project relies on the skills and dedication of employees of the Church History Department, faculty and researchers at Brigham Young University, retired scholars and other volunteers, and independent researchers and editors. Among those who contributed to the development of this volume are Linda Hunter Adams, Grant A. Anderson, Mark Ashurst-McGee, Brian P. Barton, Noel R. Barton, Christy Best, Kathryn Burnside, Jeffrey G. Cannon, Christopher K. Crockett, Joseph D. Darowski, Kay Darowski, Dorsey Ford, Amanda K. Fronk, Russell C. Fuhriman, Alison Gainer, Matthew C. Godfrey, Andrew H. Hedges, Sharalyn D. Howcroft, Emily W. Jensen, Cort Kirksey, David H. Kitterman, Viola Knecht, Jamie Layton, Constance Palmer Lewis, Michael Hubbard MacKay, Andrea Maxfield, Chris McAfee, Brandon Metcalfe, Allison Morgan, Larry E. Morris, Steven Motteshard, Sharon Nielsen, Jay A. Parry, Sarah Gibby Peris, Leslie Sherman, Alex D. Smith, Anna Staley, Nathan N. Waite, and Julia K. Woodbury.

Employees of other departments at church headquarters in Salt Lake City provided invaluable assistance. Clark D. Christensen and Tyler Humble, Information and Communications Systems Department, provided technical support. Daniel B. Hogan, Curriculum Department, advised us on a variety of editorial issues. Welden C. Andersen, Audiovisual Department, shot the textual photographs in this volume. Charles M. Baird, Materials Management Department, prepared the photographs for publication. The Revelations and Translations series of *The Joseph Smith Papers* would not be what it is without the expertise of Welden and Charley, and we are fortunate in our continued association with them.

We extend thanks for the consulting provided by Clark Evans, head of reference services in the Rare Book and Special Collections Division, Library of Congress; John Hajicek, collector of early Mormon books and artifacts; Joseph Johnstun, independent historian and past director of tourism for the city of Nauvoo, Illinois; Richard L. Saunders, curator of special collections and university archivist, University of Tennessee at Martin; and George J. Throckmorton, forensic document examiner and handwriting expert.

Management and staff at Deseret Book Company, Salt Lake City, expertly assisted with the design, printing, and distribution of this volume. In particular, we thank Sheri L. Dew, Cory H. Maxwell, Anne Sheffield, Richard Erickson, Suzanne Brady, Gail Halladay, Derk Koldewyn, Rebecca Chambers, and Vicki Parry. We thank Scott Eggers, of Scott Eggers Design, Salt Lake City, for designing the dust jacket and cover.

Finally, we express deepest gratitude to our families, without whose quiet support and strength this project could not succeed.